THE MIGHT OF NATIONS

WORLD POLITICS IN OUR TIME

THE FOURTH EDITION
MIGHT OF NATIONS

WORLD POLITICS IN OUR TIME

JOHN G. STOESSINGER

RANDOM HOUSE NEW YORK

Copyright © 1961, 1965, 1969, 1973 by John G. Stoessinger

All rights reserved under International and Pan-American Copyright Conventions.
No part of this book may be reproduced in any form or by any means, electronic
or mechanical, including photocopying, without permission in writing from the
publisher. All inquiries should be addressed to Random House, Inc., 201 East
50th Street, New York, N.Y. 10022. Published in the United States by Random
House, Inc., and simultaneously in Canada by Random House of Canada
Limited, Toronto.

Library of Congress Cataloging in Publication Data

Stoessinger, John George, 1927–
The might of nations: world politics in our time.
4th ed.

Includes bibliographies.
1. World politics—1945-   2. International
relations.   3. United Nations.   I. Title.
D843.S826 1973   327   72–8950
ISBN 0–394–31744–0

Originally published in 1961; Revised Editions, 1965, 1969.

Manufactured in the United States of America. Composed by Volt Information
Sciences, Inc., New York. Printed and bound by Halliday Lithograph Corp.,
West Hanover, Mass.

Typography by Karin Gurski Batten

Fourth Edition

987654321

To My Mother

and the Memory

of My Father

Preface to
the Fourth Edition

The post-war era has definitely ended. A new generation is in the process of redefining its international relationships. It seems almost as if a kaleidoscope had been shaken vigorously and the pieces had formed new patterns. Old enemies are smiling at one another and paying visits. Old friends are looking at one another askance. National leaders have begun the process of ideological decontamination and have settled down to serious and practical negotiations. In short, since I began work on the fourth edition of this book, the international system has changed before my very eyes.

The nature of the international struggle for power has changed dramatically. The United States and the Soviet Union no longer dominate the scene exclusively. China has entered the arena and bipolarity has given way to a triangle in which each of the three actors has aspired to the role of the lady, to be wooed by the other two. The liquidation of Western colonialism has continued at a steady pace. New nations have arisen not only from the ashes of former colonial empires, but out of the turbulence of post-colonial nationhood. The human tragedy surrounding the birth of Bangla Desh was a grim reminder that the international struggle for power did not end with the passing of the European order in the Third World. Similarly, the power struggles over the Middle East has continued with ferocity, and in Indochina, military confrontation has finally yielded to political negotiation only after a long and terrible war. The era of power politics is far from over.

The builders of international order have made significant progress since the last edition of this book appeared. Nuclear war seems more remote today than it did then. The United States and the Soviet Union have reached historic arms limitation accords. The United Nations, while not discovering new solutions to the age-old problem of war, has ventured bravely into hitherto uncharted territory, and has begun to face the imperatives of the world's deepening ecological crisis. Regional integration, too, has continued apace with Great Britain's accession to the European Common Market. The struggle toward order in the world has continued to be as persistent as the struggle for power.

I have done my best to incorporate all these developments into the present edition. In so doing, I have been confirmed in my conviction that the original conception of the book was sound. I believe that it continues to remain intact today. And I am more than ever convinced of the importance of the role of perception in world affairs.

Over the years I have had a multitude of letters about this book from teachers and students all over the world. Many of these contained suggestions for improvement which have found their way into the present edition. For all of these, I am most sincerely grateful.

J. G. S.
New York City
October 1972

Preface to
the Third Edition

The revision of a book is always a process of soul-searching. An author is forced to submit his work to the test of time, which is a writer's way of saying that he must face himself. To work on this edition was a joy as well as labor, since my conviction that the basic conception of the book is sound has deepened with the passing years.

The international struggle for power has intensified since the last edition of this book appeared. I have attempted to assess its most recent manifestations in this edition, by including accounts of the Soviet-Czechoslovak crisis and of the changing nature of NATO, an analysis of the Arab-Israeli war of 1967, and a case study of the war in Vietnam. I have also made an effort to convey the more subtle changes in the two major power struggles of our time: the partial moves beyond the cold war in the East-West struggle and the increasing momentum of the forces of anti-colonialism in the struggle to eliminate the vestiges of European rule from Africa.

It has not been a good three years for the builders of international order. The United Nations has been forced to the sidelines in the superpower conflicts over the Middle East and Vietnam. In the Middle East, a peace force had to be withdrawn, and in Vietnam, the world organization has been permitted to play only a marginal role. Yet, there has been progress too. Regional bodies in different parts of the world have grown in strength and stature and an effort has been made to stop the process of nuclear proliferation. Thus, the struggle for order in international relations continues to find its nourishment in the same soil as the struggle for power.

This writer is more than ever convinced of the importance of perception in world politics. As the reality principle has gained in strength in the relations between the United States and the Soviet Union, it has yielded to ever more dangerous misperceptions in the relations between the United States and China. I have made an effort to take note of these developments.

In preparing this revision, I was ably assisted by Mr. Sanford Balsam of The City University of New York. Miss Anne Dyer Murphy of Random House also supplied valuable suggestions. My greatest intellectual debt, however, still goes to Inis L. Claude, Jr., whose warm friendship over the years continues to be a source of strength and inspiration.

J. G. S.
New York City
October 1968

Preface to
the Second Edition

Three turbulent years have elapsed since the first edition of this book appeared. During this short span of time dramatic events have taken place in world politics. The international struggle for power has continued unabated, although the bipolar system has begun to loosen. In the West, the leadership of the United States has been challenged by a Western Europe rapidly gaining in strength; in the East, the dominance of the Soviet Union has been challenged by an increasingly belligerent Communist China. In 1962 the United States and the Soviet Union had a major showdown over the removal of Soviet offensive missiles from Cuba. In 1963 President John F. Kennedy was assassinated, and a year later Soviet Premier Khrushchev was ousted and Communist China exploded its first nuclear device. The developing areas of the world have continued to be the scene of East-West and North-South conflicts. Brush-fire wars have dotted the world map, notably in the Congo, in Vietnam, and in Cyprus.

The international quest for order too, however, has continued without letup. The United Nations has continued to evolve despite a severe financial crisis. While one peace-keeping operation had to be withdrawn from the Congo, a new one was mounted to help bring peace to Cyprus. New regional patterns have developed and the economic integration of Western Europe has made further progress. A partial

xii   Preface to the Second Edition

nuclear test ban has been signed and ratified by the majority of the world's nations. And hopes for a détente between the nuclear giants have been cautiously voiced on both sides of the Iron Curtain.

I have attempted to bring this book up to date by incorporating the events of the last three years. The conceptual structure of the book, however, has stood the test of time well and remains basically intact, although I have incorporated some refinements into the concluding chapter.

During my work on the revision I have continued to benefit from the stimulation of my students at Hunter College and Columbia University. I should also like to acknowledge with gratitude the research assistance of Mr. Ralph Hellmold and Mr. Robert G. McKelvey, both of Columbia University, and the editorial assistance of Miss Anne Dyer Murphy and Mrs. Leonore Hauck of Random House, and the services of Miss Marcia Rosenfeld who prepared the index.

J. G. S.
New York City
January 1965

Acknowledgments

It gives me much happiness to acknowledge here a small part of a great debt. I have benefited from the intellectual and moral inspiration of many scholars in the field of international relations and my debts to them cannot be repaid by a ritual obeisance.

Professor Joseph Dunner of Grinnell College provided me with a sound basis in scholarship. My graduate work at Harvard University was an inexhaustible source of enrichment. Professors Rupert Emerson, Sigmund Neumann, and Daniel S. Cheever have my special gratitude. Their counsel was a unique privilege and has remained a permanent inspiration.

My debts to colleagues in the profession are many. Professor Adamantia Pollis of Hunter College read the entire manuscript and made numerous valuable suggestions. Professor George Liska of the University of Chicago and Professor John D. Montgomery of Boston University deserve my thanks for many helpful criticisms. I am also indebted to the members of the Commission to Study the Organization of Peace, especially its chairman, Professor Arthur N. Holcombe.

My students at Hunter College and Columbia University are always challenging. No teacher could be more fortunate. Miss Marcia Rosenfeld of Columbia University provided valuable editorial assistance and prepared the index. Miss Susan Shapiro, who typed the entire manuscript and suggested numerous improvements, deserves my special gratitude. So does Dr. Otto Butz of Random House, whose conscientious and painstaking editorial work went far beyond the call of duty. I am also grateful to Hunter College for a George N. Shuster Faculty Grant to defray secretarial expenses in connection with the manuscript.

Finally, I wish to thank the man whose friendship and intellectual inspiration have been a constant source of strength: Inis L. Claude, Jr.

J. G. S.
New York City
September 1962

Contents

PART 3 The International Struggle for Order

Part 1 The Nature of International Relations

1 Introduction

The struggle itself toward the heights is enough to fill a man's heart. One must imagine Sisyphus happy.

ALBERT CAMUS *The Myth of Sisyphus*

Sisyphus, according to Homeric legend, had been condemned by the gods forever to exert his entire being toward accomplishing nothing. He was to roll a rock to the top of a mountain only to see it fall back each time into the depths. The crime that had won him this dreadful penalty was *hubris*—presumptuous ambition. His crime was greater even than that of Prometheus, who had attempted to steal the eternal fires. Sisyphus had a passion for life and refused to heed the call from the underworld when his time had come. By decree of the gods, Mercury had to come and snatch him from his joys. Upon arrival in the infernal darkness, Sisyphus managed to trick Death and put her in chains. For a time Hades was deserted and silent. Then Pluto, god of the underworld, dispatched the god of war to liberate Death. The wrath of the gods now descended on the man whose love of life and hatred of death had made him challenge the eternal laws. His rock was waiting for him.

Countless generations have breathed life into this myth. Its underscoring of man's impotence in an indifferent and often hostile universe has seemed relevant to men everywhere. In ancient and medieval times, the ever-present threat to man's existence lay chiefly in the vast and inscrutable forces of nature. Today, these physical conditions of our survival are for the most part understood and, in the Western world at least, controlled. Yet the menace to the species has, if anything, become more ominous than ever before. And, tragically, it is no longer anything preordained or mysterious that now confronts us with the possibility of our doom. It is the instruments of destruction that we have fashioned ourselves.

Nowhere would we have better reason for abandoning ourselves to a sense of hopelessness about the faith of modern man than when we contemplate the state of relations among today's nations, the great collective actors in whose hands the decisions as to whether we survive or perish ultimately rest. Who of us, in witnessing the frantic preparations for yet another world war, has not at times despaired and concluded that the entire spectacle was a manifestation of organized insanity? Who of us has not had moments in which he has been tempted to dismiss the efforts of those working for peace as a futile Sisyphean labor?

Yet it is from this very myth of Sisyphus, as the great French writer Albert Camus has told us, that humanity can take heart. For, according to Camus, the important part of the story is not really Sisyphus' ascent up the mountain. It is during his return to the plain that the hero is most inspiring. "That hour," as Camus sees it, "like a breathing-space which returns as surely as his suffering, that is the hour of consciousness. At each of those moments when he leaves the heights and gradually sinks toward the lairs of the gods, he is superior to his fate. He is stronger than his rock."[1]

In this view of Camus, therefore, Sisyphus' fate does not teach us a lesson of acceptance and resignation. Rather, it serves as a symbol of that higher courage that revolts against our fate and raises rocks even with the knowledge that this revolt may be in vain. It shows us that as long as the rock is still rolling, the struggle is neither sterile nor futile. Man says "Yes" and his effort must be unceasing.

The relevance of this interpretation of the Sisyphean myth to the present condition of international relations is obvious. In many respects, modern man has descended to unprecedented depths, yet in others he has soared to greater heights than ever before. He has not only built concentration camps and perfected weapons of mass destruction; he has also learned to control hunger and disease and has created the United

Nations. Never before have nations made such intensive prepartions to destroy one another. But at no previous time has mankind striven more desperately to avert such destruction. Our generation is involved in the fiercest struggles for power in history. Yet it also has the privilege of participating in the most determined struggle for order ever waged. If, therefore, we have cause for shame and despair, we also have grounds for pride and hope. We may never solve the problems of our human condition—in international relations or in anything else—completely and permanently. But what remains crucial for us, as it was for Sisyphus, is that we do not permit our rock to crush us.

It is the purpose of this book to contribute in whatever small measure it can to this effort. While it hopes to offer more than a mere description of our crisis-ridden international situation, it does not pretend to advance any full-scale theory of international relations. It is the present writer's judgment that until the discipline of international relations becomes more developed, a much more useful task is to review and analyze its vast and complex subject matter in terms of certain major organizing concepts.

The treatment of international relations here presented is focused in terms of three such broad conceptual principles. The first of these is the ever-present *tension between the struggle for power and the struggle for order.* Throughout the book, care is taken to emphasize that these two processes of international intercourse are always closely interrelated, that every form of relationship, even war itself, includes elements of cooperation, while every form of order, even the most tranquil condition of peace, bears within it seeds of conflict. The second and related organizing concept here employed is that of the *divergence between the images that nations entertain of world affairs and of each other and the international realities as they actually are.* This divergence between what is and what is taken to be often exacerbates the international struggle for power and slows the international struggle for order. Finally, the book is focused upon what the author believes are the two truly dominant events of our time: *the struggle of East versus West,* and *the struggle of nationalism versus colonialism.* It is chiefly with reference to the latter two struggles—and the linkages between them—that the data and analyses offered are topically organized.

The book is divided into four sections. Part I examines the nation-state system and the nature of power. Part II deals with the international struggle for power—including both the East-West conflict and the struggle between nationalism and colonialism, as well as the many relations between them. Part III undertakes a similar analysis of the political, military, and economic dimensions of the international struggle for order. And Part IV attempts a fuller development of the three key concepts, in terms of which the empirical materials presented in the body of the book are analyzed and interpreted.

The general approach to the subject is an interdisciplinary one. Nothing less will do in a field which requires both breadth and depth. The author is painfully aware of serious shortcomings in his command of both these dimensions. Yet, taking his inspiration from Camus' version of the myth of Sisyphus, he feels that the struggle to make international relations into a coherent discipline must continue—whether it in the end prove futile or not. The pages which follow constitute an effort in that direction.

REFERENCE

1. Albert Camus, *The Myth of Sisyphus and Other Essays.* New York: Knopf, 1955, p. 121.

2 The Nation-State System and the Nature of Power

Some are born great; some achieve greatness; And some have greatness thrust upon 'em.

SHAKESPEARE *Twelfth Night*, II, 5

The Anatomy of the Nation-State

Our world is made up of over one hundred political units called nation-states. There is hardly a place on this planet that is not claimed by a nation-state. Only a century ago the world still abounded with frontiers and lands that remained unpre-empted. But in our time, man can no longer escape from the nation-state system—unless he migrate to the frozen polar zones or to the stars. The nation-state has become ubiquitous. And everywhere it is the highest secular authority. It may decree that a man die; and, with no less effort, it may offer him the protection that enables him to live. When no state wants him—when man is naked in his humanity and nothing but a man—he thereby loses the very first precondition for his fellows even to be able to acknowledge his existence. Whether it be to be born, to live, or to die, he cannot do without official recognition—the recognition of a nation-state.

This modern-day fact of life is astounding when one considers that the nations that possess this inescapable power of life and death are in many ways only abstractions, figments of the human imagination. For though the power that is brought to bear to implement a nation's will is ultimately physical, the will itself is chiefly the result of human images, images about what a nation is and about why and how its will should be expressed and obeyed.

There are two principal aspects of this universal political image. In the first place, man has endowed the nation-state with a quality that it shares with no other human association—the attribute of *sovereignty*. It is indeed no coincidence that the theory of sovereignty was first formulated in the sixteenth century, at a time when the nation-state system was in process of emerging from the universalism of the medieval world. Its first systematic presentation was contained in the writings of the French political thinker Jean Bodin. Bodin's definition of sovereignty as "the state's supreme authority over citizens and subjects," set forth in his *De La République* in 1576, is still largely valid today. The nation remains the final arbiter over the lives of its citizens, leaving them recourse to no higher law. And while this is true in peacetime, it is even more totally and dramatically the case in times of war. For in the latter eventuality, the sovereign state has the right to send its citizens to their death and, through its sanction, to transform even the most brutal forms of killing into acts of patriotic heroism.

It is frequently asserted that the concept of sovereignty is about to become obsolete. We are undergoing, in the words of Robert Strausz-Hupé, a "systemic revolution." Just as the medieval church-state was destined to pass, so the nation-state system is in turn bound to yield to a different form of political organization. Another thinker has pointed out that the very core of sovereignty, the "impermeability and impenetrability" of nation-states, has been brought to an abrupt end by the advent of the atomic age:

In a symbolic way (in addition to their possible practical use for hostile purposes) satellites circling the globe and penetrating the space above any territory of the globe, regardless of "sovereign" rights over air spaces and duties of "nonintervention," serve to emphasize the new openness and penetrability of everything to everybody.[1]

There is much to be said for the argument that the first atomic weapon "blew the roof off the sovereign nation-state." It is probably true that in case of nuclear war, little sovereign impermeability would remain. But it is equally true that in the absence of violent conflict, and especially in what the state continues to be able to demand of its citizens, sovereignty remains very much intact.

The truth is that in our time sovereignty is being both strengthened and weakened. This apparent contradiction is resolved if we survey the different parts of the globe. The Atlantic Community, especially Western Europe, seems to be slowly relaxing the grip of sovereignty. In that part of the world, sovereign states are moving toward larger units of political integration and are even beginning to experiment with "supra-national" forms of organization.* But if sovereignty is "obsolete" in Western Europe, it is just coming into its own in Asia, the Middle East, and Africa. While the Atlantic Community is moving toward cohesion, these other areas are veering toward fragmentation. In fact, more sovereign states have been born in our generation than in the preceding three-hundred-year history of the nation-state system. As a result of the triumph of sovereignty among the nonwhite peoples of the earth, the membership of the United Nations has, since 1945, more than doubled. Hence, we would seem to be living in one of those rare and fascinating transitional periods in history in which mankind is at the same time looking both forward and backward. When we consider the Western world and see sovereignty beginning to be replaced by various new forms of regionalism, we see signs of the future. When we turn to the new nationalism in Asia, the Middle East, and Africa, we witness what is in effect a rekindling of the past. Until, therefore, the world has internationally evolved somewhat further, sovereignty is bound to remain an integral part of our lives.

Despite the fact that sovereignty is omnipresent in the nation-state system, it is very difficult, if not impossible, to discover where and in whom this sovereignty is actually vested. The reason for this is that the concept is essentially an abstraction that defies precise and concrete location. The problem was much simpler as long as states in international relations were identified with their absolute rulers. Louis XIV's alleged claim, "L'Etat, c'est moi," left little doubt about the locus of sovereignty. But the advent of modern forms of government, both democratic and totalitarian, complicated the task enormously. Who, precisely, is the "sovereign" United States in international relations? Is it the President, the Congress, or the Supreme Court? The American separation of powers and the principle of "checks and balances" prevent the concentration of sovereignty in any one center. Yet the very essence

---

*Throughout this book the term "supra-national" is applied to those organizations vested with certain powers previously exercised by national governments and in which decisions of the governing body are binding on the member governments and may be taken by majority vote. For an analysis of these organizations, see Chapters 11 and 13.

of sovereignty, according to Bodin, is its absoluteness and indivisibility. The Soviet Union, too, claims absolute sovereignty in international relations. But does it reside in the person of the Premier? Or in the Presidium of the Communist Party? Or, as Soviet dialecticians maintain, in the multi-national Soviet people? No easy or precise answer is possible.

Despite all its contradictions, however, sovereignty remains an essential characteristic of the nation-state system. Even if the term itself should disappear, the substance of sovereignty—the absolute authority of states in international relations—will probably survive as long as the nation-state system itself. It is sovereignty, more than any other single factor, that is responsible for the anarchic condition of international relations. Bodin conceived of sovereignty as essentially an *internal* phenomenon, "the states's supreme authority over citizens and subjects." While the advent of democratic government has rendered this power far less than absolute, no government, democratic or totalitarian, has been willing to yield major portions of its sovereignty in its relations with *other* nation-states. Hence, it would seem that sovereignty in our time is fundamentally a phenomenon of *international* relations, a fact of life in political intercourse among nations. Over three hundred years ago man created the image of Leviathan. In some parts of the world Leviathan is man's servant; in others, he remains the master. But no Leviathan yields to another except by its own consent. Sovereignty, originally no more than a political construct defining man's relationship to the state, has taken on a life of its own on the international scene. In the internal affairs of states, sovereignty has often created political order and stability. In international relations it has led to anarchy.

The second key component that has come into the making of nations has been the phenomenon of *nationalism*. In the broadest terms nationalism may be defined as a people's sense of collective destiny through a common past and the vision of a common future. (For an analysis of the anatomy of the new nationalism of Asia, the Middle East, and Africa, see Chapter 4.) In a very real sense, a nation's "personality" is its common past, or history. Empirically, a nation is merely a group of people occupying geographic space. But nations exist much more in time than in space. The history of common triumphs and suffering evokes powerful bonds of solidarity for nations large and small. Common suffering seems to be more important in this respect than are victories. The Civil War was probably the most tragic—and continues to be the most written-about—experience of the American nation. Yet both North and South have come to regard this grim American tragedy as a period of glory. The case of Israel affords an even clearer illustration. Ethnically and culturally, the Jews of Israel are certainly anything but homogeneous. Even in their religion they range from strict orthodoxy to frank agnosticism. Yet what gives Israel its national identity in spite of these differences is the common history of suffering experienced by its people in the Diaspora. Since a similar logic characterizes nationalism everywhere, it is clear that this image of a common past exercises a most crucial function. It enables the citizen of the state to share vicariously in collective greatness and to merge his own identity, often colorless and insecure, into the larger identity of the nation. It is significant that Ernest Renan's definition of a nation, advanced in 1882 at the Sorbonne, has become a classic: "What constitutes a nation," he said, "is not speaking the same tongue or belonging to the same ethnic group, but having accomplished great things in common in the past and the wish to accomplish them in the future."

The vision of a common future constitutes the second ingredient of nationalism. Here, too, man's aspirations as an individual are often projected onto the larger stage of politics and international relations. The unconscious realization that one's personal future may be bleak and devoid of larger meaning is often unbearable. Hence, as Erich Fromm has brilliantly demonstrated in his *Escape from Freedom,* man may seek compensation for his lack of personal future in the reflected glory of the nation's collective future.[2] This form of identification may manifest itself in socially constructive ways; it may also lend itself to nationalism of a more destructive kind, as it did, for example, in Nazi Germany. The process whereby the identification is generated takes place largely in the "illogical, irrational, and fantastic world of the unconscious."[3] Hence, the insights of social psychology and psychoanalysis may have a profound bearing on the study of international relations. A case study of the development of one such image of the future, that of Nazi Germany, will serve to illustrate the point.

Many scholars now believe that the Nazi image of the ultimate enthronement of the "Aryan" superman had its roots in the authoritarian structure of the German family.[4] Erik Erikson paints a convincing portrait of the German father whose frequent remoteness and tyranny over his children made the maturation process excessively difficult:

When the father comes home from work, even the walls seem to pull themselves together. The children hold their breath, for the father does not approve of "nonsense"—that is, neither of the mother's feminine moods nor of the children's playfulness. . . . Later when the boy comes to observe the father in company, when he notices his father's subservience to superiors, and when he observes his excessive sentimentality when he drinks and sings with his equals, the boy acquires the first ingredient of *Weltschmerz:* a deep doubt of the dignity of man—or at any rate of the "old man" . . . . The average German father's dominance and harshness was not blended with the tenderness and dignity which comes from participation in an integrating cause. Rather, the average father, either habitually or in decisive moments, came to represent the habits and ethics of the German top sergeant and petty official who—"dress'd in a little brief authority"—would never be more but was in constant danger of becoming less; and who had sold the birthright of a free man for an official title or a life pension.[5]

This kind of father, of course, creates for the son an unusually difficult adolescence, a period of "storm and stress," in Goethe's words, which becomes a strange mixture of open rebellion and submissive obedience, of romanticism and despondency. For each act of rebellion the boy suffers profound pangs of guilt, but for each act of submission he is punished by self-disgust. Hence the search for identity frequently ends in stunned exhaustion, with the boy's "reverting to type" and, despite everything, identifying with his father. The excessively severe *superego* implanted by the father in his son during childhood has entrenched itself like a garrison in a conquered city. The boy now becomes a "bourgeois" after all, but with an eternal sense of shame for having succumbed.

The catalytic agent that during the 1930's offered the possibility of escape from this vicious circle was Adolf Hitler. In the Fuehrer's world the adolescent could feel emancipated. "Youth shapes its own destiny"—the motto of the Hitler Youth—was profoundly appealing to a youth whose psychological quest for identity was often thwarted. Erikson points out that Hitler did not fill the role of the father image. Had he done so, he would have elicited great ambivalence in the German youth. Rather, he became the symbol of a glorified older brother, a rebel whose will could never be crushed, an unbroken adolescent who could lead others into self-sufficiency—in short, a leader. Since he had become their conscience, he made it possible for the young to rebel against authority without incurring guilt. Hermann Goering echoed the sentiments of the Hitler Youth when he stated categorically that his conscience was Adolf Hitler. Parents were to be silenced if their views conflicted with the official doctrines of the Third Reich: "All those who from the perspective of their experience and from that alone combat our method of letting youth lead youth, must be silenced."[6] The young Nazi was taught that he was destined by Providence to bring a new order to the world, *das tausendjahrige Reich,* the Aryan millennium of the superman. Young Nazi women, too, felt a surge of pride when they were told that childbirth, legitimate or illegitimate, was a meaningful act because "German women must give children to the Fuehrer." This writer recalls how, on numerous occasions, large groups of young women would march the streets chanting in chorus: "We want to beget children for our Fuehrer." National Socialism made it possible for the young to rid themselves of their profound personal insecurities by merging their identity into the image of a superior and glorious German nation. This image of a common future was well expressed in the famous Nazi marching song: "Let everything go to pieces, we shall march on. For today Germany is ours; tomorrow the whole world."

The dynamics and forms of expression that characterized the imagery of Nazi nationalism are not, of course, typical. Indeed, the precise nature of the relationship between family structure and national and international imagery varies with each nation and is in all cases difficult to ascertain empirically. Yet subtle and complex or not, its role in the genesis of nationalism is always crucial.

It would, of course, be a mistake to claim that the psychological phenomenon of nationalism and the legal institution of sovereignty are the sole foundations of a nation. There are also a number of more 'objective' ingredients that play an essential part. Most prominent among these are territorial and economic ties and the presence of common language, culture, and religion.

Clearly the very first requirement of a nation is that it possess a *geographical base,* a territory of its own. Yet it does not necessarily follow from this that attachment to the soil of the homeland primarily explains the fact of national unity. The insights of social psychology would seem to indicate that an individual may remain attached to a much more specific and limited location, such as his place of birth or the countryside where he was raised. In fact, a person may feel more "at home" in a spot in a foreign land that reminds him of his youth than in an unfamiliar locale in his own country. Moreover, powerful emotional ties to specific locales may even divide a nation. When this is the case, the nation in question tends to be vulnerable to serious disunity and, frequently, internecine strife. Yet even when strong local attachments are not present, a really active attachment to the national territory as a whole usually results only from powerful nationalistic propaganda.

Another major contributing factor to the existence and unity of a nation lies in its common and interdependent *economic patterns.* Especially has this come to be the case since the advent of modern technology and mass production, with their need for vast national markets. Yet this same economic logic has also tended to undermine the nation-state system. For why limit production and distribution to nationally protected markets? And significantly, the only genuinely "supranational" organizations in existence in our time are of a primarily economic character. (For a full analysis of these organizations, see Chapter 13.) It is therefore incorrect to assert that economic ties reinforce the nation exclusively. Modern technology and the enlargement of markets work equally for the development of economic patterns that reach far beyond national boundaries.

It is similarly difficult to generalize about the part that is played in the making of a nation by the presence of a *common language.* In many countries, as for example the United States, a common tongue is an important integrative factor. In other nations, the fact that the same common language may be spoken in many different versions definitely constitutes a divisive influence. This is very notably the case with the Chinese language, for instance, which consists of hundreds of dialects. Thus, if a native of Shanghai wants to communicate with a Cantonese, he can do so only by falling back on written Chinese or by resorting to some foreign language that both may know. Switzerland, on the other hand, with its three different major languages, has achieved a very high degree of national unity. Still other nations have hoped to increase national cohesion by resurrecting a dead language. The revitalization of the Hebrew language in Israel is a case in point. But it is safe to assume that language is a relatively minor factor in Israeli unity. At times the quest for a national language has caused endless internal friction. The attempt to make Urdu the national language of Pakistan met with bitter resistance from that part of the Pakistani population which spoke Bengali. And India, after independence, had to accept English, a "foreign" language, as its temporary *lingua franca.* Hence the role of language in the life of nations is clearly a rather ambiguous one.

Surely one of the most perplexing concepts is that of *"national character."* Few social scientists would deny that certain cultural patterns occur more frequently and are more highly valued in one nation than in another. But it is almost impossible to find agreement among scholars on precisely what these common patterns are. In other words, we are faced with the paradox that "national character" seems to be an indisputable factor but that no one knows exactly what it is. This confusion probably stems from the fact that cultural patterns continue to live as stereotypes. For example, the stereotypes of the "volatile Frenchman" and of the "materialistic American" are strictly time-bound. Only a century ago almost opposite images were current. Moreover, patterns may differ from region to region in the same country. And it is never difficult to find exceptions to the prevailing images. On the whole, it would therefore appear that though national character patterns are a fact, their uniqueness and their significance in supporting national unity vary from nation to nation.

The role of *religion,* finally, is equally two-edged. In the United States, religion has neither substantially contributed to nor detracted from national unity. In other countries, Israel for example, religion has proved a very significant factor in making for unity in national terms. Yet in certain other cases religion has played a key part in preventing national unity. Thus it was chiefly the religious friction between Moslems and Hindus that in 1947 made necessary the partition of the Indian subcontinent into two separate nations—India and Pakistan. Religions have probably tended as much to keep nations divided as to aid their unity.

In summary, then, what constitutes a nation in our time may be characterized as follows. First and foremost, it is a sovereign political unit. Second, it is a population that in being committed to a particular collective identity through a common image of past and future shares a greater or lesser degree of nationalism. And finally, it is a population inhabiting a definite territory, acknowledging a common government, and usually—though not always—exhibiting common linguistic and cultural patterns.

Having examined the structure of the nation-state, we can now focus our attention on the heart of our subject matter—the behavior *among* nations. As a first step in this larger analysis, we must devote some attention to that most crucial of all the concepts in the study of international relations, the concept of *power*.

The Nature of Power

The nature of a nation's power vis-à-vis other nations is one of the most elusive aspects of international relations. It is frequently suggested that a nation's *power* is simply the sum total of its *capabilities*. Yet such a definition fails to do the concept of power full justice. For though power always involves capabilities, it concerns other dimensions as well. Most importantly, while capabilities are objectively measurable, power must in every case be evaluated in more subtle psychological and relational terms.

The psychological aspect of power is crucial, since a nation's power may depend in considerable measure on what other nations think it is or even on what *it thinks* other nations think it is. The relational aspect of power can be illustrated as follows. Let us assume that two nations, for example the United States and the Soviet Union, are approximately balanced in their capabilities. To the extent that this condition prevails, the power of either nation vis-à-vis the other is almost nil, even though their capabilities might suffice to wipe each other from the face of the earth. Hence, because power is a relational thing, whereas capabilities are not, there may upon occasion be no correlation whatsoever between the two. Indeed, when capabilities are equal, as in a stalemate, power tends to disappear altogether. To put it crassly, when everybody is somebody, nobody may be anybody.[7] By the same token, of course, even a small increase in the capabilities of one of the two nations might mean a really major advantage in terms of its power.

Under certain circumstances there may even turn out to be an inverse correlation between power and capabilities. Just as an experienced driver would probably give a car marked "Auto School" a wide berth, a leading nation might be doubly careful not to provoke the volatile leader of some smaller nation. The United States, for example, might be more inclined to appease a Cuba armed with atomic missiles than it would a major nuclear power like the Soviet Union. That is, a weakness in the capabilities of Cuba, the instability of its leadership, might actually enhance its relative power. Indeed, as a scholar of the role of small states in international relations has pointed out, the East-West struggle has resulted in giving greater power and freedom of maneuver to small nations at the very time that their inferiority in military capabilities has vastly increased.[8]

In the above illustration of the experienced driver, of course, there is little doubt that the man in question would make it a general rule also to accord the right of way to a large truck. Similarly, a small nation is likely to do its utmost not to provoke one of the superpowers. When the chips are down, as during or in anticipation of a conflict, it is the capabilities that count. Yet this should not obscure the fact that as long as international relations are conducted peacefully and by means of diplomacy, merely cataloguing a nation's capabilities cannot by itself provide a definitive answer to the question of its actual international power. The psychological and relational aspects of power must be recognized as hardly less significant than the objectively measurable capabilities themselves.

Coming now to the analysis of the anatomy of power as a whole, including its tangible capability aspects, we find it frequently asserted that "the most stable factor upon which the power of a nation depends is geography."[9] In the words of Hans J. Morgenthau:

The fact that the continental territory of the United States is separated from other continents by bodies of water three thousand miles wide to the east and more than six thousand miles wide to the west is a permanent factor that determines the position of the United States in the world.[10]

In the opinion of other scholars, however, the advent of the atomic age and the development of intercontinental ballistic missiles have brought about the obsolescence of "territoriality." As John H. Herz has put it, "now that power can destroy power from center to center, everything is different."[11]

It would be difficult to agree with Morgenthau that *geography* is always and necessarily a crucial factor in the power of nations. No doubt the enormous land mass of the Soviet Union prevented that country from being conquered by three different invaders in three succeeding centuries. Yet there may also be circumstances in which geographical considerations are much less relevant. Thus the same Russia whose vast expanses proved the undoing of Charles XII of Sweden, Napoleon, and Hitler, was in 1904 brought low in a naval battle by tiny Japan. It would be misleading, however, to go all the way with Professor Herz and suggest that the role of geography has drastically declined. Even the coming of nuclear weapons and intercontinental missiles may be less significant in this regard than is often claimed. As many military strategists have pointed out, mutual nuclear deterrence on the part of the superpowers may result in the wars of the future being "limited" to weapons and strategies not much different from those that have been used in the past. And to the extent that this might be the case, facts of national geography, location, and topography would continue to retain very considerable importance in the balancing of international power.

Nevertheless, it would seem that, all in all, the significance of geography as a factor in the power of nations has been decreasing. Only a generation ago it was still possible for scholars to regard the influence of geography on international relations as decisive and to elevate its study into an entirely separate discipline, the "science of geopolitics." The Scottish geographer and strategist Sir Halford Mackinder, for example, in 1904 advanced the geopolitical formula that "he who rules Eastern Europe commands the Heartland of Eurasia; who rules the Heartland, commands the World Island of Europe, Asia and Africa; and who rules the World Island commands the World."[12] The determinism of Mackinder's heartland theory was matched by that of Alfred T. Mahan, an American geopolitician of the late 19th century who believed in the decisive importance of sea power.[13] Even during World War II, power calculations of nations were still influenced by geopolitical thinking. A German geographer, Dr. Karl Haushofer, deeply impressed by Mackinder's heartland theory, argued for a German-Russian-Japanese axis. He predicted a German defeat if Hitler were to attempt an invasion of the Soviet Union. Hitler not only ignored his advice but sent Haushofer to a concentration camp. Today such geographical determinism would not find the wide audience it did in the 1920's and 1930's. With the coming of the atomic age, the "science" of geopolitics has largely disappeared from the scene.

A second major element in a nation's international power is usually considered to be its possession of *natural resources*. Yet though this factor is always significant it, too, is in itself by no means decisive. For it is not primarily the possession of raw materials that makes a nation powerful; it is above all the *use* that nation is able to make of the resources it has available. Though the Arab states of the Middle East, for example, have grown rich and been extensively courted because of their large oil deposits, they have not, by virtue of this fact, become powerful nations.

What use a nation is able to make of the raw materials it possesses depends primarily on the extent of its economic and industrial development. To develop a powerful military establishment, nations today must first command an advanced technological base. How vital this requirement may be can be seen from the examples of Germany, Italy, and Japan in World War II. In the possession of strategic raw materials, all three of these countries are relatively poor. Yet because of their highly developed industry and technology, they proved able to build military machines that almost succeeded in bringing about an Axis victory. That the power of the Allies triumphed in the end is largely attributable to the fact that the latter possessed *both* an abundance of essential raw materials *and* an advanced industrial apparatus.

Since World War II a strong industrial economy has become even more important as a factor in the power of nations. This may be seen in the degree to which both the United States and the Soviet Union are admired and envied by the smaller and economically less developed countries. The two superpowers have been fully aware of this and have capitalized on it by using foreign aid and technical assistance to influence the nations in question. Though the "underdeveloped" states concerned have often felt ambivalent about the superpowers themselves, they have done their best to conduct themselves so as to induce the superpowers to give them the greatest possible amount of such aid and assistance. To the extent that this pattern has occurred, the superpowers' relative power position versus the rest of the world has, of course, grown. (For a detailed analysis of this subject, see Chapter 7.)

It is possible that the gradual dispersion of atomic energy among most of the world's nations will diminish the importance of industrialization as a power factor. The two superpowers have used atomic energy as an object of competition in the East-West struggle and have made it easier for some of their respective allies to produce nuclear weapons on their own. As a result, some nations are in the incongruous position of controlling the most sophisticated product of an advanced technology without having the supporting base of an industrial economy. A small nation equipped with atomic weapons might, through atomic blackmail, prove as powerful as one of the superpowers. Yet its advantage would be military only, and would be operative only as regards a one-shot nuclear war. It is probable that as conventional sources of energy are increasingly replaced by the harnessed energy of the atom, the economic and hence general power of nations with large uranium deposits will somewhat increase. But unless such nations also possess the advanced technology necessary to turn uranium into actual atomic energy, their initiative in the power struggle is likely to remain limited.

The same point that has been noted in regard to geography and natural resources is also true of a third major element of national power, *population.* Once again, though a nation's population is certain always to be important as a factor in its power, the actual extent of its significance depends on many other considerations as well. Though both very populous, neither China nor India was in the past considered very powerful. Indeed, as the case of China illustrates, population is primarily *potential* power. As a result, it has been possible for nations with large populations to be weak, but impossible for nations without large populations to be powerful. Though the advent of atomic weapons may diminish the importance of manpower in warfare, the Vietnamese War would seem to have shown that the foot soldier has by no means been superseded. In the future as in the past, large populations are likely to remain an important military advantage. Hitler found it necessary to import slave labor from Eastern Europe to make up for manpower shortages in Germany. An armed conflict with a nation as populous as China would prove a struggle of the most overwhelming proportions. Even though it at the time had little else but its vast population, China was at the end of World War II accorded great-power status in the United Nations.

Population becomes most important of all as a power factor when it is combined with industrialization. It is common knowledge that those countries now going through the process of industrialization are also the ones that are growing most rapidly in population. This fact, known as the "demographic transition," significantly affects a nation's power. Industrialization leads to an increase in population, which in turn may make possible further industrialization. As the case of China demonstrates once again, the potential power of population is actualized only when it is *used*, most profitably in the development of a modern industrial base which in turn makes possible a first-rate military establishment. In the view of many observers, once China succeeds in harnessing its immense population, it may in time become the most powerful nation on earth.

On the other hand, it is well to remember that population is not in itself any guarantee of power. The *will* to commit the population in battle must be present. Hence, once again the impact of a national image may be decisive. India has great manpower resources; yet, judging by the image of herself that she projects upon the world, she has been fairly reluctant, until recently, to mobilize her population for military combat. Fascist Italy, on the other hand, with a relatively small population, was whipped into a fighting frenzy by Mussolini. On balance, even in the atomic age there is still a partial truth in the nineteenth-century dictum that "God is on the side of the biggest battalions"—provided a nation has the will and the resources to mobilize them.

A fourth element of national power whose effects it is difficult to assess concerns the nature of a country's *government*. It is tempting to assume that a democratic form of government provides greater national strength than a dictatorship. Yet though the historical record does not invalidate this assumption, it certainly places it in question. The victory of Sparta over Athens is only one of many instances in which dictatorship emerged triumphant. But any analysis of this issue must remain inconclusive. There are simply too many imponderables involved to permit any easy conclusion.

It is generally assumed that a dictatorial government has its greatest advantages for national power in time of war, when centralized control, secrecy, and swiftness of execution are most important. Actually, the record does not support this conclusion. In wartime, most democracies have managed to fashion temporary "constitutional dictatorships" which quickly balanced the initial advantages of the aggressive dictator. Britain's wartime cabinet and America's reaction to Pearl Harbor are cases in point. Centralized control and self-discipline have usually been an effective counterpoise to secrecy and regimentation.

Many observers point out that democracy has a great advantage because it rests on the consent and voluntary support of the governed, where dictatorship requires coercion. While there is much truth in this oft-repeated assertion, it has been overdone. Modern totalitarianism has developed highly effective means of psychological indoctrination. Nazi Germany, Fascist Italy, the Soviet Union, and Communist China each developed a highly organized youth movement for this express purpose. In addition, "brainwashing"—a kind of psychoanalysis in reverse—was widely applied to "reactionary elements" in Communist China during the Cultural Revolution. These techniques, when coupled with the fact that modern totalitarianism deprives a population of standards of comparison in both time and space, have made possible the emergence of a new type of government: "totalitarianism with the consent of the governed." At times, totalitarian governments do not have to create popular support through these methods. The Nazi dictatorship, for example, enjoyed the fanatical support of most of the German population before 1941. Hence, a broad base of popular support as a source of power is not a monopoly of the democracies.

A dicatorship seems to have an advantage in the development of its industrial resources. Forced collectivization and industrialization of the Soviet and Communist Chinese varieties would be unthinkable in a democratic framework. In both countries there resulted a great increase in power status, albeit at the cost of millions of human lives. But the democracies have been more generously endowed with prosperous economies and this has been a balancing factor. It is probably not an accident that most modern dictatorships have tended to be "have-not" nations. A totalitarian nation with a wealthy economy might indeed have a decisive advantage.

The total record is inconclusive. Perhaps the only democratic source of power which is denied to dictatorship is the fact that most people *think* that a democracy is inherently more powerful. Even the Soviet Union and Communist China have found it necessary to camouflage totalitarian reality behind the democratic facade of a "people's democracy." The Soviet Constitution of 1936 was hailed by Stalin as "the most democratic in the world." In a world in which most of the nations of Africa, the Middle East, and Southeast Asia are uncommitted in the struggle between democracy and dictatorship, the image of democracy's greater power might be decisive. In short, democracy exerts a magnetism and possesses a kind of mystique which dictatorship cannot muster. Yet we must remember that very few of these uncommitted nations have any tradition in democratic government. If, despite this handicap, the new nations should embrace democracy, such an act might in large measure depend upon their conviction that democracy is compatible with the dictates of power.

It appears from the above that the objective or "capability" attributes of a nation's power depend, above all, on the *use* which its government makes of such physical factors as geography, population, and natural wealth. In the hands of a resourceful government, democratic or totalitarian, geography is turned to strategic advantage, and population and natural resources become twin pillars of power—military preparedness and industrialization. But as we have stated at the outset, despite their great importance these objective bases of national power are by no means the whole story. Of no less importance for a nation's power arsenal are its image of itself and, perhaps most crucial of all, the way it is viewed by other nations. To understand the latter dimension of power we must consider chiefly the factors of national character and morale, ideology, and national leadership.

We have seen earlier that the concept of *national character* is highly elusive, and that it refers to something that is constantly changing. Its relevance to power does not lie so much in its objective existence, which is still disputed by many scholars, but in the persistence of stereotypes that are imputed by one nation to another. The instability of these stereotypes themselves denies the permanence of national character. Yet that they vitally affect a nation's power nevertheless can be seen from the following situation. Before the United States had established any physical contact with Japan, the American image of the Japanese was that of a quaint, romantic, and picturesque society, almost rococo in its fragility. Hence when the Americans decided to "open" Japan to the West in the mid-nineteenth century, they simply sent Commodore Perry and a few warships to force the door. Actually, the Japan of 1850 was a rigidly stratified society that had been ruled for over two hundred years by an authoritarian military clan, the Tokugawa. Under the Western impact, Japan modernized with astounding rapidity.

For centuries, the Japanese image of China had been that of the great master. Japan's written language, its art and literature—even its political institutions—had been copied from China, though they often had to be foisted onto the Japanese scene artificially. But between 1850 and 1900, the Japanese image of China swung to the other extreme, with the West now assuming the role of teacher and master. By 1915, Japan had only contempt for China and presented its former idol with the "Twenty-One Demands," which would have turned China into a Japanese colony had the West not interceded. When in 1931 Japan invaded China, most Japanese militarists were convinced that China would crumble in a matter of weeks. By this time many Japanese regarded the Chinese as less than human.

Americans' image of Japan had also changed rapidly. The "sweet and doll-like" Japanese of Perry's day had become "leering, bespectacled sadists" who raped and murdered innocent women and children. By the late 1930's, the Japanese image of the West, especially of the United States, became that of a decadent, corrupt, and spineless society which would disintegrate in the wake of a determined military attack. This distorted perception of America was matched by a Japanese self-image of absolute superiority and invincibility. In other words, a high *national morale* now became a major power factor. If the Japanese in 1941 had perceived themselves and the United States as they really were, there would have been no Pearl Harbor. It would have been obvious that Japan could not possibly win a war against the United States; that, in short, the objective fact of vastly superior capabilities was bound to overwhelm her. It was the power of an image that precipitated the Japanese attack. The incredible feats of little Japan during World War II cannot be explained in terms of its meager objective resources, but must be attributed above all to the existence of a self-image that was translated into superior national morale. This national morale became an immense storehouse of power. A well-known student of Japan, Ruth Benedict, provides a fascinating illustration of this morale factor in her report of a Japanese radio broadcast describing the behavior of a Japanese pilot during the war:

After the air battles were over, the Japanese planes returned to their base in small formations of three or four. A Captain was in one of the first planes to return. After alighting from his plane, he stood on the ground and gazed into the sky through binoculars. As his men returned, he counted. He looked rather pale, but he was quite steady. After the last plane returned he made out a report and proceeded to Headquarters. At Headquarters he made his report to the Commanding Officer. As soon as he had finished his report, however, he suddenly dropped to the ground. The officers on the spot rushed to give assistance but alas! he was dead. On examining his body it was found that it was already cold, and he had a bullet wound in his chest, which had proved fatal. It is impossible for the body of a newly-dead person to be cold. Nevertheless the body of the dead Captain was as cold as ice. The Captain must have been dead long before, and it was his spirit that made the report. Such a miraculous feat must have been achieved by the strict sense of responsibility that the dead Captain possessed.[14]

To a non-Japanese, this story might seem like an outrageous yarn. But this writer himself heard the particular broadcast and was able to observe the reaction of Japanese military personnel in occupied Shanghai. The story was believed almost without exception. It was common knowledge that a disciplined spirit was master of the body, that indeed "a composed spirit could last a thousand years."[15] Why should it not be possible that the spirit of a man could outlive his body by a few hours if that man had made duty and responsibility to the Emperor the central tenets of his life?

The roots of national character and national morale as sources of power are probably to be found in the culture, historical experience, and social structure of nations. Once again, the insights of the social psychologist and sociologist have relevance to the study of international relations. Empirical research has not advanced sufficiently to permit definite conclusions in this vital area of study, but it has provided some important clues. And certainly the phenomena to be explained are remarkable indeed. The German social scene, for example, changed significantly between the two world wars. Is there any connection between these changes and the fact that Germany capitulated with relative ease in 1918 but fought on fanatically in 1945? If so, what is that connection? What explains the Germans' conviction in 1941 that they would dictate peace terms to Stalin in a matter of weeks? And what, on the other hand, accounted for the tremendous staying power of the Red Army? What made British morale during World War II the object of almost universal admiration, whereas France collapsed within a few weeks? What made the United States gather its resources after Pearl Harbor in an iron determination to force the enemy into unconditional surrender? The answers to these questions must await further insights into the nature of national character. What is clear is that national character and morale provide tremendous reservoirs of power.

We have seen earlier that the very essence of nationalism is a nation's image of a common past and a common future. Hence it goes without saying that nationalism vitally affects a nation's power. Under certain conditions, moreover, the vision of a common future may become an *ideology*. This occurs when a nation's image of the future includes *the notion of a dynamic evolution toward some universal utopia.* Ideology has largely become the monopoly of totalitarian nations. Napoleon's vision of universal empire was rationalized by the ideology of the French *"mission civilisatrice."* The ultimate vision of Nazi Germany was the enthronement of the "Aryan race." To accomplish this end, it became necessary for Germany to expand into ever wider areas of *Lebensraum* or "living space." The Japanese "Co-Prosperity Sphere" was based on similar assumptions. The Communists, in turn, have their own blueprint for the world, which predicts the growing influence of the Soviet Union and China. In all these cases, the nation is seen as the dynamic instrument for world-wide dominion.

It would be too simple to assert, as does Morgenthau, that ideology is simply "a flattering unction" for the concealment of imperialist expansion:

It is a characteristic aspect of all politics, domestic as well as international, that frequently its basic manifestations do not appear as what they actually are—manifestations of a struggle for power. Rather, the element of power as the immediate goal of the policy pursued is explained and justified in ethical, legal, or biological terms. That is to say: the true nature of the policy is concealed by ideological justifications and rationalizations. . . .

Politicians have an ineradicable tendency to deceive themselves about what they are doing by referring to their policies not in terms of power but in terms of either ethical and legal principles or biological necessities. In other words, while all politics is necessarily pursuit of power, ideologies render involvement in that contest for power psychologically and morally acceptable to the actors and their audience.[16]

Not only is it an exaggeration to claim that *all* politics is a pursuit of power, but the relationship between power and ideology is a much more complex and multifaceted one. In the first place, a widespread belief in the "truth" of an ideology may hasten its realization and thus become a power factor. For example, the ideological conviction of many Communists that the victory of Communism is ordained by history has added immensely to the power of the Soviet Union and Communist China. This faith in a metaphysical determinism has tended to inspire Communism with a self-image of invincibility. Second, ideology may assume an authority all its own, precisely because its adherents are convinced of its metaphysical validity. Power, in the last analysis, must rest on the capacity of physical force. Authority, on the other hand, may attain similar compliance because it is accepted as legitimate or "true." Ideology serves the peculiar function of "justifying power and transforming it into authority, thus diminishing the amount of power which must be applied to achieve compliance or to produce the desired effect."[17] Moreover, the image of an ideology's ultimate universal ideal takes on a life of its own, which even an all-powerful dictator ignores only at his own peril. This inner dynamic has been well stated by one student of ideology:

Since an important ingredient of the movement's power is the element of explicit and proclaimed purpose which furthers its seizure of political power, the fulfillment of major portions of the ideologically stated objectives becomes a necessity dictated by power, by the inner dynamic of the movement itself. It is therefore doubtful that Hitler could have survived without gradually increasing the scope of the National-Socialist revolution in Germany, or that Stalin and his regime could have maintained the New Economic Policy without ultimately losing power. . . .

A skeptical leader would run a serious risk of undermining his power if he were to allow himself to question the ideology. It is very doubtful that even Stalin could have done it.[18]

The relationship between power and ideology seems, up to a point, to be one of mutual reinforcement. Commitment to an ideology creates an image of the future which is based on the confident expectation of victory. This confidence is a source of tremendous long-range power. The enhancement of power in turn necessitates the further development and refinement of ideology along ever more ambitious lines. Theoretically, this mutual enhancement of ideology and power would end only in world domination. But if the reality lags too far behind the longed-for utopia, if the dichotomy between image and reality is too sharp, ideology begins to erode and lose its authority. It is for this reason that each Soviet Five-Year Plan has been "the final great effort" which would make entrance into the promised utopia a reality. As long as confrontation with reality does not uncover too great discrepancies, in short, as long as image and reality tend to converge, ideology remains a vast fountainhead of power. But the point of diminishing returns is usually reached when no further victories can be won and expansion is brought to a standstill.

In former times, the peculiar character of ideology with its claims of expansion toward universal power was limited to religious movements. Modern ideology has become the psychological counterpart of messianic religion. Although its ultimate goals are secular rather than supernatural, it has been able to command as much power as the most fanatical of religious movements. The implications for international relations of the presence of competing ideologies have been well stated by Hans Morgenthau:

The claim to universality which inspires the moral code of one particular group is incompatible with the identical claim of another group; the world has room for only one, and the other must yield or be destroyed. Thus, carrying their idols before them, the nationalistic masses of our time meet in the international arena, each group convinced that it executes the mandate of history, that it does for humanity what it seems to do for itself, and that it fulfills a sacred mission ordained by Providence, however defined.[19]

Ideology as a source of power is largely a monopoly of totalitarianism. A democracy may have goals or ideals but not an ideology. Since the very essence of a democracy is the principle of the right of disagreement on substantive goals, such a nation lacks the fanaticism and uniformity that lend an ideology its coherence and drive. The citizens of the United States may disagree on America's "national purpose." A totalitarian society, on the other hand, has only one official ideology. This does not mean, of course, that democracy has no resources to marshal against the aspirations of a universal ideology. As we have seen, it has other great sources of power. Besides, ideology is not *only* a source of power. It is the great overreacher of international relations. By definition, its goals are boundless and its horizons of conquest unlimited. The time must come, as it always has, when the image of a universal ideology is thwarted by an unyielding reality—when power encounters concerted counter-power. Hence each ideology carries within itself the seed of its own destruction, the hubristic assumption that power can expand without limit.

Finally, the quality of a nation's *leadership* and the image which it projects upon the world are important sources of power. If leadership is defective, all other resources may be to no avail. No amount of manpower or industrial and military potential will make a nation powerful unless its leadership *uses* these resources with maximum effect on the international scene. If the tangible resources are the body of power, and the national character its soul, leadership is its brains. It alone can decide how to apply its nation's resources. For example, the

United States before World War II possessed virtually every single attribute of a powerful nation. But it played a relatively minor role in international relations because its leadership was committed to a policy of isolation. Hence as far as American power was concerned, the advantages of geography, natural resources, industrial and military potential, and size and quality of population might as well not have existed at all, for though they did in fact exist, American leadership proceeded as if they did not.[20]

Leadership may build and save nations; it may also destroy them. The former capacity is symbolized in Winston Churchill's immortal challenge to the Nazis: "We shall fight on the beaches, we shall fight on the landing grounds, we shall fight in the fields and in the streets, we shall fight in the hills; we shall never surrender." It would be difficult to understand the power of the young American republic without reference to the outstanding leadership of its early statesmen. What would Britain have been without Castlereagh, Disraeli, and Canning? France without Talleyrand? Czechoslovakia without Masaryk? On the other hand, leadership may provide the power for national extinction. The early triumphs of Nazi Germany were the product of Hitler's mind. But the utter nihilism of the Third Reich and its final act of national suicide also grew out of Hitler's leadership. As historians have demonstrated, Hitler cast an almost hypnotic spell over Germany long after the war was considered lost by most of his entourage. His will alone resulted in the prolongation of the war at the cost of millions of lives. The German image of the Fuhrer invested him with the power of life and death.

In concluding our analysis of power, we must take note of a striking paradox: while the power gap between big and small states has never been greater, never have big states been less able to impose their will upon lesser countries. The conflicts between the United States and North Vietnam, France and Algeria, and the Soviet Union and Yugoslavia are cases in point. Part of the reason for this is, of course, the fact that whenever one superpower is engaged against a lesser state, the other superpower tends to be arrayed on the other side. Yet, the French experience in Algeria and both the French and American experiences in Indochina demonstrate that power also has a great deal to do with a nation's willingness to accept punishment. American policy in Southeast Asia failed because the threshold of suffering for North Vietnam and the Vietcong was much higher than Washington had assumed, while the American threshold was considerably lower. The United States dropped more bombs on North Vietnam than she dropped on the Axis powers during the entire period of World War II. Yet that little nation virtually fought the United States to a standstill. It seems that, with the coming of the atomic age, the power of big states has diminished while the power of small states has increased. At any rate, power can no longer be calculated simply by adding up a nation's physical capabilities. Psychology and will must be given as much weight as resources and hardware.

Now that we have analyzed the anatomy of power, we may propose the following definition: *power in international relations is the capacity of a nation to use its tangible and intangible resources in such a way as to affect the behavior of other nations.*

The Nature of Foreign Policy

We have now examined the nation as the unit of action in international relations. We have seen that it consists of both imagery and objective attributes. We have also seen that power—the nation's ability to affect the behavior of others—is more than the sum total of its attributes. It too consists of both image and reality. We yet have to see toward what *goals* this power is applied—in brief, the ends toward which a nation's foreign policy is conducted.

A nation's foreign policy is the expression of its national interest vis-à-vis other nations. To define foreign policy in this manner is, in a sense, to beg the question: What *is* the national interest? And merely to state that each nation provides its own definition is to underline the obvious. Yet might it nevertheless be possible to discover some universal guiding principle that governs the foreign policies of *all* nations? In brief, is there any one goal that is shared universally in the nation-state system?

One of the most challenging theories of international relations is that advanced by Morgenthau, who considers the central and universal goal of foreign policy to be power. Accordingly, it is always in terms of power that he views the national interest:

The main signpost that helps political realism to find its way through the landscape of international politics is the concept of interest defined in terms of power. . . . We assume that statesmen think and act in terms of interest defined as power, and the evidence of history bears that assumption out. . . .[21]

In short, Morgenthau postulates that nations will tend to use their power in the quest for further power. Moreover, he rejects as unrealistic the proposition that the national interest may be defined in terms of abstract moral principle. Rather, in his view, the national interest becomes virtually identical with national security. Excessive preoccupation with questions of morality and law is condemned as "moralism" and "legalism." These are out of place in the making of foreign policy:

Intellectually, the political realist maintains the autonomy of the political sphere, as the economist, the lawyer, the moralist maintain theirs. He thinks in terms of interest defined as power, as the economist thinks in terms of interest defined as wealth; the lawyer, of the conformity of action with legal rules; the moralist, of the conformity of action with moral principles.[22]

Morgenthau's is a brilliant exposition of a single-factor analysis. But like all such efforts, it is a *tour de force* which simply does not stand up under critical scrutiny. In the first place, we have seen that the essence of power is relational, that it depends upon comparison to be meaningful. To define the national interest in terms of the maximization of power is to assume that the goals of *all* nations are *competitive.* This is incorrect on two counts. First, many nations are interested in enhancing the power and welfare of others, rather than in competing with them. And, more important, the goals of some nations are not competitive but are *absolute,* not being defined in relation to other states at all. It is true that most of the powerful nations are competitive and seek even greater power. But can this be said with equal validity of small nations like Switzerland or Ceylon? Neither of these can be said to define its national interest primarily in terms of power. Moreover, competitive goals may change into absolute ones in the same nation. Sweden, for example, was once a powerful nation with fiercely competitive goals. But in our time, her goals are absolute and in essence unrelated to those of other nations. Hence the maximization of power is a major ingredient of the national interest, but not the only one. Nations have and always have had *both* competitive and absolute goals.

The statement that power is a vital goal of most of the world's powerful nations does not solve our problem. We have seen that the anatomy of power is highly complex. It also is an oversimplification to assert, as Morgenthau does, that a nation's foreign policy must be based *either* on national interest *or* on moral principle and *should* be based on the former. The two considerations are seldom if ever mutually exclusive. As W.T.R. Fox has aptly pointed out:

Moral principle necessarily enters into any valid formulation of national interest which must itself reconcile the desirable and the possible. Against the view that there can be no compromise, I assert that there can be no escape from compromise. This is what makes politics a vocation only for the mature, for the responsible, for the man who does not despair when he discovers incommensurate values placed in such a juxtaposition that one or another has to be sacrificed.[23]

Indeed, power and moral principle might be considered as two concentric circles. At times power is the larger and includes morality. This is true when a nation is powerful and can "afford" to act morally. But at other times, and this is equally important, morality may include power; that is, greater power may accrue to a nation from moral behavior. Or, conversely, a nation may lose a measure of its power through immoral behavior. For example, suppose the United States should break a promise to one of its allies in NATO, hence acting "immorally." The ally might leave NATO and become neutralist. The United States would thereby lose a measure of power by ignoring moral principle. (The relationship between power and morality is discussed more fully in Chapter 8.)

We see therefore that it is misleading to define the national interest in terms of any one concept. In fact, our definition of foreign policy as the formulation of the national interest is purely *formal.* To say, "Always follow the national interest!" is to devise a kind of categorical imperative. But, like Kant's famous dictum "Always treat man as an end, never as a means," the formula of the national interest is ambiguous and frequently not at all helpful when applied to a concrete situation. Simply to assert that it is identical with power is equally imprecise. Perhaps we can bring the concept of national interest into clearer focus by ascertaining the *types* of goals as well as the goals themselves which nations tend to pursue in international relations.

We have seen above a useful distinction between *competitive* and *absolute* goals. The pursuit of power, by definition, is a competitive goal. The pursuit of peace or order, on the other hand, may be defined as an absolute goal. Another useful distinction may be made between goals that are *clearly defined* and those that are *diffuse.* A clearly defined goal is shared by an entire nation or, at least, an overwhelming majority in that nation. Nazi Germany's aim to annex Austria was such a case. But most of the time it is exceedingly difficult to abstract a national goal which is common to most members of a nation. For example, does the United States have a national interest which can be objectively determined? Is the guideline of its foreign policy the maximization of power, the consolidation of economic prosperity, or the pursuit of peace? Or is it a combination of the three? Moreover, as one scholar has demonstrated, the foreign policy views of most Americans tend to fluctuate greatly and depend primarily on mood.[24] Sometimes diffuse goals may change in the direction of a more clearly defined policy. The foreign policy of France under the Fourth Republic was an example of extreme diffusion, but with the ascendancy of General De Gaulle to the Presidency, national goals were set forth with far greater clarity. A third distinction may be drawn between a nation's *declaratory* policy and its *action* policy. Often a nation's stated goals are very different from its real intentions. The Soviet slogan of "peaceful coexistence" during the Khrushchev era was a good example of declaratory policy. But it was quite possible that the Soviet leader conceived of peaceful coexistence as merely a phase in the struggle for world domination. Finally, a foreign policy may be either *static* or *dynamic.* Some nations are interested in the preservation of the status quo in international relations, while others are equally eager for change.

We may now attempt to make some general observations about the national interest. The goals of nations are subject to constant change. There is no single concept that explains the national interest. It is true that many nations use their power for the pursuit of greater power. This is especially true in the case of nations which are already powerful. But it is equally true that nations may employ their power in the pursuit of cooperation and international order. National goals may be competitive or absolute, clear or diffuse, overt or covert, static or dynamic. Beyond this it would be hazardous to generalize.

In a sense, the study of international relations is a study of the interplay of the foreign policies or of the national interests of nations. But while the architect of foreign policy tends to regard the world from the vantage point of his own nation, the student of international relations must look at the world in the round. As we have seen, the uses of national power are manifold. But two dominant themes stand out from the mosaic of international relations in our time: the struggle for *power* and the struggle for *order*. We must now address ourselves to their exposition and analysis.

REFERENCES

1. John H. Herz, *International Politics in the Atomic Age*. New York: Columbia University Press, 1959, p. 22.

2. Erich Fromm, *Escape from Freedom*. New York: Rinehart, 1941, *passim*.

3. Louis L. Snyder, *The Meaning of Nationalism*. New Brunswick, N.J.: Rutgers University Press, 1954, p. 89.

4. See the provocative analysis by Erik Erikson in *Childhood and Society*. New York: Norton, 1950, pp. 284–315.

5. *Ibid.*, p. 289.

6. *Ibid.*, p. 300.

7. Charles P. Kindleberger, "International Political Theory from Outside," in William T.R. Fox, ed., *Theoretical Aspects of International Relations*. South Bend, Ind.: University of Notre Dame Press, 1959.

8. Annette Baker Fox, *The Power of Small States*. Chicago: University of Chicago Press, 1959, p. 186.

9. Hans J. Morgenthau, *Politics Among Nations*, 4th ed. New York: Knopf 1967, p. 106.

10. *Ibid.*

11. John H. Herz, *op.cit.*, p. 108.

12. Sir Halford Mackinder, *Democratic Ideals and Reality*. New York: Holt, 1919, p.150.

13. Alfred T. Mahan, *The Influence of Sea Power upon History*. Boston: Little, Brown, 1890, *passim*.

14. Ruth Benedict, *The Chrysanthemum and the Sword*. Boston: Houghton Mifflin, 1946, p. 25.

15. *Ibid.*, p. 26.

16. Morgenthau, *op. cit.*, pp. 83–84.

17. Zbigniew K. Brzezinski, *The Soviet Bloc; Unity and Conflict.* Cambridge, Mass.: Harvard University Press, 1960, pp. 386–387.

18. *Ibid.,* pp. 387–389.

19. Morgenthau, *op. cit.,* p. 249.

20. *Ibid.,* p. 136.

21. *Ibid.,* p. 5.

22. *Ibid.,* p. 11.

23. William T. R. Fox, "The Reconciliation of the Desirable and the Possible," *The American Scholar,* Spring 1949.

24. Gabriel A. Almond, *The American People and Foreign Policy.* New York: Praeger, 1960, *passim.*

BIBLIOGRAPHY

Almond, Gabriel A. *The American People and Foreign Policy.* New York: Praeger, 1960.

———, and Coleman, James S., eds. *The Politics of the Developing Areas.* Princeton, N.J.: Princeton University Press, 1960.

Arendt, Hannah. *The Origins of Totalitarianism.* New York: Harcourt, Brace, 1951.

———. *On Revolution.* New York: Viking, 1963.

Aron, Raymond. *Peace and War.* New York: Doubleday, 1966

Barker, Ernest. *National Character and the Factors in Its Formation.* New York: Harper, 1927.

Baron, Salo W. *Modern Nationalism and Religion.* New York: Harper, 1947.

Beard, Charles A. *The Idea of National Interest, An Analytical Study in American Foreign Policy.* New York: Macmillan, 1934.

Beloff, Max. *Foreign Policy and the Democratic Process.* Baltimore: John Hopkins Press, 1955.

Benedict, Ruth. *Patterns of Culture.* Boston: Houghton Mifflin, 1934.

———. *Race: Science and Politics.* Modern Age Books, 1940.

Bruchan, Silviu. *The Dissolution of Power: A Sociology of International Relations and Politics.* New York: Knopf, 1971.

Brzezinski, Zbigniew K. *Between Two Ages: America's Role In The Technetronic Era.* New York: Viking, 1970.

———. *The Soviet Bloc: Unity and Conflict,* rev. ed. Cambridge, Mass: Harvard University Press, 1967.

Byrnes, James F. *Speaking Frankly,* New York: Harper, 1947.

Carr, Edward H. *The Twenty Years' Crisis, 1919–1939; An Introduction to the Study of International Relations.* London: Macmillan and Company, Ltd., 1946.

Christiansen, Bjørn. *Attitudes Towards Foreign Affairs as a Function of Personality.* Oslo: Oslo University Press, 1959.

Claude, Inis L., Jr. *National Minorities, an International Problem.* Cambridge, Mass.: Harvard University Press, 1955.

———. *Power and International Relations.* New York: Random House, 1962.

Cobban, Alfred. *National Self-Determination.* Chicago: University of Chicago Press, 1951.

Cook, Thomas I., and Moos, Malcolm. *Power Through Purpose.* Baltimore: John Hopkins Press, 1954.

Cressey, George B. *The Basis of Soviet Strength.* New York: McGraw-Hill, 1945.

DeGaulle, Charles. *Memoirs of Hope: Renewal and Endeavor.* New York: Simon and Schuster, 1972.

_____. *The War Memoirs of Charles DeGaulle.* Volumes I, II, and III. New York: Simon and Schuster, 1966.

de Rivera, Joseph H. *The Psychological Dimension of Foreign Policy.* Columbus, Ohio: Charles E. Merrill, 1968.

Deutsch, Karl W. *Nationalism and Social Communication.* New York: Massachusetts Institute of Technology Press and Wiley, 1953,

Duchacek, Ivo D. *Comparative Federalism: The Territorial Dimension of Politics.* New York: Holt, Rinehart and Winston, 1970.

Emerson, Rupert. *From Empire to Nation.* Cambridge, Mass.: Harvard University Press, 1960.

Fairbank, John K. *The United States and China,* rev. ed. Cambridge, Mass.: Harvard University Press, 1970.

Forward, Nigel. *The Field of Nations.* Boston: Little, Brown, 1971.

Fox, Annette B. *The Power of Small States.* Chicago: University of Chicago Press, 1959.

Gross, Feliks. *World Politics and Tension Areas.* New York: New York University Press, 1966.

Hauser, Philip M., ed. *The Study of Population: An Inventory and Appraisal.* Chicago: University of Chicago Press, 1959.

Herz, John H. *International Politics in the Atomic Age.* New York: Columbia University Press, 1959.

_____. *Political Realism and Political Idealism.* Chicago: University of Chicago Press, 1951.

Hilsman, Roger. *To Move a Nation.* New York: Doubleday, 1967.

Hinsley, F. H. *Power and the Pursuit of Peace.* Cambridge: Cambridge University Press, 1963.

Holborn, Hajo. *The Political Collapse of Europe.* New York: Knopf, 1951.

Joseph, Franz M., ed. *As Others See Us, The United States Through Foreign Eyes.* Princeton, N.J.: Princeton University Press, 1959.

Kaplan, Morton A., ed. *The Revolution in World Politics.* New York: Wiley, 1962.

Keohane, Robert O. and Nye, Joseph S., eds. *Transitional Relations and World Politics.* Cambridge, Mass.: Harvard University Press, 1972.

_____. *Soviet Foreign Policy, 1917–1941.* Princeton, N.J.: Van Nostrand, 1960.

Kissinger, Henry A. *A World Restored: Metternich, Castlereagh and the Problems of Peace, 1812–1822.* Boston: Houghton Mifflin, 1957.

Klineberg, Otto. *Tensions Affecting International Understanding.* New York: Social Science Research Council, 1950.

Knapp, Wilfred F. *A History of War and Peace: 1939–1965.* New York: Oxford University Press, 1967.

Kohn, Hans. *The Idea of Nationalism.* New York: Macmillan, 1944.

_____. *Prophets and Peoples, Studies in Nineteenth Century Nationalism.* New York: Macmillan, 1946.

_____. *Nationalism.* Cambridge, Mass.: Harvard University Press, 1938.

Lasswell, Harold D. *Power and Personality.* New York: Norton, 1948.

_____. *World Politics and Personal Insecurity.* New York: McGraw-Hill, 1935.

———, and Kaplan, Abraham. *Power and Society.* New Haven, Conn.: Yale University Press, 1950.

Lefever, Ernest W. *Ethics and United States Foreign Policy.* New York: Meridian Books, 1957.

Lippmann, Walter. *U.S. Foreign Policy: Shield of the Republic.* Boston: Little, Brown, 1943.

———. *Public Opinion.* New York: Macmillan, 1947.

Liska, George. *Imperial America.* Baltimore: John Hopkins Press, 1967.

Mackinder, Halford J. *Democratic Ideals and Reality.* London: Penguin, 1944.

Macridis, Roy C., ed. *Foreign Policy in World Politics.* Englewood Cliffs, N.J.: Prentice-Hall, 1958.

Marshall, Charles B. *The Limits of Foreign Policy.* New York: Henry Holt, 1954.

Masters, Roger D. *The Nation Is Burdened.* New York: Knopf, 1967.

Mattingly, Garrett. *Renaissance Diplomacy.* London: Jonathan Cape, 1955.

Meadows, Donella H., *et al. The Limits to Growth.* New York: Universe Books, 1972.

Merriam, Charles E. *The Making of Citizens.* Chicago: University of Chicago Press, 1931.

Modelski, George. *A Theory of Foreign Policy.* New York: Praeger, 1962.

Morgenthau, Hans J. *In Defense of the National Interest: A Critical Examination of American Foreign Policy.* New York: Knopf, 1951.

———. *Politics Among Nations: The Struggle for Power and Peace,* 4th ed. New York: Knopf, 1967.

———. *The Purpose of American Politics.* New York: Knopf, 1960.

Mowat, Robert B. *The European State System.* London: H. Milford, 1923.

Nicolson, Harold G. *Diplomacy.* New York: Oxford University Press, 1950.

Niebuhr, Reinhold. *The Structure of Nations and Empires.* New York: Scribner, 1959.

Northrop, F.S.C. *The Taming of the Nations.* New York: Macmillan, 1952.

Organski, A.F.K. *World Politics.* New York: Knopf, 1958.

Osgood, Robert E. *Ideals and Self-Interest in America's Foreign Relations.* Chicago: University of Chicago Press, 1953.

———, and Tucker, Robert W. *Force, Order, and Justice.* Baltimore: John Hopkins Press, 1967.

Padelford, Norman J., and Lincoln, George A. *The Dynamics of International Politics.* New York: Macmillan, 1962.

Rostow, W. W. *Politics and the Stages of Growth.* New York: Cambridge University Press, 1971.

Russell, Bertrand. *Power, a New Social Analysis.* New York: Norton, 1938.

Rustow, Dankwart A. *A World of Nations: Problems of Political Modernization.* Washington, D.C.: Brookings Institution, 1967.

Sapin, Burton M. *The Making of United States Foreign Policy.* Washington, D.C.: Brookings Institution, 1966.

Schlesinger, Arthur, Jr. *A Thousand Days.* Boston: Houghton Mifflin, 1965.

Sherwood, Robert E. *Roosevelt and Hopkins.* New York: Harper, 1948.

Sprout, Harold, and Sprout, Margaret, eds. *Foundations of International Politics.* Princeton, N.J.: Van Nostrand, 1962.

———. *Toward a Politics of the Planet Earth.* New York: Van Nostrand Reinhold, 1971.

Spykman, Nicholas J. *America's Strategy in World Politics.* New York: Harcourt, Brace, 1942.

Stoessinger, John G. *Nations in Darkness: China, Russia and America.* New York: Random House, 1971.

_____. and Westin, Alan F., eds. *Power and Order: Six Cases in World Politics.* New York: Harcourt, Brace and World, 1964.

Taylor, Alan J. P. *The Struggle for Mastery in Europe, 1848–1918.* Oxford: Clarendon Press, 1957.

Thompson, Kenneth W. *Political Realism and the Crisis of World Politics.* Princeton, N.J.: Princeton University Press, 1960.

Ulam, Adam B. *The Unfinished Revolution.* New York: Random House, 1960.

Vital, David. *The Survival of Small States: Studies in Small Power/ Great Power Conflict.* New York: Oxford University Press, 1971.

Yost, Charles. *The Insecurity of Nations: International Relations in the Twentieth Century.* New York: Praeger, 1968.

Part 2 The International Struggle for Power

3 The East-West Struggle

There are at the present time two great nations in the world, which started from different points, but seem to tend toward the same end. I allude to the Russians and the Americans. . . . . Their starting point is different and their courses are not the same; yet each of them seems marked out by the will of Heaven to sway the destinies of half the globe.

ALEXIS DE TOCQUEVILLE *Democracy in America,* 1835

The Roots of the East-West Struggle

The East-West struggle hovers over us all like a "brooding omnipresence in the sky." It has become so much a part of our daily lives that we have virtually come to accept it as an axiom of international relations. While its presence and fearful implications are obvious to all, its causes are far from simple. It is to these that we must first address ourselves.

It is tempting to explain the genesis of the East-West struggle purely in terms of the expansionary zeal of Communist ideology. Indeed, a fairly good case can be made for such a position. Marxism, with its prediction that the "expropriated" would expropriate the "expropriators" on an international scale, envisaged world revolution as its ultimate goal. Leninism fashioned a network of Communist parties—the Comintern—to "give history a push" and hasten the day of Communist victory. This inherent aggressiveness of the Communist ideology, emanating from the Soviet Union as its citadel and directing center, elicited protective countermeasures in the West. These, in turn, generated suspicions of "capitalist encirclement" in the Soviet Union. Suspicion begot counter-suspicion, gradually drawing East and West into a vicious circle. And thus the East-West struggle was launched.

A moment's reflection shows that this description of the "cold war," though tempting, is all too simple. It does not explain the fact that the Soviet Union on many occasions pushed forward its frontiers for reasons other than ideology. For example, it could hardly be said that the absorption of part of Poland and of the Baltic states in the wake of the Nazi-Soviet Pact of 1939 was the result of Communist ideology. Nor could it be assumed without question that the extension of American influence in Europe and Asia during World War II was purely a countermove to Communist expansion. Even a cursory inspection suggests that the East-West struggle may have some of its roots in geographic, historical, or cultural factors. This is not to say that ideology is not important. But the first and crucial question which we must ask is *how much* of the East-West struggle is rooted in the expansionary zeal of Communist ideology?

As one careful scholar of Soviet foreign policy has pointed out, it is a striking fact that Russian expansion can often be explained without reference to Marxist-Leninist ideological factors. For example,

In the Second World War the Soviets could scarcely have permitted their Anglo-American partners to extend Western influence into all sections of the power vacuum created by the Axis defeat. American expansion in both Europe and Asia has often been hesitant and reluctant. Nevertheless, the war ended with an American general in Berlin and another in Tokyo. This the Soviets could hardly afford to neglect.[1]

It is, of course, impossible to determine the exact contribution of Communist ideology to Soviet expansion. But a perusal of Soviet foreign policy suggests that ideology alone did not prompt the Soviet Union to join or to break any alliance that it would not have joined or broken on the grounds of national interest. There are indications, however, that ideology in some cases retarded the shift or speeded up the change. Certainly, Marxism compounded the difficulties besetting the Grand Alliance during World War II and contributed to its disintegration. Lenin's strategy of Communist Party infiltration, put to work so effectively in Eastern Europe following World War II, no doubt hastened the coming of the cold war. This "residual" quality of ideology has had one very important result:

. . . the Marxist-Leninist tradition has made it very difficult to reach a *modus vivendi* with the Soviets, which the Americans have been genuinely anxious to do. A belief in the inherently aggressive tendencies of modern capitalism obviously excludes any agreement except an armed truce of undetermined duration. Likewise, the acceptance of the Leninist theory makes it almost impossible to believe in the friendly intentions of American leaders.[2]

Hence, the Soviet perception of the West is to some degree, at least, colored by the lenses of ideology. And to the extent that this has been the case, the Soviet Union has, in effect, been struggling not so much with the West itself as with its ideologically conditioned image of the West.

More broadly, ideology has lent a Jekyll-and-Hyde quality to Soviet behavior vis-à-vis the West. In one sense, the Soviet Union had de-emphasized ideology and has acted as a nation among nations: it has made and broken alliances with Western nations; it has used diplomacy as an instrument of its national policy; and it has participated in the League of Nations and the United Nations. But on another level, the Soviet Union has always considered itself as the citadel of a revolutionary ideology destined ultimately to dominate the world. Thus, while ideology cannot be considered *the* cause of Soviet expansion and, hence, of the East-West struggle, it is clearly one very important cause.

There are other possible explanations for Soviet expansion that deserve analysis. First, it is often asserted that authoritarian states, by the very nature of their being, have need of an external enemy in order to deflect the frustrations of the population from the government to an external scapegoat. While there is some psychological truth in this claim, it cannot be carried too far. Authoritarian Sparta, for example, had no more expansionary zeal than its "democratic" counterpart, Athens. Nor did authoritarian Japan attack the United States in the nineteenth century; it was democratic America that forced open the door of Japan. We cannot demonstrate empirically that authoritarian regimes are by necessity more aggressive than democracies. Nor can the oft-asserted claim be validated that a good part of Soviet expansion is due to a power drive in the leading personalities of the Soviet leadership. Another explanation is sometimes sought in historical and geographic factors. Thus, some scholars maintain that Soviet expansion is merely a continuation of Tsarist aggrandizement and that certain Soviet territorial claims have their roots in the historical Russian strategic interest in warm-water ports. While it may well be that Soviet leadership derives some of its inspiration from the expansionist dreams of Tsarism, it is important to bear in mind that though history can teach by analogy, it never repeats itself exactly. The roots of Soviet expansionism must therefore equally be sought in what the men in the Kremlin believe to be the needs and opportunities of their country's contemporary situation. There is no doubt, for example, that economic factors enter into the picture. The Soviet absorption of most of Eastern Europe in the wake of World War II is generally agreed to have been dictated in some measure at least by very conscious economic considerations.

In sum, then, Soviet expansion cannot be explained in terms of any single-factor analysis. Its roots must be seen in a syndrome of forces among which are ideological and economic considerations, as well as factors of historical and geographic continuity. It is quite possible, although this cannot be demonstrated, that ideology constitutes the most important single element in this syndrome.

The temptation to explain American world strategy during and after World War II purely in terms of countermoves to Soviet expansionism is almost as great as the temptation to explain the latter exclusively in terms of Marxist-Leninist ideology. Yet here again we must beware of the pitfall of the single-factor analysis. No doubt there is much truth in such an interpretation of American policies, but it explains only part of the picture. Over a century before the cold war developed, the great De Tocqueville predicted its coming. Indeed, as one scholar has pointed out:

Well before 1945 the map of the world suggested the primacy of America and of Russia. Already by 1850 the United States formed one of the greatest land empires of the globe, stretching from the Atlantic to the Pacific and from the Canadian frontier to the Gulf of Mexico and the Caribbean Sea; already by 1800 the Russian Empire, stretching from Manchuria to Warsaw, covered over one-sixth of the entire land of our globe. Already by 1850 there were as many Russians as there were Frenchmen and Englishmen and Germans; already by 1890 there were more Americans than Frenchmen and Englishmen together; already by 1900 the United States produced more steel than any other country in the world; already during the First World War the financial wealth of the world shifted to America. Well before 1945 the United States and Russia were becoming the two largest Empires in the history of mankind.[3]

It is true that the United States had liquidated many of its possessions by the end of World War II. By 1946 the Philippines were given their independence and the remaining American possessions were being steadily prepared for self-government or statehood. On the other hand, it is quite clear that World War II had broadened the United States' perception of its strategic interests. Soon after hostilities had ended in Europe, the entire North Atlantic, from the Azores to Iceland and Greenland, had come within the sphere of American influence. And as a result of the occupation of Japan, the Pacific was transformed into what was virtually an American strategic lake. Indeed, World War II had created several power vacuums which the United States had decided to fill long before the cold war actually crystallized.

Hence, American expansion, too, must be seen in terms of a syndrome. Reaction to Soviet expansionism, while very important, is not the only factor in the picture. The analysis must also include such factors as a broadened conception of the American national interest, changing strategic goals and objectives, and economic considerations.

The East-West struggle, then, has multiple roots. Among these, Communist ideology and the American reaction to it are probably the most important. But, as we have seen, they must be weighed in conjunction with a number of others. Now that the two superpowers are caught in their circular predicament, "it is futile to argue which contestant has aggressive intentions and which has peaceable aims, since each move in the struggle calls out its countermove from the opponent."[4] A more useful function is served by analyzing the actual dynamics of the East-West struggle in our time.

The Dynamics of the East-West Struggle

PHASE ONE: THE COMINTERN AND THE WEST, 1917–1949

When the Soviet Union emerged from the Bolshevik Revolution of 1917 it was largely guided in its relations with the West by the tenets of Marxism-Leninism. Indeed, Lenin proclaimed a complete divorce from the past. The new Soviet Union was to be a revolutionary society that would spread the Communist idea to other lands, beginning with the highly industrialized nations of the West. The first three years of the new state's existence, known as the period of War Communism, were a time of great ferment. Though engaged in a murderous civil war, the Soviet Union embarked on a program of ambitious experimentation in virtually every field of human endeavor. The Communist Party assumed complete control of all political activity; the Komsomol (Soviet Youth Movement) was organized; industry was nationalized; atheism became official dogma; marriage was regarded as unnecessary; and education was completely reoriented. In its relations with the Western powers, the new Soviet government repudiated most of the debts contracted by its predecessor. It announced that within a short time the revolutionary tidal wave of Communism would engulf the West as well. According to the Soviet leaders, there were omens and portents to justify this prediction: some of the Western nations, especially England and Germany, had reached the point of "capitalist concentration," a reliable signal of impending doom. Moreover, Lenin was confident that the struggle of these nations for colonies in World War I was a final and desperate maneuver to prevent their imminent collapse. To hasten this process, Lenin instructed the Comintern, which over a period of fifteen years had been built into a formidable revolutionary instrument, to concentrate its activity on Germany and England. This network of Communist parties was controlled unequivocally though clandestinely by the Communist Party of the Soviet Union. Lenin's tenet of unquestioning obedience to the leadership of the Soviet Union was its governing organizational principle.

The West's reaction was a mixture of awe and terror. Many Western intellectuals were sincerely attracted by the bold new Soviet experiment. But the vast majority among the peoples of Western Europe and the United States recoiled from the "Red Terror." In the United States stringent security measures were taken; under Attorney-General A. Mitchell Palmer, thousands of arrests and deportations for alleged Communist subversion were made. The Western nations broke off all diplomatic relations with the new Soviet government and intervened in the civil war on the side of the Tsarist generals. In 1918, the Soviet Union stood alone, fighting a battle for survival at home and treated as a pariah abroad.

By 1920 the Soviet government faced imminent catastrophe. Not only had the Comintern failed in its international revolutionary efforts—save for brief Communist interludes in Bavaria and Hungary—but the Soviet Union itself was in desperate straits. Nationalization did not prove to be a magic formula for a country whose resources had been sapped by a destructive civil war, nor was a thorough knowledge of Marxism a substitute for technical competence in the factory and on the farm. The withdrawal of foreign investments and credits left the Soviet Union economically ostracized and on the verge of bankruptcy. Lenin was faced with a difficult dilemma: to continue the pursuit of world revolution would almost certainly lead to the destruction of the Soviet Union itself; on the other hand, to save the Soviet Union from the specter of bankruptcy would mean the betrayal of the revolutionary ideal. Lenin, shrewd pragmatist that he was, took a middle course. He announced the formula of "One step backward in order to take two steps forward." The answer was to be found in the postponement of world revolution, not its abandonment. The struggle against the West would simply be pursued by other means. Lenin announced the New Economic Policy. Under this directive the Soviet government made an about-face in both domestic and foreign affairs. Almost all industry was denationalized, *Pravda* celebrated Soviet millionaires, social mores were tightened once again, and foreign investors were reinvited to the Soviet Union. Lenin instructed the Comintern to camouflage its tactics and adopt a policy of United Front with other leftist political parties in national parliaments. The Soviet Union concluded its first treaty in 1922—with Germany at Rapallo—and expressed interest in entering nonaggression pacts with France and Czechoslovakia. It seemed as if the Soviet Union had taken its place among the nations of the world community.

The Western world greeted the New Economic Policy with tremendous relief. Most Western observers concluded that the storm and stress period was over and that the Soviet Union had come of age. It now seemed that the "Red Terror" had been but a passing phase and that the Soviet Union had abandoned its struggle against the West. This impression was strengthened when Lenin died in 1924 and a bitter struggle for the succession left the Politbureau little time or energy for the business of world revolution. Besides, both the Soviet Union and the West became increasingly apprehensive about the new threat of a remilitarized and aggressive Germany that loomed ever larger as the 1920's passed. The German Communist Party, one of the most powerful in the Comintern network, found itself without effective leadership at a time when it was embattled with the National Socialist Party for the control of Germany. The German population, harassed by the aftermath of a lost war and tormented by a galloping inflation, was ready to vote for political extremism of either Left or Right. The Nazi Party attacked the Communists as agents of a foreign power and pointed to itself as the party of true patriots. The Communist tactic of the United Front proved unavailing and in 1933 the Nazi Party assumed complete control of Germany.

The United Front technique proved equally unsuccessful in England—the second Western nation on the revolutionary timetable— when the British Communist Party attempted to use a depression in the coal industry to bring England into the Communist orbit. Instead, a Liberal-Labour coalition took power. Thus, ten years after the foundation of the Soviet Union, neither the direct subversion of the early years nor the United Front of the 1920's was able to demonstrate any territorial gains for the cause of world revolution.

Stalin's accession to power in 1928 ushered in a period of complete transformation in Soviet domestic affairs. The New Economic Policy was abruptly terminated. In its place, a rigorous Five-Year Plan was announced, mobilizing the industrial and agricultural resources of the nation in order to build "socialism in one country." Stalin saw no inconsistency between this present emphasis on national power and the future goal of world revolution. The more powerful the Soviet Union was as a national state, he maintained, the better equipped it would be to export its revolutionary ideology later. But to accomplish "socialism in one country" during the 1930's, the complexion of the Soviet state underwent profound changes. Industry was nationalized once again and agriculture was forcibly collectivized in a ruthless campaign. The Communist Party changed from a group of ideologues to a group of production experts; ability to overfulfill the Plan rather than a knowledge of Marxism-Leninism became the criterion of Party membership. The Party itself became an elite. Equality of pay was denounced as a "bourgeois superstition"; "Stakhanovites," or shock workers, were given higher wages and bonuses. In short, Stalin used Western capitalist methods to overcome the West. The goal was clear:

To slacken the tempo of industrial growth in the Soviet Union would mean to fall behind. And those who fall behind get beaten. But we refuse to be beaten! One feature of the history of old Russia was the continual beatings she suffered for falling behind, for her backwardness. She was beaten by the Mongol khans. She was beaten by the Turkish beys. She was beaten by the Polish gentry. She was beaten by the British and French capitalists. All beat her—for her backwardness. Lenin said during the October Revolution: "Either perish—or overtake and outstrip the capitalist countries; either we do it—or they crush us."[5]

In foreign affairs, Stalin continued the policy of the United Front. A growing fear of Nazi Germany prompted him to de-emphasize Communist subversion of the Western countries. In 1936 he promulgated the so-called Stalin Constitution, which he proclaimed as the world's most democratic. The Soviet Union joined the League of Nations and its representative, Maxim Litvinov, proclaimed the U.S.S.R.'s adherence to the principles of collective security. The early 1930's was a fairly inactive period for the Comintern. One attempt at revolutionary coup—in France—was foiled by the French government. The growing fear of Nazism coupled with the opportunity of at last delivering one country into the orbit of the Soviet Union prompted Soviet intervention in the Spanish Civil War during the late 1930's. When Nazi intervention on the side of General Franco seemed to assure the latter's victory, Stalin decided to aid the Loyalists to redress the balance. But, in the midst of the Spanish war, the Great Purges took place in the Soviet Union. These cost the lives of many of the country's top military leaders. The Comintern, like every other Soviet power structure, was deeply affected by this gigantic bloodletting. It took its toll also in Spain and, coupled with the neutrality of the Western powers in the Spanish Civil War, gave victory to Franco by default. The Comintern had failed once again.

By 1938, Stalin felt increasingly insecure in his temporary alliance with the West. He may even have suspected that the West aimed at encouraging Hitler to strike to the East to promote a death struggle between the Soviet Union and Germany. At any rate, the Western fiasco at Munich confirmed the Soviet leader in his suspicion that an alliance with Hitler, who had just absorbed Austria and was rapidly gaining strength, would yield greater advantages. Stalin calculated that a pact with Hitler would safeguard the Nazi dictator's Eastern flank and thus give him the green light to launch an offensive against the West. Since, in Stalin's view, Nazi Germany and the West were approximately equal in strength, a mutually exhausting war would ensue that would give the Soviet Union an opportunity to grow stronger in peace and ultimately to absorb both adversaries. Besides, Stalin reasoned, a pact with Hitler would buy time and since the Great Purges had seriously weakened the

Soviet military machine, time was most necessary. Moreover, the Soviet Union would at last be able to make some territorial gains: part of Poland and the three Baltic states of Latvia, Lithuania, and Estonia. Thus, in 1939, a strange alliance took shape between two incompatible dictators, and Marxism-Leninism was sacrificed on the altar of Machiavelli. As it turned out, Stalin's hopes were premised on a great miscalculation: it took Hitler not years but weeks to conquer most of Western Europe. By 1940, therefore, Stalin was dismayed to see himself confronted with a Nazi colossus preparing to break an alliance that had outlived its usefulness. Moreover, the ill-fated pact with Hitler had cost the Comintern many loyal followers who had been unable to accept the new dictum that the Nazis were to be the allies of the Soviet Union.

On June 22, 1941, Nazi troops crossed the Soviet border. Hitler vowed to dictate peace terms from the Kremlin within six weeks. As the Nazi forces advanced deep into Soviet territory, Soviet foreign policy became one desperate cry to the Western powers for help. The Allies responded with lend-lease supplies in late 1941, but refused to open an immediate second front in Europe. As a condition for further help, they insisted on the dissolution of the Comintern, since they thought it illogical to buoy up a government whose policy it was to subvert them. Accordingly, in 1943, the Comintern was dissolved.

Perhaps the greatest paradox of this phase of the East-West struggle is the fact that the Comintern was most successful at a time when the Soviet Union had reached its lowest ebb. The Communists, who had been suspect in the United Fronts of the 1920's and 1930's, were now welcomed. Their ruthless methods, which were formerly so feared, now proved a valuable asset in the common resistance against the Nazis. Communist Party membership swelled again all over Western Europe. As the Red Army pursued the retreating *Wehrmacht* after the victory at Stalingrad, plans were laid for the absorption of liberated territories into the Soviet orbit. During the last two years of the war, preparations were worked out for the absorption of eight Eastern European countries. In carrying out this objective, the Soviet Union generally operated in three stages: first, a genuine anti-Nazi resistance coalition was to be formed with existing socialist and peasant parties; second, the Communist Party would attempt to split the opposition parties by exploiting regional and ethnic jealousies, thereby transforming the coalition into a bogus alliance controlled by the Communist Party; and finally, a *coup d'état* would establish complete Soviet control.

While the Soviet Union was thus preparing to take over most of Eastern Europe, American and Russian armies met in the heart of Europe, near the German town of Torgau, in April 1945. This event was the prelude to the division of Germany and most of Europe into American and Russian spheres of influence. Soon after, the first open misunderstanding arose and the "cold war" began to take shape. While the West had lowered its guard, the Soviet Union established control over seven Eastern European countries whose absorption had been prepared during the last years of the war: Albania, Bulgaria, Hungary, Poland, East Germany, Yugoslavia, and Rumania. In March 1946, Winston Churchill visited the United States and delivered his famous "Iron Curtain" speech in which he warned the West of Soviet intentions. During the following year, the United States took two specific steps to counter the Soviet challenge. In March 1947, through the Truman Doctrine, the United States took over from Britain the responsibility of protecting Greece and Turkey from Communism. In June 1947 General George Marshall proposed the outline of a vast European Recovery Program at a commencement address at Harvard University. The aim of the Marshall Plan was the ultimate restoration of the economies of Europe through American aid. This aid was also offered to Eastern Europe and the Soviet Union, but Stalin refused to accept it. Relations between the Soviet Union and the United States now deteriorated rapidly. The four-power negotiations over a German peace settlement bogged down and a tougher American policy was adumbrated by George Kennan writing under the pseudonym "Mr. X" in the journal *Foreign Affairs*. Indeed, this policy of "containment" was soon to become the official American posture. In February 1948 the Soviet Union electrified the West by absorbing the eighth Eastern European country, Czechoslovakia, into the Communist orbit. In this case, all three Soviet techniques of subversion described above were employed successfully.

In the United States and Western Europe, the Communist coup in Czechoslovakia came as a most painful shock. Under its two great leaders Thomas G. Masaryk and Eduard Beneš, Czechoslovakia had during the 1920's and 1930's become the only really well-established and sophisticated democracy in Eastern Europe. Moreover, the country had been woven into the Western political community through defense alliances with Britain and France and had received a guarantee from the Soviet Union for help against the Nazi threat provided that Britain and France would fill their obligations. From the Czechoslovak point of view, however, the Munich Conference of 1938, resulting in the subsequent absorption of the country by Nazi Germany, signified a complete betrayal by the Western powers of their treaty obligations. This "Munich hangover" played an important role in the Soviet success. The eastward orientation of Czechoslovakia was given further impetus by the fact that the Red Army was permitted to liberate most of Czechoslovakia, including the capital, Prague, in 1945. Communist Party membership at the conclusion of World War II was substantial. The Party was instructed to exploit the regional jealousies between the Bohemians and the Slovaks. Capitalizing on its anti-Nazi record, the Communist Party now claimed control of the Ministry of the Interior.

By 1947 the vote for the Communist Party exceeded 40 per cent of the population and the Red Army surrounded four-fifths of the Republic. At this juncture, the United States offered economic aid to Czechoslovakia under the Marshall Plan, which President Beneš was eager to accept. Stalin informed the Czechoslovak government that he would take a grave view of Czech acceptance of American aid. When, after an agonizing debate, the Czechoslovak government decided to decline the American offer, the Soviet Union knew that the Czech ship of state was foundering and was no longer an independent entity. In February 1948 Soviet Deputy Foreign Minister Valerian Zorin arrived in Prague, ostensibly to supervise the delivery of Soviet wheat. During the next few days the Communists completed the take-over through a *coup d'état*.

The success of the Communist coup in Czechoslovakia galvanized the West into action. Twelve nations, under the leadership of the United States, formed the North Atlantic Treaty Organization (NATO), a regional defense alliance for the purpose of containing Soviet expansion. For the United States, membership in a peacetime alliance was a drastic reversal of foreign policy. The fear of the Soviet Union and her newly acquired allies now dominated political thinking in all of the Western nations. The fact that the Comintern was reconstituted by 1947 in Warsaw—although under the innocuous-sounding title of Communist Information Bureau, or Cominform—was widely interpreted in the West as a sign pointing to renewed Soviet emphasis on the goal of world revolution. The West now determined to stand fast.

The showdown came in Germany. In Berlin, the former capital, the cold war reached a point of rigidification. It will be remembered that, in 1945, Germany had been occupied by the four major victorious powers, the United States, Britain, France, and the Soviet Union. The Yalta and Potsdam Agreements of 1945 had divided Germany into four zones, three Western and one Soviet. Berlin, the former capital, was situated in the Soviet zone but was itself divided into four sectors. Under the Agreements, none of the Occupation Powers was to have the right to change the status quo without the consent of the others. In 1948, however, shortly after the absorption of Czechoslovakia, Stalin began to put pressure on the Western garrisons in Berlin. The Soviet administration suspended all communications between West Berlin and the Western zones of Germany. The object of this blockade was to turn West Berlin into an island and to starve it into submission. The American response was the famous Berlin Air Lift, which effectively countered the Soviet move by supplying the population of West Berlin from the air. In May 1949 the blockade was lifted.

By this time, the division of Germany as a whole had begun to be accepted as a long-time condition. Both superpowers attempted to absorb their zones of occupation into their respective orbits. The three Western zones emerged as the Federal Republic of Germany, with its capital at Bonn, and the Eastern zone was turned into a Soviet dependency. The vast majority of the German people, however, desired the reunification of their country.

The Western condition of German reunification was, in essence, a free election to be held in all of Germany. This was unacceptable to the Soviet Union because both East Berlin and West Berlin would probably opt for the West and thus remove the city from Soviet influence. Moreover, the population of all of Germany would probably prefer the West. Such a development would bring Germany within the Western orbit and extend Western influence to the Czech and Polish borders, thereby threatening Soviet control in Eastern Europe. The Soviet demand in return for granting German reunification was the neutralization of Germany and Western withdrawal from Berlin. These conditions seemed unacceptable to most Western statesmen. It was felt that the East German Communist government would then be in a position to absorb West Berlin through a process of strangulation. Moreover, the United States alleged that German neutrality would play into the hands of the Soviet Union, since American troops would withdraw across the Atlantic while the Red Army could be based in Eastern Europe and thus return at any moment to fill the power vacuum. Perhaps most important, the West feared that meeting the Soviet conditions would convince the Eastern European nations that they had been abandoned by the West and, hence, cause them to settle in the Soviet orbit for good.

The deadlock over Germany ended the first phase of the East-West struggle, which till then had still been characterized by large areas of maneuverability. It ushered in a period of increasing rigidity, in which each superpower stipulated conditions that were unacceptable to the other. This sort of relationship—mutually exclusive positions short of actual physical conflict—was to characterize the East-West struggle from then on.

At the very time that the Soviet Union encountered stiffened Western resistance in Berlin, the Soviet orbit also began to undergo internal changes with great significance for the East-West struggle. Indeed, the Czech coup was the last major Communist action in which Moscow was the absolute master of Communism. For thirty years, Moscow's orders had been executed without question by Communist parties everywhere. This relationship was now subjected to profound changes. In 1948, for the first time in Communist history, another Communist Party defied Moscow's authority: the Yugoslav Party under the leadership of Tito. Tito had always been a loyal Communist; he and his fellow partisans had distinguished themselves in guerrilla warfare against the Nazis, whom they had fought bravely and relentlessly. Stalin, however, let it be known that the Soviet Army had driven the Germans from Yugoslavia while the partisans had just engaged in mopping-up operations. Though Tito took a dim view of this version of events in Yugoslavia, the episode no doubt would have passed without major repercussions if Stalin had permitted the fulfillment of Tito's fond dream of organizing a Balkan Federation. It was Tito's desire to form an empire within an empire, with Yugoslavia exercising its rule over Albania and Bulgaria. Stalin not only scotched this ambition but proceeded to rebuke Tito for the slow advance toward collectivization in Yugoslavia. When Tito defended himself by pointing out the difficult conditions he had to face in coping with the local peasantry, Stalin threatened to send to Yugoslavia Soviet Communist inspectors who were to be paid out of Yugoslav funds. Tito interpreted this as an attack upon his control of the Yugoslav Communist Party and refused to follow orders. Stalin thereupon expelled Tito from the Cominform.[6] By this act of excommunication Stalin fully expected to end Tito's political revolt—and probably his life as well. But there was to be no walk to Canossa. Instead, the West immediately offered assistance to Tito's government and Stalin decided not to crush the defector by force. Tito, though continuing to identify himself as a Communist, thenceforth refused to submit to Cominform authority. He remained suspended precariously between East and West.

Later during the same year, the Chinese Communist Party came to power on the mainland of China. As we shall see in Chapter 5, this Party had been ruggedly independent of Moscow's control from its very beginnings. With its formula for the organization of Communism on a peasant, rather than an urban, industrial basis, it had come to power to the surprise of both the West and the Soviet Union. Though describing himself as a Communist, Mao Tse-tung, the political leader of the new China had, in effect, developed an ideology sharply at variance with the orthodox, Moscow-directed Communist creed. What this of course meant for Stalin was that shortly after the Yugoslav fiasco, he found himself confronted with a second and similar dilemma: should he insist on the ideological conformity of Mao Tse-tung and thereby risk the defection of China from the Communist orbit? Or should he recognize the ideological deviation of the Chinese leader and thereby encourage the development of Peking as an independent Communist power center? Stalin chose the latter course and in late 1949 the Soviet Union extended recognition to the new Communist government in China.

The Yugoslav defection and the developments in China ended Moscow's unquestioned authority within the Communist orbit. By 1949 there were three centers of Communism: Moscow, Belgrade, and Peking. In Communism's struggle against the West, this internal transformation signified both a strength and a weakness. It portended a greater threat to the West because increased ideological flexibility could be expected to inject new life into a credo threatened by petrification. On the other hand, after 1949 the Cominform was no longer able to count on the blind obedience of its membership, which had guaranteed it such swiftness of political action in the past.

In evaluating this first phase of the East-West struggle, we can come up with at least two interesting observations. The first concerns the striking number of blunders committed by the Comintern during the 1920's and 1930's. Indeed, it did not achieve its first successes until during and immediately after World War II. Nevertheless, the Western view of the Comintern during the inter-war decades for the most part remained that of an implacable foe, a kind of consummate chess master impervious to the mistakes of ordinary men. Many acts of the Comintern were seen in the West as carefully worked out and long-planned stratagems and many of its errors were interpreted as strategic retreats according to plan.

What were the reasons for this collective "inferiority complex" on the part of the West? In part, it no doubt stemmed from fear of the "built-in" expansionism of Communist ideology. But the Nazis were equally imperialistic and, moreover, were locked with the West in an all-out military conflict, which Communism never was. Yet the West was more afraid of Communist than of Nazi ideology. This may be attributable to the facts that Communism attacked private property and was a highly sophisticated ideology that offered something to almost everyone: an ultimate vision of humanitarianism and equality to the democrat; revolution to the revolutionary; a better life for the worker; and a sophisticated dialectic to the intellectual. Most important, it offered a coherent secular religion:

The dictator becomes God, the only God for that matter; and the Party becomes the church. As a variant, collective leadership becomes a sort of Trinity. The central committee and the local leaders take care of polytheistic needs. The parallels could be pressed further. The point is that all the essential mundane elements of religion except the Virgin Mother are represented.[7]

One group of students even went so far as to state that Communism by 1946 had become a "father image the like of which the world had never seen—harsh, revengeful, jealous, and unpredictable."[8] Something like this was implied by John Foster Dulles when he made the following statement in 1946:

Few men in political life anywhere act without first thinking whether they will please or displease the leaders of the Soviet Union. Never in history have a few men in a single country achieved such world-wide influence.[9]

Yet as we have seen, this "superman" image by no means squares with the record. The history of the Comintern until 1949 presents a mixture of failures and successes, of rational and irrational acts, and of much gross distortion of the facts of international life.

The second observation that deserves to be noted about this early phase of the East-West struggle concerns the difficulty of sorting out its "causes." The great importance of Communist ideology is clearly apparent; but it is equally clear that the "cold war" also grew out of the meeting between Russians and Americans in the heart of Europe at the close of World War II. Indeed, the entire pattern suggests the validity of Barrington Moore's point that it is futile to argue about the primal causes of the struggle since each move by one superpower elicited a countermove from the other. What is important is that the East-West struggle had rigidified in Europe by 1949. There was virtually no maneuverability left as power confronted concerted counter-power. Thus, it was no accident that the major arena of the East-West struggle during the next decade shifted away from Europe. And the rise of China as an independent power center in the Communist orbit helped move this arena to East Asia.

PHASE TWO: THE RISE OF CHINA

The most striking development in the context of the East-West struggle during the 1950's and early 1960's was the ascendancy of Communist China, both within the Communist orbit itself and in the power configuration vis-à-vis the West. While Western fears of Communist expansionism continued during the 1950's to concentrate mainly on the Soviet Union, the expansion that actually occurred took place not in Europe but in East Asia. Indeed, the Soviet Union was unable to absorb any territory during the 1950's while, during the same decade, the Chinese Communists fought in Korea, shared in the dismemberment of Indochina, and made expansionary moves into Tibet and India. Not only did the Soviet Union fail to score further advances in Europe during the 1950's, but it had to fight to retain control in Poland and Hungary, which had been absorbed in the 1940's. In August 1961 the erection of the Berlin Wall served notice of yet another Soviet failure: Moscow was forced to fence in its East German ally lest it emigrate out of existence. The sole Soviet territorial advance was the acquisition of a Communist foothold in the Caribbean—Cuba. But this gain was offset by the loss of face Moscow suffered when it was forced to withdraw its missile bases and offensive weapons from Cuba in 1962 and by simultaneous Chinese territorial gains in the Himalayas, Indeed, it seemed that, by the mid-1960's, the center of gravity of Communist expansion had shifted from Moscow to Peking. This transition in the East-West struggle deserves analysis.

Communist China's first participation in the East-West conflict took place in Korea. That peninsula had been partitioned at the thirty-eighth parallel shortly before the end of World War II as a result of the military disposition of Soviet and American forces. The Japanese were to surrender to American troops south of that parallel, to Soviet troops north of it. Since neither half of the country was economically viable and the partition was accepted very reluctantly by the Korean people, Korea's truncated state was seen as only a temporary *modus vivendi.* During the next two years the United States occupied South Korea, while North Korea was absorbed into the Soviet orbit. All attempts to agree on a formula for unification failed. In the fall of 1947 the United Nations took over the Korean problem and recommended free elections. But since United Nations observers were not permitted to visit North Korea, an election could be held in the southern half only. From this election there emerged the Republic of Korea as a sovereign state; the northern half retaliated by pronouncing itself a sovereign "Democratic People's Republic." During the next two years there occurred a great deal of military posturing on both sides of the parallel. Finally, on June 25, 1950, the North Korean Army attacked. The United Nations Security Council responded immediately by authorizing a "police action." During the summer of 1950 United Nations troops were in retreat, but in October they recrossed the thirty-eighth parallel, shortly thereafter capturing the Communist capital of Pyongyang and advancing toward the Manchurian border. At that point Communist China entered the conflict.

The United Nations action in Korea will be evaluated in another context in Chapter 12. What is important in the present connection is the impact of Communist China on the Korean War. It is not entirely clear why the Chinese Communists decided to intervene. Perhaps they were persuaded to do so by the Soviet Union. On the other hand, the decision may have been made quite independently and for reasons wholly their own. In the opinion of one scholar, there were two overriding reasons for the Chinese Communists' actions. One was their concern that an American-controlled Korea, along with the United States itself and a revived Japan, might develop into an alignment that could dominate all of Northeast Asia. The other was their fear that if they passively accepted an American victory in Korea, their enemies both within and outside China might be so strengthened as to imperil the Chinese Communist regime itself.[10] In any case, the entry of Communist China turned the hostilities in Korea into an entirely new war. The lines of battle seesawed for two more years, to come to a standstill approximately where they had been when the war began, with the indefinite partition of the country by the armistice agreement of 1953. North Korea thus became Communist China's first prize in the East-West struggle.

When, in 1954, the battle of Dienbienphu brought to an end the French Empire in Asia, four new entities emerged from the colony of Indochina: South Vietnam, Laos, Cambodia, and North Vietnam. As a result of the Geneva Conference of 1954, North Vietnam fell under the shadow of Chinese Communism while South Vietnam established a pro-American regime. The West, alerted to the new threat emanating from Communist China, formed the Southeast Asian Treaty Organization (SEATO), which bound together the United States, Britain, Australia, France, New Zealand, the Philippines, Thailand, and Pakistan in a military defense alliance. Yet the "Pekintern" continued its expansionary drive. In 1959 it suppressed a rebellion in Tibet, which it had "liberated" in 1950, and began moving into areas that it claimed along the Chinese-Indian border. Armed clashes between Chinese and Indian border forces occurred intermittently until the Chinese launched a major offensive in October 1962. The result of this invasion was a cease-fire giving China control over a large section of the disputed border area in Ladakh. Moreover, under SEATO's very nose, China continued its pressures on Laos and its infiltration into Cambodia.

Not only did Communist China fare better than its Soviet partner in the struggle against the West; it also made rapid strides during the 1950's on its internal Chinese home front. Most notably, Mao Tse-tung announced the "Great Leap Forward," a vast program of agricultural reform through which he planned to turn China's arable land into a series of gigantic communes far closer to the ideal of pure collectivization than their counterparts in the Soviet Union had ever been. While the Russian peasant on the typical Soviet collective farm continued to enjoy a small private plot of land—a residue of capitalism which neither Stalin nor Khrushchev had been able to eliminate—the Chinese commune aimed at the abolition of all private property. In the more advanced communes, even the bringing up of children was not left a private family matter but was put into the hands of party functionaries. Although the "Great Leap Forward" was thwarted by poor planning and repeated crop failures, these lapses did not seriously affect China's rising international power status.

As Communist China consolidated its independent position within the Communist orbit, it also began to develop an increasingly independent approach to the East-West struggle. During the late 1950's it became increasingly evident that China's attitude toward the West was more hostile than that of the Soviet Union and that the Chinese leadership showed fewer inhibitions about the use of violence than did its Soviet partners in the struggle. Indeed, Mao Tse-tung was reported to have pointed out that neither the Soviet Union nor the United States could afford an atomic war, whereas if China lost three hundred million people, there would still be over four hundred million left. By 1960 a major doctrinal divergence on the question on how best to bring the West to its knees had arisen between the two major Communist powers. Peking's apparent conviction that "capitalism" could only be defeated through war was at variance with Premier Khrushchev's doctrine of "peaceful coexistence," which postulated a Communist victory without the necessity of armed conflict. However, since both Moscow and Peking were aware of the fact that their continued unity was a crucial factor of strength in the East-West struggle, the Chinese nominally accepted Soviet ideological leadership. While the dialogue continued under the surface, the common dictates of the East-West struggle still kept it well within limits. As one scholar of Sino-Soviet relations astutely observed in 1960:

In the bargaining process between them [Russia and China], *unity* plays a role analogous to that of a hostage restraining both parties. In a situation involving the exchange of hostages, one may threaten the life of a hostage, but such threat can be effective only as long as the hostage is alive; once he is dead, the threat is meaningless. The same applies to unity. Since loss of unity is the worst eventuality for both, the weaker partner must limit his efforts at self-assertion, the stronger must limit or make oblique his countermoves.[11]

In the early 1960's the Sino-Soviet conflict entered a new and more violent phase. The doctrinal differences grew more intense as the two Communist colossi exchanged veiled insults, with the Chinese attacking "Yugoslav revisionism" and the Soviets retaliating with assaults on "Albanian adventurism." Chinese disenchantment with the Soviet leadership reached a new high when the latter withdrew its technicians from China, thus postponing temporarily China's entrance into the nuclear club. In 1962 two dramatic events brought the conflict into the open: the Cuban missile crisis and the Chinese attack on India. In the former, China attacked the Soviets for backing down before a paper tiger while Premier Khrushchev pointed out that the American tiger happened to be equipped with nuclear teeth. In the latter, the Soviet Union gave neither aid nor encouragement to the Chinese, but used its influence to bring about a rapid and peaceful settlement. The outcome of these two simultaneous crises again favored the Chinese: while Russia had to back down from one of the most serious East-West confrontations in a decade, China was achieving a major diplomatic and military victory.

By 1963 the doctrinal and "methodological" differences between the two major Communist nations began more and more to take on the coloration of a major power conflict between two great national states. Ideology began to decrease in importance as competitive nationalism began to increase. Serious border disputes broke out along the Sino-Soviet frontier over contested territory in Sinkiang and Mongolia. Communist parties throughout the world were deeply split over the issues raised by the dispute. China no longer recognized the ideological leadership of the Soviet Union and accused Khrushchev of plotting with Washington for Russo-American world domination. In 1964, two dramatic events occurred in quick succession. Premier Khrushchev was ousted by the Soviet Presidium as a "hare-brained schemer" and the Chinese exploded their first atomic device. Thus, while yet another succession crisis shook the Soviet government, China had crashed the gates of the exclusive nuclear club.

By the mid-1960's, moreover, it was clear that some of the expansionary drive of Communism had definitely shifted from Moscow to Peking. During the 1950's and early 1960's all the territorial gains for Communism, with the exception of Cuba, were made by China. This is not to say, of course, that the Soviet Union's intention to expand had disappeared or even diminished. But it met far more effective Western resistance from NATO than Communist China did from SEATO. Certainly this was true until the United States became deeply involved in the Vietnamese war. Indeed, while China made its gains against the West, the Soviet leadership had to expend its energies in maintaining control over what it had gained earlier. Moreover, Stalin's death in March 1953, marking the end of a heavy-handed personal dictatorship that had lasted since the late 1920's, triggered a rumble of discontent among the Eastern European nations. The promulgation by the United States government in 1953 of a "policy of liberation" toward Eastern Europe had already caused some ferment in those nations. When Khrushchev publicly denounced Stalin in February 1956, he opened a Pandora's box of revolts. Within the year, Poland, under the leadership of Wladislaw Gomulka, attempted to emulate the Yugoslav move for independence. The Poles demanded the removal of the Soviet secret police and military rule, tolerance for the Catholic Church, and the freedom to "travel their own road to socialism." Almost at the same time, Hungary revolted against Soviet control. The first stage of the Hungarian Revolution was patterned after the Polish precedent. But then the revolutionaries were no longer content with ideological deviation within the Cominform, but wanted to escape from Communism altogether. At this point, the Soviet Union moved in with military force and crushed the revolt. The West found itself unable to intervene because of fear of a general war. "Liberation" proved unworkable and the West had to be content with the "containment" of the Soviet Union. Nevertheless, in most Western countries the spectacle of the Hungarian freedom fighters shattered whatever still remained of the old "chessmaster concept" of the Soviet Union.

The instability of the East German regime was indicated in another manner. East Germans were voting against Soviet domination with their feet, emigrating at the rate of about 200,000 a year to West Germany via that gaping hole in the Iron Curtain, Berlin. By early 1961 the number of refugees amounted to one quarter of the total population of East Germany at that time. The danger which this loss of skilled workers and professionals represented to the East German economy was matched only by the grave political implications of the exodus. In order to retain East Germany as a dependency, Moscow was forced to turn it into a walled jail. The Berlin Wall, closing off the last gap in the Iron Curtain, was erected in August 1961.

The greatest crisis within the Soviet bloc during the 1960's, however, took place in Czechoslovakia in 1968. These events were of sufficient importance to merit detailed consideration.

For almost two decades Czechoslovakia had been an apparently tranquil nation in the Soviet orbit. Toward the end of 1967, however, many intellectuals in Czechoslovakia began to criticize the lack of literary freedom, and President Antonín Novotný, a Stalinist, found it increasingly difficult to maintain his leadership. In January 1968, Alexander Dubček, a reform-minded liberal, was appointed as First Secretary of the Communist Party of Czechoslovakia. Two months later, Novotný was forced to resign and a highly respected elderly military leader, General Ludvík Svoboda, was named to succeed him to the presidency. During the spring of 1968, the Dubček regime decided on a dramatic move: it lifted censorship of the press. As a result, on April 16, 1968, *Rudé Právo*, the Czechoslovak Communist Party organ, suggested for the first time that Soviet agents might have been responsible for the death of Jan Masaryk, Czechoslovak Foreign Minister, who either jumped or was pushed through a window in March 1948. This initiative triggered the first Soviet suspicions about developments in Czechoslovakia. In April 1968, the Dubček leadership issued a manifesto promising fuller civil rights to the Czech people, but, in order to reassure the Soviet Union, reiterated on numerous occasions that Czechoslovakia would remain Communist and a faithful member of the Warsaw Pact.

In May 1968, the Communist Party leaders of the Soviet Union, East Germany, Poland, Bulgaria, and Hungary—stung by ever more critical articles in the Czechoslovak press—began talks in Moscow about the Dubček liberalization program. Rumania stayed aloof from this conference. On May 17, Soviet Premier Aleksei Kosygin arrived in Prague for a "continuing exchange of views" as a result of which the Prague regime agreed to Warsaw Pact military maneuvers on Czechoslovak soil. Later that month, a manifesto called "Two Thousand Words" was issued by seventy Czechoslovak intellectuals. This manifesto called for, *inter alia,* the establishment of multiple poltical parties and proposed that Stalinists be purged from the Czechoslovak Communist Party. Although the Dubček leadership strongly objected to this manifesto, it was seen in the Soviet Union as a confirmation of Soviet fears that Dubček would not be able to control events and that anti-Communists were gaining ground in Czechoslovakia.

In June, Warsaw Pact maneuvers took place in Czechoslovakia and on July 9, the Dubček regime rejected a demand from the Soviet Union and its four Warsaw Pact allies for a summit meeting in Warsaw. On July 14, this summit meeting took place without the Czechoslovaks and the result was a stinging letter demanding an end to the liberalization program. On July 18, the Dubček regime rejected this rebuke and declared its intention to continue the reforms. At the end of July, on Soviet initiative, a dramatic meeting took place between virtually the entire ruling bodies of the Soviet Union and Czechoslovakia in the small Czechoslovak border town of Cierna. The Soviet leaders appeared to yield after three days of talks and on August 3, at Bratislava, Czechoslovakia, the five Warsaw Pact members and Czechoslovakia signed a "unity document" that seemed to ratify the accord reached at Cierna. Shortly thereafter, Soviet troops that had lingered in Czechoslovakia after the June maneuvers, left the country. It seemed that Czechoslovakia was the victor in its confrontation with the Soviet Union and its four allies.

Following the conclusion of the Bratislava conference, Czechoslovakia was host to three Communist leaders. On August 9, President Tito, who had supported the Dubček leadership all along, visited Prague. Two days later, however, East German Party leader Walter Ulbricht, a mainstay of Communist orthodoxy, arrived in the Czechoslovak capital and received a very cool reception. On August 15, Rumanian President Nicolai Ceausescu arrived in Prague to dramatize his regime's support for Dubček. On the following day, the Soviet press resumed its attacks on Czechoslovakia, charging that "anti-socialist forces" were stirring dangerously in the country.

During the night of August 20, the blow fell. Troops from the Soviet Union, East Germany, Bulgaria, Hungary, and Poland, crossed the Czechoslovak border in a surprise move and proceeded to occupy the country. The decision which seemed to have been the result of many months of disagreement within the Soviet leadership came as a profound shock to most of the world and virtually split the Communist movement down the middle. Rumania and Yugoslavia as well as China opposed the Soviet move, as did most of the Communist parties in Western Europe. The Czechoslovak population offered resistance through strikes, non-cooperation, and, in places, violence. The leading members of the Dubček regime, including the First Secretary himself, were arrested, but the Soviets were not able to assemble a regime of Czechoslovaks that was more to their liking. Instead, while the Czechoslovak Foreign Minister placed the case of his nation before the United Nations Security Council, representatives of the liberal Czechoslovak regime continued to meet clandestinely in Prague, virtually under the guns of the occupying powers. Three days after the invasion, the Soviet Union realized that it had to negotiate with the Czechoslovak leaders after all. Yet another confrontation now took place, this time in Moscow. The Soviet leadership and its four Warsaw Pact allies again faced the Czechoslovaks, including the aged President Svoboda and First Party Secretary Dubček himself. This time, the agreement that emerged was a compromise heavily weighted in favor of the Soviet Union. The five occupying powers insisted that their troops would remain in Czechoslovakia until the situation was "normalized," that is until, in their eyes, the threat of "counter-revolution" had disappeared. In the view of most Western observers, the Moscow agreement bordered on capitulation. Thus, the Soviet Union managed to reimpose a degree of orthodoxy on Czechoslovakia, but the price that it paid was a further fragmentation within the international Communist movement.

In the light of these events, the East-West struggle could by now no longer be considered exclusively, or perhaps even primarily, in terms of the Soviet Union and the United States. Competition *within* the two camps had become almost as important as competition *between* them. The homogeneity of the Western alliance was seriously challenged by the nationalist policies of President de Gaulle in Western Europe. In the East, China's bid for ideological leadership of the Communist camp had begun to assume the proportions of a major national power rivalry with the Soviet Union. In fact, Moscow's control was now threatened from both Left and Right. China and her Eastern European ally Albania took every opportunity to attack Soviet "revisionism" for its alleged collusion with American "capitalism." On the other side of the Communist spectrum, Yugoslavia had been free of Moscow's control since Tito's expulsion from the Cominform in 1949 and Rumania, by the late 1960's, had carved out for itself a relatively independent role in the Communist bloc including an independent foreign policy.

Thus, by the late 1960's, the bipolar system had begun to loosen even though spheres of influence continued to exist. Some observers noted a similarity in the behavior of the superpowers in their respective spheres of influence. Thus, each superpower still risked intervention by force of arms when faced with the possible loss of a nation that it considered vital to its national interests. The United States took this course in the Dominican Republic and in Vietnam, and the Soviet Union resorted to it in Hungary and Czechoslovakia. There were, however, significant differences in degree between American and Soviet patterns of intervention. While some of the policies of the Dubček regime no doubt seemed provocative to the Soviet Union, Czechoslovakia never threatened to leave the Warsaw Pact. President de Gaulle of France, on the other hand, not only frequently provoked the United States, but came close to pulling France out of the Atlantic Alliance. Yet, no American statesman seriously contemplated an invasion of France. Be that as it may, the world of the late 1960's still seemed divided into fairly well-defined superpower spheres of influence with some gray areas in between which, while remaining objects of competition, were not considered crucial.

Even after the Czechoslovak crisis, United States-Soviet relations continued to exhibit elements of both conflict and cooperation. As the

1960's drew to a close, the Soviet Union and the United States had concluded an agreement to ban the use of outer space for military purposes and had jointly proposed a treaty to halt the further spread of nuclear weapons. In addition, despite conflicting policies in Vietnam and in the Middle East, the two superpowers managed to open talks on limiting their respective missile systems, ratified a long-delayed consular agreement, and arranged for direct New York-Moscow air connections.

There were thus some hopeful signs that the United States-Soviet relationship had moved beyond the cold war into a phase of uneasy coexistence. At least it was possible to gain some perspective on those bleak two decades following World War II. In retrospect, it was impossible to see the cold war simply as a case of Soviet aggression and American response or of American aggression and Soviet response. Only the tragic elements in the developing cold war spiral were clear. But the question remains, as Arthur Schlesinger, Jr., has put it, whether the cold war was an example of Greek tragedy, " the tragedy of necessity," where the feeling aroused in the spectator is "what a pity it had to be this way"—or of Chistian tragedy, "the tragedy of possibility," where the feeling aroused is "what a pity it was this way when it might have been otherwise."[12] Perhaps the cold war could have been avoided if Stalin had not been so convinced of the imminent decline of the West and of the inevitability of a Communist victory, and if the United States had not in turn succumbed to its own forms of dogmatism and self-righteousness. In that sense, perhaps, a tragedy of possibility was transformed into one of necessity.

Chinese Communist fortunes began to suffer some significant reversals during this period. In October 1965, the Chinese-controlled Communist Party of Indonesia was purged in a bloody coup. And when President Nkrumah of Ghana was ousted a year later, the Chinese were virtually expelled from that African country.

In 1966, the beginnings of a furious internal struggle further weakened China's role on the world scene. Under the leadership of Mao Tsetung, a "Great Cultural Revolution" was launched which shook China's political structure to its very foundations. Mao, anxious that China might follow the "revisionist" example of the Soviet Union, made a concerted effort to reinfuse China's masses with the revolutionary fervor of the old Yenan days. Toward this end, hundreds of thousands of young Red Guards, who were to spread Mao's slogans across the land, were mobilized. But these efforts encountered stiff opposition by more pragmatic elements in both party and army who were more interested in consolidating the gains China had made since the ascendancy of the Communist regime than in risking these in a war with the West. The ensuing struggle for power between Mao and his opponents was somewhat reminiscent of the struggle between "Reds" and "experts" that had characterized the Soviet Union in the 1920's.

Thus, by the late 1960's, both internal and international developments had brought setbacks to China. In addition, her relations with the Soviet Union had deteriorated to such an extent that she found herself embattled in a two-front cold war with both superpowers at the same time. The stage was now set for a fundamental change in the nature of the East-West struggle.

PHASE THREE: FROM BIPOLARITY TO TRIANGLE

On July 15, 1971, President Richard M. Nixon made a dramatic announcement: China's Premier Chou En-lai had invited him to visit the People's Republic of China, and he had accepted the invitation. This terse announcement reversed almost a quarter century of the United States' China policy and provided the catalyst for major changes in the constellation of the East-West struggle.

The Soviet Union reacted to this event with considerable ambivalence. While its leaders ostensibly welcomed the imminent improvement in Sino-American relations, they were nevertheless fearful theat the new détente between China and the United States was aimed at them. Thus, they promptly invited President Nixon to visit Moscow as well and, in an effort to woo the United States and protect their flanks, became more flexible in their own negotiations with the Americans, particularly in relation to Germany and the limitation of strategic arms.

On October 25, 1971, another dramatic event took place. The People's Republic of China, excluded for over twenty years from the United Nations, was finally admitted to the world organization. The shape of things to come became manifest during China's first participation in a debate of the UN Security Council. The occasion was the Indo-Pakistan war. The Chinese delegate, Huang Hwa, spoke to the Soviet delegate, Jacob Malik, in almost the same vitriolic manner in which Mr. Malik had addressed the United States delegate twenty years earlier. In the United Nations, as well as outside of it, bipolarity had given way to triangular politics.

Machiavelli would have taken considerable pleasure in the dynamics of the Sino-Soviet-American triangle. During the 1950's, China and the Soviet Union were allies, and the United States feared the menace of a monolithic Sino-Soviet threat. In the 1960's, after the Cuban missile crisis had ushered in a détente between the Soviet Union and the United States, China began to fear the specter. of Soviet-American collusion. And in the 1970's, the Soviet leaders began to worry that the Chinese and Americans might be getting along too well. Each of the three powers had had its turn at being frozen out by the other two.

The three relationships in the triangle exhibited differing degrees of stability and instability in the 1970's. The Soviet-American relationship continued to be marked by both conflict and cooperation. The possibility of a major war between the two superpowers had become quite remote, even though serious strategic struggles continued to exist, particularly in the Middle East and on the Indian subcontinent. Significant progress was being made toward the relaxation of tensions in Europe, helped along by West German Chancellor Willy Brandt's policy of *Ostpolitik*. Soviet and American leaders had also begun to decontaminate their respective vocabularies somewhat of cold war clichés and shopworn slogans and had begun to settle down to the difficult task of negotiating outstanding differences in a serious and businesslike manner. The Moscow Summit of 1972 marked the occasion of the first arms-control agreement between the two superpowers since the end of World War II.

The Chinese-American relationship had clearly improved. After risking a major confrontation at the height of the Vietnamese war, the two countries moved gradually toward rapprochement in the wake of the Nixon visit in early 1972. Contacts at many levels short of formal diplomatic recognition were established and possibilities of trade and exchange programs were explored. For the first time in almost a quarter of a century, face-to-face contacts between the peoples of China and America became possible again. A relationship that had been based for an entire generation on fictions, anxieties, and fears once again showed signs of returning to a sense of reality. Needless to say, beasts did not turn into beauties overnight and stubborn objective differences, such as the disposition of Taiwan, remained. However, the leaders of the two nations at last began to fashion their policies less on fears and more on facts.

The Sino-Soviet relationship continued to show signs of great instability. Territorial problems and boundary disputes further deepened the conflict. The Chinese felt that the Soviet Union was the last remaining Western power which continued to occupy large areas of territory claimed by China. The fact that both China and the Soviet Union considered themselves communist nations no longer provided a unifying bond. Rather, it separated them further because each maintained that it was the only legitimate torchbearer of Marxism-Leninism. And lastly, personality factors entered the picture: Mao Tse-tung and Chou En-lai, both veterans of the Long March of 1934, recalled that, during their long struggle for power, instead of supporting them, the Soviet government had carried on diplomatic relations with the Chiang Kai-shek regime to the bitter end in 1949. In short, the Soviets had placed Machiavelli above Mao Tse-tung.

The triangle of the 1970's, amazingly enough, exhibited a striking resemblance to the balance-of-power system practiced in 1815, at the time of the Congress of Vienna. In both cases, great power politics dominated the scene: Austria, Prussia, England, Russia, and France in the early nineteenth century; the United States, the Soviet Union, China, and to a lesser degree, Japan and a gradually unifying Western Europe, in the late twentieth. Each contestant attempted to become the holder of the balance: Britain managed to do so quite successfully at the time of the Concert of Europe and the United States tried to emulate her example in the 1970's by establishing symmetrical relations with both Russia and China, thus being "wooed" by both Communist nations, in short by being the "lady" in the triangle. What remained to be seen was whether the world of Metternich and Castlereagh, with its relatively stable world order, could be transplanted into the late twentieth century, whether peace could be secured by seeking a formula for achieving equilibrium among the world's greatest powers.

As the twentieth century entered its eighth decade, the nature of the East-West struggle had changed almost kaleidoscopically. Old enemies had begun to smile at one another across the great divide and old alliances had begun to loosen. While such events are always a shock to contemporary observers, it is important to maintain a sense of historical perspective. Political friendships never last forever, and enemies may suddenly become friends. A striking comparison between the Chinese-American rapprochement of 1972 and the Anglo-French "Entente Cordiale" of 1904 may serve to make the point. Both sets of powers had a recent history of intense mutual hostility. Prior to Lord Cambon's mission to London and Nixon's trip to Peking, both France and Britain and the United States and China had envisaged each other as bitter enemies. The impetus for détente in both cases was provided by the mutual antagonism of a third country: Germany in the former case and the Soviet Union in the latter. In both cases, the power initiating the détente had recently suffered a severe military and diplomatic setback. The Fashoda crisis of 1898 had been a profound blow to French prestige. French soldiers had faced British soldiers in the Sudan and, with the full knowledge of all of Europe, had been forced to back down. The Vietnam catastrophe had had similarly destructive effects on the moral and political fiber of the United States. Finally, Germany concluded that the Anglo-French Entente was anti-German in its intent just like the Soviet leaders, despite American assurances, continued to believe that the Chinese-American détente was inspired by anti-Soviet considerations. The international struggle for power thus remains constant, but its specific manifestations are ever changing. The East-West struggle is no exception.

In addition to the metamorphoses in the East-West struggle just described, the rise of numerous new nations in Asia and Africa has further transformed the international power constellation. It is no longer meaningful to analyze the East-West struggle *in vacuo*. To perceive its place in the overall perspective of the international struggle for power, it is necessary to analyze the second great political struggle of our time: that between North and South—between Western colonialism and the new nationalism of Asia, the Middle East, and Africa.

REFERENCES

1. Barrington Moore, Jr., *Soviet Politics—The Dilemma of Power.* Cambridge, Mass.: Harvard University Press, 1950, p. 392.
2. *Ibid.*
3. John Lukacs, *A History of the Cold War.* New York: Doubleday, 1961, pp. 18–19.
4. Moore, *op. cit.,* p. 392.
5. Merle Fainsod, *How Russia Is Ruled.* Cambridge, Mass.: Harvard University Press, 1953, p. 285.
6. For a perceptive analysis of the Soviet-Yugoslav dispute, see Adam B. Ulam, *Titoism and the Cominform.* Cambridge, Mass.: Harvard University Press, 1952.
7. Robert Strausz-Hupé *et al., Protracted Conflict.* New York: Harper, 1959, p. 188.
8. *Ibid.*
9. John Foster Dulles, "Thoughts on Soviet Foreign Policy," *Life,* June 3, 1946, p. 124.
10. Allen S. Whiting, *China Crosses the Yalu: The Decision to Enter the Korean War.* New York: Macmillan, 1960, *passim.*
11. Zbigniew K. Brzezinski, "Pattern and Limits of the Sino-Soviet Dispute," *The New Leader,* September 19, 1960, p. 5.
12. Arthur Schlesinger, Jr. "Origins of the Cold War," *Foreign Affairs,* October 1967, p. 52.

BIBLIOGRAPHY

Acheson, Dean. *Power and Diplomacy.* Cambridge, Mass.: Harvard University Press 1958.

Almond, Gabriel A. *The Appeals of Communism.* Princeton, N.J.: Princeton University Press, 1954.

Armstrong, Hamilton F. *Tito and Goliath.* New York: Macmillan, 1951.

Ball, George. *The Discipline of Power: Essentials of a Modern World Structure.* Boston: Atlantic-Little, Brown, 1968.

Ball, William M. *Nationalism and Communism in East Asia,* 2d ed. Melbourne, Australia: Melbourne University Press, 1956.

Barghoorn, Frederick C. *The Soviet Cultural Offensive.* Princeton, N.J.: Princeton University Press, 1960.

———. *The Soviet Image of the United States.* New York: Harcourt, Brace, 1950.

Barnett, A. Doak. *Communist China and Asia, Challenge to American Foreign Policy.* New York: Harper, 1960.

———, ed. *Communist Strategies in Asia.* New York: Praeger, 1963.

Bass, Robert H., ed. *The Soviet-Yugoslav Controversy, 1948-1958: A Documentary Record.* London: Prospect Books, 1959.

Bergson, Abram, ed. *Soviet Economic Growth: Conditions and Perspectives.* Chicago: Row, Peterson, 1953.

Berle, Adolf A., Jr. *Tides of Crisis, A Primer of Foreign Relations.* New York: Reynal, 1957.

Blum, Robert. *The United States and China in World Affairs.* New York: McGraw-Hill, 1966.

Brzezinski, Zbigniew K. *The Soviet Bloc: Unity and Conflict,* rev. ed. Cambridge, Mass.: Harvard University Press, 1967.

———, and Huntington, Samuel P. *Poltical Power: U.S.A.–U.S.S.R.* New York: Viking Press, 1964.

Campbell, John C. *Tito's Separate Road.* New York: Harper and Row, 1967.

Cantril, Hadley, ed. *Tensions That Cause War.* Urbana, Ill.: University of Illinois Press, 1950.

Clubb, O. Edmund. *China and Russia: The "Great Game."* New York: Columbia University Press, 1971.

Cohen, Benjamin C. *The Political Process and Foreign Policy, The Making of the Japanese Peace Settlement.* Princeton, N.J.: Princeton University Press, 1957.

Dallin, Alexander, compiler. *Soviet Conduct in World Affairs.* New York: Columbia University Press, 1960.

Dallin, David J. *Soviet Foreign Policy After Stalin.* Philadelphia: Lippincott, 1961.

Davidson, Walter P. *The Berlin Blockade.* Princeton, N.J.: Princeton University Press, 1958.

Deutscher, Isaac. *The Great Contest: Russia and the West.* New York: Oxford University Press, 1960.

Dinerstein, Herbert S. *War and the Soviet Union.* New York: Praeger, 1959.

Feis, Herbert. *Between War and Peace: The Potsdam Conference.* Princeton, N.J.: Princeton University Press, 1960.

———. *The China Tangle.* Princeton, N.J.: Princeton University Press, 1953.

———. *Churchill, Roosevelt, Stalin.* Princeton, N.J.: Princeton University Press, 1957.

———. *From Trust to Terror: The Onset of the Cold War.* New York: Norton, 1970.

Fontaine, André. *History of the Cold War: From the Korean War To the Present.* New York: Pantheon, 1969.

Franck, Thomas M., and Weisband, Edward. *World Politics: Verbal Strategy Among the Superpowers.* New York: Oxford University Press, 1971.

Halle, Louis J. *The Cold War as History.* New York: Harper and Row, 1967.

Halpern, A. M., ed. *Politics toward China: Views from Six Continents.* New York: McGraw-Hill, 1965.

Harriman, W. Averell. *America and Russia in A Changing World: A Half Century of Personal Observation.* Garden City: Doubleday, 1971.

Hinton, Harold C. *Communist China in World Poltics.* Boston: Houghton Miffin, 1966.

Hoffmann, Stanley. *Gulliver's Troubles, Or the Setting of American Foreign Policy.* New York: McGraw-Hill, 1968.

Howard, Michael. *Disengagement in Europe.* Baltimore: Penguin, 1958.

Ionescu, Ghita. *Communism in Rumania, 1944-1962.* New York: Oxford University Press, 1964.

Kennan, George F. *American Diplomacy, 1900–1950.* Chicago: University of Chicago Press, 1953.

——. *Russia, the Atom, and the West.* Princeton, N.J.: Princeton University Press, 1957.

——. *Soviet Foreign Policy, 1917–1941. Princeton, N.J.: Van Nostrand, 1960.*

——. *Russia and the West under Lenin and Stalin.* Boston: Atlantic-Little, Brown, 1960.

——. *Memoirs: 1925–1950.* Boston: Atlantic-Little, Brown, 1967.

——. *Memoirs: 1950–1963.* Boston: Atlantic-Little, Brown, 1972.

Kertesz, Stephen D., and Fitzsimons, M. A., eds. *Diplomacy in a Changing World.* South Bend., Ind.: University of Notre Dame Press, 1959.

——, eds. *The Fate of East Central Europe: Hopes and Failures of American Foreign Policy.* South Bend, Ind.: University of Notre Dame Press, 1956.

Kindleberger, Charles P. *Power and Money.* New York: Basic Books, 1970.

Khrushchev, Nikita S. "On Peaceful Coexistence," *Foreign Affairs,* October 1959.

——.*Khrushchev Remembers.* Boston: Little, Brown, 1970.

Kissinger, Henry A. *The Necessity for Choice.* New York: Harper, 1961.

Klineberg, Otto. *Tensions Affecting International Understanding.* New York: Social Science Research Council, 1950.

Lall, Arthur. *How Communist China Negotiates.* New York: Columbia University Press, 1968.

Laqueur, Walter Z. *Communism and Nationalism in the Middle East.* New York: Praeger, 1957.

——. *The Soviet Union and the Middle East.* New York: Praeger, 1959.

Lefeber, Walter. *America, Russia, and the Cold War, 1945–1966.* New York: Wiley, 1967.

Lefever, Ernest W. *Ethics and United States Foreign Policy.* New York: Meridian Books, 1957.

Lewis, Flora. *A Case History of Hope, the Story of Poland's Peaceful Revolutions.* New York: Doubleday, 1958.

Liska, George. *Imperial America.* Baltimore: Johns Hopkins Press, 1967.

Loewenthal, Richard. *World Communism: The Disintegration of a Secular Faith.* New York: Oxford University Press, 1964.

McGeehan, Robert. *The German Rearmament Question: American Diplomacy and European Defense After World War II.* Urbana, Ill.: University of Illinois Press, 1971.

McVey, Ruth T. *The Soviet View of the Indonesian Revolution.* Ithaca, N.Y.: Cornell University Press, 1957.

Moore, Barrington, Jr. *Soviet Politics: The Dilemma of Power.* Cambridge, Mass.: Harvard University Press, 1950.

Morgenthau, Hans J. *Truth and Power.* New York: Praeger, 1970.

——. *A New Foreign Policy for the United States.* New York: Praeger, 1969.

Mosely, Philip E. *The Kremlin and World Politics.* New York: Vintage, 1960.

Overstreet, Gene D., and Windmiller, Marshall. *Communism in India.* Berkeley, Calif.: University of California Press, 1959.

Quester, George H. *Nuclear Diplomacy: The First Twenty-Five Years.* New York: Dunnelen, 1971.

Rapoport, Anatol. *The Big Two: Soviet-American Perceptions of Foreign Policy.* New York: Pegasus, 1971.

Remington, Robin Alison. *The Warsaw Pact: Case Studies In Communist Conflict Resolution.* Cambridge, Mass.: Massachusetts Institute of Technology Press, 1971.

Ridgway, General Matthew B. *The Korean War.* Garden City, N.Y.: Doubleday, 1967.

Roberts, Henry L. *Russia and America*. New York: Harper, 1956.

Rostow, Walt W. *The United States in the World Arena*. New York: Harper, 1960

Royal Institute of International Affairs. *The Soviet-Yugoslav Dispute*. London: 1949.

Rubinstein, Alvin Z., ed. *The Foreign Policy of the Soviet Union*. New York: Random House, 1972.

Russian Institute, Columbia University, ed. *The Anti-Stalin Campaign and International Communism*. New York: Columbia University Press, 1956.

Salisbury, Harrison E. *War Between Russia and China*. New York: Norton, 1969.

Seabury, Paul. *The Rise and Decline of the Cold War*. New York: Basic Books, 1967.

Schelling, Thomas C. *The Strategy of Conflict*. Cambridge, Mass.: Harvard University Press, 1960.

Schram, Stuart. *Mao Tse-tung*. New York: Simon and Schuster, 1967.

Schwartz, Benjamin I. *Chinese Communism and the Rise of Mao*. Cambridge, Mass.: Harvard University Press, 1951.

Schwarzenberger, Georg. *Power Politics, A Study of International Society*. New York: Praeger, 1951.

Seton–Watson, Hugh. *The East European Revolution*. New York: Praeger, 1956.

_____. *From Lenin to Khrushchev, the History of World Communism*. New York: Praeger, 1960.

Snell, John L. *Wartime Origins of the East-West Dilemma Over Germany*. New York: Hauser Press, 1959.

Speier, Hans. *The Soviet Threat to Berlin* New York: RAND Corporation, 1960.

Stimson, Henry L. and Bundy, McGeorge. *On Active Service in Peace and War*. New York: Harper, 1948.

Strausz-Hupé, Robert, *et al. Protracted Conflict*. New York: Harper, 1959.

_____, Kintner, William R., and Possony, Stefan T. *A Forward Strategy for America*. New York: Harper, 1961.

Swearingen, Roger, ed. *Soviet and Chinese Communist Power In the World Today*. New York: Basic Books, 1966.

Truman, Harry S. *Memoirs, Vols. I and II*. New York: Doubleday, 1955.

Ulam, Adam B. *The Rivals: America and Russia Since World War II*. New York: Viking, 1971.

_____. *Titoism and the Cominform*. Cambridge, Mass.: Harvard University Press, 1952.

_____. *The Unfinished Revolution*. New York: Random House, 1960.

UNESCO. *The Nature of Conflict*. New York: Columbia University Press, November 1957.

United Nations. *Report of the Special Committee on the Problem of Hungary*. 1957.

United States Department of State. *The Sino-Soviet Economic Offensive in the Less Developed Countries*. 1958.

Weintal, Edward, and Bartlett, Charles. *Facing the Brink*. New York: Scribner, 1967.

Werth, Alexander. *Russia at War 1941–1945*. New York: Dutton, 1964.

Wheeler-Bennet, John W. *Munich: Prologue to Tragedy*. New York: Duell, Sloan, and Pearce, 1948.

Whetten, Lawrence L. *Germany's Ostpolitik: Relations Between The Federal Republic and The Warsaw Pact Countries*. New York: Oxford University Press, 1971.

Whiting, Allen S. *China Crosses the Yalu*. New York.: Macmillan, 1960.

Wolfe, Thomas W. *Soviet Strategy at the Crossroads*. Cambridge, Mass.: Harvard University Press, 1964.

_____. *Soviet Power and Europe, 1945–1970*. Baltimore: Johns Hopkins Press, 1970.

Wolfers, Arnold. *Britain and France Between Two Wars, Conflicting Strategies of Peace Since Versailles*. New York: Harcourt, Brace, 1940.

_____, ed. *Changing East-West Relations and the Unity of the West*. Baltimore: Johns Hopkins Press, 1964.

Young, Kenneth T. *Negotiating with the Chinese Communists: The United States Experience, 1953–1967*. New York: McGraw-Hill, 1968.

4 The Struggle Over Colonialism

The day of small nations has passed away; the day of empires has come.
JOSEPH CHAMBERLAIN *Birmingham,* 1904

Empires have fallen on evil days and nations have risen to take their place.
RUPERT EMERSON *Cambridge, Massachusetts,* 1960

The New Nationalism

The second great power struggle of our time is being waged over the liquidation of Western colonialism. A new nationalism in Asia, Africa, and the Middle East has risen to challenge the dominance of the waning European empires. Indeed, at no time since the inception of the nation-state system have so many new states joined the world community during so short a period. Even a partial list dwarfs all previous expressions of nationalism. In Asia, we have seen emerge into sovereign national status the former colonies of four different empires; in the Middle East a number of new states have arisen, many of them profoundly hostile toward one another; and in Africa, finally, the addition of a new member to the family of nations was for several years virtually a monthly event.

We have tentatively defined nationalism as a people's vision of a common past and a common future. This definition of nationalism provides a general form, but is still lacking in content. We shall now attempt to build a more complete definition of nationalism in our time by analyzing those attributes that the new nations seem to hold in common. After examining the anatomy of the new nationalism in this manner, we shall subject its great adversary—colonialism—to a similar analysis. Only if we are clear about the nature of the two antagonists, can we understand the pattern of their interaction.

The first striking fact about the new nationalism is its peculiar vision of a common past. Its birth took place in the crucible of the declining Western empires. In the words of Rupert Emerson, "empires have fallen on evil days and nations have risen to take their place."[1] The fight that these new nations waged against Western powers was their great formative experience. As the adult person is conditioned by the conscious and unconscious memories of his childhood and adolescence, the nation-state is also conditioned by its memories—in other words, its history. This explains the fact that the world view of the new nationalism is oriented toward anticolonialism rather than anti-Communism.

This common colonial heritage of the new nations has resulted in their extreme ambivalence toward all things Western. Most of the new nationalist leaders harbor great admiration for many of the Western institutions and mores which they absorbed during the days of colonialism, but in their fight for national identity they are psychologically compelled to reject too close an identification with the West. It is not an accident that many of the leaders of independence movements were educated in Western universities as well as Western jails. Gandhi of India, Sukarno of Indonesia, and Nkrumah of Ghana are cases in point.

The psychological dependence on the colonial past sometimes reaches a point of fixation. A good example of this was Indonesia's insistence on annexing West New Guinea. The Indonesians had nothing in common with Guinea either ethnically or culturally. The only link that united them was the fact that both Indonesia and Guinea were parts of the Dutch empire. For this reason alone, it was felt, Guinea must belong to the new state of Indonesia. The hypnotic effect of the colonial past thus continues to play a vital role in the political policies of the new nationalism.

A final aspect of this psychological phenomenon is the paradoxical fact that in the very name of independence the new nationalism often tends to claim as its own many Western institutions that it absorbed during the colonial period. The following report from Nigeria shortly before independence will make this point clear:

With Nigerian independence approaching, government officials are pleading with Africans to wear clothes. Abakaliki Province officials said it would not be dignified for nature-loving Nigerians to go naked in independence as they did under British colonialism. In other provinces the people have donned clothes. But in Abakaliki not even a fig leaf, much less a loin cloth is worn. Provincial secretary J. W. Leach said Abakaliki residents must get clothes in thirty days. Any person found naked or scantily clothed will be prosecuted, the secretary said.[2]

In sum, the colonial heritage has left a deep and lasting impression. Even though sovereign national status is in the process of superseding Western colonialism almost everywhere in our time, the distinctive psychology of the former colonies, especially their emotions of "independicitis," are certain to persist for a long time to come. When one considers the fact that virtually everything that shaped colonial peoples was determined by the white West, this prediction should surprise no one. Their god was an alien god, their language was foisted upon them, and even their territorial boundaries, as in Africa, were drawn arbitrarily by Western hands. One cannot free oneself from such a past easily or without great pain.

Turning to the vision of a common future, a second important attribute of the new nationalism is the determined quest for racial equality. All the major colonial powers practiced the color bar with varying degrees of rigor. It was an inexpensive, rapid, and reliable instrument which enabled the white man to establish his political, economic, and psychological domination. There was a relative permanence in the racial line of demarcation which was absent from other lines of demarcation, such as economic status, occupation, language, or religion. It is probably not an exaggeration to maintain that the color bar, of all the attributes of colonial rule, was the one most fiercely resented. Until the end of World War II, the alleged inherent superiority of the white man was accepted almost as an axiom by the peoples under colonial dependency. This superiority, rationalized by various concepts, such as "the white man's burden" or *la mission civilisatrice,* was frequently impressed upon the African and Asian peoples by force. There is a poignant account in Gandhi's *Autobiography* of an episode in South Africa which left a lasting impression on the young man's life. The scene took place on a train to Pretoria. In Gandhi's words:

"A passenger came next and looked me up and down. He saw that I was a 'coloured' man. This disturbed him. Out he went and came in again with one or two officials. They all kept quiet, when another official came to me and said, 'Come along, you must go to the van compartment.'

'But I have a first class ticket,' said I.

'That doesn't matter,' rejoined the other. 'I tell you, you must go to the van compartment.'

'I tell you, I was permitted to travel in this compartment at Durban, and I insist on going on in it.'

'No, you won't,' said the official. 'You must leave this compartment, or else I shall have to call a police constable to push you out.'

'Yes, you may. I refuse to go out voluntarily.' The constable came. He took me by the hand and pushed me out. My luggage was also taken out. I refused to go to the other compartment and the train steamed away.[3]

Once nonwhite peoples began to win battles, the myth of the white man's invincibility began to disintegrate. This writer witnessed the process of disintegration in Asia, at a time when the Japanese war machine swept the continent and forced the English from Burma, the French from Indochina, and the Dutch from the East Indies. Although the Japanese victory was short-lived, the lesson was clear: the white man could be beaten. And when the colonialists returned in 1945, they found to their bitter surprise that they could not go home again, that indeed a relentless demand for equality rang in their ears and would not be silenced. The Japanese invasion had served as a kind of catalyst, which demonstrated that the white man could be challenged successfully. In the case of the former British colonies, sovereignty was won with relatively little bloodshed: India, Pakistan, Burma, and Malaya gained their independence through legal transfers of power. Indonesia, however, emerged from Dutch colonialism only after four years of bloody conflict; and the French colony of Indochina was liquidated only after a decade of terrible jungle warfare culminating in the disastrous battle of Dienbienphu in 1954. This battle was a major landmark in the rise of the new nationalism: it signified the first great military encounter since the Russo-Japanese war of 1904 in which a nonwhite people was victorious over the white man and made its victory stick.

The importance attached to racial equality in the new nationalist countries may also be seen in their reactions to racial problems outside their own boundaries. Preoccupation with this problem frequently distorts their perception of conditions elsewhere. The view held of the United States, for example, was never more favorable than in 1954 when the United States Supreme Court in a unanimous decision declared segregation in public schools unconstitutional. But when this decision subsequently had to be enforced at Little Rock, the United States stood condemned in the eyes of the new nationalist world. Similarly, the passage of comprehensive civil rights legislation in the United States a decade later was widely hailed, but the simultaneous racial crises were seen by many Africans as virtually a civil war. Hence, the understandable though often single-minded quest for racial equality motivating the African and Asian peoples makes it difficult for them to arrive at an objective appraisal of political forces in those parts of the world where different conditions apply. It is clear that in the perspective of the new nationalist powers, racial equality is the most important single principle of their new-found sovereignty.

The quest for equal status with the Western powers is also expressed in the economic goals of the new nationalism. Almost all of the new nations have adopted programs of industrialization, their leadership being convinced that industrialization is an essential precondition for economic development in general. As a rule, this new "industrial revolution" works in favor of centralization in both government and economy. In fact, a case may be made that rapid industrialization leads to the development of elites inimical to the democratic process. Severe splits have arisen in African and Asian societies between those who favor industrialization and those who oppose it in the name of tradition. Indeed, since such circumstances as the overpopulation of urban centers, the breakdown of kinship systems, and the breakdown of traditional handicraft economies tend in many ways to conflict with the official goal of industrialization, there is generally a great deal of such opposition. And not infrequently, the new national leadership does not shrink from resorting to undemocratic means to eradicate those who oppose it. In this struggle, there often emerge one-party machines and various other arrangements of an authoritarian nature. Former Prime Minister Nkrumah of Ghana, for example, simply sent the opposition into exile when it challenged his authority, and President Sukarno of Indonesia frankly announced the institution of "guided democracy" shortly after he came to power.

It must, of course, be admitted that the end of political colonialism does not always necessarily mean the end of economic dependency upon the former colonial power. In many cases, a new nation's financial and trading patterns are still heavily influenced by the colonial past. Ghana's cocoa crop, for example, is still marketed primarily through London, and the price of cocoa is largely determined by the demand picture in Western countries. These vestiges of colonial dependency, described by the new nationalist leaders as "neo-colonialism," are likely to persist for a considerable time, even though it is the declared policy of most of the new nations to become self-sufficient as rapidly as possible.

A third and somewhat disturbing generalization concerns the political structures which seem to be evolving in the new nationalist countries. The trend is clearly not in the direction of democratic parliamentary regimes. Most of these new nations are leaning toward some kind of authoritarian political organization. One-party governments, weak legislative bodies, and military elites are common to most. This fact simply demonstrates that the fight for national self-determination is not necessarily synonymous with a struggle for democracy. It is a curious fact that the Western conception of the new nationalism has not sufficiently grasped this truth. Instead, many Westerners have continued to expect that, after a period of tutelage in the arts of self-government under one or another of the Western powers, the new nations of Asia and Africa would quickly develop into sound and sophisticated democracies. Yet in view of the fact that most of the new nations have a centuries-long heritage of tribalism, feudalism, or autocracy, the authoritarian trend of the new nationalism is entirely consistent with their historical tradition. One cannot expect that a single generation of political independence can quickly erase centuries of political domination.

A final characteristic of the new nationalism is its reluctance to ally itself with either of the two superpowers. Most of the new nations desire to stay aloof from the East-West struggle. In Asia, India for many years considered itself the leader of this policy of nonalignment. The Indians' reasoning regarding this stand was that since their own experience had been such a unique synthesis of Asia's past and the West's present, their country might be better suited than most others to act as a mediator in the East-West struggle. In Africa, Nigeria took the lead in the adoption of such a bridge-building policy before it was convulsed by civil war in the late 1960's.

We must remind ourselves here that the term "uncommitted," when applied to the new nationalism, refers only to the East-West struggle. In the other struggle, that against colonialism, the movement is very much committed. Even in the East-West conflict, the policy of non-alignment is applied, strictly speaking, only in the avoidance of military alliances. In their political sympathies, most of the so-called uncommitted nations are much less scrupulously impartial, but tend, in fact, to lean in either one direction or the other. Ethiopia, for example, inclines toward the West, whereas Guinea, through its leader, Sekou Touré, is deeply influenced by Marxism. Others of the new nations, such as Indonesia and Burma, have flirted with both sides in the course of their brief histories.

In its attempts to gain the allegiance of the new nationalism in the struggle with Communism, the West has consistently pointed out that Western colonialism is a phenomenon of the past that is today in rapid process of dissolution. The West maintains that a far more threatening and virulent form of colonialism than that of the dying Western empires is that posed by Communism. Yet the new nations inevitably find it difficult to forget the experiences of their own history, which is the history of Western domination. And the fact remains—historical accident though it undoubtedly was—that there were no Russian colonizers in Africa, and few of them in Asia. The absorption of Eastern

Europe and Soviet military interventions in Hungary and Czechoslovakia have been geographically too far removed from most of the African and Asian nations to arouse the indignation and concern that they have in the West. Indeed, not until Communist expansionism reached their own frontiers, as in India, for example, did the new states' perception of what constitutes colonialism broaden to include the contemporary Soviet variety. It is very likely that as the new nations become more exposed to Communist expansionary goals, their views of what today is the most dangerous threat of colonialism and imperialism will come much closer to those held in the West.

The new nationalism, then, may be defined as a movement profoundly conditioned by a Western colonial past, leaning toward authoritarian political organization, and declaring as its goal political, economic, and social equality with the West—that is, sovereignty, racial equality, and a modern industrial economy.

We shall now turn to an analysis of the great antagonists of the new nationalism.

Imperialism and Colonialism

Among the nations of Africa and Asia, imperialism and colonialism are generally viewed as monopolies of the white man. This view has become so widespread that the terms "imperialism" and "colonialism" have assumed a pejorative connotation in the West itself. To call a nation "imperialistic" has come to be an indictment, and to describe a dependent territory as a "colony" is likely to be construed as an insult. In effect, the two concepts have in the Western world become the symbols of a kind of collective guilt complex. Yet as a noted historian has pointed out, the West's record in this regard is by no means as unqualifiedly deserving of condemnation as is often alleged or felt to be the case. For,

Though the brief history of Western imperialism has witnessed many injustices and cruelties, which however were in no way worse than the normal happenings in Asia and Africa before the advent of the white man, it has been on the whole a period of which the West, and especially Britain, has not to be ashamed. It would be wrong to apply twentieth century standards and principles of international law to preceding centuries. By doing that—and it should not be forgotten that these new twentieth century standards were developed by the Western world—the West suffers a bad conscience.[4]

Actually, the terms "imperialism" and "colonialism" simply denote a power relationship of one political entity over another. Imperialism describes the process of establishing that power relationship, and colonialism has to do with the pattern of domination and rule once the relationship has been consolidated. Neither is a monopoly of the white man or an exclusively modern phenomenon. Yellow peoples have dominated each other for centuries; black peoples are known to have exercised power over one another many centuries before the white man set foot on the African continent; and the history of political evolution in the West is the story of white men dominating other white men.

Historical perspective shows that these two terms have not always been in disrepute. The imperialist or colonizer of the nineteenth century was a hero to his contemporaries. Today a very different view is taken of Cecil Rhodes, for example, in both the West and in the new nations, than was taken of him two or three generations ago. The concept of colonialism has undergone a radical transformation in both time and space. The truth is, of course, that as concepts the terms "imperialism" and "colonialism" are neutral. Whether the relationship of domination they refer to is good or bad depends entirely on the values of the beholder. Power always remains power, but the values regarding what constitute desirable or undesirable power relationships are ever changing.

It is clear that, in our day, the new nationalism sees Western colonialism as its great antagonist and directs most of its energies toward destroying it. This tendency to place colonialism and the new nationalism at opposite poles may be somewhat misleading. Actually, when viewed in historical perspective, the relationship between imperialism and nationalism has not been one essentially of antagonism, but of dialectical interrelation. Frequently, as in the course of the French Revolution, imperialism has grown out of nationalism; and such imperialism, in turn, has spawned new nationalist movements, as witness the rise of nationalism against the Napoleonic Empire. Indeed, the germs of imperialism are already in evidence in the nationalism of some of the new countries. Former Premier Nkrumah's aim to create a Pan-African movement under the leadership of Ghana was a case in point. President Nasser's Pan-Arab ambitions were another. In the words of one thoughtful observer, "Nations have arisen from the ashes of empire. Must they follow the ruinous course of their cantankerous predecessors?[5]

Imperialism and colonialism in our time cannot be understood without reference to their historical development. We shall therefore begin by examining the origins of Western imperial expansion and then compare the policies of the Western colonial nations in their respective empires.

Imperialism, like most things human, cannot be explained by a single factor, although the attempt is persistently made. The Soviet explanation of Western colonialism, for example, is based on an exclusively economic interpretation. The new nationalism too, as a rule, fails to see the complexity of the truth.

Imperialism was, first of all, a function of the struggle for prestige and power among nations. During the nineteenth century the possession of colonies was a major criterion of national power. It is a remarkable fact that only a century ago over half the world's territory was ruled by European nations. Hence, when war broke out between two or more European powers, the hostilities held within them the seeds of world conflagration. The intense competition among Britain, France, and Germany for colonies in the nineteenth century was essentially the expression of a struggle for preponderance of power.

A second source of Western colonial expansion lay in the kind of secularized missionary zeal represented in Rudyard Kipling's concept of "the white man's burden." The stated purpose of this sense of mission was to bring the blessings of an allegedly more advanced civilization to the non-European areas of the world. And frequently, indeed, genuine humanitarianism did play a significant part. Yet nearly always there were important less altruistic motives. At times the Europeans' civilizing zeal largely expressed itself in a claim of self-styled superiority. On other occasions it served as a cover for what was chiefly a desire to export some particular religious cause. And not infrequently, as in the case of Cortés in Mexico, it stood simply for the universal human urge for adventure.

A further ingredient in "the white man's burden" attitude, as well as a factor of the greatest importance in itself as a contributor to the development of Western imperialism and colonialism, was the motive of economic self-interest. In its early form, this was usually referred to as "mercantilism." The primary reason for colonization by Spain, for example, was the mercantilist quest for gold—the quest for the riches of an overseas empire to strengthen the mother country's standing and power at home and among the other nations of Europe. As has already been pointed out, the Communist explanation of the genesis and dynamics of imperialism and colonialism limits itself to the various ramifications of this economic factor.

The principal Communist work on this subject is Lenin's *Imperialism, the Highest Stage of Capitalism.* This treatise, heavily influenced by J. A. Hobson's *Study of Imperialism,* published in 1902, still provides the official Soviet interpretation of Western imperialism and has gained wide currency in the newly emerged countries of Asia and Africa. It therefore deserves careful analysis. Lenin's thesis is based on the Marxist view that the economic struggle in the highly industrialized societies in Europe necessarily leads toward monopoly capitalism. As this state of affairs develops, there occurs a concentration of more and more wealth in the hands of fewer and fewer people, with an ever-growing group of dispossessed swelling the ranks of the proletariat. At the point of "capitalist concentration," the few remaining monopolists have no choice but to turn upon each other. When this stage in the struggle is reached, Lenin maintained, the capitalists discover a reprieve for themselves to stave off the inevitable doom that faces them at the hands of the masses of dispossessed. This reprieve is imperialism. The capitalists, instead of turning upon each other, now proceed to annex colonies overseas, which afford them vast new outlets for the export of capital, thus relieving their highly saturated markets and giving them a new lease on life. But this is a reprieve only, Lenin claimed, not an amnesty; imperialism is merely a last desperate maneuver by the capitalists to avert their inevitable collapse. All that this maneuver can accomplish is postponement of the inevitable. Hence, in Lenin's view, an imperialist policy pursued by a highly industrialized nation was a sure sign that capitalism in that nation had reached its final stage before decomposition.

Lenin's case is not to be dismissed lightly; it is the most important single weapon used by the Soviet Union to gain the adherence of the new nationalist countries. In an objective appraisal, it is evident that there is much truth in Lenin's view. It is true, for example, that the quest for colonies was pursued largely by the highly industrialized powers: Britain, France, Belgium, Germany, and, to a lesser extent, the United States. On the other hand, it must be pointed out that the rule of one people over another is not the monopoly of capitalist countries. The United States granted the Philippines their freedom; some industrialized countries like Sweden never actively sought colonies. In our time, in fact, Lenin's thesis could be turned with some validity even against the major noncapitalist power, the Soviet Union.

Lenin's thesis, while a brilliant *tour de force,* points up the dangers inherent in any one-factor analysis. For the fact is that the causes of imperialism and colonialism must be seen in terms of a subtle interplay among many factors, of which the economic, albeit the most significant, is only one. Nevertheless, the view of Western colonialism most often held in the new nationalist countries still closely resembles the single-factor interpretation first created by Lenin. Moreover, it is applied almost indiscriminately to all the varied forms of the Western colonial experience in Africa and Asia. All Western colonialism is thus lumped together and roundly condemned. And yet, in actual fact, there have been wide divergencies among the different types of Western colonialism. Each of the major Western powers—Britain, France, Holland, Belgium, and Portugal—evolved its own special colonial techniques. If the subject of colonialism is to be done justice, these differing techniques, and the philosophies behind them, deserve careful comparative analysis.

To begin with, the differences between the colonial policies of the two greatest Western empires, those of Britain and France, have been striking indeed. The British, as a general rule, exercised a form of indirect control over their possessions. The government operated through the existing local administrative patterns and usually permitted some degree of local participation. A Viceroy usually symbolized the might of the British Empire; but this Viceroy, though resplendent in the pageantry of his office, made it a point not to interfere in local customs and mores unless these jeopardized the interest of the Empire. This policy of indirect rule stood in sharp contrast to the French concept of direct rule from Paris, which in the early period of colonization permitted no local self-government whatever. Overseas colonies were considered as much a part of France as were Normandy or Brittany. As the British developed their concept of the Commonwealth, which in our time was gradually to supersede the Empire, they began to prepare their dependencies for ultimate self-government. As happened most notably in India, for example, the ground was laid for the eventual peaceful transfer of power by absorbing into the colonial administration more and more indigenous talent. The ultimate goal of the French colonial government, on the other hand, was the exact opposite: assimilation to the French way of life, in other words, "Frenchification." While for the British the political advancement of their dependent territories qualified them for secession and independence, similar advancement in the French colonies meant closer integration into the French way of life and greater participation in the French government. In practice, only a small group of the indigenous elite were "Frenchified" under this system. The vast majority continued to live under their own customs, recognized by the French under a separate legal code, and, as a rule, very much underrepresented in the French government. The British tended to emphasize the color bar more strongly than the French; the French might be said to have observed a "culture bar" more than a color bar. Hence, the masses tended to fare better in the British colonies but the educated elite had greater opportunities under the French system.

After the battle of Dienbienphu in 1954, French colonial policy began to emulate the British. The French Community under General de Gaulle's Fifth Republic sought to pattern itself after the British Commonwealth as a voluntary grouping no longer postulating assimilation as a necessary goal but aiming at a more flexible association. In 1958 President de Gaulle in effect offered the possibility of secession to all French dependencies save Algeria, and only one colony—Guinea—elected to sever all its ties with France. Virtually all the others elected to become independent states within the French Community. Six of these—Chad, Gabon, Senegal, the Central African Republic, the Malagasy Republic, and the Congo Republic—have participated in the Community, while the nine others have remained fairly inactive. Considering the Community's late start, it has been a moderate success.

There was, as noted above, one exception to the new French policy: Algeria. Algeria's legal status was never that of a dependency; it was always considered an integral part of France. Moreover, almost one tenth of the ten million people of Algeria were Frenchmen, known as *colons,* with large holdings and vested interests in North Africa. For these reasons, Algeria could not be neatly fitted into the emerging pattern of the French Community. The majority of the *colons* persistently demanded continued integration with France, while the indigenous population fought with equal insistence for independence. The Fourth Republic of France fell as a result of this apparently insoluble dilemma. It continued to be a severe irritant to the Fifth Republic as well, since protracted warfare over the issue steadily drained the resources of the mother country. In a bold and dramatic move, President de Gaulle in 1959 attempted to break the impasse by offering three alternatives to Algeria: integration, eventual complete independence, or voluntary association in the French Community. A year later, in a popular referendum on the Algerian question, a large majority of the population of France and her overseas territories supported the President in his offer. Himself favoring a voluntarily associated Algeria in the French Community, De Gaulle consistently attempted to use his great prestige to bring about a compromise between the demands of the long-embattled French *colons* and the indigenous Algerian peoples. At first, this policy achieved only slow and halting success. Extremism on both sides repeatedly stalled all progress. But in 1962 De Gaulle's solution prevailed and Algeria received her independence. Shortly thereafter, a mass exodus of *colons* from Algeria fundamentally changed the internal political complexion of that newly independent country.

The Netherlands, Belgium, Portugal, and Spain are known as the lesser colonial powers of the West. On the whole, their record is less enlightened than that of the major powers. For three hundred years the East Indies were one vast sugar plantation yielding enormous revenues for the Dutch government. The indigenous population was compelled to give up its land, volunteer its labor, and generally devote itself to the improvement of the economy on behalf of the Netherlands. Severe famines, a sharp population decline in the colony, and primitive labor conditions characterized the period from 1600 to 1900. Not until the twentieth century were somewhat more enlightened welfare and educational policies adopted and the rudiments of self-government introduced through advisory councils. But even this paternalism came too late. When the Japanese forced the Dutch from the Indies, they were welcomed in many parts as liberators. And even when it became clear that the Japanese form of imperialism was even harsher than that of the Netherlands, the Indies refused to join the Dutch in their struggle to get the colony back. A determined independence movement denounced both the Dutch and the Japanese with a "plague on both houses," and insisted on a sovereign state of Indonesia. This goal was realized in 1949 and motivated a major policy change on the part of the Netherlands in what remained of her colonial empire. The new concept, which evolved and was applied in Dutch island possessions in the Caribbean, was in essence the commonwealth concept: voluntary association with political autonomy in the local affairs of the dependencies. In effect, the Netherlands has emulated the British example.

The Belgian experience again is unique. From 1908 to 1960 the Congo was a major source of revenue. Until 1957 all authority over the Congo was in the hands of the Belgian government, which appointed a resident Governor-General who had the power to rule by decree. The distinctive aspect of the Belgian colonial experience was its enlightened economic and social policy. Minimum wage laws, housing and medical provisions, and a relatively high standard of living—among the highest in Africa—combined to give the colonial subjects of Belgium many benefits. Yet in the realm of government, the Belgian authorities were much less liberal. They insisted, in fact, on a policy of complete and uncompromising political paternalism. In 1959 this policy began to be confronted with rapidly spreading demands for independence. The Belgians, reversing their former policy, were quick to grant the formation of elective municipal and territorial councils. But this proved not enough, for with each new concession the Belgians made, Congolese demands increased and widened. The tide of new nationalism could not be stemmed and in mid-1960 Belgium withdrew from its colonial position altogether. Their social and economic advantages notwithstanding, the Congolese—wisely or unwisely—had insisted on complete sovereignty.

In spite of developments elsewhere, there is at least one Western colonial empire that has continued to live on with relatively little disturbance—at least until recently. That last stronghold of colonialism is Portugal, the first of the European states to acquire overseas territories and the one that will probably also be the last to have to give them up. In the two large Portuguese colonies in Africa—Angola and Mozambique—little has changed in five hundred years. The two colonies are considered integral parts of the mother country. There is highly centralized control from Lisbon, with a Minister for overseas Portugal making all policy decisions. A small indigenous elite is considered "assimilated," but the vast majority remain illiterate and rigorously integrated into the Portuguese economy. Until quite recently, the Portuguese practiced conscription of labor and forced cultivation, and, for control purposes, maintained a strict system of internal passports. Their forced-labor prison colonies had become notorious throughout Africa.[6] Today, Portuguese Africa is still without a doubt the most rigid Western colonial regime of our time.

In reviewing the Western colonial record, one is able to make several interesting generalizations. First, all the Western empires, with the exception of Portugal, have adopted the commonwealth concept of voluntary association or have come to terms with the prospect that sooner or later their colonial holdings must be liquidated altogether. It is very probable indeed that in our lifetime the story of Western colonialism will have passed into the pages of history.

Second, it is significant that at first the new nationalism was most vociferous and insistent in its demands in those dependencies, like the British, which had enjoyed the most liberal colonial regimes. The more the colonial administrators taught the colonial elite about democracy, the more the demand for democracy made itself heard. It is not an accident that the most repressive colonial regime, that of Portugal, has been the last to be troubled by political unrest. In part this may be explained by the fact that Portugal, itself an authoritarian regime, has managed so ruthlessly to insulate its African population and, hence, to deprive it of outside contacts and standards of comparison. This observation might lead a Machiavellian observer to the paradoxical conclusion that the virtues rather than the vices of the West led to the graveyard of Western colonialism. Yet this would be very shortsighted. For if, as seems the case, the disappearance of colonialism is sooner or later inevitable, there are far greater advantages—at least in the long run—in a policy of meeting the demands of colonial peoples gradually and while a spirit of mutual respect still remains. The Belgians, for example, by seeking to control and hold on to their colonial positions too uncompromisingly, in the end not only lost out completely in the Congo but reaped widespread international ill will as well. The British, in contrast, have been rewarded for their more liberal policies in India by the continuation of valuable political and economic bonds between the two countries as well as by deep admiration on the part of Western and non-Western peoples alike. Thus, it is likely that, if Portugal remains adamant on her colonies, more "wars of liberation" like the Indian invasion of Goa in 1961 will result. The 1963 Addis Ababa Conference of African nations, which agreed to use force if necessary against South Africa and Portugal, made public the writing on the wall.

The third observation that can be noted about Western colonialism is that though it is in fact in the process of liquidation, it continues to be denounced as the new nations' most mortal threat. Although, as we have seen, there have been very different types of Western colonialism, it tends to be represented and reacted to as one and the same reprehensible phenomenon. Communist expansion, on the other hand, has so far largely escaped this kind of wariness and opposition. Most of the representatives at the Bandung Conference, held in April 1955 by twenty-nine Asian and African nations in Bandung, Indonesia, had the West in mind when the Conference resolved that "colonialism in all its manifestations is an evil which should speedily be brought to an end." The suggestion by the delegate from Ceylon that the Soviet Union was practising colonialism in Eastern Europe was rejected by Prime Minister Nehru of India—the major spokesman at the Conference—who declared that there was no such thing as Soviet colonialism. There has been some modification of this attitude since the Hungarian revolution and the Communist Chinese incursions into Tibetan and Indian territory. But the primarily Western connotation of colonialism has persisted, and was reasserted at the Belgrade Conference of nonaligned nations in 1961 and again in Cairo in 1964. The United Nations, too, has been a major arena for the colonial struggle. Relentlessly, the new nationalist powers, steadily growing in numbers and strength, have demanded the "speedy and complete end of Western colonialism" in all organs of the world organization. The United Nations was unwilling to stop India from annexing the Portuguese enclave of Goa and was actually used as the vehicle for effecting the transfer of West New Guinea from Holland to Indonesia. These precedents seem to indicate that the world organization is unlikely to interfere with the liquidation of colonialism even if that liquidation may at times be accompanied by a show of force.

Finally, no discussion of colonialism would be complete without reference to the "white redoubt" in Africa: the Union of South Africa, Southwest Africa, and Southern Rhodesia. These three cases merit special consideration.

To the quarter of the South African population that is white, South Africa is a "white man's country." In their view, they settled it and developed it and are therefore unwilling to yield their control of it to the black man. Through the policy of *apartheid,* the whites have kept the African majority apart and subordinate in education, politics, economic opportunity, and social status. A succession of *Afrikaner* Prime Ministers have insisted on absolute separation between the races. Militarily and economically, South Africa has been the most powerful nation on the African continent. Ever since the decolonization process began in earnest, however, growing majorities in the United Nations General Assembly have secured resolutions branding *apartheid* as a threat to international peace and security and as a crime against humanity. The Union government has consistently ignored these resolutions as unwarranted intrusions into the domestic affairs of a sovereign state.

Efforts by the new nationalist nations in the General Assembly to wrest Southwest Africa away from the Union government's control have remained equally ineffective. After almost two decades of inconclusive litigation before the International Court of Justice (see Chapter 9), the General Assembly in October 1966 declared in a vote of 114 to 2, with South Africa and Portugal opposed, that, henceforth, Southwest Africa would be the direct responsibility of the United Nations. Implementation was another matter, however. Even though the General Assembly in 1967 decided to establish a special United Nations Council for the purpose of administering Southwest Africa, the Union government continued its policy of uncompromising opposition to any effort at internationalization.

The problem of Rhodesia proved equally vexatious. In November 1965, when the Ian Smith government broke away from Great Britain in a unilateral declaration of independence, the whites made up less than 4 per cent of the total population. This was the main reason why Britain had wanted to pave the way for eventual African rule. The Smith regime, however, stood by its policy of white minority rule. After unsuccessful efforts by the British government to end the secession, it took the case to the United Nations. In December 1966, the Security Council, in a vote of 11 to 0, imposed mandatory selective economic sanctions against Rhodesia. Although Secretary-General U Thant reported in March 1967 that 92 nations had complied with the resolution, the sanctions were not sufficient to bring down the Smith regime.

By the late 1960's, an entente had developed among the three "white redoubt" nations of South Africa, Rhodesia, and Portugal, These three nations formed a hard core of resistance to the new nationalism of Black Africa. Not only did they refuse to yield, but their white settler policies went against the trend of the times. For this reason, the specter of violence continued to hover over these last vestiges of European rule in Africa.

Perhaps the most important claim of the new nationalism is its insistence that it provides the only viable answer to Western colonialism. We are now ready to test this claim objectively. We have examined the anatomy of both the new nationalism and Western colonialism. It now remains to study their interaction. In order to gain the broadest possible perspective, we have chosen three case studies of such interaction, one from each of the major geographic areas of conflict, Asia, Africa, and the Middle East.

Nationalism and Colonialism: Patterns of Interaction

DEMOCRATIC AND AUTHORITARIAN NATIONALISM: INDIA AND PAKISTAN

The unique character of modern Indian nationalism has its roots in the tremendous power of the religions that shaped the nature of ancient Indian society. Any analysis of Indian nationalism must therefore begin with an examination of the three great religions of India: Hinduism, Buddhism, and Islam.

Ancient Hinduism was an austere doctrine subscribing to the view that the cause of all evil in the world was human desire. The path toward redemption, therefore, lay in man's capacity to extinguish desire within himself through an act of will, and thus reach a state of *Nirvana*. Hinduism conceived of life as a never-ending cycle, or *karma*. Death

simply meant passage into another incarnation of life. The form this
new incarnation would take depended on performance in the previous
one. Hence, it was quite possible for a man to pass into a lower or a
higher form of life. The standard of excellence toward which the Hindu
was to aspire was the attainment of *Nirvana,* or renunciation of desire.
Since men were by nature unequal, only a few could attain this goal.
This concept of the inequality of men was expressed in the social
structure of ancient India, the caste system. Society was divided into
four rigidly separated castes: the Brahmins, or priests, who had come
closest to the Hindu ideal; the warriors who were to defend the society;
the merchants; and the laborers. Actually, the social system was even
more complex, since each caste had numerous subdivisions. At the
bottom of the social pyramid were the outcasts, or pariahs, also known
as "untouchables."

The great inroads made by Buddhism in ancient India may be
explained largely in terms of the austerity of the Hindu doctrine. While
Buddhism, too, was directed toward the afterlife, its view of man was
much more optimistic. Under its influence, the *Nirvana* concept gradually changed from a doctrine of extinction and renunciation to a goal
not unlike the Christian paradise. The figure of the *Bodhisattva* entered
Indian life—the priest who, though entitled to enter *Nirvana,* has decided
to postpone his own entrance in order to show the way to others. Late
Buddhism, in fact, steered away more and more from the austerity of
the Hindu faith. Sometimes only a few invocations would suffice to gain
entrance to *Nirvana,* and *Bodhisattvas* frequently became deities who
played the role of "social workers," assisting their less fortunate
brethren. Despite this radical transformation of Hinduism, it must be
remembered that Buddhism was able to grow out of Hinduism because
the latter lent itself to the absorption of new forms of faith quite
readily.

The third major religion of ancient India—Islam—stands in striking
contrast to the other two. It came to India around 1000 A.D. Unlike
Buddhism, Islam was never absorbed by the Hindus. The only attribute
which Islam shares with its predecessor is its accent on the hereafter;
there the similarity ends. While the Hindu worships a pantheon of gods,
Islam is strictly monotheistic. While the Hindu structured his society
along rigid caste lines, the Moslem believed in the doctrine of the
equality of men under God. The Hindu made no effort to convert others
to his faith; Islam, like medieval Christianity, tended to proselytize by
the sword. Even the social customs differed sharply. The Hindu was
forbidden to eat beef, the Moslem was enjoined from eating pork.
Worship in Hindu temples was often accompanied by music, whereas
the Moslem in his mosque insisted on strict silence. The two religions
were virtually irreconcilable. After sections of India in the northeast
and the northwest were conquered by Moslems, the Hindus tended to

regard them as another caste to be kept rigidly separate. The religious conflict between Hinduism and Islam still exists, and is at the root of the struggle between India and Pakistan. Thus, by the time the West arrived there, India was a society politically divided, a society in which two radically different ways of life competed for the allegiance of the population: Hinduism, which was pacifist, tolerant of dissension, and absorptive; and Islam, which was militant, exclusive, and dogmatic.

British rule in India was established in the early seventeenth century through the instrument of the East India Company. In their campaigns to gain control of the subcontinent, the British followed a strategy of "divide and rule." The many satraps were played against each other until, by the late eighteenth century, most of India was in British hands.

The administration of British India presents a story full of contradictions, harmony, and conflict. The coming of the British added yet another element to the already highly complex Indian society. Christianity was brought to India, and yet the materialism of the Christian colonizers stood in stark contrast to the spiritualism of the Hindu. The individualism of the British differed sharply from the group-centered culture of India. The democratic ideal of equality seemed strange to the caste-conscious Hindu. The British tried very hard, on the whole, to harmonize these many conflicts, and sometimes succeeded.

In the pattern of indirect rule initiated by the British, a Viceroy was put in charge of colonial administration. Local customs were left intact so long as they did not present a direct threat to the British presence or radically offend the British social ethos. Thus, the British did not interfere much with the caste system, although they did insist on the abolition of the Hindu custom of suttee, the immolation of widows on the funeral pyres of their husbands. They also outlawed infanticide and "thuggee," the practice of sacrificing unsuspecting travelers in lonely mountain passes to the goddess Kali.

The British made every effort to teach the Indians about British democracy, thus shaping the thinking that later was to result in the Indians' demand for self-rule. Imported British law and contractual relationships were often superimposed upon the Indian culture. Especially in the later colonial period, indigenous talent was admitted into the civil service. On the other hand, the British often exhibited extreme insensitivity. For example, in 1857 a full-dress rebellion was started by the rumor that pig and cow fat were being used to grease cartridges in rifles to be employed by Hindu and Moslem recruits in the army. The Sepoy Rebellion of 1857 which was touched off by this incident was crushed by the British with extreme cruelty.

The economic side of the Indian colonial experience presents a similarly mixed record. The early profits made by the East India Company were enormous. The British flooded India with manufactured goods and in turn compelled the indigenous population to concentrate on the production of raw materials, thus causing an imbalance in the economy and a decline in Indian industry. On the other hand, the industrial development of India meant the development of modern roads, telegraphs, harbors, mails, and railroads. Some aspects of this industrialization did not conflict with traditional customs, but at times even helped to revive them. For example, a modern network of railroads made religious pilgrimages easier for many Hindus. Another important by-product of British colonialism was the rise of a whole new class of bankers, traders, educators, and lawyers who were to play a major role in the rise of the new India.

It is impossible to say whether modern India has benefited or suffered more as a result of its experience with British colonialism. To be sure, colonialism had many unfortunate effects. It frequently meant the exploitation of indigenous labor in order to develop the natural resources of the colony. And it resulted in the dislocation of the economy by turning the colony into a raw-material-producing area—a condition of "economic colonialism" that was to last much longer than its political counterpart. On the other hand, the British also did much to prepare India for the modern world: they bestowed upon the country an enlightened health and education program; they provided at least the foundations for a higher standard of living; and they educated an elite of future leaders.

In sum, then, India's experience with Western colonialism was by no means entirely negative. In view of this fact, combined with the pacifist faith of the Hindu religion, it is not surprising that when the nationalist reaction in India came, it followed an essentially nonviolent and democratic path.

The Indian nationalist movement was marked by the overwhelmingly powerful personality of Mahatma Gandhi. Gandhi was the spiritual father of the Indian Congress, the nationalist resistance organization under the British which, without his unifying influence, would have been destroyed by factionalism. Indeed, without the charismatic leadership of Gandhi, Indian nationalism might well have run a very different and far more violent course.

Gandhi's nationalism was rooted in the Hindu doctrine of *ahimsa*, or noninjury to any living being. This concept was translated into the political doctrine of passive resistance, or "civil disobedience," a technique of nationalist assertion that the British found very embarrassing. Gandhi, himself of humble origins, lived most unpretentiously. He used a spinning wheel to produce his few garments. He denied himself all comforts and often endured long fasts in order to find support for his causes. When, in 1930, the British imposed a heavy tax on salt, Gandhi walked 165 miles to the sea to make his own salt. His example of employing a spinning wheel led to a widespread boycott of foreign cloth. Rather than cooperate with the British, he exhorted the population to go to jail. He himself was frequently imprisoned. But always, he emphasized the nonviolent character of Indian nationalism. His rejection of bloodshed as a deplorable aberration was, indeed, the movement's most basic moral and political principle. The steady advance toward independence made by India between 1900 and 1947 was due in large measure to Gandhi's insistence on spiritual rather than physical power.

Despite his enormous influence, Gandhi was unable to forge Indian nationalism into a cohesive whole. The Congress was always viewed with suspicion by the Moslems of the colony who feared persecution at the hands of a Hindu majority once India became independent. Though he tried his utmost to do so, Gandhi never succeeded in composing the differences between the two faiths. In the end, in 1948, he was assassinated by a Hindu fanatic who found the Mahatma's dogged attempts at reconciliation unbearable.

The Moslems early developed their own nationalist organization, the Moslem League. Its leader, Mohammed Ali Jinnah, insisted on the creation of a separate state of Pakistan for the Moslem minority. The great chasm between Hinduism and Islam robbed the Indian nationalist movement of much of its effectiveness. Often the two antagonists feared each other more than they did the colonial rule of Britain. The depth of the conflict may be seen from the fact that not even the unparalleled prestige of Gandhi was able to persuade his Hindu followers to make common cause with Islam. Nor did the Moslems feel any less strongly. As their view was expressed by Jinnah:

How can you even dream of Hindu-Moslem unity? Everything pulls us apart: We have no intermarriages. We have not the same calendar. The Moslems believe in a single God, and the Hindus are idolatrous. Like the Christians, the Moslems believe in an equalitarian society, whereas the Hindus maintain their iniquitous system of castes and leave heartlessly fifty million Untouchables to their tragic fate, at the bottom of the social ladder.[7]

It is quite possible that this intense communal strife would have enabled the British to maintain control over India for an indefinite period. But World War II forced the British to make their peace with the prospect of Indian sovereignty. As a condition of India's collaboration in the war, Gandhi demanded a promise of immediate independence. When the British hedged, the Indian leader stated caustically that he was unwilling to accept "a post-dated check on a bank that was obviously failing." Even a British guarantee of speedy independence did not prevent some Indian nationalist leaders, like Subhas Chandra Bose, from throwing in their lot with the Japanese. After the conclusion of the war, it fell to the British Labour Government, which itself had always been severely critical of Conservative policy toward India, to honor Britain's pledge. But when, in 1947, Indian nationalism finally triumphed, it left the country a house divided. In spite of Gandhi's repeated fasts and prayer meetings against it, partition seemed the only practicable solution. Hence, India and Pakistan emerged from British colonial rule as two separate sovereign states.

The triumph of nationalism in India was thus severely marred by the tragedy of partition. Three staggering problems were the direct result of this tragedy. The first aftermath of partition was a gigantic population exchange, one of the most massive in history. Over seven million Hindus, fearful of persecution in Pakistan, frantically sought refuge in India, and a similar number of Moslems fled to safety from India to Pakistani soil. The integration of these millions of refugees presented an almost insurmountable problem to both of the new states.

The second problem was economic in nature. Colonial India had been an economic unit for centuries and now suddenly found itself divided into three parts: India, East Pakistan, and West Pakistan. East Pakistan, formerly East Bengal, was separated from West Pakistan by almost one thousand miles of Indian territory. These two Moslem enclaves, dating from the Moslem conquest, had in common their religion but almost nothing else—not even language. Regional jealousies and economic competition immediately rose to the surface between the two Pakistans. Worse, Pakistan and India almost at once began economic warfare. India devalued her rupee, but Pakistan refused to follow suit. Jute, an important raw material grown mostly in Bengal, now became prohibitively expensive in India. In short, the three parts of the Indian subcontinent, which for centuries had been operating as an economic entity, now found themselves in the throes of a destructive economic feud. Overshadowing all the other disputes between the two new nations was the struggle for contested territory, especially the princely state of Kashmir. India demanded Kashmir on the ground that its ruler had been a Hindu, but Pakistan claimed the state on the basis that over three fourths of the population of Kashmir was Moslem.

The political structures of Hindu and Moslem nationalism also diverged sharply after independence. India, under the leadership of Jawaharlal Nehru, Gandhi's successor, immediately embarked on the ambitious and unprecedented experiment of shaping an overwhelmingly illiterate country into an advanced democracy. The Indian national elections of 1951-1952 were indeed an impressive performance. The new Indian government spared no effort to make this election a truly democratic one, and, on the whole, succeeded admirably. The Congress Party, now pursuing a policy of gradual socialism patterned after the example of the British Labour Party, became the dominant political power, with Nehru as its undisputed leader. In foreign affairs, the new India began at once to pursue its policy of nonalignment in the conflict between East and West and continued its primary emphasis on the struggle against colonialism. Pakistan set out on a very different road. It followed the general pattern of the new nationalism by developing its political structure along authoritarian lines; yet it departed from that pattern in its foreign policy by almost immediately embracing the side of the West in the East-West struggle.

The death of Nehru in 1964, however, marked the end of the postcolonial era in India. In the elections of 1967, the Congress Party, now no longer associated by the opposition with the independence movement but rather with a stagnant *status quo,* suffered severe setbacks. Pakistan, too, changed course. While technically remaining a member of two Western alliances, SEATO and CENTO, the policies of her President, Ayub Khan, tended to remove her from the Western orbit. Relations between the two countries remained bitterly hostile. In 1965, fighting broke out along the Kashmir cease-fire line, ending later that year with another UN cease-fire. In January 1966, Soviet Premier Kosygin, at a meeting in Tashkent, persuaded both Pakistani President Ayub Khan and Indian Prime Minister Lal Bahadur Shastri to withdraw to the pre-1965 cease-fire lines in Kashmir. In 1966, Indira Gandhi, Nehru's daughter, was elected Prime Minister of India in a democratic election, while in 1969, President Ayub Khan turned Pakistan over to General Yahya Khan who placed the country under martial law.

In 1970, conditions on the Indian subcontinent deteriorated dramatically when severe tensions between East and West Pakistan erupted into open conflict. The catalyst was the worst cyclone of the century, which swept through East Pakistan, killing almost half a million people. In the aftermath of the storm, the Bengalis of East Pakistan felt that West Pakistan did not respond adequately to the needs of the victims. This sentiment led to increasingly insistent demands by the Bengalis for regional autonomy, articulated by their leader, Sheik Mujibur Rahman. During 1971, the West Pakistan government resorted to extremely repressive measures to deal with Bengali demands for autonomy. Severe fighting broke out and massive waves of Bengali refugees fled for their lives into the territory of their former enemy, India. By late 1971, the number of refugees approached the ten million mark. This flood of homeless and dispossessed people imposed a severe strain on the Indian economy and pressure mounted on Mrs. Gandhi to move toward a showdown with Pakistan.

In August 1971, India signed a defense treaty with the Soviet Union and shortly thereafter her forces crossed into East Pakistan, now renamed Bangla Desh by the Bengalis. India's objective was to sever Bangla Desh from West Pakistan, stop the flow of refugees into India, and dismember her old enemy. Indian soldiers were welcomed as liberators by the Bengalis, Pakistan was divided in half, Sheik Mujibur Rahman returned to Dacca in triumph, and Bangla Desh became a political reality. At the United Nations, the Security Council met, but repeated Soviet vetoes prevented a cease-fire until the Indian forces had attained their military objectives. China supported West Pakistan, but with little more than rhetoric. By 1972, the political complexion of the Indian subcontinent had fundamentally changed.

The above analysis suggests that independence is no unmixed blessing. The two nations that emerged from British colonialism never really managed to live in peace with one another. When, moreover, West Pakistan decided to persecute its Moslem brethren in the East, India used this event as a pretext for a war that ended in the dismemberment of Pakistan. The great powers were also drawn into the vortex of this confrontation in the Third World. The Soviet Union backed India and thus increased its influence on the subcontinent. China backed Pakistan, largely as a function of her split with the Soviet Union, and the United States "tilted" toward Pakistan, since President Nixon, on the eve of his visit to China, found it tactically advisable to do so. Neither India nor Pakistan, during its quarter century of independence, made any radical changes in its political structure. India's government remained a constitutional democracy while the two Pakistans preferred authoritarian rule. For both countries, nationalism had been a bulldozer that had pushed them into the twentieth century. They now enjoyed the blessings of self-determination, but also inherited all the travails and turbulence of the modern world. In terms of human suffering on the subcontinent, a high price had been paid for independence.

TRIBAL NATIONALISM: THE CASE OF GHANA

The most dynamic arena of the new nationalism in our time is the continent of Africa. In the course of a single generation the mounting discontent and will to independence of the peoples of Africa have resulted in the liquidation of most of three massive Western empires— the British, French, and Belgian—whose imperial rule had lasted for centuries. Only Portugal's increasingly restive colonies and a handful of minor Western enclaves remain as the rearguard of a passing age. The pacemaker of the new African nationalism was the state of Ghana, formerly known as the British Gold Coast, the first African colony to receive its independence in the twentieth century. When Ghana became a sovereign state on March 6, 1957, the frenzied shouts of jubilation celebrating its triumph sounded the death knell of the Western empires in all of Africa. The present case study will analyze the rise of nationalism in the Gold Coast which led to the creation of Ghana.

Little is known about the Gold Coast's early history. There are records of an ancient tribal kingdom by the name of Ghana, but there seems to be no continuity between it and the Gold Coast. This ancient civilization was ruled by a chief in consultation with village elders. The process of decision-making was a curious mixture of democratic and authoritarian principles. When an issue had to be decided, the chief summoned the council of elders and fully discussed all aspects of the problem. Everyone was invited to express his view. The decision itself was reached by the chief, and to question that decision was treason. If a chief consistently made bad decisions, the village elders were likely to depose or kill him and select a new chief.

This form of tribal rule might at first glance seem archaic or "primitive." Actually, however, it is not so remote from the twentieth century as might appear. It is, in fact, reminiscent of Lenin's doctrine of "democratic centralism": free discussion of policy in the Politbureau, but unquestioning adherence to it once the policy is reached. Nor is it altogether far-fetched to note the analogy between the jealousies and strife among tribal elders and the brutal struggle for successorship to Lenin that occurred in the Soviet Union in the 1920's. In view of the widespread prevalence of this type of political heritage among formerly tribal peoples, it is not difficult to understand why the new nationalism in Africa tends to lean toward authoritarian—although not necessarily Soviet—political forms. And ancient Ghana, though unique as a civilization, was typical of the rest of Africa in the sense that it had little if any tradition in political democracy.

The first Western colonizers to visit the Gold Coast were the Portuguese in search of gold. They were displaced briefly by the Dutch and finally, in the nineteenth century, firm control of the colony was established by the British. Great Britain's colonial administration of the Gold Coast was, on the whole, enlightened. Slavery, the greatest evil of Western colonialism, largely preceded the British period. It is true that the Gold Coast was turned into a single-crop economy and that the colony became a major producer of cocoa, all of which was marketed through London. In fact, the colony's entire economy was made dependent on that of the mother country. Yet on the other hand, British colonialism also accomplished a great deal that was positive. Cannibalism, ritualized murder, and tribal warfare were reduced by the British; epidemics that had scourged many of the tribes for centuries were brought under control; droughts, famines, and other disasters were dealt with by modern methods; and—not least important for the future—the country was equipped with railroads and other means of communication. Though all these benefits, to be sure, were instituted in the first instance for the convenience of the colonizers, their effect on the indigenous population was immense. Perhaps the most important of the positive by-products of British rule in the Gold Coast was education. In their educational institutions the British taught the Africans about the mother country. And once having heard about the rule of law, Magna Carta, and the Bill of Rights, the independent minds among the African

students soon began to ask themselves—and then their colonial masters—
why the British did not practice what they preached. Could the color
bar be reconciled with the rule of law? Was colonialism compatible
with the Bill of Rights? Such questions, inherent though often unantic-
ipated in Britain's colonial educational policy itself, were to become the
tinder of the Gold Coast's fiery nationalism.

Nationalism in the Gold Coast thus consisted of a combination of
factors that together became explosive. Often these factors were not
experienced as "nationalism" by the African population itself, but
found expression in their reactions to specific crises. One of the most
important of these crises was the economic one of recurrent unemployment in the colony's cocoa industry. This created much hardship among
the population and resulted in mounting bitterness against the British,
who were held responsible. Another factor was the determined leadership of Western-educated nationalists like Dr. Kwame Nkrumah. Ever
ready to use the economic crises to exact concessions from the British,
these native leaders insisted upon demand after demand without let-up.
And the more the British yielded, the more concessions were asked of
them. Indeed, the fact that Gold Coast nationalism finally triumphed—
and especially in the manner in which it did so—was once again, as in
India, due in no small measure to the flexibility of the colonial power
itself.

The earliest nationalist body in the Gold Coast under British rule was
the Aborigine Rights Protection Society. Tribal warfare among its
leaders slowed its advance, but in 1925 the British Governor appointed
some of its members to serve in native councils in an advisory capacity.
After this initial concession, the advisory councils steadily grew in
importance. In 1946 the British granted the Gold Coast a new Constitution, stipulating that the advisory councils be elected rather than
appointed. The function of the councils was still not to make policy but
to criticize and modify the decisions taken by the British. Thereafter,
however, the major concern of Gold Coast nationalism was less with the
machinery of government than with the development of native leadership that could supplant the British in operating it. The story of the
development of this leadership is primarily the drama of Dr. Nkrumah.

Dr. Nkrumah was educated at Lincoln University, in the United
States. In the course of his liberal arts training he was exposed to the
teachings of Christianity and Gandhi as well as to the system of Karl
Marx and the experiments of Franklin Delano Roosevelt's New Deal.
Aspects of all of these lessons were destined to be applied in the social
laboratory of the Gold Coast. Dr. Nkrumah returned to the colony in
1948, at a time when the Gold Coast was in the grip of riots which had
been sparked by a major crisis in the cocoa industry. Nkrumah was no
longer content merely with the existing advisory councils, but insisted
that the Gold Coast be given full Dominion status. The British

appointed an able negotiator, Sir Charles Arden-Clarke, who thought that this demand was premature. Nkrumah, following the example of Gandhi, encouraged the population to civil disobedience. As a result, he was sentenced to two years in jail. During this period he became a national hero. Africans on the Gold Coast now looked to the United States for inspiration in their cause. They adapted their own version of "John Brown's Body" and could be heard singing: "Kwame Nkrumah's body lies amouldering in jail, but his soul goes marching out." In 1951, with Nkrumah still incarcerated, Arden-Clarke decided to grant a general election. In this election the nationalist leader emerged victorious in 34 out of 38 constituencies. He was released from prison to become the first Prime Minister of the Gold Coast. By 1952 virtually all internal matters were in Nkrumah's hands, though foreign affairs, especially foreign trade, were still controlled by the British. The next four years were spent in a strenuous fight to have these vestiges of colonial rule removed. Finally, in September 1956, the British yielded and promised full independence. On March 6, 1957, Dr. Nkrumah's hour of triumph arrived.

With the battle for political independence won, the new nationalism in Ghana tended to revert to the authoritarian heritage of the ancient kingdom. Dr. Nkrumah showed little patience for the development of opposition parties, with the result that Ghana became virtually a one-party state. In fact, the most articulate leaders of the opposition were sent into exile. Statues of the independence leader were displayed prominently throughout Accra, the capital. While Western political institutions, such as a legislative assembly and a court system, continued to exist, they seemed more and more like a thin veneer superimposed on a society that firmly believed in the indispensability of its chief, Dr. Nkrumah. The Premier's philosophy of Pan-Africanism was also an echo of the ancient African kingdom.

The achievement of political sovereignty in Ghana did not immediately usher in full independence in all respects. Most importantly, the new state still had to face the problem of decolonializing its economy. In the case of Ghana, as in most of the other African colonies, the economic heritage of colonialism was harder to erase than its political counterpart. Ghana's entire cocoa crop, the country's main source of income, was dependent on British markets. Under the colonial administration, the British had incurred the wrath of the cocoa growers by keeping down prices and using the resulting profits for improvements in the colony and higher dividends for foreign shareholders. With independence won, Dr. Nkrumah became the cocoa growers' target in their demands for higher prices. But the Premier refused to yield, remaining adamant for at least three reasons: partly because the new government needed money for public education and other improvements; partly because consumption increases had to be kept below production increases so as to guarantee a healthy rate of capital formation; and partly to make possible the financing of an army which, though it might not be needed militarily, was to add to the new state's prestige. In view of this post-independence dilemma, it was suggested by some observers that Dr. Nkrumah's political authoritarianism was less a matter of choice than of necessity—that it was made necessary by the nature of the country's economic conditions and that it would remain so until Ghana's vulnerable one-crop economy was at last diversified. More specifically, these observers pointed out, if Nkrumah had permitted an unfettered opposition, its first demand would have been for higher cocoa prices, and these, if granted, would have correspondingly reduced the funds available for badly needed public improvements.

In February 1966, Nkrumah was ousted by a group of army dissidents led by Lt. General Joseph A. Ankrah. A junta with Ankrah as chairman took power and embarked on a drastic program of reform. In domestic policy, the new government resorted to severe economy measures: government ministers were cut from thirty-two to eighteen and embassies were reduced by 40 per cent. Every effort was made to cut expenditures in order to decrease the $1 billion deficit that had been incurred by the Nkrumah government. In foreign policy, the new regime expelled both the Chinese and Soviet presences from Ghana. In May 1967, it decided to participate in an arrangement with eleven other West African nations designed to maximize the exchange of goods and to eliminate customs barriers among themselves. In its general orientation, the new regime turned more to the West, but maintained its authoritarian character.

In general retrospect, an interesting overall analogy suggests itself between Ghana and the history of most of the countries of Latin America. Immediately after Portuguese and Spanish colonial rule in Latin America had disintegrated, the continent was plagued by strife, disease, and abject poverty and underdevelopment. The new republics quickly turned into dictatorships, with one strong man following another. Yet the basic problems remained. Only the gradual improvement in the standard of living and the general welfare proved capable of creating the soil in which parliamentary institutions could grow. Hence it took more than a century for independence from political colonialism to be followed by the emergence in Latin America of forms of government that could be called truly democratic.

In conclusion, the case of Ghana illustrates the dynamics of the new nationalism in several important respects. It in large measure owed its rapid success to the enlightened policies of its British colonial administrators. Once triumphant, it tended to revert to the authoritarian pattern of the past. This trend was accentuated by the fact that economic colonialism continued into the era of political independence and seemed, almost, to require some form of authoritarian rule for its liquidation. Indeed, the question of whether the new Western parliamentary institutions grafted onto ancient tribal customs will be victorious in Ghana, or whether the old tribal authoritarianism will ultimately dominate in some new form, would seem to depend above all on what happens to the new nation's economy. Finally, the Pan-African movement led by Ghana under Nkrumah suggests that the new nationalism may even bear within it the seeds of imperialism, though this time not white and Western, but by and among Africans themselves.

COMPETITIVE NATIONALISM: THE MIDDLE EAST

Perhaps the most perplexing problems raised by the new nationalism occur when it takes different and hostile forms in the same geographic area. In such cases, its energies are divided between the struggle against colonialism on the one hand and, on the other, the struggle for dominance among the emerging nations themselves. This has most notably been the case in the Middle East, which has in fact been undergoing a threefold nationalistic struggle: Arabs versus Arabs, Arabs versus Israel, and Arabs versus Western colonialism.

Modern Arab nationalism harks back to the proud tradition of the Arab Empire, which profoundly influenced medieval Europe between the ninth and the twelfth centuries. This empire, which contributed much to the advancement of science and philosophy, was eventually conquered by the Ottoman Turks and remained under Turkish rule until World War I. During this period the great Arab civilization stagnated. Only the gradual disintegration of the Ottoman Empire and the coming of Western colonialism to the Arab world reawakened the Arabs' awareness of their great and distinctive heritage. And under the impact of such events as Napoleon's expedition to Egypt, the construction of the Suez Canal, and the British military occupation of Egypt, this Arab awareness turned into an ever more conscious and militant nationalism. Hence in the Arab world, as elsewhere, the new nationalism arose in the first instance as a reaction against the establishment of Western colonialism.

Leadership in the expression of Arab nationalism was first assumed by Egypt. Though the British granted the Egyptians formal independence in 1922, this in effect amounted to little more than local autonomy, with even that being extensively qualified so as to protect continuing British interests in the country. As a result, nationalist agitation steadily grew and was kept in check only through the British-backed authoritarianism of the Egyptian monarchy.

The culmination of Egyptian nationalism came with the overthrow of the monarchy and the rise to power in 1952 of Colonel Gamal Abdel Nasser, a young officer in the Egyptian army. Nasser not only assumed the leadership of Egypt but also immediately announced himself as the self-appointed leader of the entire Arab nationalist movement, pledging his dedication to the ideal of "an Arab Nation from the Atlantic to the Persian Gulf." An all-out Egyptian-led Arab struggle was declared against both Zionism and colonialism. In addition, President Nasser promised extensive economic reforms which were to turn his nation into a modern industrial state. In 1958 Syria was absorbed into Egypt and from the union of these two countries a new nation was born, the United Arab Republic. The new Egypt seemed launched on the imperialist path.

At this juncture, Nasser's bid for leadership of Arab nationalism began to encounter competition. Much of the Arab world—Saudi Arabia, Jordan, Libya, and Morocco—was still governed by absolute monarchs. These rulers were deeply suspicious of Egypt's ambitions. Even though dynastic feuds of long standing had kept relations among some of these monarchs strained—as, for example, the feud between Saudi Arabia and King Hussein of the Hashemite Kingdom of Jordan— they presented a united front against the new nationalism of Nasser. In this struggle, however, the traditional monarchical nationalism fought a losing battle. Its most dramatic failure was in Iraq, whose King Faisal was assassinated in 1958. But though the new Iraq was now a republic, its leader, General Kassem, did not join forces with President Nasser. Instead, he developed his own ambitions to lead the Arab nationalist movement. In 1961 he threatened to annex the oil-rich kingdom of Kuwait, and was prevented only by British forces which intervened at the Sheikh's request. Nasser himself suffered a setback in 1962 when Syria seceded from the United Arab Republic. And Kassem's ambitions, in turn, were thwarted by the Baathist (Arab Renaissance) Party, which staged a coup d'etat in Baghdad in 1963 and executed the Iraqi leader. Monarchist forces also clashed with the new nationalism in Yemen when Saudi Arabian and Egyptian forces fought over that country. Thus Arab came to be set against Arab, not only in the struggle between the old and the new forms of nationalism but also in internecine warfare within the camp of the new nationalism itself. The death of President Nasser in 1970 and the ascendancy of Anwar Sadat to the Egyptian Presidency did little to alleviate this situation.

Perhaps the most important single development in the Arab world has been the rise of the Palestinian Liberation Movement. Quick to accuse their fellow Arabs of cowardice in the face of the enemy, the Palestinians have been the most uncompromising and fanatical element in the Arab world. They have been suspicious of any Soviet-American efforts at "collusion" in the Middle East and have been sympathetic to the Chinese concept of protracted guerrilla warfare. Their hostility to some of the more conservative Arab governments, such as Jordan, has been almost as fierce as their hatred for Israel. Their ultimate objective has been the reestablishment of an Arab homeland in Palestine.

Despite these profound divisions in the Arab world there developed a united front of all Arabs against at least one competing form of nationalism in the Middle East: that of Zionism. The founder of the Zionist movement was Theodor Herzl, a nineteenth-century Austrian journalist, who was convinced that in a world of recurrent anti-Semitic pogroms only the establishment of a national Jewish home could safeguard the rights of the Jewish people. Herzl and the Zionists based their case primarily on the ancient Hebraic Biblical claim to the Promised Land from which the Jews had been driven into the Diaspora. In 1917, when Palestine was a British Mandate, the British issued an ambiguously worded document, the Balfour Declaration, in which they stated that the British government "looked with favor upon the establishment of a national Jewish home in Palestine." The Zionist movement was much encouraged by this half-promise; the Arabs, on the other hand, feeling that Palestine was Arab territory which the British did not have the right to promise to anybody, were incensed. However, the destruction of six million Jews by the Nazis lent new vigor to the Zionist movement and finally, on May 15, 1948, Theodor Herzl's dream came to be realized. The new State of Israel was proclaimed a sovereign national entity.

Thereafter, the Arab-Israeli dispute turned into what was in essence a struggle between two competing forms of nationalism. It had, however, the elements of a genuine tragedy, since each side's case, though containing points of merit, did not invalidate the case of the other. For example, the Palestine refugee problem, which has been the most important single issue in the struggle, originated in two different interpretations of the same event. When the new state of Israel was established, over 800,000 Arabs left their homes. The Arab position in the matter was that these refugees were forced to flee by the Zionist troops in order to make room for Jewish settlers. The Zionists, on the other hand, claimed that the refugees fled as a result of exhortation by their own leaders, who wanted to use them as a political tool in the struggle against Israel. Approaches to a solution also differed radically. The Arabs insisted on the refugees' right of repatriation to Israel and compensation for their loss of property. Israel, on the other hand, fearing that if the refugees were readmitted they might weaken and subvert the country from within, urged that they be resettled in adjacent Arab lands. In the meantime, the refugees themselves have lived for over two decades in camps, supported chiefly by the United Nations. It is noteworthy that the political competition between these two forms of nationalism in the Middle East has been so intense that the human aspects of the refugee problem have been all but ignored. Few attempts have been made to establish the refugees' own preference between repatriation and resettlement—if, indeed, such a preference could after so many years of privation and resentment be objectively established at all.

Similar intransigence frustrated the resolution of every other Arab-Israeli dispute. Not surprisingly, therefore, the conflict resulted in countless Arab-Israeli border clashes, raids, and counterraids, and spilled over into the religious sphere in the division of the city of Jerusalem and the retention of restrictions on its places of worship.

In June 1967, open war erupted between Israel and three of her Arab neighbors—Egypt, Jordan, and Syria. In four days of lightning warfare, Israel defeated her three antagonists and captured the Sinai peninsula, the Gaza Strip, the Old City of Jerusalem, and borderlands in Syrian territory. As a condition of withdrawal Israel now insisted on direct peace negotiations with the Arab States and an end to belligerency. The Arab States, on the other hand, insisted that Israel withdraw first before any meaningful negotiations could take place. The war seemed to be but another battle in a protracted conflict.

If one considers the Arab-Israeli dispute in psychological terms, it becomes clear that, in the eyes of the Arab nationalists, Israel has become the successor to Western imperialism. Like Britain and France, Israel is an advanced Western-type democracy. It is, moreover, the only modern industrial state in the Middle East. Hence it can quite correctly be regarded as the only representative of democratic nationalism in the region. The Arab world's antipathy to the new Jewish state on these grounds was strongly reinforced when, in 1956, Israel joined Britain and France in a punitive military expedition against Egypt and when, in 1967, the United States tended to favor Israel in its confrontation with the Arabs. As a result, Israel is not only opposed as a competing form of nationalism; it is also felt to be in league with Western imperialism. This double resentment of Israel goes a long way in explaining why Arab hostility continues to be as intense and uncompromising as it is.

The Arab-Israeli struggle has also derived much of its tenacity from the fact that anti-Zionism has served as a rallying point and a unifying force among the disparate forces of Arab nationalism itself. Without the common enemy of Israel, the precarious unity of Arab nationalism might well disintegrate and internecine strife destroy its momentum altogether.

The final struggle rending the Middle East is being waged between Arab nationalism and the remnants of Western colonialism. President Nasser's nationalization of the Suez Canal in the summer of 1956 was in essence an act of national self-assertion against what the Egyptian president considered illegal colonial rule by Britain and France. The abortive Anglo-French attempt to destroy Nasser through military force in October 1956 was, in turn, an attempt to restore what the British and French considered their legitimate economic rights. United States pressure resulted in the withdrawal of the British and French and a political victory for Arab nationalism. The Suez misadventure spelled the end of British and French influence in the Middle East. In March 1957 the United States sought to fill the vacuum through the promulgation of the Eisenhower Doctrine, which pledged American military assistance to Middle Eastern countries in order to deter Communist aggression. Again, when President Nasser decided to blockade the Gulf of Aqaba in May 1967, he described this action as a general measure against imperialism and when the United States criticized the blockade as "illegal and potentially disastrous," Nasser was quick to accuse the United States itself of being an imperialist power.

An objective assessment of the record shows that Western colonialism in the Middle East is no longer a reality. Each of the great powers, however, has its own views on how the Middle East problem should be resolved and it is precisely this which has made the impasse so intractable. The United States has leaned toward Israel. The Soviet Union has supported the Arab side and even signed a defense pact with Egypt in 1971. In 1972, however, Egypt demanded the withdrawal of the Soviet military presence from her territory. The British have taken an impartial position, but the French have sided with the Arabs. And China, fearful of Soviet-American détente, has thrown her support to the most radical of the Arabs, the Palestinian guerrillas.

Arab nationalism has by now become the most explosive single force in the Middle East. But here we are faced with a curious paradox: In order to maintain its unity and drive, Arab nationalism needs the continued existence of its adversary, the State of Israel. Indeed, with Western colonialism in the Middle East now a thing of the past, the role assigned to the new Jewish state as a common enemy is undoubtedly the most crucial factor making it possible for Arab nationalism to survive at all. Ironically, therefore, if the avowed aim of Pan-Arabism—the destruction of Israel—were actually realized, it might also mean the end of a united Arab nationalism.

As diverse as the above three case studies of the interaction between nationalism and colonialism are, they permit several general conclusions. First, it is clear that the patterns of colonial rule have varied widely, that the results for the colonies have been both beneficial and harmful, but that the new nationalism continues to view the entire Western colonial experience as a monolithic and unmitigated evil. Similarly, while the record indicates that Western colonialism is in a state of probably irreversible liquidation, the new nationalism acts as though it remained a living and ever-menacing threat. Second, it is evident that the new nationalism has been strongest and most successful in those areas where colonial rule was least repressive and most enlightened politically. Third, it appears from our cases that the new nationalism, in its battle against colonialism, is seldom a cohesive force;

indeed, it seems to be able to draw its life-force not only from being an "anti-movement" directed against colonialism, but also from its confrontation with other and competing forms of nationalism. Fourth, there would seem to be a very real danger that once the new nationalism reaches its goal, it may spawn a new imperialism of its own. Finally, as colonialism passes into the pages of history, it may well be seen as the vehicle that brought the non-European peoples into the modern world, for better or for worse. Herbert Lüthy has made this point well:

> Europe's colonization of the world was neither a chain of crimes nor a chain of beneficence; it was the birth of the modern world itself. Not one of the former colonial peoples remembers it with gratitude, for it was an alien rule, but none wishes to turn back the clock and this perhaps is colonialism's ultimate historical justification.[8]

REFERENCES

1. Rupert Emerson, *From Empire to Nation*. Cambridge, Mass.: Harvard University Press, 1960, p.3.
2. *The New York Times,* July 4, 1960.
3. Mohandas K. Gandhi. *An Autobiography,* Boston: Beacon Press, 1971, p. 111.
4. Hans Kohn, *Is the Liberal West in Decline?* London: Pall Mall Press, 1957, pp. 69–70.
5. Emerson, *op. cit.,* P. 419.
6. For further reference, see the perceptive book by James Duffy, *Portuguese Africa*. Cambridge, Mass.: Harvard University Press, 1959.
7. Quoted in George McT. Kahin, *Major Governments of Asia*. Ithaca, N.Y.: Cornell University Press, 1958, p. 268, fn. 35.
8. Herbert Lüthy, "The Passing of the European Order," *Encounter,* November 1957, p. 12.

BIBLIOGRAPHY

Almond, Gabriel A., and Coleman, James S., eds. *The Politics of the Developing Areas*. Princeton, N.J.: Princeton University Press, 1960.

Astiz, Carlos Alberto, with McCarthy, Mary F. *Latin American International Politics*. Notre Dame, Ind.: University of Notre Dame Press, 1969.

Ball, William M. *Nationalism and Communism in East Asia*. 2d ed. Melbourne, Australia: Melbourne University Press, 1956.

Bandyopadhyaya, J. *The Making of India's Foreign Policy*. Calcutta: Allied Publishers, 1970.

Barber, James. *Rhodesia: The Road to Rebellion*. New York: Oxford University Press, 1967.

Barnett, A. Doak. *Communist China and Asia, Challenge to American Foreign Policy.* New York: Harper, 1960.

Baron, Salo W. *Modern Nationalism and Religion.* New York: Harper, 1947.

Birmingham, Walter, *et al. A Study of Contemporary Ghana. Volume Two: Some Aspects of Social Structure.* Evanston, Ill.: Northwestern University Press, 1967.

Black, C.E. *The Dynamics of Modernization.* New York: Harper and Row, 1966.

Bovis, H. Eugene. *The Jerusalem Question, 1917–1968.* Stanford, Calif.: Hoover Institution Press, 1971.

Campbell, John C. *The Defense of the Middle East.* New York: Praeger, 1961.

Carmichael, Joel. *The Shaping of the Arabs: A Study in Ethnic Identity.* New York: Macmillan, 1967.

Carter, Gwendolen M., ed. *National Unity and Regionalism in Eight African States.* Ithaca, N.Y.: Cornell University Press, 1966.

Cohen, Arahon. *Israel and the Arab World.* New York: Funk and Wagnalls, 1970.

Coleman, James S. *Nigeria, Background to Nationalism.* Berkely, Calif.: University of California Press, 1958.

Cremeans, Charles D. *The Arabs and the World.* New York: Praeger, 1963.

Crowder, Michael. *West Africa Under Colonial Rule.* Evanston, Ill.: Northwestern University Press, 1968.

Davidson, Basil. *The African Genius.* Boston: Atlantic-Little, Brown, 1970.

Deutsch, Karl W. *Nationalism and Social Communication.* New York: Massachusetts Institute of Technology Press and Wiley, 1953.

Douglas-Home, Charles. *The Arabs and Israel: A Background Book.* Chester Springs, Pa.: Dufour Editions, 1969.

Duncanson, Dennis J. *Government and Revolution in Vietnam.* New York: Oxford University Press, 1968.

Emerson, Rupert. *From Empire to Nation.* Cambridge, Mass.: Harvard University Press, 1960.

Erikson, Erik H. *Gandhi's Truth: On the Origins of Militant NonViolence.* New York: Norton, 1969.

Feis, Herbert. *The China Tangle.* Princeton, N.J.: Princeton University Press, 1953.

———. *The Birth of Israel: The Tousled Diplomatic Bed.* New York: Norton, 1969.

Feit, Edward. *African Opposition in South Africa: The Failure of Passive Resistance.* Stanford, Calif.: Hoover Institution, 1967.

First, Ruth. *Power In Africa.* New York: Pantheon, 1971.

Forsyth, Frederick. *The Biafra Story.* Baltimore; Penguin, 1969.

Fox, Annette B. *The Power of Small States: Diplomacy in World War II.* Chicago: University of Chicago Press, 1959.

Gann, L. H., and Duignan, Peter. *Burden of Empire: An Appraisal of Western Colonialism in Africa South of the Sahara.* New York: Praeger, 1967.

Gérard-Libois, Jules. *Katanga Secession.* Madison, Wis.: Wisconsin University Press, 1966.

Gifford, Prosser and Louis, Wm. Roger. *Britain and Germany in Africa: Imperial Rivalry and Colonial Rule.* New Haven, Conn.: Yale University Press, 1971.

Gordon, David C. *Self-Determination and History in the Third World.* Princeton, N.J.: Princeton University Press, 1971.

Halberstam, David. *Ho.* New York: Random House, 1971.

Harrison, Selig S. *India: The Most Dangerous Decades.* Princeton, N.J.: Princeton University Press, 1960.

Hobson, John A. *Imperialism.* London: Allen and Unwin, 1938.

Hopkins, Harry. *Egypt, The Crucible: The Unfinished Revolution in the Arab World.* Boston: Houghton Mifflin, 1970.

Horwitz, Ralph. *The Political Economy of South Africa.* New York: Praeger, 1967.

Howe, Russel Warren. *Black Africa: Africa South of the Sahara From Pre-History to Independence.* New York: Walker, 1967.

Hsu, Immanuel C.Y. *The Rise of Modern China.* New York: Oxford University Press, 1970.

Jordan, Robert S. *Government and Power in West Africa.* New York: Africana Publishing Corp., 1970.

Kautsky, John H. *Political Change in Underdeveloped Countries.* New York: Wiley, 1963.

Karpat, Kemal H. *Political and Social Thought in the Contemporary Middle East.* New York: Praeger, 1968.

Kertesz, Stephen D., and Fitzsimons, M.A., eds. *Diplomacy in a Changing World.* South Bend, Ind.: University of Notre Dame Press, 1959.

Kohn, Hans. *The Idea of Nationalism.* New York: Macmillan, 1944.

Lamb, Alastair. *The Kashmir Problem.* New York: Praeger, 1967.

Laqueur, Walter Z. *Communism and Nationalism in the Middle East.* New York: Praeger, 1957.

———. *The Soviet Union and the Middle East.* New York: Praeger, 1959.

Lacouture, Jean. *The Demigods: Charismatic Leadership in the Third World.* New York: Knopf, 1970.

———. *Nasser.* Paris: Editions du Seuil, 1971.

Legum, Colin and Margaret. *The Bitter Choice: Eight South Africans' Resistance to Tyranny.* Cleveland: World Publishing Co., 1968.

Levi, Werner. *The Challenge of World Politics in South and South-East Asia.* Englewood Cliffs, N.J.: Prentice-Hall, 1968.

Lichtheim, George. *Imperialism.* New York: Praeger, 1971.

Lusignan de, Guy. *French-Speaking Africa Since Independence.* New York: Praeger, 1969.

Mander, John. *The Unrevolutionary Society: The Power of Latin American Conservatism in a Changing World.* New York: Knopf, 1969.

Mboya, Tom. *The Challenge of Nationhood.* New York: Praeger, 1970.

Matthews, Herbert L. *Fidel Castro.* New York: Simon and Schuster, 1969.

Marquard, Leo. *A Short History of South Africa.* New York: Praeger, 1968.

McAlister, John T. *Vietnam: The Origins of Revolution.* New York: Knopf, 1969.

McKay, Vernon, ed. *African Diplomacy.* New York: Praeger, 1966.

McVey, Ruth T. *The Soviet View of the Indonesian Revolution.* Ithaca, New York: Cornell University Press, 1957.

Miller, J.D.B. *The Politics of the Third World.* London: Oxford University Press, 1967.

Moore, Clement Henry. *Politics in North Africa: Algeria, Morocco and Tunisia.* Boston: Little, Brown, 1970.

Mortimer, Edward. *France and the Africans 1944–1960. A Political History.* New York: Walker, 1969.

Nevakiki, Jukka. *Britain, France and the Arab Middle East, 1914–1920.* New York: Oxford University Press, 1969.

Niebuhr, Reinhold. *The Structure of Nations and Empires.* New York: Scribner, 1959.

Niven, Sir Rey. *Nigeria.* New York: Praeger, 1967.

Nye, Joseph S., Jr. *Pan-Africanism and East African Integration.* Cambridge, Mass.: Harvard University Press, 1965.

Overstreet, Gene D., and Windmiller, Marshall. *Communism in India*. Berkeley, Calif.: University of California Press, 1959.

Park, Richard L., and Tinker, Irene, eds. *Leadership and Political Institutions in India*. Princeton, N.J.: Princeton University Press, 1959.

Rivkin, Arnold. *The African Presence in World Affairs*. New York: Free Press, 1963.

Rostow, Walt W. *The United States in the World Arena*. New York: Harper, 1960.

Ruiz, Ramon Eduardo. *Cuba: The Making of a Revolution*. Amherst, Mass.: University of Massachusetts Press, 1968.

Rotberg, Robert I., and Mazrui, Ali A. *Protest and Power in Black Africa*. New York: Oxford University Press, 1970.

Safran, Nadav. *From War to War: The Arab-Israeli Confrontation, 1948–1967*. New York: Pegasus, 1969.

Schwartz, Benjamin I. *Chinese Communism and the Rise of Mao*. Cambridge, Mass.: Harvard University Press, 1951.

Shepherd, George W., Jr. *The Politics of African Nationalism*. New York: Praeger, 1962.

Shafer, Boyd C. *Faces of Nationalism: New Realities and Old Myths*. New York: Harcourt Brace Jovanovich, 1972.

Snyder, Louis L. *The New Nationalism*. Ithaca, New York: Cornell University Press, 1968.

Stevens, Richard P. *Lesotho, Botswana and Swaziland: The Former High Commission Territories in South Africa*. New York: Praeger, 1967.

Strausz-Hupé, Robert, *et al. Protracted Conflict*. New York: Harper, 1959.

——, Kintner, William R., and Possony, Stefan T. *A Forward Strategy for America*. New York: Harper, 1961.

Thompson, Scott W. *Ghana's Foreign Policy 1957–1966. Diplomacy, Ideology, and the New State*. Princeton, N.J.: Princeton University Press, 1969.

Thompson, Virginia. *West Africa's Council of the Entente*. Ithaca, N.Y.: Cornell University Press, 1972.

Treger, Peter and Burley, John. *African Development and Europe*. New York: Pergamon, 1970.

Trevelyan, H. *The Middle East in Revolution*. Boston: Gambit, 1970.

Ulam, Adam B. *The Unfinished Revolution*. New York: Random House, 1960.

United States Department of State. *The Sino-Soviet Economic Offensive in the Less Developed Countries*. 1958.

Vandenbosch, Amry. *South Africa and the World: The Foreign Policy of Apartheid*. Lexington, Ky.: University Press of Kentucky, 1970.

Wallerstein, Immanuel. *Africa: The Politics of Independence*. New York: Vintage, 1961.

——. *Africa: The Politics of Unity*. New York: Random House, 1967.

——. *The Interplay of East and West: Points of Conflict and Cooperation*. New York: Norton, 1957.

Ward, Barbara. *India and the West*. New York: Norton, 1957.

Weiner, Myron. *Party Politics in India*. Princeton, N.J.: Princeton University Press, 1957.

Wheeler, Richard S. *The Politics of Pakistan: A Constitutional Quest*. Ithaca, N.Y.: Cornell University Press, 1970.

White, Ralph K. *Nobody Wanted War: Misperception in Vietnam and Other Wars*. Garden City, N.Y.: Doubleday, 1968.

Whiting, Allen S. *China Crosses the Yalu*. New York: Macmillan, 1960.

Winslow, Earle M. *The Pattern of Imperialism*. New York: Columbia University Press, 1950.

5 The Two Political Power Struggles of Our Time

When sorrows come, they come not single spies, but in battalions.
SHAKESPEARE *Hamlet,* IV, 5

The Interdependence of the Two Struggles

The most significant characteristic of the international struggle for power in our time lies in the fact that its two principal conflicts—the struggle between the Communist and the non-Communist worlds, and that between the new nationalism of Asia, Africa, and the Middle East and the waning empires of Europe—are very closely and inseparably intertwined. At least potentially, every nation is today to a greater or lesser degree involved in both of these struggles.

This interconnection between the East-West and the nationalism-colonialism conflicts has steadily increased as each of them has intensified. In an earlier phase, the nations' energies tended to be directed to only one of the two conflicts, with their involvement in the other remaining obscured or unemphasized. Immediately after World War II, for example, the United States was inclined to perceive world affairs largely in terms of a division between East and West, between the democracies and the Communist powers. The Soviet Union, tending to share this chiefly East-West orientation, also paid comparatively little attention to the developing areas of the world. India, on the other hand, was above all concerned with the conflict between the new nationalism and colonialism, regarding the East-West struggle as of distinctly secondary importance.

The most dramatic expression of this limited perception of world affairs by the major nations involved came to center around the term "neutralism." The United States, for its part, frequently became impatient with the "neutralism" shown by the new nations toward the issues of the East-West struggle. It viewed their reluctance to join the American-led system of alliances as less than responsible and saw their inclination to abstain in voting on East-West issues in the United Nations as, at best, blindness to what was really at stake in international relations. The new nationalist countries, on the other hand, felt strongly critical of the United States' attitude of seeming detachment—politically as well as in the United Nations—in regard to the issues of the colonial struggle. India, for example, failed to understand the "neutralism" of the United States in the disputes between France and Algeria, the Netherlands and Indonesia, or Portugal and India over the disposition of Goa. It could not understand how the United States, itself once a revolutionary power, could fail to sympathize with the new nationalism against the colonial threat. From India's point of view, the colonial struggle was paramount. The United States wanted to enlist the support of India and India wanted to enlist the support of the United States. But their causes, and therefore their perceptions of the struggle, differed sharply. Each was quick to accuse the other of indifference in the battle which really mattered. In other words, the perception of each remained limited to one of the two great power struggles.

As the new nationalism continued to gain ground during the 1950's, both East and West became increasingly aware that the objectives of the new nations could no longer be ignored. Recognizing the need for allies in the prosecution of the East-West conflict, the United States and the Soviet Union alike found it in their self-interest to pay greater and greater heed to the colonial struggle. And as each searched for friends and prospective allies among the new nations, the involvement of each in the colonial struggle became more extensive. At the same time, the new nationalist powers took increasing cognizance of the East-West struggle and began wherever possible to exploit it to gain advantages in their fight against colonialism. Thus the international power struggle came more and more to resemble a game of three-dimensional chess.

In a dramatic reversal of its traditional foreign policy, the United States surrounded itself with a ring of defensive alliances against Communist expansion. It was instrumental in the forging of NATO, OAS, SEATO, and ANZUS—all of them regional military alliances. In addition, it concluded bilateral defense agreements with Japan, South Korea, Formosa, and the Philippines. Altogether, the United States became allied with forty-two nations. Moreover, though not technically a member, it pledged its support to the Central Treaty Organization (CENTO), linking Britain, Turkey, Iran and Pakistan in the common defense of the Middle East. (For an analysis of these military alliance systems, see Chapter 6.)

In its quest for allies, the United States thus made it its policy to woo both nationalist and colonial powers. On the one hand, through NATO, it found itself allied with all the great Western colonial powers—Britain, France, Belgium, the Netherlands, and Portugal. On the other, it simultaneously courted the newly emerged nations that were, or had recently been engaged in, all-out conflict with the colonial powers. As a result, prospective allies against Communism frequently tended to be incompatible and to be more fearful of each other than of the alleged common enemy, the Soviet Union. This was the situation when the United States attempted to persuade India, Indonesia, and Burma to join SEATO. These nations rebuffed the United States' overtures, in large part because they suspected the United States of sympathizing with the colonial powers in view of its alliance with them in NATO.

Most of the new nations have pursued a policy of remaining uncommitted in the East-West struggle. They have felt that such a "neutralist" course mitigated East-West tensions and, most importantly, netted them the greatest advantages in gaining their own objectives. The United States, attempting to attract both colonial and anticolonial powers into its anti-Communist defense system, has found it in its interest to pursue an equally "neutralist" policy toward the colonial struggle. For if it supported the new nationalism too strongly, it would jeopardize its alliance with its partners in NATO, and if it identified itself too closely with the colonial powers, it would incur the certain hostility of the new nationalism. Since either eventuality would accrue to the benefit of the Soviet Union, the United States has confronted most of the major colonial disputes with a Hamlet-like posture, refusing to commit itself or indicate its unqualified support for either side. It has pursued a similarly detached strategy—for similar reasons—in the struggles that have occurred among various of the new nations themselves. On the one hand, to assure the flow of essential oil to its NATO allies, it has supported such old monarchical forms of nationalism as that of Saudi Arabia. On the other, wanting above all to prevent its absorption into the Communist orbit, it has also maintained a measure of commitment to the new Arab nationalism of the United Arab Republic. At the same time, Arab hostility notwithstanding, it has recognized and supported the new Jewish state of Israel. In each case, that is, the United States has done its utmost to prevent the anticolonial nations from feeling it necessary to align themselves with the Soviet Union, and to secure the pacification of whatever disputes existed among them. The logic of the policy of pacification has been that only when differences among the new nations are reconciled, can they be persuaded to turn their attention to the East-West struggle.

The United States' desire to keep itself as attractive as possible to as diverse a group of nations as possible has not been the only obstacle standing in the way of a more consistent and forceful anticolonial posture. A further complicating factor has been America's own historical tradition in the matter of colonialism. For the fact is that the United States finds itself in the unique position of having been both an anticolonial and a colonial power. In its successful battle for independence from Britain in 1776, the United States waged the first major anticolonial struggle in modern history. This American example, along with the Declaration of Independence in which it was proclaimed, have inspired and guided nationalist leaders throughout the world and have made it difficult for them to understand American "neutralism" on the question of colonialism in our time. Yet it is no less a fact that in the late nineteenth century the United States became involved in an experience of its own as a colonial power, albeit reluctantly and with an exceedingly bad conscience. For in the wake of the Spanish-American War, the Philippines were annexed and Puerto Rico, Guam, Hawaii, and the Samoan Islands became American territories. Nevertheless, official American terminology never referred to these possessions as "colonies" nor to the United States itself as an "empire." Indeed, the effect of this bad conscience was an attempt to humanize the United States' venture into colonialism and to establish as its eventual goal the giving of self-government and independence to the areas concerned. How ambivalent were American feelings upon becoming a colonial power may be gathered from President McKinley's report of his reflections on his decision in 1898 to keep the Philippines:

The truth is I didn't want the Philippines and when they came to us as a gift from the gods, I did not know what to do about them. . . .I sought counsel from all sides—Democrats as well as Republicans—but got little help. I thought first we would take only Manila; then Luzon; then other islands, perhaps, also. I walked the floor of the White House night after night until midnight; I am not ashamed to tell you, gentlemen, that I went down on my knees and prayed to Almighty God for light and guidance more than one night.

And one night late it came to me this way, I don't know how it was, but it came: (1) that we could not give them back to Spain—that would be cowardly and dishonorable; (2) that we could not turn them over to France or Germany—our commercial rivals in the Orient—that would be bad business and discreditable; (3) that we could not leave them to themselves—they were unfit for self-government—and they would soon have anarchy and misrule over there worse than Spain's was; and (4) that there was nothing left for us to do but to take them all, and to educate the Filipinos, and uplift and civilize and Christianize them and by God's grace do the very best we could by them, as our fellow-men for whom Christ also died. And then I went to bed, and went to sleep and slept soundly. . . .[1]

By the end of the first half of the twentieth century, the United States had almost ended its entire colonial experiment. Franklin Delano Roosevelt's "Good Neighbor Policy" had replaced American intervention in Latin America; Puerto Rico had been prepared for limited self-government; and Hawaii and Alaska were ready to be absorbed as states into the Union. The Philippines received their political independence in 1946, although a high degree of economic dependence on the United States continued. The distinctive aspect of the American colonial experience was the fact that, unlike the British, French, or Dutch colonies, most American possessions, save for the Philippines, came to see as their ultimate goal not independence from the United States but full-fledged and permanent membership in the American union.

In contrast to the dilemmas faced in regard to the "colonial-anticolonial" struggle by the United States, the Soviet Union has had a comparatively easy time of it and has benefited accordingly. Communism has not had to contend with a choice between nationalism and colonialism. It has clearly and almost without exception been in the Soviet Union's interest to give unqualified support to the new nationalism in its conflict with the Western colonial powers. This policy has served the twofold purpose of winning the new nations' good will for the Soviet Union and, at the same time, of weakening NATO by hastening the dissolution of the Western empires.

Nor are the new nationalist powers any less advantage-minded in their conduct vis-à-vis the East-West struggle. They have shown themselves prepared to use whatever opportunities come their way to utilize this struggle to enhance their own positions, both in the competition among themselves and in their conflicts with Western colonialism. In July 1960, for example, Premier Patrice Lumumba of the new Republic of the Congo threatened to request the intervention of Soviet troops in order to expel the Belgians. The Soviet Union immediately responded by denouncing "Belgian imperialism," hoping thereby to widen the gulf between Belgium and the Congolese. This in turn compelled the United States to respond, though in line with its own national interest it brought its power to bear for a conciliation of the dispute. In any case, here as in numerous similar situations, the superpowers have become involved in the colonial struggle less of their own initiative than as a result of the conscious designs of the new nations themselves. Indeed, the existence of the East-West struggle has in many instances been a great boon to the newly sovereign states. Ready to be wooed by either side, and sometimes by both simultaneously, they have often acquired much greater international bargaining power than would have been possible on the basis of their own national capabilities alone. The position of the Arab States in the war with Israel in 1967, for example, demonstrated this truth.

While it may appear from the above discussion that the Soviet Union is in an incomparably better position to gain the allegiance of the new nationalist powers than is the United States, this is not entirely true. For though the Soviet Union has consistently supported the new nationalism, the record indicates that Communism—once in power—is itself inclined to look with hostility upon the politics of national self-determination. It attempted to destroy Yugoslav "nationalism"; it rigidly controlled Polish "nationalism"; it crushed the Hungarian revolt for national independence; and it was unwilling to tolerate political liberalization in Czechoslovakia. In East Asia, Communist China permitted little independence to Tibet and threatened India through a border war and Indonesia through internal subversion. Though, as we have seen earlier, the new nationalism is still hypnotized by the specter of Western colonialism, the lessons of Soviet and Communist Chinese policies have not failed to make a deepening impression.

In order to illustrate the complex pattern of interdependence of the East-West and colonial-anticolonial struggles, we shall once again employ the case study approach. Probably the best example of this interdependence in Asia may be seen in the rise of nationalism and Communism in China, the subject of our first case study. Second, we have selected the Middle Eastern crises of 1956 and 1967. Our final case will deal with the Congo crisis of 1960 in Africa. These three studies show clearly how extensively and inextricably the two great power struggles of our time interpenetrate—to the point, indeed, of being essentially merely two different aspects of a single global political drama.

The Pattern of Interdependence

THE CASE OF CHINA

Napoleon was once reported to have said, "Let China sleep; when she awakens, the world will be sorry." These were prophetic words. During the last century the impact of the colonial West first awakened China from its traditional past. That awakening has resulted in the modern

Communist regime of Peking today. The events in this development excellently illustrate how closely the two great political conflicts of our time are connected.

It is a significant fact, frequently not realized in the West, that ours is the first century in over four thousand years in which China does not consider herself to be at the center of the universe. The Chinese Empire was also known as the Middle Kingdom. For over four millennia it conceived of itself as the hub of civilization, the great school of the world—much as Athens had once considered itself to be the school of the ancient Mediterranean world. Although dynasties came and went, the political structure of the Empire remained essentially static. The Emperor, aided by a small intellectual elite, controlled the government. Insofar as the large mass of the population was concerned, this government was an amorphous force, inscrutable and unpredictable. The Emperor ruled by the Mandate of Heaven, and his edicts had the authority of the philosopher-king. The Socratic dictum "virtue is knowledge" could have been the motto of the Confucian scholars or "mandarins," whose major qualification for government office was a knowledge of the great literary classics of the Empire. Admission to government posts was not decided by imperial fiat or arbitrary violence, but through the institution of a highly formalized system of civil service examinations held in the capital. These examinations, open to all, were the first of their kind in history.

The world beyond the Great Wall of China did not hold much interest since, in the eyes of the Chinese, it was populated by barbarians. Hence, the foreign relations of the Empire were in essence tributary relationships: long caravans laden with gifts for the Emperor would weave their way across the land to the Imperial Court at Peking; the envoy would kowtow before the Son of Heaven, present the tribute, and hope for the favor of being permitted to trade with the great Empire. The arts of war and the use of violence were not held in high esteem in the Confucian ethos. The Chinese believed that since it was perfectly evident that their Empire was a superior civilization, it would be in the interest of all barbarians to learn from it rather than destroy it. The military preparedness of the Empire was therefore limited to defense against intermittent incursions by barbarians into China's territory.

This self-sufficient and almost static society had virtually no contact with the West whatsoever. The travels of Marco Polo in the twelfth century and the Jesuit mission of Father Matthew Ricci in the sixteenth were of too brief duration to create a lasting impression. The first massive Western impact occurred in the eighteenth century, when the British in their quest for more lucrative trade became intent upon establishing trade relations with the Empire. The Chinese, significantly enough, attempted to fit these British overtures into their traditional tributary framework. When, in 1793, a British trade mission led by Lord Macartney arrived at Peking, it was labelled as a tributary mission from the King of England. In exchange for the privilege of presenting his gifts, Lord Macartney was expected to kowtow, that is, to perform three kneelings and nine prostrations before the Emperor. When the British Lord objected to this procedure, he was politely requested to go home, although his tribute was graciously accepted. Shortly thereafter the Emperor sent an Imperial Edict to the King of England. This document is so significant that parts of it deserve to be quoted:

You, O King, are so inclined toward our civilization that you have sent a special envoy across the seas to bring to our Court your memorial of congratulations on the occasion of my birthday and to present your native products as an expression of your thoughtfulness. On perusing your memorial, so simply worded and sincerely conceived, I am impressed by your genuine respectfulness and friendliness and greatly pleased.

The Celestial Court has pacified and possessed the territory within the four seas. Its sole aim is to do its utmost to achieve good government and to manage political affairs, attaching no value to strange jewels and precious objects. The various articles presented by you O King, this time are accepted by my special order to the office in charge of such functions in consideration of the offerings having come from a long distance with sincere good wishes. As a matter of fact, the virtue and prestige of the Celestial Dynasty having spread far and wide, the kings of the myriad nations come by land and sea with all sorts of precious things. Consequently there is nothing we lack, as your principal envoy and others have themselves observed. We have never set much store on strange or ingenious objects, nor do we need any more of your country's manufactures. . . .[2]

There was one commodity, however, for which the British did find a market in China, and a lucrative one indeed: opium. Large quantities of opium were brought into China by traders of the British East India Company and in the early nineteenth century over one million Chinese became addicts to the poison. The Emperor became increasingly perturbed and authorized one of his mandarins to appeal to the conscience of the British ruler to discontinue the smuggling of opium into China. One of his officials, Commisioner Lin, sent a poignant note of protest to Queen Victoria in 1839, at a time when the use of the drug threatened to undermine the health of the entire population. This protest is an historic document:

We find that your country is sixty or seventy thousand li [three li make one mile, ordinarily] from China. Yet there are barbarian ships that strive to come here for trade for the purpose of making a profit. The wealth of China is used to profit the barbarians. That is to say, the great profit made by barbarians is all taken from the rightful share of China. By what right do they then in return use the poisonous drug to injure the Chinese people? Even though the barbarians may not necessarily intend to do us harm, yet in coveting profit to an extreme, they have no regard for injuring others. Let us ask, where is your conscience? I have heard that the smoking of opium is very strictly forbidden by your country; that is because the harm caused by opium is clearly understood. Since it is not permitted to do harm to your own country, then even less should you let it be passed on to the harm of foreign countries—how much less to China! Of all that China exports to foreign countries, there is not a single thing which is not beneficial to people; they are of benefit when eaten, or of benefit when used, or of benefit when resold: all are beneficial. Is there a single article from China which has done any harm to foreign countries? Take tea and rhubarb, for example; the foreign countries cannot get along for a single day without them. If China cuts off these benefits with no sympathy for those who are to suffer, then what can the barbarians rely upon to keep themselves alive?[3]

The request went unheeded and finally Commissioner Lin decided to take strong action. He issued orders to blockade British merchants at Canton and to destroy their opium. The British interpreted this seizure as an interference with freedom of trade and as an act of aggression. Instead of ending the smuggling of opium, Commissioner Lin precipitated the Opium War. This war was little more than a skirmish, settled by the Treaty of Nanking in 1842. The war itself, which signified the first violent contact between China and the West, showed how distorted were the perceptions that the two sides held of each other. The British, surprised by the weak show of resistance exhibited by the Chinese, interpreted this weakness as a surrender and proceeded to advance up the coast to occupy all the major coastal ports of China. The Chinese, on the other hand, with a few exceptions like Commissioner Lin himself, firmly believed that the British, like other barbarians before them, would recognize the self-evident superiority of Chinese civilization and behave accordingly. The Treaty of Nanking, marking the beginning of Western imperialism in China, was thus a surprise to both sides: to the Chinese because they found themselves unable to eject the "barbarians" by moral persuasion; to the British because they encountered almost no effective military resistance.

The first massive Western influence on China, therefore, was one of violent intrusion. It now remained for the West to consolidate its position in the Empire. This was accomplished through a series of arrangements known as the "unequal treaties," which gradually divested the Chinese Empire of its territorial integrity. The British were quickly followed by other Western nations, who were lured to China by the British example: French, Portuguese, and German colonizers attempted to negotiate similarly advantageous treaties with the Empire. The Empire had little choice but to grant the foreigners extensive concessions, with the result that by the mid-1840's China's sovereignty was little more than a fiction. The ominous and omnipresent threat of Western gunboats and superior military techniques were simply more than the old China could effectively resist.

The treaties which carved up China among the Western powers all had certain elements in common. First, there was the legal device of extraterritoriality. Under this system, foreigners in China were not subject to Chinese law but remained under the jurisdiction of their own governments. Many desirable sites on Chinese soil, including most residential areas in the large Chinese cities, were made inaccessible to the Chinese. Thus the Chinese suddenly found themselves in the incredible position of not being permitted to enter the choicest buildings and parks in their own cities unless permitted by a "barbarian" to do so. China's foreign trade and her customs and tariff policy were placed under the control of an Englishman, Inspector General Sir Robert Hart. One of the most anomalous consequences of this one-sided treaty system was the influx of Christianity into China. The picture of Christian missionaries attempting to repair the ravages of opium addiction caused by their conationals became a source of additional confusion.

The most important single feature of the unequal treaty system was the so-called "most-favored nations clause." Professor John K. Fairbank, a leading American authority on China, has called this "the neatest diplomatic device of the nineteenth century." The clause simply meant that all Western nations would participate in whatever any one of them could obtain. For example, if Germany was able to persuade China to give it a ninety-nine-year lease of an important port, all of the other Western powers had the automatic right to similarly favorable leaseholds. This rule of the "highest common denominator" made it a foregone conclusion that by mid-nineteenth century the entire coastal area of China, including her most important cities, were virtually in the hands of the West.

The rise of Chinese nationalism, including its culmination in the Communist revolution, must be understood in terms of this initial Western impact. During the past century, China has undergone five major convulsions: the Great Peasant Rebellion, the Boxer Rebellion, the Self-Strengthening Movement, the Nationalist Revolution, and the Communist Revolution. Each of these has been in essence a desperate attempt to regain national status, and each has its roots in the Western policy of imperialism mounted against China a little over a century ago. We shall now analyze each of these five nationalist movements.

The Great Peasant Rebellion of 1851 was one of the great social upheavals of modern times. It marked the first time in the history of the Empire that the Chinese population was politically activated *en masse.* An estimated twenty million people lost their lives in the course of this fifteen-year rebellion. Its leader, Hung, was a disappointed office-seeker. He claimed to have experienced a vision in which a venerable sage exhorted him to save humanity. Hung began to play on the population's fear of the "foreign devils" and its impatience and disgust with the tottering Empire which seemed to be at the mercy of the "barbarians." Hung vowed to unseat the bankrupt Manchu government and ultimately to eject the foreigners. He began to describe himself as "the younger brother of Jesus" and developed a philosophy incorporating tenets of Christianity and an ambitious program of agrarian reform. Millions of peasants supported his cause. Many believed that Hung had the Mandate of Heaven for a new dynasty that would displace the weak and discredited Manchus. Many peasants were also deeply fearful of the foreigners. For example, the foreigners built railroads and suspended wires in the air; when it rained, these wires would rust and reddish drops would fall onto the ground; the Chinese peasants believed that these reddish drops were the blood of the good spirits which had impaled themselves on the wires placed there cunningly by the foreign devils. A terrible famine gave the rebellion its final impetus. Millions of peasants began to advance rapidly toward Peking, led by Hung who vowed to establish his strange theocracy. By the mid-1850's, the rebels were in control of half of China. The Manchu government as well as the Western powers on the coast became increasingly terrified. In desperation the Manchus formed an alliance with the foreigners in order to present a united front against the rebels. The battle seesawed back and forth for an entire decade. Finally, the imperial forces, buttressed by modern arms and aided by foreign military leaders, were able to stem the rebellion. Hung committed suicide in 1864 and his death marked the defeat of the Great Peasant Rebellion.

This first reaction to the impact of Western imperialism is interesting for several reasons. The rebellion was the first example of popular nationalism in China and proved so powerful that only an alliance between the Manchu government and its worst enemy was able to crush it. It was in effect the first mass movement in China's history and, in historical perspective, was clearly a forerunner of the Communist Revolution.

China's second attempt to rid herself of the West was the pathetic and ill-fated Boxer Rebellion of 1900. The Manchu dynasty, which had received a new lease on life, decided on a show of force. The Boxers, fanatical members of anti-Western secret societies who believed themselves to be invulnerable, decided to besiege the foreign community in its own legations in Peking. For two months in the summer of 1900 most foreign officials were the prisoners of the Boxers. The suicidal futility of this venture became apparent when reinforcements arrived and the Western plenipotentiaries and their families were liberated. Retribution was swift: the leaders of the rebellion were executed and a heavy indemnity was exacted from the Chinese treasury. This second attempt at nationalist revolt was an utter and dismal failure.

During the second half of the nineteenth century it became increasingly clear to many Chinese intellectuals that their entire way of life was being undermined by the fire power of foreign arms and by superior Western technology. The Peasant and Boxer Rebellions, though very different, had proven equally futile because of China's backward state of military development. As a typical example of this state of affairs, in Fairbank's words "the British had used on the coast of China a shallow bottomed paddle-wheel iron steamer called the *Nemesis*. It carried swivel cannon fore and aft and was capable of moving into the wind and against the tide in a manner disastrous to China's fortunes."[4] The realization of China's inadequacy vis-à-vis the West led to the development of the so-called Self-Strengthening Movement, which spanned the latter half of the nineteenth century. The premise of the movement was a simple one: "Chinese learning as the fundamental structure, Western learning for practical use."[5] Its leaders felt that the only way of restoring the national status of China was for the Chinese themselves to utilize Western science and military techniques. In short, some of the ways of the foreigner would have to be copied in order to get rid of him. Accordingly, shipyards, arsenals, and science academies began to flourish. The Self-Strengtheners emphasized, over and over again, that this Western technology must be used to preserve Chinese values, not to destroy them. Thus, for example, Chinese students were sent to the West but were always accompanied by Confucian chaperones who made sure that these future leaders of China would not be infected by Western ideas. The fallacy of the Self-Strengthening Movement lay in its assumption that knowledge and life could be neatly compartmentalized, that one could adopt the tools of the West but totally ignore its values, that one could leap into the modern world only halfway. Inevitably, "one Western borrowing led to another, from machinery to technology, from science to all learning, from acceptance of new ideas to change of institutions, eventually from constitutional reform to republican revolution."[6] In the last analysis, the principal net effect of the Self-Strengthening Movement was to prepare the ground for the Nationalist Revolution of 1911.

One of the outstanding leaders of the Self-Strengthening Movement was Dr. Sun Yat-sen, destined to become the leader of the Nationalist Revolution. The life of Dr. Sun affords a fascinating case study of a revolutionary. He was born in Portuguese Macao, received his education in an English school, and was converted to Christianity early in life. He decided to study medicine in Hong Kong, where he came under the influence of a British missionary doctor, Sir James Cantlie. Cantlie acquainted the young Sun Yat-sen with Western ways ranging from the study of physics to the playing of cricket. Sun received his medical degree and hoped to set up practice as a surgeon in Macao. The Portuguese, however, debarred him from practice in his own country. Subsequently Dr. Sun abandoned his new profession and embarked on a revolutionary career. Between 1894 and 1911 he organized revolutionary sentiment against both the tottering Manchu dynasty and the Western powers. Like Lenin, he lived in exile with a price upon his head and relentlessly worked for the cause of revolution. At one point, in 1896, during a stay in London, he was abducted and imprisoned in the Chinese Legation for shipment back to China and certain death. He managed to inform Sir James Cantlie, who lived nearby, of his plight. Cantlie mobilized Scotland Yard and Sun was saved through British intervention. From this time onward, Sun was recognized as the undisputed leader of the Nationalist Revolutionary Movement.

It was during this incubation period of the Revolution that Dr. Sun developed his philosophy of the "Three Principles of the People": Nationalism, Democracy, and the People's Livelihood. This concept went beyond the philosophy of the Self-Strengthening Movement; Sun insisted that in order to become free China would have to borrow not only science but ideas as well. Sun's first principle of Nationalism simply meant "China for the Chinese." Democracy, as conceived by him, was to be an amalgam of American, British, and Swiss constitutional principles. And the People's Livelihood stood for a gradualist program of socialism patterned after the example of the Fabians in Britain. Armed with this synthesis of Western political thought Dr. Sun Yat-sen engineered ten revolutionary attempts against the Manchu government, all of which failed. Finally, in October of 1911, Sun went to the United States to raise funds for his cause. During his campaign he received a coded cable which he was unable to decipher because he had shipped his code book ahead. As it turned out, the cable contained news of yet another plot. This time the plot was successful. A few days later, on October 10, 1911, Sun Yat-sen read in the newspapers that a Nationalist revolution had broken out in China and that he was to be the first President of the new Republic.

It now remained for Sun to consolidate the Nationalist Revolution. This was by no means an easy task. With the collapse of imperial authority, China was now controlled by numerous warlords who were unwilling to yield to Sun Yat-sen's demand for unification under the Nationalist banner. The revolution seemed abortive. The warlords were not receptive to Sun's new ideas of parliamentary democracy, for these were wholly alien to the authoritarian tradition in which the Empire had been ruled for centuries. Moreover, they refused to reconcile their parochial interests with the national programs of the revolution. In 1912, as a result, Sun resigned as President and it seemed that the Nationalist Revolution had foundered on the rock of warlordism. Yet Sun continued to work for his ideal and, in desperation, approached the Western powers, pleading with them for aid in his struggle for national unification. The response, however, was negative, partly because a divided China was preferred by the West and partly because the energies of the great powers were primarily engaged in Europe, which was drifting toward the brink of war.

Western indifference to Sun Yat-sen during this period helped to direct the course of Chinese nationalism toward authoritarianism. Sun turned away from the West in disappointment and became increasingly disillusioned with parliamentary democracy as a way toward unification. It was no accident that when, at this critical moment in the fortunes of Chinese nationalism, another vast revolution took place—that in Russia in 1917—Sun looked toward the newly formed Soviet Union. To his amazement he saw that the Bolsheviks were able to subdue a country larger than China in a relatively short space of time, whereas China, a decade after the revolution, still lay prostrate at the mercy of the warlords. It was at this moment that Chinese nationalism began to look to Communism for inspiration. Sun Yat-sen had found Lenin.

Both Lenin and Sun Yat-sen were professional revolutionaries, yet no two men could have differed more. Sun Yat-sen was a Christian and by temperament inclined toward parliamentarianism rather than the use of violence; Lenin was a tough, shrewd revolutionary strategist who firmly believed that only a tightly organized, blindly obedient Party could accomplish the goals of revolution.

The Bolshevik success induced Sun Yat-sen to accept Lenin's advice and organize a Nationalist Party, the Kuomintang, patterned on authoritarian principles. Soviet advisors, most prominent among whom was the Comintern agent Michael Borodin, helped in the organization of the new Nationalist Party at Nanking. By 1924 the Nationalist Party apparatus was sufficiently permeated with Communists that China could have been absorbed into the Communist orbit without much difficulty. But in that year Lenin died and during the remainder of the 1920's the energies of Soviet leaders were absorbed in a brutal struggle for succession.[7] As a result, though China seemed to lie within their grasp, none of the Soviet leaders gave it much attention. As Stalin put it, when the time came, the Soviet Union would "squeeze the Chinese Nationalists like a lemon."

In 1925 Dr. Sun Yat-sen died. Unlike Lenin, who had not groomed a successor for his mantle, Sun had prepared one of his most brilliant disciples to follow in his footsteps. This man was Chiang Kai-shek, a young military leader who had been sent by Sun to the Soviet Union for study, to acquaint himself with Soviet political and military techniques. When Chiang Kai-shek took over the leadership of the Nationalist Revolution, he was quite aware of the Comintern's plans to absorb China. He decided to "squeeze the lemon" first. Using techniques that he had learned from the Communists, Chiang Kai-shek decided to stage a workers' strike. He then blamed this strike on the Communists in his own Party and used it as an excuse to purge them ruthlessly from the Kuomintang, forcing them on the famous "Long March," which was to last seven years and was to take them to the other end of China.

By 1930 Chiang Kai-shek, having assumed the title of Generalissimo, was at the zenith of his power. He had expelled the Communists and was now able to embark on his goal of unification of all of China, the first aim of the Nationalist Revolution. He announced that China was to be under the political tutelage of the Nationalist Party until conditions became stable enough to make possible the transition to constitutional democracy.

Under the leadership of the Generalissimo, the new Nationalist government made a determined effort to rid itself of the unequal treaties with the West. Chiang Kai-shek mapped out his program in his book, *China's Destiny*, in which he blamed most of the ills of China on Western imperialism. He announced a "Rights Recovery Movement" and a "New Life Movement." The former was a plan gradually to wipe out extraterritoriality, Western customs control, and the foreign concessions in the major Chinese cities. The latter was an attempt to restore the old Confucian virtues which had been displaced by the West. The Kuomintang was to serve as the instrument of the Generalissimo's will.

Chiang Kai-shek's nationalism was in essence an attempt to revive the past and the tradition of the Empire. It was a somewhat modernized version of the old imperial hope that government by Confucian precept and example would restore China to her rightful place of centrality in the comity of nations. The Party ruled in an almost completely authoritarian manner, providing little opportunity for popular participation in government. The lesson of the Great Peasant Rebellion was forgotten; once more the peasant was virtually disfranchised and little attempt was made to ease his lot through land reform. The New Life Movement was symbolic of the Kuomintang approach: the anomalous picture of old greybeards preaching the restoration of Confucius to impatient university students brimming with the excitement of new ideas and yearning for a whole new way of life.

Moreover, Chiang Kai-shek's conservative nationalist program was never really tested in time of peace. In 1931 the country was attacked by Japan and after 1937 the Nationalist government had to bear the brunt of the full fury of the new Japanese imperialism. In the face of this deadly threat, Chiang Kai-shek was compelled to suspend his domestic programs and to employ almost his entire resources in the battle for national survival. Even so, the invaders succeeded in capturing the capital at Nanking and forcing Chiang Kai-shek to relocate the seat of his government in the mountains of the interior, at Chungking.

Meanwhile, the few thousand Chinese Communists who arrived exhausted in Yenan in 1934 appeared destined for oblivion. Chiang Kai-shek had turned his attention to the Japanese and the Comintern had written them off as hopeless. But during the Long March a new and tenacious leadership had emerged which was ultimately to bring the Communists to a complete national victory. Mao Tse-tung, surely one of the most complex figures of our time—a mixture of scholar, poet, party organizer, and military strategist—took command. The redoubtable leader Chu Teh became responsible for military operations;

and Chou En-lai, the most cosmopolitan of the three, took charge of the Chinese Communists' foreign relations.

Yenan in the mid-1930's provided a privileged sanctuary to the Communists. The first American reporter to visit them there in 1936 described the startling contrast between the electric atmosphere of optimism prevailing in Yenan and the dank smell of defeat in Chiang Kai-shek's wartime capital.[8] It was during this period that Mao Tse-tung worked out the program whereby his Communist forces were to take over the leadership of Chinese nationalism. For one thing, the Chinese Communist Party completely emancipated itself from control by Moscow and thereby became the only Communist Party in the world that was independent of the Soviet Union from the very beginning of its rise to power. Mao Tse-tung embarked on an important ideological deviation by declaring that in China, Communism would have to be built on an agrarian rather than an industrial base. "Just as fish cannot live without water," he said, "Communism in China cannot survive without the support of the peasants."

The second significant aspect of Mao's program was his strategy of attempting to win the allegiance of the peasantry by capitalizing on the economic and social inadequacies of the Chiang Kai-shek government. Mao Tse-tung promised an extensive land reform program and pledged that no Communist soldier would be permitted to live off the land, that indeed the Communist soldier should be considered as the friend of the peasant. The Communists organized festivals and dances to woo the peasantry and gained thousands of recruits. Their great opportunity came in 1936. Chiang Kai-shek, badly pressed by the Japanese, was being beseeched by his officers to form a United Front with the Chinese Communists against the common enemy. When he refused, he was kidnapped by some of his own military leaders and forced to ask the Communists to join in the battle. As soon as had reluctantly agreed, the Communists sallied forth from their sanctuary and swept across the countryside, picking up nearly a half million new recruits on the way. As Chiang Kai-shek had suspected, the United Front was for the Communists largely a project in self-aggrandizement. Given minimal help by the Communist Chinese Eighth Route Army, he had to fight the Japanese alone until the entrance of the Allies into the war.

This writer witnessed the liberation of Shanghai from the Japanese by Chiang Kai-shek's forces in 1945. Seldom was there a more Pyrrhic victory; the Nationalist soldiers entered the city tattered, exhausted, and demoralized, while the Communist forces stood poised only a few hundred miles away, fresh and ready for the decisive encounter. Hence the defeat of Japan did not bring peace to Chiang Kai-shek's government. Instead of being free to implement his long-postponed programs, he was compelled to mobilize his resources to attempt to block the steadily advancing armies of the Communists. In the ensuing four years of civil war, the Generalissimo's fortunes steadily declined. Mediation attempts by the United States—first through Ambassador Patrick Hurley and then through General George C. Marshall—proved to be of no avail. Chiang Kai-shek refused to form a coalition government with the Communists because he feared their techniques of infiltration. Mao Tse-tung was equally unwilling to agree to a compromise because he was certain of ultimate victory. In addition to his program of economic and social reform, Mao Tse-tung now bitterly attacked the rampant corruption of the Nationalist government and proceeded to portray Chiang Kai-shek as a lackey of Western imperialism. The Nationalists, corroded by inflation, corruption, and defeat, finally had to quit the mainland in 1949 in a desperate scramble for refuge on the island of Formosa. The Mandate of Heaven passed from their hands. It was now the Communist Party that assumed leadership of the new nationalism in China.

The course of these Chinese developments affords some interesting insights into the interdependence of the East-West and the colonial-anticolonial struggles. It is clear that both the Nationalist and the Communist revolutions in China were in essence reactions against Western imperialism. The five upheavals in which this reaction became manifest were not isolated events but consecutive expressions of a continuing development. Indeed, so far as China is concerned, the present East-West conflict is a direct outgrowth of the long struggle of Chinese nationalism against Western imperialism—with the policies of today's Communist regime being simply its latest phase.

In the United States, which consistently supported Chiang Kai-shek, the struggle between the Nationalist government and the Chinese Communists has received much attention and aroused a great deal of emotion. It was widely believed that the two sides represented completely opposite motives and aspirations. Few Americans perceived the complex truth that the Nationalist and Communist revolutions were *both* in essence anti-Western movements and that the struggle between them was more a struggle for power between competing forms of authoritarian nationalism than a conflict between radically different ideologies. It was a measure of the extent to which Americans had failed to recognize this basic fact that during the 1950's so many people in the United States were prepared to accept the allegation that the United States had "lost" China as a result of the machinations of subversives in the American government. Though it is not within the purview of this case study to examine the problem of subversion, it must be noted that underlying this "explanation" of the recent course of Chinese history is the assumption that a handful of Americans actually had it in their power to determine the fate of the more than half billion people of China.

During the quarter century of non-relations between the United States and China, most Americans regarded Chiang Kai-shek as a soldier-saint who could do no wrong. After all, he had fought the Japanese and the Communists and was a Christian. Mao Tse-tung, on the other hand, was perceived as the Communist devil in league with Stalin. This devil image of Mao Tse-tung, so prevalent in America, helps to explain why a détente between the two nations was so long in coming. When in 1954, Secretary of State John Foster Dulles refused to shake hands with Chou En-lai in Geneva, he expressed the feelings of most Americans at the time: one does not engage in commerce with the devil. Another eighteen years had to elapse before an American President shook hands with the Chinese Premier, this time on Chinese soil. In truth, the similarities between Chiang Kai-shek and Mao Tse-tung over half a century had always been greater than the differences.

In conclusion, our case study demonstrates the continuity between the Nationalist and the Communist revolutions. The pattern is, in fact, a continuum: China's role in the East-West conflict actually grew out of the struggle between nationalism and Western imperialism. In this struggle for national self-assertion against the West, Communist China used the Soviet Union as an ally. There were, after all, striking elements of similarity between the old authoritarian nationalism of the Chinese Empire and the new authoritarian nationalism of the Russian Communists. Communism, like the Empire, saw itself as occupying a central position in the world, almost messianic in character. And Communism, too, had its "barbarians"—the West—to be treated with contempt and derision. Communist ideology was the anti-Western cement that temporarily bound the two nations together. But once China had demonstrated her new prowess to the West, she turned against the East as well. The alliance with the Soviet Union had now outlived its usefulness. And remembering that Russia, too, had in the nineteenth century joined in the predatory policies of the Western powers, China now pressed territorial claims along the Sino-Soviet border. Thus, the ultimate thrust of the Chinese revolution must be seen as directed against both East *and* West.

It is perhaps well to remind ourselves again that ours has been the only century in the past four thousand years in which China has not seen itself as the center of the universe. Is it possible that Communism may turn out to be the instrument that the new nationalism in China has forged for itself to restore China to the central place that she considers to be rightfully hers by the verdict of history? This may yet be the ultimate bearing that the two great power struggles of our time have on the fate of China.

THE SUEZ CRISIS OF 1956 AND THE ARAB-ISRAELI WAR OF 1967

Whereas our consideration of Chinese nationalism has been concerned with a relatively long historical period, our second case study focuses upon two specific and short-term events, the Suez crisis of 1956 and the Arab-Israeli war of 1967. A comparative analysis of these two events affords dramatic insights into the complexities and ambiguities of the political struggle of our time. For not only did these two crises involve the two general global struggles of East versus West and nationalism versus colonialism; in addition, they generated sharp conflicts among the Western powers and among the new anticolonial nations themselves.

The Suez crisis was precipitated in the summer of 1956 when President Gamal Abdel Nasser of Egypt nationalized the Suez Canal, abrogating, in the view of Britain and France, the International Convention of Constantinople of 1888, which had provided that "the Suez Maritime Canal shall always be free and open, in time of war as in time of peace, to every vessel of commerce or of war without distinction of flag." The Egyptian leader defended his act by stating that the Canal was within Egyptian territory and that the time had come to announce Egypt's "Declaration of Independence from Imperialism." In an emotional speech, he hailed nationalization as a symbolic act which would set Arab nationalism on its course from the Atlantic to the Persian Gulf. Britain and France, aghast at this unexpected move, lodged a strong protest against the seizure of "an international water-way" and against the violation of what the two Western nations considered to be their legal rights in the area. For Britain, as well as for Egypt, the Suez Canal was a symbol. While for Egypt it represented the growing power of the new nationalism, for Britain, control of the Canal symbolized her status as an Empire and as a world power. To the French, who blamed Egypt for supporting the Algerian rebellion against France, seizure of the Canal served as a kind of last straw. For Britain and France alike, the issue at stake was therefore not merely the rational one of safeguarding the economic rights of their shareholders in the Suez Canal Company. Far more important was their emotional reaction to the seemingly insolent and irresistible nationalism represented by the Egyptian move. The highly emotional nature of the conflict thus set the stage for a violent encounter between nationalism and colonialism.

During the weeks that followed Nasser's action the conflict broadened. Britain and France sounded out the official American reaction to the situation. Prime Ministers Eden and Mollet, contemplating the use of force against Nasser, were partially reassured by the fact that Secretary of State Dulles also appeared outraged by Egypt's action. The British and French Foreign Ministers compared Nasser's action to Hitler's behavior at Munich and stated in the strongest terms that this type of Western appeasement must not be allowed to occur again.

Secretary Dulles replied that "force was the last method to be tried, but the United States did not exclude the use of force if all other methods failed."[9] From this statement Mr. Eden inferred that the United States would, at best, present a united front with Britain and France in a show of force against Nasser and, at worst, remain benevolently neutral. Thus it seemed in the late summer of 1956 that the United States would side with the colonial powers against the new nationalism.

Britain and France now prepared for military action. They hoped to mount a lightning attack against Egypt, occupy the Canal, depose Nasser, and then negotiate with his successor from a position of strength. In the course of these preparations, it became increasingly evident to the two Western powers that they shared a common interest with Israel. The new Jewish state, harassed by border clashes and made increasingly insecure by Nasser's pronouncements "to drive Israel into the sea," could be used as the cutting edge of the Anglo-French punitive expedition against Egypt. "Collusion" between Britain and France on the one hand and Israel on the other has not been substantiated, but a great deal of circumstantial evidence points in that direction. At any rate, Israel penetrated Egyptian territory on October 29, 1956, and rapidly advanced toward the Suez Canal. On the following day the British and French bombarded Cairo. What had thus begun as an armed conflict between the two new Middle Eastern nations now assumed the proportions of a large-scale Western onslaught against the new nationalism. The United States, instead of observing a benevolent neutrality toward the British, French, and Israeli actions, took a leading role in the United Nations General Assembly in calling for a cessation of fighting and the immediate withdrawal of the Anglo-French-Israeli forces from Egypt. To the consternation of most of its Allies in NATO and to the delight of Egypt, the United States upheld the United Nations Charter against the NATO alliance. On the same day, the Soviet Union took up the Egyptian cause, and threatened to send "volunteers" to Egypt and to bomb London and Paris with rocket missiles. Thus the United States found itself in the paradoxical postion of being allied in the United Nations with its great antagonist in the East-West struggle, the Soviet Union, and of being at odds with its closest friends and allies, Britain and France. By November 6 Britain had to yield. Confronted by United Nations resolutions charging her with aggression, dismayed by the action of the United States, and troubled by an increasingly hostile opposition at home, Prime Minister Eden terminated his abortive venture. France had no choice but to follow suit, and the "gentle persuasion" of the United States resulted in the withdrawal of Israeli forces shortly thereafter. A world conflagration had narrowly been averted.

Of all the roles in the drama, that of the United States was undoubtedly the most problematical. Confronted in the most acute way

possible with the old dilemma of whether to support the colonial powers
or the new nationalism, the United States was bound to lose either way.
Her actual decision to side with Egypt inevitably alienated Britain and
France and put the most severe strains on the NATO alliance. Sir
Anthony Eden was compelled to resign, and throughout Britain as well
as France a growing body of "neutralist" sentiment became articulate.
Indeed, in the view of a number of observers, for example former
Secretary of State Dean Acheson, American policy in the crisis came
close to losing the United States its two most trusted allies and thus
exposing Western Europe to the domination of Communism. On the
other hand, if the United States had sided with Britain and France
against Egypt, its risks would have been no less heavy. The new nations
of Africa, Asia, and the Middle East would have quickly concluded that
when the chips were down the United States was at heart no less a
colonial power than its Western European allies. In disillusionment, the
new nationalism would almost certainly have veered sharply away from
the United States toward the Soviet Union. Probably the least amount
of animosity would have resulted if the United States had followed its
more typical pattern in such situations and abstained from the conflict
altogether. Yet even in this case both sides would likely have found
reason for objecting to America's role.

As one observer has pointed out, "the criticism of the American stand
came essentially to this point: the United States had chosen to behave
like a collective security power, not like an ally. In the Middle Eastern
situation, 'Uniting for Peace' had prevailed over NATO."[10] Yet the
American rejection as "unthinkable" of a Soviet proposal for joint
superpower intervention in the Middle East suggests strongly that the
American position was not determined by the abstract considerations of
the collective security ideal. There was, first, the sense of outrage that
the President and Secretary of State both felt because the British and
French had not bothered to consult their NATO ally on a matter as
important as military action in the Middle East at a time when a
national election was imminent in the United States. Second, from a
purely military standpoint, the Anglo-French punitive expedition
seemed to be foundering and thus could not be presented to the General
Assembly as a *fait accompli*. The United States, by supporting the Anglo-
French venture or even by taking a neutral view of it, would have
risked the ill will of a large majority of the UN membership and, in
addition, might have had to look on helplessly while the military action
failed or bogged down. Moreover, such an American response might
have persuaded many neutralists that the United States, by countenanc-
ing aggression in the Middle East, differed little from the Soviet Union,
which was practising aggression by crushing a rebellion in Hungary
with military force. Most important, the United States feared the

possibility of Soviet intervention in the Middle East through "volunteers" and the risk of sparking a major war through direct superpower confrontation in the contested area.

All this does not exclude the possibility that some of the reasons motivating the United States were of a genuinely moral nature. As stated by the American government, the United States acted as it did because it insisted on the principle that the same standard of international law and morality should apply to all nations, friends and foes alike. Yet even this seemingly unassailable moral reason rested upon ambiguities. It could be argued, for example, that a "moral" action might under certain circumstances eventuate in "immoral" consequences. Thus the "moral" behavior of the United States in the Suez crisis ran the risk of leading to the disintegration of NATO and the "immoral" result of opening Western Europe to Soviet domination. Conversely, if the United States had decided upon the "immoral" step of supporting the British and French military expedition against Egypt, the outcome might have been the quite "moral" one of restoring the legal economic rights of the Western powers and of reestablishing the Suez Canal as an international waterway. The point here is *not* that the United States acted either morally or immorally. It is, rather, that among other things, the Suez affair demonstrated how subtle and indeterminate the relationship between ethics and power in international relations can be. The most "moral" intentions may lead to highly "immoral" consequences, whereas on other occasions and in different circumstances the very reverse may be true.

The Soviet Union's role in the Suez crisis was much simpler. From its point of view, the only unusual aspect was its strange alliance with the United States in the United Nations. In order to dissociate itself from this somewhat unwelcome association, the Soviet Union interpreted the action of the United States not as being helpful to Arab nationalism but, rather, as a nefarious scheme to replace British and French imperialism with American imperialism. In contrast, it pointed to itself as the only true champion of the new nationalist cause. Its threat of rocket retaliation against Britain and France was designed to underline how firm its commitment to the new nationalism in fact was. From the Soviet Union's point of view, indeed, the Suez crisis constituted a great windfall in the East-West struggle: the British and French appeared to be digging their own graves in the Middle East and the United States seemed to be doing its best to help them. Thus, by appealing to the cause of Arab nationalism, the Soviet Union saw its opportunity to eject all Western influence from the Middle East and gain a foothold of its own. The fact that Israel was allied with the two colonial powers also played into Soviet hands. Typically, therefore, the Soviet Union showed itself ready to use every facet of this colonial struggle to advance its own cause in the East-West battle. And, from the melee, Communism emerged with a clear-cut gain.

The main losers in the Suez affair were clearly the two colonial powers, Britain and France. In humiliation, they had to watch Nasser snatch a political victory from a military defeat. Abandoned by their closest and oldest ally, they had to admit that they could no longer act like great powers and that, in the last analysis, their initiative in international politics depended upon the decisions of the United States. The new nationalism had inflicted a painful defeat upon them and the very issue that they had set out to rectify by force of arms—the internationalization of the Suez Canal—now seemed beyond redemption. For all practical purposes, the Suez crisis terminated Anglo-French authority in the Middle East. Suez had become another Dienbienphu.

The greatest victory in the Suez crisis was won by Arab nationalism. Nasser was now clearly master of the Suez Canal. The two great superpowers had both supported him. The prestige of the Egyptian leader reached its zenith immediately after the Suez affair. Not only did Nasser triumph in the showdown with Western colonialism, but his other great foe, Israel, had also been compelled to withdraw as a result of American pressure. The political logic of the East-West struggle, by becoming the decisive factor in the crisis, thus operated to advance the cause of Arab nationalism to greater strength and prestige than it had ever possessed or than Nasser could ever have hoped to gain on his own.

Only Israel emerged relatively unchanged from the turmoil of the Suez affair. To be sure, it had demonstrated its military superiority over the competing nationalism of Nasser, yet it was prevented from capitalizing on its advantage by strong United States pressure to withdraw. In the end, nearly all the territories it had occupied had to be given up.

When the Suez crisis was over, the world's power configuration had definitely altered. In the East-West struggle, the Soviet Union clearly had come off best. It had created a more attractive image of itself in the Arab world and had won its first foothold in the Middle East. The promulgation by the United States of the Eisenhower Doctrine in March 1957—pledging American assistance to Middle Eastern countries against Communism—was testimony to increasing American awareness of this latest Soviet gain. In the second struggle, that of nationalism versus colonialism, the winner was clearly the new nationalism. After Suez, the great-power role of Britain and France in the Middle East was clearly at an end. The Eisenhower Doctrine attempted to salvage what was left of Anglo-French influence. In the third struggle, that of nationalism versus nationalism no appreciable change occurred in the distribution of power between Arab nationalism and Zionism. Both emerged stronger from the crisis, Israel because of its formidable military prowess and Egypt owing to its political triumph over Britain and France.

One question still remains about the Suez crisis that cannot be answered with certitude but that nevertheless ought to be raised. It is quite conceivable that the events in Suez determined the course of another political struggle, thousands of miles away—that of the Hungarian revolutionaries against the Soviet Union. The simultaneity of the two upheavals may have been more than accidental. The first stage of the Hungarian revolution was completed when Imre Nagy assumed complete control of Hungary and announced on November 1, 1956, that Hungary would be "free, independent, democratic, and neutral." Soviet forces were withdrawing from Hungary and agreement seemed to be near between the Soviet Union and the new Hungarian government. On that same day, however, the British and French mounted their invasion of Egypt, which reached its climax on November 3. On that day Nagy was informed that Soviet forces, in battle formation, were steadily advancing on the capital. On the following day, Soviet armored units had broken through the defenses of Budapest and the Hungarian revolution was drowned in blood.

Is it possible that the Soviet Union, in addition to the other advantages which it derived from the Suez crisis, decided to use the Anglo-French invasion of Egypt as a pretext for deflecting attention from events in Hungary? Or, to put it in other words, would the Soviet Union have decided to let Hungary escape from Communism into a position of international neutrality if the Suez crisis had not occurred? Should we ask ourselves the somewhat ironical question of whether, because of the actions of Britain and France, the West itself was responsible for the failure of the Hungarian revolution? It is very doubtful that, in our own generation at least, we shall have the answers to these questions. What the Suez crisis did make dramatically clear, however, is that both in its origins and in its consequences the struggle for power among nations in our time has become one continuous, global, and indivisible process.

Interdependence again was the keynote of the Arab-Israeli war of 1967, although the specific alignment of forces was quite different. This time the two superpowers took opposing sides, while Britain tended to favor Israel and France leaned toward the Arabs.

The decade between the two crises had seen a bevy of border incidents but no major eruption. In early 1967, however, tension began to mount. President Nasser's Arab neighbors accused the Egyptian leader of hiding behind the United Nations Emergency Force in order to avoid a confrontation with Israel. Sensitive to this charge, Nasser demanded on May 18 that UNEF leave the positions in Sinai that it had occupied for more than ten years. It is not certain whether the Egyptian leader initiated this move primarily to assuage his Arab critics or whether he really intended to clear the field for military action. At any rate, Secretary-General U Thant complied with the demand, reasoning that UNEF could no longer remain in the area if the consent of the host government were withdrawn. Hence, the UNEF contingents were removed from Sinai, the Gaza Strip, and from Sharm El-Sheik overlooking the Straits of Tiran. Almost simultaneously, Israel, Syria, and Jordan began to mobilize their armed forces and mass them on their respective borders. On May 20, military control over the Gaza Strip reverted to Egypt and the Arab League issued a joint declaration signed by twelve of its members with only Tunisia abstaining, stating that an attack on one would be considered as an attack on all. Israel responded by calling up the reserves and on May 22 Egypt ordered total mobilization. During this early phase of the crisis the superpowers indicated their positions, but refused to become vitally involved.

The second phase of the crisis began when, on May 23, President Nasser announced a blockade of the Gulf of Aqaba, thus cutting off Israel's only southern port, at Elath. Israel immediately responded by defining the blockade as an act of war that entitled her to take appropriate action. Egypt, for her part, maintained that the Straits of Tiran were within her territorial waters and therefore could be closed to states with which she was at war.

At this juncture, the East-West struggle was superimposed upon the two competing nationalisms of Israel and the Arab states. On May 23, President Lyndon B. Johnson presented the American position. He described the blockade as "illegal and potentially disastrous to the cause of peace" and affirmed that "the right of free, innocent passage through the international waterway [was] a vital interest of the international community." The American President supported the settlement that had been reached after the Suez crisis of 1956. Since Egypt was determined to overthrow that settlement, the American position in effect came down on the side of Israel.

On the following day, the Soviet Union declared that Israel was to blame for the dangerous aggravation of tensions in the Middle East. The forces of imperialism represented by "a handful of colonial oil monopolies" and backed by commercial interests in the United States and Britain were the chief culprits behind the scene, in the Soviet view. The USSR further proclaimed its support for the Arab states in their "just struggle for national liberation against colonialism."

The other major powers—Britain, France, and Communist China—also took stands in the escalating crisis. Britain supported the United States on the right of free passage of all nations through the disputed straits; France declared herself to be "not committed in any way and on any subject" on the side of "any of the states involved;" and China, supporting the Arab cause, also accused both the United States and the Soviet Union of "strangling the just struggle of the Palestinian people."

In the meantime, the two main protagonists edged closer to the brink. On May 25, Israel's chief delegate to the United Nations, Abba Eban, flew to London and Washington in order to ascertain what the two Western powers would do to end the blockade. Both offered vague assurances but counselled restraint. On May 28, Syria and Iraq signed a military agreement calling for the cooperation of their armies against Israel—and on the following day, President Nasser announced that Soviet Premier Alexei Kosygin had sent him a pledge to guarantee the Egyptian blockade. On May 30, King Hussein, described several weeks earlier as a "Hashemite Harlot" by President Nasser, placed Jordan's armed forces under Egyptian control in the event of war with Israel. Thus, by the end of May, the brink was reached and Israel confronted the armies of Egypt, Syria, and Jordan.

On the morning of June 5, heavy fighting broke out between Israel and Egypt. In four days of lightning warfare, Israel defeated the armies of her three main Arab antagonists. In Egypt, she captured the Sinai up to the east bank of the Suez Canal and also lifted the blockade of Aqaba by capturing Sharm El-Sheik. The Gaza Strip also fell into Israeli hands. In bloody fighting with Jordan, Israel occupied the Old City of Jerusalem and all of Jordan west of the Jordan River. Finally, Israel also captured portions of Syrian borderlands from which Arab guns had harassed Israeli settlements. On June 9, the short but violent war came to a halt with a cease-fire resolution passed by the UN Security Council.

During the next phase, the conflict moved from the military arena of the Middle East to the political forum of the United Nations. Both the Security Council and the General Assembly debated the issues, the latter in a four-week emergency special session. In the world forum, Israel insisted on recognition by the Arab states and an end to belligerency as conditions of withdrawal from the occupied Arab territories. She was supported in this view by the United States. The Arab states demanded unconditional withdrawal and full reparations, and insisted that Israel be condemned as an aggressor. Soviet Premier Kosygin supported the Arab demands from the rostrum of the General Assembly. France inclined toward the Arab position and the small nations were about evenly divided. Neither superpower was able to muster a two-thirds majority for its respective position and hence the General Assembly adjourned in a mood of frustration after two resolutions calling upon Israel to rescind its annexation of Old Jerusalem were ignored. The one concrete UN measure was the dispatch of a small number of cease-fire observers to the Suez Canal.

An analysis of the changes in power constellations after the war reveals some suggestive comparisons and contrasts with the 1956 crisis. In the first place, the Soviet Union had backed a loser this time, while she had been on the winning side a decade earlier. Most of the military hardware that the USSR had shipped to the Arab states had been destroyed in the four days of war. Nor was the Soviet Union able to turn anticolonial sentiments to its advantage in the United Nations, since many of the smaller nations also identified with Israel. On the other hand, their defeat now made the Arab states more than ever dependent upon the USSR, which promptly resumed arms shipments to them.

The role of the United States was once again problematical. She was on the winning side and, superficially, her policy seemed successful. But on a deeper level, it was clear that the swiftness of Israel's victory had saved the United States from having to make some very difficult decisions. Had the war gone badly for Israel, the United States might have been forced to intervene and risk a confrontation with the Soviet Union.

Britain and France, the two main losers in the 1956 affair, this time were only marginally involved. A new power factor in the equation, however, was Communist China, which accused the United States and the Soviet Union of conspiring together in the Middle East.

Israel, which had to withdraw in 1956, this time was determined not to yield its military gains, except in exchange for an end to belligerency. This the Arabs were unwilling to concede and thus, in the view of many observers, the 1967 war had not resolved and perhaps had even exacerbated the deeper causes of the conflict.

Thus, by mid-1967, the balance of power in the Middle East had definitely altered. Although Israel had won her military victory essentially unaided, the political constellation clearly showed once again the interdependence of the two great struggles of our time. One superpower tried to exploit the Arab-Israeli war by describing it as a struggle between Arab nationalism and Western imperialism. In this effort, the USSR failed where it had succeeded in 1956 when the two superpowers found themselves on the same side. And the United States, eager to pacify the struggle, was saved by Israel's arms from the decision to intervene. Thus, the connection between the two world struggles might have widened the theater of war had the conflict between the two main antagonists been inconclusive or gone the other way.

THE CONGO CRISIS OF 1960

The Congo crisis of 1960 affords a third illuminating case study of the interdependence of the two great political conflicts of the twentieth century. Once again—this time in Africa—East confronted West and the new nationalism challenged Western colonialism. And once again all the interests, issues, and consequences involved became inextricably inter- meshed.

Belgian rule in the Congo had for fifty years been based on the assumption that conscientious concern for the physical well-being and economic needs of the indigenous population would prevent the rise of a nationalist movement. When, in January 1959, violent nationalist riots erupted in Leopoldville, the Congolese capital, it became clear that this assumption had been incorrect. The Belgian government, interpreting these riots as a harbinger of impending disaster, decided to end its colonial rule as rapidly as possible. Independence for the Congo was slated for June 30, 1960. During the last year of Belgian colonial rule, little attempt was made to prepare an indigenous elite for the imminent responsibilities of self-government. Only a handful of Congolese had enjoyed a university education and the overwhelming majority of the Congo's fourteen million people were illiterate. Most were under the impression that on Independence Day all Belgian property would simply revert to the Congolese population. As one Congolese phrased the question, "Does independence come wrapped in paper or do we get it at the bank?"[11] Thus, on June 30, 1960, the colony of the Belgian Congo was suddenly transformed into an independent nation, a new-born infant left on the world's doorstep. The government that took over the Congo was headed by President Joseph Kasavubu and Premier Patrice Lumumba. Both had been members of the Congolese Nationalist Movement. Kasavubu, the more conservative of the two, was not excessively hostile toward Belgium and the Western powers. The office of the Presidency which he came to occupy was largely an honorific post. Lumumba, the Premier, had been a more ardent nationalist than Kasavubu, and was resolved to sever all relations with Belgium after independence. Both of these men were challenged in their views by Moise Tshombe, Premier of the provincial government of Katanga. Tshombe had been financed by the Belgian government during the colonial period. He was a wealthy man, conservative, and pro-Belgian. Thus the new Congolese leadership held political views covering the entire spectrum—from Lumumba's uncompromising anticolonialism to Tshombe's pro-Belgian sentiments.

A few hours after its Declaration of Independence, the new government faced a crisis which threatened its very survival. The Congolese Army of 25,000 men, which had never had an African officer corps, rose up, demanding the ouster of its Belgian officers and pay increases for the enlisted men. Many disappointed civilians who had expected to inherit all Belgian possessions on Independence Day joined in the mutiny. During the following days the mutiny spread through the rest of the Congo. In the major cities lawlessness prevailed and thousands of Belgians fled in panic. Premier Lumumba was unable to enforce the authority of the new government and unwilling to request Belgian help for fear of fanning the flames of violence still further. On July 11 Tshombe declared that Katanga was seceding from the rest of the country and forming a new state allied with Belgium. Since Katanga Province was the wealthiest part of the Congo, possessing the former colony's richest mineral deposits, this act of secession threatened the very life of the new state. Moreover, the provincial government of Katanga requested Belgian military help in order to suppress the violence that was engulfing it along with the rest of the Congo. Accordingly, Belgian troops re-entered Katanga for the purpose of restoring order. But on the following day, the Belgian government charged that since the new Congolese government of Premier Lumumba had been unable to protect the lives and interests of the remaining Belgian population, Belgian troops would march into Leopoldville as well. When the Belgians re-entered the capital, shooting broke out between them and Congolese soldiers. At this point the Lumumba regime began to blame the riots not on the Africans but on the Belgians. The Premier accused Belgium of aggression and stated that the colonial power had conspired with Tshombe to engineer the secession of Katanga Province in order to find a justification for the reimposition of colonial rule. What had started as only a local conflict thus quickly took on the dimensions of another major struggle between nationalism and colonialism.

On July 13, 1960, members of the Lumumba regime cabled the United States government for aid but both Premier Lumumba and President Kasavubu immediately disavowed this appeal and stated that it had been meant as a request for a United Nations force composed of military personnel from neutral countries. Nevertheless, the earlier request proved enough to set off a sequence of events that overnight turned the Congo into a battleground for the East-West struggle. Soviet Premier Khrushchev immediately announced that the Congolese soldiers had been perfectly right in their mutiny against the Belgian officers. He also claimed that the United States and the Western colonial powers in NATO had conspired to send Belgian troops into the Congo to reimpose colonial status under the pretext of restoring order. United Nations Secretary-General Dag Hammarskjöld called an emergency meeting of the Security Council and urged authorization for the dispatching of a United Nations military force to the Congo. During the Council session, the Soviet Union condemned Belgian "armed aggression" and accused the United States of collusion with colonialism. The United States denounced the Soviet accusation as "outrageous and untrue." The Security Council, in an 8 to 0 vote, called on Belgium to withdraw its troops from the Congo and authorized the Secretary-General to organize a United Nations Peace Force to be patterned after the Middle East Force established during the Suez crisis of 1956. Both the Soviet Union and the United States voted for the resolution, while Britain, France, and Nationalist China abstained.

Thus, the first United Nations resolution on the Congo reflected a tenuous consensus between the superpowers: the United States was eager to interpose the authority of the United Nations between East and West and to prevent the Congo from becoming yet another battlefield in the cold war; the Soviet Union was eager to speed the withdrawal of the Belgian forces and thus to play its role as self-appointed champion of anticolonialism. The solid backing of the African states for the resolution was a signal to both of the superpowers to stand clear.

The East-West battle continued, however. Premier Khrushchev announced that the Soviet Union was considering direct intervention in the Congo. He said that this might become necessary since he had received a telegram from President Kasavubu and Premier Lumumba stating that their lives were in danger and that they might "be compelled to ask for intervention by the Soviet Union if the Western camp (did) not desist from aggression against the sovereignty of the Congo Republic.[12] The Soviet leader pledged Russia's support to Lumumba and told the West, "Hands off the Congo!" The Soviet delegation in the United Nations demanded the evacuation of the Belgian "aggressors" within three days. The United States representative, Henry Cabot Lodge, countered with the declaration that the United States "would do whatever may be necessary to prevent the intrusion of any military forces not requested by the United Nations."[13] The Security Council unanimously barred unilateral intervention and urged the speedy withdrawal of Belgian forces. In the meantime, the United Nations Congo Force was gradually replacing the Belgian troops. The two superpowers were carefully excluded from the international contingent. Troops from twenty-nine nations, including Morocco, Tunisia, Ghana, Ethiopia, Mali, Guinea, Ireland, Sweden, and India—all under the United Nations flag—were deployed throughout the Congo to prepare the way for the more arduous task of building a responsible and viable Congolese government. (For a full discussion of UNEF and ONUC see Chapter 12.)

Even while UN troops were arriving in the Congo, further complications were in the making. Tribal antagonisms erupted into local wars; South Kasai, following the example of Katanga, seceded from the central government; and Moise Tshombe not only refused to dismiss his Belgian advisers and troops, but announced that he would meet any attempt by the United Nations to enter Katanga with force.

In the light of all these developments, Hammarskjöld thought it necessary in early August to return to the Council for a clarification of his mandate. The consensus between the superpowers continued to hold. Both the United States and the Soviet Union voted for a resolution sponsored by Tunisia and Ceylon which declared that "the entry of the United Nations Force into the province of Katanga (was) necessary," and demanded the immediate withdrawal of Belgian troops from the province.[14] The resolution was adopted by a vote of 9 to 0 with France and Italy abstaining. The United States voted for the resolution with some misgivings because of the strong action against Belgium; the Soviet Union, which wanted even stronger action, had introduced a draft resolution which would have imposed upon the Secretary-General the obligation "to take decisive measures, without hesitating to use every means to that end," to remove the Belgian troops. But in the end the Soviet Union too supported the Ceylon-Tunisia resolution.

The precarious consensus between the superpowers broke down when, in the autumn of 1960, the new Congolese government disintegrated completely. A power struggle between Premier Lumumba and President Kasavubu erupted. The Soviet Union supported the Premier and supplied him with military equipment to crush the Katanga secessionist movement. The Premier, however, was deposed and a young pro-Western colonel, Joseph Mobutu, took command. As a result, the Soviet bridgehead in the Congo had to be withdrawn. Under Mobutu's rule, many Belgian administrators returned to the Congo as unofficial advisors.

The superpowers now took opposing positions on the two rival factions in the Congo government. The United States pressed the United Nations to recognize the Kasavubu-Mobutu government, while the Soviet Union continued to supply Lumumba with aircraft and trucks and accused the United Nations of partiality in the conflict. The United Nations representative in charge of this critical phase of ONUC's operations in the summer and fall of 1960 was Andrew W. Cordier, Executive Assistant to Dag Hammarskjöld. Cordier's overriding concern was to uphold the Charter and to restore law and order in the war-torn Congo. In order to stop both Kasavubu and Lumumba from inflaming popular feelings even further and to prevent the outbreak of civil war, he decided to close all Congolese airports, thereby immobilizing troops, and to shut down the national radio in Leopoldville. Three years later, N. T. Fedorenko, the Soviet delegate in the UN General Assembly's Fifth Committee, was to declare that by this action, "Cordier had adopted a decision that broke Lumumba's back" and had thus started the United Nations on its pro-Western course in the Congo.[15] Similarly, many highly placed United States officials later pointed to Cordier's decision as having "stopped the Russians." Cordier himself defended his action on the grounds that it had *not* been taken *against* one of the rival factions or *against* one of the superpowers, but *for* the law of the United Nations and the Charter.[16]

After the closing of airports and radio stations by the United Nations, the Soviet Union accused the UN of neocolonialism and proposed a draft resolution directing the UN to cease any interference in the internal affairs of the Congo and to hand over the airports and radio

stations to the central government. Only Poland supported this resolution. Ceylon and Tunisia abstained and proposed a substitute
resolution that endorsed the policies and actions of the Secretary-
General. This resolution was vetoed by the Soviet Union.[17] What
remained of consensus between the superpowers on the Council now
broke down completely and the General Assembly was immediately
called into emergency session.

The superpowers now attempted to line up majorities for their
opposing positions in the General Assembly. The United States led the
forces seeking "to affirm and strengthen the mandate already given to
the Secretary-General by the Security Council." The Soviet Union, on
the other hand, took the position that "the United Nations Command
and the Secretary-General personally have unmasked themselves as
supporters of the colonialists."[18] After intensive and often acrimonious
debate, an overwhelming majority of the Assembly supported the
Secretary-General's policy, appealed to members to refrain from unilateral action in the Congo, and created a Conciliation Commission, made
up of African and Asian representatives, to pacify the internal dissensions in the Congolese government.[19]

The fiercest battle in the Assembly was waged over the question of
who should represent the Congolese government in that body. The
Republic of the Congo had been admitted to membership on September
20, but the question of seating its representatives had been left to the
Credentials Committee. Several days later Guinea proposed that,
pending a decision of the Credentials Committee, representatives of the
Lumumba government should be seated. This proposal was supported
by Ceylon, Ghana, India, Indonesia, Mali, Morocco, and the United
Arab Republic, all of which had troops in the Congo. It was also
vigorously defended by the Soviet Union.

The Guinean proposal evoked a sharp protest from Kasavubu, who
immediately set out to plead his case at UN Headquarters in New York.
On November 8 he appeared on the rostrum of the General Assembly
and demanded the seating of his representatives. He was supported in
this demand by the United States, which claimed that the Lumumba
government had neither effective and stable control of the country nor
the ability to fulfill its international obligations. The Assembly debate
was adjourned briefly pending the return from the Congo of the
Conciliation Commission. But the West had a clear majority on the
Credentials Committee, which had been given a separate mandate after
the vote of the Congo's membership. The United States proposed the
accreditation of the Kasavubu delegation, and after two days of heated
debate the motion was adopted in Committee by a vote of 6 to 1.
Lumumba's supporters now had to bring their fight into the plenary.

The two superpowers both lobbied intensively for their positions,
especially among the African members of the Assembly. But it became

clear very quickly that the United States position was the more persuasive one. It was backed solidly by all the NATO powers, most of the Latin American states, and most of the French-speaking African members, although a considerable number of African and Asian states that had endorsed the Congo policy of the Secretary-General now balked and either abstained or voted against it. The final vote on the critical accreditation issue was 53 in favor, with 24 opposed and 19 abstentions. The United States position thus emerged victorious. The Soviet Union, in turn, now mounted a fierce attack on the Office and person of the Secretary-General. (For a full analysis of this attack, see Chapter 10.)

On February 13, 1961, it was announced that Patrice Lumumba had been killed by hostile tribesmen in Katanga. This event, which convulsed the Congo and brought it to the brink of civil war, also resulted in a partial restoration of the superpower consensus on the Security Council. On February 21 the Council passed its strongest resolution to date, urging that "the United Nations take immediately all appropriate measures to prevent the occurrence of civil war in the Congo, including . . . the use of force, if necessary, in the last resort."[20] The resolution also called for "an immediate and impartial investigation" of Lumumba's death. While the United States and the Western powers had some misgivings about the implications of the use of force, even "in the last resort," they did endorse the tough paragraphs of the resolution. The fact that most of the African and Asian states solidly supported the resolution helped persuade the United States to vote for it. France, however, decided to abstain. The Soviet Union, which by now was waging a relentless war against Hammarskjöld and the entire Congo operation, found itself almost completely isolated in this position in the General Assembly. Fearful of alienating the African states if it vetoed the "force in the last resort" resolution, the Soviet Union abstained. Thus, with the reluctant approval of one of the superpowers and the tacit consent of the other, the Security Council once again took over the political guidance of the Congo operation.

During the spring and summer of 1961 the Congo presented a picture of extreme confusion. Kasavubu had appointed Cyrille Adoula as Prime Minister of the Congolese government, but the Adoula government was unable to control the entire country. Lumumba's Vice-Premier, Antoine Gizenga, established the "legitimate government" of the Congo in Stanleyville. And ONUC forces, in their efforts to integrate Katanga into the central government, ran into mounting resistance, not only from the Katangese forces of Moise Tshombe, but from French, Belgian, and South African mercenaries. Numerous casualties were suffered on both sides. Finally, on September 17, while engaged in an effort to persuade Tshombe, the Secretary-General was killed during a night flight when his airplane crashed near Ndola, Northern Rhodesia.

Against the background of Hammarskjöld's tragic death, the Security Council met on November 13, barely ten days after the election of U Thant as Acting Secretary-General. The increasing turmoil in the Congo resulted in an even stronger resolution than that of February 21. With no negative votes and only France and the United Kingdom abstaining, ONUC was now authorized "to take vigorous action, including the use of the requisite measure of force for the immediate apprehension of all foreign military and paramilitary personnel and political advisers not under the United Nations command, and mercenaries."[21] Both superpowers strongly supported the resolution. The United Nations was now clearly committed to support Adoula's central government against the secessionist efforts of both Tshombe and Gizenga.

In early December Acting Secretary-General U Thant directed UN forces to reestablish law and order in Elisabethville, the capital of Katanga. This initiative resulted in heavy fighting. The UN moved in heavy reinforcements for an all-out offensive to gain control of Katanga. But some Western powers, notably Belgium and Great Britain, were still hesitant to see Tshombe suppressed. Apart from the considerable financial interests which both countries had in Katanga, Tshombe was seen as the only pro-Western anti-Communist, while Gizenga was seen as a serious Communist threat to the Congo, and the Central Government at best merely neutral. Even in the United States, the Tshombe regime had some supporters. Britain refused to supply bombs to the UN to be used against Katanga. The Western powers viewed the danger of Communist influence as the greater threat, while the anticolonial African and Asian nations saw Tshombe as the tool of "imperialism," and thus the major danger. The Soviet Union backed the anti-Tshombe forces.

This time the UN was determined not to stop too soon, as it had done earlier. UN forces, supported by jet fighters, pressed on, and on December 20 Tshombe signed the Kitona Agreement, acknowledging the authority of the Central Government and promising to comply with the UN resolutions requesting the removal of foreign mercenaries. But talks to implement this agreement were not begun until March 1962, and in June, after a second breakdown of discussions, it appeared that Tshombe still had no intention of ending his secession. In late July U Thant submitted a plan for the reunification of the Congo, involving a 50-50 sharing of revenues from Katangese mines, integration of the Katangese army with that of the Central Government, and the discontinuance of separate representation abroad, in return for which Katanga would receive considerable local autonomy. U Thant intimated that if this plan was not accepted economic pressure would be used, possibly extending to a complete trade and financial boycott. But neither Belgium, Britain, nor the United States wanted to allow the pressures to go beyond the economic sphere, and Tshombe's conditional acceptance of the plan sufficed to avert any economic sanctions. In October the West became preoccupied with the Cuban crisis and seemed content to let Congolese matters drag on. But the Chinese attack on India gave rise to Indian pressures to obtain the release of her troops in the Congo, numbering over 5000 men, to fight in the Himalayas. Moreover, the weakening of Premier Adoula's position because of the Central Government's inability to enforce its authority in Katanga created a need for the early settlement of the Katangese secession. Finally, ONUC was running into increasing financial difficulties.

By December 1962 the pressure for economic measures against Tshombe increased. Adoula had been requesting such measures since August, but at that time both Britain and Belgium had been opposed. Nor had the United States actively supported such a move. Now Belgium shifted its stand, in return for a promise from the Central Government to grant Katanga a larger share of the mining revenue. The United States, too, threw its support behind Adoula. But Britain and the Union Minière still refused to go along. Fighting broke out again in late December, but Elisabethville was captured by UN forces on December 28, and the important mining center of Jadotville fell a week later. At first it appeared that Tshombe was going to fight to the end and pursue a scorched earth policy which would ruin Katanga, but he surrendered his last stronghold at Kolwezi in return for a general amnesty for Katanga officials. By the end of January 1963 the resistance was ended, though the Congo's problems were far from over. The last UN troops were withdrawn in mid-1964 and the situation continued to be tense throughout that year. Ironically enough, Moise Tshombe emerged as the new Premier of the Congo after the withdrawal of the UN Forces.

The escalation of the Congo crisis may be seen in three stages. The crisis began as a local conflict among several warring factions, or competing forms of nationalism. But when the new Congolese government blamed the secession of Katanga on Belgium, the tribal struggle merged into the larger one of nationalism versus colonialism. Finally, the superpower conflict entered the picture as the last of three widening concentric circles: the Soviet Union gained its first foothold in the Congo through Lumumba and the United States felt impelled to support Kasavubu.

Once both the colonial and the East-West struggles were involved, a pattern of mutual exploitation began to appear. The various nationalist factions in the Congo saw the East-West struggle as a means to an end, and the Soviet Union used nationalism to advance the cause of Communism. Thus, the Soviet Union attempted to infiltrate the Congo by underwriting the most virulent form of Congolese nationalism. But the Congolese, in turn, by appealing to both East and West for help, sped the withdrawal of Belgian troops and placed a United Nations guarantee on the Congo's independence.

Perhaps most important was the paradoxical fact that the pattern of interdependence of the two main conflicts created a precarious consensus between the superpowers which permitted the establishment of the Congo Force. Thus the two superpowers, though their interests clashed in Africa, allowed the UN Security Council to act. The United States, interested in the pacification of the colonial struggle and the neutralization of the Congo, saw in the United Nations the most efficient instrument to attain these ends. The Soviet Union, aware of the new African nations' high regard for the world organization, dared not be cast in the role of defying overwhelming Afro-Asian majorities in the General Assembly if the Security Council were to be paralyzed by a Soviet veto. Neither superpower was enthusiastic about the Council's first two resolutions. The United States thought them too strong, the Soviet Union too weak. But both preferred them to inaction.

The defeat of Lumumba turned the Soviet Union against the Congo operation. The General Assembly had to take over the direction of ONUC from a temporarily paralyzed Council. The UN operation in the Congo now proceeded against the express and active opposition of one of the two superpowers. It is doubtful whether or not the United States would have taken a very different position if Lumumba had been victorious in the Congolese power struggle and Kasavubu had been killed in his stead. Be that as it may, the death of Lumumba and the intransigence of Tshombe in seceded Katanga restored a partial consensus between the superpowers on the Council. This consensus resulted in two of the toughest resolutions ever passed by a United Nations body. Once again they were thought to be too strong by the United States and not strong enough by the Soviet Union, but both superpowers permitted the Council to act. The UN, which at first had tried to remain aloof from the internal political struggles in the Congo, now discovered that this position had only created a power vacuum. Thus, it decided to support the Central Government against the separatisms of both Tshombe and the political heirs of Lumumba. The United States gave this policy its active—though not enthusiastic—support. The Soviet Union, in turn, backed away from its policy of active obstruction to a more flexible one of passive opposition.

The Congo crisis again demonstrates that the struggle between East and West must be considered in conjunction with the struggle between the forces of nationalism and colonialism. In essence, the United States permitted the UN to act because it hoped to neutralize a "no man's land" in Africa regarding the East-West struggle and because it was impressed with the powerful African backing for UN action. The Soviet Union permitted the UN to act because it, too, wanted to woo the Africans in the United Nations and because a veto would have brought about immediate action in the Assembly, where the Soviet Union had much less power and influence. Only when the Congo operation began to go directly against the interests of one of the superpowers was a veto cast. And when the UN's policy became more acceptable, the Soviet Union once again stood clear. In the last analysis, the peculiar linkage between the two great international power struggles made it possible for the United Nations to take action, and, after four difficult and costly years, finally to bring a solution to the problems of the Congo within reach.

. . .

Our analysis has shown that the two paramount political struggles of our time revolve around the liquidation or preservation of colonialism and the expansion or containment of Communism. Most of the world's nations are engaged in one of these two conflicts, many in both. Hence, there has emerged a web of global political interdependence, though each specific issue has produced its own unique alignment of forces.

The revolutionary upheavals in China during the last hundred years demonstrate that the Chinese struggle against Western imperialism during the nineteenth century provided the seedbed for the Communist Revolution. Indeed, in historical perspective, it becomes clear that Chinese Communism is but the most recent phase of the Chinese nationalist reaction against the coming of the West. Communist China today is of course a major factor in the East-West struggle. But it, in turn, was the end product of the Chinese struggle for self-assertion. In China, therefore, the pattern of interdependence appears as a continuum: the East-West conflict actually grew out of the struggle between Chinese nationalism and Western imperialism.

The Middle East and Congo crises also exhibit the continuum pattern, though in a much shorter interval of time. They began as local conflicts between competing forms of nationalism: the Arab states and Israel in the Middle East, and the tribal and regional jealousies among the several warring factions in the Congo. This conflict between competing forms of nationalism ushered in the next stage: nationalism versus colonialism. Thus, in the Middle East, the 1956 Suez Canal crisis precipitated a violent eruption between Arab nationalism and the two colonial powers, Britain and France. During the 1967 war, the Arabs tended to perceive Israel as the vanguard of Western imperialism backed by the United States and Britain. In Africa, the new Congolese government blamed the secession of Katanga on Belgium and, therewith, the tribal struggle merged into the larger one of nationalism versus colonialism. Finally, the East-West conflict entered the picture as the last of three widening concentric circles: in the Middle East, the Soviet Union gained a foothold in 1956, but took a substantial loss in 1967, while the United States was compelled to protect the area against

Communist expansion by promulgating the Eisenhower Doctrine in 1957 and resuming arms shipments to Israel in 1967. In Africa, the Congolese request for help to the United Nations and the almost simultaneous appeal to the Soviet Union introduced the East-West struggle into that area.

Once both political struggles were involved, the pattern of interdependence became one of mutual exploitation. Nationalists used the East-West struggle to shore up their position and the Soviet Union used the new nationalism to further its own ends. Nevertheless, the very conditions that gave rise to this multifaceted struggle for power also provided the opportunity for the strengthening of international order. The two superpowers, despite their divergent interests in the Middle East and Africa, permitted the establishment of a United Nations Peace Force in 1956 and a small team of UN observers in 1967. The struggle for power and the struggle for order both found their nourishment in the same soil.

As the twentieth century completes its seventh decade, the web of interdependence between the two great political struggles has become truly universal. The 1950's saw it expand into Asia; the 1960's saw it move into the Middle East; and in the 1970's it reaches into the remotest corners of Africa. The international struggle for power among nations in our time has indeed become a one-world struggle.

One important difference between the two struggles may suggest something about their ultimate resolution. In the East-West conflict the two sides have fought to a kind of stalemate, while in the North-South struggle the colonial powers have, for the most part, been conciliatory and the forces of anticolonialism are close to achieving victory. By and large, the issues in the former have turned on the propriety of substantive demands for change, while in the latter they have been concerned with tempo and modality of change. It is quite conceivable that the East-West conflict will still be with us in the next generation, but it is almost certain that the struggle over colonialism will pass before long into the pages of history.

REFERENCES

1. Thomas A. Bailey, *A Diplomatic History of the American People,* 4th ed. New York: Appleton-Century-Crofts, 1950, p. 520.

2. John K. Fairbank and Ssu-yu Teng. *China's Response to the West.* Cambridge, Mass.: Harvard University Press, 1954, p. 19.

3. *Ibid.,* p. 25.

4. John K. Fairbank, *The United States and China*. Cambridge, Mass.: Harvard University Press, 1958, p. 142.

5. *Ibid.*, p. 143.

6. *Ibid.*

7. For an excellent description and perceptive analysis of this period, see Conrad Brandt, *Stalin's Failure in China*. Cambridge, Mass.: Harvard University Press, 1958.

8. Edgar Snow, *Red Star Over China*. New York: Random House, 1938, *passim.*

9. *Full Circle: The Memoirs of Anthony Eden,* quoted by Herbert Feis in *Foreign Affairs,* July 1960, p. 600.

10. Inis L. Claude, Jr., *Swords into Plowshares,* 2d ed. New York: Random House, 1959, p. 460.

11. *The New York Times,* July 10, 1960.

12. *Ibid.,* July 24, 1960.

13. *Ibid.*

14. UN Doc. S/4426, August 9, 1960.

15. UN Press Release 6A/AB/842, May 22, 1963.

16. Interview with Dr. Andrew W. Cordier, March 18, 1963.

17. UN Doc. S/4526, September 17, 1960.

18. General Assembly Official Records: Fourth Emergency Session, 858th Plenary Meeting, September 17, 1960.

19. General Assembly Res. 1474(ES-LV), September 20, 1960.

20. UN Doc. S/4741, February 21, 1961.

21. UN Doc. S/PV 982, November 24, 1961, pp. 71–75.

BIBLIOGRAPHY

Badeau, John S. *The American Approach to the Arab World.* New York: Harper and Row, 1968.

Ball, William M. *Nationalism and Communism in East Asia,* 2d ed. Melbourne, Australia: Melbourne University Press, 1956.

Barnds, William J. *India, Pakistan and the Great Powers.* New York: Praeger, 1972.

Barnett, A. Doak. *Communist China and Asia. Challenge to American Foreign Policy.* New York: Harper, 1960.

———. *Communist China: The Early Years, 1949–55.* New York: Praeger, 1964.

Beal, John R. *Marshall in China.* Garden City, N.Y.: Doubleday, 1970.

Black, Cyril E., *et al. Neutralization and World Politics.* Princeton, N.J.: Princeton University Press, 1968.

Brzezinski, Zbigniew. *The Fragile Blossom: Crisis and Change in Japan.* New York: Harper and Row, 1972.

Burton, J.W., ed. *Nonalignment.* New York: James H. Heineman, 1967.

Buttinger, Joseph. *Vietnam: A Dragon Embattled,* Vols. I and II. New York: Praeger, 1967.

Campbell, John C. *The Defense of the Middle East.* New York: Praeger, 1961.

Chaudhri, Mohammad A. *Pakistan and the Great Powers.* Karachi: Council for Pakistan Studies, 1970.

Clissold, Stephen, ed. *Soviet Relations with Latin America 1918–1968.* New York: Oxford University Press, 1970.

Emerson, Rupert. *From Empire to Nation.* Cambridge, Mass.: Harvard University Press, 1960.

——. "Nationalism and Political Development," *Journal of Politics,* February 1960.

Fairbank, John K. *The United States and China,* rev. ed. Cambridge, Mass.: Harvard University Press, 1971.

Fall, Bernard B. *The Two Vietnams.* New York: Praeger, 1967.

Gittings, John. *The Role of the Chinese Army.* New York: Oxford University Press, 1967.

Gordon, King. *UN In the Congo.* New York: Carnegie Endowment for International Peace, 1962.

Guillermaz, Jacques. *A History of the Communist Party.* New York: Random House, 1972.

Gurtov, Melvin. *The First Vietnam Crisis.* New York: Columbia University Press, 1967.

Hinton, Harold C. *China's Turbulent Quest.* New York: Macmillan, 1970.

Hurewitz, J.C. *Soviet-American Rivalry in the Middle East.* New York: Praeger, 1969.

Jackson, D. Bruce. *Castro, the Kremlin and Communism in Latin America.* Baltimore: John Hopkins Press, 1969.

Johnson, Cecil. *Communist China and Latin America, 1959–1967.* New York: Columbia University Press, 1970.

Kautsky, John H. *Political Change in Underdeveloped Countries: Nationalism and Communism.* New York: Wiley, 1962.

Kertesz, Stephen D., and Fitzsimons, M.A. eds. *Diplomacy in a Changing World.* South Bend, Ind.: University of Notre Dame Press, 1959.

Klieman, Aaron S. *Soviet Russia and the Middle East.* Baltimore: John Hopkins Press, 1970.

Klineberg, Otto. *Tensions Affecting International Understanding.* New York: Social Science Research Council, 1950.

Lacouture, Jean. *Vietnam Between Two Truces.* New York: Random House, 1965.

Lacquer, Walter. *The Soviet Union and the Middle East.* New York: Praeger, 1959.

——. *The Struggle for the Middle East.* New York: Macmillan, 1969.

Landau, Jacob M. *The Arabs in Israel.* New York: Oxford University Press, 1969.

Legvold, Robert. *Soviet Policy in West Africa.* Cambridge, Mass.: Harvard University Press, 1970.

Loh, Pichon P.Y. *The Early Chiang Kai-Shek.* New York: Columbia University Press, 1971.

Martin, Lawrence W., ed. *Neutralism and Nonalignment.* New York: Praeger, 1962.

Maxwell, Neville. *India's China War.* New York; Pantheon, 1971.

McVey, Ruth T. *The Soviet View of the Indonesian Revolution.* Ithaca, New York: Cornell University Press, 1957.

Mehnert, Klaus. *China Returns.* New York: Dutton, 1972.

Nielsen, Waldemar A. *The Great Powers and Africa.* New York: Praeger, 1969.

Nutting, Anthony. *No End of a Lesson: The Story of Suez.* New York: Potter, 1967.

Olson, Lawrence. *Japan in Postwar Asia.* New York: Praeger, 1970.

Palmer, Norman D., and Shao Chuan Leng. *Sun Yat-sen and Communism.* New York: Praeger, 1960.

Polk, William R. *The United States and the Arab World.* Cambridge, Mass.: Harvard University Press, 1969.

Reischauer, Edwin O. *Japan: The Story of a Nation.* New York: Knopf, 1970.

Rowland, John. *A History of Sino-Indian Relations.* Princeton, N.J.: Van Nostrand, 1967.

Safran, Nadav. *The United States and Israel.* Cambridge, Mass.: Harvard University Press, 1963.

Sainteny, Jean. *Ho Chi Minh and His Vietnam.* Chicago: Cowles Book Co., 1972.

Schram, Stuart. *Mao Tse-tung.* New York: Simon and Schuster, 1967.

Schwartz, Benjamin I. *Chinese Communism and the Rise of Mao.* Cambridge, Mass.: Harvard University Press, 1951.

Schwartz, Harry. *Tsars, Mandarins, and Commisars.* Philadelphia: Lippincott, 1964.

Selden, Mark. *The Yenan Way in Revolutionary China.* Cambridge, Mass.: Harvard University Press, 1971.

Sen Gupta, Bhabani. *The Fulcrum of Asia.* New York: Pegasus, 1970.

Seton-Watson, Hugh. *From Lenin to Khruschev, the History of World Communism.* New York: Praeger, 1960.

———. *Neither War nor Peace.* New York.: Praeger, 1960.

Strausz-Hupé, Robert, *et al. Protracted Conflict.* New York.: Harper, 1959.

———, Kintner, William R., and Possony, Stefan T. *A Forward Strategy for America.* New York: Harper, 1961.

Thomas, Hugh. *Cuba: The Pursuit of Freedom.* New York: Harper and Row, 1971.

———. *Suez.* New York: Harper and Row, 1967.

Tuchman, Barbara W. *Stilwell and the American Experience in China, 1911–45.* New York: Macmillan, 1971.

Ulam, Adam B. *The Unfinished Revolution.* New York: Random House, 1960.

United States Department of State. *The Sino-Soviet Economic Offensive in the Less Developed Countries.* 1958.

Ward, Barbara. *India and the West.* New York: Norton, 1961.

———. *The Interplay of East and West, Points of Conflict and Cooperation.* New York: Norton, 1957.

Whiting, Allen S. *China Crosses the Yalu.* New York: Macmillan, 1960.

Wilson, Dick. *The Long March 1935: The Epic of Chinese Communism's Survival.* New York: Viking, 1972.

Xydis, Stephen G. *Cyprus: Conflict and Conciliation, 1954-1958.* Columbus,Ohio: Ohio State University Press, 1967.

6 The Military Struggle for Power

Blood and destruction shall be so in use,
And dreadful objects so familiar,
That mothers shall but smile when they behold
Their infants quartered with the hands of war.

SHAKESPEARE Julius Caesar, III, 2

The East-West Military Struggle

Since the coming of the nuclear age, it has sometimes been said that war has become rationally unthinkable and therefore impossible. This assertion is untrue. It is based on the false premise that whatever is too horrible cannot happen. And it erroneously assumes that men always act rationally and that pathological behavior—like that of Hitler—was abruptly ended with the discovery of atomic power. The truth is that atomic warfare *is* a possibility. Atomic power, like other discoveries of genius, is inherently amoral. It is merely an instrument that in itself in no way guarantees human progress. How it is used—whether for welfare or for warfare—depends entirely on human choice and direction.

The founders of the United Nations did indeed nurture the hope that the birth of the world organization would usher in a brave new world in which alliances and counteralliances, power politics and aggressive war could at last be thrown into the garbage can of history. It was widely believed that the principle of collective security, if rigorously applied, would at last render these age-old international maneuvers superfluous. The meaning of this principle was nothing less than that international relations should henceforth be governed by "the rule of all for one and one for all." There would be no more Ethiopias and no more Munichs. The overwhelming military power of the world community would be arrayed against aggression. Collective security was to be indifferent to traditional alliances, friendships, or animosities. It was to act impartially and anonymously. Indeed, it was hoped that the collective security principle would completely supersede all old-fashioned alliances.

Actually, these hopes were never realized. The Great Power veto in the UN Security Council served as a clear reminder that the United Nations was not to have the function of mobilizing collective security against major aggressors. The intensification of the East-West struggle and the post-World War II gains made by Communism in Eastern Europe starkly pointed up this limitation. By 1947 the West had found to its dismay that the principle of collective security could not in practice be applied to check further Communist expansion. In the absence of real unanimity among the Great Powers, the Security Council unanimity rule threatened to make a mockery of the collective security ideal. As a result of this blighting of the great hopes earlier entertained for the UN, there occurred a return to what Claude has called "selective security,"[1] a devolution of military responsibility for keeping the peace from the United Nations to regional and bilateral arrangements. A military struggle of unprecedented magnitude began to take shape between East and West. And in this struggle for preponderance there soon emerged a vast network of alliances and counteralliances. We shall now turn to a description and analysis of these alliance systems.

Until 1947, the United States had consistently avoided "entangling alliances," heeding the warning of her first President. But the absorption of most of Eastern Europe into the Soviet orbit elicited in the United States a profound fear of Soviet domination of all Europe. The growing conviction that the American national interest lay in the defense of Europe against Communism led to the abandonment of the "go it alone" policy. In March 1947 the President proclaimed the Truman Doctrine, offering American support to "free peoples who [were] resisting attempt to subjugation by armed minorities or by outside pressures."[2] This doctrine was applied immediately in the cases of Greece and Turkey, which were threatened by Soviet infiltration. The successful Communist coup in Czechoslovakia in the following year resulted in the traditional American policy of nonalliance being reversed altogether. In April 1949, in the North Atlantic Treaty, the United States committed itself to the proposition that a military attack upon ten Western European countries or on Canada would be considered as an attack on the United States. The NATO Treaty became the first expression of a revolutionary American policy of collective defense. In the words of President Truman, it was "the first peacetime military alliance entered into by the United States since the adoption of the Constitution."[3] Thus, ironically enough, the age of collective security ushered in for the United States an age of alliances, of checking power with counterpower. The Rio Treaty or Inter-American Treaty of Reciprocal Assistance, which the United States had signed in 1947 with her sister republics in Latin America, was not, strictly speaking, a military alliance although it was alliance-like in its external orientation. It served to transform the traditional Monroe Doctrine into a multilateral arrangement and established machinery for the settlement of hemispheric disputes.

Communist activity in the Far East, especially the outbreak of the Korean War, resulted in a quest for further allies. In 1951 the United States entered into bilateral security arrangements with Japan and the Philippines. In the same year, the ANZUS Treaty linking the United States to Australia and New Zealand was concluded. After the end of hostilities in Korea, a treaty of mutual defense with the Republic of Korea was added. The French loss of Indochina and Communist absorption of North Vietnam caused the extension of the Western alliance system to Southeast Asia in the form of the Southeast Asia Treaty Organization (SEATO), signed at Manila in 1954. SEATO included the ANZUS countries, two NATO countries (Britain and France), and three Asian countries (Pakistan, the Philippines, and Thailand). Vietnam, Laos, and Cambodia did not become signatories but were given SEATO "protection." In December 1954 the United States concluded a mutual defense treaty with the Nationalist Chinese government on Formosa.

By now, only the Middle East was excluded from the Western alliance system. In 1955 Britain, Turkey, Iraq, Iran, and Pakistan joined in the Baghdad Pact. The United States did not technically become a member, since many Arab states considered the Pact an oblique attack on Arab unity, but in effect the United States was a mainstay of the new alliance. When, as a result of the Suez fiasco, British and French authority in the Middle East reached a new nadir and Communism gained its first foothold in the Arab world, the Eisenhower Doctrine, promulgated in March 1957, attempted to salvage Western interest in the Middle East. This Doctrine suggested that the United States might "use armed force to assist any nation or group of nations requesting assistance against armed aggression from any country controlled by international Communism."[4] In the words of Secretary of State Dulles, the Doctrine had "as much effectiveness as membership in the Baghdad Pact."[5] In July 1958 Iraq seceded from the Pact as a result of an internal revolution. The alliance continued to exist, however, under the new name of Central Treaty Organization (CENTO).

By the mid-1960's the United States had bilateral or regional military alliances with forty-two nations: the Organization of American States (OAS) had twenty-one members; NATO, with the addition of West Germany in 1955, comprised fifteen signatories; SEATO included eight nations; and finally, the bilateral arrangements with Japan, South Korea, and Formosa complete the list. In addition to these formal military commitments, SEATO extended its "protection" to three Southeast Asian countries, and the Eisenhower Doctrine offered assistance to the nations of the Middle East. In a little over a decade the United States had thus changed from a "go it alone" policy to an alliance system of "going it with forty-two others."

Like the West, the Soviet Union also has sought military allies. During the years following World War II it entered bilateral security arrangements with the seven Eastern European countries that had been absorbed into the Soviet orbit. It also became a party to a multilateral alliance, the Conference of European Powers for the Assurance of Peace and Security in Europe, better known as the Warsaw Pact. This union, established in 1955, linked the Soviet Union in a military pact with its seven Eastern European allies. It was intended as a riposte to the North Atlantic Treaty and, indeed, was practically a carbon copy of NATO. Both provided that an armed attack upon one nation was an attack upon all; and in both, the commitment was to render such assistance, including armed assistance, as was deemed necessary. The Soviet rationale for the Warsaw Pact was that the inclusion of a rearmed West Germany in NATO made a Soviet defensive alliance absolutely essential. In 1950 the Soviet Union concluded another bilateral mutual assistance treaty, this one with the new Communist government on mainland China.

Both East and West have consistently described their respective military alliance systems as purely defensive in character. Thus, in the West's view, NATO was conceived as a reaction to Communist expansion, with no aggressive designs whatsoever. In the Soviet view, however, NATO was an "aggressive, imperialist bloc" of hostile nations whose military alliances extended over most of the world and who—most terribly of all from the viewpoint of the Soviet Union—went so far as to rearm West Germany. Conversely, the West has tended to think of the Warsaw Pact as a "collective Communist menace," the military arm of the aggressive design of international Communism.

By the mid-1960's two military blocs of unprecedented power and destructive capacity faced each other across a chasm of apparently unbridgeable political differences. Each claimed to be a purely defensive instrument against a war that neither wanted. Each was engaged in a gigantic arms race which was to deter the other from starting such a war. And, most important, each of the two superpowers leading the respective alliance systems had at its disposal an arsenal of atomic weapons powerful enough to devastate most of the civilized world. We shall now turn to a specific analysis of the Western and Soviet alliance systems and the relationship between them.

NATO: THE WEST'S MAIN MILITARY ALLIANCE IN THE NUCLEAR AGE

The North Atlantic Pact, concluded in 1949, bound together twelve states of the Atlantic community: the United States, Britain, France, Canada, Italy, Portugal, Norway, Denmark, Iceland, Belgium, Holland, and Luxembourg. Greece and Turkey joined the Alliance in September 1952 and West Germany's accession in 1955 brought the total membership to fifteen. The chief political arm of NATO has been its Permanent Council, composed of representatives of all the member states at the ministerial level. Its military organization consists of a Military Committee made up of the Chiefs of Staff of all NATO members. NATO's principal purpose has been the defense of Western Europe, which has been the responsibility of the Supreme Headquarters Allied Powers Europe (SHAPE). The Secretariat of NATO, like the United Nations Secretariat, has employed an international staff headed by a Secretary-General.

The United States has clearly been the leading member of the Alliance. Arnold Wolfers has aptly applied the analogy of a wheel to describe the relationship of the United States to its partners in NATO. "The friends and allies of the United States are spread out along its rim each occupying the end of a spoke, while the United States is located at the hub of the wheel."[6] Thus, danger to any allied country, Denmark or Turkey for example, would be communicated to the United States at the center but not necessarily to other states on the rim. Any action emanating from the hub, however, would affect the entire wheel. The United States has consistently viewed herself as the main "producer" of security, while casting most of her allies in NATO into the role of "consumers."

While NATO has doubtless been the most powerful of the Western military alliances, there have been problems and tensions which, at times, have seriously threatened the cohesion of the Pact. These problems have tended to fall into two categories, one political, the other military. The political tensions have arisen from divergent national aims and policies pursued by the chief members of the Alliance. The military problems have been primarily of a strategic nature raised, above all, by the unprecedented dilemmas posed by the discovery of nuclear power.

The struggle over colonialism has been responsible for some political schisms in NATO. As we have seen earlier, the United States has considered the East-West struggle as paramount, but this view has not always been shared by all of her NATO allies. The Suez crisis of 1956 illustrated this dilemma in all its stark contours. The United States voted against her two closest military allies, Britain and France, and paradoxically found herself aligned in the United Nations with the very power against which she had called NATO into existence. By preferring collective security through the United Nations to selective security via NATO, the United States seriously jeopardized the unity of the Alliance. Although Britain and France in effect had no choice but to remain in NATO, Anglo-French resentment was so considerable that a major operation had to be launched in order to retighten the bonds of the Pact. Indeed, the Suez crisis might well have led to NATO's disintegration. What if the British and French had not recoiled before the fact of a united world public opinion and had persisted—against the will of the United States—in their attempt to destroy the Egyptian government by force? Such a course might have left Britain and France no choice but to withdraw from the Alliance.

The colonial struggle, like a hydra-headed monster, has also tended to rise in other parts of the world to haunt the American leadership of NATO. Thus the United States found itself embarrassed by a protracted dispute between India and Portugal over Goa, and by another longstanding quarrel between the Netherlands and Indonesia over the disposition of West New Guinea. In both cases, NATO allies were involved. When India annexed the Portuguese enclave by force in 1961, the United States did protest, but was severely criticized by India for doing so. And when in the same year the United States voted against Portugal in the United Nations on the issue of Angola, Portugal threatened to evict the United States from its base in the Azores. Similarly, the United States was caught in the middle on the Dutch-Indonesian dispute, though in this case the conciliation attempts of an American intermediary and the peaceful transfer in 1963 of West New Guinea to Indonesia with the help of the United Nations prevented an actual outbreak of hostilities.

The colonial dilemmma at times occurs in even more complicated form. In the dispute over Cyprus, for example, three NATO powers were involved. Extremists in Greece wanted to annex the island, Turkey demanded partition, and Britain wanted to continue using Cyprus as a military base. In addition, the Greek and Turkish communities on the island itself harbored fierce resentment against each other. As a result, the American talent for mediation among its own NATO allies was tested to the limit. Nevertheless, the conflict could not be resolved in the NATO family, and in 1964 the UN Security Council dispatched a peace force to the embattled island in order to prepare the way for a solution.

The United States has had to assuage other political tensions in order to maintain the unity of the Alliance. NATO has included both allies and enemies from World War II. Residual British and French fear of Germany had to be mitigated. The United States had to make the necessity for German rearmament plausible to those powers in the Alliance that had been most exposed to Nazi aggression during World War II. This task was not always easy. One specific example will serve to illustrate the point.

In 1950 the United States thought it desirable to equip the European "continental sector" of the Atlantic Alliance for concerted self-defense. It was suggested that the Benelux countries, France, Italy, and new contingents from a hitherto demilitarized Germany should form a truly supra-national army. This European Defense Community (EDC) was to have a unified command, common uniforms, and common pay scales for the soldiers. The EDC idea incorporated both realism and vision. If constituted, such a European army would remove the traditional animosity between France and Germany; would make the necessity of German rearmament more palatable to other NATO members by subjecting West Germany's military forces to international control; and finally, it was hoped, would strengthen NATO by providing it with a truly supra-national nucleus. The battle for ratification in the six parliaments of the countries that were to constitute EDC continued from 1950 to 1954. By 1954 all the legislative bodies save the French National Assembly had given the idea their blessing and it seemed that an unprecedented experiment was about to be launched. But on August 30, 1954, the French National Assembly rejected the treaty that would have established the EDC, not because "it feared Russia less but because it feared Germany more." Most of the delegates in the French parliament voted as though the choice available to them were between German rearmament or no German rearmament. As it turned out, the choice for the French actually lay between two types of German rearmament: rearmament within EDC, which would have integrated the German forces into a larger European command; or the rearmament of Germany as a sovereign state and a member of NATO. Quite possibly, if the French Deputies had known that the United States had decided to rearm Germany in any case, the EDC treaty would have been ratified by the National Assembly. As it turned out, however, traditional French suspicion of Germany prevented the emergence of a supra-national military force within the framework of the Atlantic Pact. In the words of one French Deputy, "They raped us three times and we're not going to marry them now!" Yet half a year later a sovereign West Germany was admitted to NATO. Instead of the ambitious EDC, a more loosely organized European NATO nucleus was called into being: the Western European Union (WEU), comprising the six EDC countries as well as Britain. But WEU was a lukewarm compromise. The European Defense Community had been scuttled on the rock of traditional animosities and suspicions.

It must be pointed out, however, that since the EDC fiasco, the old World War II animosities have diminished steadily. Indeed, one of the most amazing developments within NATO has been the increasing rapprochement between West Germany and France. With General de Gaulle's accession to the French presidency in 1958, many NATO observers feared the resurgence of old tensions. Instead, the drawing together continued apace until, in 1966, the French President decided to insist on the withdrawal of NATO forces from French soil.

Finally, political schisms between the United States and her European allies have arisen from policy divergencies outside the European continent. The Vietnam war has been a case in point. Britain has reacted to American policy in Vietnam with considerable ambivalence and France has been openly critical. Most other members of NATO have expressed their reservations or disagreements. These differences have tended to strain relations between the United States and her NATO allies whenever the Vietnam question has arisen.

The second set of problems confronting the American leadership of NATO has been concerned with the challenge of nuclear power. The problem may be divided into the two related issues of atomic sharing and devising a viable nuclear strategy. So long as the United States possessed a monopoly of nuclear power, most American military thinkers tended to base NATO's primary defense against the Soviet Union upon the concept of atomic deterrence. Fear of atomic retaliation, it was hoped, would prevent Communist aggression. Sir Winston Churchill expressed this early view when he said in March 1949: "It is certain that Europe would have been communized like Czechoslovakia and London under bombardment sometime ago but for the deterrent of the atomic bomb in the hands of the United States."[7]

Secretary of State Dulles, speaking for the United States in January 1954, also placed most of his faith in the Great Deterrent, although he admitted the necessity of local defense with conventional weapons as an auxiliary factor:

Local defense will always be important. But there is no local defense which alone will contain the mighty landpower of the Communist world. Local defenses must be reinforced by the further deterrent of massive retaliatory power. A potential aggressor must know that he cannot always prescribe battle conditions that suit him. Otherwise, for example, a potential aggressor, who is glutted with manpower, might be tempted to attack in places where his superiority was decisive.

The way to deter aggression is for the free community to be willing and able to respond vigorously at places and with means of its own choosing.[8]

This policy of the Great Deterrent or reliance upon "massive retalia- tion," as it came to be called, suggested that a Soviet military attack upon any member of the alliance might be countered with a crippling atomic attack. The essence of this policy was not the stationing of American troops in NATO countries nor even the presence there of American bases, but the commitment itself. The United States intended to spread the strength of its atomic shield over the weakness of its allies and thus place them under virtually invulnerable protection.

For a time this tying of NATO to the American atomic monopoly seemed to give the West a decisive edge in its confrontation with the Soviet Union. But haunting doubts once more began to torment NATO planners. For one thing, it seemed that the "massive retaliation" strategy was highly inflexible and tended to commit the United States to a kind of "all or nothing" policy. The Great Deterrent seemed an efficient instrument in case of an all-out Soviet attack, but what if the Soviet Union should choose to provoke some more local conflict? Or if it should limit itself to aggression through infiltration? In such cases, the Great Deterrent seemed to be a disproportionate application of military force. This in turn raised the question of credibility. If a threat is to be effective, it must be believed or at least considered within the realm of the possible. Would the Soviet Union believe that the United States and NATO would unleash "massive retaliation" with atomic weapons in case of an East German attack on West Berlin, or of a Soviet attack on Britain? Or would this strategy be invoked only in case of a Soviet attack on the United States itself? Might not the Soviet Union assume that in a showdown the United States would not be able to bring itself actually to use the Great Deterrent? The problem was that the strategy of "massive retaliation" tended to leave the West too exclusively prepared for a total war—which might seem unwarranted—and too little prepared for aggression of the "nibbling" variety, which was the kind most likely actually to be encountered.

The validity of such fears as to the adequacy of "massive retaliation" strategy became apparent on three different occasions during the 1950's. Encouraged by the high hopes of the "massive retaliation" policy, Secretary Dulles announced that NATO's aim of containment of Communism was no longer sufficient. To win the East-West struggle, the Secretary declared, the United States would embrace a policy of "liberation" toward the Eastern European satellites of the Soviet Union. Whether "liberation" meant military or political or merely moral support by the United States and NATO was never clearly spelled out. The first test of the new policy occurred in June 1953 when, in a spontaneous revolutionary outbreak, East German workers and students rose against their Communist government. When Chancellor Konrad Adenauer asked the United States government whether it planned to intervene on the basis of the "liberation" policy, the answer was negative. The second test took place during the Polish uprising of October 1956. In this instance, even while the Soviet Union was weighing alternatives, Secretary Dulles announced on the radio on October 21 that, in case of Soviet military intervention, the United States would take no action.[9] The most dramatic test of the liberation formula, of course, was the Hungarian revolution of October 1956. In this case, the United States' attitude proved to be one of complete paralysis, with the liberation policy petering out in only a lame American recommendation in the United Nations to "study suitable moves."[10] These three events amply showed that since the liberation policy, coupled with the strategy of "massive retaliation," could too easily lead to World War III, it was in fact felt to be too risky to be invoked.

The possible consequences of the Great Deterrent began to cause the United States' allies concern. Of particular worry was the fact that if American protection through massive retaliation were to serve its purpose, it would have to be premised on the continuing atomic monopoly of the United States. The grounds for this fear became a reality when in August 1953 the Soviet Union exploded its first hydrogen bomb. The promulgation of the American "massive retaliation" doctrine five months later seemed anachronistic to most European military planners. Their thinking began to run something like this: "If the Americans mean what they say and unleash the Great Deterrent, we shall become an atomic rubble heap; but if they do not mean what they say and are bluffing, the Red Army will take over Western Europe without a shot. Either way, we are the losers." Thus, many NATO allies became almost as fearful of American protection as of Soviet aggression. As a result, most of America's allies began to raise their voices for "no annihilation without representation."

With the development of the new nuclear stalemate between East and West, the NATO allies' attitude toward the United States changed sharply. Suddenly, membership in the alliance seemed a provocation to the Soviet Union and hence fraught with danger. The fate of each member of the pact seemed to hinge upon decisions of the United States. To free themselves from this situation and possible danger, most of the powers became intent on developing their own defense policies independent of the United States. But sharp disagreement arose among members of the Western Alliance and within each country as to the most effective methods for establishing such policies. Some observers felt that their nations should join the "nuclear club" as rapidly as possible and thus be in a position to develop their own atomic defense policies. This could be done by stepping up the pace of national atomic research, or by appealing to the United States to share the secrets of the atom. Other observers were convinced that the road to safety lay not in the quest for atomic weapons but in a retreat from power. Since membership in NATO was now a policy entailing great risk, it was argued that the best way of enhancing the chances of survival was to withdraw from NATO and pursue a policy of neutrality.

This process of reappraisal in the capitals of Western Europe confronted the United States with renewed dilemmas of power and responsibility. While some of the NATO nations, such as Britain and France, succeeded in joining the "nuclear club," others counted on the United States to supply them with technical knowledge and materials with which to develop independent atomic arsenals. Yet for the United States to grant this request entailed serious responsibilities. It meant the dispersion of atomic power to many countries, with unforeseeable consequences. Although under the terms of the Atlantic Pact all partners were equal, in the American view some were "less equal than others"—that is, less dependable. If the United States were to decide to give atomic weapons to Norway, a democracy, would she be in duty bound to grant them also to Portugal, a dictatorship? In any case, the dissemination of atomic weapons throughout NATO might increase the mathematical chances of a war through inadvertence. This fact had to be weighed against the opposing claim that independent atomic arsenals for each member nation would strengthen the Alliance as a whole. Furthermore, if the United States were to vest nuclear power in its NATO allies, could it refuse similar requests from SEATO or OAS, and if so, on what grounds? But if the United States refused to furnish any atomic weapons at all to its allies, would the Soviet Union believe the American claim that it would protect a European ally even at the risk of exposing the United States to Soviet atomic attack? For example, if the Soviet Union were to threaten the "liberation" of West Berlin and were to warn the United States of atomic retaliation if Washington interfered, would the United States then honor its obligation to its West German partner in NATO? Or would the Soviet Union only take seriously a threat from the country that it intended to attack, in this case West Germany itself? Many observers were convinced that the Soviet Union would find only those threats of nuclear reprisal credible that came from the nation whose own survival was at stake. Hence the biggest dilemma that the United States now faced was how to respond to a Soviet attack which was limited to a particular member of NATO.[11]

The United States has continued to agonize over the dilemma of whether or not to share nuclear weapons with its NATO allies. In 1960 the first proposals to convert the entire Alliance into a nuclear striking force were put forward: General Lauris Norstad, Supreme Commander of NATO, suggested a NATO atomic force, based on an allied pool of atomic power but separate from the American, British, and French forces of the same kind. This plan was to provide an added deterrent against the Soviet Union; it was to meet allied demands for a share in the control of nuclear arms in Europe; and it was to give assurance to the NATO allies that they would have atomic arms of their own, thereby allaying suspicions that the United States might withhold nuclear defense of Europe for fear of nuclear retaliation by the Soviet Union on its own soil. A "fire brigade" of highly mobile forces equipped with tactical nuclear weapons was also proposed to deal with "brush-fire" conflicts.

The administration of President John F. Kennedy reexamined the entire problem of nuclear sharing. It came to the conclusion that, in the light of the mutually deterrent effect of Soviet and American nuclear power, the importance of conventional forces was increasing. Hence American proposals now sought to trade United States nuclear commit-ments for conventional build-ups on the part of the Europeans. For example, the United States offered to commit five Polaris missiles to NATO in return for an increase of European conventional forces to thirty divisions. Many European military thinkers were hesitant, however, and pointed out that such arrangements were too one-sided, since the United States would keep its finger on the atomic trigger. President de Gaulle of France, for example, declared that an indepen-dent national nuclear force was now more important than ever, since no one could be sure that an American President would always be willing to risk nuclear devastation by defending Europe. The United States, in turn, strongly opposed the development of national nuclear forces in Europe for fear of being drawn into a nuclear war against its will.

The dialogue continued with an American proposal, made in 1961, to create "a NATO seaborne force which would be truly multilateral in ownership and control."[12] While the Europeans were invited to partic-ipate in the establishment of policy guidelines, the United States insisted on maintaining a veto power over the use of the nuclear weapons. Hence European suspicions were far from allayed, even though in 1963 the United States proposed a multilateral NATO force of mixed crews. The Europeans' own quest for nuclear independence met with mixed results, however: in 1962 the British had to eliminate their plans for a "Skybolt missile" for technical reasons; and the French *force de dissuasion,* while of some limited military value, was widely regarded as primarily a status symbol.

The continuing dialogue over nuclear sharing has forced the United States continuously to reexamine its fundamental thinking with regard to the even more basic problem of evolving a viable strategic doctrine.

After 1956 there was almost unanimous agreement in the United States that the concept of massive retaliation had become obsolete. Leading military thinkers in the United States began to feel that the United States had added the hydrogen bomb to its arsenal in the East-West struggle without making room for its implications in American strategic thinking. Since "massive retaliation" was an all-or-nothing posture, the Soviet Union would be able to win the military struggle by installments:

If the Soviet bloc can present its challenges in less than all-out form it may gain a crucial advantage. Every move on its part will then pose the appalling dilemma of whether we are willing to commit suicide to prevent encroachments, which do not, each in itself, seem to threaten our existence directly but which may be steps on the road to our ultimate destruction.[13]

It was pointed out that the United States' capacity for "massive retaliation" had created a "psychological gap," a situation in which America's NATO allies had become convinced that they had nothing to gain from it and the Soviet leaders had begun to feel that they had nothing to fear from the threat of it. In the words of the observer cited above, "the dilemma of the nuclear age reside[d] in the impossibility of combining maximum horror with maximum certainty."[14]

It was from this type of thinking that the new strategic concept of "graduated deterrence" emerged. This concept was based on the simple assumption that to make the threat less horrible would render it more credible. The United States would not have to place itself in a position of risking its national substance every time a stand had to be taken against aggression. Instead, NATO would inform the Eastern military bloc that the West was determined to exact a price for Soviet aggression that would exceed the benefits to be gained from the act, but that such retaliation would not aim at the total destruction of the Soviet Union itself. Thus, by a kind of Benthamite calculus, each crime would be punished in proportion to its seriousness. The United States would not say to the Soviet Union: "If you march into West Berlin, we *may* do something terrible to you, even use massive retaliation." It would warn, rather: "If you march, we *shall* make you pay a price that will exceed the prize gained from your act." Exactly how and in what magnitude the more limited wars of this strategy of "graduated deterrence" would be fought of course raised many further problems of far-reaching complexity.

The great hope of the strategy of "graduated deterrence" among the members of NATO was that it should combine a minimum threat with a maximum of credibility. Thus, they looked to a wide range of weapons, including nuclear arms, in order to achieve as wide a variety of choices of retaliation as possible. This strategy, it was held, would make NATO much more flexible than it had been. For so long as every war threatened to mushroom into an all-out war, NATO allies were naturally inclined to do their best to prevent *any* action by the United States that would involve them. But with the availability of a variety of strategic alternatives, it was reasoned, this reluctance would be overcome and the Atlantic Alliance could once again function as a truly effective instrument of deterrence.

Critics of this new strategic doctrine, however, pointed out that it rested on the dubious assumption that the actions of the opposing military bloc would always be governed by rationality. They admitted that "massive retaliation" had purchased deterrence at an exorbitant risk, but expressed serious doubt as to whether a limited war in the atomic age—especially one fought with nuclear weapons—would *remain* limited. The premise of "graduated deterrence" was almost a medieval one—a kind of chivalry imposed by necessity upon the two opponents not to unleash the ultimate weapon against one another. But how would NATO know what "the other side" would actually do, and whether it would always react rationally? Even if its rationality could be counted on, would it believe NATO's "guarantee" to make the punishment fit the crime? And, most important, would not the use of "tactical" nuclear weapons by NATO result in the use of similar or more powerful "tactical" weapons by the other side, until one of the two antagonists would decide to use "strategic" atomic weapons, from which it would only be a short step to "massive retaliation"? In other words, the critics of a "graduated deterrence" strategy for NATO felt that a war in the nuclear age could *begin* as a limited war, but was likely to *end* as an all-out war. Hence, "graduated deterrence" would, sooner or later, lead to "massive retaliation" by both sides, and total destruction.

The problem of targeting also caused major concern. It was quickly realized that a "second strike counter-city" doctrine would be ineffective, since the destruction of Soviet cities would still leave the Soviet striking force intact. Nor was a "second strike counter-force" strategy completely satisfactory, since even the most careful targeting of the enemy's missile sites could not ensure the complete elimination of his nuclear bases. In the absence of any one completely adequate strategic doctrine, the United States decided to emphasize a maximum of flexibility in its defense posture, ranging from guerrilla warfare all the way up to nuclear war.

The United States leadership in NATO has not been able to resolve the fearful dilemmas created by the condition of mutual atomic deterrence that has prevailed between the two superpowers. The uncertainties and ambiguities of Alliance strategy in the nuclear age have created an extreme ambivalence between the United States and its partners, a kind of love-hate relationship, a "dialectic of dependence and counter-dependence," a constant process of asking "who needs whom most and who will defend whom?"[15] As long as the United States was safe from Soviet atomic attack, she tended to doubt the readiness of her NATO partners to fulfill their obligations in a war which would involve the two superpowers. Would France "come through" if the Soviet Union were to launch an attack upon the United States and threaten France with complete destruction unless she remained neutral? But even while the United States still possessed an atomic monopoly, some of her NATO allies feared the opposite, namely that the United States would not "come through" in case of a Soviet attack on a NATO country that was not considered "vital" to America's defense. With mutual deterrence a fact of life between East and West, the mutual suspicions between the United States and her NATO partners grew apace. Would the United States stand by the defense of France if this might mean the destruction of her own national substance? President De Gaulle believed that no American President would do this. In February 1966, the French President, in a dramatic move, announced his intention to withdraw French units progressively from the integrated NATO command. He implied that France would withdraw from NATO altogether when the Treaty would permit such action in 1969. He declared that the American deterrent was at best "indeterminate," that American military involvements in other parts of the world might drag France into an undesired war, and that, for all these reasons, the reestablishment of normal sovereign relations between France and the United States was a "necessary adaptation." While De Gaulle, in a letter to President Johnson in March, reaffirmed France's intention to fight on the side of her allies in case of attack, he nevertheless began the process of troop withdrawal. The United States deplored the French move and President Johnson found it "difficult to believe that France [would] long remain withdrawn from the common affairs and responsibilities of the Atlantic." However, in March 1967, NATO Headquarters were shifted from Paris to Brussels. The disengagement of France from NATO was now a physical reality.

The French move served to underline the fact that the world power constellation had changed. More specifically, it was an expression of French dissatisfaction with the fact that the problem of nuclear sharing was not resolved so long as the United States retained its veto over the use of nuclear weapons. All other concessions were regarded by France— and to a lesser extent Britain and West Germany—as peripheral and insufficient. The Europeans, encouraged by the French example, began to demand participation in the entire NATO decision-making process, ranging from the creation of forces to the use of ultimate weapons. Nothing short of this was likely to satisfy them.

On a deeper level, the French crisis symbolized a shift in power alignments within the Atlantic Community. For twenty years, the United States had clearly been the dominant NATO power with the other members in varying stages of dependence on it. During the 1960's, the various European initiatives subtly changed this relationship. By the late 1960's the challenge to the United States no longer lay in preserving its privileged status in NATO, but in working out meaningful patterns of partnership with its allies as a first among equals.

Despite the tensions plaguing NATO twenty years after its formation, the Alliance may be said to have succeeded in its primary task: the deterrence of the Soviet Union. After all, the "family quarrels" within NATO could be afforded only because there was now a margin of safety, namely a decrease in the likelihood of a Soviet attack on Europe. In fact, it may be argued with some validity that NATO's internal tensions were merely a signal alerting its members to the fact that the primary mission of the Alliance had been accomplished and the time had now come to knit the bonds of solidarity not only on the basis of deterrence, but on the more lasting values of building a larger Atlantic Community. While the Soviet-led invasion of Czechoslovakia in 1968 flashed a warning signal to the members of NATO not to drop their guard, this event did not arrest the gradual metamorphosis of the Alliance.

NATO, even without France, has remained the West's most powerful military alliance. In comparison with this favored position of NATO, other alliances in the West's military network have tended to play a distinctly peripheral role. SEATO, for example, despite its involvement in the Vietnamese war, has been of very limited value because only three Asian countries have chosen to associate themselves with it. These three—the Philippines, Thailand, and Pakistan—have been more in the nature of "consumers" than "producers" of Western security. The powerful countries of Asia, such as India, have abstained from SEATO, in part because of the inclusion of all the Western colonial powers in the American alliance system. Pakistan's membership in SEATO has alienated India even more. In fact, India has accused the United States of having forced her to increase armaments expenditures because of American military assistance to Pakistan through SEATO. On the whole, the creation of SEATO seems to have brought more political losses than military gains. CENTO, too, especially since the British decision in 1967 to remove its military presence from the area east of Suez, has not appreciably added to Western military strength. In fact, it has been argued that the membership of Iran, Turkey, and Pakistan has turned CENTO into a pro-Moslem rather than an anti-Communist alliance.

In an overall perspective, the United States' "collector's approach" to alliances raised many serious problems. The about-face from "no entangling alliances" to an all-inclusive alliance system often brought little more than formal unity within the Western military camp.[16] It at times placed the United States in the anomalous position of engaging in an armaments race with itself. For example, the United States supported

Pakistan as a member of SEATO, but when India armed against Pakistan, had to support India as well, for fear of endangering the latter's benevolent neutrality.

The American "greatest good by the greatest number of signatures" approach has given the Western alliance system a somewhat mechanical complexion. One thoughtful observer has gone so far as to state that SEATO has become a useless alliance from the military point of view and a harmful one politically.[17] While this view seems somewhat exaggerated, it does point up the fact that the American conception of "safety through numbers" is of dubious validity. Indeed, it seems that the United States has tended to overemphasize military defense in places where political allegiance should have been secured first. In the process, she has frequently found herself sacrificing the latter to the former. This has most prominently been the case with SEATO and CENTO, which, as a result, have been weak alliances. The strength of NATO, on the other hand, has largely lain in the fact that it has represented much more than merely a military commitment. Under Article 5 of the NATO Charter, indeed, the only legal commitment by the United States is to do what it would "deem necessary" in case of Soviet aggression. It could take no action whatever and still be within its legal rights. Yet the NATO Alliance, based on common dedication to the values of Western civilization, has remained stronger than the disruptive influences of divergent interests within it. This is not equally true of the other Western military pacts.

The root of America's difficulties as leader of the Western alliance system is to be found in the American belief that the greatest danger confronting the Western world is Communism. So long as, and to the extent that this view is not shared by all her military allies, dissensions within the Western camp continue. NATO's greater cohesion in relation to SEATO and CENTO has been attributable in large part to the overriding concern with Communism of the NATO powers. Among many of the United States' non-European allies, in contrast, other loyalties and fears have tended to predominate. In addition, the condition of mutual deterrence has convinced France and some non-European powers that the path to safety lies not in closeness to, but in distance from, the United States. In sum, the North Atlantic Pact, despite all the difficulties besetting it, has remained the West's foremost—perhaps only—effective military bulwark.

THE EAST'S MILITARY ALLIANCE SYSTEM

The two major pillars of the East's military alliance system have been the Warsaw Pact and, until the late 1950's, the Sino-Soviet Alliance.

The Warsaw Pact, concluded in 1955 as a counterpoise to NATO, committed the Soviet Union to the defense of its seven Eastern

European allies. Its Article 4—virtually a carbon copy of NATO's Article 5—commits the Soviet Union to such armed assistance as it might "deem necessary." Yet in other respects, the Warsaw Pact has differed significantly from its Western counterpart. For one thing, while the former has been geographically compact, the membership of the latter extends over a great distance. Moveover, the main difference between the two alliances lies in the fact that the Soviet Union insisted on fairly tight political bonds within the Alliance, whereas the United States was content with quite loose ones. All NATO partners have been relatively free agents, but it would be difficult to speak of Bulgaria as a sovereign equal in the Warsaw Pact. The United States has never compelled a NATO ally to remain within the Alliance by force. But what kept Hungary in the Warsaw Pact after 1956 was clearly not her freely given consent. Whereas NATO military policy has admittedly been strongly influenced by American leadership, the Warsaw Pact has been almost completely dominated by the Soviet Union. Whereas the NATO powers' share in Western security has been the subject of multilateral negotiations, Eastern Europe's contributions to Soviet security has in effect been determined by unilateral decision of the Soviet Union. Finally, the American military leadership in NATO has not been accompanied by the export of ideology, while the Soviet Union has attempted to cement the military bonds of the Warsaw Pact with the unifying mortar of the Communist creed. The invasion of Czechoslovakia in 1968 by the Soviet Union and four other members of the Warsaw Pact was an effort to impose this creed by force of arms even though Czechoslovakia, unlike Hungary, had never declared her intention to give up membership in the Pact.

Though the structural differences between the two military blocs have thus been great, the strategic problems they have faced have been fairly similar. Ironically enough, the coming of mutal deterrence has confronted the Soviet Union with strategic agonies analogous to those tormenting the United States. Dilemmas of "massive retaliation" and "graduated deterrence" have also been plaguing the Warsaw Pact nations. More specifically, the Soviet Union's problem of whether or not to give nuclear weapons to its allies has been no less difficult than the same issue confronting the United States. There has been pressure on Moscow to share its nuclear monopoly. Western rearmament of West Germany has given rise to great fears, particularly in Poland and East Germany. If they possessed atomic weapons, these nations have argued, their security would be restored. In this decision the Soviet Union, like the United States, has seen "its native hue of resolution sicklied o'er with the pale cast of thought." On the one hand, could the Soviet Union refuse atomic weapons to East Germany if the West Germans should be so equipped by the United States? On the other, what if another Tito, equipped with nuclear weapons, were to decide to leave the Warsaw Pact? And what if the Hungarians had had atomic weapons in 1956? Moreover, nationalist tendencies and de-Stalinization programs in most of the Eastern European countries have greatly reduced the degree of Soviet control over Eastern Europe. The Czechoslovak crisis of 1968 did not reverse, but probably only slowed this overall trend. In fact, some of the Eastern European countries, particularly Rumania, have tended to pursue policies fairly independent of the Soviet Union. Rumania even suggested the dissolution of the Warsaw Pact in the context of a United States-Soviet agreement on troop withdrawal from the European continent.

On the whole, the cohesion of both NATO and the Warsaw Pact has loosened. One expert has described this loosening process as follows:

Considering the over-all picture of the alliances . . . one is impressed by the similarity of the changes that have occurred in the structure of the European alliances on both sides of the Iron Curtain. The seemingly irreversible trend toward a two-bloc system that marked the immediate postwar era has been arrested, if not reversed. The uncommitted nations not only want to remain uncommitted but have, with a few exceptions, also shown the ability to do so. On the other hand, many of the European nations that are committed as allies of one or the other of the superpowers would like to join the ranks of the uncommitted nations but have, with the exception of Yugoslavia, been unable to do so. They have at best been able to move to the outer confines of the blocs to which they belong, but have had to stop there. In consequence, the two-bloc system is in the process of loosening but not of breaking up.[18]

The most formidable military instrument of the East used to be the Sino-Soviet Alliance concluded in February 1950. In this Treaty the two parties had agreed that, in case of attack on one, the other would use all means available to provide immediate military and other assistance. We have seen earlier that the Chinese Communist Party reached power without Soviet assistance and that Stalin obviously sacrificed ideological uniformity on the altar of coalition unity when he recognized the new regime upon its accession to power. This relationship had made of the Sino-Soviet Pact a genuine alliance between two equals, held together by joint interests and coordinated policies—unlike the Warsaw Pact, which was dominated by the Soviet Union.

The Sino-Soviet Alliance held fast into the late 1950's, but then began to disintegrate in the context of the widening ideological rift. As late as 1957 the Soviet Union made an agreement with Communist China providing its ally with technical atomic assistance in order to speed China's entry into the nuclear club, and in 1958 Premier Khrushchev fully endorsed the Chinese Communist claim to Formosa, pledging that "an attack on the People's Republic of China was an attack on the Soviet Union."[19]

In 1959, however, China's aggressive attitude over the Quemoy question and her incursions into Indian territory forced the Soviet Union to reconsider its policy of equipping its ally with nuclear teeth.

Moreover, China's claim that "after the next war there would be twenty million Americans, five million Englishmen, fifty million Russians, and three hundred million Chinese left," no doubt gave the Soviet Union food for thought.[20] At any rate, Russia abrogated her nuclear assistance treaty with China in 1959 and had withdrawn most of her technicians from China by 1960. There is little doubt that this action was one of the major factors contributing to the rising temperature of the Sino-Soviet dispute. It also demonstrated that the dispute was shifting from an ideological disagreement over the best method of "burying" the West to a power struggle between two competing national states. After all, ownership of the bomb by one Communist state would have been sufficient to advance the cause of world Communism. But the fact that the Chinese wanted atomic power in their own right and attained it in 1964 showed that they were eager to demonstrate their national power too—vis-à-vis Russia as well as the West. By the mid-1960's little if anything remained of the Sino-Soviet Alliance of 1950.

THE EAST-WEST MILITARY CONFRONTATION

During the 1950's, the discussion of East-West problems increasingly shifted from the political to the military realm. Evidence of this development could be seen in the growing preoccupation of the two superpowers not with matters of diplomatic substance but with propagandistic flourishes of military power. Some leading military thinkers on both sides continued to profess their desire to see the arms race ended. For example, General Lauris Norstad, Supreme Commander of NATO, said in 1957: "No military man is pleased with the present *status quo*—two armed camps sitting opposite each other. That would be a hell of a state of affairs to perpetuate."[21] Other military leaders, however, fatalistically concluded that, like other arms races before it, the East-West weapons build-up would sooner or later lead to war and that the only open question was therefore the question of what kind of war it was necessary to be prepared for: all-out, limited conventional, or limited nuclear. This vacillation between statements of hope for the best and fears for the worst tended to characterize the Eastern and Western alliance systems alike during the 1950's.

This confrontation of two opposing military blocs was commonly referred to as "bipolarity" before it was transformed in many important ways in the 1960's. In itself such a political division of the world was by no means unprecedented. Athens and Sparta, Rome and Carthage provide classic illustrations of bipolar relationships. The U.S.-Soviet bipolarity was unique, however, in that the two protagonists were equipped with weapons that in case of war would, for the first time in history, threaten the survival not only of entire propulations but of the species itself. Though it has occurred before, bipolarity has not been the normal pattern in history. More typically, the power configuration among nations has been that of a multiple equilibrium, known as "balance of power." This multiple equilibrium provided a flexible framework in which a number of nations sought to maximize their power and, at the same time, frequently switched sides so as to prevent any one from attaining preponderance. This traditional balance of power in our time gave way to what Sir Winston Churchill so aptly called the "balance of terror," a precarious balance between two superpowers, each equipped with the weapons of nuclear mass destruction. In this new situation room for maneuvering steadily lessened, with the result that there was no longer a flexible balance but, in effect, two virtually frozen and uncompromising blocs. The superpowers could only

. . . advance and meet in what is likely to be combat, or they can retreat and allow the other side to advance into what to them is precious ground. Those manifold and variegated maneuvers through which the masters of the balance of power tried to either stave off armed conflicts altogether or at least make them brief and decisive, yet limited in scope—the alliances and counteralliances, the shifting of alliances according to whence the greater threat or better opportunity might come, the sidestepping and postponement of issues, the deflection of rivalries from the exposed frontyard into the colonial backyard—these are the things of the past.[22]

Military thinkers in the West disagreed on what kind of "balance" between the two blocs would most effectively deter them from attacking one another. Some claimed that as exact an equilibrium as possible would afford the best chance for peace. Others maintained that war would be less likely if one bloc were far stronger than the other. But almost all were agreed that the threat of war was greatest in the case of a slight imbalance.[23] As Organski pointed out, most major wars of recent history occurred when the challenger had grown rapidly, but before he was quite as powerful as the dominant nation and its allies.[24]

It is clear that the atomic "balance of terror" greatly inhibited the traditionally almost casual resort to war as "a continuation of policy by other means." Sir Winston Churchill even suggested that "It may well be that we shall, by a process of sublime irony, have reached the stage in this story where safety will be the sturdy child of terror, and survival the twin brother of annihilation."[25] Sir Winston's optimism, however, seemed somewhat exaggerated. For while it is true that mutual deterrence operates as a safeguard to some extent at least, it is equally true that the closeness of the arms race between East and West meant repeated passage through the most dangerous power configuration of all, namely that of a slight imbalance.

There was a further danger inherent in the condition of mutual deterrence. The Churchillian "balance of terror" was based on the assumption that both East and West were protected through weapons that were never actually to be used. There was a serious flaw in this reasoning. Its ultimate premise involved a gigantic bluff. For on the one hand, if the nuclear weapons should actually be used, they might well end up destroying most of what they were intended to protect. On the other hand, if everyone assumed that they would never be used, they could not offer adequate protection, since the opponent could feel free to act as if they did not exist. In order to protect itself, therefore, each superpower had to be determined to use nuclear arms if necessary, and this meant that they might indeed one day be used.[26]

Perhaps the greatest peril of all inherent in the relationship of nuclear parity between the two blocs was that a nuclear war could be triggered through irrationality or inadvertence. Each side, assuming that the other intended to behave rationally, was nevertheless compelled to include in its calculations the possibility of irrational behavior by the other side. The Western bloc's view of "the Communist menace" and the Soviet bloc's conception of "the imperialist camp of the West" tended to heighten expectations of irrational behavior. Hence, policies might be based on what one side believed the other side believed, with the danger of an outcome desired by neither. Thomas C. Schelling described this problem well in the following analogy:

If I go downstairs to investigate a noise at night, with a gun in my hand, and find myself face to face with a burglar who has a gun in his hand, there is danger of an outcome that neither of us desires. Even if he prefers just to leave quietly, and I wish him to, there is danger that he may *think* I want to shoot, and shoot first. Worse, there is danger that he may think that *I* think *he* wants to shoot. And so on. "Self-defense" is ambiguous when one is only trying to preclude being shot in self-defense.[27]

If war through irrationality could be caused by incorrect expectations of what the other side may or may not do, war through inadvertence could result from a mere technical error. A misunderstanding of orders; a misinterpretation of a situation; "a speck on a radar screen caused by a meteorite or a swarm of birds could be mistaken for a plane or a missile"—all these could set off atomic retaliations almost automatically. This danger was increased by the fact that modern means of weapons delivery made a great many types of military errors irrevocable. Planes could be called back from a bombing mission, but intercontinental ballistic missiles could not. In John Herz's words, there now existed the real possibility of world destruction by mistake. Whereas war was traditionally regarded as "the continuation of diplomacy by other means," the 1950's transformed diplomacy between the two superpowers into a variety of warfare.

The problem of somehow stabilizing the precarious "balance of terror" became the overriding concern of responsible military thinkers on both sides of the Iron Curtain. Yet in view of the numerous difficulties, the task seemed almost insurmountable. Perhaps, the greatest difficulty was to make the nuclear balance work even though trust and good faith were lacking and there was no recourse to a higher authority. Schelling astutely pointed out that in having to live with this problem, our generation was at a disadvantage when compared with that of Machiavelli, for example. In the days of Machiavelli—as in many other historical periods—peace was not felt to be dependent on trust, good faith, and mutual respect in interstate relations. It was recognized as resulting no less frequently from hard and often ugly political realities. Perhaps, Schelling suggested, we too must become accustomed to such situations.

We may wish to solicit advice from the underworld, or from ancient despotisms. The ancients exchanged hostages, drank wine from the same glass to demonstrate the absence of poison, met in public places to inhibit the massacre of one by the other, and even deliberately exchanged spies to facilitate transmittal of authentic information.[28]

There was good sense in this argument. For it seemed, ironically enough, that the "balance of terror" would not really be stabilized until both sides had invulnerable retaliatory power. Once this condition prevailed, neither side—even if it struck first—could then destroy the other's ability to strike back. The "ancient wisdom" of this proposition rested on the somewhat Machiavellian assumption that the safety of weapons would increase the safety of people. Once each side knew that no blow, however massive, could destroy the other's capacity to return the blow, a greater stability would result.

The conception each side in the East-West struggle tended to hold of its own camp was one of defense against the other. The tragedy of this phase of the military struggle between East and West was in the possibility that these images could *become* reality and that the circle of suspicion and countersuspicion could precipitate a "preventive" war. If each side continued to believe that the other was its mortal enemy, this could influence behavior to such a point of rigidity and compulsiveness that the "inevitable conflict" could end up becoming a self-fulfilling prophecy.

The 1960's saw the beginning of the breakup of the bipolar system. The Sino-Soviet rift spelled the end of a monolithic Soviet bloc and the policies of President de Gaulle of France introduced powerful centrifugal tendencies into the Western camp. Most important, in 1962 a dramatic military confrontation took place between the Soviet Union and the United States which changed the entire complexion of the cold war. This turning point deserves close analysis as a case study.

THE CUBAN MISSILE CRISIS OF 1962

This crisis was the climax to the rising tensions between the superpowers during 1961. The Soviet Union's action in testing nuclear weapons of unprecedented explosive force had triggered off a major debate over fallout shelters in the United States; the erection of the Berlin Wall had made the tension almost palpable; and the memory of the abortive American-sponsored invasion of Cuba was still fresh. But as yet there had been no "eyeball-to-eyeball" confrontation. The Cuban missile crisis was such a confrontation.

In mid-October 1962 hard evidence that the Soviet Union was secretly building offensive missile bases in Cuba with headlong speed had been gathered by United States intelligence services. High-altitude photographs had disclosed a medium-range ballistic missile site near San Cristóbal and one near San Diego de los Baños. Tanker trucks, power and instrument installations, missile guidance stations, and erector launchers were clearly visible. And pictures of cylindrical shapes on incoming Soviet freighters confirmed the worst.

It is difficult to determine with certitude why the Soviet leadership made the decision to try to make Cuba an offensive missile base. First, it has been suggested that Premier Khrushchev intended to use the bases as a psychological lever to make more effective his demands for Berlin. Indeed, in the summer of 1962 Khrushchev had announced that he would postpone the Berlin issue until after the American elections. He may have hoped that President Kennedy would not dare to disclose a missile build-up during an election campaign and that he could therefore confront the United States over Berlin with the Cuban bases as a *fait accompli.* Second, the Soviet leader probably underestimated the will of the American President. The Berlin Wall, Laos, and especially the fiasco in the Bay of Pigs may have suggested to Khrushchev that Kennedy lacked resolve and would not take determined action. Third, successful installation of the weapons would give the Soviet Union an important temporary military advantage; rockets launched from Cuba could destroy American cities and knock out United States missiles and bombers on the ground in a first-strike attack, since the warning time would be critically reduced. The American weapons lead over the Soviet Union would not be cancelled but would be seriously weakened. Fourth, neo-Stalinist pressures on Khrushchev may have played a role, although this is unlikely, since Stalinism was very much on the defensive in Russia at the time and the Soviet leadership was emphasizing its policy of "peaceful coexistence" against the harsher line of Communist China. Nor is it likely that Cuban Premier Fidel Castro had persuaded the Soviet leader to install the missiles in order to prevent an American invasion of Cuba. On balance, Khrushchev probably calculated that, at best, a frightened America would go down on her knees, lose the confidence of her military allies in Europe, Asia, and Latin America, and thus give the Soviet Union a new opportunity to resume the offensive in the cold war. If the United States insisted on the removal of the bases, perhaps a barter deal could be worked out over bases in Greece and Turkey. And, even if the United States took a resolutely uncompromising stand, Khrushchev could gain favor in world public opinion by a policy of withdrawal. At the very worst, then, the *status quo ante* would be maintained, with Soviet control over Cuba intact.

The American leadership, which had hard evidence of the missile sites by October 15, now weighed its decision silently. For one week the President and his closest associates constituted themselves as an Executive Committee of the National Security Council and pondered the alternatives. The deliberations were intense but no word leaked out to the public. The President continued his preparations for the forthcoming political campaign, and as late as October 18 met with Soviet Foreign Secretary Andrei Gromyko, who professed ignorance of the offensive nature of the missile sites in Cuba.

Inside the White House and Pentagon, the War Council considered the alternatives along a kind of "escalation ladder." There developed seven possible responses in ascending order of severity: first, a sharp protest note to the Soviet Government; second, an American appeal to the United Nations Security Council; third, some form of economic retaliation against the Soviet Union; fourth, a naval blockade of Cuba; fifth, a "surgical air-strike" to eliminate the bases; sixth, invasion of the island; and seventh, direct nuclear retaliation against the Soviet Union. The War Council immediately eliminated the first three alternatives as ineffective and the last as unwarranted. The discussion centered around the alternatives in the middle range. The problem confronting the American planners was the classic one of deterrence strategy: so to combine the twin demands of capability and credibility that the Soviet leader would be checked by the actual and potential display of American power. Too little power could be interpreted as surrender, too much power as a bluff. Only controlled and flexible use of power at every step would make deterrence effective in the mind of the opponent.

An immediate invasion of Cuba was ruled out because that might have provoked the war which deterrence was designed to prevent. An air-strike at the missile bases was also rejected since Russian personnel would have been killed at the sites and such an action would have been difficult to justify by a nation that had made Pearl Harbor a symbol of infamy. A quarantine seemed to hold out the best hope for a solution. It would entail the requisite amount of strength by throwing a naval ring around Cuba, especially if it were coupled with a demand that the Soviet Union dismantle its bases there. Yet it offered the Soviet Union a way out: Khrushchev could avoid a direct confrontation by ordering his ships to change their course. Also, a quarantine would entail no violence, at least not immediately. Thus, on the evening of October 22, President Kennedy announced the American decision to impose a quarantine and added that "any nuclear missile launched from Cuba against any nation in the Western Hemisphere" would be regarded "as an attack by the Soviet Union on the United States requiring a full retaliatory response on the Soviet Union."[29] The issue was now squarely joined between the superpowers in the most dramatic military confrontation of the cold war. It was clear to participants and onlookers alike that Castro's Cuba was by now only a pawn. The United States had announced a check to the King, and the King was Premier Khrushchev.

The quarantine announcement was accompanied by an unprecedented peacetime mobilization of military power in the United States. The Polaris fleet was moved within striking range of the Soviet Union and for the first time Strategic Air Command bombers were dispersed to civilian airfields. Half of the SAC force was on airborne .alert. If necessary, the United States was ready to deliver an equivalent of thirty billion tons of TNT upon the Soviet Union. An atmosphere of impending showdown also pervaded the Soviet Union, where all military leaves were cancelled. The next seven days took the world to the brink of war.

On October 23 Secretary of State Dean Rusk obtained the unanimous support of the Organization of American States for the quarantine. The NATO allies came to the support of the United States, though with misgivings and not without reminding the United States of her behavior during the Suez crisis. The UN Security Council met in the afternoon. The United States demanded the immediate withdrawal, under international inspection, of the offensive weapons; the Soviet Union condemned the blockade as piracy and asked for its immediate termination. Neither resolution was voted on and the Security Council presented a spectacle of complete helplessness. Toward evening the Russian tanker *Bucharest* approached the blockade zone and the American destroyer U.S.S. *Gearing* steamed to meet it. Since the Russian vessel carried no contraband, it was allowed to proceed. Khrushchev claimed that the ship had not stopped; the United States claimed that the captain had acknowledged inspection. Neither side had backed down. October 24, United Nations Day, took the world a step closer to the brink. Secretary-General U Thant advanced a plan for a two-week cooling-off period to explore the issues. Khrushchev accepted the proposal at once but Kennedy rejected it on the ground that the issue of removing the missiles was not negotiable. An appeal by Premier Khrushchev to the British pacifist leader Bertrand Russell to use his influence to effect a general lowering of temperatures was also rejected as irrelevant by the United States. On October 25 Ambassador Stevenson challenged Soviet Ambassador Valerian Zorin to admit the existence of the missiles, stating that he was ready to wait for his answer "until hell freezes over."

On October 26 it was learned that several Soviet ships bound for Cuba were changing their course. But on the other hand, continued photo scrutiny of the missile bases indicated a speed-up in their construction since the announcement of the quarantine. The American offensive had to gather speed before the sites were ready and the missiles operational. President Kennedy spoke of possible "further measures" and did not rule out an air-strike at the bases. He also pointed out the numerous possibilities for accidental war if the Soviet Union would not comply. That evening a telegram from Premier Khrushchev arrived which looked like a conditional surrender. In it the Premier indicated his willingness to withdraw the missiles provided Cuba was guaranteed against invasion. This seemed like a fair offer.

On the morning of the following day, however, the White House received a second telegram from the Soviet leader which was much tougher in tone and more demanding in content. This time a deal was suggested: The United States was to dismantle her missile bases in Turkey and the Soviet Union would withdraw her missiles from Cuba.

The War Council now had to make a crucial decision. Superficially the Soviet proposal seemed reasonable. It expressed a widespread feeling among neutralists that both sides should compromise and sacrifice something. It was generally approved in the United Nations, and several distinguished Western commentators like Walter Lippmann supported it. Nevertheless, the War Council turned down the proposal. In the first place, President Kennedy felt that the first Soviet telegram reflected more clearly than the second the Soviet leader's real feelings. And second, to bargain away NATO bases under pressure would be to undermine the entire alliance and engender a Munich psychology. Each time the Soviet Union would gain a strategic advantage in the cold war, it might offer to give it up in exchange for an existing NATO base until the alliance would be totally dismantled. Thus, by turning down the barter offer, the United States in effect presented the Soviet Union with an ultimatum: remove the bases or "further measures" will be taken. The brink had been reached.

On Saturday morning, October 27, the Soviet Union "blinked" and the "eyeball-to-eyeball" confrontation came to an end. Kennedy's gamble on the first Soviet telegram had paid off. The Soviet leader reiterated his offer of withdrawing the missiles in return for an American "no-invasion" pledge. The American President accepted immediately and welcomed Khrushchev's "constructive contribution to peace." Other differences were settled in short order. Castro refused to admit on-site inspection by the United Nations to survey the dismantling of the bases, but the United States decided to forego such inspection and continued to rely upon its own aerial surveillance. The missile sites were completely stripped within a few weeks and outgoing Soviet ships laden with shrouded shapes that everyone took to be missiles brought the crisis to an end. The world had gone to the brink of nuclear hell and come back.

An analysis of the Cuban missile crisis reveals all the strengths and weaknesses of deterrence strategy. A strong case can be made for the American President's action on several grounds. Diplomatically, the action exhibited a combination of toughness and flexibility worthy of a great chess player. It never lost sight of the ultimate goal: the removal of the bases. Yet it at all times offered the Soviet leader the possibility of a retreat with dignity. Militarily, it prevented a serious upset of the distribution of power by forcing the removal of medium-range ballistic missile bases ninety miles from American shores. And historically, it was based on the bitter lesson of Munich that appeasement under pressure is the road to war.

Yet there is a case to be made against deterrence. First, it is accident-prone. Many times during those seven crucial days in October 1962 the world could have been destroyed by accident. The sinking of an American or Soviet ship could have triggered off a naval war. Indeed, an accident almost did occur. An American U-2 plane on a routine mission over Alaska on October 26 lost its bearings and headed for Siberia. Khrushchev hesitated, but in the atmosphere of crisis *might* have ordered a full retaliatory blow.[30] Second, the quarantine demonstrated that when power speaks, international law is silent. It is not difficult to see that a blockade, traditionally regarded as an act of war, does not advance the cause of world law in international relations. And finally, one should not lightly assume that deterrence will always work because it once did in a major showdown.

On balance, deterrence strategy was applied with consummate skill in the Cuban crisis. All things considered, the American President's determination was matched only by his prudence. He merely demanded the restoration of the *status quo*. Any additional demand, such as the withdrawal of Russian forces from Cuba, might have been intolerable to the Soviet Union and provoked a thermonuclear war. This feeling for nuance seems to be one of the integral requirements for a successful deterrence strategy. After all, the world's two most powerful statesmen had to make decisions that no mortal man before them ever had in his power to make. Hence, they had to speak to each other in a language the grammar of which they had to learn in action. Advisers on both sides could *clarify* the choices, but the two leaders had to *make* them. This truth was well expressed by President Kennedy when he cited the following poem:

> Bullfight critics ranked in rows
> Crowd the enormous Plaza full;
> But only one is there who *knows*
> And he's the man who fights the bull.[31]

Even Premier Khrushchev paid a grudging compliment to his opponent when he admitted to a Western diplomat: "Had I been in the White House instead of the Kremlin, I would have acted like Kennedy."[32]

A good case may be made for the proposition that the successful application of deterrent strategy by the United States in 1962 ushered in a period of quiescence in the East-West confrontation. The partial nuclear test-ban treaty concluded in 1963 was probably a result of it. Soviet-American agreement in the UN on the election of U Thant for a full five-year term as Secretary-General and on the peaceful uses of outer space also followed in the wake of "Cuba-2." And the installation of a "hot line" between the White House and the Kremlin reduced the chances of war through misunderstanding or accident. Thus, power, when prudently and judiciously applied, can give life to new elements of order, which in turn may soften the fierce edge of the power struggle among states.

In the past, great power confrontations were often accompanied by large-scale physical violence such as World Wars I and II. Yet, these conflicts often led to new efforts in international order-building, such as the League of Nations and the United Nations. The Cuban missile crisis suggests the possibility that mankind may be able to fight bloodless wars and build new institutions of order without having to pay the terrible price of nuclear conflict.

The Pattern of Interdependence in War

THE CASE OF VIETNAM

The military struggle between Western colonialism and the new nationalism has largely been decided in favor of the latter. The French were forced to leave Indochina; the Dutch, Indonesia; and the Belgians, the Congo. However, in some cases, the termination of the colonial presence on the soil of the new nations did not end the struggle, but only moved it into a new and even more violent phase. This tragic development occurred when a war between the forces of nationalism and colonialism gradually merged into a war between East and West. Such was the case in Vietnam where the interdependence between the two great struggles of our time brought about one of the most complex and terrible conflicts since the advent of the atomic age. Its importance in the context of our general analysis warrants a special case study.

The origins of the conflict go back to the end of World War II. The Japanese surrender in August 1945 had left a vacuum which two different forces now attempted to fill. On one side stood Ho Chi Minh, a typical product of the cross-fertilization of Vietnamese nationalism and European Communism, leader of the Vietminh forces, most of whom were Vietnamese nationalists with Communist leadership cadres. Ho quickly established control over much of Vietnam. There was little effective immediate competition since the Japanese had driven out the

French and the Americans had ruined the Japanese. France, however, was determined to regain her old colonial holdings in Indochina. After a number of efforts at negotiations had failed, the mounting tension culminated in November 1946 when a French naval bombardment of Haiphong touched off major hostilities. For the next eight years, France fought a bitter war against the Vietminh. With her superior firepower, she was able to hold many of the cities, but the Vietminh gained more and more of the countryside. In 1949, the French installed a Vietnamese Emperor, Bao Dai, but to no avail. France was simply unable to gain the confidence of the non-Communist Vietnamese nationalists while Ho Chi Minh organized more and more determined opposition to France under his Vietminh leadership. Thus, the Communists used nationalism more effectively against the French than the French were able to use anti-Communism against the nationalists. In short, while the war in its early phase was primarily a struggle between nationalism and colonialism, gradually it tended to take on overtones of an East-West conflict.

Between 1946 and 1949, the United States remained aloof from the war in Indochina. With the victory of Communism on the Chinese mainland, however, and the massive American involvement in the Korean war during the following year, the American attitude toward Indochina underwent a significant change. On February 7, 1950, the United States recognized the Bao Dai Government and a few months later President Truman announced that the United States would supply substantial military assistance to the French forces. By late 1950, United States aid was flowing in support of the French war effort and by 1953, this aid had reached the $500 million mark. By 1954, the United States was deeply committed to the French cause in Indochina and was paying for fifty per cent of the costs of the war.

Nevertheless, in the spring of 1954, the United States still decided against military intervention. On March 20, 1954, the French Chief of Staff, General Paul Ely, informed President Eisenhower that only massive American military intervention could save the French at Dienbienphu. This prospect touched off a vigorous debate within the American Government. Vice-President Nixon and the Chairman of the Joint Chiefs of Staff, Admiral Radford, favored prompt United States intervention. On the other hand, President Eisenhower's Army Chief of Staff, General Matthew B. Ridgway, and several members of the State Department's Policy Planning Staff, urged a policy of restraint. President Eisenhower finally decided not to intervene. He feared that the French had engendered too much popular antagonism to win the war and also felt that his Administration would get little backing from the Congress and from Great Britain for even a limited military intervention.

The Geneva Conference of mid-1954 and the formation, a few weeks later, of the Southeast Asia Treaty Organization signified the end of

French military involvement and the beginning of an American military presence in Indochina. The Geneva Conference resulted in the signing of several agreements to cease hostilities in Indochina and to establish three independent sovereign states: Laos, Cambodia, and Vietnam. The Agreement on Vietnam provided for a "provisional military demarcation line" at the seventeenth parallel. Vietminh forces were to regroup north of the line while the forces of the French Union were to regroup to the south. The line was to have military significance only and the political unification of Vietnam was to be brought about through a general election two years hence under the supervision of a neutral three-powered International Control Commission consisting of Canada, India, and Poland.

France had little choice, but her exit was made somewhat more graceful. Ho Chi Minh's Vietminh forces were dominant in more than three-quarters of Vietnam and were poised to overrun considerably more. To Ho, the terms of the Agreement were acceptable since he was convinced that the general election of 1956 would win him all of Vietnam. From his point of view, the certainty of a military victory was simply replaced by the certainty of a political victory. Both the Soviet Union and Communist China, reflecting their recently adopted line of "peaceful coexistence," applied pressure on Ho to accept the terms of the Agreement reassuring him that his victory at the polls was certain.

The United States never signed the Geneva Accords. However, in a unilateral declaration at the end of the Geneva Conference, the United States Government pledged to "refrain from the threat or the use of force to disturb" the settlement and added that it would view any violation of the Geneva Agreement with grave concern.

The general American position at the Conference remained ambivalent since, on the eve of a congressional election compaign, the maintenance of Eisenhower's domestic appeal as peacemaker in Asia was of great importance. Moreover, to block a peaceful settlement of the Indochina war would also have jeopardized French participation in European defense plans. These conflicting considerations led the Eisenhower Administration to dissociate the United States from the Geneva Agreement and to seek another solution that would prevent any further territory in Asia from falling under Communist control. The answer was the creation of SEATO. Secretary of State Dulles declared that now that the war had ended, the United States could make arrangements for collective defense against aggression and build up "the truly independent states of Cambodia, Laos, and South Vietnam." On the day the treaty was signed at Manila, by an additional protocol, its eight members designated the states of Cambodia and Laos and "the free territory under the jurisdiction of the state of Vietnam" to be under SEATO protection. The United States thus created SEATO to offset the results of Geneva. It also decided to consider South Vietnam as a separate state.

The Vietminh, on the other hand, regarded SEATO as a clear violation of the spirit of the Geneva Agreement. Ho Chi Minh saw the American position as an effort to deprive the Vietminh in the political arena of what it had gained militarily on the battlefield. Nevertheless, Ho withdrew his forces from the South, assuming that he would get enough votes there in 1956 so that he would emerge with a clear majority on a nationwide basis at election time. After all, his election in the North would be a certainty and if only a minority would support the Vietminh in the South, his election would be assured. President Eisenhower, too, thought that elections, if held on the basis of the Geneva Agreement, would lead to a Communist victory. As he put it in 1954, "Had elections been held as of the time of the fighting, possibly 80 per cent of the population would have voted for the Communist Ho Chi Minh as their leader rather than Chief of State Bao Dai."[33]

In the meantime, Ngo Dinh Diem, an American-backed Roman Catholic from a Mandarin family, began to challenge Emperor Bao Dai in the South. The United States strongly supported Diem in his bid for power and in October 1955, Diem proclaimed the establishment of a Republic of Vietnam, with himself as President.

Hence, Geneva and the SEATO Treaty meant the end of French power in Indochina and the beginnings of the American effort to enter the struggle with military might. As yet, there were no significant military encounters between Vietminh and American forces. But the issue was joined. The Vietminh now saw the Americans as following the path of French imperialism and the Americans perceived Geneva as a well-laid Communist trap to engulf all of Vietnam. The end of a colonial war merely signified the beginnings of a war between Americans and Communists. Thus, once again the continuum pattern appeared: the East-West conflict simply grew out of the struggle between nationalism and colonialism.

As the East-West conflict superseded the colonial war, the pace of battle gradually intensified. A pattern of escalation emerged by which every diplomatic failure to achieve negotiations paved the way for yet another upward step on the scale of violence.

The first such discernible move after Geneva was the American effort between 1954 and 1956 to strengthen President Diem's military establishment and Ho Chi Minh's visit to Moscow and Peking in 1955 to negotiate aid and friendship treaties with the two Communist powers. Diem declared in July 1955 that, since South Vietnam had not signed the Geneva Agreements, he was not prepared to permit elections under the conditions specified by it. He also added that there was no freedom in the North to campaign for any opposition to Ho Chi Minh. The American Government supported this view and July 1956, the date scheduled for general elections in the Geneva Accords, passed without elections being held. Ho, in retaliation, began to train Communist cadres for guerrilla war in the South. He also became the recipient of aid from the Soviet Union and China for the purpose of shoring up the economic base of the North Vietnamese state.

On December 20, 1960, a National Liberation Front was created in South Vietnam. The Front announced a ten-point program calling for the overthrow of the incumbent Saigon Government and the removal of American military advisers.

During the remaining years of the Eisenhower Administration, the United States continued to support the increasingly unpopular President Diem with military advisers. The second rung of the escalation ladder was reached in January 1961 when Hanoi announced its endorsement of the National Liberation Front in South Vietnam.

The three years of the Kennedy Administration were years of gradually deepening, though always limited, American involvement. By the time of President Kennedy's death, the United States had approximately 17,000 advisers in Vietnam though there was no direct American participation in actual combat. A further complicating factor was the increasingly oppressive nature of Diem's regime which was ultimately overthrown by a military coup in November 1963. Kennedy himself always tried to draw a distinction between American assistance to South Vietnam and Americanization of the war. "In the final analysis," he says, "it is their war. They are the ones who have to win it or lose it."[34] In the meantime, the growth of Communist insurgency in the South was rapid. The resurrected Vietminh, now called Vietcong by the Americans, infiltrated the South in increasing numbers. The National Liberation Front built a highly efficient network of political cadres which began a campaign of terror and assassination in South Vietnamese villages. By late 1963, both sides had raised the stakes and the United States, though not yet directly involved in actual combat, began to establish the necessary logistical base for the further action.

Another threshold was crossed in the summer of 1964. In July, the new South Vietnamese Prime Minister, General Khanh, delivered a major address, the keynote of which was "to the North." Two days later Nguyen Cao Ky, the commander of the South Vietnamese Air Force, announced that he was prepared to bomb North Vietnam at any time. In early August, North Vietnamese torpedo boats launched attacks on two American ships in the Gulf of Tonkin. President Johnson retaliated by bombing oil depots and other facilities in North Vietnam. On August 10, the President secured the passage of the Tonkin Gulf Resolution in Congress which authorized him "to take all necessary measures to repel any armed attack against the forces of the U.S. and to prevent further aggression." The air war had gone north of the seventeenth parallel for the first time.

The next rung on the ladder was reached in February 1965. On February 7, the Vietcong staged a night raid against American barracks at Pleiku, killing 8 Americans and wounding 126. Twelve hours later, American jets attacked North Vietnam in what was to be the first of an almost uninterrupted series of daily air attacks against the North. In the South, marines were introduced into the ground war which was now rapidly Americanized. By 1966, United States fighting units were frequently suffering higher casualty rates than their South Vietnamese allies. The Liberation Front responded to these events with its harsh five-point manifesto of March 1965 in which it refused to enter into negotiations until after American troops had been withdrawn. Three weeks later, however, Hanoi published its own "four-point program" in which it did not rule out the possibility of negotiations. In mid-May, the United States stopped its bombings of the North for five days, but no talks ensued—and the air attacks were resumed.

In February 1966, President Johnson met with the South Vietnamese leader, Air Marshal Ky, at Honolulu, where the two men underlined their solidarity against "the aggression from the North." In mid-1966, President Johnson announced that guerrilla infiltration from the North had increased at an alarming rate and that further American retaliatory action might be necessary. In June, the United States bombed the North Vietnamese capital of Hanoi and its largest port, Haiphong. In the South, American manpower had risen from 17,000 to 500,000 by 1968. There was no evidence, however, that this policy of "strategic persuasion" had deterred the Hanoi regime from sending more guerrillas to the South or the Liberation Front from attempting to infiltrate the countryside. The war had escalated in ever more violent bursts but no decisive change had occurred in the balance of power among the main belligerents.

By this time, a deep division had occurred within the United States about the American commitment in Vietnam and the future course of American foreign policy in Southeast Asia. The Administration defended its policy in Vietnam on the following main grounds: First, it defended the air attacks as "strategic persuasion" of the North to leave its neighbors to the South alone. Also, the bombing raids, in the view of the Administration, "raised the costs of aggression" and made it more difficult to send guerrillas to the South via the "Ho Chi Minh trail." Second, a withdrawal would, in the eyes of the Administration, signify a tremendous victory for the Chinese view on "wars of liberation," showing up the United States as a "paper tiger" and encouraging stepped-up aggressive moves by Communism elsewhere in the world. Third, "aggression must be stopped at the source." In the view of the Administration, Hanoi stood behind the National Liberation Front and China stood behind Hanoi. Hence China must be contained on her periphery as the Soviet Union was successfully contained twenty years earlier. A withdrawal, on the other hand, would produce a "row of falling dominoes" and bring to an end the American presence in Southeast Asia altogether.

Critics of the Administration pointed to the experience of 400,000 French troops in Indochina and wondered whether the United States could fare better in a counter-insurgency war in which a ten-to-one troop ratio in favor of the United States might be necessary for victory over the Vietcong. Opponents of the war also accused the United States of destroying the social fabric of South Vietnam—the very nation it had set out to save from Communism—through air bombardments and ground warfare. Third, the danger of Chinese or Soviet intervention on Hanoi's side took a prominent place in the view of most critics. Finally, opponents asserted that the United States still behaved as if Communism were a monolithic force that had to elicit an American response whenever a Communist regime appeared. Actually, the argument continued, Communism was now much more diffuse and each such regime should be evaluated in a specific and pragmatic manner by the United States rather than seen automatically as an attempt to extend the design of world Communism. Hence, the argument concluded, the American involvement in Vietnam would have made sense twenty years earlier as did the formation of NATO in Europe, but in the 1960's a strategic United States commitment in Southeast Asia was at best an anachronism and, at worst, a catastrophe. These differing perceptions of the nature of Communism lay at the heart of the dialogue between "hawks" and "doves" in the United States.

By 1968, the impasse over negotiations between the NLF and North Vietnam on one side and the United States and South Vietnam on the other had crystallized into a single issue: the bombing of North Vietnam. Hanoi and the Front demanded the cessation of bombings as a precondition to talks; the United States and South Vietnam demanded an end to Communist infiltration into the South as a precondition to the cessation of air attacks on the North. On March 31, 1968, President Johnson decided to stop all bombings north of the nineteenth parallel. Shortly thereafter, peace talks began in Paris between the United States and North Vietnam. At these talks, the North Vietnamese negotiators insisted on a total halt to the bombings, but the United States in turn insisted on the simultaneous reduction of guerrilla infiltration into South Vietnam as an act of reciprocity. On October 31, President Johnson ordered the complete cessation of the bombings. The Paris peace talks were broadened to include South Vietnam and the National Liberation Front. But as in Korea, the peace talks were only a prologue to the difficult business of peacemaking.

The war continued during Richard M. Nixon's presidency. The objective of the new President was "Vietnamization," or the turning over of the ground war to the combat forces of South Vietnam. Under this policy, Nixon gradually withdrew most American combat troops from South Vietnam, but a North Vietnamese offensive in 1972 prompted him to resume the air attacks on the North including Hanoi and Haiphong. He also decided to mine the major North Vietnamese ports and to interdict land routes from China to North Vietnam in order to choke off Soviet military supplies. Thus, the ground war contracted but the air war expanded and the long and tragic conflict went on. Only in late 1972 was a cease-fire finally hammered out. At long last military confrontation yielded to political negotiation.

The war in Indochina demonstrates the interdependence of the two great struggles of our time. The war had begun as a local nationalist uprising with Communist leadership cadres, but was ultimately perceived by the United States as a mortal test of wills between Communism and the West. As the "Pentagon Papers" made abundantly clear, this remained the perception of the American leadership through four successive Presidencies, even though Communism during this very period ceased to be monolithic and was breaking up into political and ideological fragments.

In conclusion, it seems that the interdependence of the two great struggles of our time tends to prolong wars. A "pure" East-West confrontation like the Cuban missile crisis had to be quickly resolved, as if by radical surgery; "pure" colonial wars, as were fought by France against Algeria or by Holland against the emerging nation of Indonesia, came to an end in less than a decade. But when an East-West conflict supersedes a colonial war, as it did in Vietnam, the complexities seem to become so enormous that peacemaking becomes a much more arduous task. Thus, a "pure" confrontation may end in horror, but a Vietnam-type war may be a horror without end.

From Balance of Power to Multipolarity

Perhaps the most enduring "law" of international relations has been the principle of the balance of power. It is generally agreed to have been operative for over three hundred years, since the emergence of the multi-state system. In its simplest form, the principle operated as follows: In the anarchic world of nation-states, each protagonist sought to maximize his safety through the enhancement of his power. In this competition, the quest for safety expressed itself chiefly in a search for allies. The safety of all was assured only if no one nation or group of nations was permitted to achieve a preponderance of power—if, in other words, a rough balance was achieved. Whenever the system threatened to break down, a "balancer" would ally himself with the weaker group of nations and thus restore the unstable equilibrium known as the "balance of power." This role was traditionally played by Great Britain.

The Pax Britannica, when seen in terms of the balance of power principle, was therefore in essence guaranteed by Britain's capacity to tip the scales by allying herself with the weaker nations against whatever state or combination of states threatened to become predominant.

In order to analyze the concept and its applicability meaningfully and unambiguously, it is necessary to make our definitions as precise as possible. In his *Power and International Relations,* Inis L. Claude, Jr., has pointed out that students of international relations have used the balance of power concept in four different ways.[35] First, and most commonly, it has been used to connote a *system* for the operation of international politics in a world of multiple states. This system can be seen as working automatically like a physical law; semi-automatically, since Britain seemed exempt from this law in her traditional role as balancer; or manually, with every actor manipulating the system through his own contrivance. Second, writers have referred to the balance of power concept as a *situation,* either of equilibrium or preponderance, between two states. Third, it has been used to describe a *policy* of equilibrium or preponderance. And finally, it has often served as a *symbol* of concern with the problem of power without substantive content. Throughout this book, the term "balance of power" will be used to describe a system of either the semi-automatic or manually operated type. The term "bipolarity," or "balance of terror," will connote the rough equilibrium of mutual atomic deterrence between East and West; and "multipolarity" will be used to describe a system of international relations in which a large number of protagonists engage in the balancing process without any one single nation playing the role of balancer.

Essentially, the balance of power system was a process of checking power with counterpower. The favorite technique used to accomplish this end was the formation of alliances and counteralliances. These unions were not permanent; those partner to them frequently switched sides whenever the maintenance of equilibrium seemed to require this. One classic example of the rapidity of such realignments was the Austro-British alliance against France and Prussia in 1740, which only a few years later changed to an Anglo-Prussian alliance against France and Austria. One of the chief alleged benefits of the balance of power system, when it operated successfully, was to guarantee the independence of small nations who were protected by the "balancer" from being devoured by the large ones. And perhaps most important, of course, the system was supposed to ensure peace in an anarchic world.

A careful scrutiny of this theory of the balance of power as almost a kind of "natural law" of classic international relations leaves one with many doubts about its actual validity. First, while the theory assumed that every nation would strive to enhance its power, it curiously viewed at least one nation—the "balancer"—as somehow exempt from this apparently universal rule. This "balancer" was seen as motivated not by national egotism but by international altruism. Since it was the British who traditionally played this balancing role, Great Britain was perceived as a sort of Olympian arbiter, allegedly above and exempt from the rules of international intercourse that governed the actions of other nations. As A.F.K. Organski has pointed out,

> The English modestly and the rest of the world credulously assigned this role to England. England has been the balancer because Englishmen believed that she was, said that she was, and the rest of the world believed them. The specifications for the role of balancer have been written with England in mind: the balancer must be a big power slightly removed from the center of controversy, preferably an island and mistress of the seas. Later, the fact that England met these specifications was used as added proof that England was the balancer.
>
> Just why England's motives should differ so from those of other nations is never explained. Why a preponderance of power in England's hands should be a balancing factor is not explained, either, nor can it be, for it is not true.[36]

Actually, of course, Great Britain's balancing strategy was as motivated by national interest as were the strategies of all the other European nations. It was grounded, above all, in two circumstances. One was the fact that as an island and the predominant naval power, Britain was likely to prove invulnerable to conquest save possibly by a state that had gained control over the whole European continent. The other was that in view of its size, population, and resources, Britain could not—as France did under Napoleon and Germany did under Hitler—reasonably aspire to win and maintain hegemony over Europe on her own. Hence her optimum strategy was to settle for the compromise policy of playing the European balancer—preventing anyone else from developing control over all of Europe by always siding against whichever happened to be the ascendant power, in alliance with the state or states that potentially, along with herself, seemed at the moment most seriously threatened.

The further assumption that nations participating in the balance of power were free to switch partners at will, like the dancers in a quadrille, also seems open to question. Could international combinations really be formed that mechanically? To be sure, alliances changed their membership in an almost kaleidoscopic fashion, but just as often the bonds of tradition and friendship made rapid shifts difficult and well nigh impossible. This has not, admittedly, been the case in countries whose governments have been authoritarian or totalitarian. Though Hitler and Stalin, for example, had denounced each other for a decade as mortal enemies, in 1939 they proved able to make a complete turnabout and, acknowledging what appeared to them to be the dictates of their respective national interests, overnight became close, if temporary, allies. However, in countries where government, including foreign policy, is directly responsible and responsive to the electorate, such a rapid shift of sides would be impossible. Any major realignment would require a lengthy period of popular rethinking and reconditioning—as the United States' difficulty in facing up to the sudden post-World War II challenges of its former ally, the Soviet Union, amply illustrates. And for the United States to go so far as to throw her weight against such long-standing friends, partners, and allies as Britain and France—even if the maintenance of the balance of power would seem to demand it—would be almost inconceivable.

The most fundamental criticism of the theory concerns the assumption that a rough equilibrium among nations generally ushered in periods of peace. It is well known that the Pax Romana was one of the longest periods of relatively undisturbed peace in the history of Western civilization. This peace was guaranteed not by a balance, but by the absolute predominance of Rome. This example may be dismissed as invalid because it preceded the emergence of the nation-state system; however, it would be difficult to disregard the century of relative stability and peace that was ushered in by the Congress of Vienna in 1815. This peace was guaranteed by the preponderant power of the combined forces of the Concert of Powers: Britain, Austria, Prussia, and Russia. Indeed, the peace was broken only when, once again, a condition of relative balance emerged at the beginning of the twentieth century. Organski goes so far as to state that "the relationship between peace and the balance of power appears to be exactly the opposite of what has been claimed. The periods of balance, real or imagined, are periods of warfare, while the periods of known preponderance are periods of peace."[37] This view, however, falls into the opposite error. Rather, the evidence seems to point to the fact that the long-alleged causal relationship between equilibrium and the attainment of peace simply does not exist.

Whatever success in maintaining peace the balance of power may or may not once have had, its effectiveness definitely ended with the emergence of bipolarity. It might be objected, of course, that bipolarity was merely another form of balance, simple rather than multiple. And it is undoubtedly true that each side has attempted to enhance its position vis-à-vis the other. But who has been the "balancer"? Britain, allegedly the traditional holder of the balance, has long since lost the independence that the role would require today—as the Suez crisis of 1956 dramatically showed. Moreover, the development of a rough equilibrium between the two superpowers may actually have increased the danger of war. Indeed, so long as the West possessed an atomic monopoly and thus a preponderance of power, there was little danger of a major war.

As we have seen earlier, bipolarity as a type of international power configuration has ample precedent. In such cases, as Organski has pointed out, wars have been most likely to occur when there was an approaching balance between the dominant nation and a major challenger.[38] Peace, on the other hand, has been most likely when one bloc has enjoyed a decided preponderance over the other. Thus, the "bipolar" wars between Sparta and Athens and between Rome and Carthage occurred at a time when the antagonists were in a condition of approaching equilibrium.

The "balance of terror" of our time differed from traditional bipolarity in the fact that it was at the same time a nuclear bipolarity. While the equilibrium between the two military blocs of East and West increased the chances of war, the condition of mutual deterrence acted as a counterweight. One side could no longer say to the other, "Do as I say or I shall kill you," but was forced into the position of saying, "Do as I say or I shall kill us both."

Recent developments indicate, however, that the bipolar international system may be nearing its end. A war between the two major superpowers is becoming increasingly remote. The arms control agreements reached in Moscow in 1972 underlined this hope. The ascendancy of China has irrevocably changed the power equation. In addition, the rise of Japan and the process of integration taking place in Western Europe have decentralized the world's power balance even further. The slow but steady process of rapprochement between Eastern and Western Europe first initiated by West German Chancellor Willy Brandt's *Ostpolitik* has made an armed clash between NATO and the Warsaw Pact countries more and more unlikely. Friendship treaties between West Germany and the Soviet Union and Poland were signed in 1970 and ratified in 1972. Finally, the loosening of NATO, as exemplified by the behavior of France and the policy of East-West reconciliation advocated by Rumania have injected centrifugal tendencies into both military camps. All this is not to say that war is impossible. Even nuclear war, though "unthinkable," still remains a possibility. In view of this fact, we must now turn to an examination of war itself as an instrument of national policy in the nuclear age.

War in the Nuclear Age

It has become almost banal to say that the nuclear age has fundamentally changed the nature of war. In the earlier days of the European state system, war among the sovereign nations of the West tended on the whole to be fought with limited means and for limited objectives. The combatants were for the most part mercenaries and the nations' "hinterlands" were usually spared extensive and direct involvement. Not until the nineteenth century did the emergence of mass ideologies begin to change war into a "total" experience involving the entire population of the countries concerned. The first of these new campaigns grew out of the French Revolution and the rise of Napoleon Bonaparte. Thereafter, the trend toward total warfare steadily gained momentum, reaching its climax in World War II. As one student of international relations has analyzed it, this new totalness of war consists of four chief aspects: it involves total populations emotionally; it involves total populations actively and physically; it is conducted against total populations; and it is fought for total stakes, to the unconditional surrender of one of the two adversaries.[39]

A nuclear war could be expected to be total in one further respect. It would come close to totally destroying the societies involved and would certainly almost totally change their way of life. For the destruction that would have to be absorbed would dwarf anything ever before experienced: "In World War II the effects of bombing were cumulative, whereas today one ten-megaton weapon represents five times the explosive power of all the bombs dropped on Germany during four years of war and one hundred times those dropped on Japan."[40] That such a catastrophe would at the very best necessitate a complete reconstitution of society, or of what might be left of society, goes without saying.

Unfortunately, our knowledge and control of the forces that cause wars remain much less developed than are the means by which war can today be waged. Though many theories have been advanced, none has offered any real breakthrough. Perhaps the most widely accepted theory of the cause of war has located its origins in human nature itself, in what the seventeenth-century English political theorist Thomas Hobbes saw as man's propensity to seek "power after power until death." As a result of this congenital human selfishness and drive for power, in Hobbes' view, mankind finds itself involved in a continuous potential chaos, a never-ending "war of all against all."

Basically the same explanation of war as an inevitable human phenomenon has been taken up by a number of contemporary writers. Reinhold Niebuhr, for example, has warned that war is bound to be with us permanently, if only because "The man in the street, with his lust for power and prestige thwarted by his own limitations and the necessities of social life, projects his ego upon his nation and indulges his anarchic lusts vicariously."[41] This same pessimistic view is shared by Hans Morgenthau, who has rejected "the essential goodness and infinite malleability of human nature" and gone on to base his entire conceptual framework of international relations on the allegedly permanent and ubiquitous nature of man's quest for power.

The chief inadequacy of this "human nature theory" of the cause of war is that it is too one-dimensional. To explain crime and war by the inherent evil of man is altogether too simple. Moreover, the theory leaves little room for acts of love, charity, and self-sacrifice. The presence of war in human society is no proof that men are bad. As

Kenneth N. Waltz has pointed out:

Maybe we have so *little* crime and so *few* wars because men, being good, adjust so amazingly well to circumstances that are inherently difficult! To say, then, that certain things happen because men are stupid or bad is a hypothesis that is accepted or rejected according to the mood of the writer. It is a statement that evidence cannot prove or disprove, for what we make of the evidence depends on the theory we hold.[42]

At the very least, the "human nature" theorists grossly oversimplify and exaggerate the causal relationship between human nature and war. Indeed, man's nature is so complex that we could use it to justify almost *any* theory. All that would be required would be to select whatever kind of behavior might seem to bear out our hypothesis.

If the "human nature" theorists see the evil chiefly in man, many modern social scientists tend to blame war on the nature of society. Sigmund Freud, in his brilliant *Civilization and Its Discontents,* challenged the facile assumption made by many optimists that the advance of civilization would bring with it the end of warfare among nations. On the contrary, Freud maintained, the more burdens the conventions of society would impose upon hapless man, the more likely it would be that his suppressed instincts would have to assert themselves in the liberating explosion of war.

Most sociologists and anthropologists tend to see the causes of war in tensions among societies, based largely on ignorance of each others' ways of life. The way to attack the problem of war is therefore to remove misunderstandings among nations by the replacement of distorted images with a fuller and more accurate knowledge of objective reality. This view is expressed in the Preamble to the Charter of the United Nations Educational, Scientific, and Cultural Organization: "Since war begins in the minds of men, it is in the minds of men that the defenses of peace must be constructed."

The hypothesis that men go to war because they are ignorant of each others' societies or have incorrect beliefs about each others' motives is as one-dimensional as the "human nature" theory. It has not been established that understanding has always promoted peace. In fact, at times nations have remained at peace with each other precisely because they had distorted images of each other. So long as the American image of Japan was that of the quaint society of Madame Butterfly, peace was not threatened. But when physical contact removed this "misunderstanding," relationships rapidly deteriorated. Conversely, France and Germany have known each other extremely well, but this knowledge has not prevented them from becoming embroiled in the bloodiest wars in modern history. Moreover, has the West been fearful of Communism's intentions because it has not understood them? Or have these fears been rooted in the fact that the West has understood these intentions all too well? Again, we are forced to admit that there is little correlation between ignorance and war—or between knowledge and peace. The fact is that two nations that know each other very well may want the same thing for equally valid reasons, and if it is impossible to satisfy the demands of both, war may result.

For the present, the most plausible explanation of the cause of war is war itself—or, rather, the expectation of war. This is another way of saying that wars occur because nothing exists to prevent them. Since the international system is in essence anarchic, states are forced to consider the possibility of war and prepare themselves for it. Through these preparations—such as arms races and military alliances—tensions increase until what is feared is actually brought about. This is not to maintain that an arms race is in itself the causal factor. It is probably more accurate to say that the tensions among states cause the arms race, which then creates even greater tensions. Modern man seems indeed to be caught in a spiral predicament.

Waltz has offered a useful distinction between an "efficient" cause and a "permissive" cause of war:

War may result because state A has something that state B wants. The efficient cause of the war is the desire of state B; the permissive cause is the fact that there is nothing to prevent state B from undertaking the risks of war. In a different circumstance, the interrelation of efficient and permissive causes becomes still closer. State A may fear that if it does not cut state B down a peg now, it may be unable to do so ten years from now. State A becomes the aggressor in the present because it fears what state B may be able to do in the future. The efficient cause of such a war is derived from the cause that we have labeled permissive. In the first case, conflicts arise from disputes born of specific issues. In an age of hydrogen bombs, no single issue may be worth the risk of full-scale war. Settlement, even on bad grounds, is preferable to self-destruction.[43]

Though each of the above "causes" of war undoubtedly plays a part, we clearly still lack a full and systematic knowledge of all that is involved. Until we have made up this deficiency—and assuming that if we knew what the factors were, we could actually control them—we can at least take heart in the fact that war and peace are not necessarily dichotomous. In reality, struggles between nations may be of many different types and intensities, ranging from hostile though nonviolent relations, such as those that have characterized the East-West struggle during the post-World War II period of the "cold war," to the total kind of nuclear conflagration that the whole world so fears and is so anxious to prevent.

We may find further encouragement in the fact that though during the past twenty years the world has witnessed a score of outbreaks of violence among nations, all of these conflicts have remained limited and in none have nuclear weapons been used. When one considers the actual list of these violent encounters this fact is remarkable indeed: the Indonesian war, the Chinese civil war, the Malayan war, the Greek guerrilla war, the Kashmir dispute, the Indochina war, the Arab-Israeli war, the Korean war, the Guatemalan revolt, the Argentine revolt, the Algerian insurrection, the Israeli Sinai campaign, the Anglo-French attack on Suez, the Muscat and Oman rebellion, the Hungarian revolution, the Lebanon-Jordan clash, the Taiwan Strait hostilities, the two Cuban crises, the dispute over Malaysia, the clash between Egypt and Saudia Arabia over Yemen, the hostilities over Cyprus, the violence in the Congo and other parts of Africa, the Vietnamese war, the 1967 war between the Arab states and Israel, and the war between India and Pakistan. To be sure, some of these were civil wars with minor international significance. Others were international conflicts over limited objectives. But at least five of them probably remained limited *only* because of the deterrent effect of nuclear power: the Korean war; the 1956 conflict of Israel, Britain, and France with Egypt in regard to Suez; the Hungarian revolution; the Cuban missile crisis of 1962; and the war in Vietnam.

Thus, to some degree at least, the Great Bomb has become both a unique threat and an unprecedented inhibition. It was the latter fact that Sir Winston Churchill sought to draw attention to when he stated that he "look[ed] forward with great confidence to the potentiality of universal destruction." And the same telling point was made by Belgium's Paul-Henri Spaak when he wrote that

Around the atomic bomb is being built a whole strategy, a whole policy, perhaps even, in outline, a philosophy. Out of our very extremity may come wisdom, out of the frightening means of destruction may come the means of assuring peace. What men in the past sought to make prevail by persuasion, by appealing to humane feelings, may in the end be achieved because the insensate machine inexorably imposes it. Technical progress may indirectly produce moral and social progress. If so, what an extraordinarily crooked road it would have been that led toward the good![44]

Nor is it true, as the cliché has it, that all arms races lead to war. Certainly, many do; but a considerable number simply fade away without a violent climax; and there have been times when the absence of an arms race made a war inevitable, such as the failure of the West to arm against Hitler in the 1930's. The point here is that arms races may have very different results under different conditions and that generalizations in this realm can easily become simplifications.

Though Spaak's and Churchill's hope in the dependability of the balance of terror is probably somewhat exaggerated, the fact is that for the first time in history mankind is preparing for a war that no one actually wants. Never, indeed, have statesmen sought alternatives to war so desperately. Their anxiousness to avoid not only its realities but even its name may be seen in their designation of the East-West struggle as a matter of "peaceful coexistence" and of the Korean conflict as a "police action." Save for the ever-present possibility of war through irrationality or inadvertence, it seems improbable that even the developing situation of nuclear multipolarity will see actual resort to thermonuclear hostilities. While military struggles are certain to continue, they will in all likelihood remain in the pattern of limited conflicts such as have characterized the period since World War II. And though the never-ending fight against the terror of wars of *all* kinds must continue, there is at least reasonable hope that whatever wars we may become involved in will be of essentially the same type as those we have known in the past.

REFERENCES

1. Inis L. Claude, Jr., *Swords into Plowshares,* 3d ed. New York: Random House, 1964, p. 243.

2. Department of State Bulletin, March 23, 1947, p. 534.

3. Harry S Truman, *Memoirs, Vol. II: Years of Trial and Hope.* Garden City, N.Y.: Doubleday, 1952, p. 241.

4. Department of State Bulletin, March 25, 1957, p. 481.

5. *The New York Times,* January 31, 1958.

6. Arnold Wolfers, "Stresses and Strains in 'Going It With Others,'" in Arnold Wolfers, ed., *Alliance Policy in the Cold War.* Baltimore: Johns Hopkins Press, 1959, p. 7.

7. Address at the Massachusetts Institute of Technology, March 31, 1949.

8. Wolfers, ed., *op. cit.,* p. 119.

9. Zbigniew K. Brzezinski, "U.S. Foreign Policy in East Central Europe—A Study in Contradiction," *Journal of International Affairs.* New York: Columbia University, Vol. IX, No. 1, 1957, p. 67.

10. *Ibid.,* p. 68.

11. Wolfers, ed., *op. cit.,* p. 136.

12. President Kennedy's address to the Canadian Parliament, Ottawa, May 17, 1961, in *Documents on American Foreign Relations 1961.* New York: Harper, 1962, pp. 272 ff.

13. Henry A. Kissinger, *Nuclear Weapons and Foreign Policy.* New York: Harper, 1957, p. 16.

14. *Ibid.,* p. 172.

15. John Herz, *International Politics in the Atomic Age.* New York: Columbia University Press, 1959, p. 175.

16. Wolfers, ed., *op. cit.,* p. 204.

17. Hans J. Morgenthau, "Alliances in Theory and Practice," in Wolfers, ed., *op. cit.,* p. 211.

18. *Ibid.,* p. 209.

19. A. Doak Barnett, *Communist China and Asia.* New York: Harper, 1960, p. 344.

20. Zbigniew K. Brzezinski, *The Soviet Bloc, Unity and Conflict.* Cambridge, Mass.: Harvard University Press, 1960, p. 403.

21. *The New York Times,* July 17, 1957.

22. Hans J. Morgenthau, *In Defense of the National Interest.* New York: Knopf, 1952, p. 50.

23. Herz, *op. cit.,* p. 154.

24. A. F. K. Organski, *World Politics.* New York: Knopf, 1958, p. 338.

25. *The New York Times,* March 2, 1955.

26. Carl Friedrich von Weizsaecker, quoted by Herz, *op. cit.,* p. 189.

27. Thomas C. Schelling, *The Strategy of Conflict.* Cambridge, Mass.: Harvard University Press, 1960, p. 207.

28. *Ibid., p. 20.*

29. U.S. Department of State, *Bulletin,* Volume XLVII, No. 1220, November 12, 1962, pp. 715–720.

30. Cited in Henry M. Pachter, *Collision Course: The Cuban Missile Crisis and Coexistence.* New York: Praeger, 1963, p. 58.

31. *Ibid.,* p. 89.

32. *Ibid.*

33. Dwight D. Eisenhower, *Mandate for Change.* New York: Doubleday, 1963, p. 372.

34. *Department of State Bulletin,* Washington, September 30, 1963, pp. 498–499.

35. Inis L. Claude, Jr., *Power and International Relations.* New York: Random House, 1962, pp. 11–39.

36. Organski, *op. cit.,* p. 286.

37. *Ibid.,* p. 292.

38. *Ibid.,* p. 338.

39. Hans J. Morgenthau, *Politics Among Nations,* 3d ed. New York: Knopf, 1960, Chap. 22.

40. Kissinger, *op. cit.,* p. 71.

41. Reinhold Niebuhr, *Moral Man and Immoral Society.* New York: Scribner, 1946, p. 93.

42. Kenneth N. Waltz, *Man, the State, and War.* New York: Columbia University Press, 1959, p. 28.

43. *Ibid.,* p. 234.

44. Paul-Henri Spaak, "The Atom Bomb and NATO," *Foreign Affairs,* April 1955, p. 358.

BIBLIOGRAPHY

Allison, Graham T. *Essence of Decision: Explaining the Cuban Missile Crisis.* Boston: Little, Brown, 1971.

Aron, Raymond. *The Century of Total War.* New York: Doubleday, 1954.

———. *On War.* New York: Doubleday, 1959.

Austin, Anthony. *The President's War.* Philadelphia: Lippincott, 1971.

Bader, William D. *The United States and the Spread of Nuclear Weapons.* New York: Pegasus, 1968.

Beaufré, André. *NATO and Europe.* New York: Knopf, 1971.

Bell, J. Bowyer. *The Myth of the Guerrilla.* New York: Knopf, 1971.

Brodie, Bernard. *Escalation and the Nuclear Option.* Princeton, N.J.: Princeton University Press, 1966.

Buchan, Alastair, ed. *A World of Nuclear Powers?* Englewood Cliffs, N.J.: Prentice-Hall, 1966.

Cable, James. *Gunboat Diplomacy.* New York: Praeger, 1971.

Cameron, Allan W. *Vietnam Crisis: A Documentary History. Volume I: 1940-1956.* Ithaca, N.Y.: Cornell University Press, 1971.

Churchill, Winston. *The Second World War.* Vols. I–VI. Boston: Houghton Mifflin, 1948–1953.

Clarke, Robin. *The Science of War and Peace.* New York: McGraw-Hill, 1972.

Claude, Inis L., Jr. *Power and International Relations.* New York: Random House, 1962.

Clausewitz, Karl von. *On War.* New York: Modern Library, 1943.

Cooper, Chester L. *The Lost Crusade: America in Vietnam.* New York: Dodd, 1970.

Dinerstein, Herbert S. *War and the Soviet Union.* New York: Praeger, 1959.

Dunn, Frederick S. *War and the Minds of Men.* New York: Harper, 1950.

Earl, Edward M. *Makers of Modern Strategy: Military Thought from Machiavelli to Hitler.* Princeton, N.J.: Princeton University Press, 1943.

Fairhall, David. *Russian Sea Power.* Boston: Gambit, 1971.

Fitzgerald, Frances. *Fire in the Lake.* Boston: Little, Brown, 1972.

Fox, William T. R. and Annette B. *NATO and the Range of American Choice.* New York: Columbia University Press, 1967.

Gann, Lewis H. *Guerrillas in History.* Stanford, Calif.: Hoover Institution, 1971.

Garthoff, Raymond L. *Soviet Military Doctrine.* Glencoe, Ill.: Free Press, 1953.

———. *Soviet Strategy in the Nuclear Age.* New York: Praeger, 1958.

Goodrich, Leland M. *Korea: A Study of United States Policy in the United Nations.* New York: Harper, 1956.

Griffith, Samuel B. *The Chinese People's Army.* New York: McGraw-Hill, 1967.

Holsti, Ole R. *Crisis Escalation War.* Montreal: McGill-Queen's University Press, 1972.

Huntington, Samuel P. *The Soldier and the State: The Theory and Politics of Civil-Military Relations.* Cambridge, Mass: Belknap Press of Harvard University Press, 1957.

Hurewitz, J. C. *Middle East Politics: The Military Dimension.* New York: Praeger, 1969.

Iklé, Fred Charles. *Every War Must End.* New York: Columbia University Press, 1971.

Janowitz, Morris. *The Professional Soldier.* Glencoe, Ill.: Free Press, 1960.

Kahin, McTurnan George, and Lewis, John W. *The United States in Vietnam.* New York: Dial Press, 1967.

Kahn, Herman. *On Thermonuclear War.* Princeton, N.J.: Princeton University Press, 1960.

———. *Thinking About the Unthinkable.* New York: Horizon, 1962.

Kaufmann, William, ed. *Military Policy and National Security.* Princeton, N.J.: Princeton University Press, 1956.

Kecskemeti, Paul. *Strategic Surrender.* Stanford, Calif: Stanford University Press, 1958.

Kennedy, Robert F. *Thirteen Days: A Memoir of the Cuban Missile Crisis.* New York: Norton, 1969.

Kissinger, Henry A. *The Necessity for Choice.* New York: Harper, 1961.

———. *Nuclear Weapons and Foreign Policy.* New York: Harper, 1957.

———. *The Troubled Partnership.* New York: McGraw-Hill, 1965.

Knorr, Klaus. *The Uses of Military Power in the Nuclear Age.* Princeton, N. J.: Princeton University Press, 1966.

Levine, Robert A. *The Arms Debate.* Cambridge, Mass.: Harvard University Press, 1963.

Liddell Hart, Basil H. *Strategy, the Indirect Approach.* London: Faber and Faber, 1954.

Luttwak, Edward. *A Dictionary of Modern War.* New York: Harper and Row, 1971.

Martin, L. W. *The Sea in Modern Strategy.* New York: Praeger, 1967.

McClintock, Robert. *The Meaning of Limited War.* Boston: Houghton Mifflin, 1967.

McNamara, Robert S. *The Essence of Security.* New York: Harper and Row, 1968.

Millis, Walter. *Arms and Men, a Study in American Military History.* New York: Putnam, 1956.

———, Mansfield, Harvey C., and Stein, Harold. *Arms and the State.* New York: Twentieth Century Fund, 1958.

Morgenstern, Oskar. *The Question of National Defense.* New York: Random House, 1959.

Nef, John U. *War and Human Progress.* Cambridge, Mass: Harvard University Press, 1950.

Neustadt, Richard E. *Alliance Politics.* New York: Columbia University Press, 1970.

Ogburn, William F., ed. *Technology and International Relations.* Chicago: University of Chicago Press, 1949.

Osgood, Robert E. *Limited War, the Challenge to American Strategy.* Chicago: University of Chicago Press, 1957.

———. *Alliances and American Foreign Policy.* Baltimore: Johns Hopkins Press, 1968.

Pachter, Henry M. *Collision Course: The Cuban Missile Crisis and Coexistence.* New York: Praeger, 1963.

Paget, Jullian. *Counter-Insurgency Operations.* New York: Walker, 1967.

Pike, Douglas. *Vietcong.* Cambridge, Mass.: Massachusetts Institute of Technology Press, 1966.

Ra'anan, Uri. *The USSR Arms the Third World.* Cambridge, Mass.: Massachusetts Institute of Technology Press, 1969.

Randle, Robert F. *Geneva 1954: The Settlement of the Indochinese War.* Princeton, N. J.: Princeton University Press, 1969.

Ridgway, Matthew B. *The Korean War.* Garden City, N.Y.: Doubleday, 1967.

Rothstein, Robert L. *Alliances and Small Powers.* New York: Columbia University Press, 1968.

Schelling, Thomas C. *The Strategy of Conflict.* Cambridge, Mass.: Harvard University Press, 1960.

———. *Arms and Influence.* New Haven, Conn.: Yale University Press, 1966.

Sheehan, Neil, *et al.,* eds. *The Pentagon Papers.* New York: Quadrangle Books, 1971.

SIPRI. *The Arms Trade with the Third World.* New York: Humanities Press, 1971.

Slessor, John C. *Strategy for the West.* New York: Morrow, 1954.

Synder, Glenn H. *Deterrence and Defense.* Princeton, N.J.: Princeton University Press, 1962.

Staley, Eugene. *War and the Private Investor.* New York: Doubleday, 1935.

Vagts, Alfred. *Defense and Diplomacy.* New York: King's Crown Press, 1956.

Van Dyke, Jon M. *North Vietnam's Strategy for Survival.* Palo Alto, Calif.: Pacific Books, 1972.

Von Rickhoff, Harald. *NATO: Issues and Prospects.* Toronto: Canadian Institute of International Affairs, 1967.

Werth, Alexander. *Russia at War 1941–1945.* New York: Dutton, 1964.

Wheeler-Bennet, John W. *The Nemesis of Power.* London: St. Martin's Press, 1954.

White, Ralph K. *Nobody Wanted War: Misperception in Vietnam and Other Wars.* Garden City, N.J.: Doubleday, 1968.

Wolf, Eric R. *Peasant Wars of the Twentieth Century.* New York: Harper and Row, 1969.

Wolfe, Thomas W. *Soviet Strategy at the Crossroads.* Cambridge, Mass.: Harvard University Press, 1964.

Wolfers, Arnold, ed. *Alliance Policy in the Cold War.* Baltimore: Johns Hopkins Press, 1959.

——, ed. *Changing East-West Relations and the Unity of the West.* Baltimore: Johns Hopkins Press, 1964.

Wright, Quincy. *A Study of War.* Chicago: University of Chicago Press, 1942.

7 The Economic Struggle for Power

My credit now stands on such slippery ground.
SHAKESPEARE *Julius Caesar,* III, 1

The East-West Economic Confrontation

There is hope that a major military conflict between East and West may be avoided. Power confronts counter-power and the condition of mutual deterrence has decreased the diplomatic influence of military force. Even in the political arena the contest has narrowed to a jockeying for limited advantage. In addition, centrifugal tendencies in both camps have infused the political distribution of power with new elements of flexibility. But a *decisive* victory is still possible in the *economic* theater of

194

the East-West struggle. Both superpowers are aware of this fact. The Soviet leadership has repeatedly asserted that its capacity to outproduce the West will usher in the victory of Communism without the necessity of military conflict. Its major weapon in this arena of the power struggle is economic and industrial competition. Hardly a day passes without exhortations in the Soviet press to "surpass the United States." A succession of "plans," ranging from five-year plans to twenty-year plans, testifies to this continuing effort. The Western nations, especially the United States, have responded to this challenge by reasserting the continued necessity to outproduce the Soviet Union and to retain healthy and prosperous economies. Indeed, East and West are engaged in a fierce industrial race.

In 1958 Premier Khrushchev proclaimed a bold Seven-Year Plan which was to give the Communist bloc greater industrial production by 1965 than the rest of the world put together. Indeed, the Soviet Premier added that by 1970 the Soviet Union would have the highest standard of living in the world and would be outproducing the United States both in absolute terms and on a per capita basis. Under the Seven-Year Plan, heavy industrial output was to increase by almost 100 per cent and light industry by 50 per cent. Capital investment and foreign trade were scheduled for a 70 per cent increase as were food, industry, and agriculture. In addition, the Plan promised an increase of at least 40 per cent in real income and the realization of a gigantic housing program.

In 1961 the Seven-Year Plan was superseded by an even more ambitious Twenty-Year Plan, which was to bring the Soviet Union to the threshold of true Communism. The new Plan, announced at the Twenty-second Congress of the Communist Party of the Soviet Union, envisaged the creation of "the material and technical basis of Communism" during the first decade and the introduction of "the principle of distribution according to need" by the end of the second.[1] Specifically, the Soviet leadership pledged itself to "surpass the strongest and richest capitalist country, the U.S.A., in production per head by 1970," and to "leave the overall volume of United States industrial output far behind by 1980."[2] Huge increases were planned for all sectors of heavy industry as well as for agricultural production. The Plan also included sharp rises in the standard of living and blueprints for the solution of the housing problem. The overall goal of the Twenty-Year Plan was clearly to make the Soviet Union the richest and most powerful nation in the world.

By the time of Khrushchev's fall, it had become clear that the ambitious goals of the Twenty-Year Plan could not be realized. Neither industrial nor agricultural production measured up to expectations. In 1966, the Kosygin government announced a new Five-Year Plan with more realistic objectives. National income was to increase by 7 per cent a year, industrial production by 8 per cent, and agricultural production by 25 per cent. The new Soviet regime also increased profit incentives for factory managers and collective farm chairmen. By the late 1960's, the Soviet economy showed marked improvements both in the industrial and agricultural sectors. Thus, central economic planning seems to remain a permanent feature of the Soviet system. Only the targets change. The challenge to the West remains. Hence, a rough projection of present Soviet economic plans into the 1980's may be useful.

There are several factors that operate in favor of the Soviet Plan. First, the mineral wealth of the Soviet Union far exceeds that of the United States. While American leadership is much concerned with the conservation of natural resources, the Soviet Union is just beginning to exploit the vast resources of Siberia and the Soviet Far East. With respect to most raw materials, the Soviet Union has the base to support larger industrial production than the United States. Second, the high degree of technological advance is an important factor in the raising of production and labor efficiency. Third, the Soviet labor force may be manipulated relatively freely. Manpower may be transferred from factories to farms and back again without serious repercussions to the economy. Moreover, strikes and similar labor crises restricting production do not exist in the U.S.S.R. Finally, and most important, the planned Soviet economy does not seem to be threatened by recessions or depressions. Indeed, as one American student of the Soviet economy has noted, in every year since 1946 Soviet industry has produced more than the previous year, and there is no reason to suppose that this steady upward movement will not continue.

On the other hand, there are also formidable obstacles in the path of the Plan. First, while it is true that the natural resources of the Soviet Union are almost inexhaustible, they are located for the most part in the thinly populated regions of the country. A large-scale migration of workers to Siberia would therefore be necessary to exploit these resources for production. Second, enormous capital investments are needed for the realization of production targets. But the Soviet government at the same time also promised a housing construction program, an increased living standard, and shorter work hours. It is questionable whether these production and consumption goals can be attained simultaneously. If they are not, consumer goods will probably be sacrificed to industrial production as in the past. Third, during the Khrushchev period, Soviet agriculture often was in serious trouble. Poor harvests frequently forced the Soviet government to purchase large quantities of wheat in Western markets in order to feed its people. In the light of these events it is most doubtful whether the highly ambitious agricultural targets can be attained. Fourth, the Plan is based on the assumption of relative internal stability within the Soviet bloc. The economies of the Eastern European countries are expected to contribute their share toward the 1970 and 1980 targets. The recurrence of an event like the Czechoslovak crisis of 1968 would seriously jeopardize the fulfillment of the Plan. Moreover, the increasing efforts made by Eastern European countries to establish closer economic ties with the West make their contributions to the Soviet Plan less and less predictable. Finally, the Soviet leadership takes for granted a very slow rate of economic growth in the United States.

Of all the "imponderables" in the equation, this last is perhaps the most important. On the one hand, the Soviet hope seems by no means unreasonable. Since 1950 the Soviet economy has been growing at a rate roughly twice that of the United States, and in 1958 the Soviet bloc for the first time surpassed the United States in steel production. On the other hand, a sense of urgency has been growing in the United States. American leadership of both parties has become increasingly convinced that the Soviet Plan represents a strategy with which the U.S.S.R. counts on winning the East-West struggle without war. The United States has realized that if, indeed, Communism should succeed in "burying" the capitalist system—to use former Premier Khrushchev's phrase—it is more likely to do so through higher production statistics than through nuclear bombardment. Hence the leadership of both major parties in the United States has shown itself deeply concerned about "staying ahead" of the Soviet Union in industrial capacity. Yet it seems questionable whether this sense of urgency can be sustained over a long period of time. In times of crisis the United States has always been able to outproduce its adversaries. The reaction to Pearl Harbor is a case in point. But the Communist challenge is unprecedented in that it is not an immediate but a long-range challenge that demands relentless, all-out effort. The Soviet hope, of course, is that the Western economies will disintegrate from maladies resulting from their own "inner contradictions." But the fact, counter to Marxist theory, is that capitalism has exhibited a high degree of resilience to the swings of the economic cycle. Techniques have been discovered whereby recessions and depressions can be mitigated or perhaps avoided altogether. Indeed, when one contemplates the tensions that exist within the Communist camp one is apt to conclude that Communism is at least as vulnerable to "inner contradictions" as are the Western nations.

Perhaps the greatest paradox of the economic struggle between East and West lies in the fact that as they have developed, the economies of the Soviet Union and of the United States have become increasingly similar. In both societies, good performance is rewarded with "capitalist" incentives. The successful Soviet factory manager or collective farm chairman is the recipient of bonuses, special funds, and numerous fringe benefits. While his standard of living is still far lower than that of an American executive—as, of course, the Soviet standard of living in general is much lower—the motives that spur him on are very similar. There remains one great difference, however, between the two systems.

In the United States, waste and inefficiency are not penalized by the government. In Communist countries, in contrast, failure to fulfill the quota may result in disciplinary action or dismissal. A serious discrepancy between target and actual accomplishment may be interpreted as sabotage and lead to internment in a labor camp.

It is very likely that over the years the economic similarities between the two societies will increase.[3] The great emphasis on production may even lead to a degree of ideological erosion. The typical Communist Party member is no longer a fiery orator or an idealistic visionary, but a calculating administrator and technocrat. The common dictates of industrial production may divest the East-West struggle of its messianic ideological character. Once universalist ideology atrophies, the fierceness of the struggle may abate. Hence, it is possible that the East-West industrial competition may in the end prove an indirect path to international order. The two great antagonists may settle for coexistence without victory or defeat. Possibly, even, the increasing similarity of their economic systems may contribute to a gradual realignment of the international struggle for power. Already the economic differences between "Communist" Russia and "Communist" China are nearly as great as those between "Communist" Russia and "Capitalist" America. How these trends will develop further is of course difficult to predict. Yet one thing seems certain: the nuclear age no longer permits a decisive military victory over one of the superpowers. The only possible victory can occur in the economic realm.

The Economics of the Two Struggles of Our Time: The "Waging" of Economic Aid

Despite the intensity of the economic competition between East and West, the two superpowers have not directed their resources and economic strategies primarily against each other. Rather, both the United States and the Soviet Union have become increasingly convinced that to win ultimate victory, they must gain the allegiance of the world's uncommitted nations. As a result, the competition between East and West for the favor of these neutralist states has steadily intensified. As one scholar has pointed out, "global politics have come to resemble more and more the domestic politics of a two-party system."[4] The uncommitted countries play the role of the often crucial independent vote. In order to win this floating vote, both parties promise prosperity and economic welfare. Both parties encourage industrialization. Both parties attempt to appeal to the vital center. The United States de-emphasizes its traditional associations with paternalistic colonialism, while the Soviet Union disclaims its revolutionary militancy. In short, both superpowers attempt to appeal to the new nationalism on whatever grounds seem most likely to elicit a favorable response. At the same time, the new nations themselves, having become fully aware of their strategic position, have increasingly used the East-West struggle to advance their own causes. In the process, economic aid has developed into a major instrument in the international power struggle and one that again clearly illustrates how extensively and intimately the two chief phases of that struggle—the East-West and the colonial-anticolonial—are interdependent. We shall now turn to an analysis of this new form of economic warfare.

Ever since the launching of President Truman's "Point Four Program" in 1949, Western, and especially American, aid to "underdeveloped areas" has been a permanent and expensive fact of life. And though it has been vociferously and continuously attacked on many grounds, few have gone so far as to suggest that it be ended altogether. Annual debates on the budget for economic aid programs have no longer challenged their basic purposes but have been confined to questions as to what sums should be allocated to them and how they ought to be administered. Examination of the growing literature on the subject shows that there are several telling motives that in fact underlie Western foreign aid policies. First, there is the economic argument— advanced in the United States as early as 1952—that the "underdeveloped lands" possess many of the ingredients of economic and strategic strength. The nature of the United States' economy has made it dependent on these areas for critical raw materials, and so the United States must participate in the continued development of these resources, a vital basis of its power. A second line of reasoning maintains that foreign aid is a tool in the East-West struggle, an important weapon in the competition with the Soviet Union for the support of the "neutralist" countries. This argument, a favorite of Congressmen "selling" foreign aid to their constituencies, assumes that economic aid buys grateful allies and is therefore a highly effective defense against Communist infiltration. Since Communism feeds on poverty, this argument holds, raising the standard of living should prove the best way to combat and prevent it.

A third ground on which foreign aid is justified is the hope that it will contribute to the establishment and strengthening of democracy, or at least prevent a state from turning to Communism. This hope is rooted not only in considerations of power. Rather, as is true of the Soviet Union as well, the United States feels flattered and reassured when it sees its own type of institutions apparently vindicated by being adopted and made to work elsewhere. If for that reason alone, it would prefer the world to be covered with as many democratic and as few Communist societies as possible.

Fourth, American foreign aid is intended to help provide a sound economic and social basis for the political stability and military strength of the United States' allies. In some areas, such as Formosa, South Korea, and South Vietnam, the aid given has gone well beyond these economic and social considerations and has frankly been designed first and foremost to build up the military effectiveness of the countries concerned. A similar logic has underlain the economic aid the United States has given to the two Communist states that to date have defied Soviet domination—Yugoslavia and Poland. The American assumption in undertaking this step was that whatever weakens Moscow's control strengthens the United States. However, this thinking has remained considerably tempered by American concern lest on major issues in the East-West struggle Yugoslavia and Poland side with the Soviet Union in spite of the aid they have received from the United States. Hence American policy in this regard has vacillated between the fear that "once a Communist, always a Communist" and the hope that "some Communists are less so than others." It is difficult to assess the effectiveness of these Western efforts to attract Communist countries. In the case of Yugoslavia, it is very likely that the prompt American offer to shore up Tito's government against Stalin after the former's expulsion from the Cominform strengthened the position of the Yugoslav leader and made it possible for him to pursue a fairly independent course. Poland, on the other hand, despite massive American aid, has in essence remained dependent upon the Soviet Union.

An impressive synthesis of most of the above arguments in favor of foreign aid was advanced by Professors Millikan and Rostow in a Report to the Senate Special Committee to Study the Foreign Aid Program.[5] As their main thesis the authors recommended that the United States employ its resources to create and encourage conditions for self-sustaining economic growth in the "underdeveloped" countries. Such growth, they held, would lead to the evolution of politically stable and viable democratic societies that could not easily be victimized by Communist promises or intimidation. The authors' premise in this argument was, of course, that there is a necessary causal connection between growing economic strength and the development of democratic values and institutions. Yet can this premise really be accepted as axiomatic? If it could—since economic development has in fact been steadily advancing in most of the uncommitted countries—would not democracy throughout the world have shown more victories, or even promises, than it actually has? It would seem, indeed, that the relationship between economic conditions and political institutions is considerably more complex than Millikan and Rostow have maintained.

The administration of American foreign aid has been highly complex. Almost 85 per cent of the annual budget approved for foreign aid has been earmarked for military equipment and defense. The other 15 per cent is designated as economic aid for development or defense support. Such support is in part military aid disguised as economic aid. In countries where American assistance pays for the development of a national power arsenal, defense support is economic aid disguised as military assistance. Hence, in practice, the distinction between "military" and "economic" aid is often not apparent. Ninety-nine per cent of the entire foreign aid budget is handled bilaterally between the United States and the recipient countries. Less than 1 per cent is channeled through the United Nations and its specialized agencies. The Congress has been very hesitant to allocate more generous funds to the UN's economic aid and technical assistance programs. The reasons for this have been several: unwillingness to yield financial control over American dollars to the General Assembly, reluctance to make the United Nations financially dependent upon any *one* power, suspicion that the United Nations was too responsive to Communist machinations, and a continuing preoccupation with immediate rather than long-range defense and security problems. This reluctance has been an important factor in causing the chronic shortage of funds that has afflicted the work of the United Nations in economic aid and technical assistance to "underdeveloped" areas.

The Soviet Union for a long period showed little interest in economic competition for the uncommitted nations. Under the iron dictatorship of the aging Stalin, its main concern continued to be with the consolidation of "socialism in one country" and Soviet hegemony in Eastern Europe. After Stalin's death, however, the new leaders were quick to see significant "built-in" advantages that the Soviet Union enjoyed vis-à-vis the West in its relations with the nations of Asia, Africa, and the Middle East. It could come to the nations that had just emerged from colonialism as the main protagonist of national self-determination; to the colored peoples of the world it could come as a partly Asian nation; in countries where the merchant had long been an object of contempt, it could emphasize its hostility to capitalism; to fledgling agricultural states yearning for modern industrial economies it could present itself as the nation that had launched the interplanetary age; and lastly, it could exploit its theory of the "inevitability" of a Communist victory by persuading the peoples of the new nations that by following the precepts of Marxism-Leninism they would have history on their side and could make the leap to progress almost through an act of faith.

The new Soviet leadership lost no time in utilizing these advantages and taking up the instrument of economic aid with a vengeance. Suddenly, Nehru was no longer an imperialist lackey, but a glorious leader of a free people. Nasser, who had been attacked as a Fascist usurper when he first rose to power, became the hero of a nation exploited by Western colonialism. Actual economic aid began to be offered by the Soviet Union in 1954, five years later than the United States. The formal occasion of this action was the extensive tour of Asia that Khrushchev and Bulganin undertook in that year. As the two Soviet leaders visited country after country, they accompanied their own offers of aid by vehement denunciations of Western aid as camouflaged imperialism in which "the flag would follow the dollar." They particularly hammered at the American policy of attaching "strings" to its aid programs and sought to convince their listeners that American aid was never motivated by a disinterested humanitarianism but was solely intended to prevent the forward march of Communism. Khrushchev and Bulganin pointed to the Soviet Union as the classic example of a nation that had attained industrialization without "imperialist aid." Hence, industrialization Soviet style—and with the aid of "good red rubles" with no strings attached—was recommended as infinitely preferable to American "gilded missiles."

The Soviet theme of anti-imperialism fell on ready ears in Asia and soon made necessary a reevaluation of American aid policy. For it was indeed true that until the mid-1950's the United States had customarily attached political conditions to its foreign economic assistance. In exchange for extensive aid to South Vietnam, for example, the United States had exerted a degree of pressure on the government of that country to install a pro-American Premier, Ngo Dinh Diem. In addition, a Vietnamese army was equipped with American weapons and training facilities, but was expected to return to resist any possible Communist aggression from the North. The Soviets branded this as an example of "Yankee Imperialism" working hand in glove with French colonialism. The result of this maneuver was that Ho Chi Minh, the Communist and anti-French leader of North Vietnam, gained a great deal of popularity, while Premier Diem was regarded in many Vietnamese circles as "l'homme d'Amerique."

In this altered situation following the appearance of the Soviets on the scene, the task of the United States became increasingly difficult. Most importantly, it now became possible for an opportunistic neutralist to "play both sides of the street" and to hold out his political friendship to the highest bidder. If the United States demanded unacceptable political conditions, the recipient was now in a position to say: "If you do not give me aid without strings, I know someone who will." One striking example of this is the history of the Aswan High Dam. In 1956, President Nasser conceived this ambitious project in order to control floods, add irrigation and provide power for his growing economy. The United States offered to finance the construction of the dam. Shortly thereafter, however, Nasser bought some armaments from Czechoslovakia and decided to recognize Communist China, whereupon Secretary of State John Foster Dulles withdrew the American offer. Contingent offers by the United Kingdom and the World Bank collapsed as well. At this juncture the Soviet Union stepped into the breach and offered to build the dam. The Egyptian President accepted the Soviet offer without hesitation and subsequently the Aswan High Dam was built with Soviet funds and Soviet engineers. Eight years later, Nikita Khrushchev visited Aswan to accept the tribute of a grateful Nasser.

The United States aid programs to "neutralist" nations now made every effort to avoid "strings" of any kind. In general, American aid—and the implied political support that inevitably went with it—was therefore placed in the hands of the ruling elites that were in fact in control. Unfortunately, however, the members of these traditional elites were often the people in the countries concerned who were most closely associated with large-scale land ownership and with the former colonial powers. Though still in control, they were actually being opposed as "reactionaries" by more and more of the people. Hence, by supporting these traditional groups, the United States tended to be popularly identified with them and to become maligned as an intruding force helping to impede social and political progress. Moreover, as a result of their support by the United States, the members of the traditional elites in question felt free in a number of instances to be less than scrupulously honest and public-spirited in their administration of American aid funds. Indirectly, this contributed even further to the unfavorable popular image of the United States. As a result, although the introduction of American money and influence aided in preparing the way for industrialization and higher popular economic expectations, the Communists frequently found themselves in the better position to mobilize the population as a whole in the pursuit of these objectives. By assuming leadership against the "conservatives" backed by the United States, Communist parties were able steadily to strengthen their positions and even, in Indonesia, for example, managed for a time to participate in government in such key roles as regular cabinet positions.

The above analysis should not convey the impression that American aid without strings has had no beneficial results. Indeed, most neutralist countries have responded very favorably to the scrupulous observance of the recipient nations' sovereign rights. But just as often it has unwittingly played into the hands of Communist interests. And as this has been perceived in the United States, the entire subject of economic aid as an instrument of policy in the East-West struggle has come under extensive reexamination. Yet almost no one has gone so far as to recommend that foreign economic aid to the new nations be stopped altogether. For though such a policy might have pleased a few economy-minded Congressmen, it would obviously have alienated the new nations whose neutrality, if not support, the United States badly needs. At best, it might align the United States with static and conservative regimes, perhaps pro-Western but growing progressively more alien to the heartbeat of their countries. Such regimes would almost certainly be unstable and probably would in the long run prove unable to resist the factions championing the example of Soviet-style industrialization.

These, then, were the horns of the American dilemma in regard to economic aid. On the one hand, continued emphasis on aid with or without strings; on the other, a policy of withdrawal; with either alternative possibly having equally disastrous consequences. The dilemma seemed even more acute because many Americans looked at Soviet aid to the uncommitted nations in largely one-dimensional terms. They wondered at the "blindness" of the neutralist leaders and their failure to see that Soviet aid missions had all the earmarks of Trojan horses. This attitude failed to take into account the Afro-Asian view of the Soviet Union. To be sure, it is difficult enough for a nation to see itself as others see it. It is far more difficult to see a second nation as a third sees it.[6] Yet this is precisely the root of the competition. The Soviet Union has been able to project itself into the thinking of the uncommitted nations somewhat more successfully than the United States. The truth is that Soviet aid has been much more attractive to many of the new nations than many Americans would care to admit. To most of the Asian and African leaders Communism is merely an alternative to democracy—an alternative, in fact, which many believe may be able to produce the desired effects more quickly. In brief, the choice from the point of view of the recipient country is *not* one between good and evil. It is not even primarily a question of Soviet *or* Western aid. Rather, it is the much more practical question of how much can be sought and "safely" accepted from either or both.

Fortunately for the United States, the "built-in" advantages enjoyed by the Soviet Union in its appeal to the Afro-Asian nations are at least partly offset in many of the countries concerned by considerable and ever-growing suspicion of Communist leadership. The Soviet Union's representation of itself as a partly Asian country, for example, has by no means entirely obscured the fact that the country is governed by white men and has frequently adopted a repressive policy toward its minority groups. The antireligious overtones of Communism are repulsive to the Hindu, Buddhist, and Moslem elements that are widely scattered throughout the neutralist countries. The totalitarian features of the Soviet Union are deeply suspect in countries like India, with a spiritual tradition of nonviolence. Finally, there are profound misgivings about Communist expansionary goals and the tactics of subversion and political domination. The Chinese incursions into Indian territory, especially, have alerted the neutralists to this danger. These handicaps frequently neutralize Communism's "built-in" advantages and have compelled the Soviet Union to administer its aid program with the utmost circumspection and the most scrupulous respect for the sovereignty of the recipient countries.

In purely quantitative terms, the Soviet aid program has spent approximately one tenth of the amount expended by the West. It should be pointed out, however, that most Communist nations share in the program. An indication of the range of these activities may be gathered from the following selective summary:

Czechoslovakia provided technical aid in the construction of a meat-processing plant and sugar refinery in Afghanistan. Sixteen Soviet experts conducted a survey of possible industrial and agricultural investment projects in Cambodia. Soviet technical experts have made studies in India of possibilities for a pharmaceutical industry, glass and electric-power plants, and heavy machinery manufacturing. Hungarian experts advised on the construction of hydro-electric and diesel stations in Indonesia. The U.S.S.R. assisted in modernization of spinning looms and mills in Lebanon. Czechoslovakia provided technical aid in the establishment of a flour mill in Paraguay. Polish engineers assisted in construction of an enamelware factory in Egypt. East German experts conducted a survey of water resources, and assisted in the construction of waterworks and water systems in the Sudan, Czechoslovakian technicians assisted in the construction of an international airport in Damascus and in the construction of an oil refinery in Syria. Czechoslovakia provided technical assistance in the construction of a cement factory in Yemen.[7]

In 1959, for example, missions from the entire Soviet bloc entered Guinea, the only African country to have seceded from the French Community. Virtually the entire economy of that new nation was affected by Communist economic aid, and only several years later did the United States enter the competition effectively.

Before we embark on a more detailed comparison of the economic aid administered by East and West, it should be mentioned that several Western nations besides the United States have made sizeable contributions. The United States has, of course, been the most important single purveyor of aid. Britain has made substantial grants—largely through the instrumentality of the Colombo Plan—to develop the economies and raise the living standards of several Asian nations. This effort has not been limited to members of the Commonwealth, but has been extended to Vietnam, Laos, Cambodia, Burma, Thailand, Nepal, and Indonesia. In addition, Britain has extended large-scale assistance to her former colonies in Africa. The same is true of France and the African members of the French Community. Most recently, West Germany has made some notable contributions to the Western program. Indeed, Germany's role is becoming increasingly important.

The effectiveness of economic aid, however, cannot be judged primarily in quantitative terms. If that were so, the economic struggle would have been won by the West long ago. In order to analyze the dynamics of the struggle correctly, we must proceed to a qualitative assessment of the several specific types of aid used by both East and West in the uncommitted nations.

Both East and West have made long-term aid commitments. While the West has poured great quantities of foodstuffs and consumer goods into the uncommitted countries, the Soviet Union has preferred to build monuments to itself. For example, the United States has shipped vast quantities of wheat to India and provided vital technical assistance in Indian irrigation projects. While American technicians and engineers were widely scattered throughout the subcontinent, the Soviets concentrated their effort in Central India. In Bhilai, the Soviets erected a giant steel mill with a capacity of a million tons of ingots. The plans for the mill were drawn up by Soviet engineers but its construction was a joint Indian-Soviet effort. A great deal of machinery and equipment was brought from the Soviet Union and the project was financed by a Soviet credit to the Indian government. The total cost of the plant exceeded $200,000,000. Most important, when construction was completed, the Soviet engineers went home and the plant belonged to the Indian government to be used for the benefit of the Indian economy. A similar example of Soviet "impact" aid was the construction of asphalt roads in Kabul, the capital city of Afghanistan. The roads were financed by Soviet credit and built with Soviet machinery under the supervision of Soviet engineers. Western aid to Afghanistan, on the other hand, has consisted largely of consumer goods.

In any objective evaluation, Western aid to the Indian and Afghanistan economies has been vital. It has been applied throughout the entire economies of the two nations, has kept them from foundering and has greatly facilitated national planning. Yet once wheat has been consumed, it is easily forgotten. The Bhilai steel mill and the modern roads of Kabul, in contrast, have a decidedly more permanent "glamor value." To the casual observer, they furnish proof of Soviet generosity. More important, perhaps, they point up the Soviet ability to make long-range commitments for the construction of specific major industrial projects. Until the establishment of the International Development Association (IDA) in 1960, the United States was severely handicapped in its long-range planning by the requirement for annual Congressional approval of most foreign aid expenditures. And it is precisely this type of long-range capital assistance that is required to guide most of the new nations over their initial planning period toward the goal of industrialization. Many Western projects of this kind must grow out of private initiative. But this means higher interest rates, a search for profit, and the continued presence of Western personnel. Western capital construction aid looks askance at waste because it is motivated at least in part by private economic considerations. The persistence of the American fixation on "private enterprise" has tended to inhibit the use of economic aid as an instrument of governmental policy. The Soviet leadership, on the other hand, considers the question of economic returns completely irrelevant. Its motives are to win the psychological and political allegiance of the new nations.

Both East and West have wooed the neutralists with lavish gifts. Once again the Western, especially the American, practice has been to give "grants" in the form of commodities and technical assistance. The Soviet bloc does not give "grants." Instead, it brings "gifts." The Soviets have been very conscious of the psychological truth that a "grant" is something a richer nation gives a poorer, whereas a "gift" is a matter between friends. Gifts from the Soviet bloc again follow the "monument" pattern. For instance, the Soviet government constructed a technological institute in Rangoon as a gift to the people of Burma. In return, Burma presented the Soviet people with "a gift of rice." This type of ceremonial gift exchange was so successful that it was frequently repeated elsewhere. The Soviets have given hospitals, sports centers, hotels, and exhibition halls to the uncommitted nations. In most instances, the recipients were permitted to demonstrate their appreciation by a gift of surplus commodities. The monetary value of the gifts from the Communist bloc countries has usually been relatively small, but their significance has far transcended their cash value. A Soviet "glamor gift" frequently receives more publicity than a multimillion dollar United States "grant" of cash, commodities, equipment, or technical assistance. An amusing by-product of East-West economic competition has been the fact that some of the neutralist countries have begun to refuse any form of economic aid at all unless it is an outright gift. Cambodia, for example, has laid down this condition: "It is perfectly happy to receive grants from any source and does so with abandon, but it refuses categorically to accept loans of any kind. Even a generous Soviet offer of a very long-term, interest-free credit was rejected on the grounds that an obligation to repay would in some way constitute an abridgment of Cambodia's sovereignty."[8] This strange pattern reached its logical extreme in the case of Indonesia. Former President Sukarno announced repeatedly that he had *rewarded* the United States by *accepting* its gifts. This curious psychological inversion has become one of the most astounding phenomena of the East-West struggle.

It is not always true that neutralist leaders prefer outright grants. Most of the larger neutralist countries are the recipients of loans from both East and West. Loans do less violence to the sense of dignity and independence of the recipients and a borrowing country feels not like an object of charity but like an equal. It is simply engaging in a normal economic exchange in which it is paying fairly for what it receives.[9] Burma even insisted on paying for its Soviet "gift" with a symbolic "gift" of rice of its own. Similarly, the Burmese premier preferred an American loan to a grant, stating that: "We prefer to pay for it, as this forms a more solid basis of friendship than acceptance of gifts."[10]

There are, indeed, several further considerations in the debate concerning gifts versus loans. For one thing, as an American expert on the subject has pointed out, "Credits are twice-blessed; they bless by maintaining the sense of dignity of the recipient when first extended, and they bless by securing the gratitude of the recipient if payments are reduced or forgiven. Grants would serve neither of these ends."[11] On the other hand, there is the important matter of the interest rate. Soviet loans typically carry an interest charge of 2 to 2½ per cent. Thus the Indian government is paying the Soviet Union 2½ per cent interest on the Bhilai steel mill. In contrast, the interest rate charged by the United States government, the World Bank, and private Western firms, usually ranges between 4 and 5 per cent. For a project comparable to the Bhilai steel mill that has been financed by the World Bank and by a United States loan, The Tata Iron and Steel Company Ltd. and the Indian Iron and Steel Company are paying the World Bank 4¾ per cent. The Soviets have emphasized their low interest rate, especially in those areas of Asia, Africa, and the Middle East where the money-lender is an object of scorn. Their purpose has been to try to portray the West as an exploiter of the poverty of the underdeveloped countries and to present their own program as one of mutual benefit. While the political elites in the neutralist nations know, of course, that a large proportion of Western aid consists of grants that need not be repaid, when loans are compared with loans the comparison is favorable to the Soviet Union. For in fact the 2 per cent interest rate strikes a delicate balance. It is high enough to safeguard the national pride and sensitivity of the new nations, yet it is low enough to seem to lend plausibility to the denunciation of the West as a rapacious Shylock. Soviet capacity to manipulate its interest rate is one of the advantages of a state-controlled economy. It would be idle to expect an American firm or the World Bank to abandon traditional investment practices and pour money into unstable developing countries without the expectation of a reasonable economic return. When funds placed in an American savings bank or government bonds yield 5 per cent or more, it is difficult to persuade Western business to extend loans abroad for 2 per cent or less.

A final matter of crucial importance concerns the method of repayment of aid credits. At first, "gold clauses" were inserted into all agreements for Western loans. In order to protect the lender from inflation, the borrower had to pledge himself to repay the credit in hard currency—American dollars or British pounds sterling. But usually hard currency was in short supply in the new nations. When Soviet credit appeared on the scene, the Russians announced their willingness to accept repayment in local currency or in the form of commodity exports from the recipient countries. This gave the Soviet Union a great advantage in the economic struggle. Burma, for example, would have liked to repay a United States loan by exporting parts of its rice surplus. But the United States was burdened with a rice surplus of its own. Moreover, the Soviet negotiators have made it a policy not to require a detailed economic justification before granting a loan for a particular development project. Whereas the Soviets have emphasized speed,

Americans have often bogged down in endless surveys and preparatory missions. As one scholar has put it: "After battling with the hardheaded bankers, skeptical lawyers and insistent economists who run Western and international aid programs, it is a welcome relief for the negotiators of the underdeveloped countries to deal with the openhanded and eager Russians."[12]

The publicity that accompanies the economic aid program of East and West has an important bearing on the overall picture. A Soviet decision to extend a loan or give a "gift" is invariably announced as a "unanimous desire of the Soviet people" to bring economic and social welfare to the developing countries. Conversely, the annual foreign aid appropriation by the American Congress is usually preceded by an acrimonious debate over the merits of the recipient. Invariably, a small but articulate minority inveighs against "the great give-away" and the pouring of American funds "down rat holes and bottomless pits." Frequently, neutralist leadership is not sufficiently sophisticated to perceive that Soviet unanimity is a fabrication or, on the other hand, that violent opponents of foreign aid are in a minority in the United States. The net result is that small Soviet gifts or loans often receive more favorable notices than do much larger quantities of Western aid.

Perhaps the crucial advantage of the Communist aid program is its claim never to have attached any "strings," economic or political, to its assistance. It was, indeed, this Soviet self-restraint that compelled the West to adopt similar policies. In the meantime, however, the fact that the West *did* attach political conditions to its early programs has given the Communist bloc a great propaganda advantage. By widely proclaiming a "no strings attached" policy, the Soviet Union has capitalized on the intense emotions of anticolonialism in the new sovereign countries. All industrial establishments constructed by members of the Soviet bloc become the property of the recipient country. By contrast, private Western companies have often constructed plants and continued to operate them for profit. While it cannot be denied that private investment has made great contributions to economic growth in many underdeveloped countries, the high interest rate has often been seen as an "economic string" leading to ultimate political dependence. The Russians, on the other hand, build their monuments and go back home. Quite obviously it would be puerile to regard the Soviet refusal to attach "political strings" as a manifestation of disinterested human-itarianism. But it would be equally naive to assume that Communist economic aid missions necessarily serve as a camouflage for espionage and conspiratorial activities. There have in fact been such cases, as in Burma in 1956, when Soviet technical personnel in Rangoon were accused of espionage, but they have been rare. On the whole, the Communist countries have established a tradition of scrupulous nonin-terference and correct behavior in the neutralist countries.

It is very likely that "economic aid without strings" is seen by the Soviet Union as the best way to achieve ultimate control. For there may well be Communist "strings" of a more hidden nature. First, a tradition of correct behavior, once established, may cause a lowering of the guard in the recipient nations. As Communist aid grows, the day may come when the economy of the neutralist country will have become dependent on the continued flow of Soviet aid. At that point political pressure may be applied: first as a gentle reminder to the recipient state that its behavior is not sufficiently "friendly"; then, perhaps, as a warning that aid might stop unless behavior became "friendlier." In short, once economic dependence is established, the withdrawal of aid may be used as a lever for obtaining political concessions. The pattern may be analogous to that of drug addiction. The neutralist country accepts the aid, fully believing that it can "kick it" at any time, only to find that it may be "hooked." It is possible, of course, that at such a critical juncture, the West might come to the rescue of a neutralist nation which has been "hooked." This, indeed, might become a major challenge to Western statecraft. The Soviets themselves have frequently played this role. For example, in 1958 the government of Pakistan was bitterly split on the question of whether the nation should accept an American loan for the construction of a new steel mill. In the midst of the heated debate the Russians stepped in and also offered to build and finance a steel mill for the Pakistani people.[13] The result, of course, was an American grant.

On balance, Soviet policy seems to subordinate immediate subversion to the more ambitious and longer-range goal of economic and political dependence. During the "infiltration" stage, the Soviet program increases the appeal of neutralism in Asia, Africa, and the Middle East since it strengthens the bargaining power of the new nations vis-à-vis the West. The likelihood that immediate conspiracy is not a factor would seem to be borne out by the fact that there is no direct correlation between Soviet foreign aid policy and the role of the Communist Party in the recipient countries. The five largest recipients of Soviet aid in the late 1960's were India, the UAR, Afghanistan, Indonesia, and Cuba, each of which received more than $300,000,000 in credits. In these five recipient countries, the Communist Party was legal in India, outlawed in the UAR, nonexistent in Afghanistan where there is no political party system under the King, virtually purged in Indonesia, and ruling in Cuba. Communist objectives are thus clearly attuned to the long run. They have been planned well and have demonstrated great sensitivity to the peculiar psychology of the new nationalism. It is here that the difference between East and West has been at its most striking. While the West has often attempted to impose conditions *before* aid was to be given, thus frequently antagonizing the recipients, the Soviet bloc has posed as a benefactor seeking no payment at all. In truth, the ultimate price may be high indeed, but will not be exacted until long *after* economic aid has been absorbed.

No analysis of Communist economic aid would be complete without a consideration of the policies of Communist China. Peking's first aid project to a non-Communist country was launched in 1956 with a grant to Cambodia. Later that year, Nepal became the beneficiary of Chinese economic aid. That small nation, fearful of political intervention, went so far as to insist that no Chinese technical personnel accompany the shipments. In September 1957 Ceylon received a grant for the improvement of rubber plantations. In addition to outright gifts, the Chinese also experimented with long-term loans to neutralist countries. Following the pattern set by the Soviet Union, Peking attached "no conditions whatever" to its aid agreements.

In the 1960's, the Chinese stepped up their aid program considerably. A large loan was granted to Burma, and trade and aid missions were established in Africa. The largest single Chinese project in Africa became the Tanzam railway for which large credits were extended to Tanzania and Zambia. Several Latin American countries became recipients of Chinese aid, in particular Peru, Chile and Guyana. In the Middle East, Iraq, Syria and Southern Yemen became beneficiaries during the 1960's.

During the turbulence of the Cultural Revolution, Chinese aid was sharply curtailed, but by the early 1970's, once again had assumed major proportions. In 1970, for example, the Chinese extended credits for $700 million to seven recipient countries including a $200 million loan to Pakistan, while Soviet aid during that year, including aid to Cuba, amounted to a total of only $600 million, which was shared by ten countries. Thus, since 1970 both Soviet and American economic aid have declined while Chinese economic aid has risen. Peking generally extends its aid on soft terms, with low or no interest rates and long-deferred repayments. In most instances, trade agreements and an exchange of trade missions accompany the aid pacts, and advisors are sent to the countries where Chinese projects are underway.

A word should be said about purely military aid. Here the United States and the Soviet Union are still the main protagonists and the pattern of interdependence between them and the new nations is striking indeed. In 1965 and again in 1971, for example, India and Pakistan fought wars in which both used American weapons that had been given to them for defense against Communism. In 1967, almost three billion dollars worth of Soviet military equipment that had been given by the USSR to the Arab states was destroyed or captured by Israel. Thus, military assistance plays a large role in the economic struggle for power. It may make the new nations more dependent on a superpower, as Egypt learned after its defeat. But the superpower, in turn, may become embroiled in the wars of its client and thus run the risk of confrontation with its superpower adversary. Once again, as in the political sphere, the pattern is one of mutual exploitation.

The Future of the Economic Power Struggle

From the above analysis, it appears to be a paradox that both East and West extend aid to the same countries with the expectation of victory for their respective political systems. The Soviet Union hopes that economic and industrial development will lead to the triumph of Communism in the uncommitted countries. The West holds the view that economic growth will strengthen democratic traditions and thus win the neutralist nations for the West. Since these mutually exclusive ends cannot be achieved by the same means, must not one of the two superpowers be fatally wrong in its policies in the economic struggle? It seems that whereas the objective of Communist aid—the inclusion of neutralist areas within the Communist orbit—is clear, Western goals in the economic struggle are often vague. Part of this vagueness is of course inherent in the nature of democracy. How can American economic aid policy be imbued with a set of substantive goals with which to compete successfully with officially imposed and managed Communist ideology? How can one make democracy into an export commodity without sacrificing the most cherished parts of its heritage— the principle of disagreement, the absence of an all-encompassing creed, and the freedom of man to think and act for himself?

A democratic system of government is most strikingly distinguished from Communist determinism in that it accepts man's freedom to reflect and choose. Communist man, it has often been asserted, is caught by the inexorable laws of the system, while democratic man has the capacity to control the social system by his own will. This distinction is fundamental to those who feel that the ideological arsenal of democracy must be equipped with a fighting faith. The export of technical "knowhow," so the argument runs, is in itself inadequate unless it is accompanied by the spiritual message of democracy—the belief in the inherent rights of the individual. While this view has a great deal of force, it does not resolve our basic problem.

The dignity of the individual, freedom of thought, the right to disagree—all these are among the most dearly held Western ideals. But even if they were exportable, would they be considered more than philosophical niceties to peoples deeply impressed with crying economic needs, the glamor of industrialization, and the prospect of being in the advance guard of mankind? The very deterministic quality that the West decries in Communism is looked to by many neutralist leaders as an asset. They see in it an almost religious, if secular, assurance that their societies can attain the millennium of progress. It is therefore open to serious question whether the export of democracy as a way of life and as a substantive spiritual message by the West to "neutralist" countries is at the moment either philosophically or psychologically feasible.

One basic reason for the relative ineffectiveness of the West in promoting democracy among the uncommitted nations is a breakdown in communication. When addressing the new nations, the West tends to define the major advantages of democracy primarily in terms of *political* liberties: freedom of speech, freedom of religion, freedom of the press, and freedom of assembly. However, most of the new nations have no tradition of democracy and tend to lean toward authoritarian forms of government. To the people in these countries the overriding concern is not political liberty but *economic* security: freedom from want, freedom from illness, freedom from hunger, and freedom from an early death. The Soviet Union conducts its aid program in a psychological framework that is more immediately meaningful to the recipients. It points to itself as the leading "socialist" country and declares the "classless society" as its avowed goal. The United States, itself deeply ambivalent about the "welfare state," is reluctant to export a kind of "international New Dealism." It would be difficult to imagine the Voice of America advertising American "socialism." Yet, the "classless" society is in fact closer to realization in the West than it is in the Communist countries. Hence there emerges a cruel paradox: the United States has all the economic benefits which the neutralist nations want, yet is unwilling to advertise them; the Soviet Union, on the other hand, is only too eager to promise advantages that it does not possess.

One possible way in which the West could deal with the Soviet bloc's economic offensive would be always to outdo the Communists and call upon them to match Western efforts. It might be argued that if the Soviet Union could be involved in such a competition its resources would be overstrained, whereas its refusal to take up the challenge would show it up as a second-class power. Such a procedure, however, would be somewhat mechanistic and would transfer an equal measure of control over Western economic aid policy to the Communist bloc, since each Soviet offer would have to elicit an automatic American counteroffer. Some observers have suggested the opposite technique. According to these, the United States should withhold aid from all countries accepting Soviet offers, or at least deduct Soviet credits from the quota of American aid. Such a policy, however, would add new substance to the oft-repeated Soviet charge that Western aid is given only to combat Communism, not to increase the welfare of the recipient. The following tale circulated by the Communists found a large audience in those neutralist nations that had been warned by the Soviet Union against Western economic aid:

An American official assessing the needs of the neutralist nations for American aid arrived in Nepal. After the usual preliminaries the official got down to business and asked the Nepalese chief of state how much money he thought he needed from the American government. A fairly modest sum was mentioned in reply. Somewhat relieved, the official mentioned that this was quite feasible. "But," he added, "you do have a Communist problem here, do you not?" "No," was the reply. Now the American appeared dubious but nevertheless promised to do his best. The Nepalese, fearing for the money, decided to ask Prime Minister Nehru of India for help. "Will you lend me two thousand Communists?" he asked him. The reply, after a minute's thoughtful silence, was disappointing: "No," said Mr. Nehru, "in this country we need every Communist we can get."*

While this story is probably apocryphal, the Soviets have often managed to brand the United States with the stigma of colonialism. Hence, any form of Western punishment for the acceptance of Communist aid might easily backfire. It has therefore been suggested that the United States try to improve the economy of a country *before* the Soviets make an offer. One of the great problems of the West in the economic struggle is that of anticipating the Soviet Union. More frequently the Soviet bloc anticipates the West, as it did in Guinea, where the West was compelled to react rather than to act. It will probably be necessary for the West, in this connection, to become less concerned with economic waste. Indeed, as one scholar has put it: "When it becomes less concerned over technical strings and economic waste, the United States Congress in particular will have caught up with the Soviets in understanding that political ends justify and often require wastefulness of economic means."[14]

There may be some areas in which the West may attach conditions with impunity. But these are few and include only those in which there exists a common interest between East and West. One of these might be the dispersion of atomic energy to the uncommitted nations. Both the Soviet Union and the United States have serious reservations about equipping the new nations with nuclear capacity as their jointly proposed nuclear non-proliferation treaty testifies. Hence it might be possible "to make both sales and grants of *conventional* military hardware to industrially less developed countries contingent on a supervised commitment by the recipient country not to produce, or seek to produce, *nuclear* weapons on its own."[15]

In overall perspective, both East and West have been forced to adopt an attitude of detachment. While the West has learned this lesson only after the "strings" attached to its aid programs had snapped, the Soviets have exhibited a deeper understanding of this psychological truth and have shown a clearer perception of their own ultimate goals. The West has had a more difficult time grasping the paradox that "a decent

---

*This story was related to the author by an Indian student at the Communist Youth Festival in Vienna in 1959.

measure of control is more likely to flow from an attitude of detachment than from one of involvement."[16]

To redress the balance, the West has begun to examine the possibility of channelling a greater proportion of its economic aid programs through the United Nations. This may indeed be a fruitful approach. The last ten years have seen a tremendous growth of the United Nations functional agencies. Numerous organs exist within the UN structure for technical assistance and aid to developing areas. The World Bank, the United Nations Development Program, the Economic and Social Council and its commissions, the Technical Assistance Board, the International Finance Corporation, the International Development Association, and a number of specialized agencies such as the Food and Agriculture Organization and the World Health Organization, all share in this work. Except for the World Bank, which commands substantial capital, these agencies subsist on fairly modest budgets. It has been suggested that an upward revision of these amounts might neutralize some of the more powerful Soviet maneuvers in the uncommitted areas and lead to a more economical use of American funds.

Aid given by the Western powers through United Nations auspices might deflate the Leninist contention that it is a disguised form of imperialism. Since the Asian and African peoples have been particularly susceptible to this kind of Soviet propaganda, the gains so derived might be considerable for the West. Emphasis upon international rather than bilateral aid might give the lie to Soviet assertions, since representatives from the governments of recipient countries sit in the councils of United Nations Technical Assistance agencies. Admittedly, the ratio would have to be revised gradually to avoid a disproportion of American funds and to allow time for the responses of other countries to the American initiative. United Nations teams, by virtue of their international composition, would assure the application of technical assistance within the cultural framework of the country to which it is given. Such teams have often prevented severe social friction, and have eased the strains of industrialization. The Food and Agriculture Organization, for example, introduced artificial fertilizers in India only after the way had been prepared by a UNESCO team that had succeeded in overcoming much social resistance. The dangerous split in societies between the pro-industrialization group and those opposed may be narrowed considerably, or even prevented, by workers who bring with them a treasury of experience from many lands—including those that have already benefited from the development process. Finally, it has been pointed out that the United States might get better results for less money by committing a greater proportion of funds to the United Nations. A truly international program would decentralize budgetary responsibilities and distribute among other nations burdens so far borne largely by the United States. Indeed, a continual outflow of gold prompted the United States in the early 1960's to ask its Western European allies to assume a larger share of the Western aid program to the developing areas.

There are, on the other hand, arguments against a greater Western use of the United Nations as a vehicle of economic aid. Many American legislators are reluctant to commit more funds to the UN. They fear, first, that United Nations aid would not woo the neutralist nations as effectively for the West as would direct American aid; they are also reluctant to relinquish control over large sums of money to the United Nations General Assembly in which the United States has only one vote. Yet these arguments are of dubious validity, since it must be remembered that, given the nature of the global economic competition, the United States no longer has a choice between maintaining control over its foreign aid funds and relinquishing it. Any attempt by the United States to impose "strings" would immediately be exploited by the Soviet Union. Hence, the real choice seems to lie between yielding up the funds directly to the nations of the developing areas or appropriating them to the General Assembly. In view of the unstable and authoritarian nature of many of the governments of the new nations, many Western observers feel that while "bilateral aid" must, of course, continue, a more generous portion of Western economic aid funds should be allotted to the world body. Such a plan might considerably mitigate the intensity of the economic power struggle and help to forge economic aid into a truly effective instrument of international order. Barring such changes, however, it is very likely that economic aid in our time will remain primarily a form of warfare in the international struggle for power.

REFERENCES

1. *The New Soviet Society,* Final Text of the Program of the CPSU; H. Ritro, New Leader paperback, 1962, pp. 114–15.

2. *Ibid.*

3. For an impressive analysis of this point, see Zbigniew K. Brzezinski and Samuel P. Huntington, *Political Power: U.S.A.–U.S.S.R.* New York: Viking, 1964.

4. George Liska, *The New Statecraft: Foreign Aid in American Foreign Policy.* Chicago: University of Chicago Press, 1960, p. 5.

5. Max F. Millikan and Walt W. Rostow, *A Proposal.* New York: Harper, 1957, *passim.*

6. Joseph S. Berliner, *Soviet Economic Aid.* New York: Praeger, 1958, p. 137.

7. *Ibid.,* p. 44.

8. Hans Heymann, Jr., "Soviet Foreign Aid as a Problem for U.S. Policy," *World Politics*, July 1960, p. 533.

9. Berliner, *op. cit.*, p. 147.

10. *The New York Times*, March 13, 1957.

11. Berliner, *op. cit.*, p. 150.

12. *Ibid.*, p. 154.

13. *Ibid.*, p. 19.

14. Liska, *op. cit.*, p. 194.

15. *Ibid.*, p. 229.

16. *Ibid.*, p. 234.

BIBLIOGRAPHY

Allen, Robert L. *Soviet Economic Warfare*. Washington, D.C.: U.S. Government Printing Office, 1960.

Asher, Robert E. *Development Assistance in the Seventies: Alternatives for the United States*. Washington, D.C.: Brookings Institution, 1970.

Bergson, A., and Kuzrets, S. *Economic Trends in the Soviet Union*. Cambridge, Mass,: Harvard University Press, 1963.

Berliner, Joseph S. *Soviet Economic Aid*. New York: Praeger, 1958.

Black, Eugene R. *Alternatives in Southeast Asia*. New York: Praeger, 1968.

Brzezinski, Zbigniew K., and Huntington, Samuel P. *Political Power: U.S.A.–U.S.S.R.* New York: Viking, 1964.

Clark, Paul G. *American Aid for Development*. New York: Praeger, 1972.

Condliffe, John B. *The Commerce of Nations*. New York: Norton, 1950.

Dennett, Raymond, and Johnson, Joseph E., eds. *Negotiating with the Russians*. Boston: World Peace Foundation, 1951.

Goldman, Marshall I. *Soviet Economic Aid*. New York: Praeger, 1967.

Goulet, Denis. *The Cruel Choice: A New Concept in the Theory of Development*. New York: Atheneum, 1971.

Hance, William A. *African Economic Development*. New York: Praeger, 1967.

Hanson, Simon G. *Five Years of the Alliance for Progress*. Washington, D.C.: Inter-American Affairs Press, 1967.

Hawtrey, Ralph G. *Economic Aspects of Sovereignty*. New York: Longmans, Green, 1952.

Hirschman, Albert O. *The Strategy of Economic Development*. New Haven, Conn.: Yale University Press, 1958.

Hitch, Charles J., and McKean, R. N. *The Economics of Defense in the Nuclear Age*. Cambridge, Mass.: Harvard University Press, 1960.

Jack, D. T. *Studies in Economic Warfare*. London: 1940.

Jacoby, Neil H. *United States Aid to Taiwan*. New York: Praeger, 1966.

Kaplan, Jacob J. *The Challenge of Foreign Aid: Policies, Problems, and Possibilities*. New York: Praeger, 1967.

Kamarck, Andrew M. *The Economics of African Development*. New York: Praeger, 1971.

Levinson, Jerome and De Onis, Juan. *The Alliance that Lost Its Way: A Critical Report on the Alliance for Progress.* Chicago: Quadrangle Books, 1970.

Liska, George. *The New Statecraft: Foreign Aid in American Foreign Policy.* Chicago: University of Chicago Press, 1960.

Massachusetts Institute of Technology, Center for International Studies. *Economic, Social and Political Change in the Underdeveloped Countries.* Senate Committee on Foreign Relations, March 30, 1960.

Montgomery, John D. *The Politics of Foreign Aid.* New York: Praeger, 1962.

———. *Foreign Aid in International Politics.* Englewood Cliffs, N.J.: Prentice-Hall, 1967.

Myrdal, Gunnar. *The Challenge of World Poverty: A World Anti-Poverty Program in Outline.* New York: Pantheon, 1970.

Pigou, Arthur C. *The Political Economy of War.* London: Macmillan and Company, Ltd., 1940.

Pisar, Samuel. *Coexistence and Commerce.* New York: McGraw-Hill, 1970.

Robbins, Lionel C. *The Economic Causes of War.* London: Jonathan Cape, 1939.

Schumpeter, Joseph A. *Capitalism, Socialism and Democracy.* New York: Harper, 1950.

Schwartz, Harry. *Russia's Soviet Economy.* Englewood Cliffs, N.J.: Prentice-Hall, 1954.

———. *The Red Phoenix.* New York: Praeger, 1961.

Stanley, Eugene. *The Future of Underdeveloped Countries, Political Implications of Economic Development.* New York: Harper, 1954.

Stokke, Baard, R. *Soviet and Eastern Europe Trade and Aid in Africa.* New York: Praeger, 1967.

Thorp, Willard L. *The Reality of Foreign Aid.* New York: Praeger, 1971.

U.S. Congress, Subcommittee on Foreign Economic Policy of the Joint Economic Committee. *New Directions in the Soviet Economy.* Hearings, 89th Congress, 2nd Session, Washington, D.C.: U.S. Government Printing Office, 1966.

Viner, Jacob. *International Economics.* Glencoe, Ill.: Free Press, 1951.

Walters, Robert S. *American and Soviet Aid.: A Comparative Analysis.* Pittsburgh, Pa.: University of Pittsburgh Press, 1970.

Ward, Barbard, *et. al. The Widening Gap: Development in the 1970's.* New York: Columbia University Press, 1971.

Wilber, Charles K. *The Soviet Model and Underdeveloped Countries.* Chapel Hill, N.C.: University of North Carolina Press, 1969.

Part 3 The International Struggle for Order

8 Diplomacy and Political Order

Diplomacy is the art of avoiding the appearance of victory.

METTERNICH

"Secret" and "Open" Diplomacy

Diplomacy may be defined as the conduct of international relations by negotiation. It is a process through which nations attempt to realize their national interests. It is, of course, not always an instrument of political order. Its object at times may be the intensification of a struggle between nations, or it may be a neutral tool that regards order as irrelevant to the pursuit of the national interest. But more often than not, diplomacy is an important instrument of political order, for the

221

very process of negotiation implies that nations settle their differences through peaceful change within the framework of a given system rather than by resorting to the overthrow of the system through violence. When a nation has decided in favor of war, the instrument of diplomacy becomes superfluous. But so long as the national interest dictates the avoidance of war, diplomacy works on behalf of peace. And since most nations feel most of the time that their policies may be realized by means short of war, diplomacy has been, and remains, a major highway to political order.

Diplomacy antedates the nation-state system by almost two thousand years. The city-states of ancient Greece had developed diplomatic intercourse to a high level. On reading Thucydides' *Peloponnesian War,* one is struck by the profound insights that the ancients had gained into the subtle arts of negotiation. If the Greeks made a major contribution to the essence of diplomacy—the accommodation of conflicting interests—the Romans' contribution was the equally important one of investing the practice of diplomacy with legal authority. The reemergence of the city-state system during the Renaissance in Italy was once more accompanied by a great burgeoning in the arts of diplomacy. Machiavelli's *The Prince* was the most famous of many contemporary discourses on the subject. The coming of the nation-state system in the seventeenth century ushered in an age of even greater diplomatic activity. This era of the so-called "old diplomacy" dominated the scene until World War I. When we contemplate the quaint practices that prevailed during these three hundred years—boudoir intrigues, powdered wigs, and "waltzing congresses"—we are tempted to smile indulgently. But before we decide that this period is of only historical and archaeological interest, we would do well to remember that the "waltzing Congress of Vienna" of 1815 ushered in a century in which there occurred not a single major international war. The diplomatic dramas in which Metternich, Castlereagh, and Talleyrand were the major actors are well worth re-reading.[1] Hence, before we turn to an analysis of the more modern techniques of negotiation, we shall evaluate the traditional methods of diplomacy.

Hans Morgenthau has defined the task of diplomacy as a fourfold one:

Diplomacy must determine its objectives in the light of the power actually and potentially available for the pursuit of these objectives. Diplomacy must assess the objectives of other nations and the power actually and potentially available for the pursuit of these objectives. Diplomacy must determine to what extent these different objectives are compatible with each other. Diplomacy must employ the means suited to the pursuit of its objectives. Failure in any one of these tasks may jeopardize the success of foreign policy and with it the peace of the world.[2]

Eighteenth- and nineteenth-century diplomacy seems to have fulfilled these conditions rather well. Few nations set themselves goals that were not commensurate with their power. Only rarely did nations make gross errors in assessing the power or the objectives of others. Underrating or overrating the power of the antagonist was the exception, not the rule. Nations constantly compared their own goals with those of others and weighed their compatibility. Since the national substance of a nation was rarely if ever threatened, it was generally possible to compromise on most outstanding issues. Sometimes nations resorted to a threat of force. But most of the time, traditional diplomacy was characterized by a spirit of compromise. The hallmark of the old diplomacy was the rule of *quid pro quo*.

The greatest success of traditional diplomacy was, as we have mentioned, the Congress of Vienna of 1815. At Vienna, the diplomats of Austria, Prussia, Britain, Russia, and France managed to negotiate their differences and as a result ushered in one of the longest periods of peace in Western history. How was this feat accomplished? In the first place, the fundamental structure of the international system was accepted by the negotiating powers as "legitimate." No nation at Vienna threatened the existence of the others with aspirations to world conquest. Nor did the Congress have to cope with the presence of any revolutionary power whose ideology dictated the absorption of the others. Each of the participants advanced limited objectives and expressed them in terms of limited territorial claims and counterclaims. This happy state of affairs provided the second condition of success, namely, that each nation found itself in a relationship of reasonable satisfaction and security vis-a-vis the others. This point has been well stated by Henry A. Kissinger in his analysis of the Vienna Congress:

Since absolute security for one power means absolute insecurity for all others, it is obtainable only through conquest, never as part of a legitimate settlement. An international settlement which is accepted and not imposed will therefore always appear *somewhat* unjust to any one of its components. Paradoxically, the generality of this dissatisfaction is a condition of stability, because were any one power *totally* satisfied, all others would have to be *totally* dissatisfied and a revolutionary situation would ensue. The foundation of a stable order is a *relative* security—and therefore the *relative* insecurity—of its members. Its stability reflects, not the absence of unsatisfied claims, but the absence of a grievance of such magnitude that redress will be sought in overturning the settlement rather than through an adjustment within its framework.[3]

The conditions that contributed to the success of the Congress of Vienna do not prevail in the modern world. Yet if we study the Vienna Congress we find that there are important insights to be gained nevertheless. These do not, of course, derive from the *conditions* of the international order in 1815. They apply, rather, to the diplomatic *conduct* by which the diplomats at Vienna pursued their objectives.

All important negotiations at the Congress of Vienna took place in private. Only the ministers and their most trusted subordinates participated in the crucial discussions. Camouflaged by the glitter of nineteenth-century Vienna and the pomp of the Habsburg Court, the diplomatic interchanges proceeded strictly behind closed doors. In our own time "secret diplomacy" has become a term of disapprobation. And to be sure, secrecy often led to extreme suspicion even among the diplomats of the earlier period. Thus, when Prince Metternich, the Austrian plenipotentiary, was told that the Russian ambassador in Vienna had died during the negotiations, he was reported to have asked: "Ah, is that true? What may have been his motive?" Yet despite its inevitable drawbacks, this method gave the statesmen of the time a priceless advantage that contemporary diplomats have largely been denied: it enabled them to conduct their negotiations in private, free from the pressures and inhibitions of constant publicity.

The "old diplomacy" fell into disrepute with the coming of the twentieth century. Liberal optimists who believed that "power politics" could be banished from the earth through the establishment of a universal League of Nations took a dim view of the old-fashioned secret diplomacy and considered it the symptom of a corrupt and bygone era. The new spirit was expressed most eloquently by Woodrow Wilson in his Fourteen Points: "Open covenants of peace, openly arrived at, after which there will be no private understanding of any kind, but diplomacy shall proceed frankly and in the public view." The advocates of the "new diplomacy" urged that not only the results of diplomacy should be made public, but that even the process of negotiation itself ought to be subject to the scrutiny of the people. The implication was that the business of diplomacy was too important to be entrusted to diplomats alone. The principles of democratic government demanded that in matters affecting the vital interests of the nation the public be kept informed and allowed to express itself at every stage of the proceedings. The reason for this, as Wilson and the proponents of "open diplomacy" saw it, was that the national interest was safer in the hands of the public than it would be if left in the hands of some elite group, no matter how well versed in the arts of negotiation the latter might be.

It is a curious irony that Wilson, the great advocate of "open diplomacy," seldom practiced it. His efforts to realize his dream—the creation of the League of Nations—were conducted with considerable secrecy. When he returned from Versailles, he confronted the American people with a *fait accompli*. The Senate's refusal to ratify the Treaty incorporating the League of Nations was in some measure attributable to the fact that the Senators had not been taken into the President's confidence during the formulation of policy. Wilson wanted the "consent," but not the "advice" of the Senate and the people. In other words, the major architect of "open covenants openly arrived at" was one of the great practitioners of "secret diplomacy." Nevertheless, the impact of the new Wilsonian conception was enormous. To a world grown deeply weary of war and the struggle for power, the prospect of a new system of international conduct that, in the words of one caustic observer, would no longer be governed by "men who were sent abroad to lie for their country,"[4] looked desirable indeed.

Yet it soon became evident that if the new diplomatic techniques dispelled some long-standing fears, they also raised some serious problems. There was little disagreement that the *results* of diplomatic negotiations should be disclosed to the people, but many observers began to question the wisdom of exposing the *negotiations* themselves to the searchlight of publicity. It was soon discovered that under such conditions an atmosphere was created that precluded genuine bargaining. It became increasingly difficult, if not impossible, for a diplomat to yield on a point, to give up a claim, or to admit that there was at least a modicum of justice on the other side when he knew that each such action would be condemned by his compatriots as an act of cowardice and as a retreat in the face of the enemy. Thus, more and more frequently, diplomacy fell victim to publicity. Diplomats came to the bargaining table with maximum demands which they defended "on principle." Positions grew brittle, compromise became the exception rather than the rule, and the negotiators tended to address the audience rather than each other. This transformation of diplomacy into an instrument of propaganda was accelerated by the rapid development of the media of communication. A diplomat who was not only exposed to the physical presence of an attentive public but had to cope with a network of television cameras as well was not likely to run the risk of looking like a fool or a knave before millions of people.

Secret diplomacy seldom involved more than a small number of negotiators. The "new diplomacy," in contrast, has through the coming of the United Nations and the various regional organizations acquired an even further complicating dimension in that most negotiations must be conducted multilaterally. Once a dispute is brought before the United Nations, for example, it becomes the business of the entire General Assembly. Representatives from more than one hundred nations express themselves on the matter while the entire world watches. Such a state of affairs is hardly conducive to effective bargaining. The issue generally is not resolved through negotiations but through attempts by the leading forces in the General Assembly to obtain a majority vote with which to defeat a recalcitrant minority. It need not be emphasized that this method frequently exacerbates differences among nations instead of composing them.

All these developments have radically changed the nature of both diplomacy and the diplomat. While a plenipotentiary attending the Congress of Vienna had large powers of discretion, the modern diplomat is frequently little more than a messenger who communicates the instructions of his government. Frequently heads of state even short-circuit their emissaries altogether by dealing with each other directly. During World War II, for example, Roosevelt, Churchill, and Stalin by no means relied solely on the talents of their diplomats. In fact, many of their most vital policy decisions were hammered out in telegrams and long transatlantic telephone conversations among themselves.

The modern phenomenon that may combine all the weaknesses of the "new diplomacy" most dramatically is the "Summit Conference." Geneva in 1955, Paris in 1960, and Glassboro, New Jersey, in 1967, became the capitals of the world while heads of state met there to air their differences. The participants found themselves cast in the role of gladiators, with the rest of humanity as their audience. While most of the onlookers desperately hoped for peace, few were willing to tolerate the kind of compromise that the attainment of real peace would have required. The unprecedented publicity led to an equally unprecedented inflexibility; the inflexibility found expression in little more than repetitive propagandistic flourishes; and in the end, the heads of state parted company: in 1955, in an "improved atmosphere" but without any concrete results; in 1960, in animosity and disillusionment; and in 1967, once again, without tangible results. There are times, of course, when a "Summit" may break the ice after many years of non-relations and frozen hostility. President Nixon's visit to China in 1972 was a case in point. While none of the stubborn problems besetting Sino-American relations were actually resolved at that historic meeting, the atmosphere between the two countries was certainly improved. Similarly, the Moscow "Summit" of May 1972 improved Soviet-American relations and marked the occasion of the first superpower arms control agreement since World War II. On balance, "summitry" may be helpful under certain very specific conditions but rarely manages to dissolve substantive policy differences.

It is clear from the above that the high hopes that were originally entertained for open diplomacy have not been warranted. Public control of the negotiating process has not necessarily yielded superior results. But it is equally clear that many of the most positive aspects of the old diplomacy have little relevance in a world in which totalitarian powers are bent on the destruction of a system that others wish to preserve. And certainly the rapid advance of technology and communications that has so radically changed the nature of diplomacy cannot be halted or reversed. It would therefore undoubtedly be a gross oversimplification to blame the deterioration of diplomatic intercourse solely, or even primarily, on the vices of open diplomacy.

It seems clear that the stubbornness of the international struggle for power has its roots not in the deficiency of diplomatic techniques but in the existence of objective and fundamental differences among the major nations. These differences are deeply rooted and would not yield easily to either secret or open diplomacy. Yet it is equally true that diplomacy, open or secret, remains a major tool of order-building which the nations continue to use in their international intercourse. The answer to our question as to the present and future status of diplomacy cannot, therefore, be found in any wholesale condemnation of secret or open diplomacy. Rather, the value of each type must be assessed, utilized, and developed according to the exigencies of each particular situation that may be confronted.

To illustrate the need for such a pragmatic application and combination of the two types of diplomacy, let us weigh their pros and cons in regard to an actual case: the problem of *apartheid* in the Union of South Africa. This question has been on the UN General Assembly's agenda almost continuously. Each year attempts are made to remedy the situation by denouncing the Union government's racial policies before the General Assembly. So far, all resolutions have foundered on the rock of domestic jurisdiction and have, if anything, tended even to harden the attitude of the government of the Union of South Africa. Yet this fact should not lead to any hasty dismissal of the technique of multilateral and open diplomacy as a waste of time. For there is no denying that multilateral diplomacy in the General Assembly has its very valuable functions. For one thing, it can secure a majority vote in the General Assembly, giving notice to the disputants that their quarrel should be settled without recourse to violence. More important, it can serve as an inducement and prelude to actual nation-to-nation negotiations.[5] Moreover, open diplomacy can find additional expression through the United Nations by utilizing that organization's numerous instruments of conciliation and mediation.[6] Thus, in the dispute over *apartheid* in South Africa, the Security Council authorized the Secretary-General to use his good offices to try to influence South African policy. Once again, however, the results were negative. In this particular case it can therefore be fairly concluded that the actual negotiating process was *not* improved through the use of open diplomacy. Though private conferences with South African diplomats would probably not have resolved the problem either, they might have avoided the increased tensions that resulted from bringing the question before the United Nations and so, perhaps, might have yielded at least some minor concessions.

In other types of situations, on the other hand, the methods of open diplomacy may be exactly what are needed. One such example was the United Nations Conference on the Human Environment held in Stockholm in June 1972. The very acuteness of the environmental crisis made open discussion of its global implications a necessity. Since what happens to the environment is everybody's business, a multilateral conference on its preservation was the proper forum for seeking agreement.

To generalize, we may say that secret negotiations seem more helpful when their function is an essentially deterrent one, such as the settlement of an international dispute. The "quiet diplomacy" of the United Nations Secretary-General, for example, has shown that in an age of "open covenants openly arrived at," the older type of diplomatic strategy may make a most important contribution. Indeed, this modern version of secret diplomacy has been a direct outcome of the failures of the new multilateralism. On the other hand, the more positive aspects of order-building, like the passage of new international legislation, lend themselves more readily to the new diplomacy. In most cases, however, effective order-building requires a discriminating and sensitive application of both principles. Hence the diplomat is clearly far from obsolete. It is only that the demands upon him have become more rigorous and that he must operate under immensely more difficult conditions. We must therefore turn from our consideration of diplomacy in general to an examination of the nature of the diplomat himself.

The best portrait of the modern diplomat is probably that painted by Sir Harold Nicolson in his classic treatise, *Diplomacy*. First among the diplomat's virtues, according to Nicolson, must be truthfulness. By this he means "not merely abstention from conscious misstatements but a scrupulous care to avoid the suggestion of the false or the suppression of the true."[7] The modern diplomat must also possess the quality of intellectual integrity. Ideally, too, he should be good-tempered or, at least, able to keep his temper under complete control at all times. A display of anger, for example, is regarded as a betrayal of weakness. When Napoleon flung his hat upon the carpet in front of Prince Metternich in June 1813, the latter knew that the Emperor's strength was ebbing. Next on the list is patience, which Nicolson considers an indispensable quality for the successful negotiator. Modesty is considered important since vanity may tempt the diplomat into imprudence. The negotiator should also bear a special loyalty to his country, a loyalty that will prompt him to tell his government what it ought to know rather than what it wants to hear. And finally, the author reminds us that he has not forgotten the qualities of intelligence, knowledge, discernment, prudence, hospitality, charm, industry, courage, and tact. He has simply taken them for granted.[8]

It is clear from the above that the combination of characteristics required of the diplomat is unusual indeed. Yet even if people who measure up to this high standard can be recruited, the measure of success they may achieve in the job of international order-building remains to the largest degree dependent upon the complex and trying conditions under which they must work.

For example, so long as even one of the negotiators dogmatically adheres to universal aspirations, diplomacy's perennial quest for compromise is bound to continue to be frustrated. When two combatants, each claiming to represent the one true secular religion, meet in the arena, there remains almost no room for accommodation at all. Both tend to invoke the authority of God or the historical process and forget that "they meet under an empty sky from which the gods have departed."[9] Proselytizing should have little room at the bargaining table. Only to the extent that the negotiator can free himself from the one-sidedness and biases of his own particular ideology is he able to think and feel himself into the position of other diplomats. Such empathy can contribute a great deal to successful negotiation. For though it in no way implies a yielding of one's own position, it makes possible the placing of questions at issue in as broadly conceived and mutually respecting a framework as possible.

The modern statesman-diplomat in a democracy faces a unique dilemma of responsibility to his nation. From this he cannot escape, whether he engages in secret or in open negotiations. Should his goals simply reflect the will of the people whose servant he is supposed to be? Or does his greater knowledge of the international scene entitle him to lead the people in some new direction if he believes that the common man's judgment is in error? Moreover, how important is domestic support, politically speaking? The experience of Woodrow Wilson and the League of Nations demonstrated that the statesman-diplomat ignores his people at his own peril. But the generation that ratified the United Nations Charter hailed this same man, repudiated only a quarter century before, as a great visionary. The fate of Wilson therefore seems to indicate that the diplomat who would also be a statesman must lead more than follow. Yet since he cannot but act on incomplete knowledge, and so can never "prove" that his vision is correct, this task may be a trying and cruel one. As Henry A. Kissinger has pointed out in his analysis of the Congress of Vienna,

The statesman is therefore like one of the heroes in classical drama who has had a vision of the future but who cannot transmit it directly to his fellowmen and who cannot validate its "truth." Nations learn only by experience; they "know" only when it is too late to act. But statesmen must act as if their intuition were already experience, as if their aspiration were truth. It is for this reason that statesmen often share the fate of prophets, that they are without honour in their own country, that they always have a difficult task in legitimizing their programmes domestically, and that their greatness is usually apparent only in retrospect when their intuition has become experience. The statesman must therefore be an educator; he must bridge the gap between a people's experience and his vision, between a nation's tradition and its future. In this task his possibilities are limited. A statesman who too far outruns the experience of his people will fail in achieving a domestic consensus, however wise his policies; witness Castlereagh. A statesman who limits his policy to the experience of his people will doom himself to sterility; witness Metternich.[10]

This observation applies with equal validity to the modern statesman. It may be argued, as Kissinger does, that the failure of American statesmen to grasp this truth has placed them at a disadvantage vis-à-vis the Soviet Union. The American diplomat wants to base his decisions on the knowledge of all the facts. But crises do not wait, and by the time all the facts are in, unique opportunities may have passed. Hence, the quest for certainty in diplomatic intercourse has at times condemned the American statesman to a "reactive diplomacy." The Communist statesman on the other hand, Kissinger maintains, has faced the fact that in diplomacy only the risks are certain but the opportunities are conjectural. He has realized that "one cannot be sure about the implication of events until they have happened and when they have occurred it is too late to do anything about them."[11]

Ethics, Power, and the Statesman

If the task of the diplomat is difficult, that of the statesman who instructs him is indeed formidable. For the latter, the greatest challenge of all concerns the role of ethics in a world of power. What is the relationship between "personal" and "political" morality? Does diplomacy leave room for morality at all? How should we judge a statesman—by his intentions or by the consequences of his actions? What should be the criterion of success for the statesman-diplomat? In short, what must concern us now is the problem of statesmanship and moral choice.

Diplomacy in the era of Woodrow Wilson looked confidently to the possibility of continuous progress in the relations among nations toward the goal of justice and brotherhood. Most contemporary observers of the "new diplomacy" were convinced that the inherent rationality and morality of man could not fail to assert themselves in diplomatic intercourse. The growth of democratic institutions would help immeasurably in this process. It was assumed, also, that statesmen would conduct diplomatic relations exclusively on a basis of goodwill and cooperation. In other words, this group of thinkers, whom we shall call the "idealists," deeply believed that it was only a question of time until a congruence would be achieved between personal and political morality. The cataclysm of World War II, however, cast serious doubts on these assumptions. It was no longer at all clear that historical progress toward cooperation among nations was inevitable. Nor was there sufficient evidence for the assertion that human nature was infinitely improvable. As a result, a second group of thinkers emerged who were no less concerned about peace and justice than were the "idealists," but who felt that the very nature of the international struggle set unavoidable limits to the moral aspirations of man. These "realists" were convinced that international behavior was governed by its own objective laws, the most important of which was an immutable struggle for power. The "idealist" who attempted to deal with international relations in terms of morality did so at his own peril. Thus, at one end of the diplomatic spectrum, the Wilsonian "idealists" hoped to infuse international behavior with high moral standards. At the other end, the "realists" contended that international relations were neither moral nor immoral. The latter, indeed, defining the relations among nations as predominantly a matter of power, saw considerations of morality as irrelevant.

A careful analysis of the dilemmas of statesmanship indicates that the dichotomy between "idealists" and "realists" is too simple. The purely "idealist" statesman would be a saint, while a purely Machiavellian one would be a beast.[12] Few statesmen, however lofty their purposes, dare to ignore the reality of power, but equally few statesmen, however Machiavellian, venture to ignore the existence of morality. The crucial difference between interpersonal and international relations is not that the former permit moral behavior, whereas the latter do not. It resides, rather, in the fact that personal behavior is usually judged by an ethic of *intention* while that of the statesman is essentially one of *consequence*. Morgenthau cites an interesting example that illustrates this point:

Neville Chamberlain's policies of appeasement were, as far as we can judge, inspired by good motives; he was probably less motivated by considerations of personal power than were many other British prime ministers, and he sought to preserve peace and to assure the happiness of all concerned. Yet his policies helped to make the Second World War inevitable, and to bring untold miseries to millions of men. Sir Winston Churchill's motives, on the other hand, have been much less universal in scope and much more narrowly directed toward personal and national power, yet the foreign policies that sprang from these inferior motives were certainly superior in moral and political quality to those pursued by his predecessor.[13]

The Suez crisis of 1956 excellently illustrates the multiple facets of this problem. President Eisenhower's decision to support Egypt and the Soviet Union against Britain and France was justified in terms of "a single standard of international morality which must be applied to friend and foe alike." This was clearly an ethic of intention. The British and French, on the other hand, justified their military expedition in terms of its ultimate consequence—the reassertion of their legal rights in the Suez Canal. This difference in interpretation of what constituted "morality" led to a great deal of bitterness and confusion. If we dig further, the problem becomes even more complex. Is not the logical extension of an ethic of consequence the dreaded formula that the end may justify the means? This was a question that the British and French found difficult to answer after the Suez affair. Conversely, cannot "moral" intentions at times lead to "immoral" consequences? To be specific, the "moral" act of President Eisenhower might have destroyed NATO and resulted in a far more "immoral" consequence—Soviet domination of Western Europe.

It should be obvious from the above discussion that power and morality are inseparable and must be so considered by the statesman. Perhaps it is helpful to think of the two as two concentric circles of which power is the larger. Morgenthau, for example, has asserted repeatedly that what he regards as a morally dubious policy of the United States in Vietnam has hurt America's power position in other parts of the world. Or to take a hypothetical example, let us suppose that the United States promises Portugal a large loan. It then decides to withdraw the offer, breaking its promise. As a result, Portugal leaves NATO and becomes neutralist. If this actually occurred, it might be said that the United States lost some of its power because it acted unethically. In some cases, therefore, power may be said to *include* morality. Of course, Portugal would base its decision on a multiplicity of factors, only one of which would be the American breach of promise. Hence, this generalization, like all others on ethics and power, is subject to exceptions. At times, indeed, morality may be the larger of the two concentric circles. Thus, America's "moral" stand in the Suez crisis won the admiration of many uncommitted nations in the East-West struggle. This friendship, although it was not expressed in terms of new military allies, no doubt added power to the international position of the United States in some parts of the world.

The subtle interdependence between ethics and power compels the statesman to engage in a process of continual balancing. He is forever having to weigh alternatives. And in this enterprise it is very rare for the merits in favor of one course of action to be clearly greater than the arguments for another. As one careful student of diplomacy has pointed out:

The merits in argument for and against an acceptable line of action never occur in ratios of 100 to 0 or even of 80 to 20. They tend rather to occur in the order of 55 to 45 or even 51 to 49. Even at best, the arguments against a line of action in foreign policy tend to be almost as weighty as the considerations in favor. Yet these small margins of difference constitute the distinction between success and failure and are all-important.[14]

Almost never is the statesman called upon to decide between a clear-cut right and a clear-cut wrong. Here international relations resemble interpersonal behavior: most decisions must be taken along a continuum of varying shades of gray. But there does remain one crucial difference: the fact that the statesman's decision may affect the lives of millions of his fellow men.

Lest all this seem a study in confusion, let us, for illustrative purposes, examine the alternatives of a decision that reversed American policy of a quarter of a century: President Nixon's trip to China in 1972.

On the positive side, there were several arguments to be made. First, the decision made it possible once again to establish relations with China on the basis of reality rather than fiction. As a result, exchange programs were planned, and journalists, intellectuals and athletes were able to visit each other's countries. Second, a modest trade relationship was begun. Third, the American move placed the Soviet Union on the defensive. Finally, the American policy reversal was decisive in seating China in the United Nations.

On the negative side, the United States paid a heavy price. In the first place, since the American President chose not to forewarn Japan of his imminent move, that nation went into "Nixon shock" and began to perceive the United States as a rather capricious ally. Second, Chiang Kai-shek on Formosa felt betrayed by the United States, and, similarly, a number of America's military allies in Asia, notably South Korea and the Philippines, developed serious reservations about the value of the American commitment. In short, critics of the move thought that the President might have confused motion with progress.

Thus, the China decision, like most major foreign policy decisions, had its benefits and its costs. Arguments for and against were balanced fairly evenly. Nor did any one side of the argument have a monopoly on ethical considerations. Each side could, and did, adduce persuasive moral arguments for its respective position.

The case of China shows that the statesman must act with the tragic knowledge that he cannot choose between good and evil but only among varying stages of evil. Indeed, whatever decision he makes, *some* evil consequences are bound to result from it. In such a situation, is it not easier to abstain from *any* decision? Yet such "abstention from evil does not at all affect the existence of evil in the world but only destroys the faculty of discriminating between different evils. The perfectionist thus becomes finally a source of greater evil."[15] This tragic condition has been painted in all its starkness by Morgenthau:

We have no choice between power and the common good. To act successfully, that is according to the rules of the political art, is political wisdom. To know with despair that the political act is inevitably evil, and to act nevertheless, is moral courage. To choose among several expedient actions the least evil one is moral judgment. In the combination of political wisdom, moral courage and moral judgment, man reconciles his political nature with his moral destiny. That this conciliation is nothing more than a *modus vivendi,* uneasy, precarious, and even paradoxical, can disappoint only those who prefer to gloss over and to distort the tragic contradictions of human existence with the soothing logic of a specious concord.[16]

The Chinese case also demonstrates that the statesman must come to grips with at least three different modes of thinking. First, he must ask the question of power: could the United States afford to ignore the increasing strength of the regime in power in Communist China? Second, the question of morality: should the United States deal with a nation which it had condemned repeatedly as an aggressor? And third, the question of law: could the United States expect China to obey the legal norms established by the international community? Morgenthau maintains that the statesman, if he is a political realist, should maintain the autonomy of the political sphere and merely ask himself the question of power.[17] This would seem too one-dimensional a view, for as we have seen, most of the time power *includes* considerations of morality and law.

We are left, finally, with the ultimate question which formed the central point of the famous controversy between Socrates and the Sophists over two thousand years ago: whose standard of morality should the statesman apply? Should he seek universal principles of justice, as did Socrates? Or should he readily admit that morality and justice are bound by time and space, as did the Sophists? If he pursues the former goal too far, he becomes a dogmatist; if he yields to the latter view too easily, he will be emasculated by a sloppy relativism. Indeed, the unending quest for meaningful choices in a tragic world is the most difficult task confronting the modern statesman-diplomat as political order-builder.

REFERENCES

1. For a perceptive analysis of the Congress of Vienna, see Harold Nicolson, *The Congress of Vienna.* New York: Harcourt, Brace, 1946, or Henry A. Kissinger, *A World Restored.* Boston: Houghton Mifflin, 1957.

2. Hans Morgenthau, *Politics Among Nations,* 3d ed. New York: Knopf, 1960, pp. 539–540.

3. Henry A. Kissinger, "The Congress of Vienna," *World Politics,* January 1956, pp. 264–265.

4. This is a statement attributed to a British ambassador, Sir Henry Wotton, cited by Sir Harold Nicolson in *Diplomacy.* New York: Oxford University Press, 1955, p. 44.

5. Inis L. Claude, Jr., "Multilateralism—Diplomatic and Otherwise," *International Organization,* Vol. XII, No. 1, 1958, p. 45.

6. *Ibid.*

7. Nicolson, *op. cit.,* p. 110.

8. *Ibid.,* p. 126.

9. Morgenthau, *op. cit.,* p. 259.

10. Kissinger, *op. cit.,* p. 329.

11. Henry A. Kissinger, *Nuclear Weapons and Foreign Policy.* New York: Harper, 1957, p. 424.

12. Morgenthau, *op. cit.,* p. 14.

13. *Ibid.,* p. 6.

14. Charles Burton Marshall, *The Limits of Foreign Policy.* New York: Henry Holt, 1954, p. 33.

15. Hans J. Morgenthau, *Scientific Man versus Power Politics.* Chicago: The University of Chicago Press, 1952, p. 202.

16. *Ibid.,* p. 203.

17. Morgenthau, *Politics Among Nations,* pp. 11–12.

BIBLIOGRAPHY

American Assembly. *The Representation of The United States Abroad.* New York: Columbia University Press, 1956.

Barghoorn, Frederick C. *The Soviet Cultural Offensive.* Princeton, N.J.: Princeton University Press, 1960.

Bell, Coral. *The Conventions of Crisis.* New York: Oxford University Press, 1971.

Bowles, Chester. *Ambassador's Report.* New York: Harper, 1954.

Bundy, McGeorge, ed. *The Pattern of Responsibility.* Boston: Houghton Mifflin, 1952.

Cecil, A. *Metternich, 1773–1859: A Study of His Period and Personality.* New York: Macmillan, 1933.

Cooper, Sir Alfred D. *Talleyrand.* New York: Harper, 1932.

Corbett, Percy E. *Law in Diplomacy.* Princeton, N.J.: Princeton University Press, 1959.

Craig, Gordon A. *From Bismarck to Adenauer: Aspects of German Statecraft.* Baltimore: Johns Hopkins Press, 1958.

———, and Gilbert, Felix. *The Diplomats: 1919–1939.* Princeton, N.J.: Princeton University Press, 1953.

Dennett, Raymond, and Johnson, Joseph E., eds. *Negotiating with the Russians.* Boston: World Peace Foundation, 1951.

Foster, J. W. *The Practice of Diplomacy.* Boston: Houghton Mifflin, 1906.

Hankey, Maurice P. A. *Diplomacy by Conference.* New York: Putnam, 1946.

Iklé, Fred Charles. *How Nations Negotiate.* New York: Praeger, 1964.

Kennan, George F. *American Diplomacy, 1900–1950.* Chicago: University of Chicago Press, 1953.

Kissinger, Henry A. *A World Restored: Metternich, Castlereagh, and the Problems of Peace 1812–1822.* Boston: Houghton Mifflin, 1957.

Lall, Arthur. *Modern International Negotiations.* New York: Columbia University Press, 1966.

Landau, David *Kissinger: The Uses of Power.* Boston: Houghton Mifflin, 1972.

Mayer, Arno J. *Politics and Diplomacy of Peacemaking: Containment and Counterrevolution at Versailles, 1918–1919.* New York: Knopf, 1967.

McCamy, James L. *Conduct of the New Diplomacy.* New York: Harper and Row, 1964.

Nicolson, Harold. *The Congress of Vienna, a Study in Allied Unity: 1812–1822.* New York: Harcourt, Brace, 1946.

———. *Diplomacy.* New York: Oxford University Press, 1950.

———. *The Evolution of Diplomatic Method.* New York: Macmillan, 1955.

———. *Peacemaking, 1919.* Boston: Houghton Mifflin, 1933.

Plischke, Elmer. *Conduct of American Diplomacy.* Princeton, N.J.: Van Nostrand, 1950.

Sherwood, Robert E. *Roosevelt and Hopkins.* New York: Harper, 1948.

Spender, Sir Percy. *Exercises in Diplomacy.* New York: New York University Press, 1970.

Thayer, Charles W. *Diplomat.* New York: Harper, 1959.

9 International Law and Political Order

Inter armis silent leges. In the clash of arms the laws are silent.
We may add that in the truce of arms the laws are heard.
WALTER LIPPMANN *The Public Philosophy*

International Relations and the Rule of Law

Between the evolution of political order among nations and the development of world law—a body of rules and principles of action which are legally binding upon states in their relations with one another—there is undoubtedly a vital connection, yet there remains wide disagreement on the nature of this connection. Many observers of the international scene feel that political order-building has to precede

236

the establishment of a rule of law; that, in fact, a legal consensus can only grow in the soil of a community based on social and political harmony. Others are equally convinced that the establishment of a rule of law can help knit the bonds of social and political order, that the promulgation of legal documents such as covenants and treaties can weave the fabric of community. The former tend to favor a "political" approach to order-building and prefer to work through the processes of political accommodation and diplomacy; the latter are inclined toward a "legal" approach and look with greater hope to the role of international law. In the present chapter we shall be concerned with this "legal" approach to political order.

The modern law of nations has its origins in antiquity and in medieval times. It has four chief roots. A first important source is the work of classical writers. The most famous of these is Hugo Grotius, frequently described as the "father of international law." His fame rests mainly in a monumental work, *The Law of War and Peace,* published in 1625 as an impassioned protest against the carnage of the Thirty Years' War. It was this treatise that laid the groundwork for the modern laws of war. A key passage in its preface sounds amazingly modern:

Throughout the Christian world I observed a lack of restraint in relation to war, such as even barbarous races should be ashamed of; I observed that men rush to arms for slight causes, or no cause at all, and that when arms have once been taken up there is no longer any respect for law, divine or human; it is as if, in accordance with a general decree, frenzy had openly been let loose, for the committing of all crimes.[1]

A second significant source of international law is custom. If certain customary practices among nations persist for a long period of time, and if no state expressly rejects them, they eventually may be absorbed into the body of international law. For example, it had long been the custom to exempt unarmed fishing vessels from war booty. Finally, in 1900, this custom came to be recognized as law.[2] This role of custom, however, illustrates a major problem of international law. Since only those practices become law that are not strongly opposed by any state, the rules that nations observe represent only a lowest common denominator. It is for this reason that international law is not only threatened by the ever-present danger of not being abided by, but it is also permanently plagued by low moral standards. The reason for this is, of course, that while international law is intended to control states, it is in effect controlled by them.

A third major source of international law derives from treaties. These have played an important role since the days of Greek antiquity. Thucydides' *History of the Peloponnesian War,* for example, speaks extensively about treaties among the city-states of the ancient Mediterranean world. The Congress of Vienna, the Versailles Settlement, the United Nations Charter, and NATO have all rested on treaties that have contributed importantly to international law. Yet, though more specific than custom and requiring the deliberate commitment of states through ratification, treaties also are often ambiguous and do not necessarily ensure just relationships among nations, for the treaty makers' first responsibility is attempting to strike a delicate balance between justice and peace. If they overemphasize the former, the peace may be lost—witness Versailles. The same is true if they lean too much toward the latter—witness Munich. An example of a successful treaty which struck a felicitous balance was the Congress of Vienna.

The fourth and final important source of international law is the decisions of courts. The contribution of international tribunals in the establishment of international law is a recent development, largely a product of the twentieth century. The most important of the judicial bodies have been the Permanent Court of International Justice under the League of Nations and the International Court of Justice under the United Nations system.

Traditionally, only states have been subjects of international law. In the absence of a higher secular arbiter, each state has tended to recognize or refuse to recognize its fellow members of the world community. The practice of recognition has followed fairly arbitrary rules of co-option which each state has developed on its own. Since the advent of the United Nations, the practice of "collective recognition" has gained currency. In the case of the birth of new states, such as Israel and Ghana, admission to the United Nations has become a kind of *imprimatur* by the world community. This rise of "collective recognition" may be a hopeful sign for the development of more uniform legal standards. Our generation has also seen the extension of international law to subjects other than states: semigovernmental organizations such as the Jewish Agency; nongovernmental organizations like the International Red Cross; international organizations such as the United Nations and its specialized agencies; and, perhaps most important, individuals, who also now have rights and duties before international law. Even stateless people have come to enjoy at least a minimum of international protection. And for the first time in history the attempt was made at Nuremberg in 1945 to bring individuals before the bar of international law.*

The question of jurisdiction over individuals demonstrates that the problem of "progress" in international law is a highly complex one. It would be too one-dimensional to state that international law advances simply by the expansion of jurisdiction. The ambiguity of the problem was demonstrated during the Nuremberg War Crimes Trials in 1945.

---

*While an attempt was made by the victorious powers after World War I to bring to trial certain German "war criminals," including Kaiser Wilhelm, these so-called Leipzig Trials were a failure.

The Nuremberg Tribunal was set up by the victorious powers—the United States, the Soviet Union, Britain, and France—to try the major leaders of the Nazi government. The indictment against them was threefold: (a) crimes against peace (i.e., planning, preparing, initiating, or waging aggressive war or taking part in a common plan to do so); (b) war crimes (i.e., violations of the rules of war); (c) crimes against humanity (crimes against civilians before or during the war). On the basis of one or more of these counts, a number of the leading Nazis were either executed or given prison sentences, while others were acquitted. However, several questions have been raised as to the legality of the Nuremberg trials. For example, since international law had never before applied to individuals, was not the Nuremberg judgment *ex post facto?* Some observers felt that the Nuremberg trials set a dangerous precedent. In a future war, would it not be possible—on the basis of the Nuremberg judgment—for the victor nation to bring to trial the statesmen of the defeated country? To take the point *ad absurdum,* if in a war between the United States and the Soviet Union the latter should be victorious, might not the victor try an American president as a "warmonger and imperialist aggressor"? Hence, it is difficult to assert with finality that the subjecthood of individuals under international law has necessarily served the cause of world order. And even if this were so beyond a doubt, it must be remembered that, before international law was able to hold individuals criminally liable, it first had to destroy the sovereignty of the nation of which they were members.

The dubiousness of the Nuremberg precedent prompted the General Assembly of the United Nations to direct its International Law Commission to formulate the principles of international law established at Nuremberg. The Commission in its findings approved the principle of individual responsibility and denied the immunity of high government officials who committed crimes in the name of obedience to orders. But the Commission was also convinced that the *ad hoc* character of the Nuremberg trials pointed up the necessity for a Criminal Chamber of the International Court of Justice. However, owing to disagreement among the major powers, an international criminal code does not yet exist. From the above example one may draw the possible conclusion that "progress" in international law is perhaps better served through the development of its "protective" rather than its "punitive" aspects.

If international law still applies largely to states, it is also primarily interpreted by states. Self-judgment as the logical adjunct of sovereignty still dominates the scene. Only minor incursions have been made into the principle of "domestic jurisdiction." The only international body with military enforcement power is the United Nations Security Council, and its power is severely curtailed through the veto of the Big Five. The rule of self-judgment also applies in questions of revision and repeal of international law. For example, the Western powers took the position that the Potsdam Agreement could only be revised with the unanimous consent of the signatories. They invoked the principle of *pacta sunt servanda*—"pacts must be observed." The Soviet Union, on the other hand, desirous of evicting the Western powers from Berlin, invoked the opposing principle of *rebus sic stantibus*—"matters have changed." Quite clearly, such an explosive political issue cannot be settled by judicial means, but can only yield to the processes of diplomacy.

In view of the tremendous obstacles in the path of international law, it is remarkable that in certain limited areas a respectable body of substantive law has in fact crystallized. International law has come to serve a useful function in the demarcation of boundaries among states; the acquisition of a "no man's land" and the regulation of minor territorial disputes fall in this category. Even in this area, however, great difficulties may arise. It has been impossible, for example, to agree upon a uniform definition of territorial waters. Similarly, each state still claims sovereignty over its airspace. International law also defines the privileges and immunities of ambassadors, of heads of state, and of their immediate entourage. Certain rules have developed on the basis of reciprocity under customary international law. Ambassadors, for example, may not be taxed and may only be sued with their own consent. High-ranking United Nations officials also enjoy "diplomatic immunity." Finally, the right of political asylum for refugees has long been sanctioned by customary international law.

The law of nations also facilitates normal and peaceful relations among nations. Numerous claims by one state against another have been settled through "good offices," mediation and arbitration tribunals, and judicial decisions. A useful body of law also exists for the purpose of regulating strained and hostile international relations. For example, under the Drago Doctrine of 1902, international law holds that the forcible collection of debts through blockade is illegal. An attempt has also been made to determine the rights and duties of neutrals in times of war. Of course, the fiercer and more "total" war has become, the more difficult it has been to define these rights and duties.

Finally, international law has attempted to come to grips with war itself. Two approaches have dominated international legal thinking. The first has been a modern version of the assumption that first guided Hugo Grotius: that war cannot be eliminated by legal means, but that its worst horrors may be somewhat mitigated through the development of laws governing its conduct. An impressive body of laws aimed at this end today exists. To name but a few: the Geneva Protocol of 1925 on the Prohibition of Chemical and Bacteriological Warfare and Poison Gas; the Geneva Convention of 1929 on the Treatment of Sick and Wounded; the Washington Pact of 1935 for the Protection of Museums and Historic Sites; the London Protocol of 1936 regulating submarine warfare; the Hague Convention of 1938 outlawing inhuman weapons; and the Geneva Convention of 1949 governing the protection of civilian populations. The observance of these laws of war has varied. International laws proved almost completely impotent during World War II, though even Hitler decided against the use of poison gas for fear of retaliation in kind. The laws of war have been observed far more scrupulously in the nuclear age. For example, owing to the fear of an atomic holocaust both sides decided to keep the Korean conflict limited and demonstrated a considerable respect for the laws of war.

The second attempt by international law to deal with war has been its legal prohibition. In 1928, in the Kellogg-Briand Pact, most states of the world "renounced war as an instrument of national policy." But no sanctions were included in the Pact against a possible aggressor. During the entire lifetime of the League of Nations, international lawyers grappled with the intricate problems of defining "aggression" and of deciding what constituted a "just," that is, "defensive" war. It was impossible to reach agreement and in the end the League of Nations Covenant in fact left certain loopholes for legal resort to war. Similarly, the United Nations Charter, while expressly outlawing war, permits the creation of regional arrangements for the purpose of collective self-defense. Hence, since the United Nations has also failed in defining "aggression," war may be legal even today.

The record demonstrates that of the two approaches, the former is more realistic. The elimination of war is clearly not a legal problem, but the most brutal effects of modern warfare may perhaps be somewhat softened through the further development of a body of laws governing its conduct. Perhaps not surprisingly, as the horrors of war in our time have increased there has also occurred a revival of concern and respect for laws concerning the waging of war.

On the whole, we must admit that the contribution of international law to the building of political order has been modest. In the first place, most international disputes simply do not lend themselves to a judicial approach since they are much too deeply involved in questions of power and prestige. Hence international law, unlike domestic law, suffers from a paucity of cases and cannot easily grow into a codified system. A second obstacle is the stubborn fact that the very states that are to be governed by international law are the sovereign masters of that law, rather than its servants. In other words, international law suffers from the lack of a centralized enforcement agency. These truths have raised the question of whether there is such a thing as international law at all. The record shows that the answer is definitely in the affirmative, yet it also shows that the main usefulness of international law is in technical and fairly noncontroversial matters. In these areas, it has crystallized into a respectable body of international rules and regulations which are invaluable aids in the normal day-to-day conduct of international relations.

As a general rule, the "legal approach" to political order-building has been most effective among those nations that are held together by a sense of political community. But law has not been able to produce this community. Rather, its existence has seemed to depend on the prior existence of a cultural and political community. Where there is no such community—as in the relations between the two superpowers—the "political approach" of diplomacy is likely to yield more fruitful results than the judicial. Indeed, the true relation between diplomacy and international law has not been one in which the latter has displaced the former, but one in which more successful diplomacy has resulted in more ungrudging consent to better laws.

The most ambitious example of the "legal" approach to political order in our time is the International Court of Justice. We shall now explore the question of whether this institution accurately reflects the role of international law in general.

The International Court of Justice

The International Court of Justice, better known as the World Court, came into existence in 1945 as part of the United Nations system. Actually, the Court was a reincarnation rather than a birth. It was the successor to the Permanent Court of International Justice of the League of Nations. The Old World Court had been one of the more successful institutions of the League. In the eighteen years of its activity, it had rendered thirty-two judgments and had handed down twenty-seven advisory opinions. The new World Court broke the continuity as little as possible. It established itself at the Hague and the statute governing its activities became virtually a carbon copy of its predecessor.

The fifteen Justices of the Court are elected for nine-year terms by a majority of votes in the General Assembly and the Security Council. The veto power of the Big Five does not apply. The Statute of the Court provides that the Justices be chosen "from among persons of high moral character who possess . . . recognized competence in international law." They should also represent "the main forms of civilization and the principal legal systems of the world." Hence, individuals rather than states are to be elected to the Court. This proviso, it was hoped, would increase the Court's impartiality. It was also assumed that the fifteen Justices would represent a wide geographic distribution and that no two members of the Court would be of the same nationality. These clauses were inserted owing to the conviction of the founders that the impartiality of the Court would have to be safeguarded as much as possible. They realized that the judicial value of the Court as an international tribunal might be totally defeated if the Justices were to be swayed by national loyalties or the political interests of particular states. On the other hand, the founders had to make their peace with the fact that judges, like other human beings, were nationals of a particular country, and that the Court might have to deal with explosive political issues on which national sentiment would run high and on which Olympian dispassionateness would be hard to achieve. One important concession was made in this direction in the Statute. If a case were to come before the Court and there was no judge of the nationality of one of the parties among the permanent Justices, that party would have the right to choose an additional *ad hoc* judge of its own or any other nationality. This right has been exercised invariably. The Court was thus an expression not only of the hope that the Justices would rise above all national allegiance and serve only the law, but also of the realization that this high level of detachment might not always actually prove possible.

The record of the World Court, while modest, indicates the nature of the relationship between political order-building and the rule of law. The Court has been involved in four different types of cases: it has dealt with both the East-West and the colonial-anticolonial conflicts; it has passed on disputes within the Western Hemisphere; and it has been called upon to interpret the legal competence of the United Nations. A closer look at some significant cases from each of these four areas will shed further light on the role of the Court.

The World Court's *cause célèbre* was the Corfu Channel case, involving two countries separated by the Iron Curtain—Albania and Great Britain. This was the only contentious East-West case ever to come before the Court. In October 1946 two British warships were sunk by mines as they passed through the Corfu Channel in the territorial waters of Albania. Forty-four British sailors were killed and the British government brought the matter before the Security Council, where a resolution that held Albania responsible for the tragedy was vetoed by the Soviet Union. Subsequently, the question of responsibility was referred by both parties to the International Court of Justice. Since there was no Albanian Judge on the Court, a Czechoslovak Justice—Judge Ecer—was appointed to the Court, which now comprised sixteen members. The British contention was that the Albanian government had laid the mines or must have known about them, that it was therefore guilty of criminal negligence, and that it should therefore be held responsible. Albania claimed that the British ships had violated her sovereignty and that her action was a justifiable act of self-defense. The Court, in an eleven to five opinion, held in favor of the British contention. As a result of this opinion, the British government requested that the Court also fix the amount of damages to be paid by Albania. Although the Albanians claimed that the Court had no jurisdiction over this part of the case, the Court held that the decision of the two parties to submit the dispute gave it the right to fix the damages as well. In a ten to six opinion, the Court held that the Albanian government must have known of the existence of the mines and should therefore pay compensation to Great Britain. The amount of the damages was fixed at $2,400,000. The six dissenting Justices contended that it had not been proved that the Albanian government knew of the mines and that Albania could therefore not be held liable. The dissenting Justices represented Egypt, Brazil, the Soviet Union, Poland, Yugoslavia, and Czechoslovakia. Albania refused to honor the decision of the Court, despite the fact that the majority opinion had been based on numerous reports by experts who had visited the localities adjacent to the scene of the incident. In thus declining to pay the amount awarded, Albania has become the first state in history to "refuse in principle to comply with the decision of the Court in a contentious proceeding to which it was a party."[3] Neither the Court nor the British government has been able to enforce the decision.

A second problem involving the East-West struggle reached the Court in November 1947 when the General Assembly requested an advisory opinion on the controversial question of the admission of new members to the United Nations. The Court was asked to pass on the question of whether a member state could make its consenting vote subject "to the additional condition that other states be admitted." The General Assembly's request for an advisory opinion on this matter grew out of the Soviet Union's proposal of a membership "package deal." This was rejected by the United States, which held that each application should be considered on its individual merits. The Court, in a nine to six opinion, upheld the American view and declared that Article IV of the Charter, stating that admission was to be open to all "peace-loving" states, was to govern admissions procedure rather than extraneous political considerations. The minority, which included not only the Soviet, Polish, and Yugoslav Justices, but also the French, British, and Canadian members of the Court, contended that the question of membership was essentially a political one and that political considerations were therefore admissible. Though the decision itself was superseded through a membership "package deal" in 1955, the fact that it witnessed three Western Justices voting with the anti-Western minority has made it of more than passing interest. What was significant was not the "rightness" or "wrongness" of the opinion of these three Western Justices but the simple fact that what they considered to be an objective appraisal of the case led them to an opinion that contravened that of their national governments at the time.

The only colonial issue to reach the Court to date has concerned the disposition of Southwest Africa, which had been a mandate under the League of Nations. The Court has been concerned with various aspects of this problem intermittently since 1950. In that year the General Assembly requested an advisory opinion on whether or not the former mandate could be administered as an integral part of South Africa. The issue aroused much interest because of South Africa's adamant refusal to place the territory under any form of international supervision. The Court, in a unanimous opinion, declared that "the United Nations [was] entitled to exercise supervisory functions over the administration of the mandate, and [that] the Union acting alone [was] not competent to modify the international status of the territory."[4] Specifically, the Court stated that the Union Government was under the obligation to submit periodic reports on the status of Southwest Africa to the United Nations. In a later case, in 1956, the Court upheld the legality of oral reports to the UN from the contested territory.

In the third round, in 1962, the Court took yet another step when, by a vote of eight to seven, it rejected South Africa's objections to its jurisdiction. On the basis of this opinion, the two plaintiffs, Ethiopia and Liberia, submitted lengthy substantive briefs. The Union of South Africa, too, submitted its defense. In July 1966, by the narrowest possible majority—a seven to seven tie being broken in favor of South Africa by the "casting vote" of the President, Sir Percy Spender of Australia—the Court dismissed the complaint against South Africa on the grounds of insufficiency of legal interest on the part of the complaining states. The reaction of the Afro-Asian group was violent. It expressed its disinclination to resort to the Court in the future and secured the passage of a resolution in the General Assembly withdrawing the right to administer Southwest Africa from South Africa and conferring this right upon the General Assembly. Defenders of the decision, on the other hand, asserted that it was better for the Court to dismiss the case than to make a decision against South Africa that would have been unenforceable. Thus, sixteen years of litigation came to an end. The Court's ultimate role in the colonial struggle, as in the East-West struggle, had been negligible.

In 1972, in a dramatic move, the UN Security Council decided to meet in Addis Ababa, Ethiopia, in order to underline the importance of the problems besetting Africa. In one of its resolutions it strongly urged a United Nations role in "Namibia"—the new African term now used for the territory of Southwest Africa—and requested the Secretary-General to travel there in order to see to it that the resolution was implemented. Secretary-General Kurt Waldheim duly went to South Africa and tried his best to persuade the Union Government but to no avail. For all practical purposes, South African control over Namibia remained intact. Four major UN organs—the World Court, the General Assembly, the Security Council, and finally the Secretary-General—had come to grief on the unyielding rock of South African sovereignty.

While the Court's role in the settlement of disputes involving the two great political struggles has been minimal, it has played a significant part in intra-regional controversies, especially within the Western Hemisphere. Here the Court has made an important contribution to political order-building. Some of these cases have been fairly technical, as for example the question of fishing rights by Britain off the Icelandic coast. Others have had greater political import. One of the most typical of these cases to reach the Court was a boundary dispute between Honduras and Nicaragua. In November 1960 the Court ruled that Nicaragua was obligated to give effect to a 1906 arbitration award settling her boundary with Honduras. This award had been made by King Alfonso XIII of Spain, who had established a boundary line that would cause the transfer to Honduras of frontier regions claimed by Nicaragua. In 1912 Nicaragua had challenged the award, and repeated attempts to settle the issue had failed. Finally, in 1957, the Organization of American States brought about an agreement between the two countries to submit the case to the World Court. The Court supported the 1906 award by a vote of fourteen to one. The dissenting vote was cast by a Colombian Justice who had been designated by Nicaragua as *ad hoc* judge for the case. The dissenting opinion held that the 1906 arbitration award was invalid because of errors made by the arbitrator. The permanent judges, however, ruled in favor of Honduras and declared that the King of Spain had been a proper arbitrator under the terms of an 1894 treaty between Nicaragua and Honduras and that Nicaragua had accepted the King's decision at the time. Nicaragua complied with the decision.

The broader significance of this case was the fact that Justices from both sides of the Iron Curtain ruled in effect that once a valid arbitration award is made in an international dispute, it becomes effective and remains so despite any lapse of time in its implementation. The judgment displayed a broad support for the principle of arbitration and laid the groundwork for the future settlement of similar international disputes.

Perhaps the most important contribution of the World Court to international order-building has been the strengthening of the United Nations as a juridical and political entity. When Count Folke Bernadotte, the United Nations mediator in Palestine, was assassinated by a Jewish terrorist group, the United Nations requested an advisory opinion on the question of whether the world organization was entitled to bring a claim against a state for damages caused to the United Nations by injuries suffered by one of its representatives while acting on its behalf. The Court, in an eleven to four opinion, held that the United Nations was entitled to claim such reparation. The majority, in a far-reaching opinion, stated that

Fifty states, representing the vast majority of the members of the international community, had the power, in conformity with international law to bring into being an entity possessing objective international personality, not merely personality recognized by them alone, together with capacity to bring international claims.[5]

Thus, the United Nations was granted a "personality" by the Court, a kind of sovereignty all its own which the majority saw implied in the Charter:

Under international law, the Organization must be deemed to have those powers which, though not expressly provided in the Charter, are conferred upon it by necessary implication as being essential to the performance of its duties.[6]

The four dissenting Justices—Egyptian, Polish, Russian, and American—held that this "implied powers clause" was not inherent in the Charter. On the strength of this advisory opinion, the United Nations claimed reparations from Israel for the death of Count Bernadotte and injuries to other United Nations personnel in the pursuit of their duties. The government of Israel has honored these claims. Thus, the Court helped to endow the United Nations with an international legal personality entitled to protect its officials by bestowing upon them the legal status of world civil servants.

In July 1962 the Court once again interpreted the United Nations Charter in a very important advisory opinion. In response to a request by the General Assembly, the Court declared, by a vote of nine to five, that the expenses of the United Nations Emergency Force (UNEF) and the United Nations Congo Force (ONUC) constituted expenses of the United Nations within the meaning of Article 17, paragraph 2 of the Charter, which declares that "the expenses of the Organization shall be borne by the members as apportioned by the General Assembly."[7]

By this opinion, the Court confirmed the General Assembly's authority to impose legally binding assessments on the member states. In effect, a two-thirds majority could now bind the entire membership, including those states that voted in the negative. In that sense, the opinion signified a tentative step toward the principle of international taxation by the world community and lent support to the principle of majority rule in international relations. It also gave the Assembly and the Security Council free rein to establish peace forces of the UNEF or ONUC type and to provide for their financing, thus underwriting the late Secretary-General Dag Hammarskjöld's conception of the UN as a "dynamic instrument" capable of executive action, in contrast to the notion of the UN as a mere "static conference machinery."

Despite the far-reaching implications of the opinion, its practical effects on the UN treasury were not too significant. The two great powers that had refused for reasons of political opposition to pay for UNEF or ONUC—the Soviet Union and France—continued to withhold payment. But thirty-one smaller states that had been in arrears for reasons of alleged financial hardship decided to clear their accounts.[8]

Any analysis of the World Court must be tempered with caution, for the number of cases that have been brought before it have thus far been few—fewer, indeed, than the number earlier submitted to the League of Nations Court. Moreover, it is difficult to determine the Court's role as an impartial arbiter in political disputes. It is true that in both East-West cases, the Justices from the Soviet bloc voted with the minority, but this fact alone is inconclusive evidence. It may be explained by political considerations but it may also be attributable to the fact that the Justices have been trained in different legal systems and rooted in different political beliefs. On the other hand, the vote of the three Western Justices in the membership case indicated a high degree of objectivity.

An obvious and irritating problem consistently plaguing the Court has been that of enforcement. The World Court has no police power by which it can actually implement its decisions against recalcitrant parties to a dispute. When Albania refused to abide by its decision and the Union of South Africa paid no attention to its advisory opinion, the Court was helpless. The Albanian fiasco even raised the question of whether it might not have been better for the Court to stay out of a dispute in which it would be unable to enforce a decision. Some observers have argued that in this instance the Court had "frozen" a quarrel rather than resolved it and that it might have been wiser to leave the matter to the political processes of diplomatic negotiations. But in numerous intra-regional cases as well as in the United Nations "personality" case, the Court was successful even without the power of enforcement. These facts lend support to the thesis that the World Court's role as a builder of global law has been limited, but that it has strengthened and solidified legal bonds in regions held together by common political and social values. The World Court by itself will probably contribute little to global order-building since its success seems to be predicated on the prior existence of such an order.

The most serious problem of the Court has not been how to enforce its decisions but, rather, how to encourage nations to avail themselves of its services. In Article 36 of the Statute (the so-called "optional clause") the Court has given states the opportunity to recognize "as compulsory, *ipso facto* and without special agreement, in relation to any other state accepting the same obligation, the jurisdiction of the Court in all legal disputes." Thirty-eight states have signed this "optional clause" and it therefore seems that any legal disputes concerning any one of them would automatically fall under the Court's jurisdiction. This, however, has not been the case, because most states have found it necessary to qualify their adherence to the "optional clause" through numerous reservations. These reservations have done much to choke off the

Court's jurisdiction, since in most cases states have tended to define almost everything as remaining "within their own domestic jurisdiction." To make matters worse, some states have reserved the right to decide unilaterally which matters were to be within their domestic jurisdiction. The United States has itself taken this attitude. It has exempted from the compulsory jurisdiction of the Court any "disputes with regard to matters which are essentially within the domestic jurisdiction of the United States of America as determined by the United States of America." Many observers interested in strengthening the Court have pointed out that a beginning could be made if nations withdrew their reservations of unilateral competence to determine which matters were to fall within their domestic jurisdiction. In the words of the Commission to Study the Organization of Peace:

There is a widespread recognition, reflected in President Eisenhower's 1959 State of the Union message, that the United States has set a bad example for other states in qualifying its ratification of the optional clause so severely as to make that ratification virtually meaningless. No amount of exhortation by American leaders in favor of promoting the rule of law in international affairs would be so effective as the simple act of transforming United States ratification of the optional clause into a genuine acceptance of the Court's compulsory jurisdiction in legal disputes. Such an act might stimulate widespread alteration of attitudes toward the International Court of Justice and pave the way for the full realization of the Court's potential as an instrument for the settlement of disputes and the clarification and development of international law. The Court has a limited but vitally important role to play in the evolution of world order, and it is essential that its opportunities for service through both decisions and advisory opinions be expanded.[9]

The plight of the International Court of Justice is a fairly accurate reflection of the plight of international law in general. The great issues of international relations—the East-West and the colonial-anticolonial struggles—have remained largely outside its purview. The reason for this is that matters of national prestige and power status have been so much involved that nations have been unwilling to submit such disputes to judicial settlement. Even if states were more inclined to submit disputes to the Court, the problem of enforcement in an anarchic world would still remain. Hitler could not be stopped by a court decision. On the other hand, the World Court has made a vital contribution to order-building in technical and fairly noncontroversial matters, and—in intra-regional disputes—even in some important political questions. Perhaps most important, it has become the constitutional arbiter of the United Nations Charter.

REFERENCES

1. *De jure belli ac pacis libri tres,* in *Classics of International Law,* Francis Kelsey, trans., *Prolegomena,* p. 20.

2. U.S. Supreme Court, 1900, *Paquete Habana and the Lola,* 175 U.S. 677.

3. Oliver J. Lissitzyn, *The International Court of Justice.* Carnegie Endowment for International Peace, New York: Marstin Press, 1951, p. 80.

4. *Ibid.,* p. 94.

5. *Ibid.,* p. 59.

6. Advisory Opinion Concerning Reparation for Injuries Suffered in the Service of the United Nations, *International Organization,* August 1949, p. 575.

7. International Court of Justice, *Certain Expenses of the United Nations (Article 17, paragraph 2 of the Charter), Advisory Opinion of 20 July 1962:* I.C.J. Reports, 1962.

8. John G. Stoessinger *et al., Financing the United Nations System.* Washington, D.C.: The Brookings Institution, 1964.

9. Report of the Commission to Study the Organization of Peace, *Organizing Peace in the Nuclear Age.* New York: New York University Press, 1959, p. 14.

BIBLIOGRAPHY

Alexander, Lewis M., ed. *The Law of the Sea.* Columbus, Ohio: Ohio State University Press, 1967.

Andrassy, Juraj. *International Law and the Resources of the Sea.* New York: Columbia University Press, 1970.

Baldwin, Malcolm F. and Page, James K., eds. *Law and the Environment.* New York: Walker, 1970.

Bozeman, Adda B. *The Future of Law in a Multicultural World.* Princeton, N.J.: Princeton University Press, 1971.

Brierly, James L. *The Law of Nations.* Oxford: Clarendon Press, 1963.

Clark, Grenville, and Sohn, Louis B. *World Peace Through World Law,* 3rd ed., rev. Cambridge, Mass.: Harvard University Press, 1966.

Corbett, Percy E. *Law and Society in the Relations of States.* New York: Harcourt, Brace, 1951.

———. *Law in Diplomacy.* Princeton, N.J.: Princeton University Press, 1959.

D'Amato, Anthony. *The Concept of Custom in International Law.* Ithaca, N.Y.: Cornell University Press, 1971.

Deutsch, Karl W. and Hoffmann, Stanley, eds. *The Relevance of International Law.* Cambridge: Schenkman Publishing Co., 1968.

DeVisscher, Charles. *Theory and Reality in Public International Law.* Princeton, N.J.: Princeton University Press, 1968.

Eagleton, Clyde. *International Government.* New York: Ronald Press, 1948.

Falk, Richard A. *Legal Order in a Violent World.* Princeton, N.J.: Princeton University Press, 1968.

——. "The Southwest Africa Cases: An Appraisal," *International Organization,* Vol. XXVI, No. 1, Winter 1967.

——. *The Status of Law in International Society.* Princeton, N.J.: Princeton University Press, 1970.

——, ed. *The Vietnam War and International Law.* Princeton, N.J.: Princeton University Press, 1968.

Glueck, Sheldon. *The Nuremberg Trial and Aggressive War.* New York: Knopf, 1946.

Henkin, Louis *How Nations Behave: Law and Foreign Policy.* New York: Praeger, 1968.

Jessup, Philip C. *A Modern Law of Nations.* New York: Macmillan, 1948.

——. *The Price of International Justice.* New York: Columbia University Press, 1971.

Katz, Milton. *The Relevance of International Adjudication.* Cambridge, Mass.: Harvard University Press, 1968.

Kelsen, Hans. *The Law of the United Nations.* New York: Praeger, 1950.

Lauterpacht, H. *International Law and Human Rights.* New York: Praeger, 1950.

Luard, Evan, ed. *The International Regulation of Wars.* New York: New York University Press, 1972.

Mangone, Gerard J. *The Elements of International Law.* Homewood, Ill.: The Dorsey Press, 1964.

Matte, Nicolas M. *Aerospace Law.* Toronto: Carswell, 1969.

Oppenheim L. *International Law,* Vols. I and II. London: Longmans, Green, 1952, 1955.

Rosenne, S. *The World Court.* New York: Oceana, 1962.

Schwarzenberger, Georg. *International Law and Order.* New York: Praeger, 1971.

Stone, Julius. "The International Court and World Crisis," *International Conciliation,* January 1962.

——. *Legal Controls of International Conflict.* New York: Rinehart, 1954.

Tung, William. *International Law in an Organizing World.* New York: Crowell, 1968.

Vyshinsky, Andrei. *Law of the Soviet State.* New York: Macmillan, 1948.

Woetzel, Robert K. *The Nuremberg Trials in International Law.* New York: Praeger, 1960.

Wright, Quincy. *Contemporary International Law: A Balance Sheet.* New York: Doubleday, 1955.

——. "The Cuban Missile Crisis of 1962," in John G. Stoessinger and Alan F. Wertin, eds. *Power and Order: Six Cases in World Politics.* New York: Harcourt, Brace and World, 1964.

10 The United Nations System and Political Order

Out of this nettle, danger, we pluck this flower, safety.
SHAKESPEARE *Henry IV,* I, 3

The Idea of the United Nations

The United Nations is the most ambitious order-building experiment in history. In one very fundamental sense, its conception is rooted in the past. Its edifice was erected in times of war, during a period of concerted effort to defeat the Axis powers. The Organization was to be called into existence "to kill another Hitler in the shell ere he become too great." The nations were to be "united" against a criminal outlaw. In that sense, the United Nations was to prevent another World War II, just as the League of Nations before it had been created to prevent another World War I. Few of the United Nations' founders at San Francisco were aware of the titanic proportions of the coming East-West struggle. The rock on which the United Nations was to stand was to be the unity of the Great Powers, who would assume among them the major responsibility for peace and order. The United Nations was ill-equipped to deal with a world in which this unity would no longer exist and ill-prepared to answer the vital question: "Who will control the controllers if they should fight among each other?" In that sense, the thinking of its founders was oriented backward in time rather than forward. The future was mobilized once more to slay the dragons of the past.

But in another, equally fundamental sense, the conception of the United Nations was broad and forward-looking. The new world organization was to be created "to save succeeding generations from the scourge of war." But how to accomplish this end when so little was known about the causes of war and the roads to peace? The answer, which found its expression in the structure of the United Nations, was at once simple and sophisticated. It was simple in its failure to anticipate some of the major causes of subsequent international conflict. But it was sophisticated in the various new trails it blazed in the pursuit of peace.

To enable it to work toward its goal, the United Nations was equipped with six major organs. The ambitious task of achieving collective security was assigned to the Security Council. Based on the assumption that peace was indivisible and that the Big Five—the United States, the Soviet Union, Britain, France, and China—could reach unanimity, the Security Council was to be the great international guardian of peace. If challenged by an aggressor, it would confront him with an incontrovertible law based on the irresistible force of the world community.

If the Security Council was thus to find the road to peace through military security, a second major United Nations organ, the General Assembly, was to utilize the time-honored technique of talking things out. It was to function as the world's forum, a Parliament of Man in embryo, a meeting-place in which all member nations were to confer on the basis of sovereign equality. The General Assembly's underlying assumption was that the rational, and sometimes irrational, airing of disputes among nations could contribute importantly to the pacific settlement of those disputes as well as to peaceful changes in the system of international relations itself.

A third principal organ, the Economic and Social Council, was created in the belief that a great deal of international strife was rooted in poverty and misery and that, therefore, the United Nations should do its utmost to help raise standards of living and improve economic conditions throughout the world. Since the founders of the United Nations saw colonialism as another frequent source of war, they felt it necessary also to employ the new world organization to mitigate the anger of dependent peoples against their colonial masters. Hence, to devise a technique whereby independence could be gained with as little bloodshed as possible, they provided a fourth major organ, the Trusteeship Council. The theory behind this latter institution was that if the colonies could be viewed as responsibilities to be shouldered, rather than real estate to be owned and exploited, the colonial nations might prove more amenable to the liquidation of their empires, with the result that violent eruptions of the struggle over colonialism might be avoided. Yet another cause of war was believed by the founders of the United Nations to lie in the absence of common legal standards among nations. For this reason, they included within the United Nations framework the World Court, which we have analyzed earlier (see Chapter 9). The purpose of the World Court was to pass on judiciable disputes and, by building on precedent, to lead in the creation of a uniform international legal system. Finally, the founders of the United Nations were convinced that the maintenance of peace required a nucleus of men and women whose loyalty was first and foremost not to any particular nation but to the entire international community. To head such an international civil service, they established a sixth major organ of the United Nations, the Office of the Secretary-General.

The United Nations was thus designed to attack the problem of war on six principal fronts, each the responsibility of one of its major organs. In addition, the struggle for international peace and stability was also to be waged in a number of more peripheral ways. These became the province of the so-called "specialized agencies." Like the United Nations' main organs, these specialized agencies were designed to serve their own particular tasks, and all of them shared the same theoretical assumption. They were based on the premise that sovereignty—the behavior of nations as though they were a law unto themselves—vastly increases the danger of war. Whereas the major organs, however, were to attempt to persuade the nations to give up portions of their sovereignty, the specialized agencies were intended to proceed more indirectly. Their purpose was to engage the nations in enterprises of common interest and thus to bring them actively together in spite of their sovereignty. The reasoning behind this method was that if the United Nations could induce nations to cooperate in economic, social, and cultural activities, giving up some of their sovereignty in these relatively noncontroversial areas, habits of collaboration and a fabric of cohesion would develop that gradually might be transferred to matters of more vital political significance. It was hoped that the nations would then yield some of their sovereignty because it had become superfluous. This indirect approach to peace of the specialized agencies, working toward international cooperation and compromise in regard to specific matters of common interest, was the technique of functionalism.[1]

The specialized agencies that were absorbed into the United Nations system can be divided roughly into two groups. The first group, whose major purpose was to broaden and facilitate communication among nations, included the Universal Postal Union (UPU), the International Telecommunication Union (ITU), the International Civil Aviation Organization (ICAO), the World Meteorological Organization (WMO) and the Inter-Governmental Maritime Consultative Organization (IMCO). Some of these, like UPU and ITU, antedated the creation of the United Nations by several decades. Others, like IMCO, did not come into existence until years after the ratification of the Charter. But all were made part of the United Nations system and all were based on the premise that good "housekeeping" and good communications among nations might decrease the dangers of war.

It is less easy to generalize about the specialized agencies in the second group. For lack of a better term they may be called the "welfare" agencies, in the sense that each was intended to improve world economic, social, and cultural conditions and thus build defenses for the peace. The oldest of these, the International Labor Organization (ILO), was to better conditions of labor throughout the world on the assumption that the equalization of labor standards was a necessary condition of peace. The Food and Agriculture Organization (FAO) hoped to raise nutritional levels and improve agricultural technology. The International Refugee Organization (IRO), conceived as a temporary agency, was to find resettlement opportunities for the uprooted and homeless of the world. It was based on the assumption that nations could make a common effort to salvage refugees from intolerance and thus learn to yield part of their sovereignty in this common enterprise. The World Health Organization (WHO) was based on the premise that ill health and epidemics might be precursors of war. Hence, the objective of this agency was to be the attainment by all peoples of the highest possible level of health. The United Nations Educational, Scientific and Cultural Organization (UNESCO) was established by the framers of the United Nations because they believed that nations' ignorance of one another's ways and lives was a common cause of distrust leading to war. Hence UNESCO was to advance understanding among nations through research and the exchange of scholars and scientists. The International Bank for Reconstruction and Development (IBRD), or World Bank, was to bind up the wounds of war through loans for the reconstruction of devastated areas and to better the chances of peace by granting loans for the development of resources in lesser-developed countries. The International Development Association (IDA), an affiliate of the World Bank, was formed to provide long-term loans at low interest rates to underdeveloped countries that could not obtain World Bank loans. The International Finance Corporation (IFC), another affiliate of the Bank, was to promote the growth of productive private enterprise in the developing countries. The International Monetary Fund (IMF) was to aid peace through the promotion of exchange stability and the use of a fund to support weak currencies. Finally, the International Atomic Energy Agency (IAEA), an autonomous member of the United Nations family, was to consecrate the energy of the atom to the cause of peace.

The idea of the United Nations evolved at San Francisco was thus a multidimensional one. But though it was much more ambitious in its conception than the comparable post-World War I project of the League of Nations, it did not attempt the impossible. The UN founders were quite aware that the members of the world organization about to be born were not ready for anything like a world government. They knew that as yet, at least, the only world government that could hold together the heterogeneous population of the earth would have to be one based on force. And this would hardly be an improvement over what already was.

In not attempting the impossible, the founders of the UN were realists. But in seeking to go to the very limits of the possible, they were also visionaries. And necessarily so, for the idea of the United Nations had to take into account the full import of the cruel paradox that, in the nuclear age, the national sovereignty of nations would have to be controlled by an international order, but that this international order would have to be created and even controlled by sovereign nations. The plan therefore had to combine the dictates of national power with those of international order. We shall now see how the United Nations as a working reality has measured up to the original conception.

The United Nations: A Balance Sheet

THE SECURITY COUNCIL AND COLLECTIVE SECURITY

The complexity of the United Nations system makes analysis a formidable task. It makes little sense to evaluate the world organization as a whole. Each organ has its distinctive goals and tools and has established its own unique record. In order to do justice to the United Nations family, each of its members must be considered separately. We shall begin with the organ that the framers of the Charter conceived as the hub of the Organization—the Security Council.

The Security Council was given extensive powers to keep the peace. It was to consist of eleven members, of which five—the United States, the Soviet Union, Great Britain, France, and China—were to be permanent.

Six nonpermanent members were to be elected by the General Assembly for two-year terms. The Charter empowered the Security Council to recommend means of peaceful settlement of disputes; if a nation committed an act of aggression, the Council would have the power to apply sanctions against the aggressor. These might range from the severance of diplomatic relations to the taking of collective military measures. With a view to the latter, there was also contemplated a Military Staff which would be permanently available to the Security Council.

It thus seemed that the principle of collective security, embodied in the Security Council, had at last acquired teeth. Since the Big Five were to dominate the Council, no aggressor would be able to challenge such an overwhelming agglomeration of power. Yet the Big Five, fully conscious of their preponderant power and their primary responsibility in keeping the peace, demanded proportionate privileges. They not only insisted on their permanent status on the Council, but also demanded that if a Council decision concerned a matter of substance and not a mere question of procedure, the majority would have to include all five of the permanent members. This was the origin of the much discussed "veto power," by which each of the five Great Powers could prevent the Security Council from taking action. This veto power deserves careful analysis.

The exact original wording of Article 27 of the Charter, which gives the right of veto, is as follows:

1. Each member of the Security Council shall have one vote.
2. Decisions of the Security Council on procedural matters shall be made by an affirmative vote of seven members.
3. Decisions of the Security Council on all other matters shall be made by an affirmative vote of seven members including the concurring votes of the permanent members; provided that in decisions under Chapter VI, and under paragraph 3 of Article 52, a party to a dispute shall abstain from voting.

The principal questions to which the veto power was to apply were the admission of new members to the United Nations, enforcement actions to meet a threat to the peace, proposals for the peaceful settlement of disputes, amendments to the Charter, and the election of a Secretary-General.

Three of the Great Powers at San Francisco—the United States, the Soviet Union, and Great Britain—insisted on the right of veto. None of them would have acceded to the United Nations without that right. China and France at first took a more flexible position, but the rigid stand of the Big Three soon resulted in their equally firm insistence on the veto rule. As a further safeguard of their sovereignty, moreover, the

Great Powers insisted that the decision as to whether a vote was to be substantive or procedural was itself a substantive question and hence subject to the veto. This meant that in theory at least, anything was vetoable that a Great Power might choose to veto. Needless to say, this possibility of the use of the veto being expanded to apply to any matter at all did not augur well for the effective functioning of the Security Council. It thus seemed that from the very beginning the Great Powers' uncompromising insistence on their sovereignty, combined with the intensification of the East-West struggle, might well turn the Security Council into a moribund agency.

It has almost become a cliché to assert that the Security Council has been paralyzed through the Soviet Union's abuse of the veto power. While there is some validity to this charge, the truth is far more complex. It is true that the Soviet Union has been responsible for approximately 90 per cent of the total number of vetoes cast. By 1972, it had cast well over one hundred vetoes. But the figures themselves do not sufficiently explain the picture. In the first place, the Soviet Union has not had a monopoly of negative votes. The negative votes of the other Great Powers were usually not classed as vetoes because others of the Big Five—as well as some nonpermanent members—voted the same way. As Norman J. Padelford has pointed out:

It is clear from the record that when the Soviet Union finds its vital interests at stake there are now no other great powers generally inclined to stand with it. Therefore the negative vote of the Soviet delegate usually becomes a sole veto, accompanied ordinarily only by the vote of whatever satellite holds a non-permanent seat on the Council. When other great powers, particularly the United States and Great Britain, find their national interests at issue they can usually persuade other permanent members to go along with them either in casting a multiple negative vote sufficient to stop a proposal without the stigma of exercising a sole veto (or near-sole veto), or to join in introducing and passing a resolution more suitable to their desires.[2]

Second, the Western powers on the Security Council have been able to make the Soviet Union appear even more obstructionist by forcing votes on issues that they knew would elicit a Soviet veto. Thus over half of the Soviet vetoes were cast against the admission of Western and Western-oriented nations to the United Nations. Italy's application, for example, was vetoed six times before that nation was finally admitted as part of a "package deal" in December 1955, as a result of which sixteen new members were permitted to join the United Nations. Finally, the Soviet Union has declared that it has been forced to use the veto extensively because of the composition of the Security Council. In the words of Premier Khrushchev in 1958:

It is common knowledge that the majority in the Security Council is composed of the votes of countries dependent, in one way or another, primarily economically, on the U.S.A. Thus, the Security Council in its present composition can not be regarded as an impartial arbiter, and that is why it has of late ceased to play the important role in the maintenance of international peace and security which devolved upon it by virtue of the United Nations Charter.[3]

It is true that when Khrushchev made the above statement, there was no member of the Security Council upon whose support the Soviet Union could count. The Soviet Union was the only communist state with a vote in the Security Council. Eight votes were controlled by military allies of the United States in NATO and SEATO. Two members—Iraq and Sweden—were neutralists in the East-West struggle. In the following year, Sweden was replaced by Italy, a member of NATO, and Iraq by Tunisia. Thus, in 1959, the composition of the Security Council began to resemble that of a Western military alliance. A good illustration of a typical case is provided by the U-2 plane episode in 1960. In May of that year, the Soviet Union brought the case before the Security Council and introduced a resolution branding the flights by American planes over Soviet territory as "acts of aggression." Two states—the USSR and Poland—voted in favor of the Soviet motion; seven states—Argentina, China, Ecuador, France, Italy, the United Kingdom, and the United States—voted against. The latter were all members of the Western alliance system. Two neutralist states—Ceylon and Tunisia—abstained.

This pattern began to change somewhat in 1966 when four nonpermanent members were added to the Security Council. The passage of a resolution now required nine affirmative votes instead of seven. Since the enlargement of the Council was undertaken primarily for the benefit of the new nations, most of which were "neutralist" on East-West issues, it now became more difficult for the United States to control the Council. In 1966, for example, when the United States attempted to have the Vietnam question inscribed on the Council's agenda, it found itself dependent upon the vote of Jordan. The move succeeded, but just barely. The days of an automatic American majority or of a "hidden veto" achieved by mobilizing this majority against a Soviet-sponsored resolution were over. United States influence was still very great, but now had to depend on bargaining and persuasion rather than reliance on an absolute majority.

On the whole, the Security Council has tended to narrow rather than expand the scope of the veto power. It established that the abstention of a Great Power was not tantamount to veto, and, in the Korean police action decision of 1950, went even further by declaring that the absence of a Great Power should merely be regarded as abstention but not as a veto *in absentia*. Perhaps most important, the potential threat inherent in the "double-veto" has not materialized. It has been used relatively sparingly.

The tendency to blame the veto power—especially its excessive use by the Soviet Union—for the decline of the Security Council is to confuse the symptoms with the causes. The membership of the Security Council reflects the two great political struggles of our time. The Great Power veto has simply been a constant reminder that, in an international system of sovereign nation-states, no important action may be taken against a major power without its consent. In fact, it may be argued that abolition of the veto might increase the danger of war, since the majority might then be tempted into precipitous action against a recalcitrant superpower. The unanimity principle has also taught the lesson that, in the nuclear age, the technique of arriving at decisions by counting votes has not been the most fortunate one for the solution of international problems. The principle of voting by majority does make sense in a homogeneous political context, but in a world of profound schisms, negotiating with the opponent rather than out-voting him may be a wiser method of intercourse. All this is not to say that the veto has been a blessing. But certainly, it has not been the unmitigated evil which some observers have made it seem to be. Indeed, many Soviet vetoes have been circumvented through action in the General Assembly or through other means.

The significance of the Security Council in the overall context of the United Nations family has gone through an interesting cycle. Briefly, what has occurred has been a threefold progression. First, beginning in the early 1950's, the Security Council began to go into eclipse as the "Uniting for Peace" procedure brought an increasing number of matters concerning international peace and security before the General Assembly. Second, the Assembly in turn, beginning in the middle 1950's, began to pass increasingly vaguely worded resolutions and thus invested the Secretary-General with greater policy-making authority. And finally, in the early 1960's, the Security Council experienced a significant revitalization. The veto power provides a very important clue to this threefold constitutional development. A closer look at the three periods is revealing.

The decline of the Security Council and the concomitant rise of the General Assembly during the first ten years of the UN's existence are well-known facts, which may be documented by several data. First, the frequency of Security Council sessions declined sharply during the first decade, and the scope of the political issues it considered narrowed considerably. In 1948, for example, the Council held 168 meetings, whereas in 1955 only twenty-three were held. Eighty-one of the vetoes cast by the Soviet Union were tallied up from 1946 to 1955. The Uniting for Peace Resolution passed in 1950 was a direct response of the Assembly—under strong American pressure and over vehement Soviet opposition—to the creeping paralysis of the Council.

Its own mandate thus broadened, the Assembly, beginning in 1955, in turn widened that of the Secretary-General. The missions of Dag Hammarskjöld to Peking in 1955, to Suez in 1956, to Lebanon in 1958, and again to the Congo in 1961 were all based on Assembly resolutions that gave the Secretary-General increasing policy-making powers. Indeed, the abortive Soviet attempt to replace the Office of the Secretary-General with a veto-bound triumvirate was in essence an effort to extend the principle of the veto into the UN Secretariat.

Beginning in 1960, one could observe a definite resuscitation of the Council. The growing membership of the Assembly made the Soviet Union somewhat more hesitant in its use of the veto. The USSR knew that if it wielded the veto on a vital matter, the Assembly would immediately step into the breach. Hence, it began to prefer to keep control over even undesirable operations rather than to relinquish the reins to an unpredictable Assembly, and now tended to abstain where it might have vetoed before. The paradoxical conclusion of this development is that the Council was revived by—of all things—the Assembly.

A cross-section of actual disputes brought before the Security Council shows a mixed record. In 1946 the Security Council urged Iran and the Soviet Union to settle a dispute through direct negotiations. The prodding was successful. In 1947 the Security Council successfully acted as midwife in the birth of Indonesia. This process lasted two years. The Security Council's role in a protracted dispute between Greece and the Soviet Union from 1946 to 1950 was inconclusive. In the struggle between India and Pakistan over Kashmir, the Security Council used the technique of mediation but was unable to reach a permanent settlement. In the Palestine dispute, Security Council mediation helped produce a cease-fire and an armistice but no final solution. On the the question of Berlin, the Security Council proved impotent. The Korean case was the Council's only authorization of collective military sanctions. The results were inconclusive. (For a full discussion of the United Nations action in Korea, see Chapter 12.) The year 1960 saw a quickening of Security Council activity. Racial trouble in the Union of South Africa led to a mild resolution encouraging the Secretary-General to employ "quiet diplomacy." A month later Argentina appealed to the Council against the abduction of Adolf Eichmann, a hated Nazi chieftain, by Israeli agents. The dispute was settled by direct negotiation. Then Cuba brought charges against the United States for "economic aggression," but these were shunted to the Organization of American States. The Soviet Union on two successive occasions accused the United States of aerial espionage. In mid-1960 the Security Council was confronted with the complex problems encountered by the newly independent Congo. In the early 1960's, while still concerned with the Congo, the Council again turned its attention to the problems raised by the *apartheid* policy of the government of the Union of South Africa, and also considered the posture of the Portuguese government in Angola. While it brought a solution for the Congo's ills within reach by 1964 (see Chapter 12 for an analysis of UN peace-keeping operations in the

Congo and the Middle East), it was unable fundamentally to affect the attitudes of the Portuguese and South African governments. In 1967, the Council managed to produce a cease-fire in the wake of the four-day Arab-Israeli war and, in 1968, a Western-led initiative to condemn the Soviet Union for its invasion of Czechoslovakia was blocked by a Soviet veto.

The composition of the Council changed dramatically with the seating of the People's Republic of China in 1971. The old bipolar tug of war between the Soviet Union and the United States gave way to a new and different constellation. This became clear during the Indo-Pakistan war of 1971 when the Soviet Union backed India and China supported Pakistan. The Security Council was paralyzed not by the familiar United States-Soviet deadlock, but by a Chinese-Soviet confrontation during which the latter cast three consecutive vetoes. In 1972 China cast her first veto in order to block the admission of Bangla Desh to the United Nations. It now seemed as if effective Council action would be possible only through concensus of the Big Three, no longer just the Big Two.

When one considers the structure and political limitations under which the Security Council must function, what is impressive is not that it has accomplished so little, but that it has achieved so much. While it has not been able to compel a Great Power to do anything against its will or to take action against a small power that has the backing of a great one, it has at times interposed the authority of the United Nations between the superpowers and thus managed to nip possible military clashes between them in the bud. The UN Operations in the Congo, initiated by the Security Council and largely directed by it, was a case in point. At times, the Council was able to make significant moves with the support of the Great Powers. The establishment of a UN peace force in Cyprus in 1964 was approved by both the United States and the Soviet Union. When China joined the Security Council in 1971, she could have vetoed the Cyprus peace force, but chose to abstain instead. Thus, there occur moments in history when the constellation among the Great Powers is favorable, and at such times the Council is capable of decisive action. At other times it is essentially a mirror of a divided world.

THE GENERAL ASSEMBLY

The General Assembly was conceived as a world forum, a talking-shop in which the world's nations were to be given the broad mandate "to discuss any questions or any matters within the scope of the Charter." It was to be the largest although not the most important organ of the United Nations. Each nation, large or small, was to have one vote. The Assembly was to have no enforcement powers but merely the authority to recommend courses of action. Like a national legislature, it was organized into committees. A survey of its seven standing committees gives a bird's eye view of the Assembly's responsibilities: two Committees on Political and Security Questions; an Economic and Financial Committee; a Social, Humanitarian, and Cultural Committee; a Trusteeship Committee; an Administrative and Budgetary Committee; and a Legal Committee. Thus the Assembly was given the power to discuss almost anything within the purview of the Charter: the maintenance of peace and security; the financial contributions of member states; the raising of economic, social, education, and health standards; the disposition of former colonies; the promotion of human rights; and the development of international law. Much United Nations activity was to be initiated in the Assembly and also was to be approved by it. The Assembly was to be the world's town meeting, but its bailiwick was to be a highly heterogeneous society of nation-states. It was to have no power of compulsion; enforcement was to be the exclusive domain of the Security Council.

When, quite early in the life of the UN, it became apparent that the Security Council—paralyzed by the unanimity rule—was falling victim to the East-West struggle, the Assembly was given certain "implied powers" through a liberal interpretation of the Charter. In 1947 the Assembly voted to create an Interim Committee, or "Little Assembly," which was to meet whenever circumstances might require during intervals between sessions of the Assembly. More important was the so-called Uniting For Peace Resolution adopted by the Assembly in November 1950. This Resolution grew out of the American conviction that the Security Council action to meet aggression in Korea had been made possible only through a fortuitous circumstance—the absence of the Soviet delegation. Hence, the United States proposed that the Assembly exercise a residual responsibility in any threat to the peace in case the Security Council was hamstrung by the veto. The Resolution contained five major provisions of far-reaching import:

1. It authorized the General Assembly to meet on short notice in an emergency in which the Security Council was prevented from acting, and to recommend appropriate collective measures, including the use of armed force when necessary.
2. It established a fourteen-nation Peace Observation Commission to observe and report on dangerous situations in any part of the world.
3. It asked all members to maintain in their armed forces special elements which could be made available for United Nations service on call of the Security Council or the General Assembly.
4. It established a fourteen-nation Collective Measures Committee to study and report on these and other methods for maintaining and strengthening international peace and security.

5. It urged all United Nations members to renew their fidelity to the United Nations, honor its decisions, and promote respect for human rights and achievement of economic stability and social progress

The Resolution became the subject of heated controversy. The Soviet Union, holding to a narrow interpretation of the Charter, declared that most of its provisions were illegal. The United States, on the other hand, construing the Charter more broadly, declared that the provisions were in accordance with its spirit and that they clearly served the need of strengthening international peace and security. The Resolution was adopted by a vote of 52 to 5, with 2 abstentions. It greatly broadened the scope of the General Assembly which, as a result of its new mandate, was able to deal with several matters of security: the Chinese military intervention in Korea, the Suez crisis of 1956, Soviet intervention in Hungary, the Lebanese crisis of 1958, and the Congo crisis of 1960. Thus, the Assembly became a backstop of the Security Council. The Charter, like a Constitution, had shown itself to be amenable to interpretation in order to keep pace with changing events.

Since its inception, the United Nations has rapidly been approaching the ideal of universal membership. It started out with fifty-one original members, and for years the East-West struggle resulted in a policy of competitive exclusion of new applicants. "Package deals" in the mid-1950's resulted in the admission of over a score of new members, and by the 1970's—following the birth of many newly sovereign states in Africa—membership in the Assembly had passed the 130 mark.

The most significant consequence of the Assembly's growing comprehensiveness has been the emergence of blocs and the development of bloc voting. The Assembly has thus tended to become one of the arenas in which the two major political struggles of our time are being waged. In fact, the Assembly has begun to take on the complexion of a multi-party system. The uneven degree of discipline within each bloc or "party" has made the picture somewhat analogous to the French Parliament under the Fourth Republic. Roughly speaking, six blocs have emerged in the Assembly: the Afro-Asian bloc (the largest but least cohesive) has at times commanded over sixty votes; the Latin American bloc has been able to muster twenty votes, the Atlantic Community eighteen, the British Commonwealth ten, and the Arab bloc ten. The most highly disciplined group has been the Communist bloc which, not including Yugoslavia, has controlled nine votes.

The vast majority of votes taken in the General Assembly have involved one or both of the two great political struggles. According to the voting rules of the General Assembly, important questions are to be decided by a two-thirds vote, and "other matters" by simple majority. In view of this fact it is clear that, under certain conditions, some blocs—singly or in combination with others—may exercise what amounts to a "collective veto" over decisions of the General Assembly. Theoretically, for instance, the Afro-Asian bloc, if united, could effectively block any important decision. In practice, however, this has not tended to occur. The Afro-Asian bloc has often been deeply divided. Also, "party discipline" has been loose and, in many instances, "crossing the floor" has become a frequent phenomenon. In this connection, it is useful to point out that in the General Asssembly—unlike a national legislature—there are not two, but three sides to a controversial question. Abstentions are freely recorded and frequently their high number has demonstrated that many nations have refused to stand up and be counted in the East-West or the colonial-anticolonial struggle.

The question of who controls the General Assembly may best be answered by looking at some important votes in the 1960's. Votes on East-West issues may be grouped into three rough categories. First, there are those in which the United States is clearly in control and only the Soviet bloc is in opposition. A resolution passed in 1962 to continue the efforts of the UN Commission for Unification and Rehabilitation of Korea (UNCURK) was a case in point. The vote was 63 in favor, 11 opposed, with 26 abstentions. On others, the United States manages to control a sizeable majority, but has to lobby intensively to attain it. Thus, in 1960 it managed to persuade most Latin American, Western European, and French-speaking African states to vote for Kasavubu rather than Lumumba to represent the government of the Congo. The vote was 53 in favor, 24 opposed, and 19 abstentions. Finally, on some crucial issues, the United States was defeated. The case *par excellence* is the issue of Chinese representation, which has come before every General Assembly since 1951. Because of its special interest, the voting pattern on this question will be analyzed in depth.

During the decade from 1951 to 1960, the issue of Chinese representation came before every Assembly under the so-called "moratorium device." Using this technique, the United States proposed each year that consideration of the question be deferred. This position was adopted by the Assembly at every session until 1960. (See Table 1.[4])

Three conclusions suggest themselves from this voting record. First, the absolute number of votes in favor of moratorium remained fairly constant during the ten years. But since the membership of the UN increased by 65 per cent during this same period, the relative number of states supporting the American position significantly declined. Second, up until 1959, the total number of votes in favor was always an absolute majority and exceeded the combined votes of those opposed, abstaining, or absent. Finally, in 1960, for the first time, the American position was in serious jeopardy when the supporters of the moratorium won by only a plurality and were in turn exceeded by the combined votes of the opposition, abstainers, and absentees.

Thus in 1961 the United States had to fight the issue on its merits

TABLE 1. General Assembly Votes on the Moratorium on Discussing Chinese Representation

Session	For	Against	Abstaining	Absent	Total
6th (1951)	37	11	4	8	60
7th (1952)	42	7	11	0	60
8th (1953)	44	10	2	4	60
9th (1954)	43	11	6	0	60
10th (1955)	42	12	6	0	60
11th (1956)	47	24	8	0	79
12th (1957)	48	27	7	0	82
13th (1958)	44	28	9	0	81
14th (1959)	44	29	9	0	82
15th (1960)	42	34	22	1	99

when the Assembly decided to consider it as an "important question." But, at the very same time, China's attack on India alienated neutralist sentiment in the United Nations. Hence during the next three years the United States was able actually to improve its position. The votes in 1961, 1962, and 1963 were 48:37:19, 56:42:12, and 57:41:12, respectively. No vote was taken in 1964. In 1965, the United States just held the line in a tie vote of 47:47:20. By 1966, the excesses of the "Cultural Revolution" on the Chinese mainland had alienated some of the Afro-Asian nations and the United States position gained again to 57:46:17. In 1967, the vote was 58:45:17, and in 1968 it was 58:44:23.

As China began to normalize her foreign relations, UN sentiment in her favor began to rise once again. The vote in 1969 was 56:48:21, and in 1970 a majority of 51 members actually voted to seat the People's Republic and to oust the Chiang Kai-shek regime, with 49 opposed and 25 abstaining. Only a previously adopted resolution that a two-thirds majority would be necessary to seat the mainland government prevented its victory that year.

The moment of truth came in 1971. The China question was being debated at the very time Presidential aide Henry Kissinger was in Peking to prepare for President Nixon's forthcoming visit to the Chinese capital. The American position at the UN reflected this shift in policy. George Bush, the United States representative, now favored the seating of the People's Republic on the Security Council but wanted to retain representation for the Chiang Kai-shek regime in the General Assembly. A majority of UN members felt otherwise. After considerable procedural wrangling, the General Assembly, in a dramatic vote taken on October 25, 1971, defeated the "important question" resolution by a majority of 59:55:17. This cleared the way to seat the representatives of the People's Republic by a simple, rather than a two-thirds majority. Such a resolution, which had in fact been sponsored by Albania for over a decade, was now passed by a large Assembly majority of 76 votes in favor, 35 against, and 17 abstentions. As of October 25, 1971, China was to be represented in all principal UN organs exclusively by the mainland government. The American honeymoon with the United Nations had definitely come to an end.

On issues of colonialism there have also been changes in voting patterns. First, the Afro-Asian members, supported by the Soviet bloc and many Latin American countries, consistently urged strong resolutions against Portugal and South Africa. At first, the United States tended to vote against such resolutions. Thus, in 1962, the Assembly, by a vote of 57 in favor, 14 opposed, and 18 abstentions, declared that Portugal's policy in Angola constituted a threat to world peace and recommended an arms embargo against the colonial power. During the same year, by a vote of 67 in favor, 16 opposed, and 23 abstentions, it condemned South Africa's racial policies and called for sanctions against the Union Government. The United States opposed both these resolutions on the grounds that the call for sanctions was ill-advised. In 1966, however, the United States supported a resolution passed by a vote of 114:2, terminating South Africa's mandate to govern Southwest Africa and declaring that the territory would henceforth be the direct responsibility of the world organization. The United States, though, was not prepared to support a resolution passed by the Assembly later establishing a special UN Council for the administration of Southwest Africa. Here it expressed its ambivalence in the form of abstention. Thus, by the late 1960's, the hard core resistance to the elimination of the vestiges of European rule from Africa was limited to the white minority regimes themselves.

At times, the East-West and colonial struggles intermesh. Such was the case in 1967 when the General Assembly met in emergency session to consider the aftermath of the Arab-Israeli war. The USSR, invoking a variant of the Uniting for Peace Resolution, had convened the session in the hope of persuading the General Assembly to embrace the Arab cause and brand Israel as an aggressor. Toward that end, the Soviet Union and the Arab states attacked Israel as a "tool of Western imperialism." The African vote, however, was deeply divided. Only about half of the pivotal African group supported a Soviet-backed resolution that would have condemned Israel and demanded her unconditional withdrawal. The other half lined up with the United States and the Latin American bloc, which sponsored a resoluton that would have linked an Israeli withdrawal to recognition of the Jewish state. Neither the United States nor the Soviet Union was able to muster a two-thirds majority for its respective position. Each superpower "neutralized" the other and thus there occurred a "jamming" of the decision-making process in the General Assembly. Half of the crucial African vote saw Israel as a protégé of Western colonialism. But the other half identified themselves with a new small nation struggling for its right to national existence. Thus, in this particular case, the anticolonial nations wrested control from the superpowers, but were unable to exercise it themselves.

An analysis of the above voting patterns demonstrates that on issues involving the East-West struggle, the United States so far has generally been able to muster majorities on matters vital to its national interest. Owing to the rise of the Afro-Asian bloc this American power is no longer automatic but has demanded increasing diplomatic and persuasive efforts. In the China vote of 1971, the United States actually found itself in the minority. In the colonial struggle the United States, owing to her tendency to abstain, has abdicated leadership in the General Assembly. The Afro-Asians are in control here, demanding rapid action. The closer they come to their goal of eliminating colonialism, the more insistent they become on erasing its last vestiges from Africa. Toward this end they are eager to push the UN's powers to their limit—and even beyond. In terms of the overall distribution of power in the General Assembly, the UN's progress toward universality has resulted in some reduction of the influence of both of the two superpowers and a corresponding net gain for the forces of the new nationalism.

Turning to the accomplishments of the General Assembly, a cross-section reveals a mixed record. It has provided opportunity for the exploration of a whole galaxy of political disputes. The forum of the Assembly has had the beneficent effect of subjecting explosive disputes to the scrutiny of world public opinion, although it has also lent itself to endless and often repetitive oratory which has frequently debased the process of deliberation. But on the whole, the Assembly has shown inventiveness and flexibility in its approach. It was able to restore the *status quo ante bellum* after the Suez crisis of 1956 and, in the process, to improvise a new instrument for policing the peace—the United Nations Emergency Force (UNEF). (For a full discussion of UNEF, see Chapter 12.)

At the same time, it found itself tragically unable to take effective action to stop the Soviet Union in Hungary in 1956 or in Czechoslovakia in 1968. Similarly it was unable to inject itself into the conflict in Vietnam. Since its sole powers were recommendatory and its only sanction that of world public opinion, it succeeded in restraining Great Britain, France, and Israel, but not the Soviet Union or the United States.

The Assembly's powerlessness to intrude into the domestic jurisdiction of states has also frequently prevented it from effective intervention in disputes. For example, the Assembly recommended in 1949 that the Soviet Union allow Soviet women who married foreigners to leave the country with their husbands. For eight years, the Soviet Union refused to heed this recommendation. Similarly, the Assembly has not been able to affect the *apartheid* policy of the government of South Africa, nor has it succeeded in changing Portugal's attitude toward her two large territories in Africa—Angola and Mozambique. On the whole, therefore, the Assembly's effectiveness in the pacific settlement of disputes has been mixed, since compliance with its recommendations has, in the last analysis, depended upon the voluntary cooperation of its members.

The work of the Assembly has not been limited merely to the handling of disputes. Great inventiveness has also been demonstrated in the area of international law-making. It was under the aegis of the General Assembly, for example, that the International Atomic Energy Agency was born. The Universal Declaration of Human Rights and the Convention on Genocide were similarly notable achievements of the General Assembly's initiative. Though the former did not become a legally binding instrument, the latter succeeded in attaining that status, albeit subject to ratification by member states. Most important, the General Assembly approved three vitally important instruments of arms control: the Outer Space Treaty of 1967; the Nuclear Non-Proliferation Treaty of 1968; and the Sea-Bed Treaty of 1971.

In addition, the General Assembly has exercised a number of important "housekeeping" responsibilities. In this capacity it has supervised the activities of the Economic and Social Council, the Trusteeship Council, and the specialized agencies. Furthermore, it has had key electoral duties. In conjunction with the Security Council, it elects the Secretary-General and the Justices of the World Court, and passes on the admission of new members. It also elects the ten nonpermanent members of the Security Council. On this last matter, feelings have often run high and "gentleman's agreements" among the competing blocs have tended to develop. The Assembly has also had the responsibility of fixing the contribution of each member state to the United Nation's budget.

The rise of the Afro-Asian bloc has brought the one nation-one vote rule under heavy fire. It has become increasingly difficult for the Great Powers, especially the United States, to accept the fact that Zambia's vote should have the same weight as that of a major power. The question has been raised whether it was resonable to expect the United States or the Soviet Union to accept decisions reached by a body in which a nation with a small and largely illiterate population and an underdeveloped economy should have the same voice as a superpower, or whether the United States, which has contributed one third of the budget, should have the same voting power as a nation with an assessment of less than 0.1 per cent. These considerations have led to many informal "weighted voting" proposals designed to bring voting power into line with the realities of political power and influence in the Assembly. These proposals have all foundered on the question of what would constitute an objective criterion for weighting. Should it be population, military strength, literacy, wealth, or other more intangible factors? Moreover, since the distribution of power among nations is in constant flux, whatever weighting was decided upon would require constant revision. For these reasons, the Assembly's system of equality has been retained despite its obvious inequities. This may, however, lead to a growing preference by the superpowers for conducting important business outside the framework of the United Nations, where they would not have to worry about the votes of uncommitted countries. In any case, it seems increasingly likely that all concerned—small powers as well as large—will have to face the fact that, in the nuclear age, voting is a poor substitute for genuine deliberation and compromise.

Perhaps the most ambitious plan of the Assembly has been the projection of its influence into territories that are quite literally uncharted. Aware that the Antarctic continent and outer space could easily become objects of the power struggle, the Assembly has moved with dispatch to provide a forum for the advancement of a novel and most important principle: that neither *terra incognita* on this planet nor in outer space should be subject to ownership or control by individual states but, instead, should be considered the domain of the international community as represented by the United Nations. The Assembly has shown wisdom by having risen to this new challenge before, rather than after, actual crises have developed. And many member states have looked with considerable favor upon the principle of United Nations jurisdiction over the fruits of man's new discoveries.

Whereas the Security Council has disappointed most of its founders, the General Assembly has, for the most part, surpassed expectations. It has demonstrated the validity of the eclectic approach to universal affairs, the method of improvising as imaginatively as possible. In most instances of Security Council failure the General Assembly has developed significant "reserve powers" with which to step into the breach. In doing so, it has developed into a formidable defender of the peace and has often exhibited truly remarkable resourcefulness and adaptability.

THE ECONOMIC AND SOCIAL COUNCIL

The framers of the United Nations Charter were profoundly impressed by the functional theory of international order-building. This conviction found its most ambitious institutional expression in the Economic and Social Council (ECOSOC). This organ was to be an instrument for coordinating an entire galaxy of functional activities, ranging from aid to needy children to technical assistance to lesser-developed areas. The common denominator of all these activities was the functional premise that the bonds of international political order could be forged more readily by first concentrating on specific common problems in the politically less formidable spheres of economic, social, and cultural affairs. It was hoped that such activities could be kept out of the arena of political controversy and that the habits of collaboration thus developed might little by little reach over into the strife-torn areas of political and even military security. In order to emphasize and facilitate this work, the Economic and Social Council became one of the principal United Nations organs.

ECOSOC was made up originally of eighteen members, elected for three years by the General Assembly. In 1966, the membership was enlarged to twenty-seven. Although the Charter contains no specific membership provisions, in practice the permanent members of the Security Council have had permanent seats on ECOSOC as well. The rest of the membership has tended to reflect the power alignments in the General Assembly, although there has been a slight imbalance in favor of the more advanced industrial states. ECOSOC is responsible to the Assembly and, in effect, has frequently served as a committee of the Assembly on functional matters. Since ECOSOC itself is not an operational organ, most of its energies have been absorbed in coordinating the numerous commissions which are under its control. There are eight such functional commissions in all. They deal with a wide variety of subject matter: transport, statistics, population, social matters, human rights and protection of minorities, status of women, commodity trade, and narcotic drugs. In addition, ECOSOC has set up a number of regional commissions: the Economic Commission for Europe (ECE) and parallel bodies for Asia and the Far East, Latin America, and Africa. There are also four special voluntary programs which depend for their support exclusively upon donations from governments and private sources: the United Nations Children's Fund (UNICEF); the United Nations Development Program (UNDP), consisting before the merger of 1966 of two separate bodies known as the Expanded Program for Technical Assistance (EPTA) and the Special Fund; the United Nations High Commissioner for Refugees (UNHCR); and the United Nations Relief and Works Agency for Palestine Refugees in the Near East (UNRWA). Finally, ECOSOC receives reports from all the specialized agencies. The difficulties in coordinating this vast array of functional bodies have therefore been enormous. In general, the job has been somewhat easier in economic than in social fields, and less trying in regional than in global matters. But ECOSOC's role as a clearinghouse for the UN's functional activities has been complicated even further through the participation in its affairs of various citizens' organizations. Among these, and enjoying consultative status in ECOSOC, have been such nongovernmental organizations as the YMCA, the YWCA, and the U.S. Chamber of Commerce.

So great has been the proliferation of functional activities under UN auspices that they virtually defy systematic analysis. Ironically, among the organs coordinated by ECOSOC there have even developed certain empire-building tendencies. In areas of overlapping activity, some agencies have claimed "sovereignty" over responsibilities to which other agencies have at the same time stoutly laid claim. And inevitably, the problem of deciding priorities is a difficult one at best. Given the inescapable realities of a limited budget, who, for example, is to determine which will be more conducive to the building of international order: the exchange of scientists or advancement in the status of women?

Perhaps the greatest of all the difficulties under which ECOSOC has labored has been that its functional organs have become embroiled in the East-West and colonial-anticolonial struggles. On the whole, it has proved impossible to insulate these organs from the storms of political controversy. The United States, which has contributed by far the largest financial share to ECOSOC's programs, has tended to be more concerned with the consolidation of its power position vis-à-vis the East than with the knitting of functional bonds between East and West. The Soviet Union has been virulent in its denunciations of "imperialist domination" of ECOSOC by the United States and has tended to follow a policy of abstention. Whenever the Soviet bloc has decided to join one of the functional organs, it has been more inclined to employ it as a platform than as a tool of community-building. The colonial struggle has also been manifest in ECOSOC. Most of the beneficiaries of ECOSOC's programming have been anticolonial powers who have been more concerned with the liquidation of colonialism than with the Western inclination to employ ECOSOC as a vehicle for winning the East-West struggle. They have also consistently demanded a more generous sharing of wealth. These developments have placed in question the validity of the functionalist thesis. Some observers have even tended to reverse the cause-and-effect sequence. Perhaps, they suggest, political harmony is not in the first instance dependent on prior economic and social cooperation. Rather, the success of functionalism itself may depend on a minimum of prior political harmony.

The ease with which the functional method may break down can be illustrated by all too many of ECOSOC's activities. One such example may be seen in what has happened with the United Nations Children's Fund (UNICEF), which was first established in 1946. The purpose of this agency was to aid needy children and adolescents in countries requiring rehabilitation. Within two years after its creation, UNICEF was in fact feeding half a million children and an equal number of mothers in Europe, the Middle East, and the Far East. Yet early in its operations, the Fund began to suffer from a chronic shortage of money. It became dependent on voluntary contributions, of which the United States paid the laregest share—over 60 per cent of the entire budget. The United States therefore soon came to wield the power of life and death over the Fund, as it did over most of ECOSOC's organs. The Soviet Union and the Eastern European countries ignored UNICEF until 1953. Only after the death of Stalin did they join and pay contributions of slightly more than 4 per cent of the total. It was clear by mid-1953 that UNICEF was not going to fail, that its popularity would increase, and that more harm to the Soviet Union would result from remaining outside than from participating. But the Communist countries largely employed UNICEF as a propaganda platform. The lion's share of financial support continued to come from the West. Millions of children were aided through UNICEF's operations and millions of mothers were saved from death. But in terms of East-West community-building the Fund's contribution has been minimal.

United Nations economic development activities are also largely coordinated through ECOSOC. The Expanded Program for Technical Assistance (EPTA) was launched in 1949 and has provided experts and equipment for the underdeveloped countries. These activities were administered by a Technical Assistance Board (TAB) composed of international officials, and the choice of EPTA projects was supervised by a Technical Assistance Committee (TAC) composed of the eighteen ECOSOC members plus six nations elected by ECOSOC from UN and specialized agency membership.

The Special Fund was set up in 1959 for the purpose of financing preparatory and "preinvestment" projects that would make it possible for technical assistance and development to yield optimum results. In keeping with its mandate, the Special Fund concentrated on relatively large projects. Its support, like that of EPTA, came exclusively from voluntary contributions. The United States was the largest donor to both EPTA and the Special Fund and consistently pledged an amount equal to 40 per cent of the total. As the UN Development Program superseded EPTA and the Special Fund, the United States became somewhat more reluctant to contribute 40 per cent, not because of any specific objections to the Program, but because of congressional pressures to reduce American contributions to the United Nations in general.

Efforts to keep the cold war out of the economic development programs have not been entirely successful. The Soviet Union at first abstained from EPTA activity, but after the death of Stalin revised its policy. Fearful of Western gains in the uncommitted countries and unwilling to concede leadership in technical assistance to the United States, the Soviet Union began to make small contributions. Although it continued to use the technical assistance agencies as propaganda forums, the Soviet bloc thus evidently saw that its interests would be served by participation rather than abstention. By following this course in EPTA, Soviet behavior in effect seemed to reverse the functionalist proposition. Rather than leading to greater political accord, the participation of the Soviet Union in joint East-West activity in economic development turned out to be inspired largely by the very lack of political accord between the Soviet Union and the United States.

The full fury of the cold war hit UN economic development programs for the first time in 1960, when Premier Fidel Castro of Cuba applied to the Special Fund for aid. Up to that time, the eighteen-member Governing Council of the Special Fund had made it a rule to keep politics out of their deliberations. Annual programs were always voted on as a package. The Soviet Union had acquiesced in projects for Formosa, South Korea, and South Vietnam, while the United States had regularly voted for projects in Communist countries like Poland and Yugoslavia. But in 1961, when the Cuban project came up for consideration before the Governing Council, the United States undertook a major diplomatic effort to stop it. In this effort it was unsuccessful. When the United States tried to round up the seven votes necessary to block the project in the eighteen-member Council, it discovered that the other members were unwilling to aid in the precedent-breaking consideration of a single project. They were afraid that this might lead the Soviet Union to force separate votes on aid to Formosa, South Korea, and South Vietnam, or Egypt on aid to Israel. There was a general concern that approval of individual projects would reintroduce political considerations and turn the Special Fund into an East-West battleground. Hence, the United States decided not to press for a vote that it could not win. In February 1963 the UN decided to go ahead with the project, a step that elicited a violent reaction in the United States Congress. Yet if the United States had pressed the issue to a showdown, it would have jeopardized a considerable number of development projects that it liked for the sake of one small one that it did not like.

Despite these disturbing incursions of the cold war into UN development activities, there has been an overall sense of remarkable progress. The General Assembly, at its sixteenth session in 1961, proclaimed a Development Decade to mobilize support for the poorer nations of the earth. A second Development Decade was announced in 1971. The UN Development Program, and the specialized agencies were seen as the chief instruments of this bold plan. What is perhaps most encouraging about the Development Program is the fact that a broad consensus exists in the United Nations on the matter of future support. No nation seriously questions its existence. The debate is over how much and how quickly it should grow. And in this debate, the vast majority of the UN membership will probably continue to support a policy of gradual expansion. In 1972, for example, the UN Development Program announced a grant of $250 million over a five-year period to assist sixteen countries in their plans for economic growth. The grants were decided by UNDP's 48-nation Governing Council and ranged from $50 million for India to $5 million each for Honduras and Costa Rica.

In December 1964, the General Assembly, prodded by the developing nations in ECOSOC, passed a resolution creating a new United Nations organ, the UN Conference on Trade and Development (UNCTAD). The main purpose of the Conference, as seen by the "Group of 77" developing nations, is to help the poor nations of the world rectify the imbalances in their international trade and thus to achieve industrialization and economic self-sufficiency. Toward that end, the Conference, which includes the entire UN membership, meets at least once every four years and its permanent organ, the Trade and Development Board, once every six months. An UNCTAD Secretariat, headed by a Secretary-General, has its headquarters in Geneva, where the first Conference convened in 1964. A second Conference took place in New Delhi in 1968 and a third in Santiago de Chile in 1972.

Thus, UNCTAD is now a regular United Nations body in which the poor regularly confront the rich and demand better terms for their economies. It has become the principal forum for negotiating commodity agreements, for example. The Conference has not remained insulated from political controversy, however. At first, the Soviet Union and the United States engaged in a kind of "aid race" for the allegiance of the poor nations, but by the 1970's the richer nations developed a tougher attitude and the aid race was gradually replaced by a silent United States-Soviet agreement not to accede to unreasonable demands. Thus, UNCTAD has highlighted the political patterns that link the East-West struggle with that of the world's poor for their place in the sun.

In 1966, the General Assembly established yet another UN organ, The United Nations Industrial Development Organization (UNIDO), with headquarters in Vienna. The structure of UNIDO was patterned on the precedent of UNCTAD and its major purpose was to promote the industrial growth of the developing nations.

The birth process of the Universal Declaration of Human Rights provides another interesting case study in functionalism as an approach to international problems. In 1946 ECOSOC directed its Commission on Human Rights to draft a Declaration on this subject. However, serious differences of opinion became evident at the very outset. The United States favored a document setting forth goals and aspirations rather than legally binding commitments. It preferred to emphasize the primacy of civil rights and political liberties. The British, on the other hand, favored a legally binding document. The Soviet Union, for its part, was unwilling to commit itself to a treaty and defended the inclusion of economic and social rights in its version of desirable goals and aspirations. Finally, the anticolonial powers agreed with this more inclusive definition of human rights but also wanted definite legal commitments. Because of these wide differences, the negotiators were unable to agree on a statement of human rights that would be binding on all. Instead, it was decided to draw up a hortatory statement of general principles that would include the aspirations of all members. What this meant, of course, was that functional cooperation was possible only by defining the function to be performed in the most general terms and only by not making the end result binding on any state. Nevertheless, when on December 10, 1948, the General Assembly adopted the Declaration without a single negative vote, it had approved the first international statement of human rights in history. Most members of ECOSOC found the Declaration so encouraging that they sought to use it as a precedent for the drafting of a legally binding Covenant on Human Rights. These efforts encountered great difficulties. The Human Rights Commission attempted to overcome these obstacles by drafting two Covenants, one on civil and political rights, the other on economic, social, and cultural rights. But even though the General Assembly approved the two Covenants, states were still unwilling to ratify and thus commit themselves to legally binding instruments. Human rights were simply too vitally political to lend themselves to the functional approach.

Though the manifold activities taking place under the roof of ECOSOC have been impressive, they have not demonstrated the functional method of working toward international order to be nearly as effective as was originally hoped. Certainly, the East-West struggle has not abated significantly as a result of the existence of the UN's functional programs. On the contrary, it has appeared more and more likely that for the functional method really to work, there is first needed a relatively favorable political climate. At any rate, there clearly seems little causal connection between the launching of global economic, social, and cultural programs and the achievement of universal political order.

The fact remains, however, that the profound original commitment to functional cooperation has resulted in a tremendous growth of such activities under the supervision of ECOSOC. Indeed, the work of the functional agencies has absorbed more and more of the United Nations' energies. ECOSOC has never enjoyed the publicity given the Security Council in its early years. Nor has it commanded the prestige more recently enjoyed by the General Assembly. Yet in the number and scope of the activities under its auspices, ECOSOC's importance in the United Nations would be hard to exaggerate. None of its activities, it is true, has vindicated the claims that were at first made for the functional method. Yet few objective observers would deny the beneficent and humanitarian effects of ECOSOC's work.

THE TRUSTEESHIP SYSTEM

The concept of Trusteeship was devised by the United Nations' founders primarily as a weapon against the struggle they anticipated over the liquidation of colonialism. If only the United Nations could turn the colonies from lucrative benefits into "sacred trusts," the quest for dependencies might die from lack of incentive. Colonial powers might develop greater inhibitions in their quest for colonies, and anticolonial powers greater patience in their struggle for independence. If, indeed, colonialism was a cause of war, then the United Nations should make as international as possible the administration of dependent areas and the process by which their colonial status finally came to be terminated. This, in general terms, was the thinking that underlay the concept of Trusteeship.

In setting up the Trusteeship System, the UN founders were able to build on the precedent of the Mandate System of the League of Nations. While the League's Mandate System had in essence been a thinly disguised technique of annexation, with its Permanent Mandates Commission controlled exclusively by colonial powers, it nevertheless represented a first tentative attempt at internationalization. The United Nations' framers were determined to expand this experiment considerably. Their first step was to dispose of the mandates that had been held by the now-defunct League System. For the most part, these were immediately turned into Trusteeships of the United Nations. Excepted from this transfer, however, were the former Middle Eastern Mandates—Syria, Lebanon, Jordan, and Israel—which were soon to achieve national independence; Southwest Africa, which was lost to the United Nations because of the stubborn refusal of the Union of South Africa to permit it to be placed under Trusteeship; Japan's Pacific holdings, which were taken over as a so-called Strategic Trust Territory by the United States; and Somaliland, which had not been a League Mandate and which was entrusted to Italy. Beyond these changes, the Trusteeship System continued very much in the footsteps of the League. Britain was to administer Tanganyika and parts of Togoland and the Cameroons; the remainder of Togoland and the Cameroons remained under France; Ruanda-Urundi continued as a Belgian Trust; to Australia were entrusted Nauru and New Guinea; and New Zealand was to administer Western Samoa. In all, the Trusteeship Council was thus to supervise eleven Trust Territories, seven of them in Africa, and a total population of fifteen million people.

The most radical departure from the League precedent was the widespread conviction among UN members that administration not only of Trust Territories but of *all* colonial possessions should be internationalized. This principle became the subject of heated controversy. The colonial powers insisted that the colonial possessions were to be under their jurisdiction exclusively, whereas the anticolonial bloc saw no further justification for the continuation of colonialism at all. The outcome of this struggle was Chapter XI of the Charter, The Declaration Regarding Non-Self-Governing Territories, which represented a modest triumph for the forces of anticolonialism. For one thing, the United Nations was no longer to use the term "colony." In its place was to be substituted the more innocuous phrase "Non-Self-Governing Territory." In addition, the colonial powers committed themselves to transmit information on economic, educational, and social conditions in their respective dependencies. The new nations pressed for the submission of political information as well, but the colonial powers insisted that this matter be left to their own discretion. Thus, when the new trusteeship system was launched, it was not only responsible for the administration of eleven Trust Territories but also, for the first time in history, possessed the power of imposing a minimum of international control over all colonies.

In composition, the Trusteeship Council was originally a fourteen-nation body, with its membership divided equally between colonial and anticolonial powers, or in United Nations terminology, "administering" and "nonadministering" powers. Australia, Belgium, France, Italy, Great Britain, New Zealand, and the United States represented the first group. The Soviet Union and China plus five other nonadministering powers made up the anticolonial bloc. As a result of the liquidation of two thirds of the Trust Territories, the size of the Trusteeship Council has diminished considerably. Belgium, France, and Italy are no longer administering powers. The transition from Trusteeship status to independence has, on the whole, been orderly. The exodus began in 1960 with the granting of independence to Cameroon, Togo, and Somalia. Tanganyika was next, receiving independence in 1961. On January 1, 1962, Western Samoa became the first independent Polynesian state and on the same day the Belgian Trust, Ruanda-Urundi, was transformed into two independent countries, Rwanda and Burundi. After 1962 only Nauru, New Guinea, and the Pacific Islands remained under the authority of the Trusteeship Council.

Each of the Trust Territories was administered under a Trusteeship Agreement. These Agreements were concluded between the administering powers and the United Nations, but in most cases the former were able to determine the nature of the Agreement. The United States, for example, insisted that the Pacific Islands be made into a "Strategic Trust Territory" under the Security Council, and therefore subject to American veto. The terms of the Agreements were approved by the General Assembly, to which the Trusteeship Council has been responsible on all important matters. Like ECOSOC, the Council has, in effect,

become a committee of the Assembly. Owing to the stronger representation of the colonial powers on the Trusteeship Council, its recommendations—especially those dealing with advancement toward self-government in the Trust Territories—have at times been criticized by the
General Assembly as lacking in vigor. Responsibility for the supervision
of Non-Self-Governing Territories, under Chapter XI of the Charter,
has not been exercised by the Trusteeship Council itself but by a
separate body, the Committee on Information from Non-Self-Governing
Territories. The membership of that Committee has been patterned
after that of the Council.

Where the Trusteeship Council was directly involved in its dealings
with the Trust Territories, its responsibilities were threefold: preparation of annual reports, examinations of petitions, and dispatch of
visiting missions. Annual reports were based on lengthy written ques-
tionnaires, to be completed by the administering powers. If the replies
seemed incomplete or unsatisfactory, the Trusteeship Council had the
right to proceed to written and oral cross-examination. On the basis of
these reports, the Council then formulated its own recommendations for
the General Assembly. These recommendations were far-reaching and
related to economic development, health services, educational facilities,
labor conditions, and the participation of the indigenous population in
the affairs of government. The Trusteeship Council also permitted the
inhabitants of Trust Territories to submit petitions on specific griev-
ances. This procedure was a radical departure from the League
precedent, since it by-passed the colonial power and established direct
contact between the Trust and the United Nations. At first this
opportunity was utilized infrequently but during and since the 1950's
the number of petitions grew considerably. A typical petition brought
before the Trusteeship Council concerned the fate of the Ewe tribe in
West Africa, who claimed that the boundary line between French and
British Togoland divided their people. The following excerpt will
convey its flavor:

> About 2 years ago both french and british government promised to have constituted a
> conventional zone for the amendment of the frontiers regulations, amidst the Ewe people.
> This problem is very hard to be solved, because it is impossible for two person to wear one
> trousers. Only their guilty conscience forced them to make this promise, but in reality they
> are unfit to complete this task just like two persons suggesting of wearing one trousers.
> Therefore we beg to have explained the things to the general assembly of the UNO
> properly; in order to have considered or rescue from this cruelty in due time.[5]

On the whole, the Trusteeship Council took such petitions very
seriously. The Council's most effective device was the visiting mission.
Every three years the Council dispatched missions to each of its
Territories. These ventures were not only of great symbolic value but
had the great advantage of actual contact with the populations of the

Territories. At times there was friction between the visiting missions and the administering powers over the tempo of advancement toward self-government. This was not surprising, since the visiting missions were generally most interested in how quickly the administering powers were eliminating themselves, whereas the latter tended to regard the Trusts as quasi-colonies. But most of these tensions were fruitful and yielded worthwhile results.

While the Trusteeship Council has been a notable success, as its overall record indicates, it has not always been able to remove the Trust Territories from the colonial power struggle. Libya, for example, became the subject of a heated political controversy among several powers eager to administer it as a Trust. Since no solution satisfactory to all seemed possible, Libya was granted her independence. This was a case in which the necessity for Trusteeship was clearly apparent but in which, owing to the disagreement of the powers concerned, it could not be worked out in practice. Of the consequences of this fact for Libya itself, Inis L. Claude, Jr., has written that ". . . in terms of the objective of the rational and orderly liquidation of colonialism, the excessive prolongation of dependence [was] hardly more unfortunate than the premature conferment of independence."[6]

In a general analysis of the United Nations Trusteeship System, several factors emerge. For one thing, while the System has had little effect on the rate at which colonies have been liquidated, it has contributed considerably to making their liquidation more *responsible*. Moreover, in view of the fact that most of the Trust Territories have already received independence, the Trusteeship Council may soon find itself without a function. Of course, a liberal interpretation of the Charter would open the possibility of bringing new Trusts under the Council's responsibility. There are still a few colonies, particularly Portuguese and South African, which might be possible candidates, although the political atmosphere in the General Assembly strongly favors immediate independence without an intermediate stage.

Yet, in these cases, Trusteeship might become a vital stage between colonial status and independence, a bridge which the United Nations might help to build. Quite possibly, some of the turmoil in the Belgian Congo in 1960 might have been avoided if the Congo had passed through a Trusteeship stage. Such a policy would, of course, necessitate some modification in the thinking of the General Assembly, but the tragic outbreaks of violence shortly after Congolese independence have demonstrated that Trusteeship might well have been a blessing for colonial and anticolonial powers alike.

Perhaps the most significant feature of the Trusteeship System has been its prophylactic quality. It has belied the facile assumption that the United Nations has been ineffective because of its inability to enforce decisions. Trusteeship has proved that effectiveness without sanctions is possible. As Claude has pointed out, it has attempted to deal with a situation *before* rather than *after* it reached the crisis stage.[7] In the Congo the United Nations was compelled to create a kind of Trusteeship after the crisis had become acute. The extension of the Trusteeship System to the more explosive of the remaining colonies might forestall repetitions of such crises and, thereby, contribute to a more rational solution of the colonial problem as a whole.

In the general struggle over the liquidation of colonialism, the Trusteeship System has played a significant, but not decisive, role. More recently, with the influx of new African and Asian members into the United Nations, the General Assembly's Trusteeship Committee has dealt more with the decolonization problems of South Africa and the Portuguese possessions than with the problems of the three remaining Trust Territories. The original concept of the Trusteeship System—to prepare the Territories for independence with all deliberate speed—has been expanded by the General Assembly to apply to *all* colonial possessions via the Declaration Regarding Non-Self-Governing Territories. On the whole, the United Nations institutions set up to deal with problems of colonialism have been successfully used by the anticolonial majority of the General Assembly in its relentless drive toward full self-determination for all dependent peoples.

THE SECRETARY-GENERAL AND THE SECRETARIAT

One of the greatest fears of the founders of the United Nations was that the new world organization would be no more than the sum of its parts—a group of delegates each loyal to his own nation and perceiving the world through the particular lenses of his own nationality. The men at San Francisco were deeply convinced that one important road to international order could be constructed by providing the United Nations with a nucleus of men and women who, for the duration of their tenure as world civil servants, would place loyalty to the world community on an equal level with their other, more parochial commitments. It was this notion of international loyalty-building that provided the basis for the Office of the Secretary-General and of his staff, the United Nations Secretariat.

The Office of the Secretary-General of the United Nations is not without precedent. The League of Nations had also made provision for such a post. Its first incumbent, Sir Eric Drummond, a British civil servant, was primarily an administrator who made it his policy to remain aloof from the political disputes that were sapping the life-blood of the League. Albert Thomas, on the other hand, the Director-General of the League's International Labor Organization, set quite another precedent. Not content with anonymous administrative responsibilities, he ventured into the uncharted land of international statesmanship and did not shrink from taking a stand on controversial policy issues. Weighing these two precedents and tending to prefer the latter, the UN architects endowed the Office of the United Nations Secretary-General with political as well as administrative powers. The Secretary-General was not only to be the chief administrative officer of the United Nations, but, in the words of the Preparatory Commission in 1945, his Office was to represent

A quite special right which goes beyond any power previously accorded to the head of an international organization. The Secretary-General more than anyone else will stand for the United Nations as a whole. In the eyes of the world, no less than in the eyes of his own staff he must embody the ideals and principles of the Charter.[8]

This conception of the Office led to the inclusion in the Charter of Article 99, which set forth the Secretary-General's significant political powers: "The Secretary-General may bring to the attention of the Security Council any matter which in his opinion may threaten the maintenance of international peace and security." The founders of the UN thus clearly intended the Secretary-General to be an international statesman, a kind of conscience of the world. In order to equip him adequately for this role, they gave him what, in some respects at least, amounted almost to the power of acting as a twelfth member of the Security Council.

The first incumbent of the Office was Trygve Lie of Norway. Lie used his political powers abundantly and frequently took positions in the conflicts among the major powers. In the early years he tended to stay aloof from the most inflammable issues of the East-West struggle but defended the interest of the world community as he conceived it by taking stands on minor political disputes. He supported the European Recovery Program and opted in favor of the partition of Palestine. Soon thereafter, however, he became embroiled in political controversies of the first magnitude. Early in 1950 Mr. Lie advocated the seating of the Chinese Communist delegation in the United Nations and provoked the extreme displeasure of the United States. Several weeks later he strongly supported American initiative in the "police action" to repel aggression by North Korea, and went so far as to label the North Koreans as the aggressors. While this action reconciled the United States, it provoked the implacable hostility of the Soviet Union. When, in late 1950, the question of Lie's reappointment came up, the United States threatened to veto the appointment of any other candidate, while the Soviet Union declared with equal conviction that it would not tolerate him. The United States prevailed upon the General Assembly to "extend" his term, but the value of Trygve Lie as peacemaker between East and West was irretrievably impaired. In November 1952, after two years of fruitless bickering, Lie resigned from the post of Secretary-General.

The experience of Trygve Lie pointed up the great dilemma, if not the inherent contradiction, of international statesmanship. The Secretary-General, to be an effective spokesman for the interests of the world community, must at times take a stand on major current political issues. But he also has to retain the confidence of all the actors in the drama. The utmost diplomatic skill and political sensitivity are needed for this task. Lie, for example, never violated the Charter. He took positions on both sides of the East-West struggle and became the object of severe criticism by both antagonists. But whereas one was willing to forgive, the other thought he had gone too far. Hence his effectiveness as a possible bridge-builder was ended.

These lessons were not lost on Trygve Lie's successor, Dag Hammarskjöld of Sweden. Hammarskjöld had been an economist and chairman of the Swedish National Bank as well as Deputy Minister for Foreign Affairs. He had never been a member of a political party and was known to have a "passion for anonymity." By background he was a civil servant, not a politician. Not surprisingly, therefore, the new Secretary-General approached his Office with somewhat greater restraint than had his predecessor. Unlike Lie, Hammarskjöld at first chose not to take overt political initiative. Public diplomacy was replaced by "quiet diplomacy." This is not to say that the increasing ferocity of the two great international political struggles left the new Secretary-General untouched. But Mr. Hammarskjöld's approach to political disputes differed in two important respects from that of his predecessor. First, he always attempted to gain authority for his actions from the Security Council or the General Assembly. Second, most of his diplomatic maneuvers were carried on behind the scenes, away from the searchlight of publicity. The former habit gained him the confidence of the major powers, while the latter made possible agreements without serious loss of face for any nation. A survey of Mr. Hammarskjöld's major activities in this respect is quite revealing.

In 1954 the Secretary-General flew to Peking to negotiate the release of eleven American airmen who were interned there as United Nations personnel. Virtually no publicity was released about the trip, but a year later the airmen were released. In 1956, during the Suez crisis, the Secretary-General was confronted with an international problem of the first magnitude. Two permanent members of the Security Council were accused of military aggression and a third, the Soviet Union, threatened them with rocket bombardment. In addition, the Arab states and Israel seemed locked in mortal combat. Mr. Hammarskjöld, under the authority of the General Assembly, equipped the United Nations with an unprecedented military instrument, the United Nations Emergency Force (UNEF), which helped to restore order to the troubled area. (For a more detailed analysis of UNEF, see Chapter 12.) By taking this action, the Secretary-General became deeply involved in the political drama being acted out in the Middle East. But as always, his decisiveness was tempered with circumspection. Mr. Hammarskjöld's declaration before the Security Council, when that body met to consider the Middle Eastern crisis, is worth quoting:

The Principles of the Charter are, by far, greater than the Organization in which they are embodied, and the aims which they are to safeguard are holier than the policies of any single nation or people. As a servant of the Organization, the Secretary-General has the duty to maintain his usefulness by avoiding public stands on conflicts between Member Nations unless and until such an action might help to resolve the conflict. However, the discretion and impartiality thus imposed on the Secretary-General by the character of his immediate task may not degenerate into a policy of expediency. He must also be a servant of the principles of the Charter, and its aims must ultimately determine what for him is right and wrong. For that he must stand. A Secretary-General cannot serve on any other assumption than that—within the necessary limits of human frailty and honest differences of opinion—all Member Nations honour their pledge to observe all Articles of the Charter. He should also be able to assume that those organs which are charged with the task of upholding the Charter will be in the position to fulfill their task.

The bearing of what I have just said must be obvious to all without any elaboration from my side. Were the Members to consider that another view of the duties of the Secretary-General than the one here stated would better serve the interests of the Organization it is their obvious right to act accordingly.[9]

This declaration, expressing Mr. Hammarskjöld's conception of his Office, not only won him the Council's confidence during the Suez crisis but also resulted in his unanimous election to a second five-year term of Office. This second term, moreover, was marked by a growing tendency in both the General Assembly and the Security Council to grant the Secretary-General broad powers for the exercise of his "quiet diplomacy." The Assembly requested Mr. Hammarskjöld to facilitate the withdrawal of foreign troops during the Lebanese crisis in 1958. In 1960, when racial violence in the Union of South Africa convened the Security Council in an emergency session, a strong resolution against the Union government would have produced a British or French veto whereas a weak resolution might have provoked a Soviet veto. But East and West and colonial and anticolonial governments alike were able to agree on a mild resolution requesting the Secretary-General to use his good offices with the Union government in order to ameliorate racial tensions.

In mid-1960, when the Belgian withdrawal from the Congo left the new republic strife-torn and threatened by Great Power intervention on the model of the Spanish Civil War, the talents of the Secretary-General were called upon once more. Acting under the authority of the Security Council, he organized a United Nations Force, excluding the Great Powers, which was to restore peace and order in the Congo until responsible self-government could be established. When the Congo was threatened by civil war through the secession of the province of Katanga, Mr. Hammarskjöld—again after securing Security Council authorization—entered Katanga at the head of the United Nations Force to prevent a major conflagration. By this time, the Secretary-General had won the respect of most observers and had established the unique political value and significance of his Office. As James Reston put it in August 1960:

In the present state of diplomatic relations between East and West, it is unlikely that agreement could have been reached between Washington and Moscow on what should be done [in the Congo]. But in the all-night debate both the United States and the Soviet Union were able to agree, as they have had to do in several crises in the past, to trust in the intervention of the U.N. Secretary-General, Dag Hammarskjöld.

This remarkable man is proving to be one of the great natural resources in the world today, and it is difficult to think of another in the field of world diplomacy who could do the job as well.

He is tireless. He is infinitely patient. He is sensitive to the slightest troublesome breeze in the world. He knows exactly what his job will let him do and forbid him from doing. And he knows when to be ambiguous; he also knows when to be precise.

When he said that the Congo was "a question of peace or war," the Security Council paid attention, because he does not use three-letter words often or carelessly.

That he has exercised these powers with such skill as to win the respect, if not the affection, of the contending states is one reason why the U.N. is now a refuge for common sense in a satanic world.[10]

As the Congo crisis developed further, however, Hammarskjöld began to run into major difficulties. Though ordered to do so by Patrice Lumumba, the deposed Premier of the fledgling republic, he refused to withdraw the United Nations Peace Force. He maintained that Lumumba did not speak for the Congo and that it was necessary for the Force to remain until peace and order were restored. This action resulted in a vehement attack on the Secretary-General by the Soviet Union, which had supported Lumumba in the Congolese power struggle. Disappointed by its setback in the Congo, the Soviet Union now accused the Secretary-General of having exceeded his authority. At the Fifteenth General Assembly, Premier Khrushchev violently attacked Mr. Hammarskjöld, demanded that his Office be abolished, and proposed that in his place there ought to be a three-man committee representing the Communist bloc, the Western bloc, and the uncommitted countries. The Secretary-General refused to resign and stated that he was no longer deferring primarily to the Great Powers—a radical shift from his position during the Suez crisis. His position was firm and clear: "I would rather see that Office (the Secretary-Generalship) break on strict adherence to the principle of independence, impartiality and objectivity than drift on the basis of compromise."[11]

The Assembly affirmed his stand by a resounding vote of confidence of 70 to 0 with the nine Soviet bloc countries, the Union of South Africa and France abstaining. While it thus seemed clear that the Soviet triumvirate proposal would not be adopted, two other suggestions were made, both with a view to curtailing the Secretary-General's powers.

Premier Nkrumah of Ghana offered a plan to equip the Secretary-General with three deputies, chosen from the East, West, and neutralist blocs, each with "clearly defined authority" in United Nations affairs. And Prime Minister Nehru of India proposed an advisory committee from different geographical areas, a sort of inner cabinet whose views and perhaps even approval would have to be sought on any important matters.

The tragic death of Dag Hammarskjöld on the eve of the opening of the Sixteenth General Assembly caused great anxiety, since the Soviet Union had a veto over the election of a successor. Actually, the Soviet leadership was quite aware that it could not get the "troika" plan through the Assembly, but hopeful that it would be able to effect a drastic cutback in the power of the Office. The United States attempted to rally the General Assembly behind its view that the Secretary-General's authority must not be compromised and that a single person be named in an acting capacity until a new Secretary-General could be elected. President Kennedy expressed this view forcefully before the assembly:

However difficult it may be to fill Mr. Hammarskjöld's place, it can better be filled by one man rather than by three. Even the three horses of the troika did not have three drivers, all going in different directions. They had only one, and so must the United Nations executive. To install a triumvirate, or any rotating authority, in the United Nations administrative offices would replace order with anarchy, action with paralysis, and confidence with confusion.[12]

A number of Soviet attempts to get support for a "troika" at the under-secretary level were unsuccessful and, on November 3, 1961, the General Assembly upon recommendation of the Security Council unanimously named U Thant of Burma Acting Secretary-General for the remainder of Dag Hammarskjöld's term.

This decision postponed the "troika" issue until April 10, 1963, when Hammarskjöld's term of office was to expire. But Soviet reservations about U Thant were apparently dispelled by his conciliatory mediation during the Cuban crisis of 1962, and he was elected to a full term, retroactive, according to his own wish, to his designation as Acting Secretary-General. The Office itself had now moved eastward from Trygve Lie of Norway, a NATO country, and Hammarskjöld of neutral Sweden, to a citizen of a neutralist country in Asia.

U Thant, though very different in background and training from his predecessor, nevertheless introduced no sharp changes in policy. Most of his energies at first were taken up with the continuing crisis in the Congo and the looming threat of bankruptcy which the Organization faced as a result of having mounted two major peace-keeping operations. Still as Acting Secretary-General he played a major role in the establishment of the UN Temporary Executive Authority (UNTEA), which supervised the transfer of West New Guinea from the Netherlands to Indonesia. And in 1964 he met a major challenge when called upon to put together a UN peace force to keep apart the warring factions on Cyprus and to prepare the way for a more fundamental solution for the problems of that tormented island.

In 1966, U Thant was elected unanimously to another five-year term. He accepted reluctantly, and only after great pressure had been put on him by many Member States, both large and small. The continuing escalation of the war in Vietnam and his own inability to bring the combatants to the negotiating table gnawed at him. Moreover, he had been unable to improve substantially the finances of the Organization. In 1967, acceding to the demand of Egypt's President Nasser, he decided to withdraw the UN Emergency Force from the Middle East, where it had been stationed for more than a decade. Though political controversies continued to surround him, he nevertheless continued to enjoy the support of most of the membership. Whatever opposition there was remained fairly passive and never reached the vehemence of the attacks that had been made upon his two predecessors. In 1971, after two full terms in office, U Thant retired from his post, the first Secretary-General to do so with the blessing of most members, whether large or small. His successor was an Austrian, Kurt Waldheim.

The election of the fourth Secretary-General was particularly significant because it coincided almost exactly with the seating of the People's Republic of China in the United Nations. Despite Cassandra-like predictions emanating from many quarters that the Chinese would make difficulties, none occurred. Mr. Waldheim received the support of the five permanent members, which made his election unanimous. During the first year of his tenure, the new Secretary-General already displayed considerable initiative. He offered the UN's good offices in the settlement of the Vietnam conflict, traveled to numerous countries on a variety of missions and worked tirelessly to put the UN's financial house in order. In 1972, after Palestinian guerrillas murdered eleven Israeli athletes at the Munich Olympics, he took the initiative in asking the General Assembly to discuss the problem of terrorism on an international scale. Already quite early in his administration it seemed that he would try to be an activist Secretary-General, but also do his best not to antagonize any of the major powers. This was a difficult task since Mr. Waldheim's constituency was both larger and more complicated than that of each of his three predecessors.

In a general evaluation of the Secretary-Generalship, it is probably fair to say, as did Trygve Lie upon looking backward on his experience, that the Office is "in many ways . . . far ahead of our times."[13] And always, it remains beset by an unavoidable dilemma. If, in the fulfillment of his duties, the Secretary-General speaks out too loudly, he will incur the wrath of one or more of the Great Powers and thus doom himself to inefficacy. Yet if he refuses to speak out at all, he dooms himself to sterility. To live under the strains of this dilemma and play the most forceful possible part in the work of the United Nations in spite of it requires a most gifted and unusual man.

If the Secretary-General is the world's chief civil servant, the United Nations Secretariat is its international civil service. This international staff has not limited its activities solely to United Nations Headquarters in New York City. Each of the autonomous specialized agencies in the United Nations family has its own Director-General and secretariat. The functions of the various levels of the Secretariat have been largely of a "housekeeping" nature. The Secretariat's responsibilities have been legion and have included the planning of conferences, the gathering of information, interpreting, and the publication of a yearbook. In all these activities the international civil servant must demonstrate scrupulous objectivity in order not to antagonize any member government. Employment policy for members of the Secretariat was laid down in Article 101 of the Charter:

The paramount consideration in the employment of the staff and in the determination of the conditions of service shall be the necessity of securing the highest standards of efficiency, competence, and integrity. Due regard shall be paid to the importance of recruiting the staff on as wide a geographical basis as possible.

It was hoped to combine the principles of merit and geography. While competence should be the main criterion, a truly international service could not be indifferent to considerations of nationality. But once a national of a member state had joined the Secretariat he was expected to take an oath of allegiance to the United Nations and not to accept instructions from any government. In other words, during the time of his tenure the world civil servant—like his chief, the Secretary-General— was expected to contribute to international order-building by developing a loyalty to the world community.

The potential and at times actual conflict between the demands of a national and a world outlook have frequently placed a great strain on members of the Secretariat and on the Secretary-General. A principal source of that strain was the United States government which, in the early 1950's, subjected American members of the Secretariat to intensive loyalty investigations. Although not a single member was convicted, large sections of the American public began to regard the Secretariat as a sanctuary for American Communists and saboteurs. The United States government exerted great pressure on Trgyve Lie to dismiss those American members of his staff who had been accused of disloyalty to the United States. The Secretary-General faced a formidable dilemma: if he acceded to the American demands, he would impugn the integrity of the international civil service; if he refused, he ran the risk of alienating a government without whose support the United Nations could hardly continue to exist. In his plight, he asked the opinion of a special committee of legal advisors. This group suggested that membership in the Secretariat in no way abrogated the loyalty a person owed to the state of which he was a citizen, and that, therefore, Lie was justified in dismissing "disloyal" Americans. Accordingly, nine American members of the Secretariat with permanent contracts who had refused to answer questions of investigating committees or had invoked the Constitutional privilege of silence were dismissed from active service. One year later, however, an Administrative Tribunal of the United Nations ruled that the dismissed employees were entitled to compensation. The General Assembly—over American opposition—voted to make amends after having requested an advisory opinion of the World Court, which supported the view of the Administrative Tribunal. Nevertheless, the U.S. Congress, in a concurrent resolution, declared that no American funds paid to the UN could be used to pay compensation to the dismissed UN officials.[14]

This episode demonstrated that in a conflict between national and world loyalty in the Secretariat, the national probably remains paramount. This is further borne out by the fact that in early 1961, the Soviet Union extended its critique of the Secretary-General to the Secretariat and demanded that the entire staff be reorganized on the basis of equal representation for "the three main groups of states—socialist, neutralist, and Western." Thus, until the international civil service can ask for and find in its members unreserved world loyalty, the Secretariat member must continue to reconcile his national and international allegiances as best he can. That a fruitful synthesis between national and world loyalty is indeed possible has been demonstrated in a classical statement by C. Wilfred Jenks, one of the early pioneers of a global civil service:

A lack of attachment to any one country does not constitute an international outlook. A superior indifference to the emotions and prejudices of those whose world is bounded by the frontiers of a single state does not constitute an international outlook. A blurred indistinctness of attitude toward all questions, proceeding from a freedom of prejudice born of lack of vitality, does not constitute an international outlook. The international outlook required of the international civil servant is an awareness made instinctive by habit of the needs, emotions, and prejudices of the peoples of differently-circumstanced countries, as they are felt and expressed by the peoples concerned, accompanied by a capacity for weighing these frequently imponderable elements in a judicial manner before reaching any decision to which they are relevant.[15]

It could justly be said of the United Nations civil service that seldom has so much been done for so many by so few. In New York, Rome, Paris, Geneva, and Vienna, there have emerged small but compact nuclei of a nascent world loyalty. They have often been threatened with disintegration but have always managed somehow to survive.

"It may be true," said Dag Hammarskjöld shortly before he died, "that in a very deep human sense there is no neutral individual, because everyone, if he is worth anything, has to have his ideas and ideals. . . . But what I do claim is that even a man who is in that sense not neutral can very well undertake and carry through neutral actions because that is an act of integrity."[16] This statement, which was made in response to Premier Khrushchev's blunt assertion that no man could be neutral, probably best expresses the philosophical conception of the international civil service.

CASE STUDY: THE UNITED NATIONS CONFERENCE ON THE HUMAN ENVIRONMENT

In June 1972, about 1200 delegates from 114 nations met for two weeks in Stockholm, Sweden, in order to produce a framework for international action to halt the deterioration of the environment and to conserve the earth's dwindling resources. The UN Conference had been four years in the making and was initiated by a 1968 resolution of the General Assembly, originally proposed by the government of Sweden. It was to be man's first global attack on the deepening environmental crisis, and it was mounted under the aegis of the United Nations.

Man has always lived in two worlds: the "biosphere," which is the world of natural things from which he draws his physical existence and the "technosphere," the world of tools and artifacts, of social and political institutions which he forged for himself. For centuries, the planet's fields and forests, its reserves of fertile soil and minerals, its oceans and rivers could carry without strain the entire freight of man's technological inventions and desires. In the last few decades, however, and with explosively increasing force in the last few years, the balance between the planet's biosphere and the technosphere has been critically affected. Man no longer lives almost overwhelmed by the scale of his environment. It is the environment that is beginning to be overwhelmed by man. At stake is nothing less than the quality of life on this planet.

From its inception the United Nations has been concerned about the quality of life for the peoples of the world, and its involvement with environmental issues dates back to the 1949 International Technical Conference on Conservation. The Stockholm Conference of 1972 was convened under UN auspices because the UN alone had the worldwide system through which an essentially cooperative and international response to the global challenge could be launched. It also provided a forum in which industrialized and developing countries could most easily meet to discuss and devise joint policies for development which would enhance, rather than injure, the shared biosphere. And finally the UN, as a continuing body, could set in motion a whole range of actions without which fragmentation and disunity would continue to mark man's approach to his global environment.

Under the leadership of Maurice F. Strong, the Secretary-General of the Conference, the delegates debated multiple aspects of a single theme: How should man control his growth to save the planet earth?

At one end of the spectrum were the advocates of a "zero-growth" world, one in which the current progressive deterioration of the environment, degrading the quality of the world's air, land, and water, would be virtually brought to a halt. It would be a world in which population would be stabilized and the consumption of raw materials held to a level not substantially greater than the production of such materials. Energy use would be compatible with the planet's long-term reserves of nuclear and fossil fuels. Those supporting this view believed that social chaos and major wars would erupt over access to the world's depleting resources unless the industrialized countries decided to arrest their heedless growth.

At the other extreme were those—largely the developing countries—who saw no need in the foreseeable future to alter the emphasis on growth. They contended that a zero-growth world would lead to the destruction of the world's economies, which must expand in order to prosper.

In this tug-of-war between "environmentalists" and "developmentalists" Secretary-General Strong took a middle course. "No growth is not a viable policy for any society today," he said. "indeed, people must have access to more, not fewer, opportunities to express their creative drives. But these can only be provided within a total system in which man's activities are in dynamic harmony with the natural order." "To achieve this," he added, "we must rethink our concepts of the basic purposes of growth. Surely we must see it in terms of enriching the lives and enlarging the opportunities of all mankind. And if this is so, it follows that it is the more wealthy societies—the privileged minority of mankind—which will have to make the most profound, even revolutionary, changes in attitudes and values."[17]

Mr. Strong's carefully charted middle course between the advocates of development and the defenders of the environment avoided a confrontation between the have and the have-not nations at the Conference. The latter feared that if the advanced countries set high environmental standards for their imports, this would seriously damage the export capabilities of poorer nations. Brazil, for example, asked to be compensated for building environmental protection devices into its new automobile plants. Lurking in the background was the suspicion of "third world" nations that the industrial countries might set limits on international pollution that would inhibit the poor nations' uphill fight toward industrialization.

The tension between the rich and the poor overshadowed the usual manifestations of the East-West struggle. The Soviet Union boycotted the Conference because East Germany was denied full participation.

China, however, was in attendance and cast her lot squarely with the have-not nations. In addition, China mounted an attack on the United States for "wanton bombing" in Vietnam. The Chinese delegate also demanded "reparation payments" from the United States and other industrialized nations. He insisted that, since the advanced countries were responsible for the largest amounts of environmental pollution to date, they owed the developing countries both reparations and assistance in development. The Chinese delegate made a major bid for the leadership of the have-not nations when he exclaimed: "We must not give up eating for fear of choking." Since the poor outnumbered the rich by a ratio of about two to one at the Conference, this statement received wide support and acclaim. When a vote was taken, however, to halt all atomic testing, China was one of the three states voting against the resolution, with the other negative votes being cast by France and Gabon.

The deliberations at the Conference were divided into six subject areas: problems of human settlements, national resources, pollution, national development, environmental organization, and environmental education. Three committees, each made up of members of all the participating delegations, dealt with two of these subjects each. All Committee decisions had to be reviewed by the Conference as a whole which in turn submitted its own report to the General Assembly.

In the end, the Conference was able to point to some very notable accomplishments. In the first place, it ratified a Declaration on the Human Environment. The first draft of this document was a delicately balanced compromise between the rich and the poor that had been hammered out in dozens of diplomatic sessions before the Stockholm meeting. In the middle of the Conference itself, however, the Chinese, claiming that they had had no part in the drafting of the Declaration, demanded that the entire document be reopened for debate. The motion was successful, and after lengthy debate a revised document was approved. The new Declaration was tilted somewhat more in the direction of those who perceived poverty as a more important problem than pollution. Like its predecessor, the Univeral Declaration of Human Rights, the Declaration on the Human Environment was binding on no one. But it was hoped that it would set a standard of environmental behavior that would be observed voluntarily by most of the membership of the United Nations.

The second concrete achievement of the Conference was a set of "action plans." At the core of these was to be "Earthwatch"—the systematic monitoring and assessment of global conditions as a basis for national measures to curb environmental abuses. Typical examples of such action plans included an appeal to all nations to minimize the release of toxic metals and chemicals into the environment; a global early-warning system designed to monitor changes in the world's climate and levels of air pollution; and action to save certain species, such as the whale, from complete extinction.

Finally, the Conference established a new environmental coordinating unit in the United Nations. This permanent new organ, consisting of a 54-member governing council, a small secretariat, and an executive director—set up under the aegis of the Economic and Social Council—was to follow up on the world community's continuing concern with the environmental crisis beyond the immediate confines of the Stockholm Conference. The financing of UN environmental activities was to be arranged through the creation of a voluntarily supported Environment Fund. Only the immediate administrative costs of the coordinating unit were to be borne by the UN's assessed regular budget.

Environmental breakdown does not respect national or ideological boundaries. It threatens capitalists and communists, the rich and the poor alike. The environmental challenge may yet prove to be the great leveller of international relations. It might even become a catalyst toward a saner world order since it may compel nations to cooperate on basic problems common to all. Perhaps the greatest achievement at Stockholm lay in the fact that more than one hundred nations found it possible to face a crisis before it had reached the point of no return and to take action on a global basis to arrest it. Most delegates sensed that the planet would survive the ecological crisis as a whole or not at all. Hence they turned to the United Nations as a logical means of action. This decision also infused new life and hope into the world organization itself. Having languished for years with the realization that it could not free the planet of most of its wars and political crises, the United Nations could now draw new strength from the hope that it might make a major contribution toward making life on this planet worth living at all.

FINANCING THE UNITED NATIONS SYSTEM

Before attempting a general evaluation of the United Nations system a word must be said about financing, especially in view of the fact that this issue threw the Organization into a major crisis in the early 1960's, and again in the early 1970's. While the United Nations was engaged in major peace-keeping responsibilities, there was never a shortage of Cassandras predicting that the Organization would end with a bang. However, during the height of the UN Operation in the Congo there existed a real possibility that it might end with a whimper. A fiscal crisis developed in the early 1960's that became a threat to the very life of the Organization. The heart of the crisis lay squarely in two operations that the United Nations had mounted to keep the peace: the United Nations Emergency Force in the Middle East (UNEF) in 1956 and the United Nations Congo Force (ONUC) in 1960.

Altogether, the UN system spends less than a billion dollars annually—or a fraction of what it takes to run the New York City government for a year. First, there is the regular assessed budget for the normal day-to-day expenses of the Organization, amounting to less than $200,000,000 a year. Second, there are the assessed budgets of the specialized agencies, which come to roughly twice that sum. Third, there are the special voluntary programs such as the Children's Fund, which subsist solely on the generosity of governments' and private citizens' voluntary contributions, amounting to approximately another $200,000,000 a year for four programs.

Finally there are the expenses for peace-keeping operations. The only major UN peace-keeping force that remained in the field in the 1970's was the UN Cyprus Force (UNFICYP). It was supported solely by voluntary contributions and cost less than $30,000,000 a year. But between 1960 and 1963 the UN Operation in the Congo (ONUC) cost the United Nations roughly $120,000,000 a year and the expenses of the UN Emergency Force (UNEF) which patrolled parts of the Arab-Israeli border between 1956 and 1967 came to approximately $20,000,000 a year. Since these two major UN peace forces had been responsible for the Organization's fiscal crisis, their financing deserves special analysis.

Never have so many people argued so much about so little money, the reason being that the financial problem of the peace-keeping operations was, in reality, a political problem. The financial crisis was first and foremost a political crisis over the proper role that the UN was to play in the national policies of its member states. And only secondarily was it a crisis over the financial burdens of UN membership.

When the General Assembly authorized the establishment of UNEF in 1956, Dag Hammarskjöld urged that a Special Account be set up to finance the Force as a collective responsibility of the entire membership. Most of the Western members supported the Secretary-General in this view, but the Soviet bloc asserted that the "aggressors" should pay, namely Britain, France, and Israel. Between these two opposing views, yet a third emerged: most of the new nations claimed that everyone should pay something, but that the Great Powers, which had special privileges under the Charter, should also shoulder special responsibilities and pick up the major portion of the bill. This "rebate formula" won the day: the costs of UNEF were assessed upon the membership, but the underdeveloped nations were given rebates of 50 per cent and the wealthier nations were invited to make up the deficits through voluntary contributions.

During the next few years, however, deficits gradually developed. The Soviet Union, for example, opposed the Force on political grounds and hence was unwilling to pay. And many of the smaller nations, though approving of the Force, claimed that they were unable to pay even their reduced assessments. By 1960, when the Congo Force was created, the problem of arrears had all the earmarks of a major crisis.

The problem of paying for the $120,000,000 ONUC budget brought the United Nations to the brink of bankruptcy. The Secretary-General once again supported the principle of collective responsibility. This time the Western nations broke ranks. France was unwilling to pay and joined the Soviet Union in its political opposition. The majority of the membership agreed to another rebate formula, but this time the reductions granted the poorer states reached 80 per cent.

The deficits now began to mount sharply. Two permanent members were unwilling to pay, and over half the membership claimed incapacity to pay. By late 1961 the UN debt approached the $100,000,000 mark, and the General Assembly was forced to take emergency action. First, it authorized a $200,000,000 bond issue and invited governments to subscribe, hoping to tide the peace forces over until a more permanent solution could be found. And second, it requested an Advisory Opinion of the World Court as to the legal status of the peace force assessments. (For a full discussion of this Opinion, see Chapter 9.) The response to the bond issue was fairly generous. By 1963 sixty governments had purchased approximately three fourths of the total subscription, with the United States buying half of the total amount. This made it possible to meet the costs of the two forces until early 1963 without having to assess the membership during that period. The Court Opinion, as we have seen in the preceding chapter, did not persuade the Soviet Union and France to clear their accounts, but did elicit payments from numerous smaller nations, totalling over $6,000,000.

With the bond money exhausted, the General Assembly had to meet in emergency session in May 1963. It appropriated an amount of $42,500,000 for the two peace forces for the last six months of 1963 and granted a 55 per cent reduction to the developing countries. In December it appropriated $17,750,000 for UNEF for 1964, but decided to allot only $15,000,000 to carry ONUC until the end of June 1964. The majority of the members were in no mood to continue massive peace-keeping operations indefinitely. The combined cash appropriations for UNEF and ONUC for 1964 amounted to less than one fourth of those appropriated for 1963.

In keeping with its increasingly conservative mood, the General Assembly gradually retreated from the principle of collective responsibility for the funding of peace-keeping operations. Thus, in 1962 the costs of the UN Temporary Executive Authority in West New Guinea (UNTEA) were divided evenly between the two direct beneficiaries, the Netherlands and Indonesia, and in 1963 the costs of a UN Observer Group sent to Yemen were split between Egypt and Saudi Arabia. And in 1964, the costs of the UN Peace Force dispatched to Cyprus had to be raised through voluntary contributions.

Finally, in 1964, the United States and the Soviet Union had a major showdown over the payments for UNEF and ONUC. The United States insisted that every Member State that was in arrears for more than two years would have no vote in the General Assembly under Article 19 of the Charter. The Soviet Union rejected this view and was supported by France in the case of ONUC. The United States, despite strenuous efforts, was unable to muster enough support in the General Assembly for its strict interpretation of Article 19. An impasse resulted that produced the famous "voteless" Nineteenth Session. Finally, in August 1965, Ambassador Arthur J. Goldberg abandoned this position, but declared that the United States, too, would henceforth reserve its right not to pay for peace-keeping operations of which it disapproved. Thus, the assessment principle, the financial bedrock of collective responsibility in peace-keeping, was, temporarily at least, defeated.

At the heart of the financial crisis was, of course, the fact that no power, least of all a great power, would adopt or easily pay for a policy that it considered inimical to its national interest. Thus, the United States supported the peace forces essentially because it found them compatible with its own national goals. Yet the question might well be raised as to what United States policy toward ONUC might have been if Kasavubu instead of Lumumba had been killed. And the Soviet Union opposed the peace forces because UNEF challenged the formation of a Soviet bridgehead in the Middle East and ONUC forced the liquidation of a Soviet bridgehead in the Congo. To sum up, the positions of the major powers had relatively little to do with finances *per se*. In the case of the middle and smaller powers, money *per se* played a far larger and, in some instances, a decisive role. Hence, while the financial crisis of UNEF and ONUC was caused primarily by the political attitude of the few, it was deepened considerably by the real or alleged financial limitations of the many.

After the seating of the People's Republic of China in the United Nations it was the turn of the United States to regard UN finances with a more penurious eye. In the wake of a popular wave of anti-UN feeling in 1972, the House Appropriations Committee, without consulting any of the organs of the United Nations, moved to reduce the American contribution to the regular budget from 31 per cent to 25 per cent. In view of the fact that, under the UN Charter, only the General Assembly had the right to determine the assessments for the regular budget, this unilateral action was widely interpreted as illegal. On sober second thought, the United States brought the question of its contribution before the General Assembly in the fall of 1972. The world body was put on notice that the United States was determined not to pay more than one quarter of the UN's regular budget.

In the last analysis, the difficulties that continue to plague the financial structure of the United Nations are largely symptoms of the great political rifts that characterize the contemporary international scene. The quest for technical formulas and legal or fiscal remedies will probably not succeed unless it is preceded by more fundamental political accommodation. Such accommodation must await a greater degree of harmony among the differing conceptions of what member states want the United Nations to be: a conference forum with no executive or legislative powers—which is the goal of those wishing to "walk backwards into the future"; an organization with very limited and carefully circumscribed executive powers—which, with variations, is the view of most member states; or an organization of increasing independence and authority—more than the mere sum total of its parts— which was the aim of Secretary-General Hammarskjöld when he first defended the financing of peace forces as a collective responsibility of the entire membership.[18]

The United Nations in Perspective

We are now ready to attempt a somewhat more general analysis of the United Nations family. A look at the record of each of the member organs shows clearly that in no case have the hopes of the United Nations' founders been realized completely. Each organ has developed a life of its own, often quite different from the original conception, and has made its own unique contribution.

The record of the Security Council is uneven. It has not attained the goal of collective security, but the Great Powers have often been able to agree on investing the Secretary-General with sweeping responsibilities for keeping the peace. The General Assembly has certainly not become the world's Parliament, but has shown a capacity for improvisation far greater than any of the UN's founders would have dared to predict. In effect, it has become collective security's second line of defense and has played a major role in the establishment and political direction of UN peace-keeping operations. It has also shown a remarkable talent for international law-making, and it continues to be the last remaining global forum in which the two great political struggles are waged in an atmosphere of parliamentarianism. Neither ECOSOC nor the specialized agencies have realized the original functionalist hope, since most economic, social, and cultural work has been too permeated with political significance. But the proliferation of functional agencies under the aegis of ECOSOC has yielded a multitude of global "good works" of unprecedented magnitude and unquestioned value. While colonial dependencies have not become "sacred trusts of civilization," the Trusteeship System has doubtless contributed to the peaceful liquidation of Western colonialism. But unless new Trusts are added, the Trusteeship Council may disappear from the United Nations family.

Much could be gained if the concept of trusteeship were applied to the more explosive of the remaining colonies. The World Court's role has been modest. It has not been able to contribute much to global order-building but has managed to consolidate the gains of international law in the Western world. Of all the United Nations organs, the Office of the Secretary-General has come closest to approximating the conception of the framers of the Charter. It has, indeed, become the repository of an invaluable new treasure—international statesmanship.

Lately, the United Nations has been the object of a great deal of criticism in many quarters. Its alleged impotence in dealing with political crises is often blamed for its declining reputation. This criticism overlooks the fact that many disputes are brought to the UN only when the crisis has become acute and violence has already erupted. Nations all too frequently "dump" quarrels into the lap of the UN when they literally no longer know what else to do. Thus, they make of the UN a kind of "receiver in bankruptcy" and then proceed to blame the Organization for that sad state of affairs. Given such adverse conditions, the UN has actually done rather well. But its task as "crisis manager" would be a great deal easier if nations submitted disputes *before* they went "critical." It is wiser to deal with crises when they are still manageable than to engage in brilliant rescue operations at the brink of disaster.

In the final analysis, the most striking characteristics of the United Nations have been its *elasticity* and *adaptability*. The League of Nations, which did not subscribe to as eclectic an approach to peace as the United Nations, crumbled after the first onslaughts. The United Nations, on the other hand, has developed multiple lines of defense against war. In its short life span it has been tested at least as severely as was the League of Nations. It has managed to respond to a multitude of challenges with amazing resiliency, an unmatched gift for innovation and improvisation, and a realistic sense of the politically possible.

What has not killed the United Nations has made it stronger.

REFERENCES

1. For a full development of the functional approach to peace, see David Mitrany, *A Working Peace System.* London: Royal Institute of International Affairs, 1946.

2. Norman J. Padelford, "The Use of the Veto," *International Organization,* June 1948, pp. 231–232.

3. Quoted by Arthur N. Holcombe, "The Role of Politics in the Organization of Peace," *Organizing Peace in the Nuclear Age.* New York: New York University Press, 1959, p. 97.

4. H. Arthur Steiner, "Communist China in the World Community," *International Conciliation,* May 1961, p. 447.

5. Petition by E. M. Attiogbe, spokesman for the Ewe tribe, cited by John MacLaurin, *The United Nations and Power Politics.* London: Allen and Unwin, 1951, pp. 354–355.

6. Inis L. Claude, Jr., *Swords into Plowshares,* 2d ed. New York: Random House, 1959, p. 369.

7. *Ibid.,* pp. 370–372.

8. Cited by H. G. Nicholas, *The United Nations as a Political Institution.* New York: Oxford University Press, 1959, p. 153.

9. United Nations Security Council, *Official Records,* Eleventh Year, 751st Meeting, October 31, 1956, pp. 1–2.

10. *The New York Times,* August 10, 1960.

11. *New York Herald Tribune,* September 27, 1960.

12. Address by President Kennedy to the General Assembly, September 25, 1961, in *Documents on American Foreign Relations 1961,* pp. 473–484.

13. Trygve Lie, *In the Cause of Peace.* New York: Macmillan, 1954, p. 80.

14. House Congressional Resolution 262, 83rd Congress, August 20, 1954.

15. Cited by Claude, *op. cit.,* p. 204.

16. Cited in Wilder Foote, ed., *Dag Hammarskjöld: Servant of Peace,* A Selection of His Speeches and Statements. New York: Harper and Row, 1962, p. 351.

17. *The New York Times,* June 11, 1972.

18. For a full analysis of the UN's financial problems, see John G. Stoessinger *et al., Financing the United Nations System.* Washington, D.C.: The Brookings Institution, 1964.

BIBLIOGRAPHY

Alcock, Anthony. *History of the International Labor Organization.* New York: Octagon Books, 1971.

Alker, Hayward R., Jr., and Russet, B. N. *World Politics in the General Assembly,* rev. ed. New Haven, Conn.: Yale University Press, 1965.

Asher, Robert E., *et al. The United Nations and the Promotion of the General Welfare.* Washington, D.C.: The Brookings Institution, 1957.

Bailey, Sydney D. *The General Assembly of the United Nations.* New York: Praeger, 1960.

——. *The Secretariat of the United Nations.* New York: Carnegie Endowment for International Peace, 1962.

——. *The United Nations: A Short Political Guide.* New York: Praeger, 1963.

——. *Voting in the Security Council.* Bloomington, Ind.: Indiana University Press, 1970.

Beichman, Arnold. *The "Other" State Department.* New York: Basic Books, 1968.

Bloomfield, Lincoln P. *Evolution or Revolution? The United Nations and the Problem of Peaceful Territorial Change.* Cambridge, Mass.: Harvard University Press, 1957.

——. *International Military Forces.* Boston: Little, Brown, 1964.

——. *The United Nations and United States Foreign Policy,* rev. ed. Boston: Little, Brown, 1967.

Boyd, Andrew. *Fifteen Men on a Powder Keg.* New York: Stein and Day, 1971.

Brook, David. *Preface to Peace.* Washington, D.C.: Public Affairs Press, 1964.

Burns, Arthur Lee, and Heathcote, Nina. *Peace-Keeping by UN Forces: From Suez to the Congo.* New York: Praeger, 1963.

Claude, Inis L., Jr. *The Changing United Nations.* New York: Random House, 1967.

_____. *Power and International Relations.* New York: Random House, 1962.

_____. *Swords into Plowshares,* 4th ed. New York: Random House 1971.

_____. "The United Nations and the Use of Force," *International Conciliation,* No. 532, March 1961.

Cox, Arthur M. *Prospects for Peacekeeping.* Washington, D.C.: The Brookings Institution, 1967.

Dallin, Alexander. *The Soviet Union at the United Nations.* New York: Praeger, 1962.

El-Ayouty, Yassin. *The United Nations and Decolonization.* The Hague: Nijhoff, 1971.

Falk, Richard A. *This Endangered Planet.* New York: Random House, 1971.

Foote, Wilder T., ed. *Dag Hammarskjold: Servant of Peace.* New York: Harper and Row, 1962.

Gardner, Richard N. *In Pursuit of World Order.* New York: Praeger, 1964.

_____, and Millikan, Max F., eds. *The Global Partnership.* New York: Praeger, 1968.

Goodrich, Leland. *Korea: A Study of United States Policy in the United Nations.* New York: Harper, 1956.

_____. *The United Nations.* New York: Crowell, 1959.

_____, and Simons, Anne. *The United Nations and the Maintenance of Peace and Security.* Washington, D.C.: The Brookings Institution, 1955.

Gordenker, Leon, ed. *The United Nations in International Politics.* Princeton, N.J.: Princeton University Press, 1971.

_____. *The UN Secretary-General and the Maintenance of Peace.* New York: Columbia University Press, 1967.

Gordon, King. *UN in the Congo.* New York: Carnegie Endowment for International Peace, 1962.

Gross, Ernest A. *The United Nations: Structure for Peace.* New York: Harper, 1962.

Holcombe, Arthur, ed. *Strengthening the United Nations:* Report of the Commission to Study the Organization of Peace. New York: Harper, 1957.

Hovet, Thomas, Jr. *Bloc Politics in the United Nations.* Cambridge, Mass.: Harvard University Press, 1960.

_____. *Africa in the United Nations.* Evanston, Ill.: Northwestern University Press, 1963.

James, Alan. *The Politics of Peace Keeping.* New York: Praeger, 1969.

Jessup, Philip C., and Taubenfeld, Howard J. *Controls for Outer Space.* New York: Columbia University Press, 1959.

Kay, David A. *The New Nations in the United Nations, 1960–1967.* New York: Columbia University Press, 1970.

Lall, Arthur. *The UN and the Middle East Crisis, 1967.* New York: Columbia University Press, 1968.

Lash, Joseph P. *Dag Hammarskjold: Custodian of the Brushfire Peace.* New York: Doubleday, 1961.

Laves, Walter H. C., and Thompson, Charles A. *UNESCO: Purpose, Progress, Prospects.* Bloomington, Ind.: Indiana University Press, 1957.

Lee, Dwight E. "The Genesis of the Veto," *International Organization,* February 1947, pp. 33–42.

Lefever, Ernst. *Crisis in the Congo.* Washington, D.C.: The Brookings Institution, 1965.

Lie, Trygve. *In the Cause of Peace.* New York: Macmillan, 1954.

Mitrany, David. *A Working Peace System.* Chicago: Quadrangle Press, 1966.

Nicholas, H.G. *The United Nations as a Political Institution,* rev. ed. Oxford University Press, 1962.

O'Brien, Conor Cruise. *To Katanga and Back.* New York: Simon and Schuster, 1963.

Riggs, Robert. *US/ UN: Foreign Policy and International Organization.* New York: Appleton-Century-Crofts, 1971.

Rosner, Gabriella. *The United Emergency Force.* New York: Columbia University Press, 1963.

Rovine, Arthur W. *The First Fifty Years.* Leyden: Sijthoff, 1970.

Rubinstein, Alvin Z., and Ginsburgs, George, eds. *Soviet and American Policies in the United Nations: A Twenty-five Year Perspective.* New York: New York University Press, 1971.

Russell, Ruth B. *The United Nations and United States Security Policy.* Washington, D.C.: The Brookings Institution, 1968.

Sewell, James Patrick. *Functionalism in World Politics.* Princeton, N.J.: Princeton University Press, 1966.

Sharp, Walter R. *Field Administration in the United Nations System.* New York: Praeger, 1961.

Steiner, H. Arthur. "Communist China in the World Community," *International Conciliation,* No. 533, May 1961.

Stoessinger, John G. "Atoms for Peace: The International Atomic Agency," in Arthur N. Holcombe, ed., *Organizing Peace in the Nuclear Age.* New York: New York University Press, 1959, pp. 117–233.

——. *et al. Financing the United Nations System.* Washington, D.C.: The Brookings Institution, 1964.

——. *The Refugee and the World Community.* Minneapolis, Minn.: University of Minnesota Press, 1956.

——. *The United Nations and the Superpowers,* rev. ed. New York: Random House, 1970.

Urquhart, Brian. *Hammarskjold.* New York: Knopf, 1972.

Virally, Michael. "Vers une reforme du Secretariat?" *International Organization,* Spring 1961, pp. 236–254.

Wainhouse, David W., ed. *International Peace Observation.* Baltimore: Johns Hopkins Press, 1966.

Walton, Richard J. *The Remnants of Power.* New York: Coward-McCann, 1968.

Wilcox, Francis O., and Haviland, Field H., eds. *The United States and the United Nations.* Baltimore: The Johns Hopkins Press, 1961.

Wilson, Thomas, W., Jr. *International Environmental Action: A Global Survey.* New York: Dunellen, 1971.

Young, Oran. *The Intermediaries.* Princeton, N.J.: Princeton University Press, 1967.

Zacher, Marc W. *Dag Hammarskjold's United Nations.* New York: Columbia University Press, 1970.

11 Regionalism and Political Order

Ours is essentially a tragic age, so we refuse to take it tragically. The cataclysm has happened, we are among the ruins, we start to build up new little habitats, to have new little hopes. It is rather hard work: there is now no smooth road into the future: but we go round, or scramble over the obstacles. We've got to live, no matter how many skies have fallen.

D. H. LAWRENCE *Lady Chatterley's Lover*

The Idea of Regionalism

Regionalism may be defined as a grouping of three or more states whose goal is the formation of a distinct political entity. A regional arrangement is a voluntary association of sovereign states that have developed fairly elaborate organizational tools to forge among them such bonds of unity. A purely military alliance among nations that do not pursue the goal of political order-building is not a regional arrangement. The Triple Entente was a purely military pact, but NATO, though primarily devised for defensive purposes, may be considered a regional arrangement since it has developed purposes other than military.

We have seen the role of regional arrangements as instruments of the international struggle for power. We shall now analyze their role as contributors to international order. Before we proceed to representative case studies, however, we must examine the concept of regionalism as a form of order-builder.

Regionalism is based on the assumption that universalism is today still premature and too ambitious. Those who feel that the time is not yet ripe for order-building on a global scale want to use regionalism as an essential steppingstone. They envisage the development of political unity within delimited geographic areas, which could then be used as building blocks in the construction of a future, world-wide political order. The classic statement of this idea is that of Clarence K. Streit who, in his *Union Now,* proposed the unification of democratic countries in order to form the nucleus for a future world government. Streit conceived of regionalism as a vital intermediate stage in an organic evolution toward the more ambitious goal of globalism. Other proponents of regionalism, however, have felt that in view of the continuing heterogeneity of the world, it as yet makes little sense to speak of a world-wide political order at all. First, they insist, a universal framework of values and a global sense of community must be developed.

Regionalist thinkers have differed not only on goals but also on methods. Some have preferred the federal approach to order-building. This approach has emphasized the necessity for participating states to yield parts of their sovereignty to a "supra-national" body. The latter would then, in effect, have some of the powers of a new state and its decisions would be binding on the member governments. The federal approach has tended to concentrate especially on the legal instruments of order-building, such as constitutions. Still other regionalists have advocated the functional method, and have pointed out the necessity for economic, social, and cultural cooperation as a prerequisite to political integration. The functionalists have tended to shy away from the formation of "supra-national" organs and, instead, have encouraged the development of as many forms of intergovernmental collaboration as possible.

We have seen earlier how little we know about the nature and the causes of war. This is, of course, simply another way of admitting how little we know about the process of political order-building. Little empirical work has been done to examine the claims of the regionalists

304 Regionalism and Political Order

in relation to world order, or the approach of the federalists as opposed to that of the functionalists. Most of the arguments advanced have been based on the dubious foundations of historical analogy, popular belief, and dogmatic preference. There is ample descriptive and analytical literature about the regional and global arrangements that already exist, but relatively little material on the *process* whereby regional orders are actually built. One of the most illuminating studies of this kind has been prepared by a group of scholars at Princeton University.[1] This study made a careful analysis of ten cases in which regional order-building had attained the level of "security-communities," a condition in which warfare among the members had become so highly improbable as to be practically out of the question. The authors distinguished between two types of "security-community": one that had resulted from a formal merger of previously independent units into a single larger unit—like the United States; and a second, of a more pluralistic nature, which retained the legal independence of separate governments. This pioneering study in the formation of "security-communities" affords some penetrating insights into the dynamics of regionalism.

The Princeton study cast serious doubt on the validity of several popular beliefs that have long served as premises for regionalist thinking. The study exploded the notion of an organic, almost automatic evolution of the world into larger units; in fact, the authors pointed out that the closer they got historically to modern conditions and to our own time, the more difficult it was to find the successful formation of "security-communities." Nor did the widely held belief that the establishment of one successful "security-community" would have a bandwagon effect stand up under scrutiny. Even more important, the authors placed in question the popular notion that a principal motive for the regional integration of states had been the fear of anarchy or of warfare among themselves. These important negative findings were matched by equally significant positive insights into the nature of the integrative process.

The authors isolated several conditions that they considered essential for the establishment of regional "security-communities." In all successful cases they found a compatibility of values and expectations among the participating units. These "common values" were most helpful when they were incorporated in similar types of political institutions, thus creating a common political "way of life." The authors further discovered that the competition between the federalist and the functionalist approaches to political order-building was largely irrelevant to the dynamics of regional integration. While they did find that the establishment of pluralistic "security-communities" through functionalism was somewhat easier than the creation of amalgamated "security-communities" through federalism, this difference was not considered crucial. What did seem decisive for the outcome was whether the integrative process was accompanied by widespread expectations and experiences of joint rewards for the participating states. In this regard, the functional technique seemed somewhat more successful, since it usually implied strong economic ties which, in the cases where regionalism proved successful, in turn led to economic rewards for the member states. Another essential condition was seen in a marked increase in political and administrative capabilities of the participating states, as well as in the presence of superior economic growth within the region. Other pre-conditions for the establishment of "security-communities" appeared to be the presence of a multiplicity of unbroken links of social communication and considerable mobility of people among the states concerned. Finally, a degree of mutual predictability of behavior was considered an essential prerequisite.

In addition to these general conditions, the authors developed the concept of "take-off," which they used to describe the conditions most favorable to the *beginning* of regional integration. The study pointed out that nations have been more likely to begin the process when they have felt strong rather than when they have seen themselves as weak. The authors also discovered that a military alliance usually turned out to be a relatively poor pathway toward building a "security-community," since "the presence of excessive military commitments—excessive in the sense that they were felt at the time to bring considerably more burdens than rewards—had a disintegrative effect."[2] Finally, the study pointed out that not all "security-communities" were "final," but that, indeed, it was possible to cross, recross, or even stand poised upon a broad threshold of integration.

This thoroughgoing study has forced us to reexamine a number of widely held beliefs about both the relationship of regionalism to world order and the dynamics of the regional order-building process in general. None of the ten cases selected for the Princeton study went beyond World War II. We shall therefore attempt to apply a similar empirical analysis to some of the representative regional political groupings of our current period. We must remember, of course, that the process of regional integration does not proceed only on a political level. Most of the existing regional entities have followed a whole range of pathways to unity. But each has tended to emphasize one approach more than others. NATO, for example, has stressed military bonds of unity; the European Coal and Steel Community and the Common Market have operated largely in the realm of economics; and the Council of Europe has stressed the principles of political association. The regional arrangements that are based primarily upon economic and military premises are discussed elsewhere in this volume. (For an analysis of military arrangements, see Chapters 6 and 12; economic arrangements are discussed in Chapters 7 and 13.) The present analysis will concern itself with those regional instruments of order-building that are *primarily* political in character.

Political Order-Building in Europe

THE COUNCIL OF EUROPE

The ideal of a politically united Europe, has its roots in antiquity. It makes its appearance in the political and philosophical literature of each major epoch in European civilization. But at no time prior to our own era had the movement for European unity been a popular one, capturing strong and widespread support. Indeed, the European idea had remained largely an abstraction, the preserve of philosophers and visionaries. Only after World War I did it enter into the thinking of statesmen and diplomats as a concrete possibility and, perhaps, even as a necessity. The Balkanization of Europe in the wake of World War I made many thoughtful observers fearful of the danger of a new struggle and so led them to look and work toward the gradual acceptance by the sovereign states of Europe of a common political mechanism. Foremost among the advocates of a united Europe was a Count of the Holy Roman Empire, Richard Coudenhove-Kalergi.[3] He first expressed his thoughts in a book, *Pan Europa,* published in 1923, and organized the first Pan-European congress in Vienna which mobilized public opinion for his ideas. The promotional efforts of the Count and his followers succeeded, in the inter-war period, in winning over several prominent European statesmen. Aristide Briand of France, one of the great European figures in the League of Nations, and Gustav Stresemann of Germany made European unity a cornerstone of their national policies. But these early efforts were doomed to failure. The death of Stresemann, the lengthening shadow of Hitler over Europe, and the incapacity of the League of Nations drove the ideal of European union into temporary eclipse. Yet even during the darkest days of World War II, statements by the most prominent European leader of the Allied Powers gave indication that the ideal would emerge with increased vitality once Europe was again at peace. As early as October 1942, Winston Churchill expressed the hope that

Hard as it is to say now, I trust that the European family may act unitedly as one under a Council of Europe. I look forward to a United States of Europe in which the barriers between the nations will be greatly minimized and unrestricted travel will be possible. We must try to make this Council of Europe into a really effective League, with all the strongest forces woven into its texture, with a High Court to adjust disputes, and with armed forces, national or international or both, held ready to enforce these decisions and to prevent renewed aggression and the preparation of future wars. This Council when created, must eventually embrace the whole of Europe, and all the main branches of the European family must someday be partners in it.[4]

It had taken a Hitler to compel Europe to take union really seriously. At war's end, Sir Winston and Count Coudenhove found massive support among the statesmen of Europe. In May 1948 an attempt was made to organize the first truly continental demonstration of unity—the Congress of Europe. This Congress, held at the Hague, was the birthplace of the Council of Europe.

It is noteworthy that each of the major European countries produced statesmen deeply committed to the "European Movement." All of them came from the border lands of their respective countries and all of them shared a cosmopolitan world view. The list of these European-minded political leaders is impressive indeed: Konrad Adenauer of Germany, staunch fighter against the tyranny of Hitler and devoted disciple of Stresemann's European policy; Leon Blum and Robert Schuman of France, who carried on the tradition of Briand; Alcide de Gasperi of Italy, who saw in unity the fulfillment of a Christian ideal; Paul-Henri Spaak of Belgium; Sir Winston Churchill, one of the grand architects of the idea but one who remained ambivalent about the role of Britain in such a venture; and finally, Count Coudenhove, the pioneer who had indefatigably prepared the way.

In January 1949 the foreign ministers of the major European powers convened and drafted the Statute of the Council of Europe. The Council's primary goal, as set forth in Article I, was to be the achievement of "a greater unity between its Members for the purpose of safeguarding and realizing the ideals and principles which are their common heritage." Progress toward unity was to proceed on several fronts. The Statute listed an extensive range of subjects that were to be within the competence of the Council. Among them were legal matters, human rights, and cultural and social questions. While no specific reference was made to political questions in the Statute, it was clearly implied that the Council was to function as essentially a political body. It was to consist of a Committee of Ministers whose members were to be the Foreign Ministers of the member states and of a Consultative Assembly whose membership was to be drawn from the legislatures of the participating countries. The original membership of the Council comprised ten states: Belgium, Denmark, France, Ireland, Italy, Luxembourg, Holland, Norway, Sweden, and Great Britain. Since then, seven more have been added: Austria, West Germany, Greece, Iceland, Cyprus, Turkey, and Switzerland. The Council's membership policy was conceived as open-ended and it was hoped that it might serve as a first step toward a United States of Europe.

It is an ancient truth that organizational realities tend to be far more modest than the ideas that underlie them. In view of its broad membership base, it is not surprising that both the Council's main organs have witnessed a continuing struggle between two quite differing conceptions of what European unity should be and how it might best be achieved. On the one hand have been the "federalists," favoring a "supra-national" organ with real powers; on the other have been the "functionalists," who have advocated the more traditional "transnational" path to unification. The former have consistently urged that the member states yield more of their sovereignty to the Council, whereas the latter have jealously sought to preserve their sovereign rights. The preferability of the "supra-national" approach has been defended by France, West Germany, Italy, and the Benelux countries, who together have come to be known as "The Six." More conservative, the "transnationalists" have been led by Great Britain, who has continued to see herself not only as a European power but, at the same time, as the leader of the Commonwealth. This British ambivalence toward Europe has been aptly expressed in a classic statement of Sir Winston Churchill: "We have our own dreams and our own tasks. We are linked but not comprised. We are with Europe, but not of it. We are interested and associated but not absorbed."[5]

The Council's organizational structure reflects a clear-cut victory for the more conservative approach. Neither the Committee of Ministers nor the Consultative Assembly has "supra-national" powers. Both are intergovernmental arrangements in which sovereignty has been entirely preserved. Any resolutions are merely recommendations and must be ratified by the participating member states before they become binding. The Committee of Ministers is the "executive" organ, consisting of one representative from each member state. In principle, these should be the respective Foreign Ministers; in practice, they have frequently been alternates. All important decisions are made unanimously, "in the belief that this procedure serves the interests of European unity better than the imposition of the will of the majority on a reluctant minority."[6] Once decisions are reached, the Ministers are to take the initiative for their adoption in their respective national governments.

The Council's deliberative organ has been the Consultative Assembly. Its membership has comprised 132 delegates, with representation ranging from three in the case of Iceland and Luxembourg to eighteen for France, Great Britain, and West Germany. The Assembly has borne only a superficial resemblance to a national parliament. Although there have developed various party groupings, the Assembly has, in effect, been an assembly of individuals rather than a body of legislators representing constituencies.

One is tempted, in the light of the above, to conclude that the Council has been little more than a debating society of European parliamentarians on vacation in Strasbourg and speaking for no one but themselves. Indeed, such a judgment could be supported by some of the facts. For one thing, the mandate of the Council has been so broad that it has frequently led to vagueness. The tendency to make unity a goal in itself has led to an absence of specific programming. Moreover, while the delegates have frequently been enthusiastic about proposals in Strasbourg, they have suffered from inertia when it came to taking up the same matters in their own parliaments. The main weakness of the Council of Europe has thus not been its lack of "supra-national" authority but its lack of a clearly defined program. The capacity to deal with everything in breadth has led to few accomplishments in depth. Nevertheless, the organization's record is not without its significant positive achievements. For example, there has developed in the Council an interesting tendency toward "transnational" party caucusing. The leaders of the Italian Center Party, for instance, have gotten along better with their political counterparts in the German and French delegations than with their respective opposition parties at home. Though the contribution of this phenomenon to regional order-building cannot yet be accurately assessed, other achievements of the Council have been more concrete. Its most significant accomplishment has been in the field of human rights. Intensive debates in both organs of the Council led to a deep concern with this subject in the parliaments of the member states. In effect, the Council of Europe thus provided a springboard for the adoption of the European Convention of Human Rights. This became a legally binding document signed and ratified by all members of the Council. The following Human Rights were to be guaranteed:

Security of persons; exemption from slavery and servitude; freedom from arbitrary arrest, detention or exile; freedom from arbitrary interference in private and family life, home and correspondence; freedom of thought, conscience and religion; freedom of opinion and expression; freedom of assembly; freedom of association; freedom to unite in trade unions; the right to marry and found a family.[7]

Implementing the provisions of the Convention, a European Commission on Human Rights was created, the first international body established by governments and competent to receive and act on individual petitions concerning violations of the rights set forth in the Convention. Moreover, there was set up a European Court on Human Rights, whose function was to be the adjudication of infringements of the Convention. These institutions have gone far beyond the purely hortatory Universal Declaration of Human Rights passed by the United Nations General Assembly. This is due mainly to the regional character of the experiment but also, in some degree, to the impetus provided by the Council of Europe. The recognition of obligations in the matter of these rights and freedoms has become the principal condition of membership in the Council.

As a working reality, the Council of Europe has fallen far short of the ambitious conception of the founders of the European Movement. But for all its vaguenes and lack of authority, it has served one vital function: it has remained the only European forum that has included countries neutral in the East-West struggle and in which, therefore, it has been possible to discuss the problems of Europe as a whole. In addition, as has already been pointed out, it has provided a meeting place for the conflicting views of European "functionalists" and "federalists." The tensions arising from these differences among the Council's members have led to fruitful and sometimes tangible results. It has, of course, remained true that the Council has been able to do no more than propose policies, leaving to its individual members the choice of adopting policies in question. Yet even this act of proposing has constituted an important encouragement to the member states to pursue their common quest of European political order-building.

NATO

NATO is not only the West's major military instrument in the East-West struggle. It has been, at the same time, intended as a major means for the advancement of European unity. In fact, it was quite clear to the founders of NATO that without strong political bonds the Treaty's effectiveness as a military alliance would be minimal. This was the reason for the inclusion in the NATO Charter of its Article II:

The Parties will contribute toward the further development of peaceful and friendly international relations by strengthening their free institutions, by bringing about a better understanding of the principles upon which these institutions are founded, and by promoting conditions of stability and well-being.

NATO includes two organs that are to contribute to political integration in the North Atlantic Community. One is the North Atlantic Council, composed of the Foreign Ministers of the member countries and concerned chiefly with military matters. Yet since the exchange of military intelligence necessary for joint planning has made it almost impossible for members of NATO to go to war against one another, the Council's work has profound political implications as well. The other politically significant NATO organ is its unofficial Parliamentarians' Conference. This Conference draws its membership from all fifteen NATO countries and acts as a consultation forum for the coordination of national policies among member states.

The main weakness of NATO's nonmilitary work has been that statesmen have tended to "inform other member countries about decisions of national policy that have already been taken unilaterally, instead of consulting them fully before making decisions."[8] (For an analysis of NATO as a military alliance, see Chapter 6.) Clearance in NATO has at times been noticeably absent during the formulation stage of policy. This became tragically clear during the Suez crisis of 1956, when Britain and France failed to consult with the United States. The divergence between American and Anglo-French policies seriously weakened the bonds of NATO and resulted in the adoption by the North Atlantic Council in 1956 of a proposal to establish a Committee of Three to study possibilities for the improvement of consultation procedures among the NATO powers. This Committee, consisting of the Foreign Ministers of Norway, Italy, and Canada, expressed the opinion that NATO had been concerned too much with problems of military strategy and too little with progress toward political unity. The withdrawal of French forces from the NATO integrated command in 1966 further weakened the Alliance. As NATO Headquarters were moved from Paris to Brussels, the prospects for strengthening political bonds in the Atlantic Community seemed to recede further into the distance.

In overall perspective, however, the political cohesion of NATO has nevertheless been quite remarkable. It is frequently forgotten that under the NATO Charter, member states are merely obligated to do what they "deem necessary" in case of an outside attack. Moreover, all policy decisions must be reached by unanimous vote. In purely structural terms, national sovereignty looms larger in NATO than in the United Nations Charter, where majority decisions are possible. Hence, as Claude has pointed out, "the flight of security-minded statesmen from the veto-bound Security Council of the United Nations to NATO was not an escape from a primitive to a more advanced form of international organization so far as voting procedures are concerned, for the North Atlantic Treaty permits a much more thoroughgoing application of the veto principle than the Charter provisions concerning the Security Council."[9] The explanation may be found in the fact that political cohesion in NATO, despite all the tensions and all the setbacks, is relatively high. For this reason, NATO as a political reality means more than the structural provisions safeguarding the sovereignty of its member states would seem to indicate.

WESTERN EUROPEAN UNION

A third major European regional arrangement that has promoted political order-building is the Western European Union (WEU), which grew out of the defeat of the European Defense Community (EDC) by the French National Assembly in 1954. (For a full discussion of EDC, see Chapter 6.) Once it had become clear that the defeat of EDC had not defeated the rearmament of West Germany, those who had opposed EDC realized to their dismay that Germany would now be rearmed as a sovereign state, rather than as part of a "supra-national" military force such as had been planned under EDC. This result seemed to most observers to be far worse. Hence, a compromise had to be found that would fall between the "supra-national" arrangement of EDC and a purely national solution. Two weeks after the collapse of EDC, German, Belgian, and Dutch leaders joined with the British to search for a substitute. Dr. Adenauer expressed the feelings of all concerned when he stated that "some kind of European community must be saved at all costs." The diplomats of The Six met in London in October 1954. The United States had declared earlier that it might have to engage in an "agonizing reappraisal" if a substitute for EDC could not be agreed upon. Under this pressure, the European statesmen resuscitated a treaty that had been superseded by NATO. This was the Brussels Treaty of 1948, which had created a joint command for British, French, and Benelux forces. The Brussels Powers agreed that this structure might be expanded to admit Germany and Italy. The latter proposal proved generally acceptable and quickly crystallized into the Western European Union, which came into force in May 1955 after parliamentary ratification by the seven member states.

In terms of "supra-nationality," WEU falls short of the defunct EDC. There is no fusion of armies nor is there a central organ with decision-making powers in matters of common defense. Each member state continues to have a national army and exercises a veto power over its disposition. WEU's central policy-making organ is its Council, composed of the Foreign Ministers of the seven member states. The more important defense questions, such as the size of the armed forces to be contributed by each member state, must be approved unanimously. But decisions on types of conventional weapons to be used are taken by majority vote in the Council. In addition to the Council, a deliberative body, the Assembly coordinates the military policies of the seven states. This Assembly has a purely advisory status and its members have usually been the same parliamentarians who also attend the meetings of the Consultative Assembly of the Council of Europe.

In sum, WEU has been a useful order-building device. It is not in any extensive sense "supra-national," nor, however, is it merely transnational. EDC would have comprised only The Six, whereas WEU includes Britain as well. In fact, Britain pledged herself to maintain military contingents in Continental Europe at all times and not to withdraw these forces against the majority will of the members of WEU. If Britain had not made this promise, the French would not have permitted German participation in WEU. It is interesting to speculate on whether the French Parliament would have ratified EDC if such a commitment of British forces had been made earlier, as part of the envisaged EDC arrangement. At any rate, it is clear that the WEU is primarily a military alliance, a kind of "little NATO" within NATO. Yet by having succeeded in attracting Britain to its purposes and activities, WEU has also made a major contribution to the European political order-building process. On the other hand, the withdrawal of French forces from NATO in 1966 has had a retarding effect on the progress of community-building in WEU.

If we apply to the Council of Europe, NATO, and WEU the criteria formulated in the Princeton study of the building of "security-communities," we see that all three rate rather high. For one thing, all three of these European regional arrangements involve nations with a fairly high compatibility of values, expectations, and political forms—even though one member, Germany, is not fully trusted by the others and another, France, still pursues highly nationalistic policies. In NATO and WEU, which are held together by the need for common security, the expectation of joint rewards is great. In the Council of Europe, which is concerned more with the goal of unity than with the achievement of tangible returns, it is almost entirely absent. Save for Portugal, moreover, all the nations concerned enjoy relatively high levels of economic development. Mobility of persons is also very considerable, being highest among the nations of WEU and lowest in NATO—owing to the rather restrictive immigration policies of the United States and Canada. On the whole, political integration is highest among The Six, somewhat lower in WEU, still quite high in NATO, and low in the Council of Europe. The crucial factor seems to be the expectation of joint rewards from the integrative process. This is present in the two military alliances but not in the Council of Europe. Yet the authors of the Princeton study have warned that though an outside military threat may provide the original impetus toward political order-building, more permanent unions derive their main support from other factors.[10] This would seem to indicate that the high degree of political integration in NATO and WEU may be transitory unless it is buttressed through specific programs that hold out to the member nations the promise of substantial and sustained rewards of a nonmilitary kind as well.

Other Experiments in Regional Order-Building

THE ORGANIZATION OF AMERICAN STATES

One of the earliest post-World War II regional arrangements to be established was the Organization of American States (OAS). The Treaty, which formalized the solidarity of the Western Hemisphere against both external and internal threats to the peace, was the culmination of a long and arduous road to inter-American political order. The highlights of this history of hemispheric relations are well worth reviewing.

The famous Monroe Doctrine of 1823 declared that the United States reserved to itself the right to act as the protector of Latin America in case of outside aggression:

We owe it, therefore, to candor, and to the amicable relations existing between the United States and those [European] powers, to declare that we should consider any attempt on their part to extend their system to any portion of this hemisphere as dangerous to our peace and safety.

In 1904 President Theodore Roosevelt interpreted the Doctrine to mean that in cases of intra-hemispheric disputes the United States could also exercise the right of "an international police power." This controversial "Roosevelt Corollary" gave rise to several instances of United States intervention in the Caribbean. In all of these interventions—in Cuba, Haiti, the Dominican Republic, Nicaragua, and Panama—the United States attempted to restore political and economic stability. However, the novel interpretation that the Monroe Doctrine not only forbade intervention from Europe but permitted United States intervention in order to forestall any *possible* European incursion, led to widespread resentment in Latin America. At the turn of the century, the Latin American nations began to exert pressure upon the United States to renounce its claims to intervene. Gradually, these efforts met with success. The Roosevelt Corollary was officially discarded in 1926, and the Good Neighbor Policy initiated by Franklin D. Roosevelt in 1933 put an end to the practice of unilateral intervention. The Axis threat to the Western Hemisphere during World War II consolidated inter-American solidarity even further. And when the Americas emerged victorious, the time was ripe for the conclusion of a regional arrangement dedicated both to the maintenance of reciprocal security and to a common effort toward political order-building.

Accordingly, delegates from the twenty Latin American nations and from the United States met in Rio De Janeiro and drafted the famous Rio Treaty—an Inter-American Treaty of Reciprocal Assistance. Article III, the heart of the Treaty, provided that "an armed attack by any state against an American state shall be considered as an attack against all American states." This provision was in essence a recognition of the fact that the Monroe Doctrine had become multilateralized. It also furnished a pattern for the NATO Charter that would be concluded two years later. The drafters of the Rio Pact, unlike the framers of NATO, were not solely concerned with protection against external aggression. Most of the members were equally eager to guard against the possibility of internal schism. The immediate reason for their apprehension was the government of Argentina, which had sided with the Axis during World War II. Argentina was the only member state which wanted a treaty only against aggression by non-American states, but its position was voted down. The Rio Treaty as first constituted in 1947 was primarily an instrument of military security against internal and external attack. A year later, at a conference in Bogota, Colombia, the Pact was further elaborated by the inclusion of provisions for political order-building. This new and sophisticated system, in the words of the then American Secretary of State, George C. Marshall, was to be "the very heart of hemispheric organization." It was named the Organization of American States (OAS).

The structure of the OAS provides for an eclectic approach to political order-building. An annual Assembly of Foreign Ministers constitutes the organization's main organ. The Foreign Ministers consider all urgent problems of internal and external security. Conference procedure for the settlement of intra-hemispheric disputes differs from that which governs cases of outside attack. The procedure adopted for the former is as follows: first, the Foreign Ministers may issue a call to the parties to cease hostilities; next, they may recommend various techniques of conciliation and mediation; they may then impose diplomatic and economic sanctions; and finally, if all the foregoing measures fail, they may recommend the use of armed force to restore order. It is significant that the first three of these provisions may be initiated by a two-thirds vote, which thereby becomes binding on all members. There is no veto. However, in the case of military enforcement measures, no state may be compelled to contribute armed forces without its consent. In the eventuality of an external threat, the arrangement is somewhat looser. The member states are obligated merely to consult with one another in order to arrive at a common policy, but each state may do what it "deems necessary" to help the victim—or not to help it.

In addition to its central organ, the OAS also works through several subsidiary bodies. There is, first, the OAS Council which is the organization's central administration and coordinating organ. Second, there is an Inter-American Economic and Social Council, but, unlike its United Nations counterpart, this is not a major organ and does not have a very extensive program. Third, an Inter-American Cultural Council, designed for the promotion of friendly relations and cultural understanding among the American peoples, is patterned after UNESCO. The OAS also enjoys the services of a very active Inter-American Council of Jurists, which roughly parallels the International Law Commission of the United Nations. Finally, OAS, like the United Nations, has its international secretariat, the Pan-American Union. This is headed by a Secretary-General who is chosen by the Inter-American Conference for a ten-year term, not subject to reelection.

A survey of the OAS structure indicates that the attention of the Organization is about equally divided between the negative function of resolving disputes and the positive task of political integration. The achievements of OAS in the former category have been considerable. In December 1948 Costa Rica complained to the Council that Nicaragua was trying to overthrow its government through revolution. The

Council blamed Costa Rica for negligence and Nicaragua for not preventing the revolutionary activity. A Committee of Five was appointed to mediate between the disputants. The effort was successful and the two parties signed a Treaty of Friendship in 1949. In 1950 Haiti accused the Dominican Republic of fostering subversion aimed at the overthrow of the Haitian government. The OAS Council found the Dominican Republic responsible and called upon it to desist from further subversive activities in the Western Hemisphere. In June 1954 a more complicated issue arose. The pro-Communist government of Guatemala charged Honduras and Nicaragua with U.S.-inspired aggression. The matter was discussed first in the United Nations Security Council, but it was decided that that body would not pursue the matter further until OAS had completed its investigation. This investigation never took place because the Guatemalan government was overthrown and replaced by a new, anti-Communist government. As a result, the matter was dropped by all concerned. In 1955 Costa Rica charged Nicaragua with fomenting a revolt. The OAS Council was successful in settling the matter through an investigating committee which made a series of recommendations that made accepted by both parties.

Four serious intra-hemispheric crises occupied the OAS in the 1960's. The first concerned the policy of subversion that had been pursued by the Dominican Republic in 1960 against Venezuela, including a plot to assassinate the Venezuelan president. The Organization decided to take a strong stand against the Dominican Republic not only in the light of this specific provocation but because it was determined to end the thirty-year dictatorship of Generalissimo Trujillo. For the first time, the OAS decided to apply sanctions against one of its members for actions against another. The punishment consisted of a collective break in diplomatic relations and of "partial sanctions," including the suspension of arms shipments. The assassination of Trujillo in 1961 radically changed the Dominican picture and in 1962 the OAS voted to end the sanctions.

The second crisis grew out of the Cuban revolution and the apparent desire of Premier Fidel Castro to turn his revolution into an export commodity. The fact that the Soviet Union had gained a firm foothold in Cuba was especially distasteful to the United States and introduced further complications. The United States wanted desperately to prevent the spread of Communism in the Western Hemisphere but was now forced to pursue this aim within the context of a multilateral Conference, rather than by a unilateral wielding of the Monroe Doctrine. The other delegates were not as openly fearful of the Cuban revolution, but expressed varying degrees of ambivalence. Nevertheless in 1962, by a two-thirds vote, the Foreign Ministers at Punta del Este declared the Marxist-Leninist foundations of Castro's Cuba incompatible with membership in the Organization of American States. Cuba was also explicitly excluded from the Inter-American Defense Board and had an arms embargo imposed upon it. In October 1962, during the missile crisis, the OAS unanimously endorsed the American naval quarantine and Argentina and Venezuela actually sent ships to help United States naval forces. The response of the OAS to the missile crisis marked the first time that any military action was taken by the Organization against a country in the Western Hemisphere.

Another precedent was set in January 1964 when the OAS took up a dispute involving the United States. Panama charged the United States with aggression after American troops had fired on Panamanian demonstrators in the Canal Zone. A more basic cause of the dispute, however, was the Panamanian demand to renegotiate the 1903 Treaty giving the United States sovereign rights in the Canal Zone "in perpetuity." The OAS found itself in a dilemma. On the one hand, it wanted to help a small sister republic, but on the other, it was loath to place the United States in the role of the accused. Thus, it constituted itself as an "organ of consultation" to look into the charges and to help the two parties in reaching an amicable settlement. The peace-keeping mechanism of the Organization was adapted to the situation in a flexible and imaginative manner.

A highly controversial situation arose in April 1965 when the United States decided to intervene in the Dominican Republic and sent in marines in order to stave off an alleged Communist coup. Proponents of the move defended it by pointing out that the United States could not afford another Castro, but critics deplored the unilateral intervention and feared the imminent end of the Good Neighbor Policy. In order to give the intervention a semblance of multilateralism, the United States in May 1965 requested an inter-American military force for the restoration of order in the Dominican Republic. The OAS Foreign Ministers, in a vote of fourteen to five, which was barely the required two-thirds majority, authorized the force. The five states opposing its creation resented what they felt to be an OAS ratification of American unilateralism. Nevertheless, the first inter-American military force entered Santo Domingo in May 1965, and thus established yet another precedent in the evolution of the OAS as an intra-hemisphere peace-keeping organ. In late 1966, after a little over a year of successful peace-keeping, the force was withdrawn from Santo Domingo.

The order-building task of the OAS has been made rather difficult because the Latin American countries and the United States have had different reasons for supporting the Organization. For Latin America, OAS implied the legal sanctification of American nonintervention in the affairs of the hemisphere. It was also seen as a device for countering the supremacy of the "Colossus of the North." And most important, the Latin American countries looked forward to economic and technical assistance from the United States. The motives of the United States were somewhat different. From the American viewpoint, the OAS was to be a vital regional alliance in the East-West struggle. In 1961 the United States, in an effort to reconcile these different perspectives, launched a massive economic development program within the context of the OAS—the Alliance for Progress.

The Alliance for Progress got off to a fairly slow start. Tensions between the United States and the Latin American members of the Alliance over American trade and aid policies retarded progress. In particular, the Latin Americans resented the requirement that American goods and services would have to be purchased with American aid funds. The United States, during the early years of the Alliance, also continued to give bilateral aid to Latin American countries. This disappointed those who preferred greater emphasis on a multilateral program of hemispheric development. Finally, in 1966, at a major conference at Punta del Este, President Johnson and eighteen other heads of state, in a "Declaration of the Presidents of America," outlined plans for a Latin American common market to be in operation twenty years hence. The foundation for this emerging common market would be laid through multinational projects, the modernization of agriculture, the development of science and technology, and the advancement of education.

The continued presence of dictatorships—notably in Cuba, Haiti, and Paraguay—has had a retarding effect on order-building. Some members have advocated the encouragement of democracy in the Western Hemisphere but others have declared that such a policy would negate the principle of nonintervention. The organization has not been able to pursue both goals simultaneously. In addition, many Latin American countries have lacked internal stability. *Coups d'état* are not infrequent. In 1961 a coup ended a thirty-year dictatorship in the Dominican Republic and in 1964 another stemmed the drift toward anarchy in Brazil. Militant insurrectionist forces continue to threaten a number of shaky democracies. In the light of these divergent patterns and interests, unity and solidarity have been expressed primarily in general statements, with more concrete steps in order-building proving difficult, if not impossible. Despite its many shortcomings, OAS remains one of the most advanced regional arrangements in the world. It alone has provisions for internal security and has acquitted itself well in this respect. On the other hand, its progress toward political integration has been far more hesitant. If we apply the criteria of the Princeton study, we notice that OAS is not blessed with a system of common values—which the authors considered one of the essentials for the building of a "security-community." However, OAS meets another key condition admirably. All its members have high expectations of concrete rewards. Although these expectations differ—being primarily military in the eyes of the United States and economic in the view of Latin America—they are nonetheless effective. At present, therefore, OAS (with the exceptions of Cuba, Paraguay and Haiti) may be considered what the Princeton group would call a "pluralistic security-community" at a low level. Further political integration would seem to depend on continuing and expanded expectations of joint rewards and on the improvement and enlargement of communications that will enhance mutual responsiveness among the members.

THE ARAB LEAGUE

The most prominent regional arrangement in the Middle East has been the Arab League. It was organized on the eve of the San Francisco Conference in 1945 and comprised seven states: Egypt, Syria, Lebanon, Jordan, Iraq, Saudi Arabia, and Yemen. The purpose of the League as set forth in its Charter was

. . . to strengthen the ties between the participating states, to coordinate their political programs in such a way as to effect real collaboration between them, to preserve their independence and sovereignty, and to consider in general the affairs and interests of the Arab countries.

In practice, "strengthening the ties" between the members of the League was a subordinate goal. There were two overriding causes for the creation of the League: first, to present a united front against the return to the Middle East of French and British colonialism; and second, to prevent the creation of a Jewish state in Palestine.

The most powerful organ of the League has been the Majlis, a Council comprising the Prime Ministers of the member states. All important decisions, including any kind of collective action, have required unanimity. Majority decisions have been binding only on those states that have voted for a particular resolution. On intra-League disputes, the Council may act by majority vote, provided the "independence, sovereignty or territorial integrity of a member are not involved." As a result of this reservation, all but very minor questions have in practice required unanimous decision. In 1950 the structure of the Arab League was developed further by the adoption of a Treaty of Joint Defense and Economic Cooperation, modeled after the NATO Pact. Like NATO, this treaty stipulated the peaceful settlement of all disputes among the members; stated that an attack upon one was to be regarded as an attack upon all; and included a statement that armed attack from the outside would be met by collective military measures. In addition, for the purpose of coordinating the economies of the Arab countries, it created an Economic Council consisting of the member states' Ministers of Economic Affairs. Finally, the Office of a Secretary-General was added whose incumbent was to be appointed by a two-thirds vote of the Council.

The formal structure of the Arab League has had relatively little to do with the actual policy-making process. In the opinion of one expert student of the Arab League:

The real activities of the League are carried on in private and secret talks and through conversations held outside regular meetings. The careful elaboration of agreements, with each stage consigned to writing—so customary in the West—is utterly unfamiliar. When the prestige of man comes into conflict with the prestige of the written word, the former prevails. Furthermore, the activities of the League are unknown and misunderstood abroad, and even in the Arab world, because the organization has been reluctant to secure publicity for its activities.[11]

The League's official purpose and its formal structure thus provide few clues to its actual goals and operations.

In its first aim, the liberation of Egypt, Lebanon, Syria, and Libya from colonial rule, the Arab League was clearly successful. When France attempted to resume control of Lebanon and Syria in 1945, the League pressed for submission of the dispute to the United Nations Security Council. When in 1946 the Security Council took up the problem, the League presented a united front and succeeded in preventing the French from returning to Lebanon and Syria. Similarly the League supported the complete evacuation of British troops from Egypt. When Egypt emerged as an independent state after seventy-two years of British rule, this victory was attributable in no small measure to the efforts of the Arab League.

Finally, the Arab League played a decisive role in securing the independence of Libya by acting as the spokesman for that new state in the United Nations. Actually, the intervention on behalf of Libya probably owed its success more to the inability of the Big Four to agree on a new status for Libya than to the inherent strength of the League itself. When neither the Big Four nor the United Nations were able to decide what to do with the former Italian territory, the Arab League's insistent pressure for independence weighed heavily in the balance. Libya became independent in 1951 and was admitted as the eighth member of the Arab League in 1953. The Sudan received its independence and joined the League in 1956, and two years later Morocco and Tunisia were admitted. Kuwait became a member in 1961 and in the following year Syria resumed her separate seat, which she had relinquished by joining the United Arab Republic. Finally, in 1962 Algeria became the thirteenth member of the Arab League. By the early 1960's it was clear that the first major political goal of the League—the emancipation of the Arab states from Western colonialism—had been achieved.

In its second major objective, the prevention of the Jewish state in Palestine, the Arab League has failed. In 1946 the League developed a common policy toward Palestine: Jewish immigration and land purchases were to be stopped; Jewish products were to be boycotted; and Palestine was to be admitted to the League as an independent Arab nation. An attempt was made to create a common front against the creation of the state of Israel by threatening a general war for the liberation of the area if the new state were to come into being. When on May 15, 1948, Israel achieved her independence, the Secretary-General of the Arab League informed the United Nations Security Council that the League was forced to intervene "to achieve peace and order and to restore the territory to the Arabs of Palestine."[12] In its war against Israel, however, the latent internecine schisms within the League quickly came to the surface. It found itself unable to coordinate the armies of its members. Since each state claimed the honor for itself, the League Council was not even able to agree on a Commander-in-Chief. "Iraq refused to accept an Egyptian commander. Egypt rejected an Iraqi General. And the Commander-in-Chief of the Jordan army was of British origin and therefore out of the question. The result was that each Arab army that entered Palestine fought on its own."[13] When in May 1949 Israel was admitted to the United Nations, the League faced complete defeat. The state that the League had vowed to destroy was not only in existence but was now recognized as an official member of the world community. The League defeat was made even more bitter when one of its members, Jordan, declared itself ready to accept the establishment of Israel and seemed intent on annexing the remaining portions of Palestine. Under the impact of total defeat the League began to disintegrate completely. Iraq and Jordan developed an increasing suspicion of Egyptian domination in the League and accused the Secretary-General, Azzam Pasha, of pro-Egyptian leanings. As a result, an innocuous former civil servant, Abdel Khalek Hassouna, was appointed to the post. Nevertheless, Iraq refused to pay its membership contribution to the League and began to look around for new allies. To the consternation of the entire League, Iraq became the keystone of the Baghdad Pact, linking it to Britain, Turkey, Iran, and Pakistan. Only a revolution in 1958 brought it back into the fold. Jordan narrowly escaped expulsion because of its flirtation with Israel. The Arab League as a regional arrangement seemed to have turned into a complete debacle.

The pattern of internal conflict among the Arab states has continued. In 1961 the United Arab Republic disintegrated and Syria seceded. Later that year, a bitter feud erupted between Egypt and Saudi Arabia over Yemen. In 1962 Syria lodged a formal complaint with the Arab League, charging that President Nasser was trying to effect a reunion of Syria with Egypt by forcible means. In 1963 Iraq's Premier Kassem was assassinated by pro-Nasser revolutionaries. In Syria the nationalistic Baath party took control. During the same year actual warfare broke out between Algeria and Morocco over the ill-defined Sahara border. After a League call for a cease-fire, a shaky truce was established.

In 1967, almost all of the above conflicts were temporarily obscured when war erupted between Israel and three members of the Arab League, Egypt, Syria, and Jordan. Again, however, there was little effective coordination among the Arab armies, although King Hussein of Jordan placed his armed forces under Egyptian command. Shortly after the war, the members of the League met at Khartoum, in the Sudan, to discuss future policies toward Israel but, once again, many of the stubborn intra-Arab rivalries came to the surface and made any concerted policy difficult.

The Arab League as a regional arrangement has not invested much energy in forging instruments of internal political order. Its sole peace-keeping operation was a joint Egyptian-Saudi Arabian military force dispatched to Kuwait in 1961 to replace British troops which had entered the newly independent country to protect it against the irredentist claims of Premier Kassem of Iraq. In addition, beginning in 1972, the League, under the leadership of its new Secretary-General, Mahmoud Riad, took on the responsibility of mediating between Palestinian guerrillas and several Arab governments, such as Lebanon, that had large numbers of guerrillas on their soil. Other nonpolitical order-building efforts have included the passage by the League Council of legislation for inter-Arab private international law, the dissemination throughout the Arab world of the language of the Koran, and the organization of several cultural, scientific, and educational conferences.

If we analyze the Arab League in terms of the criteria of the Princeton study, we encounter the strange paradox of a regional arrangement that fulfills almost none of the essential conditions of a "security-community." The absence of common values and mutual responsiveness among the members of the League is all too evident. The dynastic competition between Jordan and Saudi Arabia, the hostility between the traditional authoritarianism of the monarchies and the rampant nationalism of the new republics, the fratricidal strife within the camp of the new nationalism—all these have made a mockery of unity in the Arab League. And yet it has held together. It has held together because it has been able to offer its members the expectation of two great rewards: the liquidation of Western colonialism and the destruction of Israel. It has made a vital contribution to the achievement of the first objective and this success has solidified its bonds. Its total failure in the latter has almost brought about its disintegration, yet it seems very likely that the Arab League will continue to function so long as Israel survives. Ironically, therefore, since opposition to Israel is the one thing its members have in common, the League's cohesion appears to depend on the continued existence of the very thing that it seeks to destroy. Because of its primarily negative goals, moreover, the League has done little to advance political order in the Middle East. And, as the authors of the Princeton study have pointed out, a unity that is based chiefly on common hostility against an outside force is bound to be transitory, since it imposes too many burdens and realizes too few rewards. Hence it seems safe to say that unless the Arab League develops more positive methods of integration, it cannot make a major contribution to regional order.

THE ORGANIZATION OF AFRICAN UNITY

The Organization of African Unity (OAU) was created at the Conference of African Nations meeting in Addis Ababa, Ethiopia, in May 1963 with thirty-one independent African nations attending.

There was some disagreement among the delegates over the best method of furthering the cause of African unity. President Nkrumah of Ghana urged the creation of a unitary African state with a strong central government, but the Conference was more impressed with the more moderate proposals of Emperor Haile Selassie of Ethiopia, who quickly became the major spokesman of the majority view.

The Conference decided upon a basic Charter which listed the goals of the new Organization: freedom, dignity, and equality for all Africans; continuation of the struggle against colonialism; preservation and consolidation of the territorial integrity of the members; and the establishment of common institutions. These aims were to be pursued in harmony with the United Nations Charter.

The Conference was also able to agree on institutions for the OAU. It established, as the supreme authority of the OAU, an Assembly composed of the heads of the member states which would meet at least once every year; a Council of Ministers to meet at least twice a year, with each country having one vote and decisions to be made by simple majority; and a Secretary-General and Secretariat. In addition, a special Commission for Mediation and Arbitration of inter-African disputes was set up. The costs of the new Organization were to be met by assessing the members, using the United Nations scale as a model.

Since its inception in 1963, most of the energies of the OAU have gone into the struggle to eliminate the vestiges of Western colonialism in Africa. The heads of the member states have met at least once a year and much of their planning has centered on speeding the decolonization process. In 1964, for example, they decided to deny OAU ports and airfields to ships and planes that served South Africa. In 1965, the delegates unanimously urged Britain to use force against Rhodesia if the latter would seize independence from Britain. In 1966, the members urged the UN Security Council to adopt mandatory sanctions against the Smith regime in Rhodesia. During the late 1960's and the 1970's, two-thirds of the OAU's budget was set aside to help guerrilla activity in the "white redoubt" countries of Southern Africa.

The OAU, however, has also been increasingly concerned about peace-keeping among its own members. In 1964, for example, it established a permanent commission to arbitrate border disputes. In 1965, it arranged for liaison with the UN General Assembly. In 1966, at the OAU Council of Ministers' meeting in Addis Ababa, the members were sharply divided over the seating of the Ghanaian delegation in the wake of Nkrumah's ouster. In 1967, the OAU sent a six-man mission to Lagos in search of Nigerian-Biafran peace and Zambia agreed to serve as moderator in the border dispute smoldering between Kenya and Somalia. At the same conference, UN Secretary-General U Thant urged the OAU to pay more attention to internal peace-keeping. While in 1968, the war between Nigeria and her breakaway province of Biafra assumed the proportions of a major human tragedy, Somalia agreed to resolve its boundary dispute with Kenya. In 1972, the OAU's prestige was further enhanced when the UN Security Council held a series of meetings in Addis Ababa for the express purpose of underlining the urgency of the problems that were besetting the African continent.

While much of the momentum of the OAU is still derived from its original anticolonial *raison d'être*, it is beginning to exhibit some of the earmarks of a pluralistic security-community at a low level in its increasing role as internal peace-keeper. As colonialism recedes more and more into the past, it seems safe to predict that this latter function of the OAU will assume greater prominence in the future.

THE BRITISH COMMONWEALTH

Our final case study in political order-building deals with the British Commonwealth. This is a unique international phenomenon and defies easy definition. As one observer has put it, "If it did not exist you could not invent it."[14] The Commonwealth's uniqueness as a regional arrangement lies in the first instance in the fact that it originated not as a congeries of independent states, but as an empire. The other regional arrangements we have analyzed have attempted to build unity by forging bonds where none have existed before. The Commonwealth, in essence, represents an effort to create political unity through the dissolution of existing political bonds that have become too onerous. For this reason the roots of the Commonwealth are radically different from those of other regional arrangements.

The present membership of the Commonwealth comprises 31 states, consisting of almost one billion people. The 31 members are: Australia, Barbados, Botswana, Canada, Ceylon, Cyprus, Fiji,˙ Gambia, Ghana, Guyana, India, Jamaica, Kenya, Lesotho, Malawi, Malaysia, Malta, Mauritius, New Zealand, Nigeria, Pakistan, Sierra Leone, Singapore,

Swaziland, United Republic of Tanzania, Tonga, Trinidad and Tobago, Uganda, the United Kingdom of Great Britain and Northern Ireland, Western Samoa, and Zambia. The Union of South Africa withdrew from the Commonwealth in 1961 and became the Republic of South Africa. In addition to the sovereign states listed above, the Commonwealth also includes a number of dependencies that are in the process of transition toward sovereign status. These are several territories in Africa in varying stages of emancipation. In 1965, Rhodesia announced its "unilateral Declaration of Independence" from Great Britain, a move which the latter regarded as illegal.

It is difficult to discern what common purpose holds together this highly diversified group of states known as the Commonwealth. Very generally, however, the Commonwealth can be said to be dedicated to at least two objectives: common defense against external threats and common policies for economic betterment. The organizational structure of the Commonwealth is extremely loose. It has neither charter nor treaty and membership in it confers no legal rights and imposes no legal obligations. In terms of formal machinery, the Commonwealth is the least developed of all regional arrangements. The most important of the Commonwealth institutions is a symbolic one—the Crown. Even India and Pakistan, although republics, have accepted the Crown as a symbol of their free association in the Commonwealth. The wearer of the Crown dedicates herself equally to many different peoples and many different faiths. Yet the Crown is considered indivisible. In L. S. Amery's telling metaphor, "it is a jewel of many facets, not a string of disconnected pearls."[15] The informality of Commonwealth relations is reflected in the main political organ, the Conference of Prime Ministers. This Conference is simply an annual or biennial forum with no executive authority. Resolutions that may be passed by the Conference merely have the status of recommendations until ratified by the individual members. This procedure is analogous to that in the Committee of Ministers of the Council of Europe. The Conference is primarily a means of consultation rather than an organ for reaching decisions. But the techniques of consultation and the exchange of information among the Commonwealth countries have reached a high level of sophistication. Each member sends to each of the others a High Commissioner whose relationship to the host country is far less formal than that of the ordinary ambassador. In addition, massive exchanges of personnel in fields of mutual interest at the administrative level have helped to solidify the bonds of the Commonwealth. Common defense problems are discussed and functional matters like shipping and communications receive close attention. There also exists a Commonwealth Secretariat.

The complete absence in the Commonwealth of any pretensions to "supra-nationality" has not prevented large areas of friction among the members. Ireland preferred to leave the Commonwealth rather than discuss her differences with Great Britain. Burma decided to leave it when granted her independence. The membership of India introduced serious disputes with other members: the struggles with Pakistan over Kashmir and Bangla Desh and the perennial friction with the Union of South Africa over the question of minority rights for the local Indian population. Since 1965, Rhodesia has been in a state of revolt against Great Britain, and, in addition, most of the African members of the Commonwealth have found Britain's policy toward Rhodesia too tolerant and have advocated a more forceful course including the possible use of military sanctions.

The Commonwealth has not been able to evolve any common parliamentary or executive institutions. All such efforts have come to nought, owing to the stubborn insistence of each member on its complete sovereignty. Among the many paradoxes of the Commonwealth is the fact that whatever unity it has achieved as a regional arrangement has been attained without the development of institutional limitations on the sovereignty of its members.

Measured in terms of its own purposes, the record of the Commonwealth has been a mixed one. One of its most notable achievements has been its ability to attract into what once was an empire countries that only recently and after long and bitter struggles succeeded in emancipating themselves from colonial tutelage. All the former colonial countries that joined the Commonwealth after receiving independence did so by their own free will. In an age of colonial liquidation and widespread anticolonial emotionalism this has been a remarkable accomplishment indeed. The goal of common defense, on the other hand, has been achieved only partially. At the time of Britain's gravest crisis, during World War II, the members of the Commonwealth fought freely on her side—though some, like India, exacted a heavy price. In the post-World War II world, however, the strategic interests of many of the member countries turned elsewhere. Canada solidified its ties with the United States. Because of its racial policies, the Union of South Africa became the *bête noire* of the Commonwealth and incurred the special animosity of such formerly colonial lands as Ghana and India. Australia and New Zealand, joined in the ANZUS Treaty, looked for protection more and more to the United States than to Great Britain. And India, attempting to follow her own independent course between East and West, more and more subordinated her commitment to the Commonwealth to the dictates of her own evolving strategy of "nonalignment."

How far this dissolution of strategic ties within the Commonwealth has progressed may be seen from the voting behavior of the Commonwealth countries in the United Nations. Of all the "blocs" in the General Assembly, the "Commonwealth bloc" has been the least cohesive. In fact, owing to wide divergencies on matters of foreign policy, its members have tended to vote almost completely independently. On the crucial matter of the Anglo-French invasion of Suez, only Australia and New Zealand supported the position of the United Kingdom. Ceylon, India, and Pakistan voted against Britain, and Canada and South Africa abstained. This lack of foreign-policy consensus has been fairly typical of the so-called "Commonwealth bloc." Indeed, on any matter about which the members of the Commonwealth have strong convictions, each state can usually be expected to act strictly as it sees fit.

In its second purpose, that of improving economic relations, the Commonwealth has been more successful, although the devaluation of the British currency in 1967 sent shock waves throughout the Commonwealth. All parts of the Commonwealth, with the exception of Canada, share a "sterling area" in which trade and investment are greatly facilitated. Economic aid and technical assistance are administered under Commonwealth auspices through the Colombo Plan. This Plan has been one of the most concrete incentives for Commonwealth membership in the lesser developed areas of the world. Its projects are undertaken as a joint enterprise on the basis of local development plans and mutual consultation.

Finally, the mobility of people among the member states has been fairly high. It would be too ambitious to speak of a "Commonwealth citizenship." But in many instances, Commonwealth status facilitates the right to enter or leave member states or to qualify for naturalization. Most of the Commonwealth countries afford privileges to other members not generally accorded to citizens of foreign countries. When, for example, the government of Uganda decided to expel most of its citizens of Asian heritage, Britain made a major effort to offer these refugees new homes.

In January 1971, the Commonwealth Heads of Government met in Singapore to discuss matters of common concern. The meeting was dominated by a heated discussion over Britain's decision to resume the sale of arms and warships to South Africa which had sparked off stormy reactions among the African and Asian members of the Commonwealth. In addition, Britain's decision to enter the European Common Market was considered in terms of its economic impact on the rest of the Commonwealth. At the conclusion of the session, the Conference unanimously agreed upon a "Declaration of Principles" which reaffirmed the voluntary nature of the bonds which held the sovereign members of the Commonwealth together.

In terms of the Princeton study, the Commonwealth can hardly be considered a "security-community." The unity in political and security matters that once characterized the British Empire has been greatly weakened by powerful new centrifugal tendencies. The common commitment to parliamentarianism is threatened by the political instability of the new members in Africa. It would, moreover, be difficult to speak of the existence of common values throughout the Commonwealth. On the other hand, expectation of joint rewards has been high. Membership in the Commonwealth has brought with it concrete economic benefits through joint projects like the Colombo Plan and the unhampered flow of trade. Informal order-building has been continuous without infringements of the members' sovereignty. Perhaps the most important factor of all in explaining the Commonwealth's continuing resiliency has been the fact that rewards and the expectation of rewards have always greatly exceeded burdens and responsibilities.

Regionalism and the United Nations

The relation between regional arrangements and the United Nations has been a subject of heated controversy. Attitudes on the subject have fallen along a wide spectrum. At one extreme have been those who have defended the necessity of regional arrangements as building blocks toward globalism. Those who have advanced this view have held that regionalism is not only compatible with the United Nations but, in fact, is an essential steppingstone to the world organization's successful functioning and further development. Winston Churchill expressed this position most forcefully when he stated before the opening of the San Francisco Conference that "there should be several regional councils, august but subordinate, and these should form the massive pillars upon which the world organization would be founded in majesty and calm."[16] At the other extreme in the controversy have been those who have tended to regard regional arrangements as little more than poorly camouflaged power alliances, evil creations of an anarchic world that are wholly incompatible with the principle of collective security.

At the San Francisco Conference, the problem of regional versus global organization was one of the thorniest issues. Many prospective members of the world organization were deeply committed to regional arrangements that antedated the United Nations Charter. The Inter-American system, the Arab League, and the British Commonwealth commanded the loyalty of more than a score of the nations which assembled at San Francisco. The American republics wished to safeguard the hemispheric system, the Arab states were jealous of the rights of the Arab League, Britain had an eye on the Commonwealth, the Soviet Union wished to exempt its mutual assistance pacts from Security Council control, and most of the small states were suspicious of the Security Council because of the veto power. On the other hand, some members of the Conference were deeply committed to universalism and tended to regard regional arrangements as a menace to peace and order. The interplay among these forces produced a compromise solution that was reflected in the Charter in a grudging acceptance of the fact that regionalism was here to stay and that its existence had to be reconciled with the principle of world organization. At first, there was an attempt to make regional organizations like the OAS into operating arms of the United Nations. Very soon, however, it had to be admitted that the very *raison d'être* of the regional organs was the preservation of their autonomous status vis-à-vis the United Nations. This autonomy was expressed as the right of "collective self-defense," recognized in Article 51 of the Charter. Under this provision NATO, OAS, and the Arab League were in practice exempted from external control by the United Nations. Soviet regional arrangements found a similar escape clause in Article 53 of the Charter, permitting "collective self-defense" against "enemy states" in World War II. Thus the Charter was compelled to recognize the coexistence of regionalism and universalism.

The problem for regionalists and universalists alike has, therefore, become the quest for a viable and productive division of labor between the two forms of political organization in order to maximize progress in order-building. If we compare the order-building record of the various regional organizations with that of the United Nations, the "building-block theory" advocated by the regionalists does not hold up. The Commonwealth, which prides itself on its sophisticated consultative machinery, has on several occasions been compelled to request the help of the General Assembly. It did not succeed in solving the stubborn conflicts between India and Pakistan over Kashmir and Bangla Desh. Similarly, NATO was impotent in the three-cornered struggle involving three of its members over Cyprus, and the problem was handed over to the United Nations. The vital disagreements between the United States and Britain and France over the Suez question could not be composed within the framework of NATO. Only the OAS, with its highly developed order-building institutions, has made a creditable showing and has effectively dealt with serious disputes among its members. On the whole, NATO, the Commonwealth, and the Arab League have had to ask far more from the order-building capacities of the United Nations than they have been able to contribute to the resolution of international conflicts themselves.

If the record of the regional arrangements as independent instruments of order-building is thus not impressive, the reason would seem to lie chiefly in the fact that many of their energies have been absorbed in the two great struggles of our time. As major strategic instruments in these struggles, they have, in fact, been designed and operated so as to preserve the greatest possible degree of autonomy vis-à-vis the United Nations. This situation has, in turn, been reflected in a tendency to discuss more and more of the great international issues outside the world organization's framework. In the words of one scholar of region-alism, "The United Nations has been placed in a position of inferiority so that now the links between the regional arrangements and the world organization exist at the practical pleasure of the former."[17] This increasing habit of bypassing the United Nations on vital issues of high politics and security also troubled the late Secretary-General, Mr. Hammarskjöld, who urged a reversal of the trend:

In recent years, the main attention has been concentrated on measures designed to give a measure of security on a regional basis, in the absence of a more universal system of security. If there is now to be a serious and sustained exploration of the possibilities for cooperation on a wider basis, the world organization must necessarily gain a new dimension.[18]

The problem of achieving a balance between regionalism and globalism cannot be solved in the theoretical realm. Each situation must be examined on its own merits and requires its own particular division of labor. In order to demonstrate the complexity of the problem, let us take the example of the peaceful uses of atomic energy. Should atoms-for-peace be given to needy nations through the universal channel of the United Nations International Atomic Energy Agency (IAEA)? Or should such a program be administered through regional organs like the European Atomic Energy Community (Euratom) in Western Europe? This case study shows that each problem requires its own unique solution.

It is generally agreed that the developmental aspects of atomic energy for peaceful purposes can and should be shared among organizations at the regional as well as the global level. It would indeed be difficult to make a case for totally shifting to the International Atomic Energy Agency all of the many atomic development activities that are at present being carried out through the various regional arrangements. Yet in view of the fact that the different atomic powers maintain different safeguard criteria and insist upon different standards of inspection, the entire matter poses a most difficult dilemma: how to share atomic development activities on different levels and, at the same time, work out the responsibility for adequate and generally acceptable control?

To the donor, the regional approach to atomic development may often seem preferable to working through United Nations channels. The donor's freedom to choose the recipient and to define precisely the conditions for cooperation may even result in more extensive assistance. In the case of United Nations assistance, in contrast, the donor's influence on the recipient must proceed through the machinery of the IAEA Board of Governors and the General Conference. For this reason, United Nations assistance cannot be identified with any one country and tends to assume a more apolitical character than its regional counterpart. This explains why United Nations assistance is at times preferred by the underdeveloped countries and why regional arrangements are frequently favored by donors. Finally, as recipients like to point out, an international organization like IAEA may be better suited for atomic development by virtue of the fact that its membership includes both the advanced and the underdeveloped areas—which means that it can fulfill the function of an intermediary more satisfactorily than can a regional organization.

For certain types of atomic development and research, cooperation through regional arrangements may often be more effective than through IAEA. The Western European and the Latin American countries, for example, form regions that are reasonably homogeneous both geographically and technologically. These factors inevitably favor a regional approach to the development of atomic energy. Moreover, regionalism may also in many cases be better suited to furthering atomic research. The European Organization for Nuclear Research (CERN), founded in 1956, is composed of twelve Western European countries at comparable stages of atomic research development. Its Eastern counterpart, the Joint Institute for Nuclear Research, also founded in 1956, consists of eleven countries from the Soviet bloc. Both these organizations are based on the common experiences and goals of the countries comprising their respective regions and, undoubtedly, derive considerable scientific and technological benefits from this fact.

Agencies engaged in nuclear development will probably continue to proliferate. It is not possible to make a case for exclusively regional or exclusively global nuclear development. In the absence of a general principle, the IAEA will have to adapt itself to constantly changing patterns of development.

In the area of control, however, uniform safeguards must be imposed to avert disaster. The IAEA is in a logical position to play the coordinating role in this task. Yet it is prevented from doing so because some regional controls are less stringent than those demanded by the United Nations. Neither Euratom nor the OEEC, for example, requires certain controls that are insisted upon in the IAEA Statute. However, since the member states of Euratom are also signatories to the IAEA Statute, this obstacle need not remain altogether insurmountable.

There are three possible ways in which regional development and control functions might be brought under the IAEA. First, the nuclear powers might arrange for IAEA to take over regional programs in their entirety. This is the hope of the IAEA's Director-General but is unlikely to materialize. Second, regional arrangements might continue, with the parties requesting the IAEA to assume responsibility for the administration of safeguards. The IAEA Statute permits this, and its realization is possible. The United States has already taken the initiative in bringing some of its bilateral agreements under IAEA control. Third, the regional arrangements might cover the same broad fields of development and control as are covered by IAEA. This is the most likely development. IAEA can therefore be expected to discharge a function of piecemeal coordination, dealing with limited and specific situations as they arise from day to day. The size of reactors, division of labor in isotope research, and concrete inspection provisions are likely to be some of the typical problems of coordination that IAEA will face. The reconciliation of regionalism with globalism in atomic energy will thus become primarily a process to be managed, rather than a problem to be solved.

The case of atomic energy demonstrates the extreme complexity of the relationship between regionalism and globalism. In this particular case, the regional approach seems quite appropriate for the *developmental* aspects, whereas in the matter of *control* a world approach seems required. Each problem, however, demands its own careful study and its own particular solution. Excessive theorizing and generalizing are likely to contribute very little.

The record supports neither the "building-block theory" of regionalism nor the opposite contention that regional arrangements are necessarily antithetical to the principles of the United Nations Charter. Rather, the evidence shows that frequently the United Nations has been a second line of defense for regionalism and that sometimes regional arrangements have served as backstops for the world organization. Certainly there is ample room for both types of political order-building on the international scene.

REFERENCES

1. Karl W. Deutsch, Sidney A. Burrell, Robert A. Kann, Maurice Lee, Jr., Martin Lichterman, Raymond E. Lindgren, Francis L. Loewenheim, and Richard W. Van Wagenen, *Political Community and the North Atlantic Area*. Princeton, N.J.: Princeton University Press, 1957.

2. *Ibid.*, pp. 190–191.

3. Richard Coudenhove-Kalergi, *An Idea Conquers the World*. London: Putnam, 1953, p. ix.

4. Cited by A. H. Robinson, *The Council of Europe*. New York: Praeger, 1956, pp. 1–2.

5. Cited by Arnold J. Zurcher, *The Struggle to Unite Europe*. New York: New York University Press, 1958, p. 6.

6. Political and Economic Planning (PEP), *European Organisations*. London: Allen and Unwin, 1959, p. 132.

7. Oscar Svarlien, *An Introduction to the Law of Nations*. New York: McGraw-Hill, 1955, p. 443.

8. PEP, *op. cit.,* p. 206.

9. Inis L. Claude, *Swords into Plowshares,* 2d ed. New York: Random House, 1959, p. 199.

10. Deutsch, *et al., op. cit.,* p. 156.

11. B. Y. Boutros-Ghali, "The Arab League," *International Conciliation,* May 1954, p. 394.

12. United Nations Doc. S/745, May 16, 1948.

13. Boutros-Ghali, *op. cit.,* pp. 411–412.

14. K. C. Wheare, "The Nature and Structure of the Commonwealth," *American Political Science Review,* December 1953, p. 1016.

15. L. S. Amery, *Thoughts on the Constitution.* New York: Oxford University Press, 1953, p. 169.

16. Cited by Claude, *op. cit.,* p. 120.

17. Edgar S. Furniss, Jr., "A Re-examination of Regional Arrangements," *Journal of International Affairs,* IX (1955), 84.

18. Cited by Norman D. Palmer and Howard C. Perkins, *International Relations.* Boston: Houghton Mifflin, 1957, p. 641.

BIBLIOGRAPHY

Aron, Raymond, and Lerner, Daniel, eds. *France Defeats the EDC: Studies in an International Controversy.* New York: Praeger, 1956.

Ball, Margaret M. *The OAS in Transition.* Durham, N.C.: Duke University Press, 1969.

Barclay, G. St. J. *Commonwealth of Europe.* St. Lucia, Australia: University of Queensland Press, 1970.

Beer, Francis A. *Integration and Disintegration in NATO.* Columbus, Ohio: Ohio State University Press, 1969.

Beloff, Max. *Europe and the Europeans.* London: Chatto and Windus, 1957.

Britain in Western Europe—WEU and the Atlantic Alliance. London: Royal Institute of International Affairs, 1956.

Bromberger, Merry and Serge. *Jean Monnet and the United States of Europe.* New York: Coward-McCann, 1969.

Buchan, Alastair. *NATO in the 1960's.* New York: Praeger, 1960.

Burr, Robert N. *Our Troubled Hemisphere: Perspectives on United States–Latin American Relations.* Washington, D.C.: Brookings Institution, 1967.

Claude, Inis L., Jr. "The OAS, the UN, and the United States," *International Conciliation,* No. 547, March 1964.

Crawford, Oliver. *Done This Day: The European Idea in Action.* New York: Taplinger, 1970.

Deutsch, Karl W. *et al. France, Germany, and the Western Alliance.* New York: Scribner, 1967.

——. *The Nerves of Government.* Glencoe, Ill.: The Free Press, 1963.

——, *et al. Political Community and the North Atlantic Area.* Princeton, N.J.: Princeton University Press, 1957.

Gregg, Robert W., ed. *International Organization in the Western Hemisphere.* Syracuse, N.Y.: Syracuse University Press, 1968.

Grunwald, Joseph, *et al. Latin American Economic Integration and U.S. Policy.* Washington, D.C.: Brookings Institution, 1972.

Hall, H. Duncan. *Commonwealth: A History of the British Commonwealth of Nations.* New York: Van Nostrand Reinhold, 1971.

Ismay, Lord. *NATO—The First Five Years.* Paris: The International Secretariat, 1954.

Jordan, Robert S. *The NATO International Staff Secretariat 1952–1957.* New York: Oxford University Press, 1967.

Jose, James R. *An Inter-American Peace Force Within the Framework of the Organization of American States.* Metuchen, N.J.: Scarecrow Press, 1970.

Lacqueur, Walter. *The Rebirth of Europe.* New York: Holt, Rinehart, and Winston, 1970.

Lindsay, Kenneth. *Toward a European Parliament.* Paris: The International Secretariat, 1958.

Liska, George. *Europe Ascendant.* Baltimore: The Johns Hopkins Press, 1964.

Luethy, Herbert. *France Against Herself.* New York: Praeger, 1955.

McDonald, Robert W. *The League of Arab States.* Princeton, N.J.: Princeton University Press, 1965.

Myrdal, Gunnar. *Realities and Illusions in Regard to Inter-Governmental Organizations.* New York: Oxford University Press, 1955.

Nye, J. S. *Peace in Parts: Integration and Conflict in Regional Organization.* Boston: Little, Brown, 1971.

Pfaltzgraff, Robert L., Jr. *The Atlantic Community: A Complex Imbalance.* New York: Van Nostrand Reinhold, 1969.

Political and Economic Planning (PEP). *European Organizations.* London: Allen and Unwin, 1959.

Robertson, A. H. *The Council of Europe—Its Structure, Functions and Achievements.* New York: Praeger, 1956.

_____. *European Institutions—Co-operation: Integration: Unification.* London: Stevens, 1959.

Slater, Jerome. *The OAS and United States Foreign Policy.* Columbus, Ohio: Ohio State University Press, 1967.

Stoessinger, John G. *The Refugee and the World Community.* Minneapolis, Minn.: University of Minnesota Press, 1956.

Von Geusau, Frans A. M. Alting. *Beyond The European Community.* Leyden: Sijthoff, 1969.

Warburton, Anne M., and Wood, John B. *Paying for NATO.* London: Friends of Atlantic Union, n.d.

Woronoff, Jon. *Organizing African Unity.* Metuchen, N.J.: Scarecrow Press, 1970.

12 The Military Struggle for Order

To take arms against a sea of troubles.

SHAKESPEARE Hamlet, III, 1

Dilemmas of Disarmament

The following is a description of Hiroshima shortly after the city was destroyed by an atomic bomb in August 1945:

People are still dying, mysteriously and horribly—people who were uninjured in the cataclysm—from an unknown something which I can only describe as the atomic plague.

Hiroshima does not look like a bombed city. . . . I write these facts as dispassionately as I can, in the hope that they will act as a warning to the world. In this first testing ground of the atomic bomb . . . it gives you an empty feeling in the stomach to see such man-made devastation. . . . I could see about three miles of reddish rubble. That is all the atomic bomb left. . . . The Police Chief of Hiroshima . . . took me to hospitals where the victims of the bombs are still being treated. In these hospitals I found people who, when the bomb fell, suffered absolutely no injuries, but now are dying from the uncanny after-effects. For no apparent reason their health began to fail. They lost appetite. Their hair fell out. Bluish spots appeared on their bodies. And then bleeding began from the ears, nose and mouth.

At first, the doctors told me, they thought these were the symptoms of general debility. They gave their patients Vitamin A injections. The results were horrible. The flesh started rotting away from the hole caused by the injection of the needle. And in every case the victim died.

A peculiar odour . . . given off by the poisonous gas still issues from the earth soaked with radioactivity; against this the inhabitants all wear gauze masks over their mouths and noses; many thousands of people have simply vanished—the atomic heat was so great that they burned instantly to ashes—except that there were no ashes—they were vaporised.[1]

The bomb here mentioned, it should be noted, is now considered obsolete. Its capacity for destruction has been dwarfed by an even more total weapon—the hydrogen bomb. That this development has engendered a more intensive quest for disarmament than ever before in history is by no means surprising. Indeed, the price of failure in this quest is not likely to be merely the kind of devastation that was loosed on Hiroshima and Nagasaki. It may well be the extinction of man as the dominant form of life on this planet.

Since 1945 the issue of disarmament has assumed paramount importance and has unceasingly occupied the thinking of statesmen and technical experts everywhere. The United Nations General Assembly has dealt with it during every session and it is safe to predict that this pattern will continue. The two major antagonists in the East-West struggle have both agreed that disarmament is the most important problem facing the world today.[2] Yet, despite a strategic arms limitation treaty agreed upon at the Moscow Summit of 1972, not a single weapon, atomic or conventional, has been scrapped. Instead, we are still witnessing the fiercest and most relentless arms race in history. Why? In order to answer this question, we must analyze the disarmament dilemma in all its complexity.

If the objective of the political order-builders is a world without major disputes, the hope of those who would build order through disarmament is a world without weapons. In the view of the latter, arms races cause wars. If, as they see it, arms are permitted to accumulate, they will sooner or later be used. An arms race therefore becomes a relentless and self-propelling march to war. Both sides strain furiously to maintain or reclaim the lead. Finally, the tension reaches such a pitch that war is almost welcomed as a liberating explosion. If, on the other hand, nations are deprived of the means to fight, the proponents of disarmament maintain, wars will either cease to exist or, at worst, become relatively harmless. In the telling phrase of Maxim Litvinov: "the way to disarm is to disarm."

Here we encounter the first crucial problem. Is it true, as the advocates of disarmament hold, that arms races cause the political tensions that drive nations to war? Or are the political order-builders correct in asserting that though arms races may precipitate war, the real source of international conflict must be sought in the political tensions between nations that lead to arms races in the first place? The former tend to regard the arms race as a basic cause of war, the latter merely as a symptom of political pathology. Both groups are prepared to admit that the problem is really a circular one: that arms races breed political tensions; that these in turn lead to the development and acquisition of more destructive weapons; and that this situation raises temperatures even further—until the violent climax is reached. But the two groups differ as to the most effective point at which to intervene in the vicious circle. Those who see arms races as a basic cause of war assert the primacy of international order-building through disarmament. They maintain that halting the arms race will lead to a reduction in political tensions, which will likely result in an even further scrapping of weapons. On the other hand, a growing number of observers are defending the view that disarmament efforts are bound to fail unless they are preceded by more fundamental political accommodation. The way to disarm, according to this latter view, is not to begin by disarming but to concentrate instead on the settlement of political differences.

One of the most articulate spokesmen for the primacy of disarmament is the British Nobel Prize winner Philip Noel-Baker. This scholar attacks the thesis that disarmament can only be a consequence, never a cause, of improvement in international relations. In support of his view, Noel-Baker cites the Rush-Bagot Agreement of 1817 between Britain and the United States, which disarmed the Canadian frontier. In his view, this Agreement was a great contribution to the establishment of friendly relations between Canada and the United States. He also points to the 1922 Washington Naval Disarmament Convention, which reduced the navies of Britain, the United States, and Japan, as producing a remarkable improvement in international relations. He suggests that the Convention nipped in the bud an impending struggle for supremacy of the seas and played a major part in creating cordial relations between Britain and the United States. From these examples, the author concludes that the ending of the East-West nuclear arms race by a disarmament treaty would improve international relations, reduce tensions, and facilitate the settlement of outstanding political disputes.[3]

The opposing view is most eloquently defended by Hans J. Morgenthau. He attacks the view of the military order-builder as unrealistic. "Men do not fight because they have arms, but they have arms because they deem it necessary to fight." If deprived of weapons, nations will employ all their resources for the development of new ones. In fact, Morgenthau continues, the threat of all-out nuclear war may have been the most important single factor that has prevented the outbreak of general war in the nuclear age. The removal of that threat through disarmament might indeed increase the dangers of war. Disarmament might do away with weapons but not with the will and the technical knowledge to produce these weapons. In support of his argument Morgenthau cites the Treaty of Versailles which, in his view, was a blessing in disguise for German militarism. Disarmament compelled Germany to project its military thinking in the future, to look at problems of strategy and technology *de novo*. Far from removing German ambitions of conquest, disarmament merely equipped it to fight a second World War while France was ready merely for a repetition of World War I.[4] Hence, Morgenthau concludes, the first step toward order-building must always be political rather than military. Disarmament *in vacuo* is bound to be a failure.

In view of the sharp disagreement on the nature and significance of disarmament, it is necessary to subject the modern record of disarmament negotiations to careful scrutiny. Why did most of them fail? What was the secret of success of the few that did not? Does the record provide any clues for the crucial disarmament negotiations of our own time?

Before embarking on a survey of the disarmament record, it is useful to bear in mind a definition and three important distinctions. Central to the concept of disarmament is the term *reduction*. An actual reduction of weapons must take place before we can describe an act as *dis*armament. The first of the three distinctions is between *general* disarmament, which refers to efforts involving all nations, and *local* disarmament, which includes only a limited number of countries. The second is between *quantitative* disarmament, which concerns the reduction of all types of weapons, and *qualitative* disarmament, which concentrates upon a specific category of weapons. It is also useful to remember that the reduction of nonatomic weapons is referred to as "conventional disarmament," while "nuclear disarmament" refers to the reduction of atomic stockpiles.

In the entire history of the nation-state system up to World War II, there are on record only two disarmament conferences that proved successful. Both were local and quantitative. The first was the Rush-Bagot Agreement, concluded in 1817, limiting the naval forces of Canada and the United States to three vessels each on the Great Lakes. The Agreement resulted in the demilitarization of the United States–Canadian frontier. With certain revisions that were added during World War II, the Agreement has remained in force.

The more significant of the two successful ventures in disarmament was the Washington Treaty of 1922 for the Limitation of Naval Armaments. The aim of the Treaty was to determine ratios for the allocation of capital ships among the major naval powers. The United States and Britain were to have the largest navies, while Japan, France, and Italy were given smaller allocations. A ratio of 5:5:3:1.67:1.67 was finally established for the capital ships of the United States, Britain, Japan, France, and Italy, in that order. As a result, the three leading countries scrapped approximately two fifths of their capital ships. In regard to cruisers, destroyers, and submarines, however, the Washington Treaty failed to reach agreement. The London Naval Conference of 1930 attempted to complete the work begun at Washington by limiting the tonnage of naval craft other than capital ships. Parity for cruisers, destroyers, and submarines was agreed upon between the United States and Britain, while Japan was limited to two thirds of American or British strength. Neither France nor Italy was a signatory to the London Treaty. Italy demanded parity with France, as in the Washington Agreement. This parity France was now unwilling to grant.

The agreements hammered out so painstakingly in Washington and London were not destined to endure. In 1934 Japan demanded parity with Britain and the United States in all naval craft. When this demand was rejected, Japan abrogated the Treaty and embarked on an ambitious naval rearmament program. Hence, of the two successes on record, only the Rush-Bagot Agreement may be considered permanent. The Washington Treaty was moribund after a decade.

Unhappily, the list of failures is far longer. The pattern was set at the First Hague Peace Conference in 1899, when twenty-eight nations expressed themselves on the desirability of a reduction in armaments but were unable to agree on a specific formula. The failure was repeated by forty-four nations meeting at the Second Hague Peace Conference in 1907. As the Russian delegate put it at the time: "The question was not ripe in 1899, it is not any more so in 1907. It has not been possible to do anything on these lines, and the Conference today finds itself as little prepared to enter upon them as in 1899."[5] The next effort took place at Versailles in 1919, when disarmament was imposed upon Germany. As that nation became increasingly restive under the terms of the "Versailles Diktat" during the 1920's, the League of Nations sought desperately to keep German armaments at a minimum. Finally, a World Disarmament Conference was convened at Geneva in 1932. But that conference met under the shadow of Hitler, who was to come to power several months later. When Germany embarked on a relentless arms program in 1933, the World Disarmament Conference had to concede defeat.

Six years of World War, culminating in the ghastly spectacle of atomic destruction, convinced the founders of the United Nations that disarmament should be a permanent item on the agenda of the new world organization. Accordingly, in January 1946 the General Assembly created the Atomic Energy Commission for the specific purpose of eliminating atomic weapons from the nations' military arsenals. In addition, a Commission for Conventional Armaments was established by the Security Council in February 1947. When neither of these two organs made any progress, the General Assembly, in 1952, amalgamated them into one Disarmament Commission. This body originally consisted of the members of the Security Council plus Canada. However, each time the Commission failed to achieve a consensus, the General Assembly attempted to remedy the matter by enlarging its membership. Finally, the General Assembly itself became a forum for disarmament proposals that were thinly camouflaged propaganda maneuvers in the East-West struggle rather than serious overtures to negotiation. Premier Khrushchev's proposal for general and complete disarmament, which he made in the General Assembly in 1959, was a case in point. Since 1954, indeed, Geneva, Vienna, and Moscow, rather than the United Nations, have become the meeting places for serious negotiations. The conferences that have been held there have usually included an equal number of representatives from East and West. A typical "parity committee" at Geneva during the 1950's included Albania, Czechoslovakia, Poland, Rumania, and the Soviet Union, representing the East; and the United States, Britain, France, Canada, and Italy speaking for the West. More recently, a specially constituted "Tripartite Committee" has taken over the job.

Thus, since the end of World War II, disarmament negotiations have been a permanent phenomenon. Yet none of the many conferences that have been held—whether inside or outside of the United Nations—has accomplished the elimination of a single atomic or conventional weapon. Even the Moscow Summit of 1972 was no exception. It achieved a *limitation* on the building of additional arms, not a *reduction* of existing arms. The most intensive disarmament efforts in Western history have been a virtual failure. The only successes on record antedate World War II, and one of these was of too brief duration to be termed an unqualified success. We shall now look into the causes of this discouraging record.

One important reason for these many failures is the inherently *static* nature of all disarmament. It is a fact of international life that many nations are constantly engaged in attempts to manipulate the existing distribution of power in their favor. An increase in armaments is an obvious means to accomplish this end. The goal of disarmament, on the other hand, is in essence the freezing of a certain distribution of power which will be acceptable to some, but never to all the powers concerned. Most nations conceive of themselves as dynamic actors on the international scene, hoping to move from strength to strength. Such states will have little patience with policies that would deprive them of an important means whereby they can grow in power and stature. Indeed, one of the greatest obstacles to disarmament is the fact that nations are less concerned with what they are than with what they would like to be.

The technical counterpart of this political truth has been the enormous difficulty of *measurement*. Each disarmament conference has to grapple with this stubborn problem. Once the delegates get down to specifics, they constantly find themselves compelled to "compare apples with oranges." Which is more valuable to a military arsenal—a destroyer or a tank? How does the striking force of the American Strategic Air Command compare to the Soviet land army? How many Polaris missiles should be scrapped for each Soviet intercontinental ballistic missile? How do four million men in reserve compare to one million in active service? Precision is almost impossible to attain. Each side in the East-West struggle has advanced proposals that would leave its superiority intact or reduce that of the other side. Since both the United States and the Soviet Union conceive of themselves as dynamic contestants for supremacy, neither has been willing to accept an arms reduction that would freeze it at a level of inferiority. Salvadore de Madariaga has illustrated the point admirably through the analogy of an imaginary conference of animals at which "the lion wanted to eliminate all weapons but claws and jaws, the eagle all but talons and beaks and the bear all but an embracing hug."[6]

The crucial cause of the failure of most disarmament negotiations is, of course, the *absence of mutual trust*. In technical terms this has meant that each side has attempted to impose rigorous requirements of *inspection* and *control* on the other in order to ensure that an agreement, once reached, would not be violated. Control and inspection are to be the technical substitute for mutual trust. But this condition has invited a circular problem: each side requires control because it does not trust the other; yet, the acceptance of a control system itself demands a high degree of mutual trust. In short, whenever nations have taken the position that there can be no disarmament without security, they have had to realize that foolproof security is equally impossible. A degree of mutual confidence is necessary for *both* disarmament and security. The major powers have been unable to escape from this predicament.

The control problem proved to be an insurmountable obstacle at the very beginning of the nuclear disarmament negotiations in the United Nations Atomic Energy Commission in 1946. At that time, when the United States still had an atomic monopoly, it proposed a far-reaching control plan known as the Acheson-Lilienthal Report, or Baruch Plan. The purpose of the Plan was to ensure that atomic energy would be used exclusively for peaceful purposes. To accomplish this end, the United States proposed the internationalization of all facilities producing atomic power. All atomic plants would be owned and operated by an Atomic Development Authority that would have the powers of inspection, accounting, and licensing. The American hope was to place atomic energy firmly under international control before the Soviet Union would end the American monopoly and engage in an atomic arms race with the United States. The Plan was widely heralded as a generous offer which would place the power of the atom under the authority of a limited world government. The Soviet Union's response, however, was negative. It insisted upon the continuance of national ownership and operation of atomic plants and advanced a plan of its own which proposed the destruction of all existing stocks of nuclear weapons and a legal prohibition of their future manufacture. Only after existing stockpiles had been destroyed and a treaty outlawing nuclear weapons concluded would the Soviet Union be ready to proceed to international inspection. Most immediately, then, the impasse revolved around the problem of priorities. The United States insisted on the priority of international inspection before it was willing to undertake the destruction of its nuclear stockpiles. Control would have to come first and disarmament would follow. The Soviet Union, on the other hand, insisted on the prior destruction of American stockpiles before it was willing to allow international inspection. It reversed the sequence: disarmament must come first and control would follow.

It would seem from the above that the United States' offer was a generous one, whereas the Soviet Union's rejection was an unreasonable act of caprice. After all, the United States made its offer at a time when it had an atomic monopoly. It would therefore appear that the Soviet Union, which had not yet developed its own atomic bomb, could only gain from the internationalization of atomic power. Actually, however, the picture is considerably more complex. It is true that the American offer was an enlightened act of statesmanship. But it is equally true that, given the state of mistrust between the two superpowers, there were valid reasons from the Soviet point of view for rejecting the Baruch Plan. First and most important, the Plan would have perpetuated the American monopoly of atomic weapons. And beyond that, the Soviet Union feared that the proposed Atomic Development Authority would be dominated by the Western powers with the Eastern bloc in a permanent minority without the right of veto. In the words of Andrei Gromyko, the Soviet delegate:

The Soviet Union is aware that there will be a majority in the control organ which may take one-sided decisions, a majority on whose benevolent attitude toward the Soviet Union the Soviet people cannot count. Therefore, the Soviet Union, and probably not only the Soviet Union, cannot allow that the fate of its national economy be handed over to this organ.[7]

Most basically, Soviet suspicions grew out of the realization that only the United States would be in a position to cheat, i.e., withhold weapons from the Authority, while the Soviet Union would be compelled to accept a permanent position of inferiority. All this is not to say that the United States' offer was not farsighted. What does seem clear, however, is that its chances of acceptance would have been considerably greater if it had permitted the continuation of national atomic research in the Soviet Union.

The struggle over priorities that began in 1946 continued without letup until the Moscow Summit of 1972. The United States and the Soviet Union both agreed that a viable disarmament treaty would have to include provisions for the prohibition of nuclear weapons as well as acceptable arrangements for control. The Soviet Union consistently defended the priority of prohibition in numerous "ban the bomb" proposals. These proposals were unacceptable to the United States, which feared that the Soviet Union would not accede to control once prohibition was accepted. The United States' insistence on the priority of control, on the other hand, was unacceptable to the Soviet Union because the latter consistently tended to regard all international inspection as a form of espionage. Hence the paradoxical situation that though both powers accepted the principle of simultaneous disarmament and control, they were unable to translate it into practice. Each side continued to postpone what for it would be the greater sacrifice and, instead, encouraged the opponent to take the first step. To try to expedite matters the French in 1958 introduced the ingenious formula: "neither control without disarmament, nor disarmament without control but, progressively, all the disarmament that can at present be controlled."[8] Though this proposal met the problem in principle, it , too, could not be applied in practice.

Fundamentally, the impasse stemmed from the fact that American proposals assumed a good deal of Soviet confidence in the United States, while the Soviet counterproposals assumed an equal amount of American faith in Soviet intentions. When the two rivals realized that this premise of mutual trust did not exist, they sought substitutes in various technical requirements for inspection and control. Yet they soon concluded that even such technical devices could never be completely foolproof; cheating would continue to be possible regardless of how intricate the safeguards. Indeed, there clearly seemed no other alternative: good faith was a necessary premise for *all* disarmament negotiations and arrangements.

A further reason for the failure of disarmament negotiations may be found, paradoxically enough, in the very interest that the subject has continued to evoke in world public opinion. In the words of India's late Prime Minister Nehru:

The arms race affects us nations and peoples everywhere, whether we are involved in wars or power blocs or not. . . . There can be little doubt about the deep and widespread concern in the world, particularly among peoples, about these weapons and their dreadful consequences.[9]

The testing of hydrogen weapons on both sides of the Iron Curtain and the resulting problem of atomic radiation intensified public indignation the world over. Disarmament became the most emotional issue before the United Nations General Assembly. Not surprisingly, the rise of this passionate popular interest and involvement led both sides in the conflict to engage in "open diplomacy." Vying for the allegiance of the uncommitted countries where disarmament was a burning issue, the two superpowers turned the disarmament negotiations themselves into a weapon in the East-West struggle. Open diplomacy in the sensitive and frequently technical field of disarmament inevitably culminated in propaganda battles in which both East and West felt compelled to appeal to the audiences rather than to each other.

Each side faced a similar dilemma in the conduct of these public negotiations. The demands of security forbade the advancement of proposals which the other side found genuinely acceptable. But the power of publicity demanded that the proposals appear as reasonable as possible in order to avoid the onus of sabotaging the negotiations. Hence, a curious pattern developed that one observer aptly called the "gamesmanship of disarmament."[10] This "game" was played according to certain tacit but well-defined rules:

> Every plan offered by either side has contained a set of proposals calculated to have wide popular appeal. Every such set has included at least one feature that the other side could not possible accept, thus forcing a rejection. Then the proposing side has been able to claim that the rejector is opposed to the idea of disarmament *in toto*. The objectionable feature may be thought of as the "joker" in every series of proposals.[11]

As a result of this "game," the illusion was sometimes created that the two sides had narrowed their differences. Actually, what had happened was that each side had expanded its range of acceptable proposals to insure popular appeal, but had made equally sure that a "joker" would force rejection of the entire package. The Baruch Plan contained such a "joker": the insistence that there be no veto on the question of sanctions against violators of the control agreement. Acceptance of this "joker" would have placed the Soviet Union in a position of permanent military inferiority. Soviet proposals made similar use of the "joker" technique. A typical case was a Soviet proposal, made on May 10, 1955, in which the USSR agreed to reduce its land armies to a maximum figure desired by the three Western powers. For five years the Western negotiators had proposed a reduction of Chinese, Soviet, and American forces to one million men each, with 650,000 each for France and the United Kingdom. But as public pressure mounted and the July 1955 Summit Conference drew nearer, the French delegate to the Conference, Jules Moch, stated that "The whole thing look[ed] too good to be true." The spokesman for the United States, on the other hand, made the following, more optimistic statement:

> We have been gratified to find that the concepts which we have put forward over a

considerable length of time, and which we have repeated many times during these past two months, have been accepted in a large measure by the Soviet Union.[12]

As it turned out, Moch's suspicions were fully justified. The proposal was indeed too good to be true. The Soviet concession was made conditional upon agreement that "states possessing military, naval and air bases in the territories of other states shall undertake to liquidate such bases."[12] In other words, the Soviet "joker" was a demand for the dissolution of the Western alliance system—a condition, of course, that was completely unacceptable without prior settlement of the major political differences between East and West. It is significant, nevertheless, that despite the obviousness of this "joker," the onus for the collapse of the manpower reduction talks was placed by most observers at the Summit Conference squarely upon the United States. The public, eager for results, was hypnotized by what appeared to be a generous proposal and did not notice the "jokers." Even as astute an observer as Philip Noel Baker failed to perceive the deceptiveness of the Soviet bid. In his book, *The Arms Race,* he refers to May 10, 1955, the day of the Soviet manpower reduction proposal, as "the moment of hope," and attributes its failure directly to what he feels to have been the dogmatic unwillingness of the American State Department to disarm at all.[14]

Perhaps the really classic example of "gamesmanship" was Premier Khrushchev's dramatic proposal for "general and complete disarmament," made before the General Assembly in September 1959. In his speech, the Soviet Premier suggested that "over a period of four years, all states should carry out complete disarmament and should divest themselves of the means of waging war."[15] The Premier envisaged the dissolution of all armies, navies, air forces, general staffs, war ministries, and military schools as well as the destruction of all atomic weapons and missiles. Especially in the uncommitted countries, the publicity value of the Russian leader's speech was quite high, even though, by the late 1950's, the effectiveness of disarmament propaganda had begun to reach a point of diminishing returns. Yet as always, there was a "joker." And this time it was the vagueness of the new proposal's references to the matter of control provisions. Indeed, the most to which the Soviet Premier would commit himself was the establishment of "an international control body in which all states would participate."[16] Yet Mr. Khrushchev presumably knew full well that as far as the West was concerned, no disarmament proposal would be acceptable unless it at the same time provided for a rigorous and full-scale inspection system.

A final reason for the failure of disarmament is undoubtedly the fact that one of the two main negotiators is a totalitarian power and, as such, a closed society. It is true that the unwillingness to accept international inspection has not always been a Soviet monopoly. As Claude points out, the United States expressed similar suspicions of foreign inspection in 1919 and again in 1927.[17] But in the United States and most other Western countries, this attitude appears now to have been largely transcended. In 1958, for example, the American Institute of Public Opinion conducted an extensive poll in six nations—the United States, Britain, France, West Germany, India, and Japan—to determine the climate of opinion in regard to international inspection of disarmament.[18] The following three questions were asked:

1. Would you favor or oppose setting up a world-wide organization which would make sure—by regular inspections—that no nation, including Russia and the United States, makes atom bombs, hydrogen bombs and missiles?
2. If this inspection organization were set up, would you favor or oppose making it each person's *duty* to report any attempt to secretly make atom bombs, hydrogen bombs and missiles?
3. If you, yourself, knew that someone in [name of country] was attempting to secretly make forbidden weapons, would you report this to the office of the world-wide inspection organization in this country?

The first question simply referred to a general disarmament proposal; the second, however, raised a potential conflict of values between national and international loyalty; and the third posed the problem of conflicting loyalties in its starkest form. Hence it was expected that favorable responses would be highest to question one and lowest to question three. Actually, the overall results of the six-nation poll were striking: an overwhelmingly positive response to all three questions in all six countries. Japan ranked highest, with West Germany, India, France, the United States, and Britain following, in that order. From these results the authors concluded that "Inspection by the People was not as visionary a proposal as one might have thought."[19] This conclusion is perhaps overly optimistic, since the authors did not take into account the probable differences between people's reactions to a set of hypothetical questions and their possible reactions when confronted with an actual situation. Yet the study did permit the conclusion that a cross-section of the citizens of six democratic nations was definitely in favor of some form of international inspection of disarmament. The very fact, on the other hand, that the Soviet Union did not permit such a poll was itself indicative. Like all closed societies, it has been obsessed with the importance of national sovereignty. And, of course, national sovereignty reaches its most absolute form in matters of military security. In view of this difference in the underlying political logic of East and West, differences between the two sides on such technical matters as to whether inspection or prohibition should have priority, or as to the allocation of specific ratios, are, in the last analysis, merely surface manifestations. The really fundamental difference, rather, must be sought in the basically different characters of the two types of societies: the Western system, more "open" than that of the East, has been able to absorb at least a minimum of international authority; the Soviet Union, largely a "closed" society, has regarded all forms of foreign control as a menace and, hence, anathema.

We are now left with the crucial substantive question of whether the record indicates that order-building through disarmament is a valid approach. The evidence suggests that it is not. Disarmament seems to be not so much a means for the attainment of political order as a product of its achievement. We have seen that, as a rule, nations will be concerned with disarmament only when they are engaged in a power struggle; yet it is precisely this condition which makes the attainment of disarmament so difficult. Even the Washington Treaty of 1922 cannot be cited as an argument in favor of the effectiveness of disarmament. Most of the capital ships that were discarded under the terms of the Treaty were obsolete and would have been scrapped anyway. The vessels considered most important in a future war were cruisers, destroyers, and submarines. And significantly, it was in these three categories that the five signatory powers failed to reach agreement. In fact, it might be said that all the Treaty accomplished was a "naval holiday" in the building of capital ships that freed the energies of the five nations to engage in an arms race in the production of other naval craft that were considered more vital to the needs of modern warfare. Even if one rejects this uncharitable interpretation of the Washington Treaty, it would be difficult to regard it as a significant instrument of international order-building in view of the fact that Japan repudiated it the moment its new policy of imperialism dictated such a course. Disarmament as a direct approach to order seems feasible only when nations are interested in the enhancement rather than in the reduction of one another's strength. It is probably an exaggeration to claim, as does one authority, that because of the many technical obstacles involved, "even such inveterate friends as the United States and Britain probably could not agree on a formula of mutual arms limitation."[20] After all, the Rush-Bagot agreement of 1817 between the United States and Canada was just such a case. Yet the irony of this Agreement lies in the fact that it was probably unnecessary since it was concluded between two neighbors, both of whom by then considered war between them most unlikely.

The discouraging record of disarmament in the modern world supports the proposition that order is fundamentally not a military problem. Disarmament negotiations *per se* will not reduce the tensions between the major powers unless such efforts are preceded by at least a minimum of success in the settlement of outstanding political differences. This is really another way of saying that the problem of disarmament is not disarmament at all, but is in essence the problem of forging the bonds of political community among nations. We have seen earlier that we know little about the causes of war. Similarly, we do not know enough about the process of community-building. Why should a pilot under orders drop a lethal weapon on a defenseless city in "enemy" country, but refuse to drop it on his own? At first glance, this question may seem naive. But when one considers its human implications, it is not. For if we could answer it, the issue of disarmament would have become largely irrelevant. As an order-building strategy disarmament is chiefly concerned with symptoms. The real causes of the disease must be sought at a deeper level.

The frustrations over disarmament have led some thinkers to approach the problem in a somewhat different way: arms *control* rather than disarmament. Whereas the disarmer is primarily concerned with the actual scrapping of existing weapons, the arms controller is more interested in stabilizing the climate in which these weapons exist and in the prevention of additional arms buildups. The emphasis here is less on hardware and more on psychology. The hope is that progress can be made on issues related to disarmament, which might act as confidence-builders and ultimately lead to actual disarmament agreements. In December 1959, for example, a treaty was signed among twelve nations with claims in Antarctica demilitarizing that continent. The signatories pledged themselves neither to establish military fortifications nor to carry out military maneuvers in the Antarctic. In 1963, in the wake of the Cuban missile crisis, the Soviet Union and the United States established direct communications—a "hot line" between the White House and the Kremlin—and reached agreement on the peaceful uses of outer space. In 1964 the United States offered one of its large nuclear reactors to international inspection by a United Nations agency, and in the same year the two superpowers agreed on cutbacks in their stockpiles of fissionable materials—the raw materials for atomic weapons—thus retarding the growth of "overkill" capacity on both sides.

In 1967, the two superpowers, after lengthy negotiations, agreed to work in earnest on a formula for a treaty banning the proliferation of nuclear weapons. In January 1968, they presented a joint draft treaty on nonproliferation to the seventeen-member Disarmament Conference in Geneva. The draft treaty was designed to freeze the "nuclear club" at its membership of five: the United States, the Soviet Union, the United Kingdom, France, and Communist China. Several hurdles confronted the negotiators. First, neither France nor China was expected to sign. Second, certain "threshold" countries such as India and Israel were reluctant to sign, the former for fear of China and Pakistan and the latter because of Egypt. Finally, the matter of inspection posed formidable obstacles. Would the treaty be policed through self-inspection, regional bodies such as Euratom, or a United Nations organ, such as the International Atomic Energy Agency? These and other knotty problems defied easy solution and made progress on the treaty slow and arduous. Nevertheless, the very fact of superpower cooperation on such a sensitive issue as nonproliferation provided grounds for optimism. In June 1968, another forward step was taken when the UN General Assembly, in a vote of 95 in favor, 4 against, and 21 abstentions, gave its blessing to the draft treaty. Three nuclear and forty non-nuclear ratifications were now needed to make the document into a binding treaty. In March 1970, the nuclear nonproliferation treaty officially entered into force without the adherence of China and France.

Two other arms control treaties are deserving of mention: In 1967, the two superpowers agreed on a treaty in which each pledged itself not to militarize outer space. The treaty was approved by the UN General Assembly in 1967 and entered into force that same year. And in 1971 a similar treaty was signed in relation to the seabed and the ocean floors. It is significant to note that none of these efforts achieved an actual reduction of existing weapons, but each went a long way in preventing their further dissemination and in preventing the construction of new weapons.

In view of the current successes in arms control rather than in disarmament, two arms control treaties are included as case studies: The first will deal with the partial nuclear test ban signed in Moscow in 1963, which was the first specific symptom of the new United States–Soviet détente; and the second will describe the most significant fruit of that détente reached a decade later: the Strategic Arms Limitation Treaty of 1972.

The Cessation of Nuclear Testing in 1963

The goal of nuclear test cessation was always more modest than that of disarmament since it implied no reduction of stockpiles nor any fundamental change in the arsenals of the negotiating powers. A nuclear test ban would accomplish two things: it would limit the further development of nuclear weapons already stocked in great quantities in the Soviet Union, the United States, Britain, and France; and it would halt further contamination of the world's atmosphere through radioactive fallout.

If disarmament has been the most important general problem before the General Assembly, the cessation of nuclear weapons testing was the most crucial specific issue related to disarmament. The pressures on the nuclear powers, especially by the atomic "have-not" nations, were enormous. In 1959, for example, the General Assembly passed by overwhelming majorities four resolutions urging a moratorium on nuclear tests. These resolutions were primarily a reflection of a world-wide concern with the damage to human health if tests were to continue.

Scientists have differed widely on the amount of damage that radioactive fallout inflicts on the human system. But all agree that there are at least four areas in which *some* harm is certain to result. For one thing, it has been established that exposure to radiation shortens the human life span. In the opinion of Dr. H. J. Muller, a leading American geneticist, the shortening of the life span is "by far the most serious of the long term effects on the exposed person himself."[21] The second danger derives from strontium 90, a radioactive substance produced by nuclear explosions but unknown in nature. This by-product of atomic tests causes cancer of the bone. Opinions differ on the extent of the damage but there is wide agreement that each test results in bone cancer being incurred by a number of people. Most scientists also agree that children are more susceptible to the poison than adults.[22] Leukemia, a fatal disease of the white blood cells, has also been related to strontium 90.[23] Finally, the most far-reaching effects of fallout seem to be genetic mutations in future generations. Again, estimates vary but there is wide agreement among geneticists that nuclear tests will be responsible for a considerable number of stillbirths, embryonic deaths, and defective mutations.[24]

As a result of constant prodding by the General Assembly, the Soviet Union, in May 1955, took the initiative in seeking a test ban. During the following year the Soviet Union pressed the United States for the conclusion of a bilateral agreement. The Soviet position was that the question of a test ban could be separated from the general problem of disarmament and that controls to detect violations were unnecessary. As Premier Bulganin wrote to President Eisenhower in 1956:

It is a known fact that the discontinuation of such tests does not in itself require any international control agreements, for the present state of science and engineering makes it possible to detect any explosion of an atomic or hydrogen bomb, wherever it may be set off. In our opinion this situation makes it possible to separate the problem of ending tests of atomic and hydrogen weapons from the general problem of disarmament and to solve it independently even now, without tying an agreement on this subject to agreements on other disarmament problems.[25]

The Western powers agreed to discuss a test ban as a separate issue but flatly rejected the Soviet assertion that controls were unnecessary. In a counterproposal, the United States, Great Britain, and France suggested test cessation under an international control system. The Soviet Union declared itself willing to negotiate the vexatious matter of inspection. The next difficulty arose when the United States insisted on the need to continue testing until a cut-off agreement and a control plan had actually been negotiated. At this point, great pressure was exerted on the American government by a large majority in the General Assembly to agree to an informal test ban pending the conclusion of a formal treaty. Opinion among leading American scientists was deeply divided on this issue. On the one hand, Dr. Linus Pauling, an American Nobel Prize winner, represented a considerable body of opinion when he demanded that tests be halted immediately:

Each added amount of radiation causes damage to the health of human beings all over the world and causes damage to the pool of human germ plasm such as to lead to an increase in the number of seriously defective children that will be born in future generations. An international agreement to stop all testing of nuclear weapons now, could serve as a first step towards a more general disarmament, and the effective abolition of nuclear weapons, averting the possibility of a nuclear war that would be a catastrophe to all humanity.[26]

The case for continuing tests was largely defended by scientists in the United States Atomic Energy Commission. In the opinion of Dr. Edward Teller, a leading scientist, testing had to continue because

further tests will put us into a position to fight our opponent's war machine while sparing the innocent bystanders. One development of the greatest importance is the progressive reduction of radioactive fallout. Clean weapons of this kind will reduce unnecessary casualties in a future war.[27]

Dr. Teller's colleague in the AEC, Dr. Willard F. Libby, also justified atomic tests on grounds of national defense:

It is not contended, that there is no risk to human health. Are we willing to take this very small and rigidly controlled risk, or would we prefer to run the risk of annihilation which might result, if we surrendered the weapons which are so essential to our freedom and actual survival?[28]

While the United States was engaged in weighing the alternatives of a provisional test ban, the Soviet Union, in March 1958, announced a unilateral cessation of nuclear tests. Once again on the defensive, the United States proposed a meeting of technical experts to study the feasibility of a control system to detect violations of a test ban. This conference, attended by an equal number of scientists from East and West, took place in July 1958 and submitted a positive report, calling for three steps by which a detection system might be implemented:

1. A network of control posts around the globe. About 170 would be land-based. Of these ten would be in the United States, fourteen in the USSR, and eight in Communist China. The remaining land-based posts would be distributed on the continents and on large and small oceanic islands. Ten additional posts would be on ships.
2. Creation of an "international control organ," which would run the global system, pick the staff, select the detection devices, study

reports and generally see to it that no nation violated the test suspension agreement.

3. Use of weather reconnaissance aircraft to sample the air for radioactivity. They would rush to a suspicious area to see if a bomb had been set off or whether the tremor was due to other causes.[29]

The scientists' report, while welcomed by the negotiators, raised important new problems. What would be the composition of the "international control organ"? What would be the voting procedure? Would there be a veto? What would be the authority of the inspectors? Serious bargaining took place on all of these questions at Geneva. The West suggested a veto-free control commission to be headed by a neutral administrator. The Soviet Union, however, insisted on a three-man directorate and the right of veto. The negotiators also disagreed on the number and role of the inspectors in the field. The West demanded international and mobile inspection teams with freedom of access to any area where an illegal atomic test is suspected. The Soviet Union emphasized the primacy of self-inspection but accepted the admission in principle of "foreign specialists" from the West. Another technical problem presented itself when the United States announced that it had underestimated the difficulty of detecting underground nuclear explosions. The United States position was that such explosions would be almost indistinguishable seismographically from natural shocks such as earthquakes. Hence, the American government demanded that the number of control stations be raised from 180 to 600.

More threatening than the technical problems of an atomic test ban was the sword of Damocles of the "nth nation." The main negotiators were three nuclear powers—the United States, the Soviet Union, and Britain. But France, of course, was already developing her own nuclear arsenal, and it was estimated that in the not too distant future several new nations would join the "nuclear club": Belgium, Canada, China, Czechoslovakia, East Germany, West Germany, India, Israel, Italy, Japan, Sweden, and Switzerland.[30] Would the new atomic powers agree to be bound by a treaty to which they were not a party? France, for example, insisted on the completion of a series of tests while the Big Three were engaged in negotiations in Geneva. Far more serious, even, was the problem of Communist China. The 1958 Geneva report of the technical experts recommended that eight of the 180 control stations be placed on mainland China. If the "international control organ" were placed under United Nations authority, would it be reasonable to expect Communist China to admit United Nations control posts on her territory while she was not a member of the world organization? Even if the control organ were set up outside the United Nations framework, would Communist China consider herself bound by a treaty with nations that continued to refuse to recognize her as a legal government?

Despite the numerous difficulties, a remarkable lessening of differences occurred during 1959 and 1960, but in late 1961 the Soviet Union broke the informal moratorium and tested weapons of unprecedented explosive force. By the time of the Cuban missile crisis a test ban agreement seemed more remote than ever. Yet the resolution of that crisis seemed to convince the Soviet leadership that more could be gained from a détente with the West than from a policy of intransigence. At any rate, in July 1963 Paul-Henri Spaak of Belgium reported that Premier Khrushchev seemed genuinely interested in a test ban. A few days later, American and British negotiators, led by Averell Harriman and Lord Hailsham, respectively, arrived in Moscow to explore the seriousness of Soviet intentions. After five days of negotiations, tentative agreement was reached and a copy of the draft treaty was publicized on July 24. All nuclear tests in the atmosphere, under water, and in space were to cease, but underground tests were to be permitted. On August 5 Soviet Foreign Minister Andrei Gromyko, United States Secretary of State Dean Rusk, and British Foreign Secretary Lord Home put their signatures to the document. After a protracted debate, the United States Senate, on September 24, ratified the Treaty by a vote of 80 to 19. A large majority of the world's nations quickly followed suit and deposited their instruments of ratification. A decade of arduous negotiations had finally produced concrete results.

On the negative side, France and Communist China made a common front against the Treaty. The former was bent on its own independent nuclear force and the latter attacked the Treaty as a fraud and saw it as further proof of Soviet "softness on capitalism." Also, the test ban was only partial. Nevertheless, most observers agreed with President Kennedy's assessment of the Treaty as a step toward reason and away from war. In specific and immediate terms, it solved a major problem of public health by halting the further contamination of the atmosphere by radioactive fallout. More broadly, it was the first East-West agreement in the tensely guarded realm of military security.

The Strategic Arms Limitation Treaty of 1972

On May 26, 1972, President Richard M. Nixon and Soviet Party Chairman Leonid Brezhnev signed in Moscow two historic arms control documents which represented the culmination of almost three years of arduous strategic arms limitation talks (SALT) in Helsinki and in Vienna.

The first document was an Anti-Ballistic Missiles Treaty of unlimited duration which placed limits on the growth of Soviet and American strategic nuclear arsenals. The Treaty established a ceiling of 200 launchers for each side's defensive missile system and committed both sides not to build nationwide anti-missile defenses. Each country was limited to two ABM sites, one for the national capital, and the other to protect one field of ICBM's. Each such site would consist of 100 ABM's.

The United States already had a protected ICBM field in North Dakota and thus, under the terms of the Treaty, could add an ABM site around Washington. The Soviet Union already had an ABM site for the defense of Moscow and thus was permitted to add an ABM site to protect an ICBM field. At the time of the agreement, the Soviet Union had a total of 2,328 missiles, 1,618 ICBM's and 710 on nuclear submarines, compared with 1,710 for the United States—1,054 ICBM's and 656 on submarines.

The second concrete arms control achievement of the Moscow Summit was an Interim Agreement limiting ICBM's to those under construction or deployed at the time of the signing of the Agreement. This meant the retention of 1,618 ICBM's for the Soviet Union, including 300 large SS-98, and 1,054 for the United States, including 1,000 Minutemen and 54 Titans. The Agreement also froze the construction of submarine-launched ballistic missiles on all nuclear submarines at existing levels—656 for the United States and 710 for the Soviet Union. However, each side could build additional submarine missiles if an equal number of older land-based ICBM's or older submarine missile launchers were dismantled. The Agreement was to be in force for five years and both sides pledged themselves to "follow-up negotiations" in order to achieve a full-fledged treaty.

Both arms control instruments signed at Moscow placed no limitations on the qualitative improvement of offensive or defensive missiles, nor were ceilings imposed on the number of warheads that could be carried by offensive missiles or on strategic bombers permitted each side. Modernization of missiles, including the emplacement of new missiles in new silos, was permitted. Both sides pledged "not to interfere with the national technical means of verification of the other party," and each side retained the right to withdraw from either agreement if it felt that its supreme national interest was in jeopardy.

The two agreements managed to freeze a rough balance into the nuclear arsenals of the two superpowers. There remained "missile-gaps," of course, in specific weapons. The United States, for example, retained the lead in the technology of "multiple independently targeted reentry vehicles" (MIRV's) while the Soviet Union possessed a larger quantity of missile launchers. Nevertheless, the overall effect was one of achieving a rough equilibrium.

The process of achieving this equilibrium went through eight stages lasting almost three years. SALT 1 was held in Helsinki in late 1969 and was exploratory without any formal proposals submitted by either side. SALT 2, held in Vienna from April to August 1970, got down to specific proposals. The two superpowers agreed in principle on the terms of a defensive missile treaty which would have limited each side to 100 missiles each around Moscow and Washington. But several months later, the American delegation, fearful of Congress, backed away and advanced a new proposal which would have given the United States a 4-1 advantage. This was angrily rejected by the USSR, and it took a few more months before the original two-site 200 missile compromise was reaffirmed. SALT 3, held in late 1970, broke up in disagreement over offensive arms. SALT 4 took place in Vienna from March to May 1971 and during this period President Nixon and Chairman Brezhnev began to engage in top-secret correspondence. The result was a Soviet initiative proposing an ICBM freeze as well as an ABM treaty. SALT 5, held from July to September 1971 in Helsinki, saw further progress on the proposed ICBM freeze. SALT 6, in late 1971 and early 1972, produced the outlines of the ABM treaty and SALT 7, the last round before the Moscow Summit, led to the inclusion of submarine-based missiles in the accord. The final accords were thus the result of protracted and painstaking bargaining and negotiations.

Several conclusions are worthy of note in connection with the two Moscow agreements. In the first place, the observation made earlier with regard to disarmament, namely that a measure of political accommodation must precede agreement on a technical formula, seems to apply with equal logic to arms control. It must be remembered that Soviet-American relations had improved significantly by the early 1970's, partly due to the common determination to resolve long-standing differences in Europe and partly due to the Soviet fear of China. At any rate, the political climate had thawed considerably since the days of the cold war. Second, the SALT agreements did not depend primarily on verification to be effective. Each side knew that, if it cheated and "surprised" the other with a devastating nuclear attack, the other side, though mortally wounded, could still inflict a retaliatory blow that would be "unacceptable" to the offender. Hence, the agreements were not based primarily on mutual trust, but on the mutual capacity to absorb a first strike. Third, there was no doubt that, even if the two agreements did not qualify as disarmament, they nevertheless signified a momentous breakthrough in superpower relations and a large step toward a saner world. Finally, arms control rather than disarmament seems to be the main road toward military order in our time.

An International Police Force and Collective Security

The framers of the United Nations Charter foresaw that the elimination or even the substantial reduction of armaments would be an extremely difficult task. They had considerably greater faith in the possibility of fashioning a world in which arms would be redistributed and organized in such a way that lawbreakers could be confronted by preponderant military power. As the postwar world developed, however, the growing fury of the East-West struggle made it almost impossible for the UN Security Council really to function as the planned-for instrument of collective security. Consequently, the standing United Nations Armed Force that was envisaged by the UN founders in Article 43 was never permitted to come to life. It seemed, indeed, as though the East-West struggle would permanently prevent the creation of the one international instrument that could be most valuable of all for military order-building: a permanent and powerful international police force. What had happened, of course, was that the would-be international policemen had fallen out among themselves.

Yet if we survey the record, the East-West struggle has nevertheless not prevented the United Nations from engaging in military action to defend collective security. On four different occasions the United Nations has managed effectively to meet serious threats to the peace. The first military action under the United Nations flag was fought in Korea from 1950 to 1953. In 1956 a United Nations Emergency Force was set up to restore order in the Middle East. In 1960 a United Nations Force was given prime responsibility for insulating the newly independent Congo from the East-West struggle. And in 1964 a UN force was dispatched to Cyprus to prevent civil war between the island's Greek and Turkish communities. Each of these experiences has been unique in its highly improvised character; each has involved the UN in a most explosive situation and so has had a quality high of drama; and while all of them have fallen short of the original concept of collective security, each has made an important contribution to military order.

THE KOREAN "POLICE ACTION"

We have seen earlier that in Korea the mobilization of an international police force was made possible only through the absence of the Soviet delegate from the Security Council in June 1950. But once the Council was freed from the paralyzing veto—albeit only temporarily—it was able to organize military action swiftly and effectively. This first modern effort of international policing therefore deserves careful analysis.

On June 27, two days after the North Korean attack, the Security Council called upon all members to "furnish such assistance to the Republic of Korea as may be necessary to repel the armed attack and to restore international peace and security in the area."[31] On July 7 the Council recommended that such forces and other assistance be placed under a Unified Command under United States operational control. It also authorized the Unified Command to use the United Nations flag. The response of the member nations to this first modern experiment in collective security was encouraging. Fifteen members other than the

United States and the Republic of Korea offered to contribute troops: Australia, Belgium, Canada, Colombia, Ethiopia, France, Greece, Luxembourg, the Netherlands, New Zealand, the Philippines, Thailand, Turkey, the Union of South Africa, and the United Kingdom. In addition, thirty-seven other members offered to contribute a wide range of supplies and services, including food, clothing, medical supplies, and transportation.

Since almost 90 per cent of the non-Korean forces fighting under the United Nations flag were United States forces, and since it had been the United States that had taken the initiative in this UN action, it was only logical that the Unified Command should be primarily an American operation. Accordingly, General Douglas MacArthur was placed in charge of the United Nations Command and, for all practical purposes, the United Nations Police Force became identical with the Far East Command of the United States. South Korean troops were integrated into American companies and joint actions with other United Nations allies were conducted through liaison officers. Moreover, since the United States was bearing by far the largest share of the load, this preponderant American military role was accepted by all concerned as perfectly fair and proper.

While questions of military coordination in Korea were thus largely solved through the commanding position of the United States, the problem of providing the United Nations Force with political guidance presented almost insuperable obstacles. So long as the United Nations Forces were south of the 38th parallel, the problem was not acute. But by August 1, 1950, the day the Soviet delegate returned to the Security Council, the United Nations Forces were fast approaching the 38th parallel. A decision had to be made whether to stop at that point or to carry UN operations beyond it. In view of the Soviet Union's return to the Security Council and the consequent certainty of its veto in the matter, the decision had to be made by the General Assembly. Under American pressure, but with considerable misgivings, the General Assembly voted to authorize the entrance of United Nations Forces into North Korea. Yet in effect, this and subsequent decisions were made by the United States rather than by the General Assembly itself. In November 1950, after the Chinese intervention, there was formed a Committee of Sixteen for inter-allied consultation, but in practice the United States almost always prevailed. American domination of the international police force became most evident in the controversy involving the Commander, General MacArthur. Most of the allies, and many Americans, viewed MacArthur's intentions to bomb military bases in Manchuria as a serious provocation to the Chinese. The removal of the General from the United Nations Command did not, however, take place in deference to the wishes of the allies, but was fundamentally the result of the General's challenge to the authority of his Commander-in-Chief, the President of the United States.

This first experiment in blocking aggression through an international police force was neither an unqualified success nor a complete failure. On the negative side, it owed its activation to a fortuitous circumstance—the Soviet Union's temporary absence from the Security Council; it fell far short of a genuine collective security action; though initiated as a "police action," it developed into a limited war; instead of crushing the aggressor, it resulted in the signing of an armistice with him on the basis of equality; it was in effect chiefly an American enterprise and, aside from the forces of the Republic of Korea, involved the participation of only 36,000 combatants from the other United Nations countries; and its political direction was dominated chiefly by the United States. In fact, if it had not been for American initiative, the international police force in Korea would not have come into existence at all.

On the other hand, the Korean experience broke precedent in several important ways. It saw sixteen nations fighting as a United Nations army, under the United Nations flag, and led by a United Nations commander. Moreover, despite the disproportionate role played by the United States, its image as a United Nations action has remained largely intact. Most important, the United Nations Force succeeded in halting aggression and restoring what was in effect the *status quo ante bellum.* Even when comparing this achievement with the League of Nations' dismal failure in Manchuria in 1931, it would be an exaggeration to characterize it as a complete "success." Yet the fact remains that the United Nations Force in Korea took a big step along the road to collective security.

The greatest weakness of the Korean action was the lack of planning for the transition from military enforcement to the tasks of consolidating the peace. Though the aggressor had been thrown back, Korea remained as politically divided as before—and, ironically, along a line only a short distance from the 38th parallel where the fighting had begun. At best, therefore, the United Nations action provided a breathing spell during which political differences could once more be subjected to negotiation. This in itself was a great service. Yet the final lesson of Korea is nonetheless clear: that the pursuit of order through purely military techniques is bound to fail unless it is shored up by equally determined efforts to reach a political settlement.

Historically, the Korean experience has by no means been an unmixed blessing. In the United Nations of the 1970's, the Korean "police-action" of the 1950's was widely regarded as an historical anomaly. Moreover, since it had placed the UN at war with China, the People's Republic harbored a great deal of resentment. And perhaps most important, the history of the Korean war made it difficult, if not impossible, for North Vietnam to regard the United Nations as an impartial mediator in its war with the United States.

THE UNITED NATIONS EMERGENCY FORCE IN SUEZ

United Nations military action in the Middle East was considerably less dramatic than the Korean campaign. The UN Emergency Force that was dispatched to the troubled area never exceeded 6000 men. Moreover, UNEF was never meant to be a fighting army. Its purpose, rather, was to serve as a symbol of the UN's involvement which, it was hoped, would succeed in bringing about the neutralization of the disputed areas. Its unique achievement, in which it went importantly beyond the Korean action, was that it constituted for the first time a genuine international police force that was not dominated by any single power. In fact, all of the Great Powers were specifically excluded from it. For this reason the significance of UNEF greatly transcends its modest physical dimensions.

The father of the United Nations Emergency Force was Lester B. Pearson of Canada. When on November 2, 1956, the General Assembly was locked in acrimonious debate over British-French-Israeli action in Suez, Pearson proposed that peace and security be restored through a United Nations Force. United States and Afro-Asian approval encouraged the Canadian diplomat to draft a resolution requesting the Secretary-General to draw up a plan for the creation of an international military force to be submitted to the General Assembly within forty-eight hours. The Canadian resolution passed without a negative vote at a time when Britain and France were still bombing Egyptian territory. Secretary-General Hammarskjöld and Mr. Pearson immediately set about to improvise the Force. They decided to appoint Major General E. L. M. Burns, chief of staff of the United Nations Truce Supervision Organization in Palestine, as head of the new United Nations Command. The next vital decision concerned the composition of troops to be sent. The Secretary-General thought it wise to exclude the Great Powers from the Force. It would have been ill-advised to deputize Britain and France as United Nations policemen, since Egypt would never have agreed to admit them. If the United States were included, the Soviet Union would demand a role, and hence it was best to keep the two superpowers out altogether.

To the delight of leading United Nations officials, twenty-four members agreed to make troops available for the enterprise, with offers ranging from 1180 from Canada to 250 from Finland. However, this delight began to give way to embarrassment when, in order not to jeopardize relations with Egypt, it became necessary to reject some of the offers. For example, the Canadian contingent, especially a battalion of the "Queen's Own Rifles," resembled the British too much in appearance. Pearson tactfully decided to use them as maintenance and administrative personnel in roles where they would be least conspicuous. New Zealand troops were politely rejected because New Zealand had voted with Britain and France in the General Assembly on the Suez affair. Pakistan was considered unsuitable because it was a member of the Baghdad Pact and an irritant to India. Troops from the Soviet bloc—Czechoslovakia and Rumania—were not "rejected" but simply not "activated."[32] Finally, a contingent of 6000 troops from ten countries— Brazil, Canada, Colombia, Denmark, Finland, India, Indonesia, Norway, Sweden, and Yugoslavia—was ready for action.

The composition of the Force was very important since its admission to the contested area depended upon the permission of Egypt. Though this condition was distasteful to many members of the Assembly, it was, according to the Secretary-General, the "very basis and starting point" of the entire operation. In effect, Egypt therefore had a veto over the national makeup of the Force and could, as well, determine the length of its stay in the Suez area. On November 12 Egypt granted UNEF permission to enter. Shortly thereafter, Britain, France, and Israel were persuaded to withdraw from Egyptian territory and UNEF proceeded to neutralize the contested boundary zones. Its function became essentially that of a "buffer" between Israel and Egypt.

In May 1967, President Nasser abruptly demanded that UNEF be withdrawn from the borders which it had patrolled for over a decade. Secretary-General U Thant complied with the Egyptian demand, though with serious misgivings, and the Force was promptly removed.

U Thant's decision was a very controversial one. The Secretary-General was widely criticized for giving in too hastily to Egyptian pressure. Critics pointed out that, while it was true that UNEF's presence on the Egyptian border depended on the consent of the Egyptian government, the Secretary-General could have stalled by requesting an emergency session of the Security Council or of the General Assembly and thus gained time. The Israeli delegate to the UN, Abba Eban, stated caustically that "the umbrella was removed at the precise moment when it began to rain." The Secretary-General defended his action by pointing out that there would have been no legal basis for maintaining the Force on Egyptian soil without that nation's consent. Moreover, the Force had never been permitted to patrol on the Israeli side of the border and when the Israeli government was asked whether it would invite the UNEF troops to its side after leaving Egypt, Israel had refused to do so. Both governments were within their legal rights, the Secretary-General asserted.

A further complication in the picture was the fact that two nations that had given contingents to UNEF—India and Yugoslavia—were removing their forces even before the Secretary-General had given the order to withdraw. Moreover, several UNEF soldiers were killed by

Egyptian troops who threatened that, unless UNEF were promptly withdrawn, it would be regarded as an "army of occupation." Finally, the Secretary-General reasoned that if he did not comply with the request of a sovereign government, it might be infinitely more difficult to obtain consent for the admission of a peace-keeping force in a future crisis. Given all these conflicting considerations, the Secretary-General made his difficult and fateful choice.

An overall analysis of the UNEF experience points up a striking dilemma for any international peace force. In order to be an effective instrument of collective security and a respectable military force, it must include one or more of the Great Powers. But if it does, it is likely to find itself dominated by a Great Power, as was the case in Korea, and to suffer a proportionate loss of its international character. Hence, since in order to steer clear of the East-West struggle it must exclude the Great Powers, a truly international force can hardly be more than a "buffer." The Korean Force, organized and operated as an instrument of enforcement, came closer to the ideal of collective security in terms of its *action*. The Middle East Force, though compelled to limit itself to the task of neutralization, more closely approached the collective security ideal in terms of its *composition*. While its dependence on the sufferance of Egypt made it a fragile instrument of peace-keeping, it nevertheless helped to restore peace in the Middle East in 1956 and to maintain an uneasy truce on the Israeli-Egyptian border for over a decade.

THE UNITED NATIONS CONGO FORCE

Perhaps the most complex military challenge to confront the United Nations was the one that occurred in the Congo between 1960 and 1964. Historians may differ with Mr. Hammarskjöld's view that the United Nations' task in the Congo was the most important responsibility that the world organization had to shoulder in the first fifteen years of its lifetime, but most will agree that the Congo problem required every diplomatic and military resource that the United Nations could possibly muster.

We have seen earlier that the United Nations was first called into the infant African republic in order to take the place of Belgian troops whose sudden withdrawal had left the Congo in a state of political unrest verging on anarchy and civil war. The Secretary-General's problems in putting together a United Nations Force for the Congo resembled those that had been faced in the Middle East. Once again, the Great Powers had to be kept out of the conflict. Furthermore, it was deemed advisable mostly to employ African troops for the United Nations Force. The Secretary-General, together with UN Under-Secretary Ralph J. Bunche, appealed to the new African nations for support. The response again was encouraging: almost all the African nations offered contributions. In addition, troops were accepted from Ireland, Sweden, Indonesia, Malaya, the United Arab Republic, and India. At its high point, the Congo Force comprised over 20,000 men from twenty-nine different countries. The task of the Force became vastly more complex, however, when tribal warfare broke out between the central government in Leopoldville under Premier Lumumba and secessionist movements in the two provinces of Katanga and Kasai. The United Nations Force faced an almost insoluble dilemma: how to restore order while avoiding the charge of intervention in a civil war. As in the Middle East, the presence of the Force had to be approved by a sovereign government. But whereas, in the case of Egypt, President Nasser had retained control, the Congolese government was in a state of disintegration. The Premier and the President of the central government were locked in a power struggle. Moreover, the Soviet Union gave material help to the Lumumba government in direct contravention of the wishes of the United Nations Command and refused to pay its share of the cost of the Peace Force. Racial tension entered the picture when ex-Premier Lumumba accused the non-African contingents of the Force of being pro-Belgian. Several member states withdrew their contingents from the Force in protest against "neocolonialism."

Financial crises constantly threatened the life of the Force. Even after the General Assembly recognized President Kasavubu as the legitimate spokesman for the Congo, United Nations personnel were beaten up by Congolese and frequently had to shoot in self-defense. The UN troops were authorized to use force "only in the last resort." Some were killed. All these factors conspired to make the operation a most difficult and delicate one. While the tribal fighting was going on, the United Nations Force could do little more than protect civilians. It served as a sort of fire brigade: though unable to prevent the outbreak of civil war, it managed to keep it within bounds. Most important, the United Nations Force prepared the ground for the more difficult and complex task of restoring political stability in the Congo.

The Congo experience was a repeat performance of UNEF, with all of UNEF's difficulties vastly magnified. Again, the Force has to be improvised at a moment's notice. It, too, was dependent on the good will of a sovereign state, this time a fledgling state on the verge of collapse. Once again, the Secretary-General had to race against time in order to forestall Great Power intervention. The Force itself, once established, again was little more than a "buffer," but this time its task was not limited to patrol duty in the desert. It had to keep brutal tribal warfare in the jungle to a minimum and even to assume some of the administrative functions of government. Finally, like UNEF, the Congo Force accomplished its primary mission: it succeeded in preventing the Congo from becoming a seedbed of a general war.

A Permanent Peace Force?

The three United Nations experiences in peace-keeping just discussed were all successful in at least one sense: they restored military order and thus bought time. It is an open question as to whether they prevented general conflagrations, and it is clear that they were not examples of genuine collective security. But that their limited success provided renewed opportunity for political order-building is indisputable. This is a major accomplishment, especially since the three ventures operated under the handicap of starting out as complete improvisations.

In March 1964 yet another peace-keeping experiment was launched, this time in Cyprus. When the Greek and Turkish communities on that island found themselves unable to resolve their differences and civil war became an increasingly ominous threat, the Security Council met in emergency session and authorized a peace force. Once again, the Force was tailored to the situation. Three thousand British troops already on the island were deputized as UN policemen, and in addition Canada, Sweden, Ireland, and Finland contributed troops, bringing the total up to seven thousand men. The new Force also differed from previous ones in its financing arrangements. Since the mood was definitely set against another assessment, the $6,000,000 required for three months was raised through voluntary contributions, with $2,000,000 supplied by the United States, $1,000,000 by the United Kingdom, and the remainder by Greece, Turkey, Italy, Australia, and the Netherlands. The Cyprus Force also set a new precedent in that the Secretary-General appointed a high-level diplomat as mediator to help bring about a political settlement between the two hostile communities. By 1968, the Cyprus Force was the only major UN peace-keeping operation still in the field. It was still on active duty in the early 1970's, though its strength had been reduced to 3000 men. China's accession to the Security Council did not lead to the termination of the Force. When the Council considered the extension of the Force in 1972, fourteen members voted in favor. China, not wishing to disrupt the consensus, chose to abstain rather than to veto. Despite its voluntary financial base, the Cyprus Force had become an important military order-builder in the Mediterranean.

The fact that peace-keeping seems to have become an integral UN responsibility has convinced an increasing number of observers that an even more effective performance would be possible if a permanent international peace force were established under United Nations authority. Article 43 of the Charter, which contemplated such a Force, was never implemented because of the intensity of the East-West struggle. Yet the experiences of UNEF and ONUC leave no doubt that even a modest Force with permanent status would prove very valuable.

It is immediately apparent that such a Force would have to be a very different one from that contemplated under Article 43. The framers had assumed that concerted military action by the Great Powers would nip any conflict in the bud. Ironically, however, in the Suez and Congo crises the peace depended not on how quickly the Great Powers could be brought to the scene, but on how successfully they could be kept at arm's length. Hence, the great Powers would probably have to be excluded from a Permanent Force, at least at the beginning.

In composition, such a Force might consist of long-term volunteers recruited individually by the United Nations, with quotas for different nations. The commanding officer and other high-ranking personnel might be chosen from nationals of middle and smaller states. The Force would not be furnished with heavy arms or atomic weapons, but might have its own permanent bases and training depots. Its Commander-in-Chief would be the Secretary-General.

Proposals along these lines have been considered in United Nations circles and have received a mixed reaction. There have been several serious reservations. First, it has been pointed out that such a permanent Force would have to be very large and expensive to be able to meet different kinds of emergencies. Korea, for example, necessitated a fighting Force to repel an armed attack; UNEF was a patrol Force in the desert; ONUC had to help save a new country from anarchy and civil war; and the Cyprus Force was needed to prevent two hostile communities on an island from sparking off an international crisis. Thus, the argument runs, the *sui generis* character of each experience suggests an *ad hoc* approach. Second, few nations would be willing to commit troops to the United Nations for unspecified future operations and to give the Secretary-General the authority of Commander-in-Chief over these forces. Third, in view of the melancholy financial histories of UNEF and ONUC, it is most doubtful whether the membership would be willing to underwrite the costs of a standing UN Force.

The above difficulties suggest a more modest approach. There is a growing consensus that the next step should not be an existent UN Force, but a flexible call-up system under which members would be asked to earmark contingents for UN duty on a standby basis. By the early 1970's Denmark, Norway, Sweden, Finland, Canada, Iran, Italy, and the Netherlands had already offered to earmark units for UN use under such an arrangement. Nevertheless, the knotty problem of political control of these units remains to be solved; and, unless the nations earmarking the troops also "pay their own beat," the fiscal obstacles may prove insurmountable.

If such a standby UN Force could be established as a first step toward a permanent Force, the results would be most beneficial. Such a Force would be a most useful instrument in the struggle for military order. But its function in the general quest for order would still be a *transitional* one. As the record of disarmament and arms control negotiations has clearly demonstrated, military instruments *per se* cannot create political order. But a standby or permanent UN Peace Force would at least make a limited contribution by preparing the ground. It would thus embody the best that military order-building has to offer in our time.

REFERENCES

1. Peter Burchett, reporting for the *London Daily Express,* September 5, 1945; cited by Philip Noel-Baker, *The Arms Race.* New York: Oceana Publications, 1958, pp. 119–120.

2. A joint statement by President Eisenhower and Premier Khrushchev made at Camp David in 1959.

3. Noel-Baker, *op. cit.,* p. 86.

4. Hans J. Morgenthau, *Politics Among Nations,* 3d ed. New York: Knopf, 1960, pp. 410–411.

5. James Brown Scott, *The Proceedings of the Hague Peace Conference of 1907,* Vol. I. New York: Oxford University Press, 1920, pp. 89–90.

6. Cited by Inis L. Claude, *Swords into Plowshares,* 2d ed. New York: Random House, 1959, p. 308.

7. Security Council Official Records, March 5, 1947, p. 453.

8. Yves Collart, *Disarmament: A Study Guide and Bibliography on the Efforts of the United Nations.* The Hague: Nijhoff, 1958, p. 55.

9. Cited by Joseph Nogee, "The Diplomacy of Disarmament," *International Conciliation,* January 1960, p. 280.

10. *Ibid.,* p. 282.

11. *Ibid.*

12. Noel-Baker, *op. cit.,* p. 22.

13. Nogee, *op. cit.,* p. 286.

14. Noel-Baker, *op. cit.,* pp. 12–30.

15. General Assembly Official Records, Fourteenth Session, September 18, 1959.

16. *Ibid.*

17. Claude, *op. cit.,* p. 314.

18. William M. Evan, "An International Public Opinion Poll on Disarmament and 'Inspection by the People': A Study of Attitudes Toward Supranationalism," *Inspection for Disarmament,* Seymour Melman, ed. New York: Columbia University Press, 1958, pp. 231–250.

19. *Ibid.,* p. 234.

20. Claude, *op. cit.,* p. 308.

21. "Race Poisoning by Radiation," *Saturday Review,* June 9, 1956.

22. "The Biological Effects of Bomb Tests," *New Statesman and Nation,* June 8, 1957.

23. *The New Scientist,* May 16, 1957.

24. Noel-Baker, *op. cit.,* p. 255.

25. Cited by Nogee, *op. cit.,* p. 263.

26. *The New York Times,* January 14, 1958.

27. Cited by Noel-Baker, *op. cit.,* p. 261.

28. *The New York Times,* June 8, 1957.

29. *New York Herald Tribune,* September 1, 1958.

30. Nogee, *op. cit.,* p. 298.

31. United Nations Doc. S/1511, June 27, 1950.

32. William R. Frye, *A United Nations Peace Force.* New York: Oceana Publications, 1957, p. 23.

BIBLIOGRAPHY

American Assembly. *Arms Control: Issue for the Public.* Englewood Cliffs, N.J.: Prentice-Hall, 1961.

Bloomfield, Lincoln P. *International Military Forces.* Boston: Little, Brown, 1964.

Brennan, Donald G., ed. *Arms Control, Disarmament, and National Security.* New York: Braziller, 1961.

Bull, Hedley. *The Control of the Arms Race.* New York: Praeger, 1961.

Burton, John W. *Peace Theory: Preconditions of Disarmament.* New York: Knopf, 1962.

Claude, Inis L. "The United Nations and the Use of Force," *International Conciliation,* March 1961.

Cox, Arthur M. *Prospects for Peacekeeping.* Washington, D.C.: The Brookings Institution, 1967.

Edwards, David V. *Arms Control in International Politics.* New York: Holt, Rinehart, and Winston, 1969.

Etzioni, Amitai. *The Hard Way to Peace: A New Strategy.* New York: Collier, 1962.

Fabian, Larry L. *Soldiers Without Enemies: Preparing the United Nations for Peacekeeping.* Washington, D.C.: Brookings Institution, 1971.

Friedmann, Wolfgang. *The Future of the Oceans.* New York: Braziller, 1971

Fromm, Erich. *May Man Prevail?* New York: Doubleday, 1961.

Frye, William R. *A United Nations Peace Force.* New York: Oceana Publications, 1957.

Goodrich, Leland M. *Korea: A Study of United States Policy in the United Nations.* New York: Harper, 1956.

Harbottle, Michael. *The Impartial Soldier.* New York: Oxford University Press, 1970.

Henkin, L. *Arms Control and Inspection in American Law.* New York: Columbia University Press, 1958.

Jessup, Philip C., and Taubenfeld, Howard J. *Controls for Outer Space.* New York: Columbia University Press, 1959.

Kolkowicz, Roman, *et al. The Soviet Union and Arms Control: A Superpower Dilemma.* Baltimore: Johns Hopkins Press, 1970.

Larson, Thomas B. *Disarmament and Soviet Policy.* Englewood Cliffs, N.J.: Prentice-Hall, 1969.

Lefever, Ernest. *Crisis in the Congo.* Washington, D.C.: The Brookings Instituion, 1965.

———. *Uncertain Mandate: Politics of the United Nations Congo Operation.* Baltimore: Johns Hopkins Press, 1967.

Levine, Robert A. *The Arms Debate.* Cambridge, Mass.: Harvard University Press, 1963.

———. *The Peace Race.* New York: Ballantine, 1961.

Melman, Seymour, ed. *Inspection for Disarmament.* New York: Columbia University Press, 1958.

Noel-Baker, Philip. *The Arms Race.* New York: Oceana Publications, 1958.

Rosner, Gabriella. *The United Nations Emergency Force.* New York: Columbia University Press, 1963.

Russell, Bertrand. *Common Sense and Nuclear Warfare.* New York: Simon and Schuster, 1959.

Schelling, Thomas C. *The Strategy of Conflict.* Cambridge, Mass.: Harvard University Press, 1960.

———, and Halperin, Morton H. *Strategy and Arms Control.* New York: Twentieth Century Fund, 1961.

Stegenga, James A. *The United Nations Cyprus Force.* Columbus, Ohio: Ohio State University Press, 1968.

Stoessinger, John G. "Atoms for Peace: The International Atomic Energy Agency," *Organizing Peace in the Nuclear Age.* New York: New York University Press, 1959, pp. 117-233.

Wainhouse, David W., *et al. Arms Control Agreements.* Baltimore: Johns Hopkins Press, 1968.

———, ed. *International Peace Observation.* Baltimore: Johns Hopkins Press, 1966.

Waltz, Kenneth N. *Man, the State, and War: A Theoretical Analysis.* New York: Columbia University Press, 1959.

Waskow, Arthur I. *The Limits of Defense.* New York: Doubleday, 1962.

Wright, Quincy. *A Study of War.* Rev. ed. Chicago: University of Chicago Press, 1968.

Young, Oran R. *The Politics of Force: Bargaining During International Crises.* Princeton, N.J.: Princeton University Press, 1969.

13 The Economic Struggle for Order

It is not from the benevolence of the butcher, the brewer, or the baker that we expect our dinner, but from their regard to their self-interest. We address ourselves, not to their humanity, but to their self-love, and never talk to them of our necessities, but of their advantages.
ADAM SMITH *The Wealth of Nations*

The world since 1945 has been one gigantic experimental station in economic order-building. The functionalist hope that economic cooperation among nations might contribute to the building of political communities has led to the establishment of both universal and regional economic organizations. The picture is one of great complexity. At the universal level, there are UNCTAD and the manifold activities carried on under the roof of the United Nations Economic and Social Council. Outside the United Nations framework, the most prominent universal economic order-builder has been the General Agreement on Tariffs and Trade (GATT). With the sharpening of the East-West struggle after 1947, however, global economic order-building was severely curtailed. Efforts of this kind since that time have been chiefly of a regional nature and have taken place most notably in Western Europe. For the most part, therefore, the present chapter will be concerned with the various regional arrangements aimed at Western European economic integration. These arrangements include chiefly the Organization for Economic Cooperation and Development (OECD); the European Coal and Steel Community (ECSC); the European Atomic Energy Community (Euratom); the European Economic Community, or Common Market (EEC); and the European Free Trade Association (EFTA). Behind the façade of these prosaic-sounding names real pioneer work has been accomplished. The organizations they stand for have made significant contributions on the frontiers of international order-building. Yet they have shared only one common feature: their commitment to the economic path to order. Beyond this, each has been unique, attuned to its own particular objectives and accumulating its own special experiences.

Economic Order-Building at the International Level

Our analysis of the United Nations Economic and Social Council and of other United Nations economic activities such as UNCTAD (Chapter 10), has demonstrated that the functionalist approach to order at the global level is of dubious validity. Indeed, functionalism is not able to create a more favorable political climate, but is itself dependent on a minimum of pre-existent political harmony. This is true not only on a world-wide scale but can be shown to be the case even within the somewhat more limited, "quasi-global" dimensions of an organization such as the Economic Commission for Europe (ECE), which has been broad enough to include nations from both sides of the Iron Curtain.

The decision to set up ECE was made at the General Assembly of the United Nations in January 1946. Its main job was to be the economic reconstruction of Europe, a gigantic task in which it was assumed that East and West would fully cooperate. Accordingly, the Commission was open to all the countries of Europe. Its original membership included Belgium, the Byelorussian S.S.R., Czechoslovakia, Denmark, France, the Ukrainian S.S.R., the United Kingdom, and Yugoslavia. The United States, which was to shoulder the major financial burden of European reconstruction, was also one of the original members.

Despite the fact that ECE straddled the ideological chasm between

East and West, early discussions among its member nations were not marred by excessive disharmony. By 1947, however, it had become clear that although the European economies had made substantial recoveries, the purchase of raw materials to raise production to really adequate levels would require a great deal of foreign exchange, for which the only possible source was dollar aid from the United States. With this in mind, General George Marshall, on June 5, 1947, delivered an address at Harvard University in which he offered massive economic aid to Europe on a continent-wide basis and invited all the countries of Europe to join in a common plan for economic rehabilitation. It was widely hoped that this "Marshall Plan" would be taken up and implemented by ECE. Only the British objected strongly and suggested that Soviet membership in ECE would threaten to paralyze the organization's effective functioning. Most other official circles, however, hoped that the Soviet Union might be willing to join and that ECE would indeed become a continent-spanning recovery operation.

This dream of all-European economic cooperation through ECE was shattered in July 1947 when the Soviet bloc declined to take part in the Marshall Plan. Ostensibly, the Soviet argument was that the Plan would endanger the national sovereignty of the member states. The underlying reason for the Soviet rejection was probably fear that the participation of Eastern Europe in the recovery program would shift the European distribution of power toward the West. At any rate, the Soviet bloc's "nyet" proved the turning-point for ECE. Since it was clear that an all-European organization could not administer a program for the Western half of Europe only, the Commission seemed doomed to sterility.

However, though thus precluded from any substantial success in the functional realm, ECE has nevertheless found it possible to perform valuable technical services. Perhaps the most significant of these has been the work of its Research Division, whose highly expert staff, formerly headed by ECE's Executive Secretary, the internationally known Swedish economist Gunnar Myrdal, has been responsible for such widely respected and objective publications as the *Economic Survey of Europe*. In the view of some, ECE can also claim certain modest achievements of a more practical kind. Thus: "It has halted the decline in East-West trade, reduced the barriers to the exchange of technological information on an all-European basis and stimulated the flow of statistical information."[1] Though observers differ as to how significant ECE's contribution in the matter of East-West trade has been up to now, they agree that its role in this regard may well grow in the years to come.[2]

Considered as a whole, ECE has clearly not been able to mold a better political atmosphere between Eastern and Western Europe. However, it has not merely reflected the existing gulf between them. In addition to its outstanding technical work, it has continued to function as one of the few European organizations in which East and West meet in a common forum. And though chiefly technical matters are discussed in this forum, its value as an East-West meeting ground is considerable nevertheless.

A similar and even more paralyzing inability to combine broad international participation with the performance of substantive economic functions was suffered by the International Trade Organization (ITO), proposed by the United States in 1945. The ITO Charter was an ambitious project designed to reduce tariffs and other barriers to world trade on a global scale. In 1947 fifty-six nations convened at Havana to hammer out the basic document for the new organization which was to become a specialized agency of the United Nations. Two struggles plagued the Conference: The first was a tug-of-war between those nations that had accepted the goal of freeing trade from crippling restrictions and those more concerned with justifying their countries' restrictive practices and appending them to the Charter in the form of reservations. Second, there was the even graver obstacle to functional cooperation resulting from the East-West division. Though Czechoslovakia and Poland attended the 1947 ITO Conference, the Soviet Union's determination to turn Eastern Europe into its own isolated economic bloc clearly doomed the organization from the beginning. The final document was so full of reservations that it was almost meaningless. While fifty-three nations signed it in 1948, not a single nation has ratified it—not even the United States, its creator and champion.

The main Western proponents of ITO suspected even during the negotiations that the new organization might be stillborn. They therefore suggested that parallel negotiations take place among the leading nations of the Atlantic Community and Latin America. Accordingly, twenty-three nations met at Geneva in 1947 and drafted the General Agreement on Tariffs and Trade (GATT). This was a trailblazing document, incorporating the results of 120 sets of bilateral negotiations among the twenty-three participating nations, and embracing some 43,000 separate items. In fact, GATT affected more than three fourths of the import trade of the member states and about one half of total world imports. With ITO shelved, GATT assumed increasing importance. By 1949 all twenty-three of the original signatories had ratified the Agreement and had lowered customs duties among themselves. Since then, the membership of GATT has almost doubled. Two Communist states—Poland and Czechoslovakia—are members.

During the 1950's, GATT experienced numerous difficulties and was often eclipsed by the more cohesive regional arrangements in Western Europe. In 1962, however, the United States Congress passed the Trade Expansion Act, primarily to bring about a general lowering of tariff barriers with Western Europe. President Kennedy decided to utilize

GATT machinery for the negotiations. GATT members met in 1963 to discuss the "Kennedy round" in a preliminary manner and in 1964 serious negotiations got under way. The results were impressive. In May 1967, fifty countries with 80 per cent of the world's trade agreed to an average one-third reduction in their tariffs, as well as liberalization of agricultural trade and a program of food aid for the hungry nations. The 1967 agreement was a significant landmark in the liberalization of international trade.

In the early 1970's, in the wake of the devaluation of the United States dollar, most members of GATT expressed interest in a fundamental reexamination of the Agreement. GATT, after all, had been formed in the years when the United States had been the dominant power in world trade. The ascendancy of Japan and the progressive economic unification of Western Europe had changed all this, of course. The original purpose of GATT had been the lowering of tariff barriers. By the 1970's, tariffs were no longer the most significant hindrance to world trade. Non-tariff barriers loomed as far more important. Hence, it was likely that GATT would become one of the instruments in a more fundamental revision of the entire world trade system.

Four further quasi-global functional experiments must be mentioned. The International Monetary Fund (IMF), the International Bank for Reconstruction and Development (IBRD), or World Bank, the International Development Association (IDA), and the International Finance Corporation (IFC) are all members of the United Nations family. The IMF's major purpose is to make short-term currency loans, while the World Bank, IDA, and IFC engage in the industrial development of economically underdeveloped areas. Both the IMF and the World Bank have operated on the periphery of the United Nations system. The IMF has been fairly active, but has remained a primarily Western operation. The World Bank's work has been on a far larger scale. Numerous long-term loans have been made to Western European countries and a smaller number to the new nations of Asia, Africa, and the Middle East. Though the World Bank has certainly not furthered the functional cooperation of East and West, it has improved political conditions in other parts of the world. For example, a World Bank loan to India and Pakistan in 1960 for a common irrigation project resulted in the first political rapprochement between the two countries since the partition of 1947. The criterion upon which it bases its loans is the economic soundness of the project in question, but at times, as in the India-Pakistan case, an improvement in the political climate has been an attractive by-product. It is too early to attempt a prognosis of IDA and IFC, but it is unlikely that these agencies will become major instruments in the reduction of East-West tensions.

In the last analysis, economic functionalism at the global level has not produced the results so strongly hoped for—only GATT has shown impressive results since the inception of the "Kennedy round." ECE has been reduced to a clearinghouse for technical and statistical information. The International Monetary Fund and the World Bank and its affiliated bodies, though nominally United Nations bodies, have in practice become regional organizations. It has been at the regional level, indeed, and especially in Western Europe, that functional collaboration in economic matters has been really tested.

Economic Order-Building in Western Europe

The Soviet rejection of the Marshall Plan offer meant that the economic rehabilitation of Western Europe would have to take place in a regional framework under entirely Western auspices. Hence, for political reasons, the Economic Commission for Europe was bypassed by a new body, the Organization for European Economic Cooperation (OEEC), which was to take over responsibility for the European Recovery Program. OEEC proved to be one of the most successful functional organizations on record and deserves close analysis.

The nations which signed the OEEC Convention in April 1948 were all members of the Atlantic Community: Austria, Belgium, Denmark, France, Greece, Iceland, Ireland, Italy, Luxembourg, the Netherlands, Norway, Portugal, Sweden, Switzerland, Turkey, and the United Kingdom. Canada and the United States became associate members while the Federal Republic of Germany and Spain joined soon afterwards as full members. Yugoslavia took part as an observer. The machinery of OEEC included a Council composed of all the member governments, an Executive Committee, several Technical Committees, and a Secretariat. Thus equipped, the organization embarked on its two main responsibilities: the apportioning of American aid and the liberalization of trade restrictions in the Western European economy.

The structure of OEEC was the subject of some disagreement. The French wanted a strong executive organ with some "supra-national" characteristics. This was opposed by Britain, which insisted that the new organization remain under the direct control of the participating governments with no abrogation of sovereignty whatsoever. The British view prevailed both in form and in practice and OEEC was constituted as a purely transnational body, a conference of sovereign states in permanent session. The power of decision rested in the Council, which was bound by the rule of unanimity. It would be false to assume, however, that the unanimity rule was a hindrance to the work of OEEC. The rule resulted in a practice of careful deliberating at all levels of policy-making. In fact, when one or more states threatened to veto a decision, it was not uncommon for them to be "shamed" into agreement. A carefully prescribed procedure, including hearings and cross-examinations, made it almost impossible for a state to claim that it had been left out of the policy-making process. The veto was used only as a last resort. If a state used it too often, it found itself isolated and even ostracized. Diplomatic pressure was usually sufficient to persuade a reluctant member. On the other hand, the veto was a constant reminder to the large states that the smaller ones could not simply be outvoted but had to be persuaded. At times, the strict application of the unanimity rule even enabled the small states to exert a disproportionate amount of influence, as for example, when "a struggle over regulations concerning dried fruit among some of the smaller powers once held up far more important business."[3] But on the whole, the veto rule did not lead to paralysis; rather, it opened new avenues of improvisation and innovation. Of these, perhaps the most important was what OEEC officials came to call the "confrontation technique." The continuous process of intergovernmental consultation that went on at all levels of the organization encouraged a "European way of thinking" and an "OEEC point of view" in the permanent national delegations accredited to OEEC.[4] In making this view known to their national governments and in pressing for its acceptance, these officials imposed a moral obligation upon their governments that could not be lightly ignored. Indeed, the members of OEEC learned always to bear in mind the international consequences of national decisions. To be sure, there existed no legal obligation to do so, but long years of conditioning created a high degree of sensitivity to the interests of Europe as a whole. It may be said of most OEEC officials that this dual loyalty to their own country and to Europe seldom caused any serious difficulties. In most instances it proved possible for them to find a workable balance.

OEEC began as a "crisis organization" primarily concerned with the distribution of American aid. But as European recovery progressed, its second major responsibility, the liberalization of trade, assumed increasing importance. In this respect also, OEEC was very successful. It brought about a great increase in intra-European trade as well as in European production. The OEEC Code of Trade Liberalization resulted in the modification and withdrawal of numerous quota restrictions among the member states. A European Productivity Agency under the aegis of OEEC brought about major improvements in European industrial and agricultural productivity. Yet in the area of tariff reduction, OEEC also suffered a number of failures. Most notable among these were the major rifts that developed on the question of tariff reduction between the "Six"—France, Italy, West Germany, and the Benelux countries—and the rest of the OEEC membership. The increasing impatience of the "Inner Six" members of OEEC with the more conservative policies of the "Outer Seven" placed the organization under strain.

When OEEC went out of existence in 1960, it had demonstrated that a functional organization need not be "supra-national" to be moderately successful. The OEEC had managed to improvise a number of successful techniques of economic cooperation despite its Council's unanimity rule. The decisive factor in the organization's success, however, was not structural. It was the fact that OEEC had served two real and tangible purposes—the distribution of Marshall Plan aid and the liberalization of intra-European trade. It was these well-defined purposes that saved it from the fate of the Council of Europe, in whose case cooperation was defined much less concretely and sharply.

In 1961 the OEEC was replaced by the Organization for Economic Cooperation and Development (OECD). The new body included the eighteen OEEC members plus the United States and Canada. Its goals were described as close cooperation on economic and business cycle policy, expanded aid to underdeveloped countries, and further progress in trade liberalization. Its record since its inception has been impressive.

Neither OEEC nor its successor had any "supra-national" features. Quite early in the life of the OEEC, this absence of "supra-nationality" gave rise to disagreements and eventually prompted six member nations to launch a far more ambitious project in economic collaboration. In May 1950 French Foreign Minister Robert Schuman made a dramatic announcement. He proposed to pool the resources of the French and German coal and steel industries under a common "supra-national" authority that was to be open to other European countries. The motives underlying this far-reaching proposal were both economic and political. A rational distribution of European coal and steel throughout Western Europe would be highly desirable. But far more important was Schuman's desire to end Franco-German enmity. By the pooling of two raw materials vital for war, military conflict between Germany and France would become next to impossible. The bold conception of the Schuman Plan thus combined both realism and vision.

A month after the initial proposal, negotiations began among six European countries—France, West Germany, Italy, and the Benelux states. The moving spirit behind the negotiations was Jean Monnet, another major architect of the European idea. Monnet's hope was that economic union among the participating states would ultimately lead to political union. He envisaged a "supra-national" authority with well-defined but real powers over coal and steel. Subsequently, other sectors of the economy might be added, leading logically to the goal of political fusion. The treaty negotiations proceeded fairly smoothly, since all participating states saw great advantages in the proposal. The French feared that an uncontrolled revival of the German Ruhr industries might once again herald the start of German aggression. Hence France was willing to give up a degree of control over her own industries in exchange for some control over those in Western Germany. The Germans hoped that the Schuman Plan would greatly improve their coal and steel production, expand markets, and create new outlets for foreign investment. Italy looked forward to new capital and the possibility of relieving her population problem through emigration. The Benelux countries hoped for increased exports and a greater volume of transit trade.

The great disappointment encountered by the negotiators was the attitude of Great Britain. The Six had invited the Labour government to participate but had been turned down. The main objection on the other side of the Channel was to the proposed "supra-national" character of the organization. The British, in consideration of their unique international position and their ties to the Commonwealth, were simply unwilling to allow control of coal and steel to pass to a "supra-national" authority. Prime Minister Attlee rejected the Schuman Plan in the strongest terms:

We on this side are not prepared to accept the principle that the most vital economic forces of this country should be handed over to an authority that is utterly undemocratic and is responsible to nobody.[5]

Similarly, the Scandinavian countries, Austria, and Switzerland rejected the "supra-national" features of the proposed treaty. Thus, negotiations remained limited to The Six. The entire process took a little over two years. Italy was the last of the members to ratify, in June 1952. In September of that year the new European Coal and Steel Community, creating a single market for coal and steel for the 160,000,000 people of the six participating states, became a reality.

The structure of ECSC before the fusion of its executive with those of the other European Communities in 1967 deserves close analysis. At least one of the Community's institutions—the High Authority—possessed powers previously exercised only by national governments and some powers that even those governments did not possess. Hence, a real curtailment of national sovereignty by The Six was involved. The core and executive institution of ECSC, the High Authority, made all important decisions. This body consisted of nine members who held office for six-year terms. Eight of these were chosen by agreement among the six member governments and the ninth was co-opted by the other eight. The High Authority never included more than two members of the same nationality. In practice, ECSC's main organ was composed of two members from France, two from Germany, and one each from Belgium, Italy, Luxembourg, and the Netherlands. The ninth member always came from a country providing only one official. The members of the High Authority did not regard themselves as political spokesmen for their respective governments but as international civil servants of an independent European institution. Decisions of the High Authority were made by majority vote but, so far as the outside world was concerned, the principle of collective responsibility was observed.

The main "supra-national" features of the High Authority were threefold: first, its legal right to bypass the six national governments and to deal with the coal and steel industries of the Community directly; second, to make binding decisions in its area of competence; and third, to impose sanctions against violators. In carrying out its functions, the High Authority took the following types of action: first, it could direct the industries through decisions which were legally binding in every respect; second, it could act through recommendations; and finally, it could express opinions. Recommendations and opinions usually carried great weight but engendered no legal compulsion. Sanctions against violators of binding decisions took the form of monetary fines. Over twenty industrial enterprises in the Community were thus fined, principally for such infractions as exceeding the price ceiling, breaking price equalization schemes, and forming cartels without approval. The fines were usually light but increased in severity if violations continued. The first President of the High Authority was Jean Monnet. During his tenure, Monnet always emphasized that the federal aspects of ECSC were superior in actual power to those of the member governments. "In a sense, Monnet considered the High Authority as the repository of the European General Will, with the evil governments merely the spokesmen for the selfish particular wills."[6] In brief, the High Authority seemed to be the embodiment of "the European point of view."

It would be erroneous, however, to regard the High Authority as a kind of Platonic Nocturnal Council. There were important checks on its power. The most important of these was the Community's Court of Justice, established under the terms of the ECSC Treaty. This Court assumed its functions in January 1955. It was composed of seven judges elected for six years and served as an appellate body of redress against the High Authority when that body was accused of exceeding its jurisdiction. Both private firms and member states could appeal to the Court, which in fact became the constitutional arbiter of the Schuman Treaty. As such, the Court had the power to annul the High Authority's decisions. The record of the Court has been marked by a high degree of objectivity and independence. A large number of appeals came before it. On some occasions the Court upheld the High Authority against member governments and private enterprises. In 1955, for example, the Court rejected an appeal by the government of the Netherlands against the Authority's decision to maintain ceiling prices for coal and steel. On the other hand, the Court upheld appeals by the French and Italian governments and reversed High Authority decisions on the sale of scrap iron.

A second important check on the High Authority's power was exercised by the Council of Ministers, which was composed of the Ministers for Economic Affairs from the six member countries. The

Council was introduced as a result of pressure by the Benelux governments who were fearful that the Schuman Community's coercive authority might be too great. The Council's task was to harmonize the actions of the High Authority with those of the participating governments. In practice, the Council advised the High Authority and made sure that the interests and policies of the member countries were given due weight. It constantly confronted the High Authority with "national" points of view, thus serving as a vital link between national policy and the "European policy" of the Authority.

The High Authority also depended for advice upon a Consultative Committee consisting of producers, workmen, distributors, and consumers from the six member states. Before coming to any important decision, the Authority reviewed any proposed action with the Committee. The final institution in the ECSC structure was the Assembly. Since 1958, the Assembly has also served Euratom and the Common Market and is now known as the European Parliament. The 142 members of this body were chosen either by the respective parliaments of the six states or by popular election. The delegates were all parliamentarians and in most cases also attended the sessions of the Assembly of the Council of Europe. At least once a year the Assembly reviewed the action of the High Authority, acting very much like a stockholder's meeting. Unlike a national parliament, it had no legislative power and could not initiate policy. Its one great power was a negative one: it could remove the High Authority by a two-thirds vote of censure. This never actually occurred. In practice, the Assembly attempted to influence the shaping of policies. The most interesting development in this respect was the development of "supra-national" political parties.[7] It was not uncommon for the Socialist members from the six participating states to form a common front against the Assembly's conservatives, including even their own countrymen.

In sum, the High Authority was a "supra-national" organ with considerable power over the coal and steel industries of The Six. It must be remembered, however, that this power applied only to these two sectors of the member countries' economies and that an effective system of checks and balances was written into the Treaty. If the High Authority was the motor of ECSC, the Council of Ministers, the Consultative Committee, the Assembly, and the Court of Justice were its brakes. The total structure of ECSC was thus a unique phenomenon, falling somewhere along the continuum between a purely transnational organization and a federal government. Its High Authority certainly had far more power than the central agency of a conventional international organization, though less than is generally yielded to a federal government.

We must now assess the accomplishments of this unique functional organization. After the defeat of EDC by the French Parliament in

1954, many friends of ECSC feared that the Community would atrophy and that its "supra-national" features would not long endure. These fears proved unwarranted. The proposed common market for coal, iron ore, steel, and scrap went into effect in 1953. Apparently unconcerned about its isolation, the High Authority launched a massive program. A timetable was laid down by which all tariffs, quotas, currency restrictions, and discriminations among the coal and steel industries were to be eliminated. The High Authority tried its utmost to ensure fair conditions of competition and to eliminate monopolistic buying and selling practices. The Authority's most difficult task was "trust-busting"—implementing the anti-cartel provisions of the Treaty. Success on this front was limited because of resistance in all the six member states. French and German industrial interests especially complained that the Authority moved too quickly. Actually, on the cartel question, the High Authority's approach was quite cautious. By and large, the High Authority showed itself to be understanding of special problems and to be dedicated to making the most constructive contribution possible to the industries concerned. Investment in the coal and steel industries of The Six was encouraged. The Authority endeavored to raise loans for the purpose. And it even ventured into the social realm through research into occupational diseases, safety problems, and the harmonization of wage levels and fringe benefits.

There was some friction among the five institutions of ECSC but, on the whole, these tensions were useful rather than damaging. The system of checks and balances built into the Treaty worked very well. The four "brakes" attached to the High Authority effectively prevented the latter from assuming the proportions of a Frankenstein. Indeed, ECSC became a unique showcase of functional cooperation.

There was, however, one serious weakness from which ECSC suffered: the absence of Great Britain from its membership. Not that the participating powers did not make a determined effort to secure Britain's membership in the organization. They realized from the beginning that the absence of Britain would constitute a very serious obstacle to the building of a European economic order. And they feared that it might eventually even compel The Six to erect protective barriers against Britain and the other nations closely associated with it in economic matters. Yet both Labour and Conservative governments in Britain firmly rejected participation in any "supra-national" body that would entail a formal surrender of sovereignty. In view of their wider commitments to the Commonwealth, the British considered it ill-advised to wed themselves irrevocably to the European continent through ECSC. The net result of this policy, however, was that during the first decade of ECSC's life Britain and the Scandinavian countries increasingly became economic "outsiders" to the European Six. At first, Britain did not take ECSC seriously, but by 1960 she found herself left out of something of key economic importance. Hence, to try to remedy the situation, in 1960 Great Britain decided to launch a rival economic order-building scheme of her own, the European Free Trade Association. We shall examine this scheme in its proper context below.

On balance, ECSC demonstrated that the delegation of limited sovereign powers to a "supra-national" body could work in practice. When in 1954 the Community was left on its own through the demise of the European Defense Community, it was given a short life expectancy. Yet it not only survived, but encouraged The Six to engage in further "supra-national" experimentation among themselves. If it was possible to internationalize coal and steel, could not the same thing be accomplished in other sectors of the economy? Atomic energy, a new source of power with as yet few vested interests, might lend itself to a similar approach. This idea was to provide the seed for the new European Atomic Energy Community (Euratom). By the late 1950's it seemed to many observers that the "sector" approach to economic integration was the most effective road to international order-building that had yet been devised. The basis for this optimism was the impressive record of the European Coal and Steel Community.

The European Atomic Energy Community (Euratom) was born at a meeting of the Foreign Ministers of "little Europe" in June 1955. What Jean Monnet of France did for ECSC, Paul-Henri Spaak of Belgium accomplished for Euratom. Undaunted by the collapse of EDC and determined to "relaunch Europe," Spaak guided the draft treaty through a maze of technical committees during the summer of 1955. From this process there emerged the Spaak Report which became the basis for the Euratom Treaty. After protracted negotiations, the Treaty was signed in Rome in March 1957, and after ratification by the six member states went into effect on January 1, 1958. Therewith another sector of the economies of The Six, atomic energy, was absorbed into a "supra-national" community.

The essential purpose of Euratom was the pooling of the atomic energy resources of The Six for peaceful purposes. The Treaty steered clear of the military implications of atomic power. This limitation was inserted at the insistence of France, which wanted her defense program to remain outside of Euratom's control. Hence Euratom's main responsibilities included the development of nuclear research and the dissemination of technical knowledge; the development of uniform health and safety standards; the construction of nuclear reactors for peaceful purposes; and the development of control and inspection measures to prevent the member states from diverting Euratom-supplied nuclear materials to military purposes. The "working capital" of Euratom was supplied by the United States, which sold 30,000 kilograms of fissionable materials to the Community in 1958. Under the terms of the agreement, Euratom was given property rights over these materials. At the insistence of Euratom officials, the Community was also given the right of self-inspection by the United States government.

The structure of Euratom was made similar to that of ECSC. "Supra-national" authority was vested in a Euratom Commission which was composed of five members from different nationalities chosen on the basis of their competence. The Commission's powers with respect to atomic energy were even greater than those of the ECSC High Authority in matters of coal and steel. This difference may be attributed to three factors: first, the Euratom Treaty was highly technical, which meant that only nuclear specialists could discuss its implications in a meaningful sense; second, the Treaty was narrower in scope than ECSC and did not arouse as much resistance; and, most important, atomic energy was a relatively new field in which neither vested interests nor national habits were deeply rooted. Thus it proved relatively easy to endow the new Commission with very considerable powers.

Euratom, like ECSC, was a structure with checks and balances. It was decided to make the ECSC Assembly also the parliamentary body of Euratom. Even more significant, the ECSC Court of Justice also became the "conscience" of the Euratom Commission. The Court was given the power to remove the members of the Commission from office "for cause." In addition, the Court became the constitutional arbiter of the Euratom Treaty and was given the right to pass on the legality of Commission decisions if these were challenged by the member states.

Euratom has encountered relatively few serious obstacles. Atomic energy was still so new that the benefits to be derived from common action were greater and more apparent than in the conventional industries of coal and steel. Besides, matters of health and safety could be dealt with more efficiently through a "community approach." Second, the establishment of Euratom marked the beginning of the injection of order into the confusing array of functional organizations in Western Europe. The Court of Justice and the Assembly began to serve both ECSC and Euratom. By 1958 the "Community" of The Six had come to represent not only form but ever-growing substance. It was quite clear, indeed, that the ultimate objective of The Six was a United States of Europe via the road of economic order.

The second offspring of the ECSC was the European Economic Community (EEC) or "Common Market." This is the most ambitious functionalist scheme of our time. The idea for EEC was contained in the Spaak Report of 1956, which forcefully outlined the advantages of further steps toward economic union among The Six. The draft treaty proposed a twelve- to fifteen-year transitional period during which tariffs and quantitative restrictions for all commodities, including agricultural products, were to be eliminated among the six participating states. A single tariff schedule to be applied to outside countries was to be developed; freedom of movement for workers was also envisaged;

exchange policies were to be coordinated; a common transportation policy was to be hammered out; and common provisions for social benefits were contemplated. In brief, EEC was to become an arrangement that went much further than the abolition of tariffs and quotas among The Six, and was to be a half-way house toward complete political union.

Once again, Paul-Henri Spaak guided the project through the delicate formative stages. As in the ECSC, each of the prospective member states saw definite advantages. Only France had serious reservations and wanted to bring her overseas territories into the Community. France had great bargaining power because the other members feared her volatile Parliament. Also, the memory of the French refusal to ratify EDC was still fresh in everyone's mind. France was especially afraid of competition in the agricultural field and received numerous concessions in that area. She knew well that her participation was indispensable and used her advantage with consummate political skill. West Germany was eager to join since she perceived an opportunity for increasing markets and investment. Moreover, Chancellor Adenauer was deeply committed to "supra-nationality" among The Six, even as an ideal. Italy was most impressed by the goal of freedom of movement for workers which, she hoped, would contribute to the solution of her population and unemployment problems. The Benelux countries hoped for increased exports and transit trade. In spite of this favorable climate, negotiations at various times appeared on the point of breaking down. Finally, the EEC Treaty was signed in March 1957 and, together with the Euratom Treaty, went into effect on January 1, 1958.

The institutional structure of the Common Market was again patterned on the example of ECSC. A Commission composed of nine members chosen on the basis of "general competence" played the role of the High Authority. It was to perform its duties "in the general interest of the Community with complete independence." Its "supra-national" authority largely flowed from the power to fix and amend the timetables for freeing the various "sectors" from trade restrictions. The Assembly of the ECSC also served the Common Market and was given the power to remove members of the EEC Commission through a vote of censure. The ECSC Court of Justice was also made into a court of appeal in the framework of EEC. Thus the three "Communities" of The Six had a common Assembly and a common Court of Justice. In addition, EEC had a Council of Ministers which served as the link between the Community and the national governments. An Economic and Social Committee similar in function to the Consultative Committee of the ECSC completed the institutional picture in the early 1960's.

A dramatic structural step toward union was taken in 1967 when the three executive bodies of ECSC, Euratom, and the EEC were fused into a single fourteen-member European Commission. France, West Germany, and Italy supplied three commissioners each, Belgium and the Netherlands two each, and Luxembourg one. With this event, the pattern of a rudimentary federal structure clearly emerged among The Six.

The policy of Britain has gone through a full circle. As we have seen, Britain was unwilling to join any of the three "supra-national" experiments because of her reluctance to give up any of her sovereign power. In 1950 she was courted by The Six. But a decade later the wheel had turned full circle. In 1959, fearful of being left behind and outside, Britain began to woo The Six, but now it was the turn of The Six to be reluctant. France had consolidated relations with West Germany and no longer needed Britain to balance German power in the Community. President de Gaulle, eager for French grandeur, saw Britain rather than Germany as his chief rival in the race for nuclear greatness; and it was Britain, not Germany, that had delivered arms to Tunisia—a fact that the new French government, which viewed EEC as much "Eurafrican" as European, could not easily overlook. Nor did the other members of the Common Market show great eagerness to admit Britain to the Community.

In self-defense, Britain therefore assumed the leadership of a rival scheme of her own, the European Free Trade Association. Those European countries that were interested in freer trade but also had reservations about "supra-nationality" followed the British lead. In December 1959 Britain, Austria, Denmark, Norway, Portugal, Sweden, and Switzerland signed the Convention setting up the new Association. Britain, rejected by the "Inner Six," took the initiative in forming the "Outer Seven." The seven member states contemplated the abolition of tariffs in annual installments by 1970. This was the main goal. Unlike EEC, the European Free Trade Association did not include planning for agricultural products, transport, and labor movements. It was a far more modest venture to be approached through the traditional transnational channels patterned after the OEEC model.

It soon became apparent, however, that EFTA, with its market of 90 million people, was no match for the 170 million inhabitants of The Six. In August 1961 the British government finally decided to apply for membership in the EEC. Negotiations proved difficult because of Britain's Commonwealth and EFTA commitments, special agricultural problems, and the issue of "supra-nationality." While the British application was pending, EEC in January 1962 moved into its second stage of integration, which involved majority voting on numerous important issues. Even while compromises making it possible for Britain to join were weighed, President de Gaulle, to the dismay of the other EEC members, not to mention Britain herself, vetoed British membership in January 1963. The French President, eager to construct a

Western Europe in which France would play a leading role, was intent on excluding what he described as the "Anglo-Saxon presence" from the continent. In 1967, yet another British effort to enter the Common Market came to grief on the rock of French resistance.

The turning point for Britain came in 1969. That year, President de Gaulle was defeated in a referendum on a domestic question and was succeeded by Georges Pompidou. In 1970, Edward Heath led the British Conservatives to a resounding victory over the Labour Party. Mr. Heath took Britain's case for entry into the Common Market directly to President Pompidou and found the new French President much more receptive than his predecessor. Protracted negotiations ensued between Britain's Geoffrey Rippon and France's Foreign Minister, Maurice Schumann. Finally, in early 1972, a new chapter in European history was opened when Britain was formally admitted to the Common Market.

With Britain's accession to EEC, EFTA went into eclipse. Ireland, Denmark and Norway were invited together with Britain, but Norway refused to join. The welcome extended to Britain was generally warm since the French especially perceived Britain as a counterweight to West Germany, whose economic power was of some concern to France and to the Benelux countries. Thus, by the early 1970's the Common Market was a power to be reckoned with, a group of nine nations comprising more than a quarter of a billion people well on their way toward economic union.

Despite the serious growing pains described above, the Western European economic integration movement has already had profound effects upon the rest of the world. The reaction in the United States has been ambivalent. On the one hand, the United States welcomes a strong and united Europe as a more dependable ally in the struggle against Communism; but on the other, the United States confronts real economic power on the other side of the Atlantic which can no longer be dealt with lightly and which may force major reevaluations of economic policy. The Soviet bloc has not been able to ignore the Common Market either. Several Eastern European countries, as well as the Soviet Union itself, are exploring further possibilities of trade with the EEC. And even the more remote countries in the developing parts of the world have had to pay attention to this bold new experiment now taking place in Western Europe.

The Outlook

We are now ready for a more general evaluation of functionalism as a technique for the building of economic order. On a global scale, we have seen, the functional approach has not proved very productive. The organizations that have attempted it have, in effect, had to choose between greater scope or greater effectiveness. The Economic Commission for Europe and the General Agreement on Tariffs and Trade contained a wide membership, but were thereby prevented from any substantial accomplishment, although the latter definitely gained in significance during the late 1960's. The International Monetary Fund and the World Bank, on the other hand, have worked well and fruitfully, but in order to do so have had to limit their scope to an admittedly regional context. It therefore seems unlikely that global functionalism will achieve much success in furthering a more harmonious political climate. Attempts at such global functional organization are much more likely merely to reflect existing political differences and tensions.

Our Western European case study in functional order-building on a regional basis affords some interesting insights. For one thing, "supranationality" *per se* is not necessarily a precondition for an organization's success. The Organization for European Economic Cooperation was a singularly successful venture although it did not embody any "supranational" features. What seems to determine an organization's operational effectiveness is whether it has a concrete and tangible job to do. If it does, institutional gadgetry becomes more or less irrelevant. A vague desire for cooperation without clearly defined goals will lead to atrophy; the Council of Europe is a case in point. What distinguishes all the regional economic organizations of Europe, whether "supranational" or not, is the fact that they have clearly defined operational programs. This was true especially of the three "Communities" of The Six and certainly continues to be true of the Common Market since the accession of Britain. The integration process is also furthered by the fact that all participants have expectations of concrete economic rewards. The nature of these expectations differs from state to state, but all members hope to derive great benefits in one form or another.

The increasing complexity of the European organizational picture cries out for a measure of coordination. It is unlikely that an overall scheme or "Grand Design" will be acceptable to all the states of Western Europe in the immediate future. The ultimate objective of some Western European states is nothing less than a United States of Europe. This aim is not yet shared by others, especially Britain and France. Coordination will probably have to proceed within each of the two camps. Some progress has been made. Already, the three "Communities" share a common Assembly, a common Court of Justice, and a common Executive. These may be the forerunners of a European federal system.

Perhaps the most encouraging by-product of functional experimentation in Western Europe has been the development of a "European outlook." The constant process of consultation and the complexity of international machinery have persuaded most Western European statesmen to consider national policy decisions in the broadest possible context. Indeed, the "European outlook" is common to both the "supranational" and the more traditional organizations. On the other hand, the greatest danger inherent in this extensive experimentation is the possibility of rivalry among competing regional groupings. If these regional bodies should claim a new kind of "sovereignty" for themselves and develop into a form of regional nationalism, their purpose would be defeated. On the whole, however, the functional organizations have shown an amazing talent for improvisation and muddling through innumerable difficulties. Functionalism on a regional basis has become one of the most powerful instruments in the international struggle for order.

REFERENCES

1. PEP, *European Organisations*. London: Allen and Unwin, 1959, pp. 41–42.
2. Michael L. Hoffman, "Problems of East-West Trade," *International Conciliation*, January 1957, p. 299.
3. *Ibid.*, p. 58.
4. *Ibid.*, p. 53.
5. *Hansard*, June 27, 1950.
6. Ernst B. Haas, *The Uniting of Europe*. Stanford, Calif.: Stanford University Press, 1959, p. 456.
7. *Ibid.*, Chap. 11.

BIBLIOGRAPHY

Benoit, Emile. *Europe at Sixes and Sevens*. New York: Columbia University Press, 1961.

Clark, W. Hartley. *The Politics of the Common Market*. Englewood Cliffs, N.J.: Prentice-Hall, 1967.

Cochrane, James D. *The Politics of Regional Integration: The Central American Case*. New Orleans, La.: Tulane University Press, 1969.

Cooper, Richard N. *The Economics of Interdependence: Economic Policy in the Atlantic Community*. New York: McGraw-Hill, 1968.

Dam, Kenneth W. *The GATT: Law and International Economic Organization*. Chicago: University of Chicago Press, 1970.

Dell, Sidney. *Trade Blocs and Common Markets.* New York: Knopf, 1963.

Diebold, William, Jr. *The Schuman Plan.* New York: Praeger, 1959.

Esman, Milton J., and Cheever, Daniel S. *The Common Aid Effort: The Development Assistance Activities of the Organization for Economic Cooperation and Development.* Columbus, Ohio: Ohio State University Press, 1967.

Evans, John W. *The Kennedy Round in American Trade Policy: The Twilight of the GATT?* Cambridge, Mass.: Harvard University Press, 1971.

Feld, Werner J. *Transnational Business Collaboration Among Common Market Countries.* New York: Praeger, 1970.

Frank, Isaiah. *The European Common Market: An Analysis of Commercial Policy.* New York: Praeger, 1961.

Friedmann, Wolfgang, *et al. International Economic Aid.* New York: Columbia University Press, 1966.

Gardner, Richard N., and Millikan, Max F., eds. *The Global Partnership.* New York: Praeger, 1968.

——. *Sterling-Dollar Diplomacy. The Origins and the Prospects of Our International Economic Order.* New York: McGraw-Hill, 1969.

Haas, Ernst B. *Beyond the Nation-State.* Stanford, Calif: Stanford University Press, 1965.

——. *The Uniting of Europe.* rev. ed. Stanford, Calif.: Stanford University Press, 1968.

Jones, Joseph M. *The Fifteen Weeks.* New York: Viking Press, 1955.

Kaser, Michael. *Comecon: Integration Problems of the Planned Economies.* New York: Oxford University Press, 1967.

Keenleyside, Hugh L. *International Aid.* New York: Heinemann, 1966.

Kindleberger, Charles P. ed. *The International Corporation.* Cambridge, Mass.: Massachusetts Institute of Technology Press, 1970.

Kitzinger, U. W. *The Challenge of the Common Market.* Oxford: Basil Blackwell, 1961.

Krause, Lawrence B. *European Economic Integration and the United States.* Washington, D.C.: Brookings Institution, 1968.

Lieber, Robert J. *British Politics and European Unity: Parties, Elites, and Pressure Groups.* Berkeley, Calif.: University of California Press, 1970.

Lister, Louis. *Europe's Coal and Steel Community.* New York: Twentieth Century Fund, 1960.

Machlup, Fritz. *Remaking the International Monetary System: The Rio Agreement and Beyond.* Baltimore: Johns Hopkins Press, 1968.

Mason, Henry L. *The European Coal and Steel Community: Experiment in Supranationalism.* The Hague: Nijhoff, 1955.

Meyer, F. V., *The European Free Trade Association.* New York: Praeger, 1960.

Mitrany, David. *A Working Peace System.* Chicago: Quadrangle Press, 1966.

Myrdal, Gunnar. *An International Economy.* New York: Harper, 1956.

Nove, Alec, and Donnelly, Desmond. *Trade with Communist Countries.* London: Hutchinson, 1960.

Okigbo, P. N. C. *Africa and the Common Market.* Evanston, Ill.: Northwestern University Press, 1967.

Political and Economic Planning (PEP). *European Organisations.* London: Allen and Unwin, 1959.

Preeg, Ernest H. *Traders and Diplomats.* Washington, D.C.: The Brookings Institution, 1970.

Rahl, James A., ed. *Common Market and American Antitrust.* New York: McGraw-Hill, 1970.

Robinson, E. A. G., ed. *Economic Consequences of the Size of Nations.* London: Macmillan and Company, Ltd., 1960.

Rostow, Walter W. *Stages of Economic Growth.* Cambridge: Cambridge University Press, 1959.

Sannwald, Rolf F., and Stohler, Jacques. *Economic Integration.* Princeton, N.J.: Princeton University Press, 1959.

Scitovsky, Tibor. *Economic Theory and Western European Integration.* Stanford, Calif.: Stanford University Press, 1958.

Strauss, E. *Common Sense about the Common Market.* New York: Rinehart, 1958.

Streeten, Paul P. *Economic Integration: Aspects and Problems.* Leyden: A. W. Sythoff, 1961.

Triffin, Robert. *Europe and the Money Muddle.* New Haven, Conn.: Yale University Press, 1957.

Vernon, Raymond. *Sovereignty at Bay: The Multinational Spread of U.S. Enterprises.* New York: Basic Books, 1971.

Wightman, David. *Economic Cooperation in Europe—A Study of the United Nations Commission for Europe.* London: Stevens and Heinemann, 1956.

Wiles, P. J. D. *Communist International Economics.* New York: Praeger, 1969.

Zartman, William I. *The Politics of Trade Negotiations Between Africa and the European Economic Community.* Princeton, N.J.: Princeton University Press, 1971.

Part 4 Toward a Theory of International Relations

14 Perception and Reality in World Politics

Behold! human beings living in a sort of underground den, which has a mouth open toward the light and reaching all across the den; they have been here from their childhood, and have their legs and necks chained so that they cannot move, and can only see before them; for the chains are arranged in such a manner as to prevent them from turning round their heads. At a distance above and behind them the light of a fire is blazing, and between the fire and the prisoners there is a raised way; and you will see, if you look, a low wall built along the way, like the screen which marionette players have before them, over which they show the puppets.

I see, he said.

And do you see, I said, men passing along the wall carrying vessels, which appear over the wall; also figures of men and animals, made of wood and stone and various materials; and some of the prisoners, as you would expect, are talking, and some of them are silent?

This is a strange image, he said, and they are strange prisoners. Like ourselves, I

391

replied; and they only see their shadows, or the shadows of one another, which the fire throws on the opposite wall of the cave?

True, he said: how could they see anything but the shadows if they were never allowed to move their heads?

And of the objects which are being carried in like manner they would see only the shadows?

Yes, he said.

And if they were able to talk with one another, would they not suppose that they were naming what was actually before them?

Very true.

And suppose further that the prison had an echo which came from the other side, would they not be sure to fancy when one of the passers-by spoke that the voice which they heard came from the passing shadow?

No question, he replied.

To them, I said, the truth would be literally nothing but the shadows of the images.

That is certain.
PLATO, *"Allegory of the Cave" Republic, VII*

This book has attempted to present an analysis of international relations in our time. In so doing, we have dealt with a wide range of phenomena. For the purpose of ordering this body of material, we have employed *two key concepts.* First, and very broadly, we have analyzed world politics in terms of *the ever-present tension between the struggle for power and the struggle for order among nations.* We have seen that these two struggles are at many points closely interwoven. Indeed, the very soil which produces struggles for power also provides the nourishment for new institutions of order. Thus, World War I brought forth the League of Nations and World War II the United Nations. The Suez crisis of 1956 and the Congo crisis of 1960 led to the creation of unprecedented UN peace forces. And the Cuban missile crisis of 1962 made possible agreement on the cessation of nuclear testing. Similarly, every struggle for order among nations also involves some kind of power struggle. Witness the United Nations, the most imaginative instrument for order-building thus far devised, yet at the same time the arena for some of the most stubborn vying for power in history. The evidence suggests that self-styled realists and idealists are both wrong: power alone is no reliable guide through the landscape of international politics, nor is the quest for order. The relationship between power and order in world politics is inherently dialectical in nature. Fundamentally, therefore, these two pervasive struggles must be recognized as two sides of a single coin.

Within this broad and general conceptual framework, we have introduced a specific substantive theme as our second key concept: *the linkage between the triangular East-West struggle involving China, Russia, and the United States, and the struggle between nationalism and colonialism.* The pattern of interdependence between these two great conflicts of our time is woven into the entire fabric of contemporary international relations. *The struggle for power and order may be seen as the essence of international relations everywhere and always. The East-West struggle and the struggle over colonialism provide its particular form of expression here and now.*

To these two organizing concepts which deal with the substance of world politics we may now add a third which concerns a further vital dimension of international relations: *the frequent and highly significant differences between the way nations perceive one another and the way they really are.* For the titanic struggles among the nations of our time are not only waged on the basis of objective realities. They are also fought out in the realm of imagery and illusion. It is the thesis of this concluding chapter that there are often great gaps between *perception* and *reality* in world politics and that these integrally affect all aspects of international relations, deeply exacerbating the international struggle for power and seriously slowing down the international struggle for order.

The assumption underlying this thesis is that to some degree, at least, international relations are what people think they are; or, to put it in other words, that, under certain conditions, men respond not to realities but to fictions that they have themselves created. To say that there are no objective problems in world politics would be gross exaggeration. But the stage of world politics lends itself all too easily to the development of wide gaps between what that reality is and the way it is perceived. And because of this fact, perception probably plays as important a role in international relations as does objective reality itself.

Before we can analyze the significance of perception in international relations, we must define it and search out its origins. Perception in international relations may be defined as the total cognitive view a nation holds of itself and of others in the world. As such, it is a most complex phenomenon and includes both reality and distortion. There is little doubt that many nations much of the time see themselves and others the way they really are; but it is equally certain that many nations much of the time see themselves and others in stereotyped unidimensional ways. Nationalism and ideology contribute much to seeing other nations as "bad" and one's own as spotless. Stereotyped images on one side elicit similar ones on another, often compounding the distortion. Even worse, if one believes a stereotype long enough it may become reality by setting in motion the mechanism of the self-fulfilling prophecy. Thus, if a nation believes that another is its implacable enemy and reiterates this often enough, making it the guideline of its national policy, it will eventually be right.

Our first task, then, is to isolate those factors in a nation's overall perception that are distorted; to extrapolate from the composite picture of reality and illusion the elements of illusion. Here we encounter a major difficulty. Throughout this book, we have referred to nations as if they were cohesive entities speaking with a single voice on the world scene: "The United States agreed," "the Soviet Union feared," "India proposed." Such statements, while unavoidable in an analysis of international relations, tell only part of the story. The next crucial question we must ask ourselves is *who* in "the United States agreed," *who* in "the Soviet Union feared," and *who* in "India proposed." Put differently, *who* is it that speaks for nations in world politics? To answer this question, we must analyze the nature of public opinion and its impact on a nation's decision-making process in international relations. Then, we must attempt to differentiate between those decision-makers and "influencers" who tend to perceive the outside world in terms of preconceived images and stereotypes and those who evaluate their environment more in accordance with objective reality.

It would, of course, be folly to attempt a generalized answer that would be true for all nations. Fortunately, excellent studies have been made of the impact of public opinion and of stereotypes on the foreign policy-making process of three different types of nations. Walter Lippmann's study, *Public Opinion,* and Gabriel Almond's *The American People and Foreign Policy* are both classics dealing with the American scene.[1] Alex Inkeles' *Public Opinion in Soviet Russia* gives us a revealing picture of that aspect of the Soviet Union.[2] And Gabriel Almond and James S. Coleman have edited and contributed to a study on *Politics of The Developing Areas* which provides many valuable insights into the public opinion and decision-making process of the emergent nations.[3] A comparative analysis of these studies yields much valuable information on the role of distorted perception in world politics.

It was Walter Lippmann who first subjected perception in American politics to a scrupulous analysis. In his trailblazing study, he pointed out that, for most people, "the world they have to deal with politically is out of reach, out of sight, out of mind."[4] Hence, the only reaction they can have to an event that they can neither reach, see, nor care about is one conditioned by their mental predisposition toward that event. Almond further refined this theme and applied it more specifically to Americans' reactions to matters of foreign policy. He discovered that only a small segment of the American public—the elite—is able to grasp the complex realities of international relations. This group consists largely of interest groups, professional organizations, and government officials. A second layer of American public opinion he identified as the "attentive public," those people who, while not themselves experts, continuously expose themselves to information on matters of world politics. The vast majority of Americans, however, Almond discovered, respond to matters of foreign policy largely on the basis of "mood." They tend to exhaust their emotional and intellectual energies in private pursuits and thus approach problems of world politics with a perfunctory attitude. Moreover, they feel that "they cannot affect foreign policy anyway," and that, therefore, a serious investment of time and energy is not worthwhile. As a result, this "mass public" tends to respond to the complex reality of world politics with simplified and frequently distorted images. It has replaced the real environment with a "pseudo-environment" largely compounded of prejudices and stereotypes.

As a result of these observations, it follows that the "mass public" is to some extent responsible for distorted American perceptions of world politics. Most scholars feel that this "mass public" exerts a great deal of influence through its electoral powers. Lippmann argues, however, that such control, to be beneficial, must emanate from a broadly educated public. If the mass public continues to perceive public policy in terms of "pictures in their heads," Lippmann sees the coming of a functional derangement between the mass of the people and the government in which "the people will have acquired power which they are incapable of exercising, and the governments they elect will have lost power which they must recover if they are to govern."[5] Carl J. Friedrich, on the other hand, has greater faith than Lippmann in the good political sense of the "common man."[6] Be that as it may, it is clear that as a result of "mass public" influence, *some* degree of distortion enters the American perception of world politics, and that when "the United States speaks" in world affairs, its position is therefore to *some* degree colored by images which depart from reality.

It is subject to serious doubt, however, whether Lippmann and Almond are justified in locating the source of distortion primarily in the "mass public." The record of American foreign policy suggests the possibility that distortions may also originate in the elite. The relationship between the "mass public" and the elite seems to be a highly complex one. At times the interaction between the two may further compound distortions. At other times, the elite may serve as a "corrective" and educate the "mass public." But on some occasions, and this is no less important, the "mass public" may have a sounder perception than the elite. It was the policy elite surrounding the American President in 1961, for example, not the mass public, that misperceived the situation in Cuba that in turn led to the fiasco of the Bay of Pigs.

At any rate, the gaps between perception and reality that exist in the United States view of world politics are not readily attributable to any one segment of the American people.

Studies of public opinion in Soviet Russia also suggest great distortions in the Soviet perception of world politics. But while in the United States it is difficult to locate the source of these distortions, in the Soviet Union, the main locus may be identified as the elite—the Communist Party. As we have seen in an earlier chapter, Communist ideology to some degree colors the lenses through which the Soviet regime perceives the world. These lenses are distributed to the "mass public" in the Soviet Union through cadres of professional agitators who do their best to ensure that the "new Soviet man" will perceive world politics through the reddish prism of Communist ideology. Ideology thus provides a kind of "built-in" distortion. As Inkeles points out in a striking analogy, this effort is only partially successful:

The figure most apt for describing the state of Soviet public opinion is that of a forest fire. On the broad peripheral front the blaze rages in full intensity. Here is found a thin line of convinced and confirmed Communists. But behind this line comes a much larger area, which has already been swept by the flames and which now boasts only glowing embers. This is the line of the half-believers, which includes some party members as well as the nonparty supporters of the regime. And beyond that there lies a still broader sweep of the burned-over timber, in which here and there a spark still glows but which is predominantly cold, ashen, and gray. The work of mass persuasion is the wind which fans this blaze. But like the wind in the forest fire, it not only spreads the flames but hastens the burning, and behind the line of flames and embers it can only stir up little swirls and eddies of ash.[7]

Thus the Soviet Union, too, is bound to perceive world politics to *some* extent in terms of distorted images and stereotypes. Since these are rooted primarily in Communist ideology, the width of the gap between perception and reality in Soviet foreign policy is determined by the degree to which the Soviet leaders themselves uncritically accept the doctrine with which they so relentlessly proselytize the rest of the world. Yet here, too, a *caveat* is necessary. There may be times at which commitment to Communist ideology may clarify rather than distort reality. For example, a convinced Communist was probably better able to predict the coming decline of Western colonialism than many non-Communists, though he would not have expected the colonial powers to be as acquiescent as they have been with respect to decolonization. The overall record suggests, however, that the elements of distortion in the Communist world view are far greater than the elements of clarification.

It is an open question to what extent personal contact between national leaders and peoples reduces the power of distorted imagery. It is difficult to say whether Nikita Khrushchev's visit to America in 1959 confirmed or reduced whatever false perceptions he might have had of the United States. The visit was probably too brief to make a deep impression either way. Similarly, one cannot say with certitude whether

President Nixon's visits to China and to the Soviet Union in 1972 displaced clichés about "Communism" that he might have believed with more realistic perceptions of Chinese and Soviet life. Probably the visits helped to decontaminate the minds of American, Soviet, and Chinese leaders of shopworn slogans at least to some extent since they were all vitally interested in establishing new relationships with one another, and thus were more responsive to reality.

The emergent nations present yet a third pattern of the impact of public opinion on the foreign policy-making process. As several expert students of the developing nations have pointed out, there is a minimum of contact between the government elite and the "mass public" in most of the new nations:

There exists a wide gap between the traditional mass and the essentially modern subsociety of the Westernized elite. The latter controls the central structures of government and essays to speak and act for the society as a whole. This elite subsociety is the main locus of political activity and of change in the society at large.[8]

There are exceptions to this pattern, of course. India, for example, is a democracy in which there exists an intimate connection between public opinion and the government elite. But in most cases, the new nations have evolved authoritarian forms of government in which a high degree of alienation between the "mass public" and the government is typical. Hence, the pattern differs from that of the United States, since, in the developing nations, the "mass public" is, politically speaking, relatively powerless. It also differs from the Soviet and Chinese models since the leadership, as a general rule, does not make a concerted attempt to indoctrinate the population with an ideology. It would be erroneous to assume, however, that the leadership of the new nations has a completely accurate perception of world politics. As we have seen earlier, the attitudes of most of the new nationalist leaders are deeply colored by their colonial past. In their case, the memory of colonialism persists much longer than the fact. Once again, therefore, *some* distortion does result. To put it as precisely as possible, the degree of divergence between perception and reality in the new nations' view of world politics is determined by the degree to which the memory of colonialism outlives the reality.

Now that we have at least a tentative insight into the nature of public opinion and its effect on a nation's perception of world politics, we may attempt to propose a tentative answer to the following important question: Which element in a nation's population is most responsible for the degree of distorted imagery that affects its government's perception of the international scene?

In our analysis of three different examples, we have seen that the governments of the United States, of the Soviet Union, and of most of the emergent nations are all subject to some degree of distorted perception. In the United States, it is difficult to identify the precise source of distortion. It may be found in a subtle interplay between the "mass public" and the elite in which each may act on the other as either a reinforcing or a corrective agent, depending upon the specific circumstances. In the Soviet Union and in China, the locus of distortion is more easily identifiable as the Communist Party elite which, to some degree at least, perceives the world through the lenses of what it defines as Marxism-Leninism. The Soviet or Chinese "mass public" has little chance to act as a corrective, but tends to absorb at least some of the Party ideology, thus compounding the distortion. In the emergent nations of the authoritarian type, where there is relatively little contact between the elite and the "mass public," the source of distorted imagery is usually the leadership itself.

Of the three cases studied, the United States is probably least susceptible to distorted imagery. There is no "built-in" distortion through a prescribed ideology. Moreover, the very complexity of the American foreign policy-making process provides a kind of check-and-balance system which prevents extreme distortions from being translated into policy. The "built-in" quality of Communist ideology, on the other hand, no doubt injects considerable distortion into Soviet and Chinese perceptions of world politics. But it would be misleading to assume that this ideological factor always and under any circumstances produces a distorted image of the outside world. After all, it is not demonstrable that the Soviet or the Chinese leadership uncritically accepts the Marxist-Leninist conception of international relations. While it is difficult to generalize about the emergent nations, it seems fairly safe to say that those with authoritarian forms of government also experience a good deal of distortion, falling somewhere along the spectrum between the Soviet Union, China, and the United States.

Now that we have examined the nature of the perception factor in the anatomy of a nation, we may proceed to an analysis of some of the major gaps between perception and reality in present-day world politics.

The two main political power struggles of our time are being fought on the dual plane of perception and reality. First, if we consider the East-West struggle, it is obvious, as we have seen earlier, that a great number of objective differences exist which defy easy solution. But to a considerable degree, the conflict also takes place in the realm of distorted imagery. On the Soviet side, the main cause of this distortion is Communist ideology. Quite early in the Soviet Union's life, the ideological factor generated a distorted self-image of historically ordained invincibility. It was also responsible for a perception of other nations that did not tally with reality. Thus, the Soviet Union tended to view the West, through Marxist-Leninist lenses, as being engaged in an effort to impose "capitalist encirclement" on the Soviet Union. Indeed, the Soviet leadership began to believe that it understood the West better than the West understood itself and as a result struggled not so much with the West as with its image of the West.

The West, in turn, became seriously affected by Soviet imagery and, despite a number of striking blunders committed by the Comintern during its first thirty years of operation, tended to perceive the Soviet Union as a kind of chess master on the world scene. The West's self-image, in turn, approached a collective inferiority complex. This "superman" view of Communism and the inferiority complex that followed made the West more fearful of the image of the Soviet Union than of the Soviet Union itself. Indeed, the hypnotic spell that the Soviet Union was able to cast over the West became one of that nation's greatest assets in the struggle. It resulted in a "psychological lag," in the sense that the West remained hypnotized by the Soviet Union at a time when most of the inroads into the Western orbit were being made by Communist China. In sum, the net result has been a twofold distortion. The two superpowers have struggled not only *with each other,* but also *with their perceptions of each other.* This divergence between perception and reality exacerbated the conflict enormously.

Only when the cold war abated during the 1960's and the desire for détente grew on both sides of the Iron Curtain, did the old stereotypes finally give way to more realistic perceptions. By the 1970's, the Soviet Union and the United States had entered a relationship that included elements of *both* conflict and cooperation. As cooperation grew, so did the willingness and the capacity on both sides to perceive complex realities rather than to remain wedded to simple-minded and one-dimensional clichés. Policies began to be shaped less on shadows and fears and more on facts.

The struggle over colonialism also bears the stamp of distortion. Although the record demonstrates that Western colonialism is largely a phenomenon of the past, the new nationalism acts as if it were very much alive. Indeed, as we have seen, in the life of the new nations the past often lives on with a fierce intensity. Although our three case studies of interaction between nationalism and colonialism (Chapter 4) demonstrated that the colonial experiment was a very diversified experience, ranging from outright exploitation to the bestowal of generous benefits, the new nationalism always regarded, and still regards, the entire colonial record as an unmitigated evil and fails to differentiate among the many varying shades of the spectrum. Our case studies also failed to support the conception held by most leaders of the new nationalism that their movement was antithetical to imperialism. Indeed, we have seen that the new nationalism may readily become a seedbed for a new form of imperialism. Hence, the struggle over colonialism, too, is intensified by great divergencies between perception and reality.

No less affected by this type of distortion has been the relationship between the two political struggles for power. Engagement in one of the two major conflicts has tended to obscure an accurate perception of the other. The United States has perceived the world primarily in terms of East and West; Ghana, on the other hand, has seen the great divide between Black and White. The United States has often been uncommitted in the struggle between nationalism and colonialism and has frequently been accused of "neutralism" by the new nationalist powers. But the new nations have been equally uncommitted in the East-West struggle in which the two superpowers have perceived *them* as "neutralists." In short, the perceptions of the major protagonists have largely remained limited to only *one* of the two great political struggles. However, each protagonist has been sufficiently aware of the struggle in which he has not seen himself directly involved to exploit it for his more conscious purposes. Thus both the Soviet Union and the United States, though primarily concerned with the East-West struggle, have consistently striven to gain support for themselves by seeking to play the most advantageous possible role in the colonial struggle.

The divergencies between perception and reality in the political power struggle of our time thus boil down to this: though both titanic conflicts are inseparably connected and are being waged simultaneously, those involved in the East-West struggle see the world chiefly in terms of this dichotomy, and those engaged in the colonial struggle see *that* conflict as all-important. Moreover, similar distortions characterize the views of each other held by the protagonists in each of the two struggles separately. And in every case, the imagery tends to depict the "enemy" as a more deadly threat than the objective record would seem to justify. As a result, the political struggle is greatly intensified in all its aspects.

The gap between fact and fiction has been even more dangerous in the military realm. Until the Cuban missile crisis of 1962, the United States and the Soviet Union have held the most extreme images of one another. The United States was convinced that "conquering the world for Communism" was the sole motivation of the Soviet alliance system. On the basis of this view it sought to arm itself with an irresistible destructive capacity through the policy of "massive retaliation." When this posture was criticized as too exclusively nuclear-minded, it began to experiment with an image of Benthamite rationality through the more flexible policy of graduated deterrence. The Soviet Union, for its part, developed an image of the West of "imperialist aggression and encirclement" bent upon the destruction of Communism. Logically enough, the view each side held of its own camp was one of defense against the other.

The great danger in the military struggle between the United States and the Soviet Union during the cold war period lay in the possibility that the extreme image that each side held of the other might have *become* reality, and that the circle of suspicion and countersuspicion might have precipitated a "preventive" war. If each side had continued to believe that the other was its mortal enemy, this view might have influenced behavior to such a point of rigidity and compulsiveness that the "inevitable conflict" could have become a self-fulfilling prophecy. Fortunately, the missile crisis cleared the air between the superpowers, at least to some extent, and introduced a larger measure of reality into their relations.

As the element of distorted perception decreased somewhat in United States-Soviet relations, it grew apace in the relations between the United States and China. The Korean War and the conflict in Vietnam accelerated this process and by the late 1960's a vicious spiral had been set in motion. Both China and America began with the *a priori* assumption of the other's implacable hostility; the power of this conviction caused all the adversary's actions to be interpreted as confirming the validity of the original assumption; hence, the adversary was found hostile *a posteriori* as well, since his actions had "proved" that the original assumption was correct. The very actions that the Chinese perceived as an American plot to encircle them were perceived by the Americans as necessary measures to forestall Chinese aggression. Confronted by a series of American policies that appeared to them to "prove" American enmity toward them, the Chinese embarked upon an increasingly virulent "Hate America" campaign that the United States in turn took as "proof" of *their* implacable hostility toward America. What seemed patently provocative to one appeared obviously defensive to the other. In this tragic spiral of reciprocally negative reinforcement, the borderline between real and imagined threats tended to blur and finally disappear altogether.

It is easy to see why political accommodation would be well nigh impossible under such conditions. On a deeper psychological level, such mirror devil images are the stuff that holy wars are made of. For to each side in the conflict, the enemy is not quite human and it becomes difficult, if not impossible, to identify with any part of him. Hence, each adversary is left with his fears and terrors which are in no way allayed by their failure to materialize. Such fears, however, can call forth a reality as terrible as the most anguished nightmare. This was the peril of the encounter between China and America. With the visit of President Nixon to China in 1972, the danger began to diminish. As in the case of the Soviet Union a decade earlier, the moment of greatest peril seems to have passed, but not without coming very close to the abyss.

The United States and the Soviet Union are still engaged in a relentless economic struggle with each other. Each covets the distinction of being the world's leading industrial power. This economic competition has led to a curious paradox: in the imagery of each superpower, the economic system of the antagonist is alien, pernicious, and to be eradicated. In reality, the exigencies of competition have led to a high degree of mutual emulation which, in turn, has made the economies of the Soviet Union and the United States increasingly alike. The hostile images dictate further competition but this competition will probably increase the objective similarities between the two economies still further. It is therefore possible that the common dictates of industrial production may divest the East-West struggle of some of its messianic ideological character. Once global ideology atrophies, the fierceness of the struggle may abate. Hence the gap between perception and reality in the economic realm is a danger chiefly in the short run. In the long run—assuming that the two great antagonists settle for coexistence without victory or defeat—it may actually prove a force making for order.

Yet both superpowers are aware that at least in the economic realm a decisive victory is still possible in the East-West struggle. They have become convinced that such as victory can be won by gaining the allegiance of the world's uncommitted countries. Both sides have therefore waged the economic struggle with the weapon of foreign aid. In this competition, too, images have greatly diverged from realities. Both superpowers, aware of the sensitivities of the new nations, have attempted to project an image of selflessness and generosity. The secret of success in the economic struggle seems indeed to lie in the realm of imagery. Not only must each of the superpowers learn to see itself as the new nations see it, but it must learn how the new nations perceive the other "enemy" superpower. It is difficult enough for a nation to see itself as others see it; it is far more difficult to see a second nation as a third sees it. Yet this ability is turning out to be of the utmost importance in the economic competition for the new nations. The Soviet Union has been able to project itself into the thinking of the uncommitted nations somewhat more successfully than the United States. And China, which has tended to cast her lot with the world's poor and yet has found it possible to give away large quantities of economic aid, has done even better than the Soviet Union. Both China and the Soviet Union have frequently been able to exploit the anticolonial images of the new nationalism to their own advantage. In its reaction to the "blindness" of the neutralist leaders in accepting Communist aid the United States has failed to comprehend a most basic fact: that to most of the new nations, Communism is not an unmitigated evil, but merely an alternative to democracy—an alternative, in fact, that, as they see it, may quite possibly produce the desired results faster. Moreover, the West has tended to define democracy primarily in terms of political liberty. In countries without a tradition of democracy, this has often seemed like a luxury commodity. The Soviet Union, on the other hand, has tended to emphasize economic security, a more meaningful concept in countries where this is the overriding concern.

Aware of their strategic position in the East-West struggle, most of the new nations have developed an often rather inflated self-image. This has led to curious psychological inversions—almost an "upside-down" world. At times, the new nations have "rewarded" one of the superpowers by accepting its gifts or loans. Because of the peculiar constellation of world politics, and the interdependence of the two great political struggles, the power of the new nations has vastly increased. So long as the two superpowers continue to believe that the uncommitted countries may vitally affect the distribution of power, this strange divergence between perception and reality is likely to persist.

In sum, then, an analysis of the political, military, and economic aspects of the international struggle for power reveals that, on the whole, there exist great divergencies between perception and reality. In the political realm, these divergencies exacerbate the fierceness of both the East-West struggle and the struggle over colonialism. This is also largely true, or at least it was, until very recently, in the military arena. Only in the economic struggle is the picture more mixed. There the gap between perception and reality seems to work in the direction of cooperation as well as of conflict.

The relationship between perception and reality has also affected the international struggle for order. In the political realm, the United Nations is a case in point. Public opinion studies show that, in the United States, for example, the "mass public" and even the "attentive public" tend to evaluate the United Nations fairly indiscriminately. There is little awareness of differences among the major organs of the world organization. It is either praised or condemned as a whole. Images swing all the way from cynical disillusionment through apathy to an exaggerated "panacea" view. Yet the record of the United Nations demonstrates that it is quite impossible to generalize about the world organization in its entirety. The performance of each of its major organs and specialized agencies has been different. In other words, in the imagery of the United States there is little or no awareness of the United Nations' most important characteristic: its elasticity, and the fact that it is working on many fronts and with varying degrees of effectiveness at one time. The unfortunate result of this one-dimensional image is to encourage all-too-quick disillusionment by making the failure of some one UN organ, such as the Security Council, seem like a failure of the organization *in toto.* Hence, American support of the United Nations has tended to be based on the very unstable factor of popular oversimplification. This gap between perception and reality has thus slowed the development of a firm and dependable basis of support for the United Nations.

Such distortion also extends to specific institutions of the United Nations. The veto power of the Big Five in the Security Council affords an interesting example. In the Soviet view, this power saves the USSR from being continuously outvoted in an organization consisting largely of non-Communist nations. The United States, while equally adamant on maintaining the veto power, holds the view that the Soviet Union has used it excessively and thus crippled the organization. Neither of these views tallies with the record. The truth is that only a few of the many Soviet vetoes cast in the Security Council have been final. Many of them have been circumvented through action taken in the General Assembly under the Uniting for Peace Resolution or otherwise.[9] Thus, the view that the veto can paralyze the world organization as a whole—a view held by the Soviet Union, the United States, and most of the new nations—does not square with the facts.

The tug-of-war between regionalists and globalists, too, has relevance to our thesis. Typically, regionalist thinkers conceive of globalism as either premature or altogether unworkable. Internationalists, on the other hand, have developed an image of regional arrangements as harmful roadblocks on the path to world order. Neither perception leaves room for what the record demonstrates: that frequently globalism has served as a second line of defense for regionalism and that regional arrangements have served as backstops for the world organization. Certainly, there is ample room for both types of political order-building on the world scene. In this case, the gap between perception and reality has sometimes led to unnecessary friction between the two approaches and thus slowed down the advance toward political order.

A serious divergence exists in the military realm of political order-building. The widespread view that arms races cause wars has led to a passionate popular demand for disarmament everywhere. This, in turn, has led to a propagandistic corruption of diplomacy in disarmament negotiations because diplomats have been compelled to address a world audience instead of engaging in the exacting business of searching for a technical disarmament formula. As we have seen earlier, the popular assumption that arms races cause wars is very oversimplified. The record shows that an arms race is merely the symptom of a deeper pathological condition. It is very likely that the search for a technical disarmament formula is bound to fail unless it is preceded by a more fundamental political accommodation. The same observation may validly be made of arms control, as the arduous road to the Moscow Summit of 1972 amply demonstrates. Indeed, the history of disarmament and arms control negotiations supports the proposition that order is fundamentally a political, not a military problem. This gap between the simple popular image of disarmament and the complex reality has caused a great deal of cynicism, disillusionment, and waste of energy.

The economic field alone has escaped serious distortions. The functionalist hope has largely been vindicated by the record on the regional level. Within the framework of Western Europe, two basic conceptions of economic order-building have developed, both of which have enjoyed a measure of success. "Supra-national" and more traditional intergovernmental organizations alike have mushroomed. Wherever a concrete task had to be accomplished, the record has been good, regardless of the formal structure of the organization. Since a well-defined task has existed in most instances, serious gaps between perception and reality have been avoided. One interesting development is worthy of mention: the widely prevalent conception that a clear line of demarcation may be drawn between national governments and international organizations no longer seems to be valid. Recent developments, chiefly in Western Europe, indicate that the two are beginning to blend into one another. Indeed, some regional organizations, like the European Communities, come close to exercising powers previously enjoyed only by national governments. Whether these groupings will justify the fear of the globalists and develop into a kind of regional nationalism remains to be seen. For the present, accomplishments have largely kept pace with expectations. Hence, an unusual congruence exists between perception and reality in economic order-building in Western Europe.

In conclusion, then, the gaps between perception and reality have exacerbated the fierceness of the international struggle for power and have also done much to slow down the advance toward international order. In view of this fact, it seems of the utmost importance for students of international relations to expose themselves to the work of scholars in the area of human perception—sociologists, social psychologists, and even depth psychologists. This is not to say that the objective realities of world affairs should in any way be neglected. Yet since these are as vast and difficult to contend with as they are, the least we can hope for is that they not be rendered even more complex and inaccessible to reason by our unsubstantiated preconceptions. The perils of our age demand our every effort to see and deal with the world as it really is. Once again man must escape from Plato's Cave, in which he perceives only shadows instead of realities. Only when our reason thus acquires passion will we remove the Sword of Damocles which has been suspended for far too long over our tormented world.

REFERENCES

1. Walter Lippman, *Public Opinion.* New York: Macmillan, 1922; Gabriel Almond, *The American People and Foreign Policy.* New York: Harcourt, Brace, 1950.
2. Alex Inkeles, *Public Opinion in Soviet Russia.* Cambridge, Mass.: Harvard University Press, 1950.
3. Gabriel Almond and James S. Coleman, *The Politics of the Developing Areas.* Princeton, N.J.: Princeton University Press, 1960.
4. Lippmann, *op. cit.,* p. 29.
5. Walter Lippmann, *The Public Philosophy.* Boston: Little, Brown, 1955, p. 14.
6. Carl J. Friedrich, *The New Image of the Common Man.* Boston: Beacon Press, 1950, *passim.*
7. Inkeles, *op. cit.,* p. 323.
8. Almond and Coleman, *op. cit.,* p. 535.
9. For a complete analysis of this point, see John G. Stoessinger, *The United Nations and the Superpowers.* New York: Random House, 1965, pp. 3–20.

BIBLIOGRAPHY

Aron, Raymond. *Peace and War.* New York: Doubleday, 1966.

Boulding, Kenneth E. *The Image.* Ann Arbor, Mich.: University of Michigan Press, 1956.

Cantril, Hadley. *The Human Dimension: Experiences in Policy Research.* New Brunswick, N.J.: Rutgers University Press, 1967.

Carr, Edward H. *The Twenty Years' Crisis, 1919–1939: An Introduction to the Study of International Relations.* London: Macmillan and Company, Ltd., 1946.

Fox, William T. R., ed. *Theoretical Aspects of International Relations.* South Bend, Ind.: University of Notre Dame Press, 1959.

Friedrich, Carl J. *Inevitable Peace.* Cambridge, Mass.: Harvard University Press, 1948.

Harrison, Horace V., ed. *The Role of Theory in International Relations.* Princeton, N.J.: Van Nostrand, 1964.

Herz, John H. *International Politics in the Atomic Age.* New York: Columbia University Press, 1959.

Hoffmann, Stanley, ed. *Contemporary Theory in International Relations.* Englewood Cliffs, N.J.: Prentice-Hall, 1960.

Jouvenel, Bertrand de. *Sovereignty, an Inquiry into the Political Good.* Cambridge: Cambridge University Press, 1957.

Kant, Immanuel. *Eternal Peace,* in C. J. Friedrich, *Inevitable Peace.* Cambridge, Mass.: Harvard University Press, 1948.

Kaplan, Morton A. *System and Process in International Politics.* New York: Wiley, 1957.

Kennan, George F. *American Diplomacy 1900–1950.* Chicago: University of Chicago Press, 1953.

———. *Realities of American Foreign Policy.* Princeton, N.J.: Princeton University Press, 1954.

Lenin, Vladimir I. *Imperialism, the Highest Stage of Capitalism.* New York: International Publishers, 1939.

Lieber, Robert J. *Theory and World Politics.* Cambridge, Mass.: Winthrop, 1972.

Liska, George. *International Equilibrium, a Theoretical Essay on the Politics and Organization of Security.* Cambridge, Mass.: Harvard University Press, 1957.

Machiavelli, Niccolo. *The Prince and the Discourses.* New York: Modern Library, 1950.

Mahan, Alfred T. *The Influence of Sea Power Upon History, 1660–1783.* Boston: Little, Brown, 1898.

Mitrany, David. *A Working Peace System.* Chicago: Quadrangle Press, 1966.

Morgenthau, Hans J. *Dilemmas of Politics.* Chicago: University of Chicago Press, 1958.

———. *Scientific Man vs. Power Politics.* Chicago: University of Chicago Press, 1946.

———, and Fox, William T. R. "National Interest and Moral Principles in Foreign Policy," *American Scholar,* Spring 1949.

Niebuhr, Reinhold. *Christianity and Power Politics.* New York: Scribner, 1940.

———. *The Irony of American History.* New York: Scribner 1952.

———. *Moral Man and Immoral Society: A Study in Ethics and Politics.* New York: Scribner, 1932.

Osgood, Robert E., and Tucker, Robert W. *Peace, Order and Justice.* Baltimore: Johns Hopkins Press, 1967.

Pfaltzgraff, Robert L., Jr. *Contending Theories of International Relations.* New York: Lippincott, 1971.

Rosecrance, Richard N. *Action and Reaction in World Politics.* Boston: Little, Brown, 1963.

Rosenau, James N. *International Politics and Foreign Policy: A Reader in Research and Theory.* Glencoe, Ill.: The Free Press, 1961.

———, ed. *Linkage Politics: Essays on the Convergence of National and International Systems.* New York: Free Press, 1969.

Snyder, Richard C., *et al. Decision-Making as an Approach to the Study of International Politics.* Princeton, N.J.: Princeton University Press, 1954.

Sterling, Richard W. *Ethics in a World of Power, the Political Ideas of Friedrich Meinecke.* Princeton, N.J.: Princeton University Press, 1958.

Stoessinger, John G. *Nations in Darkness: China, Russia, and America.* New York: Random House, 1971.

Toynbee, Arnold J. *War and Civilization.* (From *A Study of History.*) New York: Oxford University Press, 1950.

Waltz, Kenneth N. *Man, the State, and War: A Theoretical Analysis.* New York: Columbia University Press, 1959.

Wolfers, Arnold, and Martin, Lawrence W., eds. *The Anglo-American Tradition in Foreign Affairs.* New Haven, Conn.: Yale University Press, 1956.

Wright, Quincy. *A Study of War,* rev. ed. Chicago: University of Chicago Press, 1968.

———. *The Study of International Relations.* New York: Appleton-Century-Crofts, 1955.

Yost, Charles. *The Insecurity of Nations: International Relations in the Twentieth Century.* New York: Praeger, 1968.

Appendix
The Charter of the United Nations

THE CHARTER OF THE
UNITED NATIONS

We the peoples of the United Nations determined

to save succeeding generations from the scourge of war, which twice in our lifetime has brought untold sorrow to mankind, and

to reaffirm faith in fundamental human rights, in the dignity and worth of the human person, in the equal rights of men and women and of nations large and small, and to establish conditions under which justice and respect for the obligations arising from treaties and other sources of international law can be maintained, and

to promote social progress and better standards of life in larger freedom,

and for these ends

to practice tolerance and live together in peace with one another as good neighbors, and

to unite our strength to maintain international peace and security, and

to ensure, by the acceptance of principles and the institution of methods, that armed force shall not be used, save in the common interest, and

to employ international machinery for the promotion of the economic and social advancement of all peoples,

have resolved to combine our efforts to accomplish these aims.

Accordingly, our respective Governments, through representatives assembled in the city of San Francisco, who have exhibited their full powers found to be in good and due form, have agreed to the present Charter of the United Nations and do hereby establish an international organization to be known as the United Nations.

Chapter I/Purposes and Principles

ARTICLE 1

The Purposes of the United Nations are:

1. To maintain international peace and security, and to that end: to take effective collective measures for the prevention and removal of threats to the peace, and for the suppression of acts of aggression or

other breaches of the peace, and to bring about by peaceful means, and in conformity with the principles of justice and international law, adjustment or settlement of international disputes or situations which might lead to a breach of the peace;

2. To develop friendly relations among nations based on respect for the principle of equal rights and self-determination of peoples, and to take other appropriate measures to strengthen universal peace;

3. To achieve international cooperation in solving international problems of an economic, social, cultural, or humanitarian character, and in promoting and encouraging respect for human rights and for fundamental freedoms for all without distinction as to race, sex, language, or religion; and

4. To be a center for harmonizing the actions of nations in the attainment of these common ends.

ARTICLE 2

The Organization and its Members, in pursuit of the Purposes stated in Article 1, shall act in accordance with the following Principles.

1. The Organization is based on the principle of the sovereign equality of all its Members.

2. All Members, in order to ensure to all of them the rights and benefits resulting from membership, shall fulfil in good faith the obligations assumed by them in accordance with the present Charter.

3. All Members shall settle their international disputes by peaceful means in such a manner that international peace and security, and justice, are not endangered.

4. All Members shall refrain in their international relations from the threat or use of force against the territorial integrity or political independence of any state, or in any other manner inconsistent with the Purposes of the United Nations.

5. All Members shall give the United Nations every assistance in any action it takes in accordance with the present Charter, and shall refrain from giving assistance to any state against which the United Nations is taking preventive or enforcement action.

6. The Organization shall ensure that states which are not Members of the United Nations act in accordance with these Principles so far as may be necessary for the maintenance of international peace and security.

7. Nothing contained in the present Charter shall authorize the United Nations to intervene in matters which are essentially within the domestic jurisdiction of any state or shall require the Members to submit such matters to settlement under the present Charter; but this principle shall not prejudice the application of enforcement measures under Chapter VII.

Chapter II/Membership

ARTICLE 3

The original Members of the United Nations shall be the states which, having participated in the United Nations Conference on International Organization at San Francisco, or having previously signed the Declaration of United Nations of January 1, 1942, sign the present Charter and ratify it in accordance with Article 110.

ARTICLE 4

1. Membership in the United Nations is open to all other peaceloving states which accept the obligations contained in the present Charter and, in the judgment of the Organization, are able and willing to carry out these obligations.

2. The admission of any such state to membership in the United Nations will be effected by a decision of the General Assembly upon the recommendation of the Security Council.

ARTICLE 5

A Member of the United Nations against which preventive or enforcement action has been taken by the Security Council may be suspended from the exercise of the rights and privileges of membership by the General Assembly upon ◆the recommendation of the Security Council. The exercise of these rights and privileges may be restored by the Security Council.

ARTICLE 6

A Member of the United Nations which has persistently violated the Principles contained in the present Charter may be expelled from the Organization by the General Assembly upon the recommendation of the Security Council.

Chapter III/Organs

ARTICLE 7

1. There are established as the principal organs of the United Nations: a General Assembly, a Security Council, an Economic and Social Council, a Trusteeship Council, an International Court of Justice, and a Secretariat.

2. Such subsidiary organs as may be found necessary may be established in accordance with the present Charter.

ARTICLE 8

The United Nations shall place no restrictions on the eligibility of men and women to participate in any capacity and under conditions of equality in its principal and subsidiary organs.

Chapter IV/The General Assembly

Composition

ARTICLE 9

1. The General Assembly shall consist of all the Members of the United Nations.

2. Each Member shall have not more than five representatives in the General Assembly.

Functions and Powers

ARTICLE 10

The General Assembly may discuss any questions or any matters within the scope of the present Charter or relating to the powers and functions of any organs provided for in the present Charter, and, except as provided in Article 12, may make recommendations to the Members of the United Nations or to the Security Council or to both on any such questions or matters.

ARTICLE 11

1. The General Assembly may consider the general principles of cooperation in the maintenance of international peace and security, including the principles governing disarmament and the regulation of armaments, and may make recommendations with regard to such principles to the Members or to the Security Council or to both.

2. The General Assembly may discuss any questions relating to the maintenance of international peace and security brought before it by any Member of the United Nations, or by the Security Council, or by a state which is not a Member of the United Nations in accordance with Article 35, paragraph 2, and, except as provided in Article 12, may make recommendations with regard to any such questions to the state or

states concerned or to the Security Council or to both. Any such question on which action is necessary shall be referred to the Security Council by the General Assembly either before or after discussion.

3. The General Assembly may call the attention of the Security Council to situations which are likely to endanger international peace and security.

4. The powers of the General Assembly set forth in this Article shall not limit the general scope of Article 10.

ARTICLE 12

1. While the Security Council is exercising in respect of any dispute or situation the functions assigned to it in the present Charter, the General Assembly shall not make any recommendations with regard to that dispute or situation unless the Security Council so requests.

2. The Secretary-General, with the consent of the Security Council, shall notify the General Assembly at each session of any matters relative to the maintenance of international peace and security which are being dealt with by the Security Council and shall similarly notify the General Assembly, or the Members of the United Nations if the General Assembly is not in session, immediately the Security Council ceases to deal with such matters.

ARTICLE 13

1. The General Assembly shall initiate studies and make recommendations for the purpose of:

a. promoting international cooperation in the political field and encouraging the progressive development of international law and its codification;

b. promoting international cooperation in the economic, social, cultural, educational, and health fields, and assisting in the realization of human rights and fundamental freedoms for all without distinction as to race, sex, language, or religion.

2. The further responsibilities, functions, and powers of the General Assembly with respect to matters mentioned in paragraph 1 (b) above are set forth in Chapters IX and X.

ARTICLE 14

Subject to the provisions of Article 12, the General Assembly may recommend measures for the peaceful adjustment of any situation regardless of origin, which it deems likely to impair the general welfare or friendly relations among nations, including situations resulting from a violation of the provisions of the present Charter setting forth the Purposes and Principles of the United Nations.

1. The General Assembly shall receive and consider annual and special reports from the Security Council; these reports shall include an account of the measures that the Security Council has decided upon or taken to maintain international peace and security.

2. The General Assembly shall receive and consider reports from the other organs of the United Nations.

ARTICLE 16

The General Assembly shall perform such functions with respect to the international trusteeship system as are assigned to it under Chapters XII and XIII, including the approval of the trusteeship agreements for areas not designated as strategic.

ARTICLE 17

1. The General Assembly shall consider and approve the budget of the Organization.

2. The expenses of the Organization shall be borne by the Members as apportioned by the General Assembly.

3. The General Assembly shall consider and approve any financial and budgetary arrangements with specialized agencies referred to in Article 57 and shall examine the administrative budgets of such specialized agencies with a view to making recommendations to the agencies concerned.

Voting

ARTICLE 18

1. Each member of the General Assembly shall have one vote.

2. Decisions of the General Assembly on important questions shall be made by a two-thirds majority of the members present and voting. These questions shall include: recommendations with respect to the maintenance of international peace and security, the election of the nonpermanent members of the Security Council, the election of the members of the Economic and Social Council, the election of members of the Trusteeship Council in accordance with paragraph 1 (c) of Article 86, the admission of new Members to the United Nations, the suspension of the rights and privileges of membership, the expulsion of Members, questions relating to the operation of the trusteeship system, and budgetary questions.

3. Decisions on other questions, including the determination of

additional categories of questions to be decided by a two-thirds majority, shall be made by a majority of the members present and voting.

ARTICLE 19

A Member of the United Nations which is in arrears in the payment of its financial contributions to the Organization shall have no vote in the General Assembly if the amount of its arrears equals or exceeds the amount of the contributions due from it for the preceding two full years. The General Assembly may, nevertheless, permit such a Member to vote if it is satisfied that the failure to pay is due to conditions beyond the control of the Member.

Procedure

ARTICLE 20

The General Assembly shall meet in regular annual sessions and in such special sessions as occasion may require. Special sessions shall be convoked by the Secretary-General at the request of the Security Council or of a majority of the Members of the United Nations.

ARTICLE 21

The General Assembly shall adopt its own rules of procedure. It shall elect its President for each session.

ARTICLE 22

The General Assembly may establish such subsidiary organs as it deems necessary for the performance of its functions.

Chapter V/The Security Council

Composition

ARTICLE 23

1. The Security Council shall consist of fifteen Members of the United Nations. The Republic of China, France, the Union of Soviet Socialist Republics, the United Kingdom of Great Britain and Northern

Ireland, and the United States of America shall be permanent members of the Security Council. The General Assembly shall elect ten other Members of the United Nations to be non-permanent members of the Security Council, due regard being specially paid, in the first instance to the contribution of Members of the United Nations to the maintenance of international peace and security and to the other purposes of the Organization, and also to equitable geographical distribution.

2. The non-permanent members of the Security Council shall be elected for a term of two years. In the first election of the non-permanent members after the increase of the membership of the Security Council from eleven to fifteen, two of the four additional members shall be chosen for a term of one year. A retiring member shall not be eligible for immediate re-election.

3. Each member of the Security Council shall have one representative.

Functions and Powers

ARTICLE 24

1. In order to ensure prompt and effective action by the United Nations, its Members confer on the Security Council primary responsibility for the maintenance of international peace and security, and agree that in carrying out its duties under this responsibility the Security Council acts on their behalf.

2. In discharging these duties the Security Council shall act in accordance with the Purposes and Principles of the United Nations. The specific powers granted to the Security Council for the discharge of these duties are laid down in Chapters VI, VII, VIII, and XII.

3. The Security Council shall submit annual and, when necessary, special reports to the General Assembly for its consideration.

ARTICLE 25

The Members of the United Nations agree to accept and carry out the decisions of the Security Council in accordance with the present Charter.

ARTICLE 26

In order to promote the establishment and maintenance of international peace and security with the least diversion for armaments of the world's human and economic resources, the Security Council shall be responsible for formulating, with the assistance of the Military Staff Committee referred to in Article 47, plans to be submitted to the Members of the United Nations for the establishment of a system for the regulation of armaments.

Voting

ARTICLE 27

1. Each member of the Security Council shall have one vote.
2. Decisions of the Security Council on procedural matters shall be made by an affirmative vote of nine members.
3. Decisions of the Security Council on all other matters shall be made by an affirmative vote of nine members including the concurring votes of the permanent members; provided that, in decisions under Chapter VI, and under paragraph 3 of Article 52, a party to a dispute shall abstain from voting.

Procedure

ARTICLE 28

1. The Security Council shall be so organized as to be able to function continuously. Each member of the Security Council shall for this purpose be represented at all times at the seat of the Organization.
2. The Security Council shall hold periodic meetings at which each of its members may, if it so desires, be represented by a member of the government or by some other specially designated representative.
3. The Security Council may hold meetings at such places other than the seat of the Organization as in its judgment will best facilitate its work.

ARTICLE 29

The Security Council may establish such subsidiary organs as it deems necessary for the performance of its functions.

ARTICLE 30

The Security Council shall adopt its own rules of procedure, including the method of selecting its President.

ARTICLE 31

Any Member of the United Nations which is not a member of the Security Council may participate, without vote, in the discussion of any question brought before the Security Council whenever the latter considers that the interests of that Member are specially affected.

ARTICLE 32

Any Member of the United Nations which is not a member of the Security Council or any state which is not a Member of the United Nations, if it is a party to a dispute under consideration by the Security Council, shall be invited to participate, without vote, in the discussion relating to the dispute. The Security Council shall lay down such conditions as it deems just for the participation of a state which is not a Member of the United Nations.

Chapter VI/Pacific Settlement of Disputes

ARTICLE 33

1. The parties to any dispute, the continuance of which is likely to endanger the maintenance of international peace and security, shall, first of all, seek a solution by negotiation, enquiry, mediation, conciliation, arbitration, judicial settlement, resort to regional agencies or arrangements, or other peaceful means of their own choice.

2. The Security Council shall, when it deems necessary, call upon the parties to settle their dispute by such means.

ARTICLE 34

The Security Council may investigate any dispute, or any situation which might lead to international friction or give rise to a dispute, in order to determine whether the continuance of the dispute or situation is likely to endanger the maintenance of international peace and security.

ARTICLE 35

1. Any Member of the United Nations may bring any dispute, or any situation of the nature referred to in Article 34, to the attention of the Security Council or of the General Assembly.

2. A state which is not a Member of the United Nations may bring to the attention of the Security Council or of the General Assembly any dispute to which it is a party if it accepts in advance, for the purposes

of the dispute, the obligations of pacific settlement provided in the present Charter.

3. The proceedings of the General Assembly in respect of matters brought to its attention under this Article will be subject to the provisions of Articles 11 and 12.

ARTICLE 36

1. The Security Council may, at any stage of a dispute of the nature referred to in Article 33 or of a situation of like nature, recommend appropriate procedures or methods of adjustment.

2. The Security Council should take into consideration any procedures for the settlement of the dispute which have already been adopted by the parties.

3. In making recommendations under this Article the Security Council should also take into consideration that legal disputes should as a general rule be referred by the parties to the International Court of Justice in accordance with the provisions of the Statute of the Court.

ARTICLE 37

1. Should the parties to a dispute of the nature referred to in Article 33 fail to settle it by the means indicated in that Article, they shall refer it to the Security Council.

2. If the Security Council deems that the continuance of the dispute is in fact likely to endanger the maintenance of international peace and security, it shall decide whether to take action under Article 36 or to recommend such terms of settlement as it may consider appropriate.

ARTICLE 38

Without prejudice to the provisions of Articles 33 to 37, the Security Council may, if all the parties to any dispute so request, make recommendations to the parties with a view to a pacific settlement of the dispute.

Chapter VII/Action with Respect to Threats to the Peace, Breaches of the Peace, and Acts of Aggression

ARTICLE 39

The Security Council shall determine the existence of any threat to the peace, breach of the peace, or act of aggression and shall make recommendations, or decide what measures shall be taken in accordance with Articles 41 and 42, to maintain or restore international peace and security.

ARTICLE 40

In order to prevent an aggravation of the situation, the Security Council may, before making the recommendations or deciding upon the measures provided for in Article 39, call upon the parties concerned to comply with such provisional measures as it deems necessary or desirable. Such provisional measures shall be without prejudice to the rights, claims, or position of the parties concerned. The Security Council shall duly take account of failure to comply with such provisional measures.

ARTICLE 41

The Security Council may decide what measures not involving the use of armed force are to be employed to give effect to its decisions, and it may call upon the Members of the United Nations to apply such measures. These may include complete or partial interruption of economic relations, and of rail, sea, air, postal, telegraphic, radio, and other means of communication, and the severance of diplomatic relations.

ARTICLE 42

Should the Security Council consider that measures provided for in Article 41 would be inadequate or have proved to be inadequate, it may take such action by air, sea, or land forces as may be necessary to maintain or restore international peace and security. Such action may include demonstrations, blockade, and other operations by air, sea, or land forces of Members of the United Nations.

ARTICLE 43

1. All Members of the United Nations, in order to contribute to the maintenance of international peace and security, undertake to make available to the Security Council, on its call and in accordance with a special agreement or agreements, armed forces, assistance, and facilities, including rights of passage, necessary for the purpose of maintaining international peace and security.

2. Such agreement or agreements shall govern the numbers and types of forces, their degree of readiness and general location and the nature of the facilities and assistance to be provided.

3. The agreement or agreements shall be negotiated as soon as possible on the initiative of the Security Council. They shall be concluded between the Security Council and Members or between the Security Council and groups of Members and shall be subject to ratification by the signatory states in accordance with their respective constitutional processes.

ARTICLE 44

When the Security Council has decided to use force it shall, before calling upon a Member not represented on it to provide armed forces in fulfillment of the obligations assumed under Article 43, invite that Member, if the Member so desires, to participate in the decisions of the Security Council concerning the employment of contingents of that Member's armed forces.

ARTICLE 45

In order to enable the United Nations to take urgent military measures, Members shall hold immediately available national air-force contingents for combined international enforcement action. The strength and degree of readiness of these contingents and plans for their combined action shall be determined, within the limits laid down in the special agreement or agreements referred to in Article 43, by the Security Council with the assistance of the Military Staff Committee.

ARTICLE 46

Plans for the application of armed force shall be made by the Security Council with the assistance of the Military Staff Committee.

ARTICLE 47

1. There shall be established a Military Staff Committee to advise and assist the Security Council on all questions relating to the Security Council's military requirements for the maintenance of international peace and security, the employment and command of forces placed at its disposal, the regulation of armaments, and possible disarmament.

2. The Military Staff Committee shall consist of the Chiefs of Staff of the permanent members of the Security Council or their representatives. Any Member of the United Nations not permanently represented on the Committee shall be invited by the Committee to be associated with it when the efficient discharge of the Committee's responsibilities requires the participation of that Member in its work.

3. The Military Staff Committee shall be responsible under the Security Council for the strategic direction of any armed forces placed at the disposal of the Security Council. Questions relating to the command of such forces shall be worked out subsequently.

4. The Military Staff Committee, with the authorization of the Security Council and after consultation with appropriate regional agencies, may establish regional subcommittees.

1. The action required to carry out the decisions of the Security Council for the maintenance of international peace and security shall be taken by all the Members of the United Nations or by some of them, as the Security Council may determine.

2. Such decisions shall be carried out by the Members of the United Nations directly and through their action in the appropriate international agencies of which they are members.

The Members of the United Nations shall join in affording mutual assistance in carrying out the measures decided upon by the Security Council.

If preventive or enforcement measures against any state are taken by the Security Council, any other state, whether a Member of the United Nations or not, which finds itself confronted with special economic problems arising from the carrying out of those measures shall have the right to consult the Security Council with regard to a solution of those problems.

Nothing in the present Charter shall impair the inherent right of individual or collective self-defense if an armed attack occurs against a Member of the United Nations, until the Security Council has taken the measures necessary to maintain international peace and security. Measures taken by Members in the exercise of this right of self-defense shall be immediately reported to the Security Council and shall not in any way affect the authority and responsibility of the Security Council under the present Charter to take at any time such action as it deems necessary in order to maintain or restore international peace and security.

Chapter VIII/Regional Arrangements

1. Nothing in the present Charter precludes the existence of regional arrangements or agencies for dealing with such matters relating to the maintenance of international peace and security as are appropriate for regional action, provided that such arrangements or agencies and their

activities are consistent with the Purposes and Principles of the United Nations.

2. The Members of the United Nations entering into such arrangements or constituting such agencies shall make every effort to achieve pacific settlement of local disputes through such regional arrangements or by such regional agencies before referring them to the Security Council.

3. The Security Council shall encourage the development of pacific settlement of local disputes through such regional arrangements or by such regional agencies either on the initiative of the states concerned or by reference from the Security Council.

4. This Article in no way impairs the application of Articles 34 and 35.

ARTICLE 53

1. The Security Council shall, where appropriate, utilize such regional arrangements or agencies for enforcement action under its authority. But no enforcement action shall be taken under regional arrangements or by regional agencies without the authorization of the Security Council, with the exception of measures against any enemy state, as defined in paragraph 2 of this Article, provided for pursuant to Article 107 or in regional arrangements directed against renewal of aggressive policy on the part of any such state, until such time as the Organization may, on request of the Governments concerned, be charged with the responsibility for preventing further aggression by such a state.

2. The term "enemy state" as used in paragraph 1 of this Article. applies to any state which during the Second World War has been an enemy of any signatory of the present Charter.

ARTICLE 54

The Security Council shall at all times be kept fully informed of activities undertaken or in contemplation under regional arrangements or by regional agencies for the maintenance of international peace and security.

Chapter IX/International Economic and Social Cooperation

ARTICLE 55

With a view to the creation of conditions of stability and well-being which are necessary for peaceful and friendly relations among nations based on respect for the principle of equal rights and self-determination of peoples, the United Nations shall promote:

a. higher standards of living, full employment, and conditions of economic and social progress and development;

b. solutions of international economic, social, health, and related problems; and international cultural and educational cooperation; and

c. universal respect for, and observance of, human rights and fundamental freedoms for all without distinction as to race, sex, language, or religion.

ARTICLE 56

All Members pledge themselves to take joint and separate action in cooperation with the Organization for the achievement of the purposes set forth in Article 55.

ARTICLE 57

1. The various specialized agencies, established by intergovernmental agreement and having wide international responsibilities, as defined in their basic instruments, in economic, social, cultural, educational, health, and related fields, shall be brought into relationship with the United Nations in accordance with the provisions of Article 63.

2. Such agencies thus brought into relationship with the United Nations are hereinafter referred to as specialized agencies.

ARTICLE 58

The Organization shall make recommendations for the coordination of the policies and activities of the specialized agencies.

ARTICLE 59

The Organization shall, where appropriate, initiate negotiations among the states concerned for the creation of any new specialized agencies required for the accomplishment of the purposes set forth in Article 55.

ARTICLE 60

Responsibility for the discharge of the functions of the Organization set forth in this Chapter shall be vested in the General Assembly and, under the authority of the General Assembly, in the Economic and Social Council, which shall have for this purpose the powers set forth in Chapter X.

ChapterX/The Economic and Social Council

Composition

ARTICLE 61

1. The Economic and Social Council shall consist of twenty-seven Members of the United Nations elected by the General Assembly.

2. Subject to the provisions of paragraph 3, nine members of the Economic and Social Council shall be elected each year for a term of three years. A retiring member shall be eligible for immediate re-election.

3. At the first election after the increase in the membership of the Economic and Social Council from eighteen to twenty-seven members, in addition to the members elected in place of the six members whose term of office expires at the end of that year, nine additional members shall be elected. Of these nine additional members, the term of office of three members so elected shall expire at the end of one year, and of three other members at the end of two years, in accordance with arrangements made by the General Assembly.

4. Each member of the Economic and Social Council shall have one representative.

Functions and Powers

ARTICLE 62

1. The Economic and Social Council may make or initiate studies and reports with respect to international economic, social, cultural, educational, health, and related matters and may make recommendations with respect to any such matters to the General Assemby, to the Members of the United Nations, and to the specialized agencies concerned.

2. It may make recommendations for the purpose of promoting respect for, and observance of, human rights and fundamental freedoms for all.

3. It may prepare draft conventions for submission to the General Assembly, with respect to matters falling within its competence.

4. It may call, in accordance with the rules prescribed by the United Nations, international conferences on matters falling within its competence.

ARTICLE 63

1. The Economic and Social Council may enter into agreements with any of the agencies referred to in Article 57, defining the terms on which the agency concerned shall be brought into relationship with the United Nations. Such agreements shall be subject to approval by the General Assembly.

2. It may coordinate the activities of the specialized agencies through consultation with and recommendations to such agencies and through recommendations to the General Assembly and to the Members of the United Nations.

ARTICLE 64

1. The Economic and Social Council may take appropriate steps to obtain regular reports from the specialized agencies. It may make arrangements with the Members of the United Nations and with the specialized agencies to obtain reports on the steps taken to give effect to its own recommendations and to recommendations on matters falling within its competence made by the General Assembly.

2. It may communicate its observations on these reports to the General Assembly.

ARTICLE 65

The Economic and Social Council may furnish information to the Security Council and shall assist the Security Council upon its request.

ARTICLE 66

1. The Economic and Social Council shall perform such functions as fall within its competence in connection with the carrying out of the recommendations of the General Assembly.

2. It may, with the approval of the General Assembly, perform services at the request of Members of the United Nations and at the request of specialized agencies.

3. It shall perform such other functions as are specified elsewhere in the present Charter or as may be assigned to it by the General Assembly.

Voting

ARTICLE 67

1. Each member of the Economic and Social Council shall have one vote.

2. Decisions of the Economic and Social Council shall be made by a majority of the members present and voting.

Procedure

ARTICLE 68

The Economic and Social Council shall set up commissions in economic and social fields and for the promotion of human rights, and such other commissions as may be required for the performance of its functions.

ARTICLE 69

The Economic and Social Council shall invite any Member of the United Nations to participate, without vote, in its deliberations on any matter of particular concern to that Member.

ARTICLE 70

The Economic and Social Council may make arrangements for representatives of the specialized agencies to participate, without vote, in its deliberations and in those of the commissions established by it, and for its representatives to participate in the deliberations of the specialized agencies.

ARTICLE 71

The Economic and Social Council may make suitable arrangements for consultation with non-governmental organizations which are concerned with matters within its competence. Such arrangements may be made with international organizations and, where appropriate, with national organizations after consultation with the Member of the United Nations concerned.

ARTICLE 72

1. The Economic and Social Council shall adopt its own rules of procedure, including the method of selecting its President.
2. The Economic and Social Council shall meet as required in accordance with its rules, which shall include provision for the convening of meetings on the request of a majority of its members.

Chapter XI/Declaration Regarding Non-Self-Governing Territories

Members of the United Nations which have or assume responsibilities for the administration of territories whose peoples have not yet attained a full measure of self-government recognize the principle that the interests of the inhabitants of these territories are paramount, and accept as a sacred trust the obligation to promote to the utmost, within the system of international peace and security established by the present Charter, the well-being of the inhabitants of these territories, and, to this end:

a. To ensure, with due respect for the culture of the peoples concerned, their political, economic, social, and educational advancement, their just treatment, and their protection against abuses;

b. to develop self-government, to take due account of the political aspirations of the peoples, and to assist them in the progressive development of their free political institutions, according to the particular circumstances of each territory and its peoples and their varying stages of advancement;

c. to further international peace and security;

d. to promote constructive measures of development, to encourage research, and to cooperate with one another and, when and where appropriate, with specialized international bodies with a view to the practical achievement of the social, economic, and scientific purposes set forth in this Article; and

e. to transmit regularly to the Secretary-General for information purposes, subject to such limitation as security and constitutional considerations may require, statistical and other information of a technical nature relating to economic, social, and educational conditions in the territories for which they are respectively responsible other than those territories to which Chapters XII and XIII apply.

Members of the United Nations also agree that their policy in respect of the territories to which this Chapter applies, no less than in respect of their metropolitan areas, must be based on the general principle of good-neighborliness, due account being taken of the interests and well-being of the rest of the world, in social, economic, and commercial matters.

Chapter XII/International Trusteeship System

ARTICLE 75

The United Nations shall establish under its authority an international trusteeship system for the administration and supervision of such territories as may be placed thereunder by subsequent individual agreements. These territories are hereinafter referred to as trust territories.

ARTICLE 76

The basic objectives of the trusteeship system, in accordance with the Purposes of the United Nations laid down in Article 1 of the present Charter, shall be:

a. to further international peace and security;

b. to promote the political, economic, social, and educational advancement of the inhabitants of the trust territories, and their progressive development towards self-government or independence as may be appropriate to the particular circumstances of each territory and its peoples and the freely expressed wishes of the peoples concerned, and as may be provided by the terms of each trusteeship agreement;

c. to encourage respect for human rights and for fundamental freedoms for all without distinction as to race, sex, language, or religion, and to encourage recognition of the interdependence of the peoples of the world; and

d. to ensure equal treatment in social, economic, and commercial matters for all Members of the United Nations and their nationals, and also equal treatment for the latter in the administration of justice, without prejudice to the attainment of the foregoing objectives and subject to the provisions of Article 80.

ARTICLE 77

1. The trusteeship system shall apply to such territories in the following categories as may be placed thereunder by means of trusteeship agreements:

a. territories now held under mandate;

b. territories which may be detached from enemy states as a result of the Second World War; and

c. territories voluntarily placed under the system by states responsible for their administration.

2. It will be a matter for subsequent agreement as to which territories in the foregoing categories will be brought under the trusteeship system and upon what terms.

ARTICLE 78

The trusteeship system shall not apply to territories which have become Members of the United Nations, relationship among which will be based on respect for the principle of sovereign equality.

ARTICLE 79

The terms of trusteeship for each territory to be placed under the trusteeship system, including any alteration or amendment, shall be agreed upon by the states directly concerned, including the mandatory power in the case of territories held under mandate by a Member of the United Nations, and shall be approved as provided for in Articles 83 and 85.

ARTICLE 80

1. Except as may be agreed upon in individual trusteeship agreements, made under Articles 77, 79, and 81, placing each territory under the trusteeship system, and until such agreements have been concluded, nothing in this Chapter shall be construed in or of itself to alter in any manner the rights whatsoever of any states or any peoples or the terms of existing international instruments to which Members of the United Nations may respectively be parties.

2. Paragraph 1 of this Article shall not be interpreted as giving grounds for delay or postponement of the negotiation and conclusion of agreements for placing mandated and other territories under the trusteeship system as provided for in Article 77.

ARTICLE 81

The trusteeship agreement shall in each case include the terms under which the trust territory will be administered and designate the authority which will exercise the administration of the trust territory. Such authority, hereinafter called the administering authority, may be one or more states or the Organization itself.

ARTICLE 82

There may be designated, in any trusteeship agreement, a strategic area or areas which may include part or all of the trust territory to which the agreement applies, without prejudice to any special agreement or agreements made under Article 43.

ARTICLE 83

1. All functions of the United Nations relating to strategic areas, including the approval of the terms of the trusteeship agreements and of their alteration or amendment, shall be exercised by the Security Council.

2. The basic objectives set forth in Article 76 shall be applicable to the people of each strategic area.

3. The Security Council shall, subject to the provisions of the trusteeship agreements and without prejudice to security considerations, avail itself of the assistance of the Trusteeship Council to perform those functions of the United Nations under the trusteeship system relating to political, economic, social, and educational matters in the strategic areas.

ARTICLE 84

It shall be the duty of the administering authority to ensure that the trust territory shall play its part in the maintenance of international peace and security. To this end the administering authority may make use of volunteer forces, facilities, and assistance from the trust territory in carrying out the obligations towards the Security Council undertaken in this regard by the administering authority, as well as for local defense and the maintenance of law and order within the trust territory.

ARTICLE 85

1. The functions of the United Nations with regard to trusteeship agreements for all areas not designated as strategic, including the approval of the terms of the trusteeship agreements and of their alteration or amendment, shall be exercised by the General Assembly.

2. The Trusteeship Council, operating under the authority of the General Assembly, shall assist the General Assembly in carrying out these functions.

Chapter XIII/The Trusteeship Council

Composition

ARTICLE 86

1. The Trusteeship Council shall consist of the following Members of the United Nations:

a. those Members administering trust territories;

b. such of those Members mentioned by name in Article 23 as are not administering trust territories; and

c. as many other Members elected for three-year terms by the General Assembly as may be necessary to ensure that the total number of members of the Trusteeship Council is equally divided between those Members of the United Nations which administer trust territories and those which do not.

2. Each member of the Trusteeship Council shall designate one specially qualified person to represent it therein.

Functions and Powers

ARTICLE 87

The General Assembly and, under its authority, the Trusteeship Council, in carrying out their functions, may:

a. consider reports submitted by the administering authority;

b. accept petitions and examine them in consultation with the administering authority;

c. provide for periodic visits to the respective trust territories at times agreed upon with the administering authority; and

d. take these and other actions in conformity with the terms of the trusteeship agreements.

ARTICLE 88

The Trusteeship Council shall formulate a questionnaire on the political, economic, social, and educational advancement of the inhabitants of each trust territory, and the administering authority for each trust territory within the competence of the General Assembly shall make an annual report to the General Assembly upon the basis of such questionnaire.

Voting

ARTICLE 89

1. Each member of the Trusteeship Council shall have one vote.

2. Decisions of the Trusteeship Council shall be made by a majority of the members present and voting.

Procedure

ARTICLE 90

1. The Trusteeship Council shall adopt its own rules of procedure, including the method of selecting its President.

2. The Trusteeship Council shall meet as required in accordance with its rules, which shall include provision for the convening of meetings on the request of a majority of its members.

ARTICLE 91

The Trusteeship Council shall, when appropriate, avail itself of the assistance of the Economic and Social Council and of the specialized agencies in regard to matters with which they are respectively concerned.

Chapter XIV/The International Court of Justice

ARTICLE 92

The International Court of Justice shall be the principal judicial organ of the United Nations. It shall function in accordance with the annexed Statute, which is based upon the Statute of the Permanent Court of International Justice and forms an integral part of the present Charter.

ARTICLE 93

1. All Members of the United Nations are *ipso facto* parties to the Statute of the International Court of Justice.

2. A state which is not a Member of the United Nations may become a party to the Statute of the International Court of Justice on conditions to be determined in each case by the General Assembly upon the recommendation of the Security Council.

ARTICLE 94

1. Each Member of the United Nations undertakes to comply with the decision of the International Court of Justice in any case to which it is a party.

2. If any party to a case fails to perform the obligations incumbent upon it under a judgment rendered by the Court, the other party may have recourse to the Security Council, which may, if it deems necessary,

make recommendations or decide upon measures to be taken to give effect to the judgment.

Nothing in the present Charter shall prevent Members of the United Nations from entrusting the solution of their differences to other tribunals by virtue of agreements already in existence or which may be concluded in the future.

1. The General Assembly or the Security Council may request the International Court of Justice to give an advisory opinion on any legal question.

2. Other organs of the United Nations and specialized agencies, which may at any time be so authorized by the General Assembly, may also request advisory opinions of the Court on legal questions arising within the scope of their activities.

Chapter XV/The Secretariat

The Secretariat shall comprise a Secretary-General and such staff as the Organization may require. The Secretary-General shall be appointed by the General Assembly upon the recommendation of the Security Council. He shall be the chief administrative officer of the Organization.

The Secretary-General shall act in that capacity in all meetings of the General Assembly, of the Security Council, of the Economic and Social Council, and of the Trusteeship Council, and shall perform such other functions as are entrusted to him by these organs. The Secretary-General shall make an annual report to the General Assembly on the work of the Organization.

The Secretary-General may bring to the attention of the Security Council any matter which in his opinion may threaten the maintenance of international peace and security.

ARTICLE 100

1. In the performance of their duties the Secretary-General and the staff shall not seek or receive instructions from any government or from any other authority external to the Organization. They shall refrain from any action which might reflect on their position as international officials responsible only to the Organization.

2. Each Member of the United Nations undertakes to respect the exclusively international character of the responsibilities of the Secretary-General and the staff and not to seek to influence them in the discharge of their responsibilities.

ARTICLE 101

1. The staff shall be appointed by the Secretary-General under regulations established by the General Assembly.

2. Appropriate staffs shall be permanently assigned to the Economic and Social Council, the Trusteeship Council, and, as required, to other organs of the United Nations. These staffs shall form a part of the Secretariat.

3. The paramount consideration in the employment of the staff and in the determination of the conditions of service shall be the necessity of securing the highest standards of efficiency, competence, and integrity. Due regard shall be paid to the importance of recruiting the staff on as wide a geographical basis as possible.

Chapter XVI/Miscellaneous Provisions

ARTICLE 102

1. Every treaty and every international agreement entered into by any Member of the United Nations after the present Charter comes into force shall as soon as possible be registered with the Secretariat and published by it.

2. No party to any such treaty or international agreement which has not been registered in accordance with the provisions of paragraph 1 of this Article may invoke that treaty or agreement before any organ of the United Nations.

ARTICLE 103

In the event of a conflict between the obligations of the Members of the United Nations under the present Charter and their obligations under any other international agreement, their obligations under the present Charter shall prevail.

The Organization shall enjoy in the territory of each of its Members such legal capacity as may be necessary for the exercise of its functions and the fulfillment of its purposes.

ARTICLE 105

1. The Organization shall enjoy in the territory of each of its Members such privileges and immunities as are necessary for the fulfillment of its purposes.

2. Representatives of the Members of the United Nations and officials of the Organization shall similarly enjoy such privileges and immunities as are necessary for the independent exercise of their functions in connection with the Organization.

3. The General Assembly may make recommendations with a view to determining the details of the application of paragraphs 1 and 2 of this Article or may propose conventions to the Members of the United Nations for this purpose.

Chapter XVII/Transitional Security Arrangements

ARTICLE 106

Pending the coming into force of such special agreements referred to in Article 43 as in the opinion of the Security Council enable it to begin the exercise of its responsibilities under Article 42, the parties to the Four-Nation Declaration, signed at Moscow, October 30, 1943, and France, shall, in accordance with the provisions of paragraph 5 of that Declaration, consult with one another and as occasion requires with other Members of the United Nations with a view to such joint action on behalf of the Organization as may be necessary for the purpose of maintaining international peace and security.

ARTICLE 107

Nothing in the present Charter shall invalidate or preclude action, in relation to any state which during the Second World War has been an enemy of any signatory to the present Charter, taken or authorized as a result of that war by the Governments having responsibility for such action.

Chapter XVIII/Amendments

ARTICLE 108

Amendments to the present Charter shall come into force for all Members of the United Nations when they have been adopted by a vote of two-thirds of the members of the General Assembly and ratified in accordance with their respective constitutional processes by two-thirds of the Members of the United Nations, including all the permanent members of the Security Council.

ARTICLE 109

1. A General Conference of the Members of the United Nations for the purpose of reviewing the present Charter may be held at a date and place to be fixed by a two-thirds vote of the members of the General Assembly and by a vote of any nine members of the Security Council. Each Member of the United Nations shall have one vote in the conference.

2. Any alteration of the present Charter recommended by a two-thirds vote of the conference shall take effect when ratified in accordance with their respective constitutional processes by two-thirds of the Members of the United Nations including all the permanent members of the Security Council.

3. If such a conference has not been held before the tenth annual session of the General Assembly following the coming into force of the present Charter, the proposal to call such a conference shall be placed on the agenda of that session of the General Assembly, and the conference shall be held if so decided by a majority vote of the members of the General Assembly and by a vote of any seven members of the Security Council.

Chapter XIX/Ratification and Signature

ARTICLE 110

1. The present Charter shall be ratified by the signatory states in accordance with their respective constitutional processes.

2. The ratifications shall be deposited with the Government of the United States of America, which shall notify all the signatory states of each deposit as well as the Secretary-General of the Organization when he has been appointed.

3. The present Charter shall come into force upon the deposit of ratifications by the Republic of China, France, the Union of Soviet Socialist Republics, the United Kingdom of Great Britain and Northern Ireland, and the United States of America, and by a majority of the other signatory states. A protocol of the ratifications deposited shall thereupon be drawn up by the Government of the United States of America which shall communicate copies thereof to all the signatory states.

4. The states signatory to the present Charter which ratify it after it has come into force will become original Members of the United Nations on the date of the deposit of their respective ratifications.

ARTICLE 111

The present Charter, of which the Chinese, French, Russian, English, and Spanish texts are equally authentic, shall remain deposited in the archives of the Government of the United States of America. Duly certified copies thereof shall be transmitted by that Government to the Governments of the other signatory states.

IN FAITH WHEREOF the representatives of the Governments of the United Nations have signed the present Charter.

DONE at the city of San Francisco the twenty-sixth day of June, one thousand nine hundred and forty-five.

Index

443

About the Author

Born in Austria, John G. Stoessinger grew up in China and came to the United States in 1947. He received his B.A. from Grinnell College and his M.A. and Ph.D. from Harvard University. Professor Stoessinger is currently Professor of Political Science at The City University of New York at Hunter College and Director of The City University's Institute on the United Nations. He is also serving as Director of the Political Affairs Division of the United Nations. He has taught at Harvard, M.I.T., Wellesley, and Columbia, and he has received an Honorary Doctor of Laws degree from Grinnell College. From 1960 to 1967 he was Visiting Professor of International Relations at Columbia University, and in 1969 he led the International Seminar on International Relations at Harvard University.

In 1963 the first edition of *The Might of Nations* earned Professor Stoessinger the Bancroft Prize for the best book in international relations published in 1962. He is also the author of *The Refugee and the World Community* (1956), *Atoms for Peace: The International Atomic Energy Agency* (with Arthur N. Holcombe, 1959), *Financing the United Nations System* (1964), *Power and Order: Six Cases in World Politics* (1964), and *The United Nations and the Superpowers* (1965 and 1970). His latest book, *Nations in Darkness: China, Russia, and America* (1971), was chosen by the Book Find Club as its February 1972 selection.